Off the Beaten Path

Off the Beaten Path

A Travel Guide to More Than
1,000 Scenic and Interesting Places
Still Uncrowded and Inviting

Reader's Digest

The Reader's Digest Association, Inc.
Pleasantville, New York

A READER'S DIGEST BOOK

Copyright @ 2003 The Reader's Digest Association, Inc.

Editor: Susan Byrne
Project Coordinator: Vicki Fisher
Contributing Editors: Barbara Booth, Ellen McCurtin, Sean Nolan, Melissa Virrill
Contributing Writers: Mysia Haight-Hoogsteden, Julienne Marshall
Contributing Copy Editor: Mary Connell
Editorial Assistance: Fran Guerin, Jessica Kovler
Senior Design Director: Elizabeth Tunnicliffe
Senior Designer: George McKeon
Senior Project Designer: Eleanor Kostyk
Contributing Designer: Martha Grossman
Production Technology Manager: Douglas A. Croll
Indexer: Andrea Chesman

Executive Editor, Trade Publishing: Dolores York
Director, Trade Publishing: Christopher T. Reggio
Vice President & Publisher, Trade Publishing: Harold Clarke

The acknowledgments and credits that appear on page 375 are hereby made a part
of this copyright page.

Special thanks to Ken Kraus, Media Relations Manager, Utah Travel Council

Picture research by Carousel Research, Inc.
Laurie Platt Winfrey
Van Bucher
Cristian Peña

ISBN 0-7621-0424-4

Note to Our Readers
The information for this book was gathered and carefully fact-checked by Reader's Digest
researchers and editors. Since site information such as dates and hours is always subject to
change, you are urged to check the facts presented in this book beforehand to avoid any
inconvenience.

Address any comments about *Off the Beaten Path* to:
    The Reader's Digest Association, Inc.
    Adult Trade Publishing
    Reader's Digest Road
    Pleasantville, NY 10570-7000

rd.com For more Reader's Digest products and information, visit our web site.

Printed by C&C Offset Printing Co. Ltd., Hong Kong

1 3 5 7 9 10 8 6 4 2

Introduction

America's travelers enthusiastically embraced the first edition of *Off the Beaten Path,* a unique guide to more than 1,000 of our country's most undervisited, must-see destinations. Now completely revised, meticulously updated, and bigger and better than ever, this exciting new edition is sure to please the guide's legions of fans as well as newcomers to its pages.

As in the first edition, we set out to find the most interesting places, coast to coast, that most travelers overlook. Many of the destinations included in these pages are literally off the beaten path. Others are in towns or on main routes but have an unusual appeal: museums featuring old locks, teapots, or antique cars; grand homes with elaborate interiors; historic inns; and much, much more. Well-known places, including national parks, are featured, but the areas highlighted are less frequented by travelers and are interesting in their own right. Each attraction is unusual and compelling, no matter where it is located.

HOW THE BOOK WAS DEVELOPED AND REVISED

In the first edition, our editors studied the map and history of every state and made a list of intriguing places that were geographically out of the way or that had subject matter beyond the mainstream. They also chose sites in all parts of each state.

For this revised edition, we asked tourist boards in each state to confirm that each one of the original sites was still indeed off the beaten track and asked for their suggestions of new, unspoiled gems. We then culled through thousands of brochures, leaflets, and web sites in order to select almost 200 new sites that met the original criteria: appealing and overlooked attractions that travelers shouldn't miss.

Once we had settled on the final list of attractions, we sent the newly written or revised entries to the relevant sites, where all information was confirmed by a staff member or volunteer or by the state tourist board staff.

Every site includes up-to-the-minute tourist information. Every fact has been checked and rechecked. We have included nearly 400 evocative new photographs and all-new, detailed state maps. For your travel convenience, this new edition also includes phone numbers and web sites, where available, at the end of each entry.

We are very proud of this scrupulously researched and revised edition. But careful as we have been, it is possible that you will encounter the unexpected somewhere along the way. Things change: Roads deteriorate or close, opening hours and admission charges are adjusted, services may be curtailed, web site addresses get renamed, places may close down. But if you use this guide in the spirit of adventure (and call ahead to confirm the details of your trip), you are sure to develop a newfound excitement and admiration for this great country of ours.

—THE EDITORS

Information at end of entries

Symbols (below) are shown when relevant. Opening times, such as Mon.-Fri., Apr.-Oct., are inclusive—meaning Monday through Friday, April through October. Road directions are not given in the text when the location is obvious on the map.

- Picnicking
- Camping/Tenting
- Camping/RV Camping
- Swimming
- Walking/Hiking
- Bicycling
- Canoeing/Rowboating
- Fishing
- Sight-Seeing/Bird-Watching
- Horseback Riding
- Skiing/Cross-Country Skiing
- Winter Activities
- Scuba Diving /Snorkeling

Contents

MAPQUEST

0 50 100 150 200 250 Miles
0 50 100 150 200 250 Kilometers

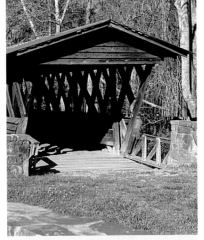

Clarkson Covered Bridge in Bethel. *Built in 1904, it is one of the largest in the state and spans a 50-foot-deep gorge (see page 11).*

(see page 11)

Alabama

Whether exploring ancient caverns or space travel, visitors have plenty of activities to pick from in the Cotton State.

Ancient American Indian culture can be explored here in one of the oldest sites of human habitation, a cave discovered by amateur archaeologists just 50 years ago. More geological wonders can be found in Rock Bridge Canyon, and in Dismals Canyon, complete with its own tiny glowworms.

Inviting hiking trails beckon visitors in a number of parks, including one going over the highest point in the state. Pioneer times are represented by a covered bridge and a lively museum village. Some surprising attractions include a fabulous display of mounted African wildlife and, at the headquarters of a paper company, an exceptional art collection and a lovely formal Japanese garden.

1 Madison County Nature Trail

Exit from U.S. Rte. 231 to east on Weatherly Rd., turn right on Bailey Cove Rd., then turn left on Green Mountain Rd. Go to top of mountain and turn right on S. Shawdee Rd.

Set high above the city of Huntsville—atop aptly named Green Mountain—this network of paths in a charming 72-acre park offers the opportunity to observe nature in the southern Appalachians firsthand. On the north side of the 17-acre Sky Lake, along the walking trail, you will come across the original cabin of Charles Green, the homesteader for whom Green Mountain was named.

Overall, about two miles of well-managed trails circle the lake and lead beyond into a woods filled with loblolly pines and hardwoods, like white oak, mockernut hickory, red maple, and black locust. Along the way, some 500 species of trees and shrubs are labeled and identified. You'll also find the state's largest and oldest champion elm tree. One side trail is marked in braille for the blind.
Open year-round except Christmas and New Year's Day.
(256) 883-9501
www.co.madison.al.us

1 Madison County Nature Trail. *A log home constructed in about 1810 greets visitors along a southern Appalachian trail.*

2 Russell Cave National Monument

3729 Country Rd. 98, Bridgeport
Discovered by amateur archaeologists in 1953, this ballroom-sized cavern is one of the oldest sites of human habitation in North America. The excavations done here have revealed much about ancient American Indian life and culture in the Southeast. A boardwalk allows visitors to experience what it must have been like to enter the cave thousands of years ago.

A small band of nomadic American Indians discovered the cave about 8,500 years ago and took shelter in it. For about 6,000 years after that, it was used almost continuously as a winter refuge by the American Indians who survived by hunting and foraging. Later people, who had evolved a more complex lifestyle, used the cave as a winter hunting camp. From about A.D. 1000, however, when American Indians had begun to practice agriculture and live in villages, the cave was used only occasionally as a shelter.

A small museum at the visitors center displays weapon points and other tools found at the site.

A short, easily walked trail takes you through the oak-hickory forest, which served as the food supply for these early people.

With permission from park rangers, experienced, properly equipped spelunkers can also explore the adjacent cave system, which has several miles of passageways and caverns, including such attractions as Waterfall Passage. The park's 310 acres of natural terrain offer trails for hikers.
Open daily except Christmas.
(256) 495-2672
www.nps.gov/ruca

3 U.S. Space and Rocket Center
15 miles east of I-65 at Exit 15 on I-565, Huntsville
At this state-of-the-art interactive museum, people of all ages can experience zero gravity, maneuver through space, and travel with astronauts—just like at space camp. Out-of-this-world experiences include a step inside the G-Force Accelerator, where bodies actually rise up off their seats, and a genuine blastoff—180 feet straight up in 2.5 seconds—courtesy of the Space Shot. There is even a "Mission to Mars," packed with astounding sights, sounds, and physical sensations.

The museum also features dozens of hands-on learning exhibits. Visitors can sit inside an authentic Apollo Command Module and check out the $200 million Blackbird, the sleek U.S. Air Force spy plane that flew coast to coast in less than 68 minutes. Or, they can delve into the technology behind the world's first ballistic guided missile and view the latest in high-tech

weaponry, including futuristic soldiers armed with particle beam guns. For the youngest aspiring astronauts, a tot-sized space station offers rockets for crawling into. And for those who prefer to sit back and be awe-inspired, the Spacedome Theater projects footage of planets, galaxies, and other cosmic amazements, filmed in space by astronauts, onto a 67-foot domed IMAX screen.

Outside the museum, visitors can stroll through what astronaut John Glenn calls the finest rocket collection in the world. Rocket Park boasts more than 1,500 pieces of space hardware, including a Mercury-Redstone rocket like the one that launched Alan Shepard, and the first Saturn V rocket built for NASA. At the neighboring Shuttle Park, visitors can walk right under the world's only "full-stack" shuttle.

Alternatively, experience life on Mars in the Olympus Moons Mining Colony. While there, scale a replica of the largest volcanic crater in the solar system, in addition to climbing a 25-foot-high wall. Note: The climb can be strenuous so take caution when climbing.
Open year-round except Thanksgiving, Christmas, and New Year's Day. Admission charged.
(256) 837-3400
www.spacecamp.com/ museum

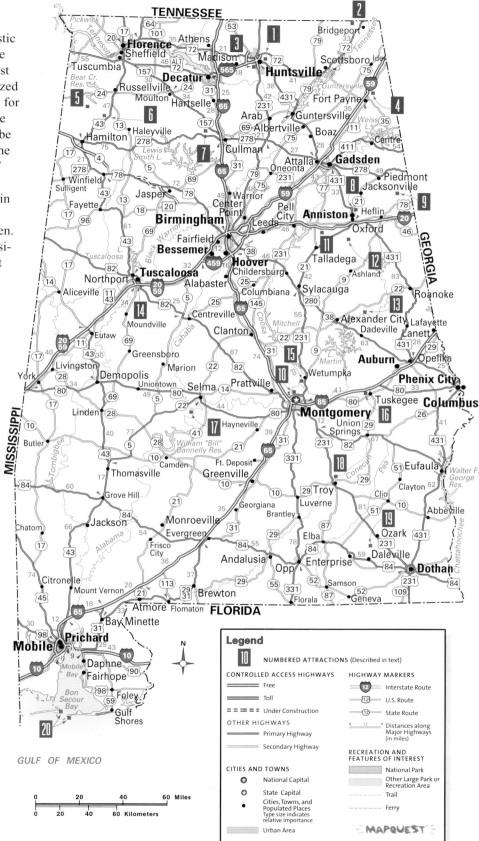

4 DeSoto State Park Resort
Fort Payne

This elaborate complex of recreational and lodging facilities is the nucleus of a 3,000-acre park that stretches for 10 miles along the Little River, the only river in the country to flow its entire course on a mountaintop. The park is named for the Spanish conquistador Hernando de Soto, who in 1540 was the first European to explore the region. Situated on the wooded, undulating terrain of Lookout Mountain, the resort has cabins and camping areas as well as a lodge and an Olympic-size pool.

The area is magnificently scenic. Miles of hiking trails lead to mountain streams, miniature cliffs, mossy glens, and waterfalls. Among the most striking features to be encountered along the paths are huge, picturesquely weathered boulders. The park is also noted for its flowering shrubs, and expanses of rhododendron and mountain laurel can be seen at their peak bloom from mid- to late May. A profusion of wild azaleas festoons the Azalea Cascade Trail with delicate clusters of bloom.

Other parts of DeSoto State Park also offer outstanding attractions. At DeSoto Falls, a few miles north of the resort, the Little River takes a 100-foot plunge into a large green lake before continuing its descent through a wide, leafy gorge. At Little River Canyon, now owned and operated by the National Park Service, the deepest canyon east of the Mississippi, the river makes another spectacular plummet. But the main attraction is the 16-mile-long canyon itself, which, with a depth of some 700 feet, is the deepest chasm east of the Rockies. A two-lane drive hugging the western edge of the rim

6 Dismals Canyon. *Rainbow Falls cascades down a canyon where trees, shrubs, and vines swarm over weathered rocks.*

provides good views. Legend holds that de Soto searched for gold in the caves along its cliffs.
Open year-round.
(256) 845-0051
www.desotostatepark.com

5 Rock Bridge Canyon
Hodges

This site takes its name from an impressive 80-foot-long, 100-foot-high natural rock bridge (one of the largest in the country) that spans a small, wooded box canyon with sheer sandstone walls. The best view of the bridge is from the canyon floor, which is reached by heading uphill from the parking area and turning right at the point where the trail forks. The canyon itself is littered with boulders, the debris of the rockfall that created the bridge. Picnic tables are set here, close to a waterfall cascading over a jumble of rocks.

The left fork of the uphill trail leads to the top of the bridge. The path winds through thick groves of mountain laurel, up steps cut in the rock, and then through a cleft in the rock to a high open place with eye-level views of the trees growing from the floor below. A short, somewhat precarious descent brings you onto the bridge. Along the path you pass a ladder reaching up to a cave.

An even more adventurous trail, steep and difficult in places and slippery when wet, leads from the parking area down to a small, dark green lake and then through woods and along the foot of cliffs to a waterfall and the remains of an old mill. Along the way are fine rockscapes and woodland scenery.

The best time to visit is in April- to mid-May, when the mountain

laurel and tulip trees bloom and the tall umbrella magnolias open their 12-inch flowers, filling the air with delicious fragrance.
Open year-round. Admission charged.
(205) 935-3663
www.ohwy.com/al/r/robrcaho.htm

6 Dismals Canyon
Hwy. 8, Phil Campbell

Locally, this site is known simply as The Dismals. But the visitor should not be put off by the gloomy-sounding name or the unimpressive entry area. In truth, the site is a small canyon with an imposing mixture of luxuriant vegetation and intricately eroded cliffs that have won it recognition as a registered natural landmark.

Starting at a waterfall, the 3/4-mile-long walking trail follows a boulder-strewn stream and wanders through labyrinthine clefts. Farther on, the canyon widens, and its sheer walls are pocked with hollows, marked with striations, and sometimes curiously rippled.

Everywhere, an exuberant, varied growth of trees, shrubs, and vines swarms over weathered, tumbled rocks. Even the stark rock walls of the canyon support pockets of ferns or dizzy ascents of vine.

A possible explanation for the chasm's odd name is that early settlers may have been struck by the subdued quality of the light, which is often blocked by the cliffs and filtered through a canopy of trees. (Among them are some of the country's tallest Canadian hemlocks.)

In any case, it is a place that leads one to observe the ways that the implacable canyon walls check the growth of vegetation. During the summer night tours allow visitors to discover "twinkle-in-the-dark" Dismalites, tiny glow-worms that "turn on" when it's pitch-dark. Dismals Canyon also offers a picnic spot and swimming in Dismals Branch, a natural limestone pool.

Open Mar.–Nov. Admission charged.
(205) 993-4559

www.dismalscanyon.com

7 Clarkson Covered Bridge
Hwy. 278, Bethel
Built in 1904 and rebuilt in 1922 after a flood, this bridge was carefully restored in 1975 in preparation for America's bicentennial celebration the following year.

One of the largest covered bridges in the state, it is 270 feet long, and it spans the 50-foot-deep gorge of Crooked Creek, supported on a foundation of four cut stone piers. It has a cedar shingle roof and clapboard siding, but its most interesting architectural feature is the latticework of timbers that support the bridge. This design, the Town Lattice, named for its inventor, Ithiel Town, was not only sturdy but also economical and easy to build.

The bridge is set in a small, charming park with a millpond. The mill itself is now a private home. A quarter-mile trail loops through a woodland of oak and mountain laurel and returns across a plank walk on top of the millpond dam.

Open year-round.
(256) 734-3369

www.cullmancountyparks.com

8 Anniston Museum of Natural History
Two miles north of Anniston at the junction of U.S. Rte. 431 and State Hwy. 21
This remarkable museum includes outstanding collections of mounted animal specimens from North America and Africa. A bird collection was prepared by the 19th-century ornithologist William Werner, who was a pioneer in the cyclorama style of presentation. The 400-specimen collection, which was assembled between 1870 and 1910, offers a rare opportunity to see now-extinct species such as the heath hen and the passenger pigeon.

The even more striking African collection is the gift of a local resident who spent years collecting in Africa. Some exhibits concentrate on aspects of animal behavior. Others are panoramic re-creations of the continent's natural environments, such as a Sahara desert landscape complete with oryx, Barbary sheep, and desert snails and a marshland scene with hippos and egrets. The most outstanding display is a diorama of a grassland showing a giant baobab tree towering over an elephant, a rhino, a giraffe, and many smaller mammals and birds.

Recently opened is the "Ancient Egypt" exhibit hall, featuring 2,300-year-old Egyptian mummies and mounted specimens of animals representing deities.

Next to the Anniston Museum is the Berman Museum. Here you will find an arsenal of weapons and works of art spanning 3,500 years. Many of the objects in the seven diorama-style exhibit halls belonged to prominent historical figures, such as Jefferson Davis, Napoleon, and Emperor Charles V.

Both museums open daily Memorial Day–Labor Day. Closed Mon. rest of year. Admission charged at each.
Anniston: (256) 237-6766
Berman: (256) 237-6261

www.annistonmuseum.org
www.bermanmuseum.org

9 Coleman Lake Recreation Area and the Pinhoti Trail
Off Rte. 78, Heflin
Located near the northern tip of the Talladega National Forest, the Coleman Lake Recreation Area lies at the end of a long road that winds through the woodland. A grove of tall pines is dotted with picnic tables set invitingly apart. A section of lakeshore is roped off for swimming, and a bathhouse with showers is on a nearby hill. Bass, shellcrackers, and bluegills are caught in many inlets, and trails circle the lake and lead across wooded hills.

The lake is also the current northern terminus of Alabama's longest hiking route, the Pinhoti Trail. In Creek, *pinhoti* means "turkey's home," and the hiker does indeed have a chance of seeing wild turkeys. The 110-mile trail, marked with a blaze that looks like a turkey track, runs mostly along a ridge system in the center of the Talladega National Forest, and it passes through some of the finest wild scenery in the South, skirting the shores of lakes and crossing mountains. Since roads intersect the trail at several points, you can sample it without an overnight outing.

The Pinhoti's ultimate destination is the Benton McKaye Trail in Georgia, which then connects to the Appalachian Trail. The Pinhoti was designated a National Recreation Trail in 1977, and there are many who would like to see it grow to 220 miles in length.

Spring and fall offer the best weather and are when this area is generally free of crowds.
Coleman Lake Recreation Area open Apr.–Jan. Pinhoti Trail open year-round.
(256) 463-2272

www.southernregion.fs.fed.us/alabama

8 Anniston Museum of Natural History. *A diorama of an African grassland features an elephant dwarfed by a giant baobab tree in the background.*

10 Montgomery Zoo
Coliseum Parkway

Spanning 40 acres of inviting landscape, this popular local zoo is home to more than 200 distinct species, many of which are endangered. Five realms comfortably accommodate more than 500 animals from Africa, Asia, North America, South America, and Australia.

Throughout, natural and hidden man-made barriers replace the iron and concrete of conventional zoos. This allows visitors to get a

10 Montgomery Zoo. *White Bengal tigers can be found here.*

sense of how animals actually live together in the wild, while keeping predators at a safe distance. Lions and cheetahs intently watch their prey (and humans) from rock outcroppings, while tigers take a dip in their own backyard pool, and birds of assorted feathers fly free.

Visitors can also hop aboard a miniature train for a narrated ride past most of the exhibit environments, complete with a trip around the zoo's eight-acre Crystal Lake for a glimpse of native turtles and waterfowl.

Among other highlights, the zoo includes a reptile house, a renovated monkey island, a bald-eagle exhibit, and two white Bengal tigers. Staff and trained volunteers regularly provide live animal demonstrations. In addition, the zoo hosts ZooBoo at Halloween and the Holiday Lights Festival in December.

The Montgomery Zoo is also involved in species repopulation programs—one of which has released more than 17 golden eagles in Alabama and surrounding states—and offers various programs with an emphasis on education and wildlife conservation.
Open year-round except Thanksgiving, Christmas, and New Year's Day. Admission charged.
(334) 240-4900
www.montgomeryzoo.com

11 International Motorsports Hall of Fame & Museum
3198 Speedway Blvd., Talladega
Established by Bill France, the founder of the National Association for Stock Car Auto Racing (NASCAR), this impressive five-building complex owned by the state is a racing enthusiast's dream. Adjacent to the Talladega Superspeedway, the fastest racetrack in the world and home of the DieHard 500 and Winston 500 races, it attracts shoulder-to-shoulder crowds during race weeks. Enormous showrooms display over 125 racing machines, all in mint condition and valued at over $25 million. In addition to record-setting cars raced by legends, the collection features muscle cars, antiques, and classics, as well as assorted motorsports memorabilia dating from 1902.

From Sam Packard's 1946 Mercury to Bill Elliott's 1985 Thunderbird, the cars offer a riveting trip through racing history. A special room honors the remarkable men behind the wheels, with lively biographical profiles of each of the nearly 100 International Motorsports Hall of Fame inductees—including Henry Ford, Enzo Ferrari, Mario Andretti, Jackie Stewart, Bobby Unser, and, most recently, Jacky Ickx—as well as the winners of the coveted Driver of the Year Award.

Serious racing devotees will want to take a detour to the McCaig Wellborn Research Library, the most complete motorsports library in existence—housing more than 14,000 books and periodicals, over 10,000 photos, plus a state-of-the-art computer system that is able to retrieve even the most obscure racing facts in a flash.

Beyond cars, there's the Cougar Cat Gentry Turbo Eagle, a 54-foot offshore powerboat acclaimed for setting a world-record speed of 148.238 miles per hour in 1987; Bobby Allison's Aerostar, a one-of-a-kind plane powered with Allison turboprop engines; and the Budweiser Rocket Car, a missile on wheels—39 feet long and just 20 inches wide—that broke the sound barrier in 1979 with a record run of 739.666 miles per hour. The price of admission also includes a guided van tour of the world-famous Superspeedway, unless the track is closed for testing or racing events.
Open year-round except Thanksgiving, Christmas, and Easter. Admission charged.
(256) 362-5002
www.motorsportshalloffame.com

12 Cheaha State Park
Hwy. 281, Delta
This lovely 2,719-acre woodland park occupies the upper slopes of Cheaha Mountain; at 2,407 feet it is the highest point in Alabama. Although you can reach the summit via a short and scenic park road off Rte. 49, you can take Rte. 281—Talladega Forest Scenic Highway—17 miles to the park.

The narrow blacktop road crosses fields on the valley floor and then immerses you in pine-scented woods, passing small rushing streams. A stone tower at the summit gives a fine view to distant farmlands, mountain ridges, river valleys, and lakes.

Five hiking trails, totaling seven miles, reveal a diversity of wildlife and panoramic views. There's also a six-mile mountain bike trail, and the park is the halfway point in the Cheaha Century Challenge, a 110-mile touring bike race held every May. Additional trails wind through the surrounding Talladega National Forest. At and near the crest of Cheaha are picnic areas, campsites with hookups and magnificent scenery, a lake with a white sand beach, cabins, a hotel with 30

■ International Motorsports Hall of Fame & Museum. *More than 125 racing machines, dating from 1902 and in mint condition, are on display at the museum established by NASCAR founder Bill France.*

rooms, and several hiking trails, both short and long.
Open year-round. Admission charged.
(256) 488-5111 or (800) 610-5801
www.dcnr.al.us

13 Horseshoe Bend National Military Park
Daviston
One of the earliest and most crucial clashes between the U.S. government and the American Indian took place on this site in March 1814. The battle of Horseshoe Bend not only ended the fighting in the nearly two-year Indian Creek War but it also broke the power of the American Indians in what is now Alabama, Georgia, and Mississippi.

The battle pitted two strong, shrewd leaders against each other: Andrew Jackson, commander of the American forces and future president, and Menawa, a powerful Upper Creek chief. Menawa and his warriors had turned the small peninsula formed by this horseshoe-shaped loop in the Tallapoosa River into a military stronghold.

With the river providing protection on three sides, Menawa and his warriors built a formidable log and earthen barricade across the fourth. In the end, however, Menawa's 1,000 or so warriors, the barricade, and the river could not save the Upper Creek Indians from Jackson's army of 3,000 men and 500 Cherokee allies.

The wounded Menawa escaped, but more than 800 of his warriors

died in battle; 49 of Jackson's men died and 157 were wounded.

The small museum in the visitors center contains weapons, historic documents, a diorama showing the storming of the barricade, and an illuminated map tracing troop movements and battle phases. The three-mile drive through the battlefield includes stops at the hill from which Jackson fired 50 cannon rounds at the barricade.

Another stop is at the mound on which the Creek prophets (medicine men) performed their prebattle dance and assured the Creek warriors that they would be immune to the effects of the army's weapons.

The park has a picnic area at the edge of the river, a launching ramp, and several miles of walk-

ing trails. The best times to visit are spring and fall.
Open daily except Christmas and New Year's Day. (256) 234-7111
www.nps.gov/hobe

14 Gulf States Paper Corporation National Headquarters
1400 Jack Warner Parkway, Tuscaloosa
The corridors and conference rooms of this modern corporate headquarters have been transformed into a rich museum by the varied and extensive art collection that is displayed on their walls, along with artifacts from various primitive cultures, bronze and porcelain sculptures, and Oriental artwork.

The highlights of the exhibit are from the collection of American art gathered by the corporation's retired chairman, Jack W. Warner. It features several hundred paintings by a number of distinguished American artists, including Mary Cassatt, Thomas Cole, Frederic Church, Childe Hassam, Frederic Remington, and Andrew Wyeth. A number of Basil Edes wild-bird portraits are among the most popular pieces.

The headquarters also contains a serene and stately Japanese garden with pavilions and a pond. Designed by David Engel, one of America's foremost landscape architects, it is modeled on a garden in the Katsura Imperial Villa in Kyoto, Japan. Visitors are invited to view both the art collection and the garden in guided tours offered each hour on the hour.
Open weekends only, 1–5 P.M.
(205) 562-5000
www.gulf-states.com

15 Fort Toulouse–Jackson Park
Wetumpka

In 1717, when this region was part of French Louisiana, the French built a fort here near the strategically vital junction where the Tallapoosa and Coosa rivers form the Alabama River. The fort—which was named for Louis XIV's son, the Count of Toulouse—was primarily a trading post where American Indians exchanged pelts for guns and household items. The only serious conflict at this remote outpost came from within, when bored, ration-short soldiers mutinied. The fort was washed away, and in 1751 it was rebuilt and ringed by a palisade of pointed logs.

The French lost the French and Indian War—and the fort—in 1763. It was an overgrown ruin in 1814, when Major General Andrew Jackson ordered a new, much larger fort to be built nearby. The Treaty of Fort Jackson, signed here that year, marked the formal end of the bitter and protracted Creek War. From the fort, Jackson began his campaign to protect the Gulf Coast from the British—a campaign that ended with their defeat in the battle of New Orleans.

Artifacts found on the site are displayed in the visitors center. The 164-acre park also offers a picnic area, a campground, and a launching ramp. Bass, bream, catfish, and crappies are among the fish that can be caught in the two rivers flanking the park. In a 30-acre arboretum the local shrubs and trees are labeled for identification along well-tended trails. Benches are placed along the way, offering welcome rest in this humid but lovely subtropical environment. The weather is most comfortable in spring and fall.

15 Fort Toulouse. *Troops re-create the battles that were once waged here.*

Fort Toulouse and Jackson Park offer living history programs, providing insight into the American Indian and military history of the site and the lifestyle during the 18th and 19th centuries.
Park and visitors center open year-round; campground open Apr.–Oct. Admission charged.
(334) 567-3002
**www.living-history.net/Fort/
FortToulouse.html**

16 Tuskegee National Forest
Watch for signs on Rte. 186.

In the mid-1770s one of America's first artist-naturalists, William Bartram, passed through here on an epic journey, recording the flora and fauna of the Southeast. Today the 8½-mile Bartram National Recreation Trail is a major feature of this protected woodland.

It is fitting that the pathway was named for a naturalist, since this is terrain that has been beautifully and successfully reclaimed by nature. Most of it is former farmland that was purchased in the 1930s by the government in a program aimed at moving farmers away from their unprofitable, eroding land. The only signs of the former farmlands are peach, plum, and nut trees that are surprisingly encountered in the midst of the renewed wilderness.

With only 11,000 acres, this is the smallest of Alabama's national forests. The Forest Service has deliberately avoided building extensive recreational facilities so that it can be enjoyed primarily as a primitive experience. The Bartram Trail is easily accessible from two trailhead parking areas and at several in-between points where it crosses forest roads. Hikes of various lengths are possible, and the terrain is gentle and rolling. A viewing tower and blind allow close-up observation of songbirds, rabbits, turtles, frogs, and waterfowl on the beaver pond.

Tuskegee National Forest has a sizable number of deer, turkeys, quail, and other wildlife, and they attract many hunters in season. The Taska Recreation Area, just off Route 29, has picnic tables and grills and a replica of the log cabin birthplace of Booker T. Washington, founder of nearby Tuskegee University. Visitors are advised to bring drinking water.
Open year-round.
(334) 727-2652
www.r8web.com/alabama/

17 Old Cahawba
Located at the confluence of the Alabama and Cahawba rivers. From downtown Selma, take Hwy. 22 west 8.6 miles. Turn onto Country Road 9 and follow 5 miles to Cahawba.

A gift from President James Monroe to the new state of Alabama, Cahawba was built up from the wilderness to become the state's first capital city in 1820. Political power then shifted northward and Tuscaloosa captured the state capital title. Yet, thanks to its plum location as a distribution point for cotton, the town quickly recovered and thrived. On the eve of the Civil War, more than 3,000 people called Cahawba home. Sadly, its glory days were short-lived. During the Civil War, the Confederate government seized the railroad in the center of town and established a prison for captured Union soldiers in its place. Between 1863 and 1865 more than 5,000 prisoners of war were locked in decrepit buildings surrounded by a towering brick fortress. In 1865 a flood overwhelmed the town. Businesses and families fled. By 1900 virtually all of the buildings had burned, collapsed, or were dismantled. Cahawba was a ghost town.

Today, Cahawba is an important archaeological site and a place of picturesque ruins. Archaeologists from the Alabama Historical Commission are busily working to uncover the town's historic past and restore its natural beauty. At the Welcome Center, exhibits feature many historical finds, along with vintage photographs of homes and businesses once located in Old Cahawba. After this introduction, visitors are invited to explore the landscape of ruins and relics. Throughout, interpretive signs bring Cahawba's fascinating remnants and forgotten people again to life. Columns and chimneys recall distinguished houses. Water still flows through the old ornamental wellheads. Prison artifacts offer solemn reminders of the ravages of war. Three cemeteries tell the surprising stories of the diverse residents of this Southern antebellum community.

(334) 872-8058

www.selmaalabama.com/
cahawba.htm

 Pioneer Museum of Alabama
U.S. Hwy. 231, Troy

Packed with over 12,000 artifacts, the museum shows visitors how early settlers lived in Alabama. Exhibits include a re-created covered bridge, hearthside cooking samples in a log cabin, an authentic wood-burning-style locomotive, and American Indian artifacts.

This remarkably lively folk museum is chock-full of items once used by this area's farmers and townspeople. The museum is a community undertaking, and its collection owes its striking variety and completeness to the local citizens and merchants who scoured their attics, basements, stockrooms, barns, and outbuildings and donated their finds.

The grounds are of equal interest with a typical two-part log cabin with authentic furnishings, a windmill, a covered well with a pulley and bucket, and a country store fully stocked with period goods, including suits, shoes, patent medicines, bone buttons, penny candies, and plug tobacco. A shed for reducing syrup is in the picnic area. Also featured is a working smokehouse, an actual log crib from the 1850s, and several pieces of Civil War memorabilia. A breathtaking nature trail with herbs, vegetables, and heirloom

roses is here for guests to enjoy. With a small donation, visitors can bring home stone-ground cornmeal or grits from the gristmill.

Open Mon.–Sat. and Sunday afternoon. Admission charged.

(334) 566-3597

www.pioneer-museum-org

U.S. Army Aviation Museum
Fort Rucker

The entrance of this Army base declares it to be "The Heart of Air Assault," and over 160 military aircraft have been put on display here to prove it. The exhibit includes not only attack aircraft but also planes that were used for such key support activities as observing the enemy, taking aerial military photographs, moving troops, delivering supplies, and evacuating the wounded. The highly technologically sophisticated AH-64 Apache used in Desert Storm in 1991 is displayed here,

and the exhibit details various functions, such as refueling the aircraft in a tactical desert environment. In adjacent outdoor areas there are aircraft from many eras, dating back to Piper Cubs used as scout planes in World War II.

The predominant aircraft is the helicopter, which was first used in Korea in the 1950s and became the workhorse of the U.S. Army in Vietnam. The helicopter used by Presidents Eisenhower and Kennedy is also on display, as are a novel one-man backpack helicopter and a collapsible helicopter that fits in a crate.

Open Mon.–Sat. and Sunday afternoon except major holidays.

(334) 598-2508

www.armyavnmuseum.org

Fort Gaines Historic Site and Fort Morgan Historic Site

"Damn the torpedoes! Full speed ahead!" shouted Admiral David Farragut as his Union fleet ran between the blazing gun batteries

Fort Morgan Historic Site. *As it did during the Civil War, a cannon still guards the water that leads into Mobile Bay.*

of these two forts and across the line of deadly torpedoes (mines) strung between them.

The twin forts, Fort Gaines on Dauphin Island and Fort Morgan on Mobile Point, guarded the neck of water that leads into Mobile Bay. By entering the bay and seizing control of it in August 1864, Farragut sealed off Mobile, the only remaining Confederate port on the Gulf. The forts quickly fell to the Union forces.

Built in the early 1800s, the two thick-walled brick structures are constructed in the classic five-sided design with pointed bastions, or blockhouses, projecting from each corner. Walking on the ramparts and through the cryptlike, barrel-vaulted rooms below provides a good overview of the fortifications and their defenses, including the furnaces where cannonballs were heated red-hot so that they would set fire to wooden ships. Visitors can also see the sites of bakeries, blacksmith shops, and officers' quarters.

Fort Morgan has a museum with weapons, shells, uniforms, and other military relics and documents.

The peninsula on which Fort Morgan stands is popular with bird-watchers; more than 350 species have been sighted. Beaches, picnic areas, a fishing pier, and a nature trail are further attractions.

A ferry that runs regularly during the day permits both motorists and pedestrians to travel between the forts.

Both sites open year-round. Admission charged at each. Fort Gaines: (251) 861-6992 Fort Morgan: (251) 540-7127

Mount McKinley in Denali National Park. *The highest peak in North America, it is usually wreathed in clouds (see page 18).*

Alaska

Essence of wilderness: mountains, valleys, and fjords; realm of glaciers, icebergs, bears, and eagles—where nature reigns supreme.

For most residents of the Lower 48, all of Alaska is off the beaten path. But the relatively few roads and accessible places are all in fact quite well known. Facilities are limited, and reservations should be made well in advance.

What people come for is the indescribably magnificent scenery, the abundance and variety of wildlife—on land and sea and in the air—and the near-mystical aura created by such vast reaches of wild, uninhabited space. Hikers can explore many facets of the wilderness—from tide pools to rain forests and glaciers—and observe unparalleled concentrations of the dominant birds and animals.

Excellent museums document the history of the state and feature the totem poles, masks, and other ceremonial objects for which the native peoples are justly famous. The early Russian presence is evidenced by some handsome churches; the gold rush days are recalled; and historic military installations can be visited, as well as a lush valley where 75-pound cabbages are the norm.

1 Kotzebue

A tour of this Inupiaq town north of the Arctic Circle includes a visit to its colorful waterfront, an introduction to the surrounding flowery tundra, and a visit to the Nana Museum.

The museum, one of the state's most sophisticated, helps to explain and maintain the unique Inupiaq traditions. Authentic Inupiaq dances are given, and visitors can participate in a lively blanket toss. This seemingly playful exercise originated as a technique for lifting hunters up to look for game in the flat, treeless terrain. Outside are a replica of an Inupiaq sod igloo and the frame of a skin boat.

In the same building as the museum is a factory where people carve blocks of jade into jewelry, figurines, and other items. The jade is quarried at distant Jade Mountain by a local corporation and barged to Kotzebue.

The museum building also contains the National Park Service offices from which Kobuk Valley National Park, the Noatak National Preserve, and Cape Krusenstern National Monument are administered.

Each of these wildernesses can be reached by aircraft from Kotzebue.

In the Kobuk Valley National Park are archaeological sites that provide evidence of human

1 Kotzebue. *In this Inupiaq town north of the Arctic Circle, where it's still as cold as the glacial period, ice fishing is a way of life.*

habitation 12,500 years ago. Here, where the climate and archaic flora still approximate the glacial period, the Great Kobuk Sand Dunes cover 25 square miles, with dunes up to 125 feet high and summer temperatures sometimes reaching 100°F.

Noatak National Preserve contains the largest complete river system in the United States to remain unaltered by man; it has been declared a UNESCO International Biosphere Reserve.

At Cape Krusenstern National Monument are some 114 beach ridges laid down successively over the past 5,000 years, each one a repository of artifacts that together form a chronology of Eskimo culture in Arctic prehistory.

Nana Museum: Third Avenue. In summer, May 15–Sept. 15; winter, by appointment.
(907) 442-3441
www.museumsusa.org/data/museums
Kobuk Valley National Park:
(907) 442-3760
www.nps.gov/noaa
Cape Krusenstern:
(907) 442-3760
www.nps.gov/cakr

ALASKA

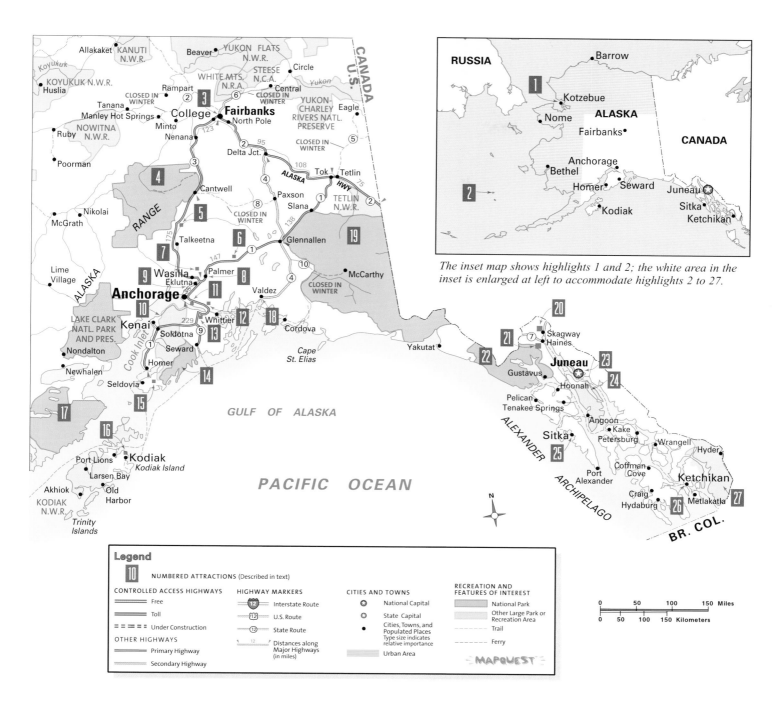

The inset map shows highlights 1 and 2; the white area in the inset is enlarged at left to accommodate highlights 2 to 27.

Legend

NUMBERED ATTRACTIONS (Described in text)

CONTROLLED ACCESS HIGHWAYS
— Free
— Toll
=== Under Construction

OTHER HIGHWAYS
— Primary Highway
— Secondary Highway

HIGHWAY MARKERS
Interstate Route
U.S. Route
State Route
Distances along Major Highways (in miles)

CITIES AND TOWNS
National Capital
State Capital
Cities, Towns, and Populated Places Type size indicates relative importance
Urban Area

RECREATION AND FEATURES OF INTEREST
National Park
Other Large Park or Recreation Area
Trail
Ferry

MAPQUEST

Pribilof Islands

2 More than a million fur seals on the beaches and 2.5 million seabirds on easy-to-observe nesting cliffs comprise one of the most wondrous wildlife spectacles in North America. Two of the volcanic Pribilof Islands, St. Paul and St. George, 270 miles out in the Bering Sea, are inhabited by Aleuts, whose ancestors were brought here by Russians to kill seals for their pelts.

Today the Aleuts provide food and lodging for tourists, who fly in on days when the fog is not too thick for landings. Blinds are available from which to watch the bull, cow, and pup seals interact, all barking and roaring loudly.

Neither is it quiet on the cliffs, where bird-watchers have close-up views of unafraid black-legged kittiwakes, tufted and horned puffins, red-faced cormorants, common and thick-billed murres, and three species of auklet. The red-legged kittiwakes, which also nest on the cliffs, are rarely seen away from the Pribilofs.

Accessible early June–late Aug.
(907) 562-7380

www.southwestalaska.com

3 University of Alaska

Fairbanks. From University Ave., which becomes Farmers Loop Rd., turn into campus on Taku Dr. Large Animal Research Station is Mile 1 Yankovich Rd., reached by way of Ballaine Rd. from Farmers Loop.

Modern sculpture, a Russian blockhouse, a totem pole, hard-rock mining equipment, and a nature trail surround the university museum. Here superb exhibits explain aspects of Alaska's wildlife, geology, and history, as well as the culture and crafts of the native peoples.

A unique display is an ice age bison that was well preserved in permanently frozen ground for 38,000 years before it was unearthed by gold miners. The museum also has the state's largest display of gold.

Other ice age creatures still very much alive—musk oxen, moose, caribou, and reindeer—are pastured at the university's Large Animal Research Station. These animals can be watched from an elevated platform that gives an unobstructed view of the area. Binoculars are recommended.

The subarctic agricultural research gardens of the university experimental farm demonstrate the productiveness possible when there are 20 hours of summer daylight. Sandhill cranes can be seen feeding in the experimental fields.

University open 9 A.M.–7 P.M. year-round. Museum open daily except Thanksgiving, Christmas, and New Year's Day.
Admission charged.
(907) 474-7581
www.uaf.edu

4 Denali National Park and Preserve. *A moose takes a drink at Wonder Lake in what has become Alaska's best-known attraction.*

4 Denali National Park and Preserve

Alaska's best-known attraction, this park was created as Mount McKinley National Park in 1917, primarily to protect the Dall sheep and other wild animals.

Mount McKinley, the highest peak in North America (20,320 feet), is usually wreathed in clouds, but this remains one of the nation's most magnificent parks.

Wildlife can be seen almost anywhere along the road, but there are no guarantees. To avoid undue disturbance of the animals, private vehicle access is limited. The best way to see the park is via an inexpensive shuttle bus from the park entrance. Visitors are encouraged to stop first at the visitors center. Along the 90-mile park road, which traverses a glorious natural tapestry of stunningly colorful tundra wildflowers and offers marvelous scenery, visitors may spot Dall sheep on Igloo Mountain, grizzlies (brown bears) at Sable Pass and many other sites, moose along the eastern section of the road, and caribou. A visitor may also spy Alaska's state bird, the willow ptarmigan, or a golden eagle. It is a rare privilege to see wolves, but other canines—the park's sled dogs, used for winter patrols—demonstrate their work three times daily from Memorial Day to Labor Day.

Open year-round. Park road passable only in summer and early fall.
(907) 683-2294
www.nps.gov/dena

5 Denali State Park

George Parks Hwy. (Hwy. 3)

The Athabascan word for Mount McKinley is *Denali,* "the high one." The peak itself was named in 1896 for the presidential nominee William McKinley, but this 324,420-acre park—almost one-half the size of Rhode Island—is called by its American Indian name.

From the highway bisecting the park, particularly from the Ruth Glacier overlook, you can see the snow-mantled upper slopes of the great mountain and its companion peaks and the many glaciers flowing from them. But in the summer, clouds veil Mount McKinley's soaring summit most of the time.

Nonetheless, with the perpetual snow line at just 8,000 feet, the other white-topped peaks of the Alaska Range create magnificent views along the highway and park hiking trails. Byers Lake is the center of most recreation in the park. A five-mile trail circles the lake and provides hiking access to another scenic path up Curry Ridge. Black bears and grizzlies inhabit the park, together with moose, wolves, and smaller mammals such as foxes, lynx, and beavers. Bears can be troublesome along Troublesome Creek Trail, when they gather here for the salmon that spawn in July and August. All posted precautions regarding bears should be carefully followed.

Open year-round except mid-July–Aug. due to bears in the area.
(907) 745-3975
www.dnr.state.ak.us/parks/units/denali.htm

6 Sheep Mountain

Mileposts 107 to 123 on Glenn Hwy.

Dall sheep, cousins of the Rocky Mountain bighorn, are easy to spot here, for in spring and summer their white coats stand out sharply against the green vegetation or rust and yellow rocks of this highly mineralized mountain just north of the highway.

The sheep are most numerous in early and late summer. If you don't have a good pair of binoculars, you might want to use the viewing telescope at Sheep Mountain Lodge (Milepost 113.5).

From Caribou Creek (Milepost 107) a hiking trail winds up the 6,300-foot mountain, and you can look down on the valley from the sheep's perspective. Road passable year-round.

(907) 822-3461

www.state.ak.us/adfg/wildlife/geninfo/viewing/sheepmt.html

7 Independence Mine State Historical Park

Wasilla—17 ½ miles along Fishhook-Willow Rd. (3 ½ miles unpaved) from Glenn Hwy.

Hard-rock mining—in this case wresting ore from the heart of a mountain—is a difficult operation, as evidenced by these gold mine buildings, ruined and reconstructed, perched above the treeline in the Talkeetna Mountains.

The first lode claim in the Willow Creek Valley was staked in 1906 in the quartz veins high along the west side of Fishhook Creek and became the Alaska Free Gold (Martin) Mine; nearby claims, which were staked on the east side of Granite Mountain in 1908, became the Independence Mine.

By 1938 both mines were controlled by the Alaska-Pacific Consolidated Mining Company. In 1941, its biggest year, the 200-man camp produced gold worth $1,686,790 (in today's dollars, worth $17 million). Second only to Juneau's AJ Mine in producing hard-rock Alaskan gold, Independence brought forth a total of 10,300 pounds before closing in 1951.

In 1980 new gold mining nearby stimulated the creation of the state historical park here and the renovation of the existing buildings. The red-roofed mine manager's house, restored to its 1942 appearance, has old photos, artifacts, a simulated gold mine tunnel, and displays showing how the gold was extracted, milled, and shipped. Other buildings include mess halls, bunkhouses, the sheet-metal shop, and the old assay office, now a hard-rock mining museum.

Park open year-round. Visitors center open only during the summer, 11 A.M.–7 P.M. daily.

(907) 745-2827

www.dnr.state.ak.us/parks/units/indmine.html

8 Matanuska Valley

Palmer

Nineteen hours of summer sun and loamy soil promised rich harvests when the federal government established the Matanuska Valley Colony in 1935. In May of that year, some 200 families who had lost their farms in the economic turmoil of the Great Depression were selected to go north to build new lives. Most of them came from Minnesota, Michigan, and Wisconsin, where they were assumed to have become familiar with farming in very cold climates. Some of the colonists failed, but others were successful. Many of the latter, or their children, still live in the Matanuska Valley, and a few are still on their original farms. Some of the original structures from the pioneer colony, including a church and a typical barn, have been moved to Colony Village on the Alaska State Fairgrounds at Palmer.

More significant as a memorial are the lush crops flanking the country roads backed by rugged mountains. If you happen to be there for the state fair in August, you'll see Matanuska Valley cabbages weighing in at 75 pounds or more. The Matanuska Glacier, one of Alaska's largest, can be viewed from Mile 103 on the Glenn Highway, 58 miles east of Palmer.

Accessible by road year-round.

(907) 745-2880

www.palmerchamber.org

8 Matanuska Valley. *The Matanuska Glacier, one of Alaska's largest, can be viewed from Mile 103 on the Glenn Highway.*

9 Eklutna Historical Park and Heritage Center

Eklutna

The name of this small Dena'ina Athabascan Indian village means "mouth of river between two hills," but today it is tucked away beside the active Glenn Highway. Here is the St. Nicholas Russian Orthodox Church, the second oldest in Alaska, built in Anchorage in the 1830s and later moved to its present location. What makes this place especially distinctive are the brightly painted "spirit houses" that mark the graves in the churchyard. Some of the little structures are multistoried and some have glass windows; they contain a variety of objects that belonged to the deceased but have no letters or dates to identify the dead person. Rather, each spirit house follows a particular family's design, and this is how parishioners know who is buried where. A tiny, hand-hewn log prayer chapel also stands in the churchyard.

(907) 688-6026

www.eklutnainc.com

ALASKA

⑭ Kenai Fjords National Park. *The Kenai mountains rise above a lake in the park, which is the gateway to nearly 670,000 acres of glaciers.*

⑩ Kenai National Wildlife Refuge

Soldotna

This refuge used to be called Kenai National Moose Range. Although the name has changed, there are still thousands of these fascinating animals (the largest of which can weigh 1,400 pounds) roaming the area. They are most commonly seen along the Swanson River and Skilak Loop roads (both gravel), and smaller roads that branch from the Sterling Highway.

Thousands of lakes spangle amid this wilderness of nearly 2 million acres. Many, such as Bottenintnin Lake, reflect the Kenai Mountains, glacier-accented peaks on the refuge's boundary with Kenai Fjords National Park. Large, graceful trumpeter swans glide across the lakes, and the haunting call of the loon can be heard.

Dall sheep and mountain goats are common above a marked observation point near Kenai Lake, on the Sterling Highway east of the refuge boundary. Beluga whales are often seen from Fort Kenay Overlook, above the mouth of the Kenai River in the town of Kenai.

Waterproof boots are suggested for hikers, for many of the 200 miles of trails are often swampy. Berry picking is popular in late summer and fall. Designated canoe routes wind along the refuge river and lake system, and chartered floatplanes provide access to some of the lovely remote lakes.

Open year-round. Visitors center open year-round also.
(907) 262-7021
http://kenai.fws.gov

⑪ Anchorage Coastal Wildlife Refuge

New Seward Hwy. (Hwy. 1), 12 miles south of downtown Anchorage
This bird-watching area within Alaska's largest city is host to trumpeter swans, bald eagles, Canada geese, ducks, gulls, terns, and shorebirds, as well as mink, muskrats, and salmon. Migrating birds make spring the best time to visit, but wildlife enthusiasts with cameras and binoculars will likely be rewarded at any time of the year.

The refuge attracts its many species of birds primarily because there are four distinct habitats within the 2,300 acres. Geese are drawn to the salt marsh along Turnagain Arm (an inlet of spectacular beauty). Mallards and other ducks flock to the freshwater marsh created in 1917, when the Alaska Railroad was constructed and its roadbed became a dike. Muskegs in the transition area between marsh and dryland harbor snipe, grouse, and sandpipers. Such deciduous trees as birch, alder, willow, and cottonwood support warblers, thrushes, and other songbirds in the wooded areas. And of course these habitats each support a distinctive community of plants. The refuge is served by Anchorage's bus system, and there are turnouts overlooking Potter Marsh.
Open year-round.
(907) 267-2182
www.state.ak.us/local/akpages/fish.game/
wildlife/region2/refuge2/acwr.html

⑫ Crow Creek Mine

Along Crow Creek Rd., which branches off Alyeska ski area road 1.9 miles from its junction with Seward Hwy. (Hwy. 1)
Placer gold mining began in Crow Creek around 1895; at its peak the area produced more than 700 ounces per month. Although owner Cynthia Toohey maintains that there is still more gold available than ever was removed, her mine has not been operated commercially in more than 20 years. Visitors from all over the world, however, still pan for "color" here, and half-ounce nuggets may still be found glittering in the gravel. All the necessary gold-panning equipment can be rented at the mine.

Listed on the *National Register of Historic Places,* the mine preserves its original equipment and buildings, which were the first non–American Indian structures in the Anchorage area. Today the rugged authenticity of the site is softened somewhat by the mine's beautiful flower gardens. They splash bright color against the dark greens of the surrounding spruce and hemlock rain forest—a welcome function today, but one the old-timers, feverishly panning for color of another kind, would probably have found incomprehensible.
Open daily 9 A.M.– 6 P.M., May 15– Sept. 15. Admission charged.
(907) 278-8060
www.crowcreekgoldmine.com

⑬ Chugach State Park

This awesome wilderness in the Chugach Mountains, almost half a million acres of jagged peaks and alpine meadows, lakes, glaciers, and marshy tidal flats, shelters an abundant variety of wildlife. Its outstanding trails include part of the Old Iditarod Trail, used by dogsled teams to speed diphtheria serum to Nome in 1925. The segment of the trail outside the park is part of the course for the grueling Iditarod Dogsled Race, held annually in commemoration. Although the trails are easily accessible from heavily populated Anchorage, they are sufficiently numerous to remain peaceful even in summer.

Wildlife here includes beluga whales seeking fish in Turnagain Arm and mountain goats scaling the nearby precipices. Telescopes at the Eagle River Nature Center (reached from the Glenn Highway) focus on surrounding steep slopes where Dall sheep and black bears are normal sightings. Moose are plentiful, and there is a salmon-viewing deck a short way down a fine nature trail that begins at the attractive log visitors center.

The altitude in the park ranges from sea level to 8,000 feet, and the annual rainfall is from 70 inches in the east to 15 inches in the west. The resulting climatic zones nurture an astonishing and beautiful variety of trees, shrubs, wildflowers, lichens, and mosses.

Open year-round.
(907) 345-5014
www.dnr.state.ak.us

14 Kenai Fjords National Park

The gateway to the almost 670,000 acres of glaciers, mountains, ice fields, and some of the world's most spectacular coastline is the picturesque town of Seward. The park offers easy access to the groaning spires and ice-blue tongues of Exit Glacier, as well as to Bear Glacier, the largest of the more than

36 named glaciers flowing from the broad Harding Ice Field, and a popular destination for kayakers.

But the main attractions here are the deep, narrow fjords, which can be viewed on daylong boat trips from Seward. From scenic Resurrection Bay the boats pass tide-carved Three Hole Arch and enter Aialik Bay, where bald eagles dive for fish. At Chiswell Islands, in the Alaska Maritime National Wildlife Refuge, as many as 50,000 seabirds may nest, including black-legged kittiwakes, tufted and horned puffins, and black oyster catchers with carrotlike bills. Sea mammals often seen in the fjords include harbor seals and Steller's sea lions, killer and humpback whales, porpoises, and sea otters.

Park open year-round. Boats run mid-May–mid-Sept.; fare charged.
(907) 224-3175
www.nps.gov/kefj

15 Kachemak Bay State Park and State Wilderness Park

Homer
Wild and undeveloped, this 370,000-acre park offers majestic peaks, glaciers, and forests, and a rugged coastline with tides among the highest in the world. Access is by boat or floatplane from the fishing community of Homer, across the bay.

Perhaps the best introduction to the park's ecology is on a boat tour conducted by the China Poot Bay Society to its Center for Alaskan Coastal Studies. Twice daily a tour boat leaves Homer for a 45-minute ride to Gull Island, nesting site for thousands of puffins,

murres, gulls, and cormorants. On the way sightings of sea mammals (sea otters, seals, porpoises, whales) are common. The tour pauses near such sights as a bald-eagle nest in a spruce tree atop a wave-battered cliff.

At the center in Peterson Bay, a naturalist leads an exploration of pools teeming with life—giant

15 Kachemak Bay State Park. *An Alaskan king crab is part of the bounty of Kachemak Bay, one of the world's best producers of seafood.*

sunflower starfish, bright sea anemones, sea urchins, and moon snails—all revealed by a 15- to 28-foot drop of the tide. At high tide the tour ascends to trails in the rain forest and archaeological sites of ancient Tanaina Indians. The boat back to Homer may pause while the crew pulls up crab pots to harvest some of the bounty of Kachemak Bay.

Park open year-round. Boat runs summer only; fare charged.
For reservations write P.O. Box 1247, Homer, AK 99669 or call
(907) 235-7024
www.alaskastateparks.org

16 Fort Abercrombie State Historical Park

Off Rezanoff Dr. East, Kodiak
Alaska's largest island has attracted

a variety of invaders. The Alutiiq people were subjugated by Russian fur traders in 1784. In 1867 America broke tradition by buying the island from Russia, along with the rest of Alaska. Another invasion threatened when the Japanese attacked Pearl Harbor on December 7, 1941. As a result, the buildup of a new naval base, started in 1939, moved at a faster pace. Fort Abercrombie became one of the three main coastal defense installations on Kodiak Island.

Concrete bunkers, gun pits, and a massive eight-inch gun barrel, occasionally shrouded in Kodiak's ghostly fogs, are all that remain of this installation, where rust and the Sitka spruce rain forest now mount an invasion of their own. Although the site had little charm for the 8,000 soldiers stationed in Kodiak, its green, mysterious mood, a small meadow vibrant in summer with wildflowers, the crash of waves, and the cries of seabirds echoing from the cliffs below appeal to visitors today. Lake Gertrude is stocked with rainbow trout and grayling; rock bass can be caught near its outlet into the Pacific Ocean.

The Baranof House Museum, built around 1793 near Kodiak's harbor, and a Russian Orthodox church on the hill above preserve the Russian heritage here. A drive south of town along the island's only road reveals an extremely lovely stretch of rugged coast.

Open year-round.
(907) 486-6339
www.ptialaska.net/~kodsp/ftaber.html

17 Katmai National Park and Preserve

Fly from Anchorage to King Salmon, then hop a floatplane to Brooks Lodge on Naknek Lake.
On June 6, 1912, Novarupta Volcano exploded from the flank of Mount Katmai, scattering seven cubic miles of ash and pumice around the Northern Hemisphere and filling the nearby Ukak River valley 700 feet deep with ash; the

17 Katmai National Park and Preserve. *A grizzly bear gets ready to feast on some of the abundant salmon in Brooks Falls.*

summit of Mount Katmai collapsed, forming a caldera that now holds the blue waters of Crater Lake.

This was the second largest eruption in recorded history, but because of its remote location, there were no known casualties. Expeditions over the next few years explored the region, including the steaming Ukak River valley, which was named Valley of Ten Thousand Smokes. The area, made a national monument in 1918, has been enlarged into a national park

and preserve. The ash has cooled now, the fumaroles are depleted of their water vapor, and the valley no longer smokes.

Beyond the sheer vast beauty of the wilderness, the major attraction here is perhaps the great number of grizzly bears that come in the summer to feast on the abundant salmon. On their protein-rich diet, these magnificent, dangerous animals can attain a weight of

900 pounds; they are common around Brooks Lodge and the nearby Park Service campground during the July and late August salmon runs. Visitors should pay careful attention to the advice available in Park Service leaflets about how to behave in bear country.
Open daily June–early Sept.
Fees for van and plane tours.
(907) 246-2100
www.nps.gov/katm

18 Valdez

Port Valdez is one of the most northerly ice-free harbors in the Western Hemisphere, and huge tankers come here from around the world to take on oil at the marine terminal of the 800-mile trans-Alaska pipeline. At its completion the pipeline was the most expensive structure ever built by private endeavor, and one can visit its impressive terminal on two-hour bus tours from Valdez.

Set at the end of an 11-mile fjord, Valdez Arm is encircled by the dramatically sawtoothed peaks and shining glaciers of the Chugach Mountains. Sea otters and seals are common in the inlet, and kittiwakes, puffins, and bald eagles are abundant.

Valdez is also a terminus for a state ferry, the *E. L. Bartlett,* which crosses Prince William Sound past Columbia Glacier. This, the second largest tidewater glacier in Alaska, is retreating rapidly and drops many icebergs into the sound. A private tour boat, the *Glacier Queen,* also makes this run and detours to observe wildlife, including the large nesting colony of kittiwakes near the town of Whittier. Several campgrounds are found near Valdez.
The Bartlett *sails Valdez–Whittier daily except Tues. and Thurs. mid-May–mid-Sept; Valdez-Cordova two to four days a week year-round. Boat and pipeline terminal tours in summer only.*
Fees charged.
(800) 770-5954
www.valdezalaska.org

19 Wrangell–St. Elias National Park & Preserve

This is our largest national park, overwhelming in its size (its 13.2

million acres stretch north for 170 miles from the Gulf of Alaska) and in the wild, astonishing grandeur of its scenery.

Wrangell–St. Elias, Kluane National Park in Canada, Glacier Bay National Park, and Tatshenshini-Alsek Park in British Columbia are together a United Nations World Heritage area. Among them they include 10 of the continent's highest peaks and the greatest wealth of mountains, canyons, and glaciers in North America. The park's highest peak is the towering 18,008-foot Mount St. Elias, the second highest peak in the United States.

Road access to the wilderness is from Slana in the north and from Chitina in the west. From Slana the normally well-maintained gravel road crosses the tundra to Nabesna, a small mining settlement. Inquire at the Slana Ranger Station about conditions on this lovely 45-mile trip, which requires some stream fording.

About 10 miles off Nabesna Road is Tanada Lake, where the fishing, especially for grayling, is as rewarding as the scenery and the views of wildlife. The hiking trail to the lake may be muddy and difficult, and the easiest access is by charter floatplane. A lodge and cabins are available in summer.

From Chitina the dirt road toward McCarthy runs for 65 miles (five hours) through superb scenery along an old railroad route. Vehicles with high clearance should have no trouble in summer, though flat tires can be a problem on such back roads. Good highways follow the western and northern borders of the park and offer spectacular views of shield and strato volcanoes: Mount Drum, more than 12,000 feet high, and Mount Wrangell,

ALASKA

 Wrangell–St. Elias National Park & Preserve. *An ice cave is part of the astonishing scenery at Bagley Ice Field.*

more than 14,000 feet.

Summers are cool and can be rainy and foggy. July is the warmest month, but the mosquitoes can be out in force. August may have even more rain but fewer bugs.

Open year-round. For information on accommodations and charter flights in the park, write Superintendent, Wrangell–St. Elias National Park and Preserve, 106.8 Richardson Hwy., P.O. Box 439, Copper Center, AK 99573. (907) 822-5234

www.nps.gov/wrst

20 Klondike Gold Rush National Historical Park

Skagway

When gold fever struck in 1897–98, some 20,000 to 30,000 adventurers came through Skagway to brave the Chilkoot and White Pass trails on their way to the Klondike goldfields. They suffered immense hardship, many died, and only a very few got rich. But Skagway prospered, as did nearby Dyea at the head of the trail that crosses the Chilkoot Pass into Canada.

The park commemorating the gold rush includes the Skagway Historic District, Dyea (now in ruins), and the American portion of the Chilkoot Trail, as well as Pioneer Square in Seattle, where so many dreamers made plans for the trip north. For many the dreams ended here in Skagway, where some 80 saloons and gambling halls and the notorious "Soapy" Smith and his cronies

were all willing and able to relieve the unwary of their grubstakes.

The aura of those days pervades the Skagway Historic District, with its boardwalks and old false-fronted buildings. A walking tour includes the restored railroad depot (home of the park visitors center), the Mascot Saloon, Goldberg's Cigar Store, and the Arctic Brotherhood Hall, whose Victorian façade is uniquely embellished with thousands of bits of driftwood.

The Skagway Museum in the city hall houses relics of pioneer days and the gold stampede. The native cultures in Alaska are represented by the arts and crafts of the Eskimos, Aleuts, Athapaskans, and the coastal Tlingit and Haida Indians.

The Chilkoot Trail, open when weather permits, is an extremely strenuous 33-mile hike that takes from three to five days and is recommended only for the most experienced backpackers. There are, however, several other hiking trails into the hills outside of Skagway.

Historic district open year-round. (907) 983-2921

www.nps.gov/klgo

21 Fort William H. Seward

Haines

With the gold rush and a growing salmon industry, Alaska's population doubled in the 1890s. In 1903 the U.S. Army began construction of a fort at Haines on land that was deeded to the government by the Presbyterian Board of National Missions. It was dedicated the following year as Fort William H. Seward, honoring the Secretary of State

whose folly it had been to purchase Alaska from the Russian government in 1867.

The first contingent of soldiers arrived in September, and the fort then became the regimental headquarters for all of Alaska. In 1922 it was renamed Chilkoot Barracks to avoid confusion with the town of Seward.

World War II saw new military installations in Alaska, and Chilkoot consequently became an induction center and rest camp. Years later it was deactivated in favor of newer, more strategically placed installations.

Now on the *National Register of Historic Places,* its stately white buildings and nine-acre parade ground, backed by the awesome, towering peaks of the Chilkat Range, still form an imposing sight. Several buildings have been put to new uses, such as an artist's studio and crafts workshop (where you can actually see totem poles being carved). Totem Village, with its totem poles and a Tlingit tribal house, is the home of the well-known Chilkat Dancers, who perform traditional dances of the Northwest Coastal Indians.

The Haines area is noted for its eagles. At the 48,000-acre preserve, about 20 miles up the Haines Highway, as many as 3,500 bald eagles, the largest gathering in the world, feed on the spawning salmon. Although the best time to see them is from October through January, they are also numerous in spring and early summer.

Fort open year-round. (800) 458-3579

www.haines.ak.us

22 Glacier Bay National Park and Preserve

Gustavus

This primeval wilderness of more than 1.3 million acres is accessible from Juneau or Haines. It is a short flight from Juneau to Gustavus and a 10-minute bus ride to the lodge and headquarters at Bartlett Cove. From Haines, it takes about 45 minutes by air.

Sixteen glaciers feed into the inlets of the bay, and there are daily boat trips to the glacier "snouts," precipitous ice cliffs that "calve" 220-foot-high bergs into the tidal inlets.

Park naturalists explain how glaciers are formed and how they advance and retreat. In this area most of the ice is now retreating (200 years ago it was up to 4,000 feet thick here), and in its wake have come many seabirds and such mammals as mountain goats, brown and black bears, marmots, river otters, mink, harbor seals, whales, and porpoises. Black bears are most readily observed on the floatplane "flightseeing" trips from the lodge or while on a day cruise. Also near the lodge are trails leading through the moss-draped rain forest to the beach: Be sure to bring waterproof footwear and rain gear.

Among the birds that favor the forest are grouse, woodpeckers, thrushes, and golden-crowned kinglets, but overall more than 200 species have been observed. When the 25-foot tides in Bartlett Cove are out, they reveal a fascinating variety of starfish, sea urchins, and other tide-pool creatures.

Open year-round. Glacier Bay Lodge open late May–late Sept. For reservations, write Glacier Bay Lodge, 107 West Denny Way, Suite 303, Seattle, WA 98119.

(800) 451-5952 or (907) 297-2230

23 Juneau

Long before 1880, when Joe Juneau struck gold here, the Tlingit Indians knew the area, with its spectacular scenery and plentiful fish. Today a cosmopolitan port where bears roam freely within a 10-minute walk of the state capitol, Juneau offers a unique mix of cultural and wilderness attractions.

The Alaska State Museum reflects the area's diversity with displays on wildlife, the region's Indian and Russian heritage, and the gold rush of the 1880s and 1890s. At the octagonal St. Nicholas Russian Orthodox Church, built in 1894, you can see handsome icons and other church relics. The U.S. Forest Service desk at Centennial Hall gives information about hiking, camping, and other outdoor recreational opportunities and has logging, fishing, and mining displays.

Tour buses run to Mendenhall Glacier, making it one of the continent's most accessible ice fields. Its cold blue face rises some 100 feet above the waters of Mendenhall Lake. Telescopes at the nearby visitors center enable you to get a detailed look at the glacier and, with luck, a view of mountain goats atop Mount Bullard in the distance. Hiking trails lead back into the woods. Arctic terns perform aerial acrobatics during the spring nesting period, and in autumn bald eagles fish for salmon in nearby Steep Creek.

For information about "salmon bakes" (uniquely Alaskan seafood feasts), scenic plane rides, charter fishing, Glacier Bay tours, and other area activities, check with the visitors center in Centennial Hall, 101 Egan Drive.

(888) 581-2201

www.traveljuneau.com

24 Admiralty Island National Monument

Juneau

The Tlingit Indians call this island *Xootsnoowu*—"Bear Fortress"—and certainly the name is apt. Almost 100 miles long and 30 wide, the island is indeed a unique place of thick forest, lakes, streams, inlets, estuaries, bogs, alpine meadows, and snowcapped peaks rising above the treeline. Relatively few trails penetrate its nearly 1 million acres, and there are no roads of significant length. Most travel is by boat.

The island's dominant residents are some 1,500 huge Alaskan brown bears. Frequently bears can be observed fishing near a viewing stand at the mouth of Pack Creek. Some 500 to 600 bald eagles are hatched here annually, more than in the entire lower 48 states. Deer, seals, sea lions, and river otters are often seen. The waterways yield an abundance of fish, crabs, and shrimp.

The jumping-off spot for visiting the bear viewing area is Juneau, where visitors can charter floatplanes for the journey to Pack Creek. Visitors who are traveling with outfitter guides can also go by kayak or in outfitters' boats.

Because the island is a remote and vast wilderness, careful preparations should be made before you visit. Forest cabins on Admiralty can be reserved through the National Recreation Reservation

22 Glacier Bay National Park and Preserve. *Boat trips are offered daily to the precipitous ice cliffs that calve 220-foot-high bergs into the tidal inlets.*

Service at (877) 444-6777.
Open year-round.
(907) 586-8800
**www.fs.fed.us/r10/tongass/districts/
admiralty/packweb**

25 Sitka

In 1804 Alexander Baranof, the manager of a Russian fur trading company, burned the Tlingit Indian fort here and reestablished the Russian colony the Tlingits had destroyed two years earlier. Sitka became the foremost city on the North American Pacific Coast, the capital of a colonial empire founded on sea otter pelts. Eventually, however, overhunting ruined the fur trade, and in 1867 the Russians sold Alaska to the United States for $7.2 million in gold. The official transfer took place on Castle Hill, overlooking Sitka's harbor, on October 18— Alaska Day, celebrated annually in Sitka with five days of pageant and ceremony.

Today Sitka retains much of its czarist and Tlingit heritage. Russian cannon face the harbor from atop the Castle Hill National Historic Site, and the colorfully costumed New Archangel Dancers perform Russian folk dances at the Harrigan Centennial Hall. St. Michael's Russian Orthodox Cathedral dominates the downtown area, and the Bishop's House, built in 1842 for Alaska's first Russian Orthodox bishop, is maintained by Sitka National Historical Park. Within the park is the site of the Tlingit fort and a lovely two-mile forest trail lined with magnificent totem poles. Crafts and artifacts of the Tlingits and other regional tribes are displayed at the park's Southeast Alaska

Indian Cultural Centers. The park's visitors center features exhibits on Sitka's history, and a world-famous collection of tribal masks is found at the nearby state-run Sheldon Jackson Museum.
Park open year-round except Thanksgiving, Christmas, and New Year's Day.
(907) 747-5940
www.sitka.org

26 Tongass Historical Museum and Totem Heritage Center

Ketchikan. Museum at 629 Dock St.; Heritage Center at 601 Deermount St.
Anyone interested in Northwest Indian art should not miss the excellent collections in these museums. The material in the Tongass Historical Museum is largely from three highly creative peoples: the Haidas, Tlingits, and Tsimshians. The totems, tools, baskets, and ceremonial objects displayed here are among the best of their kind. Also shown are exhibits related to the history of the town of Ketchikan.

In the Totem Heritage Center some 30 totem poles, house posts, and fragments from Tlingit and Haida villages can be seen in their unrestored state. These great totems, carved from the trunks of red cedar trees, indicate personal status and clan relationships and serve as memorials. They are unique to the Pacific Northwest and are widely celebrated for their emotional power and strength of design.

The center conducts workshops where established native artists teach the traditional skills of carving, basketry, and engraving.
Museum open daily May 1–Sept. 30; Wed.–Fri. 1–5, Oct.1–Apr. 30 except Thanksgiving and Christmas. Heritage

25 Sitka. *The Coast Mountains shelter Sky Boat Harbor in a city that retains much of its Russian and Tlingit heritage.*

Center open daily May 15–Sept. 30; Tues.–Fri. 1–5, Oct. 1–May 14.
(907) 225-5900
Historical Museum:
www.city.ketchikan.ak.us/ds/tonghist/index.html

27 Misty Fiords National Monument

Ketchikan
Nearly 13 feet (that's 156 inches) of precipitation drench Misty Fiords annually, adding to the abundant water provided by melting glaciers and ice fields. The fiords are narrow ocean inlets carved by ice age glaciers. The nearly vertical granite cliffs lining their shores tower to a height of 3,000 feet. Cloud-wreathed waterfalls spangle amid the soaring precipices.

All but the steepest slopes are covered by an evergreen rain forest broken only by glacially excavated lakes and muskegs. Even above the tree line (2,000 to 3,000 feet

above sea level), the land is covered with shrubs and grasses that provide summer pasture for Sitka black-tailed deer. Other wildlife includes bears, bald eagles, and mountain goats, and the waters abound with trout, salmon, sea lions, porpoises, and whales.

Most visitors arrive by boat or floatplane from Ketchikan, about 30 air miles away. There are no roads, but seven short hiking trails penetrate the rugged terrain of this 2.3-million-acre wilderness. The U.S. Forest Service maintains 14 rustic cabins scattered throughout the monument.
Monument accessible year-round but lakes not accessible in winter. For information and cabin reservations, contact Southeast Alaska Discovery Center, 50 Main St., Ketchikan, AK 99901.
(877) 444-6777
(907) 228-6220
www.fs.fed.us/r10/tongass/

Boyce Thompson Arboretum State Park. *Here the desert blooms year-round (see page 30).*

Arizona

Ghost towns and prehistoric ruins are juxtaposed with forests of cacti, Joshua trees, and petrified logs.

For centuries this seemingly arid land was home to semi-nomadic agrarian people who built cliff dwellings and other communities; although these now stand in ruins, they still evoke a sense of wonder.

The architectural heritage of the early white settlers is of another character. There are a few towns where the aura of the rough-and-ready miners still prevails.

Nature's bold design is revealed in sizable tracts of the dramatic saguaro cactus, the organ-pipe cactus, and the Joshua tree. These and many other fascinating desert plants are displayed in an excellent arboretum. There are also inviting canyons, where desert plants and lush greenery grow almost side by side. Further visual delights create a great display of erosional sculpture and a forest of trees turned to stone.

1 Navajo National Monument
Rte. 564, Kayenta

Although the Navajos became one of the most powerful tribes in the Southwest, they are relative newcomers, migrating south from their Canadian homeland in the 1400s. Sometime later they discovered the ruins of villages built by the Anasazis and moved in.

A half-mile trail (open year-round) leads to an overlook with a fine view of Betatakin ("ledge house" in Navajo) across the canyon. Nestled in a great alcove in the face of a sheer sandstone cliff, it looks like a fairy-tale setting, rosy-colored and tucked into its niche as if put there by the hands of a giant. You can visit the ruin itself only on guided tours conducted by park rangers. Tours are given from May through September. The outing requires a strenuous four- to five-hour round-trip hike; keep in mind that the elevation here is 7,300 feet.

The ruins of Keet Seel ("broken pieces of pottery" in Navajo) are even more remote and are open only from Memorial Day through Labor Day. The trail is an arduous eight miles. You can go and return in a day or camp near the ruins overnight. Only 20 people per day are allowed to visit the site, and permits and reservations are required.

Inscription House, the other ruin here, has become so fragile

3 Hubbell Trading Post National Historic Site. *The oldest in the Navajo Nation, this continuously active trading post sells Navajo, Zuni, and Hopi crafts, along with groceries and supplies.*

that it is closed to the public. The visitors center museum presents the history and lifestyle of the Navajos with a slide show and various displays.
Park and visitors center open daily except Thanksgiving, Christmas, and New Year's Day.
(602) 672-2700
www.nps.gov/nava

2 Canyon de Chelly National Monument
Headquarters 3 miles east of Chinle on Rte. 7

Of all the spectacular canyons in Arizona, Canyon de Chelly is in the eyes of many the most breathtakingly beautiful. Two scenic roadways branching from the monument headquarters lead to overlooks offering magnificent views of deep, vertical-walled canyons, sandstone spires towering from 700 to 800 feet, the Rio de Chelly flowing through the winding valley floor, and the mellow Anasazi ruins snugly sheltered along the face of the cliffs.

Since Navajos live and farm within the monument, visitors are allowed in some areas only when they are accompanied by an authorized guide. An exception is the White House Trail, which zigzags down the cliff to the canyon floor 600 feet below. Impossible though it seems from above, the path is perfectly safe, provided you are wearing appropriate shoes.

For a close-up view of Anasazi cliff dwellings, wade across the Rio de Chelly and follow a path along the river for about 100 yards. You'll find some ruins at the base of the cliff near the river's edge. Overhead you'll see the White House ruins (so-called because one of the houses is finished with a white plaster) perched on a deep ledge in the towering wall of sandstone. The climb back up the cliff is a little arduous, but the entire adventure is memorable. Check at the visitors center for flash-flood warnings before you begin the trek. Hiking trips and four-wheel-drive excursions can be arranged. Reservations should be made in advance.
(928) 674-5500

www.nps.gov/cach

3 Hubbell Trading Post National Historic Site
Rte. 264, Ganado
A visit to the trading post on this 160-acre homestead evokes its heyday, when the post was the social center for Navajos.

Established in the late 1870s by John Lorenzo Hubbell, it is the oldest continuously active trading post in the Navajo Nation. Now owned by the National Park Service, it sells not only groceries and other supplies but also Navajo, Zuni, and Hopi crafts—turquoise and silver jewelry, rugs, blankets, and baskets. Both English and

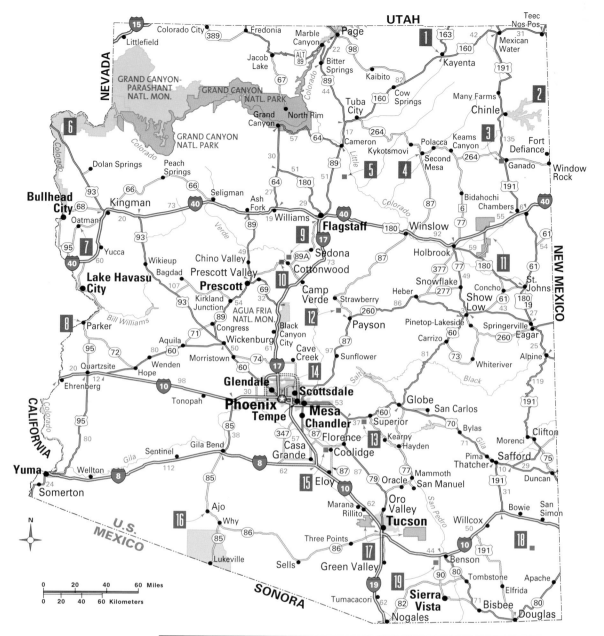

Navajo are spoken.

You can take a self-guiding tour of the compound to see the bunkhouse, storage buildings, corral, barn, and the yard, with its assortment of old buggies and farm equipment. Free guided tours are given of the Hubbell home, which looks much as it did 100 years ago. It has rough-hewn timbered ceilings and

is filled with excellent American Indian craftwork.
(928) 755-3475

www.nps.gov/hutr

Open daily except Thanksgiving, Christmas, and New Year's Day.

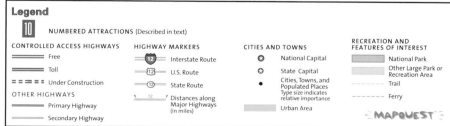

4 Hopi Cultural Center
Second Mesa

The Hopis are believed to be descendants of a farming people who first settled in the Southwest some 1,500 to 1,600 years ago. Today the Hopi villages, a fascinating mixture of modern technology and ancient architecture, are centered on three towering desert mesas.

The Hopi Cultural Center at Second Mesa has a museum that also serves as an informal visitors center for the entire reservation. The displays recount the tribe's long history, from the earliest times through the Navajo, Spanish, and American invasions of its homeland.

One of the most popular exhibits concerns the kachinas, deities central to the Hopi religion. Exquisite craft displays include examples of Hopi bridal clothes and finely wrought jewelry pieces, pottery, and basketry. Both the museum and the nearby Hopi Arts and Crafts Guild offer opportunities to observe various craftsmen at work.

Tours to various Hopi villages are available. Inquire at the museum to find out which places welcome tourists.

Museum open daily, but the schedule may be erratic from Nov.–Jan. Admission charged.
(928) 734-2401
www.hopionline.com

5 Wupatki National Monument
Flagstaff

In 1064 a nearby volcanic eruption sent clouds of ash and cinders into the sky, causing the local Sinagua people to flee. The ash settled over 800 square miles, and when the Sinaguas returned, they found that the ash retained moisture, improved the soil, and made their farms more productive. The area attracted American Indians from neighboring regions and became a cultural melting pot. Wupatki grew to be a major pueblo, eventually rising to four stories in some places and containing more than 100 rooms. But less than 100 years later the residents were forced to leave again, probably because of severe drought. By 1225 Wupatki and the surrounding villages had been abandoned.

At the 56-square-mile Wupatki National Monument you may tour the pueblo ruins and see the amphitheater, the ball court, and several typical rooms. A roadway leads to other archaeological sites, among them several fortified pueblos, and continues 18 miles to Sunset Crater National Monument, the site of the volcanic eruption in 1064. Mineral deposits around the crater's rim give the upper slopes the glowing coloration of a sunset—from which the crater takes its name. Although no hiking is allowed on the volcano's cone, a one-mile loop trail leads through the lava beds. A campground is maintained near the visitors center.

Monuments open year-round; visitors centers open daily except Christmas. Campground open year-round.
(928) 679-2365
www.nps.gov/wupa

6 Hualapai Valley Joshua Trees
Turn east off Rte. 93 onto Pearce Ferry Road for Dolan Springs

Believe it or not, these odd-looking prickly trees are members of the lily family. They can grow to 40 feet and bear beautiful greenish yellow or cream-colored flowers in spring. According to legend, the Mormons gave the tree its biblical name because its form, with upraised branches, suggested the prophet Joshua at prayer.

You'll spot the first Joshua trees slightly beyond Dolan Springs. As you continue, the trees become larger and more frequent until finally, some 20 miles down the road, you'll find yourself in a veritable forest. The strangeness of the scene is enhanced by the spectacular backdrop of the Grand Wash Cliffs. There are facilities, but you are otherwise on your own in the desert's solitude. The elevation is about 4,000 feet, so the heat is not oppressive. The area is named for the Hualapai American Indians, who have a reservation nearby.

(928) 767-4473
www.dolansprings.com

7 Oatman

Founded in 1906 on the western slopes of the Black Mountains, Oatman was an important mining town and served as the business center for several surrounding communities. By 1931 the area is said to have had 15,000 inhabitants, to have produced 1.8 million ounces of gold, and even to have engendered its own stock exchange. In 1942 the mines were closed for good.

The town has become something of a tourist center, with cafés, artists' studios, craft shops, and snack bars now occupying many of the original buildings. Along Main Street, which stretches up a hillside, there are boarded-up entrances to the old mines, and wild burros, descendants of those brought by the first prospectors, roam the street looking for handouts. Gunfights are staged on the weekends in this authentic old-Western town. Film companies, taking advantage of the spectacular mountain scenery and the turn-of-the-century buildings, have produced several movies here, including *How the West Was Won.*

From the main highway, the 28-mile drive to Oatman includes eight miles of rough mountain road with sharp switchbacks that can be treacherous if one is distracted by the scenery.

(928) 768-6222
www.gazetteg.com/rt66

7 Oatman. *This early 18th-century mining town now serves tourists and artists.*

8 Colorado River Indian Tribes Museum

Second Ave. and Mojave Rd., Parker

Four different tribes live on the Colorado River Indian Reservation, which spreads into California. The Mojaves, Navajos, Hopis, and the southern Paiutes, known here as Chemehuevis, share a tract of nearly 300,000 acres. The purpose of the museum is to depict the characteristic lifestyles, histories, and cultural attributes that distinguish the varied heritages of these four.

Costumes and models of the traditional homes of each tribe are shown, along with historic artifacts. The nearby ghost town of La Paz has contributed some pieces from long ago. Among the outstanding crafts displayed are Mojave beadwork, Hopi kachina dolls, Navajo rugs, and Chemehuevi baskets. Many crafts are for sale.

Open Mon.–Fri. except holidays.
(928) 669-9211, Ext. 1335
www.crittourismarraz.net

9 Tuzigoot National Monument
Clarkdale

Atop a barren ridge 120 feet above the Verde Valley are the ruins of a town constructed by the Sinagua—farmers and artisans who moved into the valley about A.D. 900. Around 1000 they began building the pueblo at Tuzigoot (an Apache name meaning "crooked water") using stone and clay. Originally it housed about 50 people, but by 1300 it had grown to 11 rooms and accommodated a population of 270. Even at this point there were few doorways; the rooms were entered by ladders through hatchways in the ceilings. The

village flourished for another 100 years before the Sinaguas abandoned the valley; their descendants were probably absorbed by pueblos to the north.

The small visitors center displays an extensive collection of artifacts recovered from the site. A furnished reconstruction of a typical pueblo room vividly portrays Sinagua daily life. An easy quarter-mile loop trail leads from the visitors center to the ruins, where the interior of the pueblo may be viewed.

Open year-round except Christmas.
Admission charged.
(928) 634-5564
www.nps.gov/tuzi

10 Jerome State Historic Park

Once a booming mining town at what was thought to be the richest copper deposit in the world, Jerome is now a booming ghost town. After the last large mining operation closed in 1953, a few residents stayed on and kept the town alive. Today its Main Street attracts tourists with craft shops, art galleries, and cafés behind its picturesquely weathered and dilapidated storefronts.

Begin your visit at the Jerome State Historic Park. This hilltop estate was the home of James S. "Rawhide" Douglas, the owner of one of the two major mines. Exhibits in the museum here tell the entertaining story of a town that went from boom to bust about as often as other towns elect mayors—mine claims, money crises, great finds, great losses, price crashes, fires, and buyouts were commonplace.

Historic photographs trace

11 Petrified Forest National Park. *Petrified logs rest on sandstone pedestals in Blue Mesa.*

Jerome's development from a tent camp to a town of 15,000 with an opera house, theater, baseball fields, churches, and plenty of saloons. A model depicts the mines and shows almost 90 miles of tunnels below.

The short drive from the highway to Jerome is magnificently scenic, and from the town's precarious perch on the steep slopes of Cleopatra's Hill, there are panoramic views across the valley.

Museum open 8 A.M.–5 P.M. daily except Christmas. Admission charged.
(928) 634-5381
www.pr.state.az.us/parkhtml/jerome.html

11 Petrified Forest National Park

The park's geological story began over 225 million years ago, when pinelike trees were carried by waterways here and buried in the silt of a huge flood plain. The silica-rich waters slowly penetrated the logs' cell tissue. Eventually the silica hardened, turning the logs into a stony substance aglow with a rainbow of colors. An upthrusting of the earth's crust, followed by millions of years of erosion, created the area's magnificent sandstone buttes and exposed the logs.

Rainbow Forest Museum, at the southern end of the 28-mile road traversing the park, has exhibits explaining the area's geological and human history. Extraordinary specimens of petrified logs may be seen along the half-mile Giant Logs Trail, just behind the museum. A half-mile trail leads to Agate House, the colorful ruins of a pueblo built from petrified wood, and Long Logs, where the ancient timbers have remained remarkably intact. Also included in the park's 93,533 acres is the multihued Painted Desert.

One of the most beautiful areas is Blue Mesa, 12 miles north along the park road. Here erosion has left the petrified logs resting on sandstone pedestals. Trails lead from the mesa top to the desert floor.

A mile farther up the road is Puerco Pueblo, built around A.D. 800. The half-mile loop trail will take you past the partially excavated site.

Open daily, except Christmas.
Admission charged.
(928) 524-6228
www.nps.gov/pefo

12 Tonto Natural Bridge State Park

Off Highway 87, just 10 miles north of Payson

Tucked away in a tiny valley surrounded by a forest of pine trees, Tonto Natural Bridge is a rare geological wonder. In the making for thousands of years, it is believed to be the largest bridge in the world built entirely of sedimentary rock.

Formed from layers of lava and purple quartz sandstone and supported by limestone aquifers, the bridge stands 183 feet high over a 400-foot-long tunnel that measures 150 feet at its widest point. This amazing work of natural architecture was officially discovered in 1877. A prospector, David Gowan, stumbled across the bridge while being chased by Apaches. After hiding in one of the bridge's several caves for three days, Gowan emerged to explore the surrounding green valley and promptly claimed squatter's rights.

Today visitors can stand on top of the bridge or hike down below to revel at its impressive size and stunning beauty. Hikers can choose from three trails.

For those eager to settle temporarily, the park's Historic Lodge offers a full dining room and 10 guest bedrooms.

Open year-round. Entrance fee.
(928) 476-4202
www.pr.state.az.us/parkhtml/tonto.html

13 Boyce Thompson Arboretum State Park

Rte. 60, west of Superior

This collection of cacti and other hot-climate plants was started in the 1920s by William Boyce Thompson, a mining magnate.

 Tonto Natural Bridge State Park. *Hikers can take Pine Creek Trail for a close-up view of a rare geological wonder: a sedimentary rock bridge.*

The 323-acre living museum has become an outstanding botanical garden and research center containing over 3,000 species of plants from around the world.

More than two miles of intersecting paths, most of them level and easy, wind through the gardens, and the scenery changes dramatically as you walk. Desert plants, including yuccas, palo-verdes, chollas, and a towering 200-year-old saguaro cactus, seem almost out of place when you encounter the lush vegetation around tiny Ayer Lake or the pomegranate, olive, and Chinese pistachio trees clustered along a stream. A shady eucalyptus grove provides a pleasant resting place and picnic area.

The plants are delightfully fragrant, and at practically any time of year some of them are in bloom. The best time to visit, however, is from October to May. In summer the temperature here can reach a sizzling 110°F.

Open daily from 8 A.M.–5 P.M. except Christmas. Admission charged.

(520) 689-2811
http://arboretum.ag.arizona.edu

14 McCormick-Stillman Railroad Park

7301 E. Indian Bend Rd., Scottsdale

Miniature trains, modeled after actual equipment at a scale of five inches to a foot, wind through this 30-acre park on a seven-minute trip past the station house, a water tower, and road-crossing signals—all at the same scale. Passengers are carried for a nominal charge.

Standing exhibits include a full-sized 1907 Baldwin steam engine, a 1914 Pullman baggage car that saw service on the Santa Fe Railroad, and the *Roald Amundsen*, a 1928 Pullman luxury car used by visiting VIPs, including U.S. presidents. Two reconstructed turn-of-the-century railroad stations serve as shops for memorabilia.

Open daily year-round except Thanksgiving and Christmas.

(480) 312-2312
www.therailroadpark.com

15 Casa Grande Ruins National Monument

Coolidge

One of the most mysterious of the Southwest's Indian ruins, Casa Grande was built around 1350. Clearly it served an important purpose. The three-story earthen structure sits like a crown on a high foundation at the center of a walled village, and the placement of windows in the upper stories suggests that it may have been used in part as an astronomical observatory. But beyond that, its function is lost in the past.

The building was constructed by the Hohokam, proficient farmers who built more than 600 miles of canals to irrigate their crops of corn, cotton, squash, and beans. They lived in small villages of one–room mud dwellings and were known for their earth-colored pottery and their skill in carving stones and shells. About a century after Casa Grande was built, they abandoned their Gila Valley villages for reasons unknown.

On display at the visitors center are ceramics, implements, jewelry, and other artifacts found here. A self-guiding hiking trail leads through the ruins of Casa Grande and the surrounding village. The ruins of a second Hohokam village, which includes a ball court, can be viewed from the picnic area of this 472-acre park.

Open year-round except Christmas. Admission charged.
(520) 723-3172
www.nps.gov/cagr

Organ Pipe Cactus National Monument

Ajo

Organ pipe is an apt name for a cactus whose slender stems curve upward in clusters to an average height of 15 feet. During May and June the creamy white flowers at the ends of the branches bloom at night and attract the nocturnal insects required for pollination. The red egg-shaped fruit matures in July, splitting open as it ripens to disclose the black seeds that are consumed by many of the hundreds of species of birds observed here. Fruit that drops to the ground provides food for many types of animals. The park, 500 square miles of Sonoran Desert, is this rare plant's northernmost habitat.

Ajo Mountain Drive, a 21-mile loop, and the 51-mile Puerto Blanco Drive wind through the southern section of the monument. Along each route there are picnic areas. The park has several hiking trails, some through the desert and others into the Ajo Mountains.

Open year-round except Christmas.
(520) 387-6849

www.nps.gov/orpi

Saguaro National Park, Rincon Mountain District

Tucson

The giant saguaro cactus, with its huge upright arms extending from a sturdy trunk, may after some 200 years reach a height of 50 feet. Literally thousands of these giant saguaro cacti fill the Sonoran Desert here in the eastern section of the national park's two units.

The saguaros are a great boon to desert birds. Woodpeckers drill holes in the fleshy arms for nests, which are often used later by screech owls, purple martins, and sparrow hawks.

The plants and creatures of the desert can be studied closely on an eight-mile drive that loops through the heart of the saguaro forest and also on a one-mile nature trail near a sheltered picnic area. Over 50 miles of hiking and horseback-riding trails traverse a 58,000-acre wilderness and ascend to the summits of the fir-forested Rincon Mountains at an altitude of 8,700 feet.

Open year-round. Admission charged.
(520) 733-5153

www.nps.gov/sagu

13 Boyce Thompson Arboretum State Park. *This living museum, started in the 1920s by a mining magnate, offers acres of desert vegetation.*

Chiricahua National Monument

Willcox

Strangely beautiful pinnacles, towers, spindle-thin columns, spires, and balanced boulders are so huddled together here that they seem almost surreal.

For centuries this area was part of the Chiricahua Apache homeland. The range in altitude here, from about 5,000 to more than 7,000 feet, helps to create a hospitable environment for a wide assortment of plants. Mexican pinyon pines, Apache pines, and Douglas firs thrive on the upper slopes; Arizona sycamore and wildflowers mark the course of the canyon streams, while yucca and cacti grow in the meadows.

The monument has 17 miles of hiking trails, a 24-site campground, and picnic areas. Of historic interest is the Faraway Ranch, a pioneer homestead that was a working cattle and guest ranch. From here a paved, six-mile scenic drive leads through a maze of canyons to Massai Point, which offers exquisite views of the surrounding valleys and has an exhibit building where displays describing the region's dramatic geology may be seen.

Park open year-round; visitors center open 8 A.M.–5 P.M. daily except Christmas. Admission charged.
(520) 824-3560

www.nps.gov/chir

Kartchner Caverns State Park

9 miles south of I-10, off State Hwy. 90, Exit 302

Millions of years ago, rainwater began to penetrate tiny cracks in Arizona's towering Whetstone Mountains. Interacting with minerals, the water gradually solidified into formations. In 1974 two young cavers exploring the abundant limestone hills at the base of the mountains followed the trail of a narrow crack. To their amazement they uncovered an extraordinary "living" cave—with formations in a dazzling array of sizes, shapes, and colors, dropping down thousands of feet and still growing.

Visitors can walk through this amazing underworld and revel at its impressive "speleothems." Kartchner Caverns is home to many unique formations, from the tiny and delicate to the massive. Within its walls, explorers will glimpse the first cave sighting of "birds nest" needle quartz formation, the tallest and widest column in the state of Arizona, and the longest soda-straw formation in the United States, measuring 21 feet plus 2 inches. In addition to pointing out the cave's distinctive features, tour guides share highlights from its prehistoric past and active present. Paleontologists have declared the cave a treasure trove of local fossil history, thanks to finds including the skeletons of an 80,000-year-old Shasta ground sloth, a 14,000-year-old horse, and an 11,000-year-old bear. Today, the cave serves as a nursery roost for over 1,000 female cave myotis bats.

Once outside the cave, visitors can stretch their legs on a scenic trail. The park also offers food vendors, picnic areas, and camping sites.

Open year-round. Entrance fee.
(520) 586-4100

www.pr.state.az.us/

Buffalo National River. *One of the most scenic rivers in the United States, the Buffalo can be explored by canoe or kayak in a half-day trip or a 10-day expedition (see opposite page).*

Arkansas

In addition to the expected pleasures found in the Ozarks and along the rivers, there are further delights—historic and otherwise.

Most surprising—and possibly even rewarding—is a state park where you can dig for diamonds and keep what you find. Oil is another treasure rendered from Arkansan earth, and a natural resources museum provides its story.

Two historic towns offer such highlights as superb antebellum homes, the place where the notorious bowie knife was forged, and a fine stern-wheeler steamboat. Battlegrounds, an incredible cavern, a magnificent wilderness river, and the courthouse of the famous Hanging Judge Parker are additional attractions.

1 Pea Ridge National Military Park

10 miles east of Rogers on Hwy. 62

In the early phase of the Civil War, the Union forces in Missouri, intent on controlling that state, drove the pro-Confederate troops there into neighboring Arkansas. Inevitably, when the Southern forces attempted to move back into Missouri to capture the vital crossroads city of St. Louis, the two armies clashed. After a raging battle at Pea Ridge, the Confederate soldiers, low on ammunition, were forced to retreat, and Missouri was saved for the Union.

A seven-mile self-guiding automobile tour on an excellent paved road takes you to the scenes of that struggle, including Pea Ridge, which overlooks the battlefield, and the restored Elkhorn Tavern, a focal point of much of the fighting. An eight-mile hiking trail also makes a loop of the region. A 28-minute film depicting the famous battle is presented at the visitors center.

Apart from its historic interest, the park is a scenically inviting place to explore, with its rugged bluffs, verdant valleys, the meandering Little Sugar Creek, and woods filled with maidenhair ferns and massive wild grapevines. The park is home to deer, coyotes, and bears, which have been reintroduced to the area.

1 Pea Ridge National Military Park. *The scene of a raging Civil War battle is now a park. Visitors can view scenes of the battle at the visitors center or explore the wildlife sanctuary.*

Open year-round except Thanksgiving, Christmas and New Year's Day.
(479) 451-8122
www.nps.gov/peri

2 Withrow Springs State Park
Huntsville

Bordered by towering bluffs along the War Eagle River, this secluded 786-acre retreat contains everything associated with the Ozark mountain region: a magnificent wilderness of ridges and valleys, wildlife, woodlands, and a small creek fed by clear springs.

The sparkling waters of the War Eagle River nourish the life of the park, providing an excellent canoe run and fine fishing for catfish, bream, perch, bass, and goggle-eye. Hikers have three scenic trails to explore. The three-quarter-mile Dogwood Trail, named for the area's most prevalent tree, makes a loop along ravines and ridges in heavily wooded terrain. The moderately difficult War Eagle Trail begins at a bridge, climbs up a 150-foot hill to a bluff that lets you look down to the river 200 feet below, and then continues on to a large cave with an underground stream. The trail is about a mile long and requires back-tracking. The Forest Trail follows an old roadway through a hardwood forest and connects with a paved highway that leads back to the campground, a trip of about 2½ miles.

Canoes can be rented, and a swimming pool, tree-shaded picnic grounds, and several camping sites are provided.

Open year-round.
(479) 559-2593
www.arkansasstateparks.com

3 Buffalo National River
Harrison

One of the most scenic rivers in the United States, the Buffalo has miraculously escaped alteration or impairment by civilization. To keep it that way, it has been designated a national river for 135 miles of its 150-mile length. It is protected by the National Park Service, which also administers a 95,000-acre strip of wilderness bordering its serpentine course.

As it winds through peaceful valleys and beneath huge limestone cliffs, rushing over rapids and slipping through placid pools in its journey from headwaters in the Boston Mountains to its junction with the White River, the river tumbles over 2,000 feet.

The Buffalo is especially popular with canoeists and kayakers, who can enjoy a half-day trip or a 10-day, 120-mile expedition. The upper river, from Boxley to Ponca, is normally navigable only after substantial rainfalls.

Canoes and kayaks can be rented, with transportation provided to and from any of the 20 access points. Picnic areas and

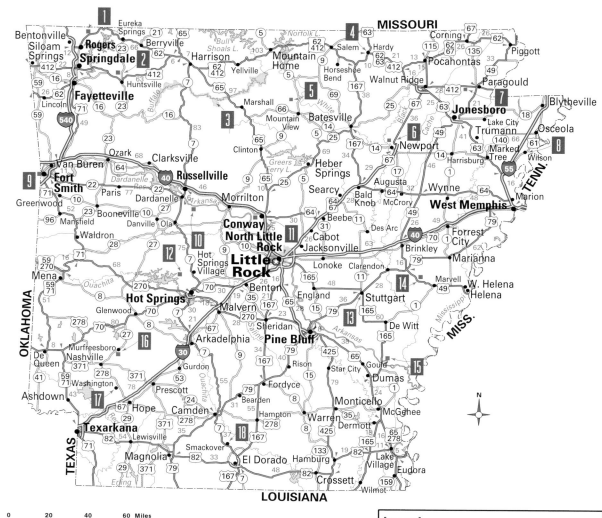

Legend

10 NUMBERED ATTRACTIONS (Described in text)

CONTROLLED ACCESS HIGHWAYS
— Free
— Toll
= = = = = Under Construction

OTHER HIGHWAYS
— Primary Highway
— Secondary Highway

CITIES AND TOWNS
⊙ National Capital
⊙ State Capital
• Cities, Towns, and Populated Places Type size indicates relative importance
Urban Area

HIGHWAY MARKERS
12 Interstate Route
12 U.S. Route
12 State Route
12 Distances along Major Highways (in miles)

RECREATION AND FEATURES OF INTEREST
National Park
Other Large Park or Recreation Area
— Trail
— — — Ferry

campsites are scattered along the river. Some 160 kinds of fish have been found in the Buffalo; the most popular with fishermen are smallmouth bass, goggle-eye, perch, bream, and catfish.

Several hiking trails and old abandoned roads give access to the canyons, hollows, bluffs, forests, and meadows of the surrounding Ozark wilderness, which has changed little in character in the last century.

In this richly varied environment some 1,500 different plant species come into flower between late January and late autumn. The Lost Valley Nature Trail, which follows Clark Creek as it skirts waterfalls, towering fern-clad cliffs, a natural bridge, and a 200-foot cave, is especially rewarding. The dense forests are home to deer, beavers, red foxes, coyotes, and a great variety of native birds.

River guidebooks, maps, and other information may be obtained at the Pruitt, Silver Hill, and Buffalo Point information centers and at the park headquarters in Harrison.

Open year-round.
(870) 429-2502
www.nps.gov/buff

4 Old Hardy Town
*Located at the juncture
of U.S. Rtes. 62 and 412*
On the *National Register of
Historic Places,* this charming
small town looks much as it did
during the Model-T days. Since
the 1920s, it has grown only in
spirit: Hardy's total population is
about 600. Centered on Main
Street, the town's business district
consists of three square blocks.
Among its 43 buildings are three
churches and dozens of vintage
craft nooks and antique shops. In
fact, Old Hardy Town prides itself
as the "Antique and Craft Capital
of the Arkansas Ozarks." Quaint
shops feature the work of local
artisans, including handmade
musical instruments like wooden
flutes and mountain dulcimers.
Local musicians often gather at
the Main Street Gazebo to play
time-honored favorites from the
Ozarks region.

Formally established in 1883,
Hardy got its start in a heavily
timbered, sparsely populated area.
The town gained prestige as the
county seat in 1894 but remained
tiny. By 1900 its residents numbered just about 600. During the
next couple of decades, thanks to
an economic boom and the expanding railroad, Hardy built up a small
but thriving downtown business
district, including general stores,
two cafés, two livery stables, and
a livestock sale barn. In 1982 a
devastating flood severely damaged
most of the downtown buildings.
After the flood the nostalgic townspeople made a pledge to restore
Hardy to its old town glory.

Hardy is now home to two
museums. The Vintage Motorcar
Museum boasts a private collection
of more than 50 classic vehicles,
from a 1908 Sears Runabout to a

1981 DeLorean. The Veteran's
Military Museum commemorates
all of the major conflicts in
U.S. military history, from the
Revolutionary War to Desert
Storm, with uniforms, artifacts,
photographs, firearms, and even
a helicopter. Just one block off
Main Street the cool, clear waters
of Spring River beckon with the
promise of excellent fishing, as
well as canoeing and swimming.
**http://members.tripod.com/~hardyar/
index1.html**

5 Blanchard Springs Caverns
Mountain View
Because some of the more
enchanting caves here were not
discovered until the 1960s, this
magnificent underworld system
isn't yet as well known as New
Mexico's Carlsbad Caverns,
though it is in many ways just
as spectacular.

Visitors to this subterranean
marvel have a choice of three
tours. Along the easier, the

Dripstone Trail, you pass through
the aptly named Cathedral Room,
an enormous chamber whose size
is accentuated by a play of light
on a number of dazzling rock
formations, and the stunning Coral
Room, found in 1963.

The Discovery Trail is a taxing
100-minute walk, including
700 steps, and is open only from
Memorial Day through Labor Day.
Commensurate rewards include
seeing the bubbling origin of
Blanchard Springs and the haunting
Ghost Room.

The caverns are located in
an unspoiled area of the Ozark
National Forest near Sylamore
Creek, a pristine white-water
stream claiming one of the few
old-fashioned swimming holes
left in this part of the country.
A recreation area at the cavern
site offers camping.
*Open year-round. Admission charged.
(870) 757-2211*
**www.fs.fed.us/conf/ozark/recreation/
bsc.html**

5 Blanchard Springs Cavern. *Dazzling rock formations can be explored in the
enchanting caves and trails of this underworld system.*

6 Jacksonport State Park
Newport
The romance of the Old South
and the boisterous steamboat days
lives on in this small, pretty park
along a sweeping bend of the
White River. Jacksonport began as
a shipping point in the early 1800s
and later became a busy steamboat
port. Its glory days came to an end
in 1891, when a new railroad line
made nearby Newport the center
of commerce and the county seat.
From that time Jacksonport
steadily declined. All of its buildings have vanished, many destroyed
by floodwaters, except for the
old Jacksonport Courthouse, which
was refurbished following a
1997 tornado.

The stately courthouse, built
in 1872 on a high, sturdy foundation
of Arkansas limestone, has been
restored and included on the
*National Register of Historic
Places.* It is now the focal point
of the park, housing a museum of
memorabilia and relics that trace
the history of the community
through the steamboat era. Other
exhibits show local architecture
and a 19th-century courthouse and
clerk's office—complete with
12 jurors' chairs. Moored at the
steamboat landing across the levee
from the courthouse—and maintained as though ready for a week's
cruise—is the *Mary Woods II,* a
white double-deck stern-wheeler.

Campsites and picnic tables
are pleasingly situated on an open,
grassy expanse along the river
beneath a scattering of shade trees.
The 154-acre park also boasts a
sandy swimming beach, a boat
ramp, a small woodland, and a
lovely pecan grove.
*Park open year-round. Courthouse open
Tues.–Sun.; steamboat open Tues.–Sun.,
May–Labor Day, weekends Apr. and*

Sept.–Oct. Admission charged.
(870) 523-2143
www.arkansasstateparks.com

7 Crowley's Ridge State Park
Paragould

Crowley's Ridge, a geological curiosity, is an erosional remnant left when the Mississippi and Ohio rivers retreated westward, probably at the end of the last ice age. Rising like an island 100 to 200 feet above the flatlands, the sandy ridge is from 1 to 10 miles wide and runs for 210 miles from Helena, Arkansas, to Cape Girardeau in Missouri. Built on the slopes of the ridge, where the Quapaw Indians once camped, this 301-acre park is an old-fashioned summer getaway with a great spring-fed swimming hole, a productive fishing lake (bass, catfish, crappie, bream), a network of leafy trails, and plenty of places to picnic, camp, watch birds, and play ball. Along the Dancing Rabbit Trail, a name of Quapaw origin, you'll sway your way over two swinging bridges.

Benjamin Crowley, for whom the park is named, settled here following his participation in the War of 1812.

Open year-round.
(870) 573-6751
www.arkansasstateparks.com

8 Hampson Museum State Park
Wilson

Persons interested in America's past, in particular the ancestors of the American Indian, will find the Hampson Museum an especially rewarding one. Its enormous collection of artifacts—some 41,000 items, including remarkably beautiful ceramics, stone tools, weapons, human and animal effigies, and skeletal remains—serves to portray the culture of the farming and mound-building people who lived in this area from about 1350 to 1650 and who then seemed to disappear.

There are usually 300 exhibits on display at any one time, and many of them were excavated by Dr. James K. Hampson in the 1920s and '30s on his family plantation, Nodena (five miles from Wilson), where a palisaded village with two pyramid mounds once existed.

The small park, which is right in the village of Wilson, also offers a pleasant picnic area and a playground.

Open Tues.–Sat. and P.M. Sun. year-round except Thanksgiving, Christmas Eve, Christmas, and New Year's Day.
Admission charged for museum.
(870) 655-8622
www.arkansasstateparks.com

7 Crowley's Ridge State Park. *The forest holds a network of leafy trails to explore, with plenty of places to picnic, camp, or watch birds.*

9 Fort Smith Museum of History and Fort Smith National Historic Site
Rogers Ave.

Fort Smith's colorful frontier saga began when it was established by the U.S. Army in 1817 as a border post between Arkansas and Indian Territory. The area's dramatic events of that time are highlighted in the museum, which also displays pioneer relics, Indian beadwork, and military artifacts. Large murals depict the fort in its heyday. A well-equipped drugstore with an operating soda fountain of 1920–40 vintage serves up a fine scoop of nostalgia. On the Old Fort property, across the parking lot from the museum, is the historic site. A well-preserved courthouse and jail and a reconstructed gallows recall the reputation of a famous resident, U.S. Judge Isaac C. Parker. In sentencing 160 outlaws to death, Parker became known as the Hanging Judge, earning credit in the process for bringing law and order to this freewheeling frontier.

Museum: Closed Mon. in the summer, closed Sun., Mon. otherwise.
Admission charged.
(479) 783-3244
Historic site: Open daily 9 A.M.–5 P.M.
(479) 783-3961
www.fortsmith.org

10 Holla Bend National Wildlife Refuge

From Dardanelle take Rte. 7S and turn left on Cty. Rte. 155.
This 7,050-acre sanctuary is actually an island that was formed in 1954 when the U.S. Army Corps of Engineers cut a new channel for the Arkansas River across a deep bend in the old channel.

Located on a main flyway of migrating birds, the refuge, with its ponds and lakes, is a wintering home for some 5,000 Canada geese and at least 35,000 ducks. Up to 40 bald eagles can be seen sojourning here from November to March. Permanent residents include herons, egrets, gulls, and terns. Alligators are numerous in these waters, which mark the creature's northernmost range.

More than a fourth of the refuge is farmed, and a portion of each year's crop of corn, milo, and other grains is left in the fields for the birds.

You can observe the entire sanctuary by following the eight-mile self-guiding, all-weather drive. Fishing is good, primarily for bream, crappie, bass, and catfish. A boat ramp is located on Lodge Lake, Long Lake, and Old River Channel.

Open year-round.
(479) 229-4300
www.gorp.com/gorp/resource/us_nwr/ar_holla.html

⑪ Cadron Settlement Park

5 miles west of Conway on Hwy. 54; left on 319

This site, blessed with good spring-water, forest cover, and a natural harbor where Cadron Creek flows into the Arkansas River, was first used in the late 1770s as a trading post by Spaniards bartering with the local Osage Indians. With the Louisiana Purchase of 1803 the United States acquired Arkansas, and several years later a number of families settled here. Gristmills and a tannery were built, and a general store was opened. In 1820–21 Cadron vied with Little Rock in a contest to become the territorial capital and lost. When the railroad passed it by, the little river town finally died.

In 1972 the U.S. Army Corps of Engineers undertook the building of Cadron as a recreation area. An imposing two-story blockhouse has been reconstructed on the site of the original building.

An easy-to-moderate hiking trail wends through this quiet region of hills and bluffs. Named for the Cherokee Chief Tollantusky, who lived at Cadron from 1809 until his death in 1818, the trail underlines the importance of the settlement as it follows at various points the Butterfield Stagecoach Road, the Toad Suck Ferry Road, and the Old Military Road.

Open year-round.
(501) 329-2986
www.swl.usace.army.mil/parks/toadsuck/cardonsettlement.html

⑫ Lake Ouachita State Park

Mountain Pine

The park is nestled in the pine-covered hills bordering the eastern end of Lake Ouachita (pronounced

⑫ Lake Ouachita State Park.
Mini-caves and earthquake remains can be examined by boaters along this man-made lake.

Wash-i-taw), the state's largest man-made lake. This site offers camping, boating, waterskiing, swimming, and fishing along the lake's 975 miles of shoreline. Fishermen come for bass, bream, rainbow trout, and pike.

Boaters taking the Geo-Float Trail can examine a number of the area's unusual geologic features, including mini-caves and earthquake remains, while landlubbers can strike out on two hiking trails that wander through the lush woodlands of the 365-acre park.

Since the late 1800s vacationers have been lured by the Three Sisters natural springs that are said to have curative powers. Today the springs are no longer used as the park's water supply but are still open as a historical display.

Open year-round.
(501) 767-9366
www.arkansasstateparks.com

⑬ Stuttgart Agricultural Museum

921 E. Fourth St.

From the name, one could accurately surmise that the town was founded by German immigrants. This fascinating museum complex preserves the farm equipment, household antiques, and other relics of the prairie farm culture that developed here in the years after the Civil War.

Funds to build the museum were donated by local farm families, who also contributed all the items on display, among them some impressive 19th-century steam-powered farm machinery. Local craftsmen have also built replicas of a 1914 schoolhouse, the old community firehouse, complete with the refurbished 1926 fire engine, a fully furnished 1880 prairie home, a scaled-down model of an 1896 Lutheran church, and the façades of stores that once existed here.

Among the charming and unexpected exhibits is a collection of musical instruments and music boxes that entertained the great-grandparents of the women who run the museum today, and one of the largest game call collections in the United States.

Open Tues.–Sat. year-round except major holidays.
(870) 673-7001
www.stuttgartarkansas.com/stuttgart/directories/museums.html

⑭ Louisiana Purchase State Park

South of Brinkley

In 1815, 12 years after the Louisiana Purchase, a team of government surveyors blazed two big sweet gum trees in a trackless swamp in eastern Arkansas. Those marks were the starting point for the monumental task of determining the bounds of that addition to the United States.

Though the blazed trees are gone, 37.5 acres of the headwater swamp have been preserved as a state park. A 950-foot-long boardwalk leads through the area to a marker designating the initial point for the entire survey. A stroll offers a close-up view of this natural environment, where you can find the uncommon swamp cottonwood tree, the golden prothonotary warbler, and the little brown-and-green amphibian called the tree frog.

Much of the lower Mississippi River valley was once wooded swampland like this, and you get a fleeting sense, without having to get your feet wet, of how overpowering this landscape must have seemed to those surveyors who came to chart it.

Open year-round.
(888) 287-2757
www.arkansasstateparks.com

⑮ Arkansas Post National Memorial

Gillett

Called the birthplace of Arkansas, the small settlement of Arkansas Post was established in 1686 by Henri de Tonti on a grant given him four years earlier by his chief, the great French explorer La Salle. The trading post was probably abandoned a few years later, but in the early 1700s profitable trade with the American Indians revived interest in the region, and Arkansas Post was rebuilt.

Becoming an American village in 1803, Arkansas Post grew into a bustling frontier town, and in 1819 it was made the first territorial capital of Arkansas. But it faded away when the government moved to Little Rock in 1821.

During the 1700s and 1800s Arkansas Post was relocated within a 35-mile area numerous times because of floods and the river's instability. Several of these sites are within today's 747-acre memorial park. A setting of quiet beauty at the meeting point of the White, Arkansas, and Mississippi rivers, it probably looks much as it did in Tonti's time. Self-guiding trails help re-create the past.

The park is also a fine wildlife preserve and a magnificent spot for bird-watching, as it was for John James Audubon. A lake yields large bass and catfish, and a boat-launching ramp just beyond the park gives access to both the White and Arkansas rivers. The visitors center has some first-rate archaeological, historical, and wildlife exhibits.

Park open year-round.
(870) 548-2207
www.nps.gov/arpo

16 Crater of Diamonds State Park
Murfreesboro
Here's a unique chance to combine fun and profit by prospecting in the only significant diamond deposit in North America. Plus, you get to keep any stones you find.

Best known for diamonds, the area (an eroded volcanic pipe) also yields amethyst, agate, jasper, quartz, and other semiprecious stones. A 37-acre field is deep-plowed regularly to expose new earth. Though generally you must dig for stones, diamonds are occasionally found lying on the surface, sparkling in the sun.

Many of the diamonds are of an industrial quality, but every year visitors turn up hundreds of gems of significant quality and value, and some lucky prospectors carry away diamonds ranging from 2 to 5 carats. The largest ever found, the Uncle Sam, was 40.23 carats.

The first diamond from this area was found in 1906, but for various reasons commercial mining has never been successful here, and in 1972 the field was made part of an 888-acre park along the piney banks of the Little Missouri River. Some tips: Wear a hat because there's little shade. Bring boots or overshoes because the plowed earth is usually muddy. The park visitors center has digging equipment available to rent, or visitors can bring their own. The staff will identify and certify any stones you unearth. Diamonds are most often found a few days after a heavy rain, so the best time to look for them is during the rainy season from February through June.

Park open year-round. Admission charged for diamond field.
(870) 285-3113
www.arkansasstateparks.com

17 Old Washington Historic State Park
Washington
The town of Washington was a frontier jumping-off place for people streaming into Texas and the Great Southwest in the first half of the 19th century, but after the Civil War it declined and today has fewer than 300 people.

In 1958 a few residents began restoring some of the beautiful antebellum homes. That project has expanded to cover practically the entire town and includes a variety of public buildings. Highlights here now include the village smithy, where the knife used by Col. James Bowie was designed (a resident knifemaker gives demonstrations); a cotton gin; the old county jail; the 1836

courthouse, now a museum; and the 1832 Williams Tavern Restaurant.

Today all of this is a historic state park. An interesting two-hour tour of the restored area conducted by guides in period costumes gives you an overall sense of strolling back into the 19th century. During the Frontier Day Festival—in late September—the townspeople dress in old-time garb, and 19th-century crafts, music, and food are featured.

Historic buildings open daily except major holidays. Charge for tours.
(870) 983-2684
www.arkansasstateparks.com

18 Arkansas Museum of Natural Resources
Smackover
The French called the area *sumac couvert*—"covered with sumac." To American ears those words sounded like "Smackover," though its history has less to do with sumac than petroleum. Smackover was the scene of a wild and woolly oil boom during the 1920s, when great oil strikes were made in

southern Arkansas. After that it faded to a kind of uneventful small-town respectability. You'll see no evidence of the old shoot-em-up, strike-it-rich excitement, and though just about every cow pasture and vacant lot in this area has one of those woodpecker-looking oil rigs silently pumping away, few local residents know much about the colorful history of the petroleum industry or all the nuts and bolts of how it works.

This museum gives visitors a historical view and practical understanding of the oil business. Giant antique derricks and a working well are among the outdoor exhibits tucked into a pretty section of pinewoods along scenic Route 7, just north of town. In the visitors center you'll find a gift shop, archives, and some excellent exhibits documenting those hectic boom times.

Open Mon.–Sat. and P.M. Sun. year-round except major holidays.
(870) 725-2877
www.cei.net/~amnr

17 Old Washington Historic State Park. *The Hempstead County Courthouse, built in 1874, now functions as a visitors center and gift shop.*

Anza-Borrego Desert State Park. *Only the toughest plants survive in this section of the Colorado Desert (see page 47).*

California

For all its popularity as a travel destination, the Golden State still has many interesting and attractive out-of-the-way places to savor.

A variety of intriguing landscapes and sculptural forms, including spatter cones, lava tube caves, and lavacicles, owe their existence to volcanism. Other fanciful shapes, in clay, sandstone, and tufa, were sculpted by the forces of erosion. The sea has also shaped the land, and along the coast are tide pools to inspect and sandy stretches where nature's portable bounty of agates, shells, driftwood—and clams—can be gathered. Rocky coves are inhabited by seals and sea lions; and from the headlands whales and porpoises can be seen. On the sea-girt Channel Islands one is literally surrounded by these denizens of the deep.

Among the remarkable variety of trees that grow here are redwoods, the largest living things; bristlecone pines, the oldest living things; and the strange and wonderful Joshua trees.

Birds can be seen by the millions, along with great expanses of wildflowers, and two interesting species of elk. Mankind's contributions—from tools 200,000 years old to submarines—are also to be contemplated.

1 Prairie Creek Redwoods State Park

Orick

Driving north on Route 101, travelers are almost certain to notice the sudden appearance of the majestic Roosevelt elk roaming Boyes Prairie near the park headquarters and visitors center.

A display at the center features a month-by-month account of the life cycle of this magnificent creature—the largest wild animal in California. Like the elk, the rest of the area's flora and fauna tends to call forth superlatives, and other equally elaborate displays do them justice: An entire room is devoted to the ecology of the mighty redwoods, for instance.

The 14,000-acre park is a preserve for these trees *(Sequoia sempervirens),* the tallest species on earth. Some specimens here soar 300 feet. They and their companion plants can be seen close-up on more than 30 trails that range from easy to strenuous, and from one-tenth of a mile to seven miles long. Some lead down to Gold Bluffs Beach. The James Irvine Trail, for example, is a four-mile hike through redwoods and a lush undergrowth of hemlock, laurel, and alder. It connects with the Fern Canyon Trail, where eight species of ferns cling to the steplike ledges of the canyon wall. Frogs and Pacific giant salaman-

 Prairie Creek Redwoods State Park. *More than 30 trails lead visitors through redwood trees that rise like temple columns in this 14,000-acre park.*

ders inhabit the streambed here. A herd of elk roams the beach and should be given a wide berth. They are wild and unpredictable. You can camp at the beach or near park headquarters at Elk Prairie.
Open year-round. Admission charged. (707) 464-6101, Ext. 5301
www.parks.ca.gov

2 Patrick's Point State Park
Trinidad

Land meets sea here with dramatic results. The fringes of this headland, covered with evergreen forests and berry- and wildflower-carpeted meadows, are battered and fragmented. Worn offshore rocks called sea stacks bear testimony to the thundering, pounding force of the ocean.

In the tide pools of the "crash zone" between surf and cliff, you can find sea anemones, starfish, mussels, and snails. The surf's ceaseless throb is occasionally interrupted by the hoarse, hollow call of the California sea lions, which congregate on the rocks in great numbers.

Plenty of trails crisscross the park. Rim Trail, which begins at

the campground, is an agreeable two-mile walk that affords good views of the coastline and a reconstructed Yurok Indian village. In spring and fall you can watch for gray whales. Agate Beach Trail leads down from the campground to Agate Beach, a sandy crescent. The ocean is too cold and treacherous for swimming, but this is a happy hunting ground for agate and driftwood collectors. You can fish for rockfish off the rocks at the south end of the beach. There are several more trails, most of them steep descents to the shore or climbs to spectacular lookouts.

Open year-round. Admission charged.
(707) 677-3570

www.parks.ca.gov

3 Lava Beds National Monument

Off Rte. 139, south of Tulelake

A vast, majestic stretch of high desert ringed with purple mountains, the monument preserves the special beauty and strangeness of land marked by volcanic activity. From the northeast entrance the park road winds through scrubby sagebrush and rolling hills dotted with juniper and finally with stands of yellow pine. Jagged lava rocks, deep orange in color, lie amid the wispy sage. As the road climbs, one sees the distant snowy peaks of ancient dead volcanoes. The sky is deep blue, and the wind is scented with sage and cinders.

At the visitors center near the southeast entrance, information is available on the area's turbulent volcanic origins and its plant and animal life, and a rock display illustrates the variety of minerals found here. An interpretive trail in the adjacent, illuminated Mushpot Cave explains lavacicles, spatter cones, balconies, and other formations found in the monument's 436 lava tube caves. More than 30 of these are accessible from Cave Loop Road, which begins at the visitors center. If you want to explore them, the center will lend you portable lights.

The terrain provided refuge for the Modoc Indians in the Modoc War of 1872–73, an American Indian rebellion whose history is recounted at the visitors center. Petroglyphs 4,000 to 6,000 years old, found on cliffs, remind one that to the Modocs this area was the center of the world.

While you are here, take the Wildlife Refuge Tour along the northeast edge of the monument: The route overlooks Tule Lake in the Klamath Basin National Wildlife Refuge, frequented by literally millions of waterfowl in autumn. Falcons and other predators congregate along the cliffs here, including the largest number of bald eagles south of Alaska.

Open year-round except Thanksgiving and Christmas.

(530) 667-2282, Ext. 232

www.nps.gov/labe

4 Modoc National Wildlife Refuge

Alturas

An expanse of golden desert with a managed system of marshes, lakes, and ponds, this 7,000-acre refuge on the Pacific Flyway is specifically designed for waterfowl, and it's a bird-watcher's delight. But even the most avid birder will want to take time to savor the desert air and lively landscape surrounded by low mountains.

While geese, herons, ducks, egrets, and a variety of shorebirds and warblers are most frequently seen here, some 220 species have been recorded. A drive around Teal Pond is a good way to see them at close range. Grassy, tufted islets dot the pond, and herons and egrets often stand motionless along their shores. Great numbers of whistling swans may also be seen gliding on the placid blue waters.

The refuge is the summer home for the largest population of sandhill cranes in California. This wading bird with blue-gray body and bright red patch on the head grows to about four feet tall and is easy to spot. If birding is your special interest, April and September are the best times to see the greatest number of species.

Among the mammals seen here year-round are rabbits, muskrats, minks, raccoons, coyotes, and mule deer. Fishing is allowed in Dorris Reservoir, and part of the refuge is set aside for seasonal hunting.

Open year-round.

(530) 233-3572

www.r1.fws.gov/modoc

5 Whiskeytown-Shasta-Trinity National Recreation Area

A delightful haven for birders and hydrophiles, this nationally managed recreation area features four lakes, each offering distinct opportunities for wonder and fun.

Whiskeytown Lake is a man-made reservoir, with 3,200 surface acres of water, inviting swimming, scuba diving, waterskiing, boating, and fishing.

The lake was created by diverting water through tunnels and penstocks from the Trinity River Basin to the Sacramento River Basin. Just beyond its shores, Shasta Bally Mountain towers at an elevation of 6,209 feet. The intrepid can reach its summit on foot, as well as by bicycle, on horseback, or by four-wheel-drive vehicle.

Nearby, Shasta Lake boasts 370 miles of beautiful forested shoreline, which hosts dozens of osprey nests and the state's largest population of bald eagle nests on a single body of water. Trinity Lake

5 Whiskeytown-Shasta-Trinity National Recreation Area. *Boaters on Shasta Lake might spy a bald eagle since there are so many nests here.*

and Lewiston Lake support an abundance of birds, including at least a dozen pairs of nesting bald eagles, and assorted wildlife ready for watching.

No visit to the area—named Whiskeytown after a team of donkeys lost its footing on a local trail and spilled a load of whiskey into a nearby ravine—would be complete without stopping to view the historical remnants of the California Gold Rush of 1849, highlighted throughout the lakeside parks.

Open year-round except for Shasta Bally Mountain, which is closed to climbers in winter. Entrance fee.

(530) 246-1225

www.nps.gov/whis

6 William B. Ide Adobe State Historic Park

Off I-5, at 21659 Adobe Rd., Red Bluff

Visitors to this park are invited to step back to 1852 and experience what life in Northern California must have been like then. Shaded by two towering specimens of Sacramento Valley oak, this 1850s home is a focus for year-round programs aimed at giving visitors a firsthand feel for pioneer life.

William Brown Ide, fresh from Illinois, served as the leader of the short-lived Republic of California from June 14, 1846, when a small band of American settlers revolted against Mexican rule, until July 10, when the republic was declared a U.S. protectorate.

The state acquired the compound in 1951, embarking on extensive restoration of the low-roofed main house, carriage house, well, and smokehouse.

Throughout the summer months, visitors can view various craft demonstrations, such as brick-making, candle-making, blacksmithing, quilting, and woodworking. Pioneer skills and crafts are also demonstrated.

Open year-round.

(530) 529-8599

www.ohwy.com/ca/w/wmidehsp.htm

7 Feather Falls Scenic Area

From Rte. 162, east of Oroville, turn right on Forbestown Rd.; continue to Feather Falls turnoff on left.

Gleaming as a glass skyscraper, the three tiers of Feather Falls plunge 640 feet into a valley cut

into the Sierra foothills. The easiest way to see the falls is to follow the signs to the scenic overlook at Bald Rock. Even from this vantage point, the base of the falls is hidden by a jutting granite hillside.

For another perspective, hikers can take the steep, rocky but well-marked trail leading through sparse manzanita and pine chaparral to a point overlooking the churning green water at the base of the falls. Count on an afternoon to make the seven-mile round-trip.

The scenic area, which encompasses 15,000 acres in the Plumas National Forest, includes a number of other hiking trails, scenic spots, and campgrounds. The three branches of the Feather River (whose middle fork is fed by the

falls) afford some of the most challenging whitewater rafting in the state. Downstream are calmer stretches that are fine for canoeing and swimming.

Open year-round.

(530) 534-6500

www.r5.fs.fed.us/plumas

8 Montgomery Woods State Reserve

At Ukiah, off Rte. 101, take State St. to Orr Springs Rd.

Montgomery Woods is a fine place to see giant redwoods in their primeval state. A clearing ringed with the largest trees—10 to 15 feet in diameter—opens about four-fifths of a mile along the steep loop of Memorial Grove Trail, which begins at the reserve pullout. From a carpet of their red-brown needles, redwoods rise like temple columns, and any stage designer would envy the hazy amber light and vivid green of the ferns in this setting. Silence is deep, civilization distant. Camping is prohibited in the 1,142-acre reserve, but there are picnic tables near the creek that border the trail.

An added aspect of the woods' appeal is the pleasure of getting there. Orr Springs Road winds through barren, rocky areas with views of rolling hills and pasturelands and glimpses of the Napa and Mendocino valleys. Narrow, steep, and full of hairpin turns, the road is an exciting experience, but one should not attempt it with a trailer or mobile home in tow.

Open year-round.

(707) 937-5804

www.parks.ca.gov

9 Armstrong Redwoods State Reserve

Off Rte. 116 north of Guerneville
This 805-acre reserve, dense with the noble coast redwood, was established in the 1870s by Col. James B. Armstrong, an early lumberman and conservationist. It is seen at its best from Pioneer Trail, which begins at the entrance.

The first of the remarkable specimens here is the Parson Jones Tree—at 310 feet it's taller than an upended football field. Next comes Burbank Circle, a ring of smaller trees "only" 8 to 10 feet in diameter. But the Armstrong Tree, farther along, is more than 1,400 years old, soars 308 feet, and measures 14 1/2 feet across.

If the frequent rain so vital to the redwoods keeps you in the car, you can still see many of the grove's landmark trees from the road.

Beyond the reserve picnic grounds the narrow road continues into the Austin Creek State Recreation Area. Here the changing altitudes in the 5,683-acre park induce changing vegetation, climaxing at the higher and drier levels in laurel, manzanita, madrone, conifers, and oak.

Below them spreads a magnificent view of the redwoods and coastal mountains. Twenty miles of trails offer lots of exploring. Some allow horseback riding. Camping and hiking facilities are excellent, birds and other wildlife abundant, and wildflowers are splendidly profuse in the spring. The rainy season lasts from November to April.

Reserve and recreation areas open year-round. Admission charged.
(707) 869-2015
www.parks.ca.gov

10 Tomales Bay State Park

Turn right on Pierce Pt. Rd. off Rte. 1 beyond Inverness.
From clearings in the dense, aromatic undergrowth above the sandy crescent of Heart's Desire Beach (at the end of Pierce Point Road), there are endless views beyond the circling gulls and hawks to the golden hills across the bay. If you don't mind chilly water, you can swim here at the surf-free beaches, then warm up with a hike along the Johnstone Trail at the northeast end of the beach: a corridor lined with huckleberry, oak, giant fern, and braids of green lichen. Or take the Indian Nature Trail at the west end to Indian Beach, where with a California fishing license you can dig for littleneck clams and the occasional giant four-pound horseneck.

Off Route 1 on the way into the park, stop at the Bear Valley

10 Tomales Bay State Park. *Cattle get the best view as they graze near the shore of Tomales Bay north of San Francisco.*

Visitors Center for a wealth of information on the history, plants, and wildlife of Tomales Bay. A word about the weather: Vital for sustaining the park's abundant vegetation through the March–September dry season are the picturesque but chilly fogs that roll in the rest of the year.

Open year-round. Admission charged.
(415) 669-1140
www.parks.ca.gov

11 San Francisco Maritime National Historical Park and Museum

Located at the west end of San Francisco's Fisherman's Wharf
For avid sailors and vicarious seafaring adventurers, the Hyde Street Pier offers a fascinating sail back through time. On the Hyde Street Pier, landlubbers can tour an impressive fleet of historic vessels, including the 1886 square-rigger *Balclutha,* the 1890 steam ferry *Eureka,* the 1907 steam tugboat *Hercules,* and the 1914 paddlewheel tug *Eppleton Hall.*

Visitors can also experience what life was like for submariners during World War II when they step aboard the USS *Pampanito,* a fully restored floating exhibit, now a national landmark.

Continuing the journey, the park's collection of more than 100 small craft, both traditional and trailblazing, provide a lively introduction to boat building and the maritime trades.

Built as a project of the New Deal's Works Progress Administration, the maritime park museum is a work of art in itself. Inside, mast sections, jutting spars, and authentic ship figureheads are arranged among the colorful fish and gleaming tiles of renowned muralist Hilaire Hiler's expressionist vision of Atlantis. Also, *Mermaid,* the one-man sailboat that transported a daring solo adventurer across the Pacific Ocean from Japan in 94 days, is displayed on the balcony. Along with detailed ship models, intricate works of scrimshaw, and whaling guns, the museum features video presentations and interactive exhibits. The Steamship Room illustrates the technological evolution of wind-to-steam power.

In addition, the park offers frequent historical re-creations and interpretive programs christened with names like "When Battleships Were Tricky." Visitors might catch a demonstration of rigging, a class in navigation or woodworking, or a rousing concert of sea chanteys. There are also activities designed especially for kids. The voyage culminates at the Maritime Store, managed by the nonprofit San Francisco Maritime National Park Association, offering a wide range of maritime-related books, games, and videos, ship plans and models, a selection of maritime folk music, and other "gifts of the sea."

Open year-round. Entrance fee.
(415) 561-7100
www.nps.gov/safr

12 Pinnacles National Monument
On Rte. 146 east of Soledad

It's a surprise, driving through the gentle coastal hills of Monterey and San Benito counties, to come suddenly upon the jagged red spires and rugged canyons of Pinnacles National Monument. The rich soil here, on the weathered remains of an ancient volcano, helps support a variety of plant and animal life, and the Pinnacles' high, open terrain is well suited to hiking. There are over 30 miles of tended trails against a backdrop of the endlessly changing hues and textures of eroded volcanic rock. "Wilderness treks" are for experienced hikers, cave trails for would-be spelunkers (don't forget a flashlight). Scaling the Pinnacles' sheer pink cliffs, however, demands experience and specialized equipment.

Several trailheads are accessible from Bear Gulch Visitor Center, where excellent annotated maps are available. The Moses Spring Self-Guiding Trail, for instance, climaxes with a visit to the Bear Gulch Reservoir. Hikers who want even more of a challenge can take High Peaks Trail, a two-mile ramble among the higher reaches.

Heat can be intense in season, and weekends are crowded. The most relaxed times to use the trails are weekdays.

Open year-round. Admission charged.
(831) 389-4485
www.nps.gov/pinn

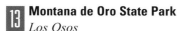

13 Montana de Oro State Park
Los Osos

This stretch of seaside marine terrace is known as the Mountain of Gold for the blaze of orange and yellow California poppies and monkey flowers that carpet its easy contours when spring arrives (in mid-April).

At water's edge the land crumbles into cliffs that plunge into an abundance of rocky inlets and tide pools along the four miles of shoreline in this 8,000-plus-acre park. At one point the shoreline edges inward to form a crescent pebble beach, a good place to set off on an investigation of the rocks and pools, but the water is too cold and rough for swimming.

The beach itself is littered with treasures: driftwood, colored pebbles, bull kelp (a seaweed whose air-bubbled stems explode with a loud crack when stepped on). The tide pools teem with snails, limpets, sea anemones, and hermit crabs. Whale spotting is a favorite pastime from November to March, and the area is a wintertime stop for migrating monarch butterflies, which can turn entire trees into fluttering fantasies.

Add to all this year-round good weather, good picnic and camping facilities, a network of easy trails—and tonic sea air mingled with the restorative scents of coastal sage and pine.

Open year-round.
(805) 528-0513
www.parks.ca.gov

14 Channel Islands National Park. *Anacapa Island, just a 95-minute boat ride from the coast, offers a chance to hike, camp, kayak, fish, or snorkel—but you have to bring your own food and water.*

14 Channel Islands National Park
Access from Spinnaker Dr., Ventura

The park's mainland visitors center—which is in Ventura—provides an enticing view of what to expect here and it's well worth a visit. It adjoins a dock from which commercial boats depart regularly for Anacapa and Santa Cruz islands and occasionally for Santa Rosa, San Miguel, and Santa Barbara islands.

The islands, rarely crowded, offer an unrivaled opportunity to observe the overwhelming diversity of marine, bird, animal, and plant life sustained in the park and the surrounding National Marine Sanctuary. Any list of what to look for would be encyclopedic, but most people come to see the seals and sea lions, pelicans, and foxes, as well as the porpoises and dolphins. Most whales may be seen offshore from December through March; humpbacks and blues can be seen in the summer.

Anacapa is only a 95-minute boat ride from the coast; Santa Cruz island lies 20 miles south. Visitors can hike, kayak, camp, dive, or fish. When snorkeling in the coves, visitors can see spiny sea urchins, bright sea stars, and brilliant orange garibaldi. Dress to ward off penetrating sea spray and hot sun, and bring your own food and water.

Boats go to Anacapa and Santa Cruz (weather permitting) year-round; to Santa Barbara, Santa Rosa, and San Miguel, summer only. Fare charged.
(805) 658-5730
www.nps.gov/chis

15 Tule Elk State Reserve

Off Stockdale Rd.,
Buttonwillow

Oil derricks may seem to be the only things moving in the lazy heat that lies over the cotton fields for so much of the year in this area. But then you come to Tule Elk State Reserve, where small, shaggy elk are seen grazing.

Given the top-heavy three- by four-foot span of mature antlers on adult bulls that measure only four feet from hoof to shoulder, no wonder they seem to move somewhat gingerly. They also often click their antlers in a dancelike rhythm, or otherwise communicate in strange blowing sighs or grunts.

There are some 35 of these engaging animals in the reserve herd, but tule elk were once so plentiful in the formerly rich San Joaquin Valley flood plains that English explorer Sir Francis Drake described them as appearing to "flow from the foothills to the seas."

Then 19th-century ranchers encroached on their grasslands, and hunters and traders shot them for fur, food, and tallow. By 1874 their numbers were down to a single pair. Intensive conservation efforts, however, have increased the population to a reassuring 3,000.

The elk are sensitive to too much scrutiny, so quiet is advisable when viewing them. Some of the best viewing can be had in the summer, when they love wallowing in their water hole, or in the cool spring, when they are friskier.

Open year-round.
(661) 764-6881
www.parks.ca.gov

16 Mono Lake Tufa State Reserve. *Calcium carbonate (tufa) formations rise out of this 700,000-year-old lake, creating a fantasy landscape.*

16 Mono Lake Tufa State Reserve

Lee Vining

Author Mark Twain called the fantasy landscape of Mono Lake a "sullen, silent, sail-less sea," and indeed the 700,000-year-old lake is three times saltier than the ocean and has a forbidding mien.

It is fed by melting snow and underwater springs and is dotted with dramatic and intricately filigreed white limestone towers, knobs, and spires, produced when calcium-laden fresh water wells up through alkaline lake water, precipitating calcium carbonate, or tufa.

As the lake level drops (through natural evaporation), and as freshwater sources are diverted to provide drinking water for the Los Angeles area, the lake bed's tufa formations are exposed.

No fish can live in the concentrated minerals and salts of Mono Lake, but brine shrimp and alkali flies thrive in the trillions. They provide food for the thousands of gulls and other migratory birds that flock here in spring and summer.

The lake's South Tufa area features a one-mile nature trail that clearly explains the lake and its peculiarities. Other attractions in this immense reserve (17,000 acres) include exceptionally buoyant swimming at nearby Navy Beach, boating, and if you arrive at the right time—dusk, say— a glimpse of the awesome alpenglow, the strange phenomenon of reflected light that bathes the High Sierra with rose and gold.

Open year-round.
(760) 647-6331
www.parks.ca.gov, or
www.monolake.org

17 Ancient Bristlecone Pine Forest

Big Pine

Suspended eerily on the rugged slopes of the White Mountains, at an altitude of 10,000 or more feet, is a stand of one of the planet's oldest living trees: the Great Basin bristlecone pine *(Pinus longaeva)*. The most ancient specimen is the 4,700-year-old Methuselah, which stands in a grove of pines that has been growing here for 4,000 years or more. The exact location of the tree is kept confidential in order to protect it.

Twelve miles farther along the road that crosses the forest is the world's largest bristlecone pine. Here in the Patriarch Grove, at 11,000 feet, is the Old Patriarch itself, which measures more than 36 feet in circumference.

The bristlecones' tortured shapes reflect the barren, windswept conditions amid which they persevere, jutting out from the mountainside like bleached bones or driftwood. Many branches appear dead, while others are thickly furred with green needles. Drippings of clear, bluish sap perfume the air. For all the seeming aridity of the land, there are lovely stands of wildflowers in the Patriarch area in August.

In most weather conditions the steep road to the forest provides breathtaking views across Owens Valley to the sheer white face of the Sierra Nevada. But after big snowfalls, cars must turn back at the Sierra Vista lookout, which is at an elevation of 10,000 feet. In good weather take advantage of miles of trails and picnic grounds beautifully sited in and around this great forest.

Open year-round, but road closed to vehicles beyond the Pinyon picnic area (elevation 7,500 feet), Dec.–early May. (760) 873-2500

www.r5.fs.fed.us/inyo/vvc/bcp

17 Ancient Bristlecone Pine Forest. *This tree's tortured shape reflects the barren conditions that it has endured for the past 4,000 years.*

18 Wildrose Charcoal Kilns and Mahogany Flat, Death Valley National Park

Off CA Hwy. 190, take either Emigrant Canyon Rd. or Panamint Valley Rd.

From Wildrose campground a narrow and sometimes difficult gravel track climbs through Wildrose Canyon to Thorndike Campground at 7,400 feet, near which looms a strange colony of what look like giant beehives or prehistoric dwellings. These are the Wildrose Charcoal Kilns, 10 perfectly aligned stone-and-mortar structures some 30 feet in diameter at the base and rising to a height of about 25 feet. They were built in the 1870s to turn local juniper and pinyon pine into charcoal for the lead and silver ore smelters near the Modoc and Minnietta mines.

Nobody has used the kilns for at least a century, but their sooty, conical interiors remain architecturally and acoustically fascinating. When you speak inside one, the echo seems to come from many places at once, and you can still smell the odor of burnt wood.

A mile beyond the kilns lies Mahogany Flat (with campground), the site of a forest of sinewy mountain mahogany, and the trailhead for the strenuous seven-mile hike to Death Valley's highest point, Telescope Peak (11,049 feet).

Open year-round, weather conditions permitting; check with park ranger. High-clearance vehicles recommended. (760) 786-3200

www.nps.gov/deva

19 Red Rock Canyon State Park
Mojave Desert

The smoothly sculpted clay, sandstone, lava, and cliff formations in the canyon form a natural divide between the Sierra Nevada and the Mojave Desert. At Red Cliffs Preserve (on the eastern side of Route 14, which runs for about seven miles through the park), erosion has carved the stone into corrugated ripples whose shades range from pristine white to peppermint candy reds. The colorful rock formations in the park served as landmarks during the early 1870s for freight wagons that stopped for water. The entire area is a geological treasure house, but rock hounds may be happiest in Opal Canyon (first right after Red Cliffs Preserve). Many movies have been filmed here, including *Jurassic Park*.

At Red Cliffs, where the bluffs crumble into dunes, Joshua trees offer shelter to the ubiquitous jackrabbits. Much rarer and well worth looking for are desert tortoises, the official state reptile. You can glimpse them here from March into June, when they venture out of their burrows morning and evening.

On the opposite side of the highway from Red Cliffs loom the appropriately named and colonnaded White House Cliffs. A campground nestles beneath their white walls, and Hagen Canyon Preserve Trail—for hikers only—commences at the nearby ranger station. There are, however, many other sandy tracks suitable for horses, and a few are open to cars.

Despite such easy accessibility, the park's reaches are usually so invitingly empty that it's hard to believe Los Angeles's teeming millions are only a few hours away from you.

Open year-round. Admission charged. (661) 942-0662

www.calparksmojave.com

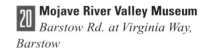

20 Mojave River Valley Museum
Barstow Rd. at Virginia Way, Barstow

Situated at the heart of the Mojave region, the museum is packed with a miscellany of objects related to valley history and geology. There's a large section devoted to the Calico Early Man Archaeological Site discoveries, including

200,000-year-old chipped stone tools. Dr. Louis Leakey, among others, believed that the Mojave may be one of the earliest sites of human habitation in the New World, and until his death in 1972 he supervised the Calico dig.

Material from other archaeological sites is on display, including the 15-million-year-old bones of a three-toed horse at the Barstowian fossil beds and the teeth of a 15-million-year-old camel. There are also objects from the Chemehuevi Indian culture, and a gruesomely fascinating case containing the remains of a mysterious "headless horseman" and the rusting weapons that apparently belonged to him. Collections of precious and semi-precious stones provide milder excitement for rock lovers (the mineralogy exhibits also include borax miners' tools and artifacts).

A block from the museum is the Barstow Way Station, an information center where tours of the Calico Early Man Site can be arranged.

Open year-round.
(760) 256-5452
http://mvm.4t.com

21 Providence Mountains State Recreation Area and Mitchell Caverns Natural Preserve

For 16 miles leading north from Route 40, on Essex Road, a glistening blacktop is the sole evidence of human intrusion into this windswept desert vista, rimmed on the horizon by the jagged Providence Mountains. The views as you climb have a calm, eerie quality and a rare dimension of spaciousness and mystery. The road ends at a campground and visitors center up 4,330 feet.

From here tours of the Mitchell Caverns are conducted by a ranger who points out interesting features along the three-quarter-mile trail, which is steep but offers fantastic scenery. Steel gates in the mountainside, designed to let bats in and out but to restrict people to the tours, admit visitors to two of the caverns, illuminated to set off the calcite formations.

Most of the park's 5,250 acres are open for hiking, and in this clear atmosphere many amateur astronomers set up their telescopes for days at a time. But remember that water is scarce and the nights are cold. Wildflowers are a major attraction in March and April, but the desert blooms in September, too. Checklists of the area's plants, birds, amphibians, and reptiles are available. Rattlesnakes are common, so be on the lookout.
Open year-round. Cave tours daily, mid-Sept.–mid-June.
(760) 928-2586
www.parks.ca.gov

22 Joshua Tree National Park
Twentynine Palms

Here is the very essence of the desert: clear skies; crisp, clean, sparkling air; and some half-million acres of fascinating landforms, plants, and animals. The area is in fact the conjunction of two deserts—the Colorado to the east and the higher, cooler, and moister Mojave in the western part of the monument, where the Joshua trees grow.

These strange trees—with their shaggy bark resembling a pelt of rough fur and their contorted branches bearing clusters of spiny leaves—could hardly be imagined, but once seen, they can never be forgotten. Great jumbled mounds of gigantic rounded boulders appear randomly among the trees, adding to the surreal character of the landscape.

Don't miss Keys View, at the end of a paved road from Ryan Campground. Here a serene expanse of purple and gray mountains fills the horizon, the valleys below lost in olive and amber shadow.

At the park's northeast entrance is the Oasis Visitor Center, where there is indeed an oasis—Twentynine Palms. From the center a road heads south through the Colorado Desert, where cholla cactus and scarlet-flowering ocotillo thrust their thorny limbs above patches of creosote bushes, the prevailing form of plant life here. Near the south entrance a four-mile trail beginning at Cottonwood Spring (a man-made oasis that bird-watchers will find rewarding) leads to Lost Palms, the largest of the park's five oases. There are nine campgrounds, mainly in the central section of the park, and a variety of hiking trails. Water is scarce, so bring your own.
Open year-round.
(760) 367-5500
www.nps.gov/jotr

23 Torrey Pines State Reserve and State Beach
San Diego

Torrey pines, which grow only here and on Santa Rosa Island, far to the north, cover the reserve's rocky headland like dense green jade set against golden sandstone. They extract moisture from fog and mist through exceptionally long needles and have an extensive root system that holds them firm against the fierce Pacific winds. Mojave yucca and mission manzanita also thrive here. The sandy track of Razor Point Trail, which begins near the handsome old adobe visitors center, winds its fragrant way seaward among a

Torrey Pines State Reserve and State Beach. *Torrey pines hold firm to the rocks as the ocean pounds away at the bluffs below.*

 Anza-Borrego Desert State Park. *At this enormously varied park, flowers and cacti carpet the desert floor.*

profusion of trees and other plants.

From the smooth red stone of Razor Point itself, the loftiest spot in the reserve, there are spacious views of the pines, Los Penasquitos Marsh, and the graceful sweep of the beach—protected and warm the year-round. Another path descends rugged yellow cliffs to Flat Rock, sometimes frequented by surfers. Dolphins can often be seen from the beach, and in season (December through March), gray whales.

Open year-round. Visitors center open 9 A.M.–5 P.M. daily. Parking fee.
(858) 755-2063
www.parks.ca.gov

24 Anza-Borrego Desert State Park
Borrego Springs
Only the toughest plants and animals survive in this 600,000-acre section of the Colorado Desert,

with its bleached sands and desolate landscape of eroded ridges. The campground in the Bow Willow area makes an agreeable headquarters: Never crowded, it's only about 10 miles from the park's southern entrance. You can stroll in any direction through open sand and savor unimpeded vistas beneath the dome of a turquoise sky.

Nearby trails, more ambitious, skirt the Carrizo Badlands on the park's eastern edge or, to the west, lead into Bow Willow Canyon along the route the Kumeyaay Indians followed to the uplands in the spring. Evidence of these vanished people (their village sites and petroglyphs) is scattered throughout the park.

Just north of Bow Willow Canyon, near Mountain Palm Springs, the scene changes at the Palm Bowl, where a magical ring of more than 100 palms could be a vision from the *Arabian Nights*.

Look for rare specimens of the squat elephant tree near here, too: It has the gray, wrinkly appearance of an elephant's trunk.

If you drive still deeper into the park, stop at Agua Caliente Hot Springs, which are fed into scrupulously clean, covered swimming pools, or penetrate northward as far as the elaborate visitors center at Borrego Springs. It's an excellent introduction to exploring the rest of this vast and enormously varied park.

Open year-round.
(760) 767-5311
www.parks.ca.gov

25 Avalon on Catalina Island
22 miles off the coast of Los Angeles
This island is a magical getaway that can be reached from Los Angeles in less than an hour by boat or 15 minutes by helicopter. Your first stop should be Santa Catalina Island Interpretive Center, an interactive museum nestled in a large canyon at an elevation of about 500 feet. Visitors can learn about the ocean, marine life, his-

tory of the island, and its flora and fauna while listening to recordings of whales and dolphins. Hiking trails begin next to the center.

Remote, seldom-seen parts of the island's rugged interior can also be explored. An off-road, guided tour in a large four-wheel-drive vehicle takes you along mountain ridges and through a canyon, with views of isolated coves, 2,000-foot peaks, and the Pacific Ocean.

You can check out the American bald eagle habitat at Middle Ranch, where restoration projects and conservation efforts around the island are on display. On the way, stop at the Catalina nature center, with its native plant garden, and at the Airport-in-the-Sky, which sits on two leveled mountain peaks at an elevation of 1,600 feet. During the tour, passengers are likely to spot wild buffalo, introduced to the island by a film production company in 1924.

Museum open daily.
Tours: (310) 510-2000;
Interpretive Center: (310) 510-2514
www.visitcatalina.org/press.htm

 Avalon on Catalina Island. *After hiking the island's many trails and exploring its interior, visitors can also kayak to secluded beaches and coves.*

Rifle Falls State Park. *East Rifle Creek takes a spectacular plunge in a remote mountain area (see opposite page).*

Colorado

The splendor of the Rockies, vast sand dunes, and ancient American Indian ruins blend with memories of mining camps, pioneers, and the Santa Fe Trail.

In one grand wilderness straddling the Continental Divide and studded with magnificent peaks, there are 200 miles of hiking and horseback trails. In other areas trails traverse foothills and prairies, canyons and mesas.

Watery settings include a reservoir, a spectacular falls, and a 15,000-acre lake that is shared with New Mexico. The Great Sand Dunes, in their unlikely inland location, are the tallest in America.

American Indian culture is recalled by some 11th-century dwellings and a museum devoted to the Utes, the last Indians to roam freely here. Other museums document the lives of the soldiers, miners, farmers, and ranchers who settled this rugged land.

1 Mount Zirkel Wilderness, Routt National Forest

Easiest access: at Steamboat Springs take Cty. Rte. 129 north 19 miles to Clark, then follow Seedhouse Rd.
Visitors to this 160,000-acre wilderness will find nature's splendor and solitude in its most primeval magnificence. Spreading along the Continental Divide, the area contains more than a dozen peaks around 12,000 feet high, more than 65 small lakes—many of them too remote to be named—and countless cascading streams. The terrain includes stands of spruce, pine, and quaking aspen.

However, in 1997 an unusually strong windstorm blew down some four million trees, triggering a spruce beetle epidemic, which is killing many trees. Because of this, the fire danger here is high, so be sure to check with the U.S. Forest Service for restrictions before hiking or riding on some of the 200 miles of trails.

Elk and deer graze in the meadows during summer. Anglers will take brook, rainbow, and cutthroat trout. Two campgrounds are maintained by the Forest Service.
Open year-round but often inaccessible in winter; campgrounds usually open June–Sept.
(970) 879-1870
www.fs.fed.us/r2/mbr/rd-hpbe

1 Mount Zirkel Wilderness, Routt National Forest. *Gelpin Lake reflects the magnificence of the Rockies in this 160,000-acre wilderness.*

2 Lory State Park

Off Rte. 287, Bellvue
A former cattle ranch, this 2,500-acre park is true Rocky Mountain high country, ranging in elevation from 5,000 to 7,000 feet. In a dramatically scenic setting sagebrush and prairie grassland valleys are flanked by orange sandstone hogback ridges. Moving upward, slopes covered with low-growing mountain shrubs give way to imposing ponderosa pine forests with patches of bare rock.

The varied vegetation provides habitats for many animals. Wild turkeys, red-tailed hawks, and blue grouse are often sighted, as are the mule deer and Abert squirrels with their long, tufted ears.

The park has 25 miles of trails, open to both hikers and horseback riders, and tent camping is permitted at six backcountry sites along them. A cross-country horse jumping course is also available. Trail enthusiasts can hike the routes up Arthur's Rock, which rises to 6,780 feet. This promontory provides a breathtaking view of Fort Collins and its surroundings.
Open year-round. Admission charged.
(970) 493-1623
www.coloradoparks.org

COLORADO

3 Overland Trail Museum

U.S. Rte. 6, east of Sterling

In the 1860s the Overland Trail was one of the most heavily used routes in the nation. Long lines of covered wagons and frequent runs by the coaches of the Overland Stage Line carried settlers and adventurers westward by the thousands. The starting segment of the trail along the South Platte River here was notable as an easy-to-follow natural highway with a sure supply of water and game.

The stone structure that houses the museum is a replica of an old fort, a stronghold established for protection from American Indians. The "village" behind the main structure is composed of several buildings from pre-1915, including a one-room school-house, a general store, a black-smith shop, a country church, a barn, and a barbershop. The west-ward-bound emigrants are com-memorated by a collection of household items they carried with them, including an 1861 sewing machine and a handsome hand-carved cherry rocker. The cattle business that later flourished on the vast surrounding plains is recalled with displays of spurs, chaps, saddles, one of the world's largest collections of branding irons, and an array of early farm implements.

The area's earliest history is represented by cases of mastodon and mammoth bones and Ameri-can Indian arrowheads.

Open year-round; call for Sunday and Monday seasonal hours. Admission is free but donations are accepted.
(970) 522-3895

www.sterlingcolo.com/recreation/ museum.html

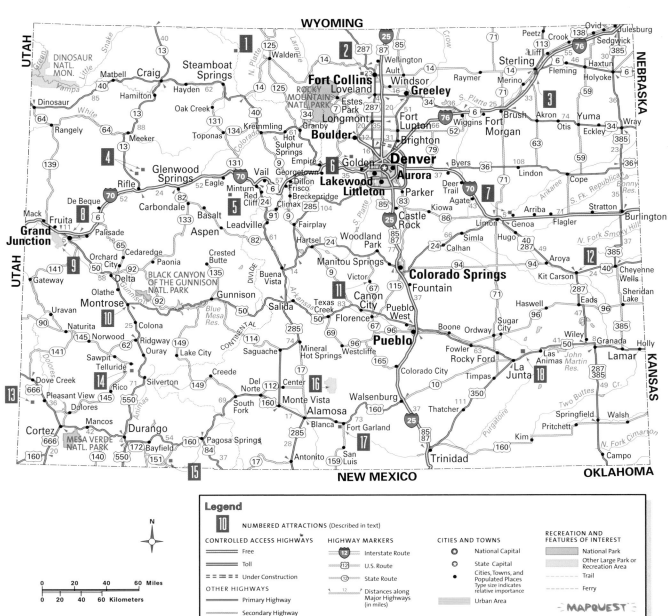

4 Rifle Gap and Rifle Falls State Parks

This remote mountain area has two state parks, and—surprisingly in this dry region—the most notable feature of each is water. The reservoir in Rifle Gap is a 350-acre lake created by the damming of East and Middle Rifle creeks in 1965. The other part is Rifle Falls, where East Rifle Creek takes a spectacular plunge.

Filled with mountain runoff, the reservoir has clear turquoise water that makes it an inviting place to swim, boat, sail, and water-ski. Anglers are likely to catch walleyes, bass, pike, perch, and trout. The trout come from a hatchery just five miles up the road that is open to visitors.

About four miles north of the reservoir, Rifle Falls State Park not only has an impressive trio of

90-foot cascades side by side, but its limestone cliff has a number of small caves, the largest about 90 feet long and 25 feet high. The caves' walls and ceilings are covered with an amazing pattern of small crisscrossing stalactites.

Open year-round. Admission charged.
(970) 625-1607

www.parks.state.co.us

⓼ Dinosaur Journey. *Visitors check out a tyrannosaurus at the Museum of Western Colorado's Dinosaur Valley.*

⓹ Sylvan Lake State Park

Eagle, 1500 Brush Creek Rd., off Hwy. 6 west

For anyone craving an authentic taste of Colorado's rugged natural beauty, this incredibly scenic park is the perfect stop. Not only nestled in the heart of the Rocky Mountains at an impressive elevation of 8,500 feet, it's also surrounded by the White River National Forest. This unspoiled alpine retreat boasts miles of pine, fir, blue spruce, and juniper amid great formations of glacial rock and sandstone. Migratory and resident birds include the raven, golden eagle, and the mountain bluebird.

Ideal for hiking, picnicking, taking breathtaking photographs, or simply relaxing, the park also contains a shimmering 40-acre lake. Anglers will revel in the bounty of trout. And for winter enthusiasts, there's ice fishing as well as cross-country skiing, snowshoeing, and snowmobiling.

Sylvan offers cabins and campsites for rent, with accommodations for tents, trailers, and RV units.

Open year-round. Entrance fee.
(970) 328-2021
http://parks.state.co.us/sylvan

⓺ Golden Gate Canyon State Park

13 miles northwest of Golden

Lumberjacks, settlers, and miners with pack animals in tow once trudged the network of trails crossing this rugged mountain terrain. For hikers who follow in their footsteps today, this is the jewel of Colorado parks, a place of quiet forests, rushing streams, and magnificent scenery. The mountains—green and fragrant with spruce, pine, and fir, and spangled in early autumn with the bright yellow of quaking aspen— are the domain of mule deer, elk, black bears, bobcats, and mountain lions. Golden eagles and red-tailed hawks soar above.

Some 12,000 acres are covered by 35 miles of trails, ranging in length from just over a mile to nearly six miles. Some are strenuous, with steep climbs, but other trails proceed easily along valley floors and ridges and may be used for horses. The best vista, however, is not far from the road: Panorama Point offers nearly a 100-mile view of the towering Continental Divide.

Reverend's Ridge Campground has such amenities as hot showers; Aspen Meadows Campground is for tents only.

Open year-round.
Golden Gate: (303) 582-3707
Reverend's Ridge: (800) 678-2267
Admission charged.
www.coloradoparks.org.

⓻ Tower Museum

Take Exit 371 from I-70 at Genoa; continue half a mile west.

One of the first things a visitor to this offbeat 22-room museum encounters is a puzzling array of some 20,000 artifacts. Anyone who can identify 10 in a row gets an admission refund. Few people today, however, can recognize such items as a buggy-whip holder, a buffalo cud, and a magician's knife. But it is fun to try, and it is a good introduction to the truly eccentric nature of the place and its collection.

The 75-foot wooden tower and the sprawling complex of rock rooms at its base are the brainchild of C. W. Gregory, sometimes known as Colorado's P. T. Barnum. He put up the tall structure to attract visitors and dubbed it the World's Wonder View Tower; from its knoll-top site it offers a spectacular view extending into six states on a clear day.

The museum's chief attractions, however, are its collections of archaeological materials, antique items, and oddities. These include 75,000-year-old mammoth bones, 8,500-year-old buffalo bones, 20,000 Indian arrowheads, a thousand paintings by the American Indian princess Ravenwing, and collections of old firearms.

Open year-round. Admission charged.
(719) 763-2309

⓼ Dinosaur Journey

Fruita

More than 140 million years ago, colossal creatures thrived on the warm, humid plains of what is now the American West. Over time, however, these beasts were trapped and buried under layers of sedimentary rock, but their bones have survived as fossils.

Today, Fruita, a glowing carat in the "Dinosaur Diamond" of western Colorado and northeastern Utah, is world famous for its wealth of dinosaur excavation sites, fossil trails, hands-on archaeological activities, and state-of-the-art exhibits. The area lays claim to more than 30 dinosaur species.

From downtown Grand Junction, off I-70, eager explorers can easily find their way to Dinosaur Journey. Visitors can also view the genuine bones of a stegosaurus, allosaurus, and other members of long-extinct species, and tour a working paleontology laboratory where scientists are restoring and preserving the fossils of dinosaurs found in nearby quarries.

The adventure continues out on the nearby dinosaur trails. Riggs Hill, a three-quarter-mile trail, marks the site of the world's first brachiosaurus, discovered in 1900. Dinosaur Hill, a mile-long trail, boasts the quarry of the 70-foot-long apatosaurus. The Trail

Through Time, about 30 miles outside of town within the Rabbit Valley Research Natural Area, features a camarasaurus skeleton and a glimpse of a quarry in action. While there, visitors can sign up for a five-day expedition, providing a crash course in geology and hands-on excavation experience.

Before returning to the modern world, explorers can grab a bite downtown at Fruita's Dinosaur Pizza, which specializes in exotic-sounding dishes like the swinasaurus—a perfectly harmless sandwich with ham substituted for dinosaur meat.

Open year-round. Entrance fees.
Fruita Visitors Bureau: (970) 858-9335
Dinosaur Journey: (970) 242-0971
www.dinosaurjourney.com

9 Colorado National Monument
Fruita

The wild vastness and beauty of this series of canyons and mesas have been preserved, thanks to local Grand Valley residents led by John Otto, a turn-of-the-century maverick who campaigned tirelessly for a national park.

Sculpted by wind and rain and ancient seas over millions of years, the magnificent formations of orange, yellow, and red sandstone can be enjoyed not only by campers and backpackers but by day visitors. The 23-mile Rim Rock Drive that snakes through the park can be covered on a short outing. The road is narrow, with precipitous drop-offs, but it offers excellent vantage points.

Longer trails proceed across mesas and zigzag up and down the canyon walls. Golden eagles, turkey vultures, and several hawk species are among the birds that swoop overhead. Spring and fall are the best times for hiking. In

the summer heat, a hat and a supply of water are essential. Overnight backpackers should register at the visitors center and ask about restrictions.

Open year-round. Admission charged.
(970) 858-3617
www.nps.gov/colm

10 Ute Indian Museum
17253 Chipeta Dr., Montrose

The Utes were a diverse, widely scattered people who lived throughout the Rockies, in Colorado as well as Utah, the state named for them. They are believed to be the only tribe native to Colorado; the Cheyennes and other Plains tribes were pushed westward into the state by white settlements.

In the late 1800s and early 1900s Thomas McKee, a photographer, lived among the Utes, documenting their lives in pictures and acquiring artifacts. His collection is effectively displayed in this small but fascinating

museum run by the Colorado Historical Society.

In one of the two galleries, you'll find traditional and ceremonial items used by the various branches of the tribe. An interactive computer kiosk interprets the Bear Dance, the oldest of the Ute ceremonies, and you can see a replica of a Ute wickiup dwelling.

The second gallery features famous Utes, most notably the great chief Ouray, who led the tribe in signing a treaty with the United States in the 1860s. Ouray's wicked-looking horn-handled knife and a beaded buckskin shirt made for him by his wife, Chipeta, are on display.

Open daily May–Oct.; Mon.–Sat. Nov.–Apr. Admission charged.
(970) 249-3098
www.coloradohistory.org

11 Victor

Located only six miles from Cripple Creek, this once-thriving

10 Ute Indian Museum. *A replica of a dwelling used by the Utes, believed to be the only tribe native to Colorado, stands at the museum in Montrose.*

mining town, which was the site of a world-renowned gold strike in the 1890s, now has a population of about 600 rather than the thousands it had at its peak. Head frames used to hoist ore from the ground and rock dumps are the only visible remains of the 400-odd mines that filled more than 70 trains per day with ore.

But the many structures that are still standing speak with a hushed eloquence of the town's prosperous past. Mining has not totally disappeared from Victor. The largest gold mine in the state is again producing ore, and here you can see firsthand the intensive labor that went into gold mining during the 1890s.

Most of the buildings are brick, and many date from 1899, when Victor was rebuilt after fire leveled the original wooden structures. Among them are a school, a hotel, a railroad station, fraternal lodges, and the city hall. There are also the remains of a mine where gold was found while the foundation for a hotel was being dug.

A museum displays mementos of the town's colorful past, along with items relating to the well-known newscaster Lowell Thomas, who grew up here. The town's even more famous son was the prizefighter Jack Dempsey, who worked in the mines and trained for his early fights in the old jail.

Visitors who want a close-up view of the mines should stick to public roads and trails; old mine workings are common in the hillsides and are dangerous.

Open year-round.
(719) 689-2284
**www.tellercountyrdc.com/
victorchamber.html**

Kit Carson Museum

302 Park St., Kit Carson

This museum's name is somewhat misleading. It is not dedicated to the legendary Western hero but rather to the town here that was named after him. In its glory days more than a century ago, Kit Carson was a thriving railhead, a town of Western legend with saloons, dance-hall girls, and a six-shooter on every hip. But little survives from that town, which burned to the ground, and the museum's collection concentrates on the relatively quiet high-plains farming and grazing center that replaced it.

The museum is housed in a 1904 Union Pacific depot and station master's house, still furnished with an old-fashioned telephone, a telegraph key, and signal levers. Several displays re-create late-19th-century rooms with period furnishings and costumed mannequins. There is a small doll collection and another of farm implements ranging from horse-drawn planters to harrows and hay rakes. Among the other diverse items that outline the community's history are American Indian arrowheads and grindstones, a bear trap, branding irons, and a caboose stove, all donated by townspeople.

Open daily Memorial Day–Labor Day.
(719) 962-3306

Lowry Pueblo

For centuries the ancestral Puebloan Indians dominated the Four Corners region (the meeting place of Utah, Colorado, Arizona, and New Mexico), where they built pueblos and cliff dwellings. But long before the time of Columbus, they migrated, leaving

Lowry Pueblo. *Built on a mesa around the end of the 11th century, Lowry Pueblo probably accommodated 100 people in its three dozen rooms and nine ceremonial chambers.*

their homes behind. One of these habitats is Lowry Pueblo, part of the Canyons of the Ancients National Monument, a complex of three dozen rooms and nine kivas, or ceremonial chambers, built on a mesa around the end of the 11th century. Probably it accommodated a farming community of about 100 people, but it was abandoned after 50 years or so, and its stone walls were not discovered until the 20th century.

Now a national historic landmark, the pueblo is open to visitors. The unique feature at Lowry is the painted kiva, now protected with a roof. Its plastered walls are neatly painted with a cloud motif. At the Anasazi Heritage Center, visitors can find photo exhibits and a virtual reality tour of village life.

Open year-round.
(970) 882-4811
www.co.blm.gov

Lizard Head Wilderness Area

Telluride

Straddling the spectacular snow-capped San Miguel Mountains, this 41,000-acre preserve encompasses some of Colorado's most impressive peaks. Three rise more than 14,000 feet; several others, over 13,000 feet.

Although mining once made a brief foray into the basins, this wilderness remains a land of unspoiled beauty and a delight for backpackers and mountain climbers who want to experience real wilderness in the high Rockies.

No vehicles are allowed in the area. Trailheads for the five established hiking routes can be reached along forest roads leading off Route 145. The most popular is the Navajo Lake Trail, which cuts through meadows and forests of spruce and aspen and then climbs steep switchbacks before it descends to the lake. Backpackers are asked to camp in preexisting campgrounds in the interest of

environmental protection. Detailed topographical maps are essential and can be obtained at local book and sporting goods stores. The high mountains can be difficult and dangerous. And even on lower pinnacles, a climber should be prepared for razor-edge ridges above the timberline and permanent snowfields near the summits.

Snow remains on some trails until mid-June, and the temperature can drop below freezing on mid-summer nights. Heavy downpours are common on summer afternoons. The preserve can also be explored by day hikers staying at nearby campgrounds. Most areas have little or no firewood, so bring a cook-stove. Horseback riders are welcome once the trails are fully dry, around the end of June.

Open year-round but usually inaccessible in winter.
(970) 327-4261
www.fs.fed.us/r2/gmug

Navajo State Park

Arboles

Fed by melting snow, Navajo Lake is a giant reservoir with some 15,000 acres of sparkling turquoise water. More than three-quarters of the lake is in New Mexico, backed up against a dam about 20 miles to the south. This Colorado state park—located on the lakeshore close to the state line—offers perfect access to the water and to all the water-sports activities that it invites. Indeed, the park boasts a quarter-mile-long boat ramp, the largest in the state. It also has a good marina and dock where boats can be rented. Waterskiing, sailing, and wind-surfing are all popular, as well as fishing. There is also a small, unguarded inlet for swimming.

Miles of outstanding hiking areas along the San Juan and Piedra rivers are available. Ducks, geese, songbirds such as thrushes and meadowlarks, and lizards are among the most commonly observed wildlife.

Park open year-round. Admission charged.
(970) 883-2208
www.coloradoparks.org
www.parks.state.co.us

16 Great Sand Dunes National Monument and Preserve

Mosca
The "Great" in the name of this fascinating natural phenomenon is more than appropriate. Not only are these ever changing dunes ranked as the tallest in North America but the dune field stretches impressively over 30 square miles of high mountain valley floor. The vast expanse of sand was formed over millions of years by the action of shifting waterways in the San Juan Mountains.

The park itself includes the main dune field nestled at the foot of the rugged Sangre de Cristo Mountains. Because of the mountains, the sand here is caught in a wind trap, and in spots 750-foot-high dunes are formed that look like miniature mountains.

Not surprisingly, this unusual park appeals to sand skiers as well as to hikers, backpackers, and campers, who stay in a campground in an area of junipers and pines at the dunes' edge. Some visitors venture onto the dunes at night with flashlights in hopes of spotting the kangaroo rats and the giant sand-treader camel crickets that manage to survive in this arid environment.

The best weather is generally in spring and fall. In summer, even though the air temperature is moderate, the sand can get uncomfortably hot. The park tends to be crowded on Memorial Day weekend with visitors from the region.

Park and campground open year-round.
(719) 378-2312
www.nps.gov/grsa

17 Fort Garland Museum
Rte. 159
For a quarter of a century, beginning in 1858, this remote frontier garrison provided protection from the Ute Indians for settlers in the San Luis Valley. It was opened only a few years after the first pioneers arrived and was abandoned when the Utes were forced to settle on a reservation.

The fort's array of low adobe structures housed up to two companies of 100 men each. But it is best known for being the last command (1866–67) of the famed Kit Carson, then a colonel with the 1st New Mexico Cavalry.

At the restored fort, the commandant's quarters have been set up to look as they did during Carson's stay, and a life-size diorama shows him meeting with Utes in his office. In the officers' quarters and enlisted men's barracks, dioramas illustrate the Spanish conquest of the region, the early fur trade, an army pack train, and a stage holdup. There are also displays of uniforms, weapons, flags, and the Mexican woolen cloaks known as serapes.

Open daily. Admission charged.
(719) 379-3512
www.coloradohistory.org

18 Bent's Old Fort National Historic Site

La Junta
Hard on the heels of the first American explorers, trappers and traders eagerly extended their range into the high plains and mountains of the Southwest. Among the trading posts that sprang up in their wake, the most important was this one, which was built in the early 1830s by two Missouri brothers, William and Charles Bent, in partnership with a reputed French nobleman, Ceran St. Vrain.

Located on the Mountain Branch of the Sante Fe Trail, a fairly safe route following the Arkansas River, the adobe fort soon became a major hub for trade radiating south to Santa Fe and Mexico, as well as west to the Pacific and north into Wyoming.

For years the three men controlled a huge commercial empire. But a sequence of events—the Mexican War, the decline in trade,

the death of Charles Bent, the departure of St. Vrain, and a cholera epidemic—led William Bent to abandon the fort in 1849. Tradition holds that Bent was so irked by the army's refusal to buy the fort that he blew it up.

This national historic site is a reconstruction of the post as it appeared in its heyday in 1846. Within thick, high walls an open plaza is ringed by furnished living quarters, warehouses, workshops, and even a billiard room.

Inside the fort you can view the 20-minute documentary film *Castle of the Plains.* Self-guiding tours are also available. Staff members dressed as trappers, American Indians, and Mexicans demonstrate frontier activities.

Open year-round. Admission charged.
Call for updated schedule of events.
(719) 383-5010
www.nps.gov/beol

18 Bent's Old Fort National Historic Site. *This reconstruction shows the adobe fort that served as a hub for trade in southeast Colorado in the 1840s. It now houses living quarters, warehouses, and even a billiard room.*

Sharon Audubon Center. *A fall trip to the center's 2,000 acres of woodlands can overwhelm visitors with eye-popping color.*

Connecticut

Gracefully spanning the centuries, the Constitution State is a pleasure to explore, from charming small towns to centers of technology.

The Audubon Center here is one of the best of its kind, as is the collection of early-day tools at the Sloane-Stanley Museum. Connecticut's contribution to Yankee ingenuity is acknowledged in the Lock Museum and the American Clock & Watch Museum. A colonial copper mine, which also served as a prison, is now open for visitors. Further examples of the variety available here include an American Indian museum, a castle, dinosaur tracks, a museum of contemporary art, an opulent mansion, and some appealing historic houses.

1 Sharon Audubon Center
325 Rte. 4, Sharon

Here on 2,000 acres of woodlands, ponds, open fields, and marshes is a microcosm of 19th-century Connecticut. Habitats for the great variety of plants and wildlife found here are fast disappearing.

The property, donated by Mrs. Clement R. Ford, includes the Ford home, which now houses the center's offices, library, classrooms, and display areas.

Among the exhibits are specimens of the local plants and flowers as well as live turtles, frogs, snakes, crows, and raptors, all found nearby. The center has over 11 miles of scenic hiking trails.

At the Children's Adventure Center, a "please touch" table invites inspection of fur, bark, and animal bones, while silhouettes of birds suspended from the ceiling show their various sizes and shapes.

Workshops, nature classes, films, guided field trips, training programs and internships, and seasonal bird counts are all part of the center's program. And in early spring, visitors can watch the making of maple syrup with sap collected from local trees.
Open year-round.
(860) 364-0520
www.audubon.org/local/sanctuary/ sharon

1 Sharon Audubon Center. *Canada geese float on a misty pond within the center's 2,000 acres, which boast more than 11 miles of scenic hiking trails.*

2 Sloane-Stanley Museum and Kent Furnace
Rte. 7, Kent

Eric Sloane, the late Connecticut artist and writer, started this museum as a tribute to the ingenuity and craftsmanship of the early settlers in New England. It houses his extensive collection of tools made by these inventive Yankees for the seemingly countless outdoor chores, as well as household equipment. The objects range from pots and baskets to axes and wheelbarrows. Several of Sloane's still lifes are shown, along with the objects portrayed.

The property and the barn that houses the museum were donated by the Stanley Works of New Britain to celebrate its 125 years as a maker of hand tools, then turned over to the state of Connecticut's Historical Commission.

Next to the museum Sloane built a small cabin, using only old tools, local lumber, and stones— referring to an 1805 farmboy's diary as a guide. The cabin has an unusual chink-log chimney, a dirt floor, bottle-glass windows, and a small herb garden in the dooryard.

During the 19th century this was the site of the Kent Iron

CONNECTICUT

Furnace. Down a slight slope from the museum are the ruins of the sturdy granite structure, with its Gothic arch.

The museum is set on a wooded hillside overlooking the Housatonic River. Although the foliage in summer is so dense that the river is lost to view, the shady rise is an ideal setting for the picnic tables scattered there.

Open Wed.–Sun., mid-May–Oct.
Admission charged.
(860) 927-3849

www.chc.state.ct.us

3 The Aldrich Museum of Contemporary Art

258 Main St., Ridgefield
The contrast between the traditional exterior of the pre-Revolutionary building and the contemporary art it contains is an unexpected pleasure here. The museum, founded about 40 years ago by Larry Aldrich, a collector of contemporary art, is known for its exhibits focusing mainly on major trends in today's art world and the works of undiscovered artists.

Behind the museum, on a sloping lawn surrounded by flowering trees and shrubs, are sculptures. The terrace overlooking the garden is a pleasant place to sit and view the collection.

The museum presents three major exhibitions and six or seven smaller ones every year. Widely respected educational and cultural programming complements the exhibition schedule.

Open Tue.–Sun. year-round.
Admission charged.
(203) 438-4519

www.aldrichart.org

4 Lockwood-Mathews Mansion Museum

295 West Ave., Norwalk
LeGrand Lockwood, who had grown up in Norwalk and left home, returned as a millionaire in 1864 and built the grandest house in town, a magnificent 62-room mansion on a hill overlooking the Norwalk River.

With towers, turrets, arches, and iron grillwork on the rooftop, the granite building resembles a European castle overlaid with Victorian elegance. The four-story house, whose interior is decorated with exceptionally fine frescoes, marble carvings, etched glass panels, marquetry, and parquetry, has a skylighted rotunda 42 feet high. Many of the rooms open onto a balcony that surrounds this great hall. Sweeping up from the rotunda to the balcony is the main stairway, whose carved walnut banister has an elegant inlay of boxwood in the Greek key design. A peacock of blue stones inlaid in a garland of marble decorates one of the mansion's 25 fireplaces.

Shortly after the house was completed, the Lockwoods lost their fortune, and the Charles D. Mathews family of New York bought the estate and occupied it for more than 60 years.

Open Wed.–Sun., or by appointment, mid-Mar.–Jan. Admission charged.
(203) 838-9799

www.lockwoodmathews.org

5 Boothe Memorial Park and Museum

5774 Main St. Putney, Stratford

On a hill overlooking the Housatonic River, this park is maintained as a memorial to two eccentric bachelor brothers, David and Stephen Boothe, who willed the property to the town of Stratford.

Within the 32 acres of their estate is an amazing collection of 20 buildings. Included is a Dutch windmill, a blacksmith shop, a miniature lighthouse, and a pagoda-like redwood cathedral.

A 77-foot clock tower and belfry known as the Anniversary Tower houses family heirlooms gathered from cousins far and near, along with the family genealogy. Boothe Homestead Museum gives tours from 11 A.M. to 1 P.M. Tuesday through Friday and weekend afternoons.

Walking trails wind through the park to the various exhibits and to a rose garden and a sundial set in a circle of stones. Picnic tables under the trees overlook the river.

Open daily June 1–Oct. 1.

(203) 381-2046

www.ohwy.com/ct/b/boomempm.html

6 Southford Falls State Park

175 Quaker Farms Rd., Southbury

The waterfall that gives the park its name is on Eight Mile Brook, which flows eight miles from Lake Quassapaug to the Housatonic River. The plunging and cascading falls once drove a waterwheel that powered a sawmill, a gristmill, and a fulling mill for finishing wool cloth. Almost all that remains of these 19th-century industries is a grindstone, a part of the sluice-way, and a few foundation walls.

5 Boothe Memorial Park and Museum. *The Boothe brothers willed their 32 acres to the town of Stratford, which turned them into a memorial park and museum.*

Several trails loop through the woods, along the stream, and above the falls to Papermill Pond, formed by a dam across the brook. Here a quiet, woodsy expanse has picnic tables and barbecue pits. The pond, stocked with trout, is popular with fishermen. A mile-long loop trail leads to a lookout tower, which can be climbed for an overview of the park.

A picturesque covered bridge spanning the stream near the bottom of the falls is a replica of a laminated arch structure designed in 1804 by Theodore Burr, a well-known early American bridge builder.

Open year-round.

(203) 264-5169

www.dep.state.ct.us/rec/parks/ ctparks.html

7 Lock Museum of America

230 Main St., Terryville

In the 19th century the Connecticut Yankees' mechanical skills were convincingly demonstrated by their work as locksmiths. With a nucleus of some 5,000 old locks donated by the Eagle Lock Company of Terryville, the Lock Museum of America opened in 1972.

News of the museum spread quickly among collectors, and donations began to pour in. Ten years later, when more space was needed, a permanent home for the collection was built.

Every one of the locks in the original 5,000 was manufactured in Connecticut during the 19th century. Today's collection, numbering more than 23,000, represents manufacturers from all across the country, and although the emphasis is still on antique locks, many from the early 20th century are included.

Thousands of keys and other related objects are on display, and the museum library includes lock catalogs from many early American lock manufacturers.

Thomas Hennessy of Bristol, a well-known collector of locks and author of books on the subject, is the museum's curator.

Open Tues.–Sun., May–Oct.

(860) 589-6359

www.lockmuseum.com

8 New England Carousel Museum

Located at 95 Riverside Ave., Rte. 72, Bristol

For centuries kids of all ages have delighted in the carousel. Yet what Americans now know and adore as the merry-go-round was not created for child's play. In its earliest incarnation the carousel helped noblemen train for jousting and even for war, providing rounds of target practice in "lancing" the brass ring. Many years later carousels became a favorite pastime of elite, wealthy grown-ups, who sipped champagne astride gilded steeds.

This delightful museum is filled with such fascinating facts about the ride's history and folklore, as well as its unique craftsmanship and art. Situated in a beautifully restored 33,000-square-foot brick building, it's also home to the country's largest collection of antique carousels. Inside, carousel fans can wander among the pretty painted horses (and the occasional pigs, cows, ducks, lions, tigers, and giraffes) at their leisure or take a wonderfully informative guided tour.

In addition to carousels and their animals, the museum showcases an antique Wurlitzer carousel organ that plays tunes on old-fashioned punched music rolls, an exhibit on how wooden carousel horses were traditionally created, and an array of carousel art and decoration.

Children can sign up to create a carousel-themed craft to take home. And for adults eager to own their very own carousel pet, the museum's showroom sells full-sized resin reproduction horses. On-staff experts also make carousel horses, as well as restore carousel creatures of all varieties.

In the center of nearby Hartford, the museum manages an antique beauty—the Bushnell Park Carousel. Created in 1914 by Solomon Stein and Harry Goldstein, the artistic merry-go-round was rescued from an Ohio amusement park 60 years later and painstakingly restored. The huge three-row carousel sports 36 jumper horses, 12 stander horses, two chariots, and a Wurlitzer 153 bend organ. Visitors to the lovely, revitalized downtown area can take a memorable spin for a mere 50 cents.

Open May–Oct. Admission charged. The Bushnell Park Carousel is closed on rainy days.
(860) 585-5411
www.thecarouselmuseum.com

9 American Clock & Watch Museum

100 Maple St., Bristol
Before they were electrified, digitized, mass-produced, and taken for granted, clocks and watches were objects of beauty and wonder. This museum pays tribute to that earlier era. Here you will see an exceptional collection of American timepieces, including jeweled watches, alarm clocks, and wall clocks—many still running.

The museum is housed in an 1801 building called the Miles Lewis House. The addition of the Ebenezer Barnes Wing, whose paneling comes from a 1728 house of that name, extends the museum into an authentic early American sundial garden.

The collection includes examples from early American clockmakers, many of whom lived in Bristol and nearby towns, as well as timepieces of the 20th century.

Among the exhibits are hundreds of watches displayed in glass cases, several early shelf clocks lined up on a wall in the summer kitchen of the old mansion, and a mirror clock, flanked by two banjo clocks, hanging above an antique chest.

The Edward Ingraham Memorial Wing is dedicated to Bristol's clockmaking history.

Open Apr.–Nov. Closed Easter and Thanksgiving. Admission charged.
(860) 583-6070
www.clockmuseum.org

9 American Clock & Watch Museum. *An exceptional collection of American timepieces, made when clocks and watches were objects of beauty and weren't mass produced, can be seen at the museum.*

10 Old New-Gate Prison and Copper Mine

115 Newgate Rd., East Granby
The mine, the first of its kind in the American Colonies, was opened in 1707 by a group of Simsbury citizens, and it continued in operation under various lessees, including Governor Belcher of Massachusetts, for more than 65 years. At the height of its productivity, more than 20 miners worked here.

Although there had been several attempts to smelt copper ore in America, a new British law prohibited it, and the ore from this mine was shipped to England for processing. After two valuable consignments of copper were lost at sea, it was decided that shipping was uneconomical, and the mine was closed in 1773.

In that year the Connecticut colony designated the copper mine as a prison for burglars, horse thieves, robbers, and counterfeiters and named it for the infamous Newgate Prison in London. In 1776 New-Gate became the first state prison in America. During the American Revolution a number of Tories were sent here. About 50 years later, when the prison at Wethersfield was built, New-Gate was closed.

There are self-guiding tours through the tunnels where military prisoners were confined. The one original building still standing is the guardhouse, where some cells exist and exhibits are shown.

Across the street is Viets Tavern, which stood at this location well before the mines were converted to a prison, and was the home of the first prison warden. Mine temperatures range in the low 50s, and sweaters are recommended.

Open Wed.–Sun., mid-May–Oct. Admission charged.
(860) 653-3563
www.chc.state.ct.us

11 Somers Mountain Museum of Natural History and Primitive Technology

332 Turnpike Rd., Somers
What you will see here is the result of one man's consuming interest in the subject of American Indians. Founder James R. King created a museum of unusual scope. He started collecting artifacts at the age of 8, and his interest grew. He studied and lived on a number of reservations from Alaska to Mexico. The collection includes objects from every major North American Indian culture and is so extensive that only about half of it can be shown here at any one time.

The displays are remarkably varied, such as beadwork and the porcupine-quill work that preceded it; wampum, including stone wampum from 300 B.C.; arrowheads from Canada and from every state in the continental United States; war bonnets; weapons; peace pipes, some of them around 2,000 years old; papoose carriers; saddles made of buffalo bone and hide; and the newspaper, dated July 6, 1876, from Bismarck, Dakota Territory, that reported the dramatic news of Custer's last stand.

The gift shop sells contemporary American Indian handicrafts. These include such traditional items as beadwork, barkwork, totem poles, and moccasins.

Open Apr.–Dec.
(860) 749-4129
www.somersmountain.org

Dinosaur State Park

 Located at 400 West St., off Interstate 91, Rocky Hill

In the late 1960s, during a routine excavation for a new building, workers accidentally uncovered 2,000 early Jurassic Period fossil tracks. Made by a nameless carnivorous northeastern dinosaur nearly 200 million years ago, the tracks average a foot in length. Fifteen hundred of the ancient footprints have been buried for preservation. The remaining 500 have been designated a Registered National Landmark and enclosed beneath a geodesic dome for family viewing.

Under the dome, visitors will also find formidable life-sized Jurassic and Triassic dioramas, a reconstruction of a geologic formation, highlights from the discovery of the tracks, and sundry interactive displays.

Outside the dome, 21st-century explorers can walk the grounds once strolled by prehistoric giants. In addition to ample spots for picnicking, the park features more than two miles of nature trails. Nature enthusiasts will also enjoy the park's unique arboretum. It contains more than 250 species of trees, shrubs, and vines, with a commitment to growing representatives of plant families that thrived during the Age of the Dinosaur.

An added attraction for visitors is the ability to make actual casts of dinosaur tracks (from May 1 until Oct. 30). You must bring your own supplies, however.

Open year-round. Admission charged.
(860) 529-8423

www.dinosaurstatepark.org

13 Gillette Castle. *Overlooking the Connecticut River, this 24-room Victorian stone dwelling was designed by its first owner, stage actor William Gillette.*

Gillette Castle

13 *67 River Rd., East Haddam*

Towering atop a bluff overlooking the Connecticut River, this majestic castle rivals the famed medieval abodes of Europe. Recently restored to its original glory, the 24-room Victorian stone dwelling was meticulously designed by William Gillette, the actor renowned for his stage portrayal of Sherlock Holmes.

Until his death in 1937, Gillette called the colossal structure, complete with an authentic stone parapet, home. In fact, he spent most of his last 20 years here, living alone as a near recluse. Today the castle and its surrounding 184 acres comprise the state's most scenically impressive and tranquil public park, welcoming all romantic travelers.

Inside the castle, visitors will find a treasure trove of distinctive details. Each of the 47 intricately carved wooden doors features a unique mechanical locking device, including a lock shaped like an owl whose wings spread when the key turns. Twisting passages wind in and out of rooms reflecting Gillette's imaginative personality. In addition to five bedrooms, six baths, and an expansive third-floor suite, the castle houses a library, an art gallery, and a collection of Sherlock Holmes memorabilia.

After strolling through the interior, visitors can explore the amazing exterior architecture and enjoy breathtaking views of the countryside and river.

Open year-round. Admission charged for the castle's visitors center.
(860) 526-2336

www.friendsctstateparks.net/
parksgillette_castle.htm

The Thankful Arnold House

14 *On the corner of Hayden Hill and Walkley Hill Rds., Haddam*

The house as it stands today has a remarkable unity, considering the history of its construction. Built in 1794–95, the place had only two rooms and a loft, all stacked against the chimney wall. It was bought four years later by Joseph Arnold, a descendant of one of the founders of this community on the Connecticut River, after his marriage to Thankful Clark.

In their 15 years of marriage before Joseph died at age 49, the Arnolds had 11 children, and the house, as can be imagined, had to be expanded. The additions, made about 1798 and 1810, brought the structure to its present size.

Thankful lived here for 26 years after the death of her husband, and the house was known locally as hers. All told, it was occupied by members of the family for more than 150 years.

The pumpkin-colored dwelling, which New Englanders call a bank or hillside house, has three stories in front and two on the slope at the back. Its restoration in the 1960s was sponsored by Isaac Arnold, a direct descendant, who turned it over to the Haddam Historical Society. The house, furnished with period pieces, is the society's headquarters and museum.

Open year-round, Mon.–Wed.
Call ahead for guided tours.
(860) 345-2400

www.thankfularnold.com

Thomas Griswold House

15 *171 Boston St., Guilford*

The white clapboard saltbox, built about 1774 by Thomas Griswold III for his two sons, stands on a gentle rise called the Griswold Ledge above the Old Post Road.

It started as a double house of the classic saltbox design and for almost 200 years was lived in by the Griswold family. In 1958 Robert Griswold DeForest sold the property to the Guilford Keeping Society, an organization dedicated to the preservation of the town's historic beginnings, and the Griswold House became the society's headquarters.

Through the years many changes had been made, with an ell, dormer windows, a shed, and a porch added. The society undertook a complete restoration in 1974, returning the saltbox to its original design.

During the restoration the 10-foot-wide kitchen fireplace was opened and was found to have two beehive ovens as well as a warming oven. Other features include a double-batten door, a round-back Guilford cupboard, and a few pieces of the original Griswold furniture, among them a 1760 cherry lowboy and a ladderback "Pilgrim" chair.

The surrounding gardens contain only plants available before 1820.
Open Tues.–Sun., mid-June–Oct. 1; Oct., weekends only.
(203) 453-3176
www.thomasgriswoldhouse.com

16 Mashamoquet Brook State Park

Rte. 44, Pomfret
These rolling hills were once the territory of the Mohegan Indians, who were forced out by early settlers. An occasional arrowhead or well-trodden footpath remains as a poignant reminder of the time when this land was theirs.

Two color-coded trails wind through the park's 960 acres—a three-mile Red and a four-mile Blue—taking hikers over terrain that is sometimes steep and rocky.

17 Mashantucket Pequot Museum & Research Center. *This state-of-the-art complex dramatically brings to life the tragedies and triumphs of the Pequot people.*

A self-guiding nature trail crosses a swampy area formed by an old beaver dam. The beavers are gone, but the results of their diligent work are plainly visible.

Mashamoquet Brook, a trout stream that flows through the park and joins Wolf Den Brook, is stocked twice a year. Picnic tables are set under evergreens beside the brook.

For cross-country skiing the area north of Wolf Den Drive is best. At man-made Bypass Pond, there's a sandy beach.
Park open year-round; camping late Apr.–Columbus Day. Admission charged weekends and holidays in summer.
(860) 928-6121
www.dep.state.ct.us/rec/parks/ctparks.html

17 Mashantucket Pequot Museum & Research Center

On the Pequot Trail, off Rte. 214, in Mashantucket
In the 16th century the Pequot tribe numbered some 8,000 strong and inhabited 250 square miles

of prime land in southeastern Connecticut. By 1637, however, the tribe's fortune drastically changed when a brutal war with English colonists slaughtered many of its members and sentenced survivors to a life of either slavery or exile.

More than 300 years later, in the 1970s, many tribal members began moving back to Mashantucket to reclaim their homeland and restore their native culture to its former pride. Tribally owned and operated, this state-of-the-art 308,000-square-foot complex dramatically brings to life the tragedies and triumphs of the Pequot people.

The museum's best exhibit is a re-creation of an authentic 16th-century Pequot coastal village. Visitors will step back in time and experience the everyday life of tribal members, circa 1550. The village includes 12 wigwams, a sweat lodge, dugout canoes, stone tools and weapons, hand-woven cattail sleeping mats, and food storage pits.

Throughout the village, 51 life-

size, perfectly lifelike figures, handcrafted from casts of American Indians, capture Pequot men, women, and children partaking in daily activities.

In addition to its strikingly real village, the museum offers a gallery devoted to telling the "creation stories" of four different tribes, enhanced by videos and native masks, art, and beadwork.
Open year-round, six days a week. Closed Tuesdays. Admission charged.
(800) 411-9671
www.mashantucket.com

18 Lyman Allyn Art Museum

625 Williams St., New London
The museum, founded in 1932, was built in memory of Lyman Allyn, a prosperous New London whaling captain, by his daughter, Harriet U. Allyn. The original building, a large granite structure with a pillared entrance, has been enlarged several times and now has 10 galleries for the permanent collection and four for changing exhibits.

Its primary focus is on paintings by Connecticut artists such as Willard Metcalf and William Chadwick, other American artists, and antique Connecticut furniture. The museum also has 17th- and 18th-century regionally crafted silver and pewter.

The Allyn home, an 1826 Federal stone building now called the Destion-Allyn House, is on the museum grounds and has been renovated and furnished with outstanding 19th-century furniture.
Museum open year-round, Tues.–Sun. except major holidays; house open by appointment. Admission charged.
(860) 443-2545
http://lymanallyn.conncoll.edu

Lewes Historic Area. *Several of the town's notable old houses, some dating back to the Revolutionary War, are open to visitors (see page 63).*

Although about half of the perimeter of this long, narrow state is bounded by water—the Delaware River, Delaware Bay, and the Atlantic Ocean—there's an engaging diversity of attractions to be enjoyed here. There are forested hills, beaches, meadows and marshes, and historic homes and gardens. And in one 16,000-acre wildlife preserve more than 300 species of birds may be observed. The Lewes Historic Area recalls the town's venerable past. Included here is a charming small church built more than 300 years ago.

Delaware

In this small state, bounded by water but with an excellent network of roads, there are still many places to explore.

1 Brandywine Creek State Park
Wilmington

Named after the small river that almost bisects its 933 acres, this park has open meadows, hills, wooded trails, a floodplain, marshland, and a majestic stand of tulip poplars, some of them 190 years old, in an area known as Tulip Tree Woods.

The park also contains Delaware's first two nature preserves. For dedicated birders, one hilltop offers a superb vantage point for viewing migrating hawks in late autumn as they follow the course of the Delaware River southward.

Guided walks are led by members of the park's nature center, which also features films and displays. One can also hike independently along 14 miles of nature trails, play some Frisbee, have a picnic, or fly kites.

The river is open to canoeists, and fishermen can angle for crappies, bluegills, rock bass, and—in spring—trout. Several bridle paths through groves of tulip, beech, and oak trees invite riders, and in winter the park attracts sledders and cross-country skiers. Primitive camping facilities are also available for youth groups.
Open year-round. Admission charged. (302) 577-3534
www.destateparks.com

■ Brandywine Creek State Park. *Brandywine Creek cuts through a state park filled with tulip poplars, beech, and oak trees that contrast brilliantly with the water. Fishermen can catch crappies, bluegills, rock bass, and trout.*

2 Nemours Mansion and Gardens
Rockland Rd. between Children's Dr. and Rte. 202, Wilmington
Designed to emulate a Louis XVI chateau and named after his family's ancestral home in France, Nemours is the former residence of renowned philanthropist Alfred I. Du Pont. Built between 1909-10, the mansion is exquisitely furnished and beautifully preserved. Its 102 rooms feature fine period antiques, rare Oriental rugs, and tapestries and paintings dating back as far as the 15th century.

Surrounding the striking villa, the 300-acre estate boasts extensive and truly magnificent formal French gardens, which have been assiduously cultivated to express old-world elegance. In addition, the grounds offer expertly planted conservatories, fountains, natural woodlands, and an old-time water tower.

Guided tours are the only way to see the estate. Taking a minimum of two hours, tours include a series of rooms on three floors of the mansion, followed by a bus tour of the gardens—with stops at Du Pont's personal billiard room and bowling alley. Visitors will leave with a vivid sense of what it was like to live on a grand scale at the beginning of the 20th century.

Open May–Dec. Admission charged.
No children under 12 admitted.
Reservations recommended.
(302)-651-6912

www.nemours.org

3 White Clay Creek State Park
Newark

You can look into Pennsylvania and Maryland from this pleasant park nestled in the northwestern corner of Delaware, where the three states come together. Their meeting point, known as The Wedge, was once popular with bandits, who could quickly escape the law of one state by crossing the boundary into another. The park has only 425 acres but seems more spacious, partly because it rises to about 300 feet—which is high for Delaware—and offers long views of the surrounding countryside.

Hikers can explore valleys and impressive rock outcrops on 25 miles of trails. The Milestone Trail shows where grindstones were once quarried from the exposed boulders. In the spring fishermen like to cast for trout from the banks of a creek that runs alongside the park. A small pond also offers good fishing. And in winter the slopes provide fine tobogganing.

The park has a primitive campsite, available to youth groups, and a picnic area.

Open year-round. Admission charged.
(302) 368-6900

www.destateparks.com

4 Read House and Gardens
The Strand, New Castle

This handsome red brick mansion, one of the finest examples of Federal architecture in the United States, was built in 1804 by George Read II, a prominent Delaware lawyer whose father was a signer of the Declaration of Independence. George Read married his cousin, Mary Thompson, and they brought up their seven children in this house.

Situated on the banks of the Delaware River, the 22-room, 14,000-square-foot mansion is known for its elaborately carved woodwork, handsome relief plasterwork, and delicate fanlights. Its second owner, William Couper, who bought the property in the 1840s, added the garden, which encompasses 1.5 acres. The garden is divided into three sections: a formal parterre flower garden, a specimen garden, and a kitchen garden.

The property was bought in 1920 by Mr. and Mrs. Philip D. Laird, who refurbished the house and furnished it in Colonial Revival style. They extended their taste for Colonial Revival to the garden as well, adding the formal brick paths. The Lairds were also instrumental in preserving the historic district of New Castle, settled by the Dutch in 1651.

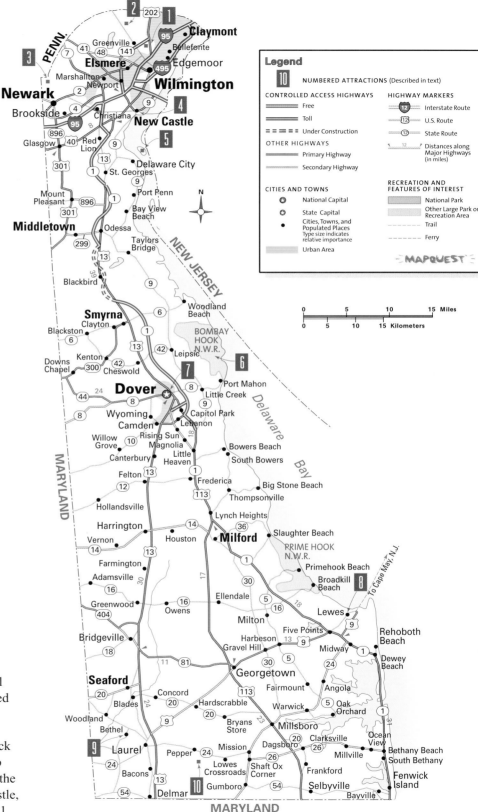

When Mrs. Laird died in 1975, the estate was donated to the Historical Society of Delaware, and the house has since been restored to its original Federal-style elegance. In tribute to Mr. and Mrs. Laird, three rooms are maintained just as they furnished them.

Guided tours of the mansion are conducted by the historical society. Also available are guided walking tours of New Castle, including visits to three of the town's 18th-century buildings.

Open Tues.–Sun. except holidays, Mar.–Dec.; Jan.–Feb., weekends only, with weekday tours by appointment.
(302) 322-8411
www.hsd.org/read.htm

5 Fort Delaware State Park

Located on Pea Patch Island in the Delaware River across from Delaware City

Accessible only by ferry, this distinctive state park—and one of Delaware's oldest—offers a journey back in time. The park's impressive Union Fortress dates back to 1859. Originally built to protect the ports of Wilmington and Philadelphia, it served as a prison during the Civil War, housing as many as 12,000 Confederate soldiers.

Inside the massive granite-and-brick structure, visitors will discover an authentic military city, going about the business of everyday life in 1864.

Hands-on demonstrations and interactive programs abound. Highlights include a crash course in the blacksmith trade, an eye-opening look at the workload of a laundress, a stop at the officers' kitchen for a whiff of freshly-baked bread, and a lesson in the lost art of loading and firing a giant

seacoast cannon. In addition, kids can get in line for an infantry drill, and the whole family can sign on for a personal tour of the fortress.

Conducted by tradesmen, craftswomen, business proprietors, socialites, activists, and generals of the day, tours include a boxed lunch and souvenir Civil War paperwork. When the sun goes down, fearless history buffs can cap off their visit with a ghost tour.

Beyond the fortress, Pea Patch Island offers many national treasures. Marked by remote marshes, it is the largest Atlantic Coast nesting ground north of Florida for wading birds and the summer home to nine different species of herons, egrets, and ibis. A hiking trail and observation tower offer opportunities to see these beautiful birds in flight. Visitors are encouraged to bring a lunch to enjoy on the spacious, grassy picnic area. Tables and grills are provided, and soft drinks, water, and snacks are available from the fortress.

Open year-round. Admission charged.
(302) 834-7941
www.destateparks.com

6 Bombay Hook National Wildlife Refuge
Smyrna

Kahanasink Indians were the first known occupants of this appealing sprawl of marshland, tidal stream, freshwater ponds, and timbered swamps. In 1679 the Indians sold part of the area to Dutch settlers from New York, who hunted birds, trapped muskrats, and cut salt hay from the marshes.

Bombay Hook now encompasses 15,978 acres and is one link in a chain of waterfowl refuges established in the 1930s along major migratory routes. Some 300 species have been observed since the refuge opened. Waterfowl abound, especially in March and November; shorebirds, wading birds, and songbirds are most evident during May, August, and September. Others for whom this is a haven include owls, hummingbirds, woodpeckers, and several varieties of vultures and hawks.

Short walking trails and a long, winding automobile trail lead through the area, which is a habitat for foxes, river otters, beavers, and varieties of turtles, snakes, salamanders, and frogs. An

information center is open on weekdays during spring and fall.

The Allee House, also in the refuge but reached from Route 9, is a superbly preserved mid-18th-century plantation home.

Refuge open year-round;
Allee House open weekends from
1–4 P.M. during spring and fall.
(302) 653-6872
http://bombayhook.fws.gov

7 John Dickinson Plantation
Dover

One of America's founding fathers, John Dickinson grew up in this spacious brick home that looks across cultivated fields to the St. Jones River. Dickinson was often called "the Penman of the Revolution" for the many pamphlets and articles he wrote about American independence. After the Revolution he served in the legislatures of both Delaware and Pennsylvania and was among the framers of the Constitution.

The house, built in 1740 by Dickinson's father, Samuel, is not as grand as Monticello or Mount Vernon, but it provides an insight into the comfortable lifestyle of a prosperous colonial landowner.

In 1804, when much of the interior of the building was destroyed by fire, a document listing the contents of the house was found. Several of the original pieces are on display today in the rooms. Members of the staff give presentations in costume as characters from that era and provide tours of the reconstructed outbuildings and a slave/tenant house.

Open daily except Mon. and holidays.
Closed Sun. in Jan. and Feb.
(302) 739-3277
www.destatemuseums.org/jdp

5 Fort Delaware State Park. *Built in 1859 to protect the ports of Wilmington and Philadelphia, Union Fortress is now home to a Civil War–era museum.*

Lewes Historic Area

Two Dutchmen purchased this spot in 1629, giving it the poetic name Zwaanendael—Valley of the Swans—even though the nearest valley is miles away. The Dutch had no lack of competitors in the area, and during the next 150 years they endured a series of confrontations, raids, and takeovers.

The first settlers, who arrived in 1631, were wiped out by American Indians. After the Dutch sent replacements, a contingent of Swedish newcomers tried to capture the area. The British also constantly argued with Holland over ownership of the whole territory. And because the town was an important seaport, the most frequent visitors for a time were buccaneers, among them Capt. William Kidd, who reputedly buried his treasure here.

Shortly after Pennsylvania annexed Delaware in 1685, the town received its present name (pronounced Lewis) from Quaker leader William Penn.

Visitors to Lewes can retrace its colorful past in the historic area, to the left off Route 9 as you enter the town. The Zwaanendael Museum, built in 1931 and modeled after the town hall in Hoorn, Holland, has a number of exhibits illustrating Lewes's heritage.

Several notable old houses, part of the Lewes Historical Society, are open to visitors. The Cannonball House, which was shelled by the British during the Revolution, still has in its foundation the cannonball for which it was named. A blacksmith shop, plank house, creamery, a doctor's office, the ferry house, and the Burton-Ingram House, which contains a marine museum, have all been carefully restored.

10 Trap Pond State Park. *The lake beckons fishermen with perch, catfish, bass, pickerel, and sunfish. Rowboats, canoes, and paddleboats are available for rent.*

St. Peter's Church, part of which dates to 1681, is a gem; and along Pilottown Road there are several fine old homes, most of which are privately owned. Guided tours of the historic area are offered Monday, Wednesday, Thursday, Friday, and Saturday mornings.
Museum open year-round, Tues.–Sun. Admission charged for tours.
(302) 645-7670
www.historiclewes.org

Historic Bethel on Broad Creek

The history of this picturesque little town and its role in early American shipping began in 1795, when Capt. Kendall M. Lewis built a small dock here on Broad Creek, a tributary of the Nanticoke River.

The dock became the busy center of the town, whose primary industry was transferring cargoes from large ships to shallow-draft scows that could reach the towns that were farther upstream on Broad Creek.

In 1869 a shipyard was constructed in Lewisville, as the town was called, and five years later the first vessel to be built here was launched.

In 1880 the town's name was changed to Bethel—"the sailor's retreat" (according to the Bible)—and in 1889, when the flat-bottomed Chesapeake Bay sailing ram was designed here, Bethel's reputation as a shipbuilding town was assured.

Although the shipyard was dismantled in the 1940s, the historic town remains a colorful place to see. A small museum displays local maritime artifacts.
Museum open year-round, Tues.–Fri. July, Aug., and Dec., weekends also.
(302) 875-9319

Trap Pond State Park
Laurel

This wooded park surrounds a small, attractive lake where fishermen angle for perch, catfish, bass, pickerel, and sunfish. Rowboats, canoes, kayaks, paddleboats, and small sailboats are available for rent, and boat owners can launch their own.

Circle the entire park on the self-guiding five-mile Boundary Trail, or hike along the pine-forested trails that surround the park. Several species of birds make their home here, including the great blue heron, the bald eagle, and the elusive pileated woodpecker.

The Cypress Point Trail takes you to the watery world of the bald cypress, where you will find the northernmost stand of these Southern trees, and through groves of dogwood, sweet gum, holly, myrtle, and magnolia.

A sandy beach and a lakeside picnic grove shaded by tall loblolly pines are popular spots, especially on summer weekends. Campsites, beneath a canopy of pines, are offered on a first-come basis.
Park open year-round; facilities available Apr.–Oct.
(302) 875-5153
www.destateparks.com

Canaveral National Seashore.
On this 13-mile span of unspoiled sand, beachcombers can search for lightning whelks and angel wings (see page 68).

Florida

The beaches and man-made wonders are all well known; among the surprises are battlefields and archaeological displays.

When one thinks about the Civil War, Florida does not readily come to mind. It was, however, the site of two hard-won victories for the Confederacy, and you can learn about the details at the Natural Bridge and Olustee battlefields.

The Sunshine State seems an unlikely place for the re-establishment of the buffalo—a prototypical symbol of the Western plains. But at Paynes Prairie the living evidence can be seen on the hoof. At Mulberry Phosphate Museum, another kind of evidence recalls animals that can't be reintroduced, such as the mastodon and the saber-toothed tiger. Among other highlights are some fine parks, wildlife preserves, and memorials to a prolific inventor and a much-loved writer.

1 Blackwater River State Park

3 miles north of Harold
This 590-acre preserve is a good example of Florida's enlightened policy of public-land management. The objective of the Florida Park Service is to maintain—and re-create where necessary—the plant communities and ecological systems that prevailed in the area before the first Europeans arrived in the early 16th century.

The Blackwater is one of the few remaining sand-bottom rivers in the Southeast, and despite the darkish color of the tannin-stained water, it is one of the cleanest. The water contrasts dramatically with the pristine white of the ever-changing sandbars deposited on the curves and oxbows of the meandering river.

The Blackwater, understandably, is a great favorite for both canoeing and swimming, with its fine sand beaches. Other features are the nature trails and a boardwalk across a swamp to a picnic area, where you find the state's champion Atlantic white cedar, a noble tree indeed.

The ecological systems here include the river floodplain, with swamps, sandbars, and oxbow lakes; the pine flatwoods, dominated by slash pine with an understory of blackberry vines, blueberry bushes, and gallberry; and the high pinelands that support longleaf pines, turkey oaks, and sweetleaf. White-tailed deer and gray fox may be seen in the woods, and the river otter roams the floodplain.
Open year-round.
(850) 983-5363
www.dep.state.fl.us/parks/index.asp

2 Grayton Beach State Park

County Rte. 30A, Grayton Beach
A superb mile-long beach of brilliant white sand awaits visitors to this interesting park. Behind the beach, high barrier dunes stabilized by sea oats and scrub overlook the clear green and azure waters where dolphins are sometimes seen. The appeal to swimmers is obvious.

Fishermen may surf cast, primarily for pomano, whiting, and king mackerel. Western Lake, behind the dunes, is popular for boat fishing; its brackish water supports both fresh and saltwater species.

For those interested in wildlife, there is the 40-minute Barrier Dune Nature Trail. It provides markers keyed to entries in a trail guide booklet explaining the many phenomena of the shoreline

 Grayton Beach State Park. *The white sand and clear waters of the Gulf of Mexico beckon visitors to abandon their bikes and take a stroll.*

ALABAMA

Century
Gonzalez
Milton
Pensacola
Warrington
Fort Walton Beach
GULF ISLANDS NATL. SEASHORE
Niceville
Crestview
De Funiak Springs
Graceville
Marianna
Panama City
Callaway
Lynn Haven
Blountstown
Quincy
GEORGIA
Monticello
Madison
Jasper
Tallahassee
Crawfordville
Perry
Live Oak
Lake City
Lake Butler
Baldwin
Jacksonville
Jacksonville Beach
Fernandina Beach
Port St. Joe
Carrabelle
Apalachicola
Mayo
High Springs
Green Cove Sprs.
Palatka
St. Augustine
Palm Coast
Flagler Beach

GULF OF MEXICO

Deadman Bay
Cross City
Chiefland
Bronson
Cedar Key
Dunnellon
Ocala
De Land
Eustis
Ormond Beach
Daytona Beach
Port Orange
New Smyrna Beach
Crystal River
Inverness
Leesburg
Sanford
Orlando
Titusville
Cape Canaveral
Merritt Island
Brooksville
Spring Hill
Dade City
Cocoa
Kissimmee
Melbourne
Palm Bay
Sebastian
Palm Harbor
Dunedin
Lutz
Lakeland
Winter Haven
Vero Beach
Clearwater
St. Petersburg
Tampa
Lake Wales
Ft. Meade
Fort Pierce
Port St. Lucie
Bradenton
Wauchula
Avon Park
Sebring
Stuart
Sarasota
Lake Placid
Jupiter
Venice
Arcadia
Okeechobee
Port Charlotte
Englewood
Punta Gorda
La Belle
Pahokee
West Palm Beach
Fort Myers
Cape Coral
Clewiston
Belle Glade
Delray Beach
Sanibel
Immokalee
Coral Springs
Boca Raton
South Bay
Fort Lauderdale
Bonita Springs
Naples
BIG CYPRESS NATL. PRES.
Hollywood
Marco
Ochopee
Hialeah
Miami Bch.
Miami
Coral Gables
Homestead
Florida City
Ponce de Leon Bay
Key Largo
Tavernier
Islamorada
Florida Bay
Florida Keys
Marathon
Big Pine Key
Key West

ATLANTIC OCEAN

FLORIDA

Legend

NUMBERED ATTRACTIONS (Described in text)

CONTROLLED ACCESS HIGHWAYS
Free
Toll
Under Construction

OTHER HIGHWAYS
Primary Highway
Secondary Highway

CITIES AND TOWNS
National Capital
State Capital
Cities, Towns, and Populated Places
Type size indicates relative importance
Urban Area

HIGHWAY MARKERS
Interstate Route
U.S. Route
State Route
Distances along Major Highways (in miles)

RECREATION AND FEATURES OF INTEREST
National Park
Other Large Park or Recreation Area
Trail
Ferry

MAPQUEST

0 20 40 60 Miles
0 20 40 60 Kilometers

ecosystem, such as shifting sands, dune building, plant pruning by wind and salt spray, and decomposition and recycling.

Raccoons and alligators are common sights throughout this 2,200-acre expanse of salt marshes, slash pines, and palmettos. In the summer loggerhead turtle nests may be found on the beach. The park has three sheltered picnic

areas, cabins, and a campground. Although the sites are close together, dense scrub separates them and gives privacy.

Open year-round. Admission charged. (850) 231-4210;

For reservations, call:

(800) 326-3521

www.floridastateparks.org

3 T. H. Stone Memorial St. Joseph Peninsula State Park

Port St. Joe

A long barrier extending north between St. Joseph Bay and the Gulf of Mexico, this 2,516-acre park will appeal to a wide range of interests. Its miles of fine natural beach are good for swimming and fishing. The fall is best for catching large redfish, sharks, bluefish, and flounder, while spring is excellent for pompano, whiting, and speckled trout.

Three walkovers placed among the high palmetto-dotted dunes provide panoramic views of pristine terrain similar to that encountered by the first Spanish settlers to arrive in this area.

These vantage points are popular with birders interested in the vast array of resident and transient species found here. Besides the many brown pelicans, willet, and great blue and green herons, more rarely seen species include white pelicans, magnificent frigate birds, American golden plovers, and Acadian flycatchers, according to the season. In autumn this park is one of the best places in the country to observe monarch butterflies and migrating hawks, including the rare peregrine falcon.

On the bay side numerous salt marshes of needlerush and cordgrass nurture populations of fiddler and blue crabs, horse conchs, sea turtles, diamondback terrapins, and the inevitable alligators.

Near the Gulf beaches are two separate camping sites; more primitive camping is available in the 1,750-acre wilderness preserve at the northern end of the park. On the bay side are a boat basin and a launching ramp. The park also offers picnic grounds and two nature trails, which present

chances to spot bobcats or otters, plus many shore and wading birds. The park's name honors the first postmaster of Port St. Joe.

Open year-round.
(850) 227-1327
www.dep.state.fl.us/parks/index.asp

4 Olustee Battlefield Historic State Park

Off U.S. 90, east of Olustee

This site commemorates Florida's major Civil War battle. In February 1864 a Union force of 5,500 men, who were charged with severing enemy communications and food supplies between east and west Florida, clashed here in an open pine forest with nine Confederate regiments. The Southern soldiers, although slightly outnumbered, forced their foes to retreat after a five-hour fight. The events of the day and other aspects of Florida's role in the Civil War are explained in a small interpretive center. A self-guiding trail through the 270-acre battle site begins with a recorded 10-minute "you-are-there" account by one "Private Bedley Jackson of the 28th Georgia Regiment."

Open year-round.
(386) 758-0400
www.dep.state.fl.us/parks/index.asp

5 Natural Bridge Battlefield Historic State Park

Natural Bridge Rd., Tallahassee

Of particular interest to Civil War buffs, this site illustrates the crucial role the lay of the land can play in military strategy. In early March 1865, Union Gen. John Newton and Naval Com. William Gibson mounted a two-pronged advance

toward Tallahassee. Newton landed his troops and headed north, but Gibson's gunboats ran aground in the St. Marks River. When word reached Tallahassee, the limited Confederate forces were quickly reinforced by volunteers—recuperating veterans, men of 70, and boys as young as 14.

When Newton encountered stiff resistance at Newport Bridge, he opted for a surprise attack across a nearby natural bridge. This move had been anticipated by Confederate Gen. William Miller, who entrenched his forces there. The Confederates repelled three Union attacks within 12 hours. Deciding the battle had been lost, Newton retreated. Southern pride still warms to this moment of victory, for it left Tallahassee the only Confederate capital east of the Mississippi never to have been occupied by Union armies.

Within a small, quiet area shaded by oaks and scrub pines, stone markers and a monument commemorate participating regiments and Confederate officers. Tablets

provide battle details, and some of the original earth breastwork is still visible. A picnic grove contains tables and grills.

Open year-round.
(850) 922-6007
www.floridastateparks.org

6 Amelia Island

Florida's northeastern shore, 15 miles east of Interstate 95, 30 minutes from Jacksonville International Airport

Graced with 13 miles of beautiful beaches, lush forests, and a unique, colorful history, Amelia Island is the perfect spot for collecting seashells, riding mountain bikes, or taking a quick trip back in time. In spite of its turbulent past and waves of industrialization and modernization surrounding it, the island remains a quaint and authentic Victorian seaport village. It's also productive: Nearly 80 percent of Florida's Atlantic white shrimp are harvested in Amelia's waters.

4 Olustee Battlefield Historic State Park. *A cannon stands as a reminder of Florida's biggest fight of the Civil War, waged in February 1864.*

Discovered by a Frenchman in 1562, the island was soon claimed by the Spaniards. Its only town, Fernandina Beach, was named for King Ferdinand VII. Later, when Spain swapped Florida for Havana with England, British loyalists took control and christened the island Amelia, in honor of King George II's daughter. In the mid-1930s the founders of Afro-American Life Insurance bought 200 acres on the island's southern end. Known as American Beach, this property became an ocean-front haven for African Americans during the Jim Crow era. Today American Beach is the first stop on Florida's Black Heritage Trail.

While basking in the island's distinctive past and character, visitors can swim, sail, kayak, or even go horseback riding on the beach—one of only a handful of places in the United States where this exhilarating activity is permitted. Kelly Seahorse Ranch provides horses and expert guidance. The intrepid can also take a wild boat ride, through the Intra-coastal Waterway to Cumberland Island, where wild horses play. Along the way, amid the salty marshes, they just might get to meet an Atlantic bottlenose dolphin. (*800) 226-3542*

www.ameliaisland.org

7 Florida Lighthouse Tour

South on I-95 and U.S. 1, following the coastline from St. Augustine to Pensacola
With more than 1,800 miles of coastline, Florida has long been a natural beacon for lighthouses. The state's impressive collection—30 still standing proud—includes some of the nation's oldest and

1 Florida Lighthouse Tour. *Ponce de Leon Inlet, the second-tallest lighthouse in the nation and one of the few still working, glows near Daytona Beach.*

tallest. Many invite visitors to step inside and climb their spiraling staircases to the top for the reward of a dazzling panoramic view. Others, conveniently located in public parks, encourage appreciation from a short distance.

The best way to see all of Florida's lighthouses is to hit the road. Spanning the coastal highway from St. Augustine to Pensacola, the complete tour takes about five days. The first stop is the famous St. Augustine Lighthouse. Built in 1874, this 165-foot lighthouse is the state's oldest and most recognizable, recently restored to its early glory. Next, near Daytona Beach, comes the 175-foot Ponce de Leon Inlet, the second-tallest lighthouse in the nation and one of the few still busily working.

Farther on down, just south of downtown Miami on Key Biscayne, stands the bright red Jupiter Inlet. This cheerful lighthouse is famous for surviving a slew of assaults, from hostile Seminoles to a fierce hurricane. Near the end of the trail, on Florida's West Coast, St. Mark's Lighthouse beckons from a 65,000-acre national wildlife sanctuary for alligators, birds, and deer.

Last but certainly not least is the Pensacola Lighthouse. Built in 1858 on the grounds of the Pensacola Naval Air Station, this structure has braved lightning strikes, a tornado, and an earthquake but continues to operate.
http://users.erols.com/lthouse.htm

8 Paynes Prairie Preserve State Park

Micanopy
If the Seminole Indian King Payne (who was killed in a battle with American settlers near the Georgia border in 1812) could have imagined that the white man would name a prairie in his honor, he would have been doubly surprised—because in his time this basin was a vast lake.

It was also a lake when explorer Hernando de Soto saw it in about 1540, and there was water here when naturalist William Bartram visited the site in 1774. But the water has had a way of coming and going in this huge, saucerlike basin because of a sinkhole in one corner.

From time to time the sink would fill with debris, and the water would rise and remain. Years later the sinkhole would become "unplugged," the water would

drain away, and the area would revert to savanna. In 1892 a small steamer plying the lake was stranded when the water disappeared. Since then the basin has been a treeless prairie.

In 1970 some 18,000 acres here were purchased by the state, and preservation of the prairie and its historic function as a habitat for wildlife was assured. A program is now in operation to perpetuate the ecosystem that Bartram observed and recorded. American buffalo have been reintroduced, and efforts are being made to breed native scrub cattle similar to the Andalusian stock brought to Florida by Spanish settlers.

A fine panoramic view of the prairie can be enjoyed from a 50-foot observation tower. The birding is superb. A list of 241 species seen here is available at the visitors center. Also listed are 27 mammals, 41 reptiles, and 20 amphibians native to the area. An audiovisual program explains the purpose and scope of the activity here, and Indian artifacts are on display. The region was inhabited as early as 10,000 B.C.

A recreation area at Lake Wauberg and Sawgrass Pond is popular for picnicking, kayaking, boating, and fishing. In addition, the preserve has several miles of riding trails and a corral. On Saturdays from November through April, buffalo and other wildlife are best seen during guided observation walks. Ranger-led hikes are also available on most Saturdays during this time.
Open year-round.
(352) 466-4100

www.dep.state.fl.us/parks/district2/ paynesprairie/index.asp

9 Cedar Key Museum State Park
Cedar Key

Many small museums owe their existence to the energy and enthusiasm of just one individual, and this one is such an example. Much of the material here was assembled by the late Saint Clair Whitman, a dedicated naturalist, collector, and former resident of Cedar Key. Along with artifacts dating from 6000 B.C. to the Colonial period, the museum houses a display of late 19th-century glassware, old bottles, exhibits that chart local history, and Whitman's extensive collection of seashells.

The town of Cedar Key has had its ups and downs. It was a bustling community in the 19th century and an important Confederate port during the Civil War. The lumbering industry boomed for a brief period, as did shipbuilding and associated activities. Today Cedar Key is a quiet town but one worthy of exploring.

The museum documents the lumbering era in particular with an excellent collection of photographs and tools. Also on view: mementos of the fishing, oystering, and sponge industries, and the brushes and brooms of a palm fiber industry. The latter enterprise was swept away by the advent of plastics.

Open year-round. Closed Tues.–Wed.
Admission charged.
(352) 543-5350
www.floridastateparks.org

10 Marjorie Kinnan Rawlings Historic State Park

West on Rte. 325 from U.S. 301, Cross Creek

Readers familiar with author Marjorie Rawlings will recognize this setting as having pervaded much of her work. An unknown writer when she moved here in

1928, Mrs. Rawlings committed herself to this small, remote community. Three years passed before she sold her first story. But as the people and environs of Cross Creek fueled her creative fire, she eventually penned her most famous work, *The Yearling,* which won her a Pulitzer Prize.

A typical Cracker homestead, designed for optimum cross-ventilation, the house consists of three board-and-batten units connected by porches and shaded by wide overhangs and the surrounding orange and magnolia trees. A 45-minute tour takes you through the farmyard and into the house. The park has two loop walking trails through the woods and farmyard.

Grounds open year-round. House closed Aug.–Sept. Admission charged.
(352) 466-3672
www.dep.state.fl.us/parks

11 Merritt Island National Wildlife Refuge. *This quiet setting is home to 19 endangered species, most notably the Southern bald eagle and manatee.*

11 Merritt Island National Wildlife Refuge and Canaveral National Seashore
Titusville

The history of Merritt Island extends from prehistoric times to the space age. Inhabited by Indians since about 7000 B.C., the island in recent years has rocketed to renown as the site of the John F. Kennedy Space Center, with which the refuge and seashore share a border.

The seashore spans 13 miles of unspoiled golden sand between Apollo and Palyalinda beaches. You may hike this distance, stopping to swim and beachcomb, gathering such seashells as lightning whelks and angel wings. Other possibilities are shellfishing, crabbing, and surf casting for pompano, bluefish, and other species. Boating, canoeing, and fishing are also enjoyed at the adjacent Mosquito Lagoon. (Bring insect repellent.)

The refuge can be explored by car along two nature drives or by foot via five hiking trails. Either way, the range of wildlife is stunning. Many of the 310 bird species that have been observed here make their nests on the refuge, including great blue and green herons, snowy egrets, anhingas and black skimmers, and pie-billed grebes.

The refuge is also home to 19 endangered species, most notably the Southern bald eagle and manatee. Porpoises and whales are occasionally glimpsed offshore, and large tracks of sea turtles are frequently seen on the sands.

The Canaveral information center offers a slide show on the history of this tidal area and the wildlife it supports. Other programs include ranger-led weekend canoe trips for bird-watching, and excursions in June and July to watch the turtles nest and lay eggs.

Merritt Island: Open year-round.
(321) 861-0667
http://merrittisland.fws.gov
Canaveral: Open year-round.
(321) 867-4077
www.nps.gov/cana

12 Fort Foster State Historic Site
U.S. Rte. 301, south of Zephyrhills

The log fort and the wooden bridge spanning the Hillsborough River are reconstructions of the originals that were built here in 1836 during the Second Seminole War, often said to be the most costly American Indian war in U.S. history. The fort was built to safeguard the bridge and thereby maintain communications along the Fort King Military Road from Tampa Bay to what is now known as Ocala.

Twice the Seminoles attempted to burn the bridge and failed. The frontier bastion remained garrisoned until June 1838, and during the last few months its commander was Gen. Zachary Taylor, who later became the 12th U.S. president. The Second Seminole War officially ended in 1842, but seven years later the Seminoles threatened again, and the fort was briefly reactivated.

The fort may be visited only by joining one of the tours leaving at 2 P.M. Saturdays and 11 A.M. Sundays from the visitors center in Hillsborough River State Park, where the fort is located. It is a quarter-mile trip by van and takes you to a shelter 900 feet from the site.

From there you continue on foot along the old Fort King Military Road to the fort. Re-enactors in the uniforms of those 2nd Artillery soldiers who manned the fort in 1837 explain the events of that time and the life of the artillerymen posted there.

Hillsborough River State Park, which is noted for its beautiful, lush scenery, flanks 10 miles of riverfront, with some 3,000 acres of hardwood hammocks, pine flatwoods, and marsh.

The river and its rapids attract fishermen, and the park also has a pond, trails, and canoe rentals.

Historic site open weekends; admission charged. Park open year-round.
(813) 987-6771

www.myflorida.com

Mulberry Phosphate Museum
Mulberry

Housed in an authentic 1899 train depot, the history of the local phosphate industry is on display here. When the ice age began, the animals that had found plentiful food and warm weather died away. Their remains petrified and left a fossil record of prehistoric Florida, along with an abundant supply of a mineral called phosphate.

Upon entering the museum, you'll see a display of butterflies from all over the world. A variety of fossils and bones, excavated from the phosphate pits in Florida's "Bone Valley," fill the museum's first room.

A mastodon, a woolly mammoth, a saber-toothed cat, and a giant ground sloth are included, as well as an 18-foot baleen whale skeleton, thought to be 10 million years old.

Open year-round, Tue.–Sat.
(863) 425-2823

Gilbert's Bar House of Refuge Museum. *The U.S. government built this house as a way station for shipwrecked passengers. Now restored, it's a museum filled with antique nautical equipment and lifesaving devices.*

14 Elliott Museum and Gilbert's Bar House of Refuge Museum
Hutchinson Island, Stuart

Step back into yesteryear with a visit to these disparate museums. They are only about a five-minute drive apart, and both are worth seeing.

Among the fascinations at the Elliott Museum are the replicas of 19th-century shops—an ice-cream parlor, an apothecary shop, a shoe store, a millinery, and a combination general store and post office—each complete with display items and original fixtures. Among the exhibits featured is a furnished dollhouse of the Victorian period, lead soldiers, a collection of clocks and watches, classic automobiles, and glassware.

These numerous themes reflect the various interests of the late Harmon P. Elliott, who built the museum in memory of his father, Sterling. Both were prolific inventors; between them they obtained more than 220 patents. The father's knot-tying machine, patented in 1881, is one of the more intriguing innovations on view here.

Nearby is Gilbert's Bar, a rocky shallow shoal named for the pirate Don Pedro Gilbert, who plagued the Atlantic Coast and the Caribbean until 1835, when he was hanged in Boston for his nefarious deeds. His Florida hangout near present-day Stuart was the site of many shipwrecks, which prompted the U.S. government to build 10 "Houses of Refuge" along the coast. These houses functioned as way stations for shipwrecked passengers and provided shelter and food until they could be sent on their way to other destinations. Gilbert's Bar House of Refuge served until 1945 and is the only house still in existence.

Now completely restored and included on the *National Register of Historic Places,* the clapboard house contains some fine Victorian furniture and an array of antique nautical equipment, woodworking tools, and memorabilia.

On display are such lifesaving devices as a Lyle gun used to fire lines from shore to ship and a breeches buoy. A surfboat recalls some of the hazards accepted by the men who made sea rescues.

Elliott Museum open daily; admission charged.
(772) 225-1961

http://elliottmuseum.goodnature.org.
House of Refuge Museum open daily except holidays; admission charged.
(772) 225-1875

15 Corkscrew Swamp Sanctuary
Naples

Extending over an 11,000-acre wilderness of pine flatwoods, wet prairie, swampland, and typical hardwood hammocks, this haven for wildlife and native plants may be enjoyed on foot by means of an incredibly beautiful 2¼-mile-long boardwalk overhung by Spanish moss.

The sanctuary is the home of the nation's largest surviving stand of virgin bald cypress trees, many of which are now 700 years old.

Among the many sights to be savored are lettuce lakes, cypress knees, floating tussocks, water hemlock, strangler fig, ferns and lilies, brilliant hibiscus, royal palms, and various epiphytes (plants such as the tree-growing butterfly, cigar, and clamshell orchids that grow on other plants).

Cardinals, red-shouldered hawks, and rare birds known as limpkins make their homes here, as well as the country's largest colony of wood storks. In addition there are the familiar alligators, Florida water snakes, mosquito fish, and turtles.

A 34-page field guide describing what you'll see on the self-guiding boardwalk tour can be purchased. A 14-minute audio-visual introduction to the sights and sounds of Corkscrew is held at Swamp Theater in the new Blair Center. The sanctuary is managed by the National Audubon Society.

Open year-round.
(239) 348-9151
www.audubon.org/local/sanctuary/corkscrew

16 Collier-Seminole State Park
Naples

This 6,430-acre park is named for Barron Collier, who was an early settler in the area, and for the Seminole Indians. Many Indians whose ancestors fought in the Second Seminole War still live in the area.

Self-guiding and conducted walks on the nature trail (nearly a mile long) reveal an interesting environment common to the coastal wilderness of Yucatan and the West Indies.

Here, too, is the rare Florida royal palm, with its distinctive lime-green upper trunk. The mangrove and cypress swamps, pine flatwoods, tidal creeks, and salt marshes shelter a broad range of wildlife.

An observation platform permits an elevated view of ospreys, spoonbills, bald eagles, wood storks, and other colorful birds. With patience and luck, elsewhere in the park you might even glimpse the rare Florida panther, the Florida black bear, or the manatee, which are observed a few times a year.

Visitors may also explore the park on a 13½-mile round-trip canoe trail to the northernmost tip of the Ten Thousand Islands. The rivers and bays provide chances to fish for snook, mangrove snapper, and redfish.

A replica of an 1840s blockhouse serves as an interpretive center, with photo exhibits of native plants and animals and a review of Collier's achievements as a pioneering developer in the area. In the winter, campfire slide shows outline park activities. Canoes may be brought in or rented. A reminder: Insects are a problem in summer.

Open year-round; admission charged.
(941) 394-3397
www.dep.state.fl.us/parks/index.asp

17 Biscayne National Park
East of Homestead, off U.S. Rte. 1

This oceanic expanse of 173,000 acres encompasses most of Biscayne Bay, the Keys, and living coral reefs south of Miami. It's one of the largest marine preserves in the United States. The waters are turquoise and crystal-clear, making it ideal for fishing, boating, snorkeling, scuba diving, and marine-gazing in general.

The most obvious way to explore this watery paradise is by boat. Visitors can launch their own at one of the county marinas, or take one of the tours available from Convoy Point, the mainland information center. A 1½-hour excursion in a glass-bottomed boat gives you a marvelously colorful view of the reefs and grassy meadows, as well as lobsters, turtles, sponges, and exotic tropical fish lurking there. For an even better view, you may wish to try snorkeling.

To savor the special appeal of a subtropical island, you can take a 50-foot excursion boat to one of the park's 44 islands seven miles offshore. Elliot Key offers an opportunity to stroll through a tropical hardwood forest and along the rocky shoreline, while Boca Chita Key harkens back to a time when the area was millionaire Mark Honeywell's personal retreat. His private lighthouse affords one of the park's best views.

At the Dante Fascell Visitor Center, several videos and

15 Corkscrew Swamp Sanctuary. *Rare birds known as limpkins make their home in this swamp sanctuary, managed by the National Audubon Society. Cardinals, red-shouldered hawks, and wood storks also abound.*

 Biscayne National Park. *One of the largest marine preserves in the United States, these waters provide snorkelers with the best view of living coral reefs, sponges, and exotic tropical fish.*

exhibits familiarize visitors with local wildlife and history. Picnic tables with grills are located along the shore beside sea grape and mahogany trees. Here you can watch brown pelicans, double-crested cormorants, herons, terns, and gulls seeking food offshore.

Snapper, pompano, striped bass, and groupers are the fish most often snagged, but blue crabs and shrimp are also taken. Lobstering is permitted on the ocean side of the Keys, but the bay is a sanctuary for that prized shellfish.

Open year-round. To make reservations for a boat excursion, call:
(305) 230-7275.
www.nps.gov/bisc

18 Fakahatchee Strand Preserve State Park

A strand is a regional name for the long, narrow drainage channels, or sloughs, that develop in the mangrove swamps. The Fakahatchee is the largest of many such strands in the Big Cyprus Swamp.

This tract in southwest Florida,

about 20 miles long and three to five miles wide, harbors some 46 species of orchids, the greatest such concentration in North America. One, the catopsis, is found only here. The preserve also contains the largest number of rare Florida royal palm trees and the only known mix of bald cypresses and royal palms in the world.

In addition to bald eagles and American alligators, the strand is a home for mangrove fox squirrels, eastern indigo snakes, Everglades minks, black bears, and white-tailed deer. Infrequent sightings have been made of the rare wood stork and the Florida panther.

The preserve maintains a 2,000-foot boardwalk, seven miles to the west on U.S. Route 41. Booklets available from a box describe the highlights of the 19 suggested stops on the walkway, which is wide enough for wheelchairs.

A three-hour guided wade through swampland to see its rare plants can be arranged at the main office for parties of at least four; reservations must be made one week in advance.

For guided-wade reservations, call (813) 695-4593. Open year-round.
(239) 695-4593
www.dep.state.fl.us/parks/index.asp

19 Flamingo Area, Everglades National Park

Flamingo, on the shore of Florida Bay, is the center for sightseeing in the southern sector of the primeval Everglades. Visitors have their choice of foot trails, canoe trails, and privately operated cruises to take in the magical beauty of this environment.

Of the four walking trails suitable for families and children,

Snake Bight Trail (four miles round-trip) is the most popular. You can walk it or bike it. The trail unwinds beneath the umbrella of a hardwood forest inhabited by some 345 bird species and nearly 100 kinds of butterflies, including such rarities as the dingy purple wings, least Florida skippers, mimics, and byssus skippers.

The park is host to Seminole bats, nine-banded armadillos, black bears, Everglades minks, and bobcats. It is the only place in the world where alligators and crocodiles exist side by side. On the Rowdy Bend, Bear Lake, and Christian Point trails you can see other facets of this unique ecological system.

Seasonally, four cruises ply the local waterways, two of them along scenic Florida Bay, where at low tide you can expect to see brown pelicans, egrets, great blue herons, and other large birds scouting the shoreline for food. (The flamingo, however, is rarely seen.) For those more intrigued by the inland waterways and plant life, a pontoon boat makes sorties into the Everglades wilderness.

Canoeists can take any of five different trails. If time is no problem, you can tackle the 100-mile Wilderness Waterway, which takes you through the backcountry between Everglades City and Flamingo. Canoes, skiffs, kayaks, bicycles, and fishing gear may all be rented. Ranger-guided canoe tours are available seasonally.

For reservations, call (239) 695-2945
for ranger-led tours in season.
Open Dec.–Mar.
Admission charged.
www.nps.gov/ever

Okefenokee National Wildlife Refuge. *A pine forest stands at the edge of this mysterious land that is home to the alligator, black bear, and bobcat (see page 79).*

Georgia

The history of the Empire State of the South is a tapestry of colorful threads— some of which lead back to prehistoric times.

The Mound Builders left their mysteries, as they did elsewhere, and—not surprisingly—the war that weighed so heavily on the South is tellingly memorialized. Remarkable, however, is the variety of other highlights here. These include a gold-rush museum; state parks with great scenery, fishing, and birding; museums that recall the demands and pleasures of 19th-century life; a classic crossroads inn; and the plantation where, one might say, Brer Rabbit and Brer Fox were born.

The "trembling earth" of the Okefenokee Swamp is another world, as are the barrier islands that helped protect the Georgian colony from the fury of the Atlantic.

1 Cloudland Canyon State Park
Off Rte. 136, Trenton

Over millions of years Sitton Gulch Creek has carved a large gorge through the western edge of Lookout Mountain, so that today the difference in elevation between the highest and lowest point is more than 1,000 feet. Spectacular scenic views of rugged rock faces, ridges, valleys, and two waterfalls—including one that spills for almost 100 feet over layers of sandstone and shale— await outdoor enthusiasts who visit this 2,300-acre area.

The forest is lush with hemlock, dogwood, holly, mountain laurel, and rhododendron. Hikers and nature lovers will enjoy the Rim and Waterfall trails through thickly wooded mountain terrain frequented by cardinals, red-tailed hawks, barn owls, and pileated woodpeckers. Gray foxes and white-tailed deer are often seen, and occasionally a bobcat is spotted.

The park offers several picnic areas and a playground. There are accommodations that range from rustic cabins with fireplaces and screened porches to family camping areas and more remote primitive sites accessible only by foot.
Open year-round.
(706) 657-4050
www.gastateparks.org

1 Cloudland Canyon State Park. *From atop the mountains, visitors have the best view of the thickly wooded forest frequented by cardinals, hawks, owls, and woodpeckers.*

2 Dahlonega Courthouse Gold Museum Historic Site
Dahlonega

The word that gold had been found here in Cherokee country in 1828 sparked a stampede of prospectors and soon led to the illegal annexation of much of the American Indians' ancestral land. In less than 10 years more than $1.7 million in gold had been shipped to the Philadelphia mint alone, to say nothing of the ore and nuggets that were marketed in other ways. Among the new districts created from the Cherokee Territory, in Georgia's lovely mountains, was Lumpkin County. Dahlonega, which takes its name from a Cherokee word meaning "precious yellow," became the county seat.

Today a handsome 1836 brick building, which served for nearly 130 years as the courthouse here, contains many interesting reminders of the local quest for riches. A 23-minute film preceded by a short talk introduces visitors to the region's history. Exhibits and paintings trace the tragic removal of the Cherokees and illustrate the methods of gold mining, milling, and refining practiced in the area.

Gold nuggets and coins, a working miniature model of a stamp mill, and a chart showing Georgia gold-production totals from 1832 to 1942 are among the many fascinating displays here. Visitors can pan for gold here as well.

Open year-round except Thanksgiving, Christmas, and New Year's Day. Admission charged.
(706) 864-2257

www.gastateparks.org/historic

3 Travelers Rest Historic Site
Rte. 123, east of Toccoa

In the early 1800s Georgia's Tugaloo River valley, once inhabited by the Cherokee Indians, became a busy crossroads for stagecoach and riverboat travelers.

In 1833 Devereaux Jarrett, an enterprising local plantation owner, bought a small wayside inn, built around 1815, and expanded it into a long, rambling structure with eight rooms on the ground floor and five above—large enough to accommodate an inn, a store, a post office, and a home for the Jarrett family. It became known as Traveler's Rest and served as both an inn and home until 1877; it was held by the Jarrett family until 1955.

Now restored to its mid-19th-century appearance as a combined plantation hall and hostelry, it is paneled throughout with wide unpainted pine planks and contains many original pieces, including a round table with a Georgia marble top, an 1840s cherry plantation desk, and a handsome 1840s walnut corner cupboard. Traveler's Rest was recognized as a National Historic Landmark because of its fine architecture, including a 90-foot porch and hand-numbered rafters.

Also of interest in this colorful place is an original second-floor post office. Down the hall you can stay in one of three common bedrooms with a tin tub and two beds (each large enough for three guests), reminding us of the differences in the provisions for travelers then and now.

The outbuildings, situated among white oaks and American holly, include a smokehouse, nanny's cabin, and a loom house.

Open Thurs.–Sat. and P.M. Sun. except Thanksgiving and Christmas. Admission charged.
(706) 886-2256

www.gastateparks.org

4 Etowah Indian Mounds Historic Site

Cartersville, off Rte. 113
For 500 years, from A.D.1000 to 1500, Etowah Indians flourished here. Along the river that now carries their name, they built a village with two public squares, or plazas, dominated by three great earthen mounds with flat platform tops and several lesser mounds.

As many as several thousand Etowah people may have lived here. The plazas, made of packed red clay, were gathering places for the villagers and other American Indians from the valley, who came for commerce, important festivals, and burial ceremonies conducted by the priest-ruler. The largest of the platform mounds (63 feet high, with a platform one-half acre in extent) is believed to have supported a temple that may also have been the priest-ruler's residence. Excavations of one of the smaller platform mounds have revealed the burials of more than 500 of the tribal elite.

Today the great mounds loom in eerie silence above a plaza overgrown with field grasses. Traces of the moat and the borrow pits from which earth was taken for mound construction can still be seen. If you climb the steps to the top of the highest mound, you will see on the eastern horizon a deep notch in the Allatoona mountain range. At the time of the summer solstice (about June 22) the sun rises through this notch, a phenomenon that may have figured into Etowah rituals.

Near the entrance to the 54-acre site is the Etowah Archaeological Museum, which has artifacts, slides, and a diorama showing the lifestyle of the Etowah, who were of the widespread Mississippian culture.
Open Tues.–Sat. and P.M. Sun. except Thanksgiving and Christmas. Admission charged.
(770) 387-3747
www.gastateparks.org/historic

5 Southern Museum of Civil War and Locomotive History

I-75, Exit 273 west to Cherokee Street, Kennesaw
In 1862, Union spies under the command of James Andrews stole a locomotive called the *General* despite the watchful eyes of guards at nearby Camp McDonald in what is now downtown Kennesaw. The ensuing Great Locomotive Chase is dramatized at this museum through film, exhibits, and the *General* itself. Visitors follow the footsteps of the conductor as he gives chase on foot, by handcar, and with three commandeered locomotives.

The construction of steam locomotives and other machinery in the South is depicted in a factory reproduction featuring two locomotives in various stages of assembly. Superior turn-of-the-century craftsmanship is highlighted by an array of wooden machine patterns and a video of the casting process. This unique collection includes archives and exhibits that detail the business transactions of the Glover Machine Works.

A member of the prestigious Smithsonian Affiliations program, the museum integrates Smithsonian artifacts and collections into its exhibits, educational initiatives, and research programs. Special events include Civil War re-enactments, an annual Big Shanty Festival, and other festivals, held at the Depot across the street.
Open daily except Easter, Christmas, and New Year's Day.
(770) 427-2117
www.southernmuseum.org

6 Stone Mountain Park

16 miles east of downtown Atlanta, off U.S. Hwy. 78
This 3,200-acre park is home to the South's greatest natural wonder and answer to Mount Rushmore. Visitors will stand in awe of the world's largest mass of exposed granite with the world's largest relief carving.

The Memorial Carving immortalizes three of the Confederate's most distinguished Civil War heroes: Jefferson Davis, Robert E. Lee, and Thomas "Stonewall" Jackson. Towering 1,683 feet above sea level, Stone Mountain covers 583 acres.

At the Skylift station, visitors can hop aboard a Swiss cable car for an 825-foot ride up to the mountain's top. Upon arriving, they'll be greeted by breathtaking views of Atlanta and the Appalachian Mountains. Back down at the mountain's base, visitors can hop aboard a diesel engine locomotive for a scenic five-mile excursion, departing from a scale replica of Atlanta's Main Train Depot, circa 1870. Visitors can also take a detour back in time to a place called Crossroads, which recaptures a small Georgia town from the 1870s, featuring hands-on demonstrations in candlemaking, blacksmithing, and glassblowing. Hungry tourists can sample the best of down-home Southern cooking at Miss Katie's sideboard restaurant.

Visitors can also explore the park's woodlands, lakes, streams, and miles of nature trails. In addition, the park offers opportunities for tennis, golf, and fishing. Picnicking is available in two public areas. Camping is welcome, and there are guest rooms available at the Stone Mountain Inn.
Open year-round except Christmas. Entrance fee.
(800) 317-2006; (770) 498-5690;
www.stonemountainpark.com

4 Etowah Indian Mounds Historic Site. *Steps lead to the top of an Etowah mound, which was a burial site of more than 500 of the tribal elite.*

6 Stone Mountain Park. *A laser show projected on the world's largest mass of exposed granite draws a crowd at this 3,200-acre park.*

7 Washington Historical Museum

308 E. Robert Toombs Ave., U.S. Rte. 78, Washington
In 1780 the Georgia Legislature voted to set aside 100 acres in Wilkes County for a town to be named Washington, in honor of the general. The little town prospered as cotton plantations and tobacco farms appeared, and the simple houses and log cabins were replaced by antebellum homes.

The house that serves as the Washington Historical Museum was built in 1835 or 1836 and acquired 20 years later by Samuel Barnett, Georgia's first railroad commissioner, who added the front rooms, hallways, and the staircase. Now owned by the city of Washington, the house has been restored to its mid-1800s condition. Elegant in its simplicity, this "upcountry" two-story white frame dwelling mainly reflects local events and customs from the cotton plantation era

through the advent of the railroads in the period 1835–55. Many rare and unusual articles can be seen here, including a 1790s cotton gin and a number of 19th-century South Carolina pottery jars, some of which were made and signed by Dave the Slave. Also in the collection are feather-edged earthenware dishes that were carried as ballast by ships from England.

Many of the period furnishings in the museum were donated by residents of Washington; among the choice pieces are an 1855 Weber piano and Belter furniture of carved rosewood.

The second-floor Civil War collection displays wartime memorabilia, including original newspapers, an 1861 Ballard breech-loading carbine, and Jefferson Davis's camp chest, sent to him by English sympathizers in 1865.
Open Tues.–Sun; closed Thanksgiving, Christmas, and New Year's Day. Virtual tour available for handicapped visitors.

First floor is handicapped-accessible. Admission charged.
(706) 678-2105
www.washingtonwilkes.com

8 Uncle Remus Museum

Turner Park, Eatonton
The fortuitous friendship of a talented printer's apprentice on a plantation newspaper and the black slaves who shared with him their folktales has given us the classic characters of Brer Rabbit, Brer Fox, Sis Goose, and the other critters of the Uncle Remus stories.

The author, Joel Chandler Harris, was born in Eatonton, and the slaves, "Uncle" George Terrell and "Uncle" Bob Capers, worked on the plantation of Joseph Addison Turner, who was the publisher of a small newspaper and gave Harris his first job at age 13.

Two connected slave cabins house the museum. Here, in these simple log structures, the world of Tar-Baby, the Laughing Place, and the brierpatch is brought to life by whimsical dioramas and other exhibits. At one end of the cabin is a replica of Uncle Remus's fireplace, around which are displayed the various 19th-century household articles mentioned in the tales. On one wall hangs a large portrait of Uncle Remus and Joseph Sydney Turner, the Little Boy in the stories and the son of Joseph Addison Turner.

First editions of many of Harris's works, including his stories of the Old South and the Reconstruction days, are exhibited, and copies of his and other children's books are on sale.
Open Mon.–Sat. and P.M. Sun; closed Tues. Sept.–May. Admission charged.
(706) 485-6856
www.ohwy.com/ga/u/uncremmu.html

9 Magnolia Springs State Park and Aquarium

Off U.S. Hwy. 25, Millen
This delightful spring might not be so well known had it not been for one of the horrors of the Civil War. The notorious conditions at Andersonville Prison led to the construction of Camp Lawton, a 42-acre stockade, where good water and plentiful timber were available. More than 10,000 Union troops were held in the camp in 1864, and vestiges of the fortifications can still be seen on a hill by the main entrance to Magnolia Springs State Park, a 1,071-acre recreation area that now includes the site.

The park is named for a spring with a prodigious flow of ice-cold water bubbling up to form a 15-foot-deep pool so clear that aquatic plants on the bottom are plainly visible. A large picnic area, with shelters, tables, and grills, is set among loblolly pines near the spring, overlooked by a boardwalk and observation deck.

A lake can be fished for bass, crappies, catfish, and bream, and a launching ramp and boat dock are provided. The park also offers a supervised swimming pool, hiking and biking trails, rental cottages, and many tent and trailer sites with water and hookups.

On the Woodpecker Woods Nature Trail seven different species of woodpeckers may be observed. Highlights on the trail are identified in a free booklet.

A freshwater aquarium displays various fish, turtles, and alligators.
Open year-round.
(478) 982-1660
www.gastateparks.org

10 Port Columbus National Civil War Naval Museum

1002 Victory Dr., Columbus

The warships of the Confederate Navy, established in 1861 to defend the Southern coasts and rivers, were built with limited funds and little skilled help; there were few experienced sailors to man them. To preserve the history of this unlikely seagoing force, the museum was opened in 1970, featuring the remains of two important ships. The ironclad CSS *Jackson* (named for the capital of Mississippi) was built at the Confederate navy yard here in Columbus. The 130-foot sail-and-steam-powered gunboat *Chatta-hoochee* was built at Saffold, Georgia.

The CSS *Jackson,* representing one of the new Civil War naval designs, was sheathed with four inches of iron plate and equipped with six Brooke rifles. But the 225-foot warship was still unfinished when the Union forces captured Columbus in 1865. Set on fire and cut loose from its moorings in the Chattahoochee River, the ill-fated ship burned to the waterline 30 miles down-river.

The gunboat *Chattahoochee* began its career under the command of Lt. Catesby Jones, who had been captain of the *Merrimack* in its famous battle with the *Monitor.* The ship was damaged by a boiler explosion in 1863 and was scuttled in the river when the war was over.

Sections of these two ships, recovered from the Chattahoochee in the early 1900s, are displayed in the museum. In the museum are artifacts from the two vessels, several ship models, weapons, and other Civil War memorabilia. On board the 87-foot-long replica

CSS-*Albemarle,* a battle simulator re-creates naval combat. Visitors are treated to interactive exhibits that illustrate one of the most innovative periods in the country's naval history.

Open daily; closed Christmas.
Admission charged.
(706) 327-9798
www.portcolumbus.org

11 Providence Canyon State Park
Lumpkin

The farmers who scratched a hard living out of the soil here 170 years ago didn't know about contour plowing, cover crops, and crop rotation and would be astounded at the erosion they started with their mule-driven plows.

Under the grass and sod lies a deep layer of red clay called the Clayton Formation. Underneath it is the Providence Formation,

11 Providence Canyon State Park. *At the rim of Georgia's "Little Grand Canyon," visitors can peer down gullies that drop 150 feet.*

whose susceptibility to erosion is dramatically demonstrated by the gullies, some 150 feet deep, which began to form generations ago in the white, pink, and purple strata.

This scenic area, which contains 16 canyons, dominates the 1,109-acre park. It serves as a colorful backdrop for wild plants and shrubs, including the rare plumleaf azalea, whose flowers, ranging in color from orange to various shades of red, bloom from July to September. Other indigenous plants include verbena, maypop, wild ginger, and prickly pear.

The three-mile Canyon Rim Trail, with 20 overlooks, winds past clumps of sumac and stands of hickories and slash pines, where raccoons and opossums might be seen and hawks circle overhead. Visitors are amazed at the 43 breathtaking colors of Georgia's

"Little Grand Canyon." The park also has primitive campsites, a group shelter, and two picnic shelters. The Interpretive Center offers two dioramas, a live beehive, and exhibits showing the park's history.

Geologists say that because of the claylike, erosion-resistant soil underlying the Providence Formation, the canyons will not get deeper, but the sides of the canyons will continue to erode. Visitors are warned not to cross any barriers at the canyons' rims.

Open daily.
(229) 838-6202
www.gastateparks.org

12 Little Ocmulgee State Park and Lodge
2 miles north of McRae

This popular park is busy in the summer and especially so on weekends. But with 1,277 acres and a 265-acre lake to enjoy, one can usually find some areas that are off the beaten path; and in the off-season there's plenty of elbow room. The two hiking trails—one about two miles long and the other a little shorter—are not crowded at any time of year. They both loop through a landscape of dogwood, pines, oaks, and hickories. In April the woods are spectacular with the dazzling bloom of wild azaleas.

Sharp-eyed observers may see bluebirds, cardinals, mockingbirds, four species of woodpeckers, wood ducks, and elegant egrets.

Raccoons, deer, squirrels, and alligators reside in the park; on guided tours through the sandhills, visitors can catch a glimpse of a gopher tortoise.

Paddleboats and canoes are available for rent, and a launching ramp is provided. Fishing is popular in these waters, where largemouth bass, crappies, shellcrackers, and large bluegills abound. Near the beginning of a quarter-mile canoe trail, a buzzard roost in a cypress swamp can be seen. A 30-room lodge and restaurant, a large camping area with hookups, a swimming pool (which is likely to be crowded in good weather), a playground, two tennis courts, and an 18-hole golf course all contribute to the popularity of this outstanding recreational area.

Open year-round.
(229) 868-7474
www.naturallybusiness.com

13 Blue and Gray Museum
Municipal Building, Fitzgerald

With a collection that includes both Northern and Southern mementos of the Civil War period, this museum reflects the strange beginnings of the town of Fitzgerald.

In the early 1890s, when hostility between Yankees and Southerners was still deeply felt, P. H. Fitzgerald, an Indiana newspaperman and former Civil War drummer boy, became concerned about aging Civil War veterans, who found the cold Northern winters difficult. Fitzgerald dreamed of a settlement in a milder climate for these retired Union soldiers. In newspaper editorials he told of his hopes, and the response was so great that he began a campaign for funds.

In 1895, with the approval of Georgia's governor, Fitzgerald used the money he had raised to purchase 100,000 acres of pineland in the heart of Georgia. People began to arrive by wagon, train, steamboat, and on horse-

back; Confederate veterans also joined the colony. The town that quickly developed was named Fitzgerald. Some Southern antipathy toward the project was diminished when streets were named in equal numbers for Confederate and Union generals.

In the ensuing years the families of the Blue and the Gray have donated many reminders of the Civil War period to the museum, which occupies a turn-of-the-century railroad depot. Among the items are a drum from a New York State regiment, a muzzle-loading rifle of the 4th Illinois Cavalry, an 1863 land grant signed by President Lincoln, a key to Andersonville Prison, a Confederate flag, and the mortar and pestle used by Jefferson Davis's physician.

Open P.M. Mon.–Fri., year-round.
Admission charged.
(229) 426-5069
www.fitzgeraldga.org

14 Thronateeska Heritage Center
Albany. Driving west on Rte. 82, turn right onto Washington Ave.; continue to Roosevelt Ave., then turn right.

The museum, which takes its name from a Creek word meaning "place where flint is picked up," is devoted to artifacts that reveal the history and the natural environment of southwest Georgia, in addition to showcasing aspects of the entire United States. It is housed in a 1913 railroad station that is now on the *National Register of Historic Places.*

Exhibits change frequently at the museum, so be sure to call in advance to find out what will be displayed during your visit.

On permanent display is the Model Train Exhibit, the only collection of its type in southwest

Georgia. Housed in an actual railroad baggage car, the exhibit details a trip from the city to the country.

Also on the grounds are the Weatherbee Planetarium and the Science Discovery Center, truly making a trip here one that will please the entire family.

Open P.M. Thurs.–Sat. year-round.
(229) 432-6955
www.heritagecenter.org

15 Kolomoki Mounds Historic Park
6 miles north of Blakely, off Rte. 27

This 1,300-acre park is both a recreational area and a mystery-shrouded archaeological site where seven mounds dating from A.D. 250 to 950 have been preserved. Kolomoki, with its mounds, plaza, and outlying villages, was an important population center for perhaps as many as 2,000 people.

The largest of the mounds, known as the Temple Mound, rises from a base 325 feet by 200 feet to a height of 56 feet and is believed to have had two distinct platforms at the top, each with a

structure, which may have been a temple. Two smaller mounds proved on excavation to be burial mounds. One excavated mound is now housed by the museum; from a platform you can look down into the archaeological dig. The museum interprets events that took place at Kolomoki with a short film, dioramas, and exhibits of artifacts.

The two lakes in the park, together with Kolomoki Creek, offer fishermen ample opportunities for catching bass, crappies, bream, and catfish. Rowboats may be rented, and there is a boat-launching ramp, but motors are limited to 10 horsepower.

Hikers on the two short nature trails may see white-tailed deer, foxes, bluebirds, cardinals, hawks, and possibly an alligator. The park also has a swimming pool, two picnic areas, and a 43-site campground.

Park open year-round. Museum open Tues.–Sat. and P.M. Sun. Admission charged for museum.
(229) 724-2150
www.gastateparks.org/historic

15 Kolomoki Mounds Historic Park. *An excavated mound shows an ancient burial site dating from A.D. 250 to 950.*

16 Seminole State Park
Donalsonville

Named for the American Indians who lived in this region before white settlers came, this 604-acre park is best known for water sports—boating, waterskiing, canoeing, and swimming.

Seminole Lake, the main feature here, is a favorite with fishermen. Its shallow waters with beds of stumps and grass contain more species of fish than does any other lake in Georgia. The lake is also reputed to have the best large-mouth bass fishing in the United States. Experienced anglers who come here maintain that live bait is the best for bass. Also caught here are crappies, jack, bream, catfish, and yellow perch. Duck hunting is also popular.

Picnic tables, some beneath shelters, are located along the lakefront. Rental cottages and tent and trailer campgrounds, shaded by longleaf pines, poplars, sweet gums, and cedars, also give a view of the lake. Pioneer camping is available in the more remote sections of the park. Be alert: Signs leading to the park can be confused with signs for the Lake Seminole launching ramp, which is not on park property.

Open year-round.
(229) 861-3186
www.gastateparks.org

17 Thomasville

The effect of the Civil War on this small town in southern Georgia was unpredictably beneficial. In 1861 the Atlantic and Gulf Railroad, with its terminus at Thomasville, was built to move men and supplies north to support the Confederate Army. The railroad's major contribution to the South, however, was the postwar transportation of wealthy Yankees, who came here to escape the rigors of Northern winters. A number of luxurious resort hotels were established, and wealthy families from Chicago, Cleveland, Philadelphia, and New York built winter cottages here. Thus, the town became a fashionable social center.

The Northerners bestowed upon Thomasville a heritage of eclectic architecture that the local citizens have fortunately managed to preserve. The houses are a charming mélange of plantation, Greek Revival, Neoclassical, Georgian, Victorian, Queen Anne, and bungalow styles. A walking tour includes 35 interesting homes, a number of which are on the *National Register of Historic Places* and some open to the public.

16 Seminole State Park. *Skeletons of oak trees stand in the shallow waters of Seminole Lake, which contains more species of fish than any other lake in Georgia.*

In the heyday of the large resort hotels, a popular wooded area by the railroad tracks was called Yankee Paradise. Today the 26-acre area is more circumspectly called Paradise Park. A stately symbol of preservation here is the 300-year-old "Big Oak," some 70 feet high and twice as broad at the crown—the largest live oak tree east of the Mississippi. Thomasville is also an agricultural center, and the farmers' market is the largest in the state.

Open Mon.–Sat.; closed last week in Sept. and major holidays. Admission charged. For tour information, call the Welcome Center at (800) 704-2350.
(229) 226-7664
www.thomasvillega.com

18 Fort McAllister Historic Park
9 miles east of Richmond Hill on Spur 144

An interesting blend of history and recreation is combined in the park's 1,724 acres of high ground salt marsh, forest, and riverfront. The focal point, Fort McAllister, was built here at the mouth of the Great Ogeechee River in 1861 to protect Savannah during the Civil War.

The earthen fort withstood eight battles with Union gunboats from June 1861 to March 1863. It was finally taken from the landward side in hand-to-hand fighting by the troops of General Sherman at the end of their epic march to the sea. A walking tour with interpretive plaques encompasses the fortification, with its central parade ground, reconstructed magazine, and reproduction cannons. A printed tour guide describing 21 locations helps bring to life the drama and intensity of the action here.

A new museum displays dioramas of the final battle, early photographs of the fort, and Confederate uniforms. Machine parts and artifacts recovered from the wreck of a Confederate blockade runner contribute to an interesting collection. On summer weekends Civil War lectures and demonstrations in firing small arms are given by staff members.

A picnic area with tables, shelters, and a playground is located along the riverfront beneath tall slash pines.

Nearby Savage Island, accessible by a causeway, offers a camping area for tents and trailers, rental cottages, and a nature trail among palmettos, water oaks, magnolias, and other native trees, some festooned with Spanish moss. A boat ramp is provided, and fishermen try for whiting, flounder, mullet, shrimp, and crabs. Care should be taken in the wooded areas to avoid poisonous snakes.

Open daily except Thanksgiving and Christmas.
(912) 727-2339
www.gastateparks.org

19 Sapelo Island Reserve
Reached only by ferry from Meridian. Tickets must be purchased at the Sapelo Ferry and Visitor Center, 8 miles northeast of Darien, off Ga. Hwy. 99.

This small barrier island, with its uplands, wetlands, marshes, and combination of fresh and salt water, harbors an impressive array of birds, mammals, and fish. In the many marsh areas—carpeted with smooth cordgrass and black needlerush—green herons, clapper rails, and ruddy turnstones may be seen, as well as minks and raccoons. Purple marsh and fiddler crabs, oysters, white shrimp, mullet, and anchovies also find sanctuary here.

American Indians had occupied the island for some 4,500 years before English colonists began to arrive in the 1700s. During the next few centuries the island changed hands repeatedly as the French, Spanish, and British fought for control. In 1934 R. J. Reynolds purchased most of the island and assisted in establishing the University of Georgia Marine Institute. After Reynolds's death the state acquired some 8,000 acres from his widow and created the Reynolds Wildlife Refuge. You can also visit the Reynolds mansion and see the restored working lighthouse.

A 30-minute ferry ride takes visitors to the island, where buses tour the marshland, dunes, and wildlife management areas. It is advisable to take insect repellent. Half-day trips are offered two or three times a week year-round. All-day tours, which include a nature walk, are scheduled once a month from March to October. Tour reservations should be made two to four weeks in advance.

For ferry schedule and further information, call (912) 485-2299. Fee charged.

www.sapeloislandreserve.org

⟨20⟩ Cumberland Island National Seashore

From Rte. 40 in St. Marys, turn right at waterfront to visitors center. This historic sandspit, the southernmost of Georgia's sea islands, has been inhabited for some 4,000 years. In the 16th century the Spanish built a fort here to protect their Florida holdings. Their religious faith was buttressed also—by the establishment

of a Franciscan mission and the conversion of many Timucan Indians. The Spanish called the island San Pedro.

In the 18th century, the present name was proposed by a local American Indian who had visited the Duke of Cumberland in England. Gen. James Oglethorpe, founder of England's Georgia colony, accepted the suggestion.

There were no further significant developments until after the Revolutionary War, when Gen. Nathanael Greene bought a large tract of land on which his widow built an imposing mansion. After the Civil War, Andrew Carnegie's brother built a handsome home, which still stands. Greyfield Inn, a mansion built for Lucy and Thomas Carnegie's daughter in 1900, is presently furnished as it was at the turn of the century.

This small island, about 17.5 miles long and three miles across at its widest point, supports a fascinating range of ecological zones, each with its own population of plants, birds, and animals. The

⟨20⟩ Cumberland Island National Seashore. *Sea oats sprout up from the dunes and help stabilize the grasses and the sand here.*

beach is spangled with shells and frequented by shorebirds that follow the tides. Where the soil is deepest, a maritime forest of oaks, magnolias, red bay, and various pines is established.

The sloughs and ponds are home to alligators, otters, and minks; wild horses, said to be descended from those brought by the Spanish, may also be seen.

The island has walking trails and camps for backpackers (reservations required). A museum displaying American Indian artifacts interprets the island's history.

Open daily Mar. 1–Nov. 30; closed Tues. and Wed., Dec. 1–Feb. 28. For ferry schedule and reservations (suggested), call (888) 817-3421.

www.nps.gov/cuis

⟨21⟩ Suwannee Canal Recreation Area, Okefenokee National Wildlife Refuge

7 miles south of Folkston, on Hwy. 121

Although a foothold has been established on the edge of this mysterious land, mankind comes as a stranger. This is the rightful realm of the alligator, black bear, bobcat, opossum, muskrat, and otter. It is home to lizards, turtles, toads, snakes, and salamanders. Some 40 kinds of fish and 230 species of birds are native to this region.

Many of the plants seen here are unique to the prairies, waterways, and forests of the Okefenokee Swamp. The tannic acid in the vegetation stains the slow-moving water a rich brown. This does not affect the fish—bass, bluegills, catfish, and pickerel are regularly caught.

The area contains numerous islands and lakes, and prairies cover about 400,000 acres. A variety of wading birds, such as herons, ibises, and cranes, can be seen here.

This fascinating environment can be enjoyed from a variety of perspectives: on the hiking trails; the boardwalk over the bogs; guided after-dark tours; and from the observation towers. A restored homestead suggests the character of early-day life in the swamp.

To explore the 11-mile Suwannee Canal, one can rent a boat with outboard motor. For a wilderness canoe trip lasting up to five days, reservations must be made two months in advance. Insect repellent to fend off mosquitoes and deerflies is needed from April through October. The interpretive center provides an overview of the sights and activities to be savored.

Open year-round. (912) 496-7836

http://okefenokee.fws.com

Akaka Falls. *Set within a deep forest, the falls plunge 442 feet down black volcanic rock surrounded by tropical foliage and flowers (see page 87).*

(see page 87)

Hawai'i

For all the similarity of their volcanic origin and temperate climate, each of the five main islands has a character all its own.

Although Hawai'i is a tourist haven, there are still interesting out-of-the-way places to see. On each island there are beautiful beaches, scenic water-falls, and hiking trails, as well as lookouts and viewpoints that reveal panoramas ranging from the merely spectacular to the breathtaking. Some of the waterfalls are reached by inviting trails, and some offer the pleasure of a swim in the pools at their base.

Four of the islands have outstanding botanical gardens where a remarkable variety of plants and birdlife can be enjoyed. Museums present the natural history and cul-ture of the islands, and one has a fascinating eclectic collection of artifacts.

Bringing one from the ancient to the more recent past are petroglyphs, a temple site, a royal retreat, and lava flows that wreaked various kinds of havoc.

KAUAI—The Garden Isle

1 Ke'e Beach and Kalalau Trail

Ke'e Beach, at the very end of Route 56, is protected by an off-shore reef and, unlike other beaches in the vicinity, provides safe wading, swimming, snorkeling, and scuba diving even in winter.

Ke'e is part of Ha'ena State Park, a scenic wildland that includes the Waikapalae and Waikanaloa wet caves containing pools of glowing green water. Hawaiian legend says that chiefs of old used to gather here.

There's much to see, and you can camp, but the real attraction is Kalalau Trail, used since prehis-toric times to reach Kalalau Valley, 11 miles away. Beginning at Ke'e Beach, the trail follows the spec-tacular Na Pali Coast. You can backpack and make an overnight stop at Kalalau, or settle for a day trip to Hanakapi'ai Beach.

Side trails lead to waterfalls and lush valleys, and hikers won't go hungry or thirsty: The way is lined with delicious wild yellow guavas. The coast is treacherous; swimming is not recommended, and in wet weather hiking the entire trail calls for caution.
Open year-round.
(808) 274-3444

www.hawaiiweb.com

1 Kalalau Trail. *This magnificent trail follows the rainbow of color along the Na Pali Coast, and you can eat delicious wild yellow guavas along the way.*

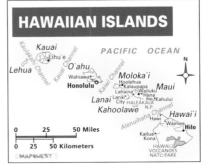

HAWAIIAN ISLANDS

PACIFIC OCEAN

Kauai
Lihu'e
Kaulakahi Channel
Kauai Channel
Kaiwi Channel
Lehua
O'ahu
Wahiawa
Hoolehua
Kalaupapa
Moloka'i
Honolulu
Lahaina
Wailuku
Kahului
Maui
Lanai
Hana
Lanai City
HALEAKALA N.P.
Kahoolawe
Kahoolawe
Alenuihaha Channel
Hawi
Waimea
Hawai'i
Kailua Kona
Hilo
HAWAI'I VOLCANOES NATL PARK

0 25 50 Miles
0 25 50 Kilometers

MAPQUEST

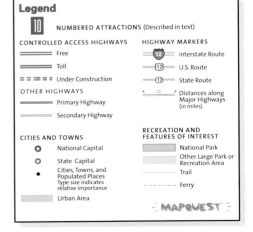

Legend

10 NUMBERED ATTRACTIONS (Described in text)

CONTROLLED ACCESS HIGHWAYS
Free
Toll
Under Construction

OTHER HIGHWAYS
Primary Highway
Secondary Highway

CITIES AND TOWNS
⊙ National Capital
⊛ State Capital
• Cities, Towns, and Populated Places Type size indicates relative importance
Urban Area

HIGHWAY MARKERS
⑫ Interstate Route
⑫ U.S. Route
⑫ State Route
12 Distances along Major Highways (in miles)

RECREATION AND FEATURES OF INTEREST
National Park
Other Large Park or Recreation Area
Trail
Ferry

MAPQUEST

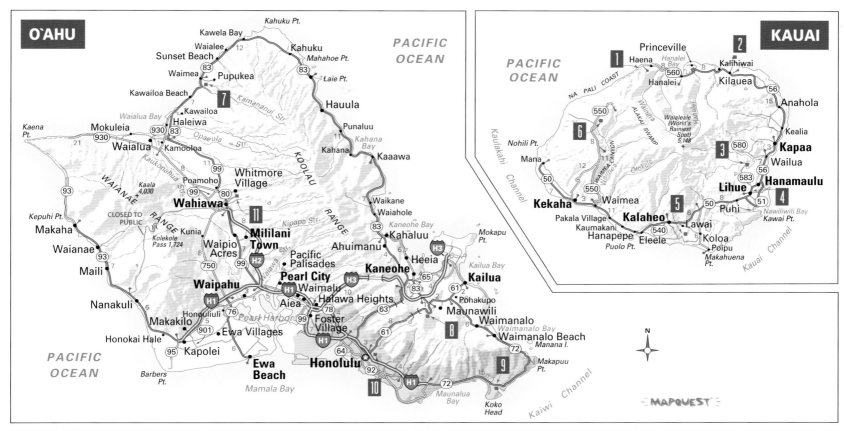

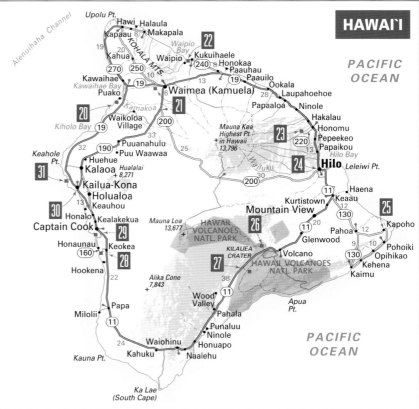

2 Kilauea Point Wildlife Refuge and Lighthouse

Located on the northern tip of Kauai. From Lihu'e, drive north on Hwy. 56 for approximately 23 miles to the town of Kilauea. Turn right on Kolo Rd., then left on Kilauea Rd. to the entrance of Wailua Falls.

Blanketing one of the most spectacular sections of coastline on the main islands, this 203-acre stretch is on the forefront of Hawai'i's efforts to protect its wildlife. Working with volunteers, the U.S. Fish and Wildlife Service has restored coastal habitats to provide the state's indigenous seabirds with a safe and beautiful home. Not only does this refuge welcome the official state bird, the nene (Hawaiian goose), but it offers a haven to two of the most distinctive endangered endemic mammals: the Hawaiian monk seal and the Hawaiian hoary bat.

For a bird's-eye view of the seabirds against a dramatic backdrop of steep cliffs plunging into the ocean, visitors can climb to the tower of Kilauea Lighthouse. Built in 1913 and named to the *National Register of Historic Places,* the lighthouse stands as a monument to Hawai'i's colorful past and natural splendor.

From the shore below, visitors might catch spinner dolphins at play or experience the majestic grace of the humpback whale. Each December through April, these magnificent animals migrate from Alaska to Hawai'i to mate, give birth, and rear their huge babies.

Open year-round except Christmas and New Year's Day. Admission charged.
(808) 828-1413

www.kilauea-point.com

3 Wailua Falls. *The double torrent drops 80 feet to a clear pool below. The plunge is especially dramatic after a heavy mountain rain.*

3 Wailua Falls

At the end of Hwy. 583, Kapaia

Even if you knew there was a natural wonder on the scale of Wailua Falls in the vicinity, you'd never dream this prosaic little road past a Buddhist cemetery and through four miles of waving sugar cane would be the way to reach it. The double torrent that feeds the falls (*wai* means "fresh water," *lua,* "two") drops 80 feet to a flower-ringed pool. The plunge is especially dramatic after heavy mountain rains—a comparatively frequent occurrence, since 5,000-foot Mount Waialeale, which dominates the center of Kauai, is considered the wettest spot in the world, with a yearly rainfall of almost 500 inches.

Unfortunately, there's no safe way to climb down to the base of the falls, so your view is limited to what can be seen from just one place. However, the next time you catch a rerun of *Fantasy Island,* note the opening shots: Filmed from a helicopter, they give a different perspective of this lovely cascade.

Open year-round.

www.kauai_hawaii.com

4 Kauai Museum

4428 Rice St., Lihu'e

The informative and well-organized material here includes exhibits on the history of both Kauai, the "garden island," and the nearby "forbidden isle" of Niihau. You'll find almost everything worth knowing about the islands' natural history and Hawaiian culture before Westerners came. The displays range from poi-pounding tools to weapons. Recorded history begins with Captain Cook's landing on Kauai at Waimea in 1778, moving through the little-known Russian attempt to dominate the island, and finally to the impact of Protestant missionaries.

Other periods covered include the islands' plantation heyday (when labor was imported from Japan and elsewhere), the Hawaiian monarchy, and contemporary times. There is one unexpected exhibit worth a detour: a collection of bowls made from the calabash gourd. The work of local artists is frequently shown here.

Open Mon.–Sat. Admission charged.
(808) 245-6391

www.kauai.qpg.com

5 McBryde Garden, National Tropical Botanical Garden

Lawa'i. Tours depart from Poipu. Exit south off Rte. 50 onto Rte. 520 and west onto Lawa'i Rd. to visitors center across from Spouting Horn.

Your tour begins when you board a tram at the visitors center to begin your descent into the Lawa'i Valley. Entering the gardens on what was once a sugar cane train railbed, visitors are treated to panoramic views of the valley and adjacent bay. Your self-guiding walking tour of the McBryde Garden includes the Spice of Life trail, Bamboo Bridge, the Ancient Plants of Polynesia, and a Walk Among the Natives.

The 252-acre McBryde Garden is home to the world's largest collection of native Hawaiian plants, the most endangered group of plants in the 50 states. The spectacular specimens include Brighamia species, which were nearing extinction on the extremely steep and inaccessible cliffs of the islands until botanists suspended themselves by ropes nearly 3,000 feet above the ocean and became human pollinators in order to save these plants.

Also in the Lawa'i Valley and adjacent to McBryde Garden is Allerton Garden. Guided walking tours of this enchanting private estate are offered by reservation and include a tram ride into the valley from the visitors center.

The National Tropical Botanical Garden is a nonprofit institution, with active programs in tropical plant research, conservation, and education. Now comprised of four gardens and three preserves in the Hawaiian islands, the organization is supported by donations and grants.

Open daily. Admission charge.
(808) 742-2623
www.ntbg.org

🚶 🔭

6 Koke'e State Park

90 minutes from Lihu'e Airport, off Rte. 550 or 552
At nearly 4,000 feet, the park's 4,345 acres are considerably cooler than lower elevations, and rainfall can be heavy, which accounts for the different character of the scenery here. Pines and other temperate plant life replace palms and tropical vegetation. Along the road there are views from Koke'e's luxuriant green surroundings into red-walled Waimea Canyon, and at the northernmost point of the park Kalalau Lookout affords a sweeping overview of Kalalau Valley.

The park contains several trails, some leading into the 30 square miles of Alakai Swamp. Birdwatching is excellent, and in August and September you can catch trout. From June to August delicious Koke'e plums are here for the picking, and all year long there are lilikoi (passion fruit) and guavas.

Just outside the park headquarters museum, note the Polynesian jungle fowl begging for handouts: They're descended from birds that Polynesians brought from Tahiti and now survive only on Kauai.

Open year-round.
(808) 335-9975
www.aloha.net/~inazoo/kokee.html

🛆 🚐 🚶 🚲 🐟 🔭 🏇 🐴

O'AHU—The Gathering Place

7 Pu'uo Mahuka Heiau State Monument

Exit Hwy. 83 at Pupukea Homestead Rd.; continue 7/10 mile and exit right onto unmarked road; continue 7/10 mile to the temple.
The isolation of this ruined sacrificial temple, a state historical site and one of O'ahu's largest and oldest structures, simply serves to make its ties to Hawai'i's pagan past more tangible.

The wooden statues of the old gods may have been destroyed here in 1819, when the old religion was abolished, but ancient customs survive. You'll note, for instance, that people still leave offerings—fruits, vegetables, and flowers—on a wooden lele altar.

Kukaniloko Birthstones in Wahiawa is the recognized site on O'ahu for the birth of royal children. Interpretive signs and brochures are available at Pu'uo Mahuka Heiau.

www.hawaii.gov/dlnr/dsp

8 Nu'uanu Pali State Wayside

Off Pali Hwy. 61; follow signs at Nu'uanu Pali Summit.
Although this dramatic view over the mountains, hills, and bays of windward O'ahu is at its magnificent best in the morning, you might want to time your visit for lunch or later to avoid the crowds and tour buses. The viewing platform, enlarged to accommodate the crowds, also detracts from the area's original wilderness atmosphere, so descend to the ledge just below it (about 1,000 feet above sea level).

Because the lookout is at a low point in the Koolau Range crest, trade winds drive so forcefully through the gap that you can virtually lean into them. There are stories of would-be suicides blown right back onto the top of the *pali* (cliffs), and when the wind is from the opposite direction, it can be dangerous. When the battle of Nu'uanu was fought here in 1795, pitting Kamehameha I against Kalanikupule, king of O'ahu, whole battalions of warriors (estimates range from 400 to 10,000) were said to have been driven—or blown—over the pali.

Open year-round.
(808) 587-0300
www.hawaii.gov/dlnr/dsp

🪑 🚶

9 Hanauma Bay Nature Preserve

100 Hanauma Bay Rd.
What makes this beach unique are shallow waters filled with rock and coral that provide shelter for hundreds of varieties of colorful reef fish. With a snorkel mask you can observe them even at wading distance. Toss out a morsel of bread, and whole schools will swim up within reach.

Snorkel- or scuba-equipped divers can venture out for even more spectacular fish-watching. It goes without saying, of course, that neither fish nor coral can be taken from this protected area.

Many tourists speeding along Kalanianaole Highway (Route 72) miss this ravishing spot. The locals know about it, though, so it's best to avoid weekend visits. But if you come with a mask and a snorkel on a winter weekday, be prepared for a marvelous experience. The almost perfectly semicircular beach and bay are what remain of a volcanic crater breached by the sea thousands of years ago. But be warned: The descent to the beach from the parking area is steep.

Open year-round except Tuesdays.
Admission charged.
(808) 396-4229
www.aloha.com

🪑 🏊 🚶 🚭

9 Hanauma Bay Nature Preserve. *Colorful reef fish are here for the viewing (but not catching) from these shallow waters filled with rock and coral.*

10 Puʻu Ualakaʻa State Wayside

Round Top Dr., Honolulu

Many *malihini* (newcomers) miss this glorious view because it's not easy to find. But look for Makiki Street on a detailed map, and you'll see that it connects from a scenic drive to this mountaintop wayside. A second, longer route—Tantalus Drive—begins farther west off Puowaina Drive. Honolulu residents usually ascend by one drive and descend by the other. The heights tend to be much cooler than the lowlands, and the wayside is an ideal spot to visit on a hot summer day.

When you get here, the expected facilities make it seem like just another park: trees, grass, picnic tables, comfort stations. But then there's the view: No other area open to the public boasts anything like it. The city is spread out before you, from Pearl Harbor and the airport in one direction to Diamond Head and Koko Head in the other.

Puʻu Ualakaʻa (known locally as Round Top) means "hill of the rolling sweet potatoes." It got its name, according to the story, because Kamehameha I ordered sweet potatoes to be planted here—and when they were dug up, they rolled down the hill.

Open dawn to dusk year-round.
(808) 587-0300

11 Wahiʻawa Botanic Garden

California Ave., Wahiʻawa

This verdant, secluded—and educational—haven is missed by the many tourists who go as quickly as possible through Wahiʻawa, an "army town" near the famous Schofield Barracks, which, it must be admitted, is not one of the island's most attractive settlements. It is worthwhile, however, to stop and see the splendid collection of plants in the botanic garden.

In the 1920s the wooded gulch in which the garden is situated was used by the Hawaiʻi Sugar Planters' Association as a nursery and for forestry experiments. In 1950 the 27-acre plot was turned over to the city and county of Honolulu, and although the area is still being developed, it's a charming and informative place to visit. Following the self-guiding tour folder, you enter past Australian tree ferns 40 feet tall and native tree ferns *(hapuʻu)* whose stalks are covered with a wool-like substance *(pulu)* once exported for pillow and mattress stuffing. Other native plants in the Hawaiʻian Garden range from hibiscus (the state flower) to loulu palms. The last of the indicated stops (No. 23) is given over to a collection of small plants and vines of the aroid family, ranging from the decorative anthurium to the edible taro. As you might imagine, birds abound in this garden environment.

Open daily except Christmas
and New Year's Day.
(808) 621-7321
www.cohonolulu.us/parks

MOLOKAʻI—The Friendly Isle

12 Kalaupapa National Historical Park

This settlement on Molokaʻi's north shore lies some 2,000 feet below "topside," which is what residents call the rest of Molokaʻi. The difficulty of reaching it was one reason why the leprosy victims, who were treated by the Belgian priest Father Damien, were exiled here in the 19th century. Today fewer than 50 former patients remain, living amid touching

12 Kalaupapa National Historical Park. *The remote settlement on Molokaʻi's north shore served thousands of leprosy patients in the 19th and 20th centuries. Today fewer than 50 former patients remain.*

reminders of Father Damien and his mission. To visit this settlement, one needs permission from the state of Hawaiʻi Department of Health and must be 16 or older. Tour sponsors can make the necessary arrangements.

A steep trail leads down from Palaau State Park, and there's also a mule train that wends its way down 1,700 feet—one of the highest seacliffs in the world. But there's reliable air-taxi service from Molokaʻi Airport, and charter flights are available from Oʻahu and Maui. In order to view the park, you must be with a registered tour group or make arrangements with the park service.

Once you've reached this remote but beautiful spot, a guided tour, on foot or by mule, is the only way to see the historic sites in the village where the remaining residents now live, the virtually deserted hospital, and the abandoned buildings from the days when thousands were treated here. The affliction,

now called Hansen's disease, can be controlled by modern drugs.

On the eastern side of the peninsula, you'll find Father Damien's church, St. Philomena's, a grassy cemetery, and a monument to the heroic priest who, in his service to the patients, contracted the disease and died here. This is Kalawao, the original site of the colony, and the park here is an ideal place to lunch (bring your own) as you contemplate the dramatic 3,000-foot-high cliffs along Molokaʻi's windward shore.

Open year-round except Sundays.
(808) 567-6802
www.nps.gov/kala.molokai
For mule rides, call (800) 567-7550.
www.muleride.com

13 Molokaʻi Museum & Cultural Center

Located on the left side of Hwy. 470, between Kualapuʻu and Kalaupapa Lookout

In 1848 Rudolph Wilhelm Meyer, a German immigrant, came to the lush, idyllic island of Moloka'i to work as a surveyor. Before long he married Moloka'i's high chieftess, Kalama, and took charge of managing the island's largest ranch settlement. In 1878 he built the R.W. Meyer Sugar Mill, now considered the oldest sugar mill in Hawai'i and listed on the *National Register of Historic Places.*

Although sugar cane is no longer widely grown or harvested on the island, the R. W. Meyer Sugar Mill invites anyone with a taste for homegrown history to learn all about the process—up-close and in action. The mill has been fully restored, complete with an operational steam engine. On a tour of the plant, which takes about an hour, knowledgeable guides explain, step by step, how the cane was transformed into sugar and molasses.

Next door to the mill at the museum complex, visitors can take a self-guiding tour through a treasure trove of local history, industry, and culture. Along with personal memorabilia from the Meyer family, exhibits offer a vivid sense of the everyday life of a 19th-century plantation worker. In addition, changing displays and artifacts range from authentic hula instruments to 18th-century fishing-net weights, from antique stone weapons to vintage hand-crafted toys and games.

Throughout, Moloka'i's scenic beauty, relaxed pace, and small-town character come alive, with its local main street looking exactly as it did in the 1940s.
Open year-round Mon.–Sat.
Nominal charges for museum and sugar-mill tour.
(808) 567-6436
www.hawaiiweb.com/molokai/html/sites/
rw_meyer_sugar_mill_museum.html

St. Joseph's Church
Kamalo

Father Damien ministered to needs beyond those of the Kalaupapa leprosy colony. He also built five churches for his parishioners on Moloka'i's uplands, or "topside," and made his ecclesiastical rounds by horseback. St. Joseph's, built in 1876, is a white one-room building with a churchyard that contains several graves. One small but poignant stone is incised partly in Hawaiian: "Margarita Kameekua, *hanau* Honolulu March 1, 1914, *make* Kamalo February 27, 1915." *Hanau* means "born," and *make* means "died."

A lifesize black metal statue of Father Damien stands just outside the tiny church, which, like St. Philomena's at Kalawao, is kept in good repair but used only for special occasions. Farther east along Route 450, near Mapulehu Stream, is Our Lady of Sorrows (1874), another of Father Damien's topside churches.
Open year-round.
(808) 553-5220

🔲 St. Joseph's Church. *Built in 1876 by Father Damien, the Belgian priest who ministered to victims of leprosy, the church is now used only for special occasions.*

MAUI—The Valley Isle
🔲 D. T. Fleming Beach Park
Honokahua

Nearby Kapalua Beach used to be called Fleming Beach (in honor of a local ranch manager, David T. Fleming) until the name was reassigned to this county beach farther north along Route 30. Although confusion about the names has kept the park off the beaten path, it has long been a favorite with locals. Fleming is one of the most convenient of the rugged area's picturesque beaches, with showers, barbecue grills, and picnic tables—at least one of which always seems to be available (on weekdays, anyway). There's even a public telephone.

Winds ruffle the ironwood and palms at the top of a sandy crescent, which slopes down to meet usually gentle ocean swells for good swimming. When the waves pick up, body and board surfers turn out in force. Stay on the beach, though, when heavy winter waves roll in, setting up rip currents and undertows. And when you stroll

the beach, wear rubber sandals *(zoris)*: Fallen ironwood cones can be rough on bare feet.
Open year-round.
(808) 661-4685
www.co.maui.hi.us

🔲 Puohokamoa Falls and Kaumahina State Wayside Park
Falls parking area is at an unmarked pull-off along Hwy. 360 two miles west of Kaumahina State Wayside. Look for a green picnic table and low stone wall.

Visitors tend to drive right by this site, unaware of the lovely falls, which cannot be seen from the road. Park and follow the sometimes muddy path. You can eat yellow guavas that may be seen along the way, but avoid the oily kukui (candlenuts), which the ancient Hawaiians used for light—and as a strong laxative.

There's another table, and a barbecue pit at the falls, but no drinking water. If you decide to refresh yourself in the pool at the base of the falls, be prepared to find yourself a target of tourists' cameras. If picnicking is a must and the tables at the falls are taken, drive a little farther to Kaumahina, where there are plenty of facilities and good views of the ocean and Keanae Peninsula. Watch for the *hala* (pandanus) tree and several types of eucalyptus (including the shaggy paperbark). At least one African tulip tree may be in bloom.
Open year-round.
(808) 984-8109
www.hawaiiweb.com

17 Pua`a Ka`a State Wayside
On Hwy. 360, about 38 miles east of Kahului

Pua`a Ka`a is a delightfully intimate park with two modest 25-foot waterfalls. A paved pathway takes you across the top of the first falls, then leads along a stream to the second. Both tumble into pools that are fine for swimming, though few visitors seem to take advantage of this opportunity.

Both pools are bordered by picnic tables, and conveniently situated a little farther along the road, near a second parking lot, are restrooms. The road crosses a small bridge, and if you walk across, you can see still more falls and pools, though they're not really a part of Pua`a Ka`a Wayside. *Pua`a ka`a* is an ancient Hawaiian name meaning "rolling pig."

Tropical foliage is abundant here: banana palms, guava trees (often bearing ripe, ready-to-eat fruit), heliconia flowers, ferns, African tulip trees, red and green varieties of *ti* plants, and the giant-leaved *ape-ape*.

Open year-round.
(808) 984-8109
www.hiohwy.com/p/puakaa

18 Helani Farm
Off Rte. 360 about a mile west of Hana

The beneficence of the Hawaiian climate is beautifully demonstrated here. H. F. Cooper established these gardens as a wholesale nursery in 1975; now he has opened them to visitors, who are free to wander the five-acre lower gardens along paths called Main Drag or Six Bridges to Heaven. The 65-acre upper gardens are also open but are of primary interest to botanists, horticulturalists, and plant collectors.

The specimens, tropical and subtropical plants and trees from throughout the world, are generally well marked. But Cooper has added his own twist to the expected common, genus, and species names. Here you will find aphorisms, Bible and poetry quotations, or anonymous quotes he feels ought to be passed on to visitors. Near a bed of spider lilies, for instance, we learn that "Knowledge is power only when it is translated into direct and positive action."

In addition to the plants and flowers, there's a pond of Japanese carp *(koi)*, whose churnings and gulpings are in noisy contrast to the peace that reigns in the rest of this quiet place, where the only other sound is likely to be the rhythmic clatter of bamboo blowing in the wind.

Picnic facilities and restrooms are located in the lower gardens.
Open year-round. Admission charged.
(800) 385-5241
www.helanitropicalflowers.com

19 Tedeschi Vineyards
Off Rte. 37, Ulupalakua

Few tourists heading for Haleakala National Park think of stopping off in the cool, bucolic up-country region, and thus they miss the green, rolling ranchland and the surprising experience of Hawai'i's only true wine country.

Pardee Erdman, owner of Ulupalakua Ranch, has turned over 20 acres to Emil Tedeschi to raise grapes, make wine, and run a tasting room. All who stop are invited to try a glass of Maui Blanc, a "light, dry pineapple wine," which was the first Tedeschi product in 1977.

When Emil and Joanne Tedeschi moved here from California's Napa Valley in 1974, they and their partner Erdman entertained high hopes of reviving the island's wine industry. These have been fulfilled. An award-winning sparkling wine they produced was served at President Reagan's inauguration.

Visitors can tour the property, where Hawaiian royalty threw lavish parties when it was used as a cattle ranch and sugar mill. Or they can tour the winery, where the wines are available for purchase.
Open year-round.
(808) 878-6058
www.mauiwine.com

HAWAI'I—The Big Island
20 Puako Petroglyph
Take the Puako turnoff from Hwy. 19 and continue 3 miles; the path to the petroglyphs connects with the road about 100 yards before road's end.

In keeping with their reputation as one of Hawai'i's major mysteries, the cryptic inscriptions left by the ancient Hawaiians aren't easy to find, let alone decipher. Stick figures, boats with sails, warriors with weapons, circles within circles continue to elude the anthropologists who study them.

Follow a natural trail system posted with signs that leads to the petroglyphs. Don't make rubbings from the stone carvings (replica petroglyphs are provided for this purpose). Damaged petroglyphs are displayed so visitors can see the consequences of mistreating these treasures. Make the trip early or late in the day, when temperatures are lower and longer shadows make the carvings easier to distinguish.
Open year-round.
(808) 886-1655
www.123hawaii.net/attractions

21 Kamuela Museum
West of Waimea near junction of Rtes. 250 and 19

The appeal of this family-owned museum lies in the fact that it looks like someone's home, with objects selected and juxtaposed by personal preference. It's a delightful hodgepodge in which the discerning visitor can expect to find something of interest: a rare example of the temple idols that were supposed to have been destroyed by royal and

19 Tedeschi Vineyards. *Visitors to the vineyards are treated to views like this as well as a glass of Maui Blanc, a light, dry, pineapple wine.*

HAWAI'I

missionary edict long ago, or paintings and furnishings from Iolani Palace, the residence of the royal family at Honolulu.

A unique Hawaiian object is the ancient canoe buster, a hammer designed specifically to put an invader's fleet out of commission.

The collection, some 50 years in the making, was assembled by Albert K. and Harriet K. M. Solomon. Mrs. Solomon is a descendant of John Palmer Parker, founder of the Parker Ranch on land granted by Kamehameha I.

Open year-round. Admission charged.
(808) 885-4724

22 Waipi`o Valley

In a state whose islands seem to provide panoramic vistas at every turn, here on the Big Island it is easy to miss the spectacular view across Waipi`o Valley. It is, however, worthwhile to take the nine-mile Route 240 to Waipi`o Valley Lookout.

From this vantage point you can see the island's largest valley some 2,000 feet below. This was once home to the ancient Hawaiian kings—and to as many as 50,000 Hawaiians, who gradually abandoned the valley settlements for fear of tidal waves. Many kings were buried here. Because of their "divine power," it was believed that no harm would come to those who lived in the valley.

The steep, narrow road down to the valley is restricted to vehicles with four-wheel drive, but there's an hourly shuttle tour into the valley from Kukuihaele. Further down, you can walk along the black sand beach.

Open year-round; charge for shuttle tour.
(808) 961-5797

23 Akaka Falls State Park
Rte. 220, Honomu

You reach the park after a six-mile drive west, passing through the little plantation town of Honomu and its fields of sugar cane. Here in a setting of tropical foliage and flowers is Akaka Falls, which plunges a sheer 442 feet down black volcanic rock, and its neighbor, Kahuna Falls, which tumbles about 100 feet. They are visible from a slippery, sometimes steep but paved pathway that loops a half-mile through deep forest greenery. Rest benches are set among ginger (notice the magnificent torch ginger), orchids, heliconias, azaleas, and birds-of-paradise.

Where the path begins, there are giant monkeypods sheltering picnic tables. But the spectacular drop of Akaka Falls is the big attraction here. No swimming is allowed, and it would be difficult indeed to make your way to the base of either falls.

Open year-round.
(808) 974-6200
www.hawaii.gov/dlnr/dsp/hawaii.html

24 Lyman Museum and Mission House
Haili Street in downtown Hilo

In 1832 David and Sarah Lyman, devout Protestant missionaries, traveled by boat from New England to the Sandwich Islands, now called Hawai`i. They had been married for all of 24 days before leaving on the six-month voyage. In 1839 they built a house in Hilo, with a school for young Hawaiian men nearby. It would remain their home for life.

Over the years, the house became a center of culture and communication, hosting members

22 Waipi`o Valley. *Ancient burial caves are located in the sides of the steep cliffs of this valley, once home to Hawaiian kings and as many as 50,000 people.*

of Hawaiian royalty and notables such as author Mark Twain. Nearly 100 years later, in 1931, descendants of David and Sarah established a museum to honor their pioneering work.

The oldest wooden structure on the Island of Hawai`i, listed on both the *State* and *National Register of Historic Places,* the Lyman Mission House has been fully restored. Featuring furniture, tools, and everyday items used by the Lymans and other early missionary families, it inspires visitors to reflect on what it meant to live 5,000 miles from home, with no running water or electricity, and with no understanding of the language or local customs, guided by a fervent commitment to a sacred duty.

Next door, the Lyman Museum houses a superb collection of fine art, artifacts, and seashells and minerals showcasing the natural and cultural history of Hawai`i. The Island Heritage Gallery celebrates the spirit and traditions of native Hawaiians, as well as vital immigrant groups, including Japanese, Chinese, Korean, and Filipino people. The Earth Heritage Gallery focuses on the island's flora and fauna, ecosystems, and geological formations, with striking collections of minerals and seashells.

The Kaha Ki`i o Hawai`i (Artists of Hawai`i) Gallery presents regularly changing exhibits from the museum's extensive collection of original paintings and drawings by 18th-, 19th-, and 20th-century Hawaiian artists. Volcanoes are just one of the wide-ranging subjects. The museum also includes a collection of art and artifacts from ancient China—with items dating back as far as 1500 B.C.; an interactive astronomy center, with slides of the world-class observatories atop Mauna Kea; and a gift shop.

Open Mon.–Sat. Closed major holidays.
Admission charged.
(808) 935-5021
www.lymanmuseum.org/index.html

25 Kapoho

Follow Rte. 132 east from Pahoa to the junction with Rte. 137.

The Hawaiian Islands were created by volcanic action. This is the positive side. On the negative side is the destruction that has been—and may still be—wrought. In January 1960, for example, the community of Kapoho all but disappeared under a flow of molten rock. Known today as the Ghost Village, it is interesting not for what you see here but for what you don't.

Road signs still show the way to the village, but once you're there, all you find jutting from the black, dusty lava is an occasional fragment of corrugated metal roof. Continue through the intersection of Routes 132 and 137 toward the ocean, and on your left is Kapoho Cemetery, where, as the wind whistles through a stand of ironwood, you can contemplate the few graves that weren't overrun.

As recently as 1990 another lava flow wiped out the famous black sand beach at Kaimu on the southern coast.

Farther along the road to the ocean stands Kumakahi Lighthouse. Inexplicably, the lava flow stopped just short of the lighthouse, encircled its base, and pushed on to the ocean. Thus, as if to compensate for the destruction of a village, it added half a square mile to the island's land surface.

The six-foot-high edge of the frozen flow is a thought-provoking sight. But as is usually the case in Hawai'i, the lava moved slowly (here it flowed from the Fast Rift Zone, which runs from Kilauea Volland to the sea). Residents had ample time to remove their belongings, and no lives were lost.

www.aps.gov/havo

26 Kipuka Puaulu

Mauna Loa Rd. NW, off Rte. 11

The northern edge of Hawai'i Volcanoes National Park has a quiet 100-acre oasis that provides a habitat for a number of unusual plants and birds, native and imported. This haven was created when a lava flow parted and came together again, sparing a 100-acre island of forest in between (*ki-puka* is the Hawaiian name for this phenomenon).

Note, however, that Kipuka Puaulu's woodland isn't in its primeval state. There's an interesting mile-long, self-guiding loop trail. You'll see the giant koa, papala kepau, mamani, and thickets of pilo trees.

The birds flitting through the treetops include exotics like the Japanese white-eye and melodious laughing thrush, and such natives as the wrenlike *elepaio* and the `amakihi, i`iiwi, and `apapane—three members of the nectar-gathering honeycreeper family. You may not see all of them, but you will certainly hear their chatter.

Open year-round.
(808) 985-6000
www.nps.gov/havo

27 Ka`u Desert Trail

Accessible by foot from the Mauna Iki trailhead on the east side of Hwy. 11

A half-hour trek from Hwy. 11 brings you to the spot where in 1790 a hapless band of Hawaiian warriors and their families were overtaken by a volcanic eruption as they moved through the Ka`u Desert. Overcome by poisonous gases, they were trapped by the heavy fall of ash, which soon

28 Pu`uhonua o Honaunau National Historic Park. *Wooden images stand in the sanctuary used as a mausoleum for the Kamehameha dynasty, as well as a place of refuge in ancient Hawaiian culture.*

turned to mud and later hardened.

Some of their footprints are preserved about a mile before Mauna Iki Trail joins Ka`u Desert Trail. Many of the prints are eroded, others covered and uncovered by shifting sands. Especially poignant are prints that were obviously made by a fleeing child.

It's reassuring to know that in modern times only one person has been killed by a volcanic eruption in Hawai`i: a photographer who took one too many chances as he tried to record an eruption in 1924.

Open year-round.
(808) 985-6017
www.nps.gov/havo

28 Pu`uhonua o Honaunau National Historic Park

On the island of Hawai`i, 22 miles south of Kailua-Kona

Spanning 180 acres of idyllic oceanfront land, this heavenly park preserves a revered place of refuge and profound significance in ancient Hawaiian culture. According to the belief of island natives, a visit to a pu`uhonua had the power to shelter those fleeing from battle, as well as absolve those who broke a *kapu*—one of the sacred laws that governed everything from fishing to social status. To break a *kapu* was to incur the wrath of the gods, with potential consequences from lava flows to *tsunamis,* not to mention certain death for the offender. Upon reaching this sanctuary, *kapu*-breakers were purified by a priest and spared further punishment.

Meticulously restored to reflect the site's spiritual and historical importance, the royal compound includes exquisitely carved wooden images, the structure used as a mausoleum for the Kamehameha dynasty, and the impressive wall—stretching 1,000 feet long, 10 feet high, and 17 feet wide—built stone by stone without mortar to designate and safeguard the pu`uhonua area.

Beyond its sublime natural beauty and mana, or spiritual power, the park is graced with abundant interactive cultural opportunities. On a 30-minute self-guiding trail you will see many archaeological sites, including reconstructed burial temples and canoe sheds. Watch your head, as the ceiling is low, and flashlights are recommended. Ask at the visitors center for a backcountry trail guide.

Visitors might also observe a traditional wood carver busy at his time-honored craft, carving ki`i, or wooden images, out of one solid piece of native wood. Or, they might play a checkerlike game of skill known as konane.

Open year-round. Admission charged.
(808) 328-2288
www.nps.gov/puho/pphtml/
contacts.html

29 Kealakekua Bay State Historical Park

Today Kealakekua Bay, on the Kona Coast, is a marine reserve and a state underwater park: a popular place for snorkeling and scuba diving, with glass-bottomed boat tours for the less athletic.

But in 1779, when the bay was an important anchorage, it achieved undying notoriety as the place where Capt. James Cook was killed. It is ironic that the great navigator who discovered Hawai`i for the Western world and who was honored as a god by the Hawaiians should die at their hands in a skirmish over a stolen boat.

The Captain Cook Monument, an obelisk on the northwest side of the bay, marks the spot where he fell. It's reached only by boat, though you may drive almost up to the beach on the bay's south shore.

From here you can walk to the ruins of Hikiau Heiau. It was at this temple that Cook conducted (for a member of his crew) the first Christian burial service in the islands.

Accessible year-round.
(808) 974-6200
www.hawaii.gov/dlnr/dsp/hawaii.html

30 Kamakahonu and the Ahu`ena Heiau

On the grounds of the King Kamehameha's Kona Beach Hotel, off Aliz Dr., Kailua
It was to this 11-acre compound of land, beach, and bay—a kind of retreat for the Hawaiian highborn, or *alii*—that King Kamehameha I and his court came shortly after leaving Honolulu in 1812. They made it the center of the islands' civil and religious government. With the assistance of the Bishop Museum in Honolulu, the precincts have been restored to an approximation of their state during the years 1813 to 1819, when the king and his priests ruled from here.

In the background you can see one of Hawai`i's most historic sites: Ahu`ena Heiau, an ancient temple rebuilt by Kamehameha, who dedicated it to Lono, god of peace, prosperity, and agriculture.

Kealakekua Bay State Historical Park. *This bay, now a popular place for snorkeling, achieved notoriety as the place where Capt. James Cook was killed in 1779 in a skirmish over a stolen boat.*

But at the king's death in 1819, when his favorite wife Ka`ahumanu became regent for his son Liholiho (Kamehameha II), the temple and all it stood for was destroyed, including the *kapu* system of taboo. In 1820 the first Christian missionaries were welcomed.

Open year-round.
(808) 329-2911, ask for the Hawaiian Culture Center
www.konabeachhotel.com

31 Kaloko-Honokohau National Historical Park

Visitors center located ocean side of Queen Ka`ahumanu Hwy. 19, 3 miles north of Kailua-Kona, 3 miles south of Kona International Airport
Until the early 20th century, this national park was a thriving Hawaiian community, created to preserve, interpret, and perpetuate traditional Hawaiian culture.

Among the many archaeological sites and features within the park are petroglyphs, heiau (religious platforms), a one-mile restored section of the ancient mamalahoa trail, house sites, fishing shrines, canoe landings, and fishponds.

The park is restoring the massive wall of Kaloko fishpond and the fish traps at Ai`opio. Sea turtles regularly bask on the beaches of Honokohau Bay, and the park is home to three endangered water birds. You can hike, fish, and picnic (no fires or glass) in the park, and swimming and snorkeling are safe in the waters of Honokohau Bay.

Open year-round.
(808) 329-6881, Ext.1
www.nps.gov/kaho

Idaho

The Gem State offers recollections of its vigorous past, a wondrous variety of places to visit, and a chance to dig for garnets and opals.

Snake River Birds of Prey National Conservation Area. *A bald eagle surveys the land (see page 94).*

The ghost towns stand as poignant reminders of the soaring hopes, hard labor, and broken dreams of those who came here to make their fortune. On a positive note is a town that survived those days and now, having returned to vibrant life, retains only the charm of its ghostly aura. The oldest structure in the state was built to serve God, not Mammon, and (with or without heavenly intervention) is beautifully preserved.

Some of the wonders in these parts seem to have been touched by the supernatural: Here are sand dunes in an unlikely place, waterfalls that spring from a canyon wall, a surreal cityscape of huge megaliths, a cave where mounds and pillars of "ice" never melt, and where the fossil remains of creatures from an ancient tropical sea remind us that the face of the earth is ever changing. Not so surprising, but with great appeal, are the rivers, lakes, hot springs, canyons, wildlife and wildflowers, and a park that boasts 38 different historic sites.

1 Priest Lake State Park
Coolin

The park's three campgrounds give access to an aqueous jewel: a 19-mile-long sapphire-blue mountain lake. Priest Lake takes its name from the indefatigable Jesuit missionary Pierre Jean De Smet, who in 1846, according to legend, became the first white man to see it. The surrounding forest is so thick that until logging roads were put through in the 1950s, most travel through here was by boat.

Fishing is excellent, with Mackinaw and rainbow trout among the likely catches. The lake's several remote, undeveloped islands, at once peaceful and intriguing, all invite exploration.

Just north of Priest Lake is Upper Priest Lake, a wilderness area accessible only by boat or foot trail. The two lakes are connected by a meandering two-mile stream known locally as the Thoroughfare, which provides an enjoyable and picturesque route for a day trip by powerboat or canoe from the Lionhead Campground at the northeastern end of Priest Lake.

A three-quarter-mile hiking trail beginning at the Indian Creek Campground, located near the center of Priest Lake's eastern shore, leads through a cedar forest to a promontory from which there are magnificent views. There are also longer backpacking trails into the Selkirk Mountains. The area is accessible in the winter and offers miles of snowmobile and cross-country ski trails.

Indian Creek Campground open year-round; day-use fee charged. Lion Head and Dickensheet campgrounds open May–Sept.
(208) 443-2200
www.idahoparks.org

2 Old Mission State Park
Take exit 39 off I-90, Cataldo

The former Jesuit mission that is

2 Old Mission State Park. *This former Jesuit mission was built about 150 years ago, combining European style with rough-hewn logs from Idaho's forests.*

the focal point of this park is the oldest building in Idaho. It was built between 1850 and 1853 by members of the Coeur d'Alene Indian tribe under the direction of Father Anthony Ravalli, and its design reflects a pragmatic blend of Old World ideals and the building materials available in the Idaho wilderness.

The walls of the mission are rough-hewn logs covered with a wattle and daub lattice. In 1865, after a sawmill was built on the mission's grounds, siding and interior paneling were added, which made the walls 18 inches thick. European-style chandeliers were fashioned from tin cans, and wooden altars and crosses were painted to imitate gilt and marble. Many of the wall hangings were made of cloth from the Hudson Bay Trading Post, and others were made by painting newspapers. A thriving Coeur d'Alene farming village was established at the mission, and many American Indians lived here until the tribe was forced onto a reservation in 1877. The park also contains the old parish house (1887) and two original cemeteries.

Open year-round. Admission charged.
(208) 682-3814

www.idahoparks.org

3 Wallace

To visit this remarkably preserved town is to step back to the turn of the century and be immersed in the aura of a time gone by. Indeed, the entire downtown district, a virtual compendium of architectural styles, is listed on the *National Register of Historic Places.*

One can take a self-guiding walking tour of 38 historic buildings constructed between 1890 and 1930: small-town banks, hotels, lodges, churches, stores, offices, and homes in styles including Victorian commercial, neoclassical, Renaissance revival, and art deco. The tour can be done in about 45 minutes, but there is a wealth of finely crafted detail to linger over, and many of the interiors are as fascinating as the exteriors; anyone particularly interested in architecture could spend several hours exploring the town's buildings in great depth.

Wallace has long been a mining and trade center, and the Wallace

District Mining Museum here should not be overlooked. It has an interesting collection of old mining tools, equipment, rock samples, and memorabilia, as well as informative dioramas and displays showing various mining methods.

Museum open daily most of the year.
Admission charged.
(208) 556-1592
Wallace Chamber of Commerce:
(208) 753-7151

www.historic-wallace.org

⑤ Nez Perce National Historical Park. *The U.S. Army was defeated here in the first engagement of the Nez Perce war in 1877 at White Bird Battlefield.*

④ Heyburn State Park

6 miles east of Plummer on Hwy. 5

From a roadside vantage point about two miles inside this 8,000-acre park, you can view a sight so strange that it seems almost impossible: a river flowing between narrow natural levees as it crosses another body of water. What you are looking at is part of "the river between the lakes," a section of the St. Joe River that seems miraculously, like Moses, to divide the waters of not only one but four separate lakes.

Actually, the explanation for this mind-boggling view is simple. In 1906 a dam was built at Post Falls on the Spokane River. The backwaters from the dam inundated the low-lying land around the St. Joe River, creating a series of shallow lakes along its banks. Since the St. Joe was here before the lakes were formed, it does divide

their waters, but it doesn't have to perform any miracles to do it. The park offers interpretive luncheons and dinner cruises that take visitors up the river.

Wild rice in these shallow lakes makes this an outstanding habitat for waterfowl, and the bass, pike, trout, and kokanee attract not only anglers but also a large colony of ospreys in the summer. The park has camping and picnic areas, beaches, lodges, and boat launches. There is water access to Lake Coeur d'Alene. Hikers on the extensive system of trails are rewarded with spectacular views.

You might want to try a day trip from Heyburn to the Emerald Creek Garnet Area, which is 24 miles south of St. Maries. For a small fee you can dig for garnets here. In addition to a strong back, you'll need a shovel, a bucket, and a mesh screen to sift and wash the stones.

Heyburn open year-round. Emerald Creek open Memorial Day–Labor Day; closed Wed. and Thurs.
Heyburn: (208) 686-1308
Emerald Creek: (208) 245-2531
www.idahoparks.org

⑤ Nez Perce National Historical Park

Rte. 95, Spalding

For centuries the Nez Perce Indians have lived in the valleys of the Snake and Clearwater rivers. In 1805 they welcomed the explorers Lewis and Clark and told them of the great water route to the Pacific along the Snake and Columbia rivers.

The tribe lived in relative peace with the influx of American settlers until gold was discovered on tribal lands in the 1860s, and the U.S. government proposed to limit the American Indians to

a reservation one-tenth the size of the territory they had been guaranteed.

The war of 1877 eventually led to the defeat of the Nez Perce people. Their brilliant leader, Chief Joseph, is famous for the lucid eloquence with which he expressed the finality of his people's tragic surrender: "From where the sun now stands, I will fight no more forever."

The park comprises 38 separate historically significant sites that are scattered over four states, most of them within the Nez Perce reservation. These sites commemorate not only the Nez Perce people but also explorers, missionaries, traders, and gold miners.

The park headquarters at Spalding has a visitors center that offers films and interpretive talks and includes a museum portraying the Nez Perce culture with beautiful examples of the Indians' dress, beadwork, and other artifacts as well as early photographs.

Within a short drive of Spalding, you can see the various sites of the 1836 mission, a gristmill, the early Indian Agency, and Fort Lapwai. If you're headed south on Route 95, you might pause below Grangeville to enjoy Camas Prairie and the spectacular scenery of White Bird Battlefield, where the U.S. Army was defeated in the first engagement of the Nez Perce War. In the surrounding area camping, boating, swimming, hiking, and fishing are available.

Visitors center open daily except Thanksgiving, Christmas, and New Year's Day.
(208) 843-2261
www.nps.gov/nepe

6 Wolf Education and Research Center

Located on the Nez Perce Reservation in Winchester

Spanning 300 acres of pristine, protected tribal land at the juncture of three national forest systems, the Nez Perce Reservation is one of the largest homes to a single wolf pack in the United States. Within a 20-acre enclosure of rolling timberland with meadows and streams, the Sawtooth Pack of six to eight wolves lives in as natural an environment as possible within a captive world.

Visitors get the rare opportunity to observe and learn about wolves in their natural habitat from two observation decks or between two fences on guided walking tours. By educating people about their kind, these gray wolves serve as ambassadors for their wild cousins.

Committed to enhancing the public's awareness of wolves as a distinctive and threatened species, the nonprofit center conducts extensive research on the characteristics and habits of wolves and on how they interact with their environment. To further this goal, the wolves of the Nez Perce have been featured in TV documentaries.

At the center, visitors also get a chance to see the all-but-vanished wilds of Idaho. Amid vast woodlands and shimmering streams, wild turkeys, hawks, owls, elk, and deer roam the land.

Nearby, situated on the edge of a former millpond, Winchester Lake State Park offers a chance to learn more about the wolves. The Wolf Education and Research Center sponsors programs at the park's amphitheater, including videos, movies, and slide shows about wolf reintroduction programs, as well as a "wolf box," where visitors can learn more about the biology of the wolf.

On the park's grounds, a mile or so safely distant from the wolves, campers can still occasionally hear the call of the pack, particularly on calm, moonlit nights.

Open daily Memorial Day–Labor Day. Guided tours by reservation only, with fee charged.
Open Sept.–May by appointment only. Group/school tours available.
(208) 924-6960
www.wolfcenter.org

7 Leesburg

Exit U.S. Rte. 93 at Williams Creek Rd., about 5 miles south of Salmon. Follow signs for Cobalt; watch for the sign to Leesburg.

Although the Civil War was over when gold was discovered in these mountains and veterans streamed into the area, regional feelings still ran high. Former Union soldiers settled about a quarter-mile to the north and called their community Grantsville, while the former Confederates established Leesburg in honor of Robert E. Lee. Almost nothing of the Union village remains, but the Leesburg town site, with some 15 log structures, is listed on the *National Register of Historic Places.*

Leesburg is situated high in the mountains above the Salmon Valley, and the journey to it makes an interesting day trip. The two-lane road from Salmon is flanked with spectacular scenery as you move from picturesque farmland upward along a series of switchbacks to an elevation of 6,000 feet.

Midway there is a wooded picnic area and, a mile and a half farther on, a pleasant campground. Most of the drive is along a relatively smooth road of compacted dirt and gravel.

Open year-round, but may be inaccessible by car Nov.–May or after heavy rains.
(208) 756-3342
www.sacajaweahome.com

6 Wolf Education and Research Center. *Visitors can observe wolves in their natural habitat on acres of protected tribal land.*

8 Custer

The remains of mines and mining camps are scattered throughout the land of the Yankee Fork in the Challis National Forest, where gold and silver were found during the last quarter of the 19th century. By the 1890s Custer was the region's central town, with a peak population of 600 to 700 and a mill that crushed some $12 million worth of ore.

Today, not many of the abandoned town's structures still stand, but the ruins of several other buildings are all labeled and still evoke their spirited past. The schoolhouse and the Empire Saloon now serve as a museum, whose displays tell the story of various Yankee Fork mines.

Outdoor exhibits show the tools and equipment used for panning, dredging, and placer and hardrock mining. An interpretive center offers displays and audiovisual programs of the historic area.

The ghost town of Bonanza, just to the south, is also of interest. On the way, you'll pass the Yankee Fork gold dredge, which was used to extract the last of the area's retrievable gold in the 1940s and early 1950s. Former workers give tours of the dredge and explain its operation. Nearby, the U.S. Forest Service runs four campgrounds along the road leading from Sunbeam to Custer.

Interpretive center open year-round. Custer Museum open Memorial Day through mid-Sept. Gold dredge open daily Memorial Day–Labor Day. Fee charged for gold dredge tour.
(208) 838-2201
www.scenic-idaho.com/custer.htm

9 Spencer Opal Mines

Headquarters: north end of Main Street, Spencer

Unlike most gems, opals have no crystal structure; rather, they are a solidified silica jelly. A regular array of holes between the microscopic globules of silica creates a diffraction grating, which breaks white light into the rainbow of color that plays upon the stone's surface.

Here in Spencer is a different kind of mine, run by the Stetler family since 1968. Rockhounds can collect material for their own hobby or jewelry-making.

Visitors are charged $5 per pound of opal-bearing material to dig through a stockpile. The ore is hauled to the site from the mine, which is eight miles away. There are no guarantees, but visitors often find opals worth many times the cost of the dig.

Anyone can join in, and visitors are encouraged to bring their own hammers, chisels, and safety glasses, or they can be rented there.

For the serious rockhound, the mine is open on holiday weekends for digging at a daily rate of $30. Contact the mine for specific dates.

A store, mini-mart, and café are also available.

Open daily May–Sept.
(208) 374-5476
www.mineralnews.com/nwlocal/ idlocalities.html

10 Harriman State Park

North of Ashton

Many Idahoans still call this the Railroad Ranch, the name the estate had for over 75 years as a summer retreat for New York's rich, railroad-owning Harriman family (especially Roland Harriman) and their wealthy colleagues. An area of high-mountain sage and grass meadows flanking the meandering Henrys Fork of the Snake River—and the habitat of such big game as moose, elk, antelope, and black bears—it was a private hunting preserve and a working ranch where the owners enjoyed their version of roughing it and playing cowboy.

Given to the state by the Harrimans, the 11,000-acre park was opened in 1982. The park and the adjoining 7,000 acres of national forest form a vast refuge rich in wildlife, which can be viewed along the park's 23 miles of hiking trails. In addition to the many large animals, a number of waterfowl thrive here, including the rare trumpeter swan, a year-round resident.

In summer the ranch's log buildings may be toured, and the old ranch roads are open to horses and bicycles. There is outstanding trout fishing, with flies only, on Henrys Fork. In winter cross-country skiing is excellent. No camping is permitted, but there are campgrounds nearby.

Open year-round. Vehicle entry fee charged.
(208) 558-7368
www.idahoparks.org

11 Craters of the Moon National Monument

Arco

At first glance this 618-square-mile park appears to be a stark and forbidding wasteland of black rock as desolate as the moon itself. But it is actually a fascinating geological wonder—a barren area complete with spatter cones, fissure vents, cinder gardens, and lava flows, with tunnels, caves, and the molds of trees that were once encased in molten lava. Sixty lava flows lie within the crater's lava field, ranging in age from 15,000 to just 2,000 years old. All of this is the work of more than two dozen lava vents as well as eight major eruptions.

Many of the most intriguing features can be seen along a seven-mile loop drive. From this drive there are trails leading to points of special interest. In addition, a hiking trail runs south for three miles to the Great Rift, which is a long fissure.

The trail ends near Echo Crater, where many backpackers camp for protection from the area's often harsh winds. Overnighters should obtain a free permit at the visitors center. Throughout the park, use care when going off the trail. Carry drinking water on hikes and a flashlight to explore the caves.

The best time to visit is mid-June, when the wildflowers bloom. Later in the summer the heat-absorbing black lava can become uncomfortably hot.

Open year-round. Admission charged.
(208) 527-3257
www.nps.gov/crmo

12 Snake River Birds of Prey National Conservation Area

Best auto access: Take Exit 44 off I-84 (Meridian Exit) and continue south to Kuna. Follow Swan Falls Rd. from Kuna to Swan Falls Dam.

Nearly half a million acres along a remote 80-mile section of the Snake River have been declared a protected habitat for one of the densest populations of nesting birds of prey anywhere in the world.

Over 700 pairs of raptors, as birds of prey are called, nest here annually—14 different species in all, including some 200 pairs of prairie falcons, 30 pairs of golden eagles, and even a few turkey vultures and Swainson's hawks. In addition, bald eagles, peregrine falcons, ospreys, and several other species stop here during migration.

11 Craters of the Moon National Monument. *A river of molten rock once flowed like water here. When it hardened, it created a geological wonder.*

Binoculars are a must for viewing the birds, which can be seen most easily during the courting and nesting period from mid-March through June. After that, high summer temperatures and the scarcity of food drive many birds to other areas. With advance reservations, local wilderness outfitters offer canoe and raft trips along the Snake River, providing visitors with a vivid sense of the raptors' wild domain.

For information, call the Bureau of Land Management in Boise: (208) 384-3300.

Open year-round.

www.birdsofprey.blm.gov

13 Celebration Park
Southwest of Kuna, in Birds of Prey National Conservation Area

At Idaho's only archaeological park, visitors get a chance to bask in the area's unspoiled beauty while learning about its fascinating natural and cultural history. A short hiking trail leads the way past petroglyphs carved on massive boulders. Other trails link to scenic sites, such as Halverson Lake, a small pond nestled along a canyon wall, and eventually converge at Swan Falls Dam. A onetime railroad bridge built in 1897 and restored for bikes and feet only provides one of the few crossings over the Snake River.

As the park's interpretive center reveals, Idahoan archaeology is a treasure trove of diversity. Thousands of years ago, Idaho was home to people who traversed the landscape in search of wild game and edible plants. About

12 Snake River Birds of Prey National Conservation Area. *A golden eagle swoops down over the Snake River (inset). Thirty pairs of golden eagles nest in this protected habitat every year, along with many other birds of prey.*

200 years ago, Lewis and Clark made their historic trip through Idaho with a Shoshone woman, Sacajawea, as their guide. About 160 years ago, hundreds of immigrants traveled through Idaho on rugged, dusty trails on their way out west. In the 1880s, Idaho attracted Chinese people to work on its railroads and Basque people to raise sheep in its vast deserts.

In addition to scenic viewing, hiking, and captivating lessons in local history, the park offers opportunities for picnicking, boating (sail, canoe, and motorized), and camping (primitive).

Open year-round.

(208) 384-3300

www.id.blm.gov/recreation/sites/celebration.htm

14 Silver City
In 1863 Michael Jordan discovered gold along the creek that today bears his name and started a rush of prospectors into the Owyhee Mountains. Besides gold, the miners found rich slabs of silver.

Silver City boomed and quickly became the county seat. According to conservative estimates, over $40 million in silver was taken from the area. By the early 1900s, however, those glory days were over.

Today approximately 75 stark and weathered buildings of this historic mining town still stand on the rugged hillsides. The once colorful streets were the scenes of several gunfights. In the former drugstore one can still inspect

14 Silver City. *One of the buildings of this historic mining town still stands to greet visitors.*

old-time pharmaceutical and medical equipment.

Silver City's centerpiece now, just as it was in the 1860s, is the five-story Idaho Hotel. With advance reservations you can spend the night here in a room with original furnishings. Family-style meals are served. Wood stoves provide heat in some rooms.

Dominated by the 8,000-foot War Eagle Mountain to the south, the surrounding countryside offers ample opportunity for recreation. Abandoned mills, mine shafts, old town sites, and half a dozen historic cemeteries are spread throughout the area. Jordan Creek is still panned for gold, although most people now prefer to fish. Snowmobiling and cross-country skiing are popular in the winter.

Visitors should note that few supplies are available in Silver City. Gasoline, food, water, and other necessities should be purchased before driving in. Also, the dirt road from Route 78 is rather rough and trailers are not recommended. Allow an hour or more to complete the 23-mile journey. Heavy snow can fall as early as October, and the road may be impassable as late as Memorial Day. Check with the Owyhee County sheriff for road conditions early or late in the season.

Generally open June–Nov. and by special arrangement in the winter. Admission charged for some buildings.
(208) 384-3300
For road conditions, call (208) 495-1154.

www.wildernet.com

For Idaho Hotel reservations call (208) 583-4104.

www.stepintohistory.com/states/id/silver_city.html

Bruneau Dunes State Park
20 minutes off I-84 near Mountain Home

The two enormous mountains of sand that form this park's centerpiece are in striking contrast to the high, flat plateaus that dominate the landscape here. Covering some 600 acres of the 4,800-acre park, the picturesque dunes give way at their base to lakes and marshland, creating an interesting ecological anomaly.

Eagle Cove, where the dunes stand, was formed by the meandering Snake River about 15,000 years ago. The sand was blown in from the surrounding plateau and trapped by opposing winds, which still keep the dunes from moving far or dramatically changing their shape. The lakes and marsh began to form in 1950, when a nearby reservoir caused the underground water table to rise.

Climbing the dunes is the park's chief attraction. At first glimpse the tallest dune, which is 470 feet high, does not seem particularly challenging. But the hike through shifting sand with no firm footholds and no well-trod trail is surprisingly strenuous. It can also be fun, and the crest offers rewarding views. Sand skiers will find the dunes especially inviting. In summer the sand can be extremely hot and dry, and it's best to climb in the early morning or late afternoon. The climb is predictably gritty; cameras and food should be sealed in plastic bags.

Wildlife here includes waterfowl, and coyotes are common. Fishing (from nonmotorized craft) is mostly for largemouth bass and bluegill. May and June are the best months for wildflowers and flowering shrubs, including the vivid primroses, penstemons, and tamarisks.

17 City of Rocks National Reserve. *The orange aspen trees contrast with the stark gray of what pioneers called "wild and romantic scenery."*

The park also offers Idaho's only public observatory, featuring the Obsession telescope, a custom-made 25-inch reflector that allows the viewer to see the rings of Saturn or the Owl Nebula.
Open year-round. Observatory presentations given at dusk Fri. and Sat., Mar.–Nov. Admission charged.
(208) 366-7919
www.idahoparks.org

Thousand Springs
Best viewed from Rte. 30, north of Buhl

The dozen or more waterfalls that spout suddenly from the wall of the Snake River Canyon here were long a puzzle to geologists as well as laymen. Now scientists believe that their source lies 150 miles to the northeast, where the Big and Little Lost rivers vanish into the lava beds that cover much of the region. Increased greatly in volume by melting snow and seepage, the underground streams course through the porous lava until they reach this canyon and plunge into the Snake River.

The springs assume a dramatic variety of forms—wispy curtains, slender columns, foamy, rushing cascades, and raging torrents. Binoculars are helpful—and a telephoto lens for photographers—since the viewing area is across the river at a commercial resort. The viewing area, however, is open and free to the public, and visitors are welcome to use the picnic tables without charge. The resort also offers a swimming pool, hot baths, boat ramps, and camping facilities.

Trout thrive in the cool, clear, aerated water pouring from the springs, making this the state's prime area for trout fishing. Facilities for boaters and campers are available all along this beautiful stretch of U.S. 30, justly known as the Thousand Springs Scenic Byway. The area has other spectacular cascades, at Twin Falls and Shoshone Falls, as well as the picturesque gorge of the Malad River and the remarkable Balanced Rock.
Open year-round.
(208) 837-4631
www.hagermanchamber.com

City of Rocks National Reserve
4 miles west of Almo

These huge natural megaliths, silently dominating the plain like a procession of brooding and forgotten prehistoric gods, are as breathtakingly startling to visitors today as they were to pioneers traveling to California in the middle 1800s.

Numerous pioneer diaries comment on the "wild and romantic scenery . . . all manner of fantastic shapes . . ." which held the visitors "spellbound with the beauty and strangeness of it all." Many immigrants, their individual fates now lost to history, were moved to leave their names marked with axle grease on these ancient stones. Perhaps, confronting the frailty of their own lives on the difficult way west, they sought to connect themselves with something timeless.

Among the hundreds of rocks found here—some formations are 2.5 billion years old—30 are so strikingly evocative that they have been given colorful names, such as Squaw and Papoose, Giant Toadstool, King on the Throne, Kaiser's Helmet, and Devil's Bedstead. A descriptive pamphlet and map, giving the names of many of the formations and the best angles from which to view them, is available at the visitors center in Almo.

The area is remote and undeveloped, and the access road has a rough, unpaved surface that may be inaccessible in inclement weather or during the winter months.
(208) 824-5519
www.idahoparks.org

18 Fort Hall Replica

10 miles north of Pocatello off Interstate 15

Fort Hall was once a fur-trading center and a rest stop for pioneers making the journey west. It was built in 1834, on the Snake River along the Oregon Trail, by Nathaniel Wyeth, an explorer and fur trader and progenitor of the artists N. C., Andrew, and Jamie Wyeth. The ruins of the fort were destroyed by floods in the 1860s, and this full-scale replica was completed in 1966, 13 miles from the original site, in Ross Park.

Enter Fort Hall through its huge wooden gates and you find yourself back in the 1800s. Experience the flavor of that bygone era in the reconstructed blacksmith's shop, carpenter's shop, trading post, company mess hall, and living quarters.

Just outside the fort walls, the Bannock County Historical Museum highlights the history of Pocatello and Fort Hall. Pocatello junction, also adjacent to Fort Hall, is a replica of a small railroad town as it was in 1893. At Ross Park Zoo, a short walk from the fort, buffalo and elk still roam.

The Fort Hall Indian Reservation, home to the Shoshone-Bannock tribes, is on the site of the original Fort Hall. Each year on the second weekend in August the reservation hosts a traditional American Indian festival, with rodeo, games, stunning craft work, and dramatic dance competitions.

Open daily mid–Apr. to end of Sept.
Fort Hall: (208) 234-1795
Reservation: (208) 478-3700
www.pokey.net/forthall/index.shtml

19 National Oregon/California Trail Center

Located at the corner of U.S. Highways 89 and 30, at Clover Creek in Montpelier

Sitting on the very spot where travelers would camp to rest their animals, stock their larders, and prepare for the next leg of the journey west, this center celebrates Idaho's part in the pioneer trails of 150 years ago.

On its way through Idaho, the Oregon/California Trail crossed deserts, mountains, and rivers. The trail was winding, arduous, and treacherous. If a valley was 10 miles wide, so was the trail. If a ford was less than a foot in diameter, so was the trail.

This living history museum captures the trailblazing experience with a main-floor exhibit area that dramatically re-creates the historic Clover Creek Encampment, where real people come alive as wagon train captains, mountain men and their women, traders, and scoundrels. Complete with the feel of prairie dust and the smell of meat, dumplings, and beans boiling for dinner, visitors can learn how the pioneers felt about their epic trek and its everyday challenges.

Nearby, a 99-seat theater, patterned after an 1860s playhouse, features short films and a multimedia show highlighting a variety of Idaho trail sites. The main floor also houses an authentic mercantile and gun shop, an art gallery showing the trail-themed paintings of Idaho native Gary Stone, and a gift shop boasting the best in period Western souvenirs.

One floor up, a state-of-the-art computer lab provides hands-on learning experiences geared to pioneers of all ages. The ground floor is home to the Rails and Trails Museum, reflecting how the local area's past was intertwined with the Union Pacific. A rare treat for railroad buffs, artifacts include a cuspidor, an order hoop, and the bell from the ping-pong steam engine. Next door, the Daughters of the Utah Pioneer Exhibit displays many items brought into the valley by wagon, courtesy of courageous women. The floor's final display is dedicated to preserving the early history and unique folklore of Montpelier and the Bear Lake valley.

Open year-round. Admission charged.
(800) 448-2327 or (208) 847-3800
www.oregontrailcenter.org

19 National Oregon/California Trail Center. *Wagon parts litter the trail that led pioneers west in the 1840s and 1850s at Three Island Crossing, the point in the Snake River where gravel bars made it possible to get teams and wagons through to the other side.*

20 Minnetonka Cave

West of St. Charles

More than a half-mile of well-lighted paths and stairways (448 steps) leads through nine subterranean rooms, the largest more than 300 feet long and 90 feet high. In the cave giant limestone stalactites and stalagmites glisten like melting wax.

Despite this ephemeral appearance, the cave's formation took thousands of years. Water absorbed carbon dioxide as it slowly filtered through the ground, forming carbonic acid, a solution that dissolves limestone into calcite. As this solution dripped through cracks and fissures in the stone, large caverns were gradually hollowed out and filled with calcite deposits—the bizarre formations you see today. Marine fossils from a prehistoric tropical sea are embedded in the walls of the cavern.

Tours are approximately 90 minutes. The pathway, damp in some places, is gently graded; however, there are spots where you'll need to climb fairly steep stairs. Warm clothing should be worn, since the temperature inside stays at 40°F. Picnic and camping areas are a few minutes' drive away.

Open daily mid-June–Labor Day.
Admission charged.
(208) 847-0375

Illinois

The appreciation of nature is obvious here, along with the imprint of the region's first inhabitants, early settlers, and young Abe Lincoln.

Mississippi Palisades State Park. *Named for the Hudson River Palisades, the resemblance is striking (see page 100).*

When Abraham Lincoln was a state legislator, he was influential in the development of canals and railroads, and a preserved section of each is now used for recreation. At the reconstruction of his father's farm, where Lincoln often visited, you'll see and hear the dress and dialect of the 1840s. Another reconstruction of log cabins, a restored Mormon community, a little-changed Victorian village, and an American Indian ghost town provide further historical insight.

Historical collections are housed in two handsome mansions, and other places are dedicated to a fascination with nature.

1 Apple River Canyon State Park

Off Rte. 20, 6 miles north of Stockton

The cool, clear waters of Apple River flow through the center of this lovely park, gently but steadily cutting through masses of limestone, dolomite, and shale as they have done for thousands of years. In the canyon, vertical cliffs now rise 150 feet above the small stream. Flowering plants, shrubs, and some 14 different kinds of ferns grow in the crevices of the rock face, transforming it into a hanging garden. Elsewhere the river eddies between sloping banks canopied by cottonwoods, black willows, hackberry, and sycamores.

For nature lovers and amateur geologists the 297-acre park has special interest. It is in a small region that was untouched by glaciation, and it apparently served as a refuge for many plants that did not survive the glacial period in most parts of Illinois. As a result, several exquisite relict plants are found here, including the bird's-eye primrose, the flower-of-an-hour, and the jeweled shooting star.

In more recent times the region was prized for its deposits of lead. American Indians dug it out for exchange with French traders 300 years ago, and in the 19th century, settlers established profitable mines here.

2 Illinois Railway Museum. *Many of the more than 200 engines and cars here have been restored and are fully operational along some four miles of track.*

Five hiking trails wind among the wooded hills, providing an opportunity to enjoy lush vegetation; a chance to amble alongside streams and springs; and possibilities to spot deer, small mammals, hawks, pileated woodpeckers, and the occasional bald eagle.

Wildflowers splash the park roadsides from spring into fall. The river is stocked with rainbow trout in early April. Family camping is popular in winter.
Open year-round except Christmas.
(815) 745-3302
http://dnr.state.il.us

2 Illinois Railway Museum

Olson Road, Union

At this museum, railroad buffs can steam into the past along some four miles of track aboard old coaches pulled by locomotives. Vintage streetcars also make a loop, stopping at the car barns that house elevated trains, mail and baggage cars, and a wide range of antique trolleys.

More than 200 engines and cars recall the charm and excitement of railroading in days gone by. Much of the equipment has been restored and is fully operational. Of special interest is the 1889 Nevada Northern private car *Ely,*

with paneled and mirrored bedrooms and a plush sitting room.
An elevated railroad car from
Chicago still displays 1907 adver-
tisements for chewing gum, while
another veteran of Chicago's busy
traffic—a "Green Hornet" streetcar—harks back to the 1940s,
when there was a popular radio
program of the same name.

Frequent departures from an
authentic depot are announced by
stationmasters, and the trains are
staffed by uniformed engineers,
conductors, and trainmen. One
of the interpretive charts translates
the intriguing code of "whistle
talk," while another explains why
the expansion of the railroads had
created a need by 1883 to divide
the country into standardized time
zones. Special events include a
Fourth of July Trolley Pageant.
*The museum is closed end of Oct.–
Mar. 31. Open daily Memorial Day–
Labor Day, Sun. in Apr. and Oct.,
weekends in Sept. after Labor Day and
in May. Trolleys run when museum is
open; steam trains only on weekends and
holidays. Admission charged.*
(800) 244-7245
www.irm.org

🛱

3 Volo Bog State Natural Area
Ingleside

Visitors to this 1,200-acre wilderness area can find themselves on
shaky ground: The main attraction
here is a so-called quaking bog
about 50 acres in extent, designated
a national natural landmark. The
bog is a deep, spongy mat of vegetation and roots, and if you were
to tread directly on it, the sensation would be similar to that
of walking on a water bed. To
preserve it, visitors are required,
however, to stay on the half-mile

loop trail, which starts at the
visitors center. The wet areas are
crossed by a boardwalk resting on
plastic foam pontoons.

Fourteen stops along the trail
permit close-up inspection of an
unusually rich plant life, which
changes from area to area because
of the changing light, temperature,
and humidity. In the tamarack
forest you'll find buckthorn, quaking aspen, winterberry, and several
types of fern. As for the stinging
nettle and poison sumac, look but
don't touch. Both are illustrated
in the seasonal trail guides.

Rose pogonias and bog tway-
blades are among the six kinds of
wild orchids thriving here, along
with marsh cinquefoils, starflowers,
Indian pipes, and other wildlings.
More than 200 species of birds are
frequently seen, including cranes,
herons, white-winged crossbills,
yellow-headed blackbirds, and
ruby-crowned kinglets.

Summer programs include
guided bird and wildflower
excursions and a "Bats Are
Beautiful" walk to an old
barn, where hundreds of these
mosquito-eaters literally hang out.

*Trail open year-round. Visitors
center open Wed.–Sun., Memorial
Day–Labor Day; weekends and
state holidays remainder of year.
Entire area closed Christmas and*
New Year's Day.
(815) 344-1294
http://dnr.state.il.us

🛱 🥾 🔭

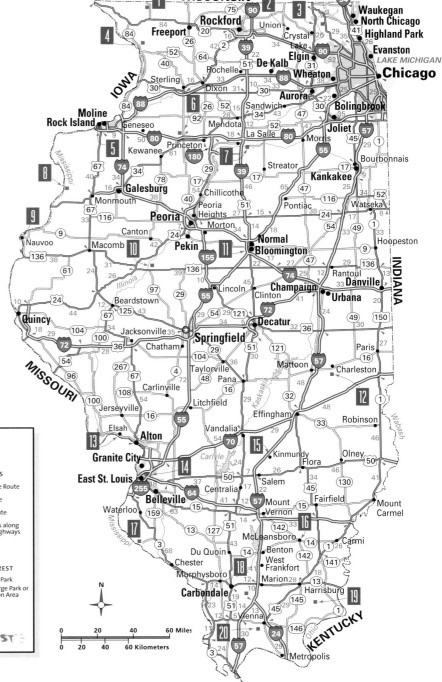

4 Mississippi Palisades State Park

Savanna

This hilly 2,500-acre park was named for the Hudson River Palisades, and the resemblance is striking, with a dramatic limestone bluff dominating the region and overlooking the Mississippi.

The recreation area offers 13 miles of hiking trails, some with steep climbs from river level to overlooks that reward you with sweeping views, especially magnificent at sunset. There are also less demanding trails, and if you don't want to hike, you can drive to Lookout Point to enjoy the scenery.

Thick growths of oak, ash, and hickory provide a fertile haven for wild turkeys, deer, and many kinds of songbirds. In spring and summer, violets, lobelias, and other wildflowers carpet the valleys and slopes, and many kinds of ferns grow rampant in the ravines.

Of particular note among the unusual rock formations are Indian Head, etched by ages of erosion, and Twin Sisters, two rock columns suggestive of their name. In all, this majestic setting encourages climbers to challenge the many limestone walls, seamed by centuries of wind and rain.

An adjacent private concession provides river access to boating and fishing. Anglers here try for catfish, walleye, and northern pike. In winter the slopes and trails are used for cross-country skiing and sledding.

Open year-round.
(815) 273-2731
http://dnr.state.il.us

5 Black Hawk State Historic Site

Off Rte. 5, Rock Island

Those who fish the creeks and hike the trails of this 207-acre park follow the footsteps of the Sauk and Mesquakie Indians, to whom this region was once home. The park is named for one of the Sauks' greatest leaders.

You'll find an activities center in the limestone lodge, one of those many built-to-last structures erected by the Civilian Conservation Corps during the Great Depression. The park itself occupies the site of a former recreation and amusement area. Highly popular at the turn of the century, it boasted the first figure-eight roller-coaster west of Chicago.

The essence of that era is captured by a photo display in the Hauberg Museum, a part of the lodge. The museum is otherwise devoted to portraying the lifestyle of the Sauk and Mesquakie Indians. Among the objects on view are a bark house, containing articles of everyday use, and a bust of Black Hawk copied from a life mask.

About half the park is a nature preserve where hackberry, hickory, and oak trees provide a canopy for rue anemone, wild orchids, trilliums, and some 30 other kinds of wildflowers. More than 100 bird species have been identified, and migrations fill the sky in spring and autumn.

Annual events include bird and wildflower walks in the spring, and geology and archaeology outings in October. Cross-country skiing is also popular.

Open daily except Thanksgiving, Christmas, and New Year's Day.
(309) 788-0177

6 Hennepin Canal Parkway State Park

Sheffield

Completed in 1907, this canal linked the Mississippi and Illinois rivers as part of an interstate waterway connecting the East Coast with the Upper Mississippi Valley. It was a project that would have won the approval of Father Louis Hennepin, the French cleric who explored this region in the late 1600s. But although the canal embodied a number of innovative designs, it was never the right size for commercial traffic. In 1951 the

6 Hennepin Canal Parkway State Park. *The canal wasn't the right size for commercial traffic, but it is perfect for hikers, boaters, and fishermen.*

U.S. Army Corps of Engineers finally closed it to commerce and in 1970 turned it over to the state of Illinois for recreational use.

The main part of the canal runs between Milan on the Mississippi River and Bureau Junction on the Illinois, while a feeder canal about 30 miles long links it with Rock Falls to the north. The canal corridor—which extends for about 100 miles and ranges from 380 feet to a mile in width—offers a pleasant venue for hikers, bikers, boaters, fishermen, and picnickers.

Marked trails along a multi-purpose surface on the old towpath run for more than 90 miles from the region of Bureau Junction to Colona to Rock Falls, with several boat ramps and designated primitive campsites available at intervals between. Bass, bullheads, channel catfish, and bluegills are caught in the waters of the canal, which are seldom deeper than five feet.

The entire parkway offers 264 points of access, so if you don't want to hike, you need not walk very far to reach the canal's banks. In winter the towpath is used for snowmobiling, and a 4$\frac{1}{2}$-mile trail in the visitors center area (near Sheffield) is groomed for cross-country skiing. Exhibits in the visitors center include a photographic display of the canal's construction and its early use.

Park open year-round; visitors center open daily except Christmas and New Year's Day.
(815) 454-2328
http://dnr.state.il.us

ILLINOIS

7 Starved Rock State Park
Utica

According to a legend from the 1760s, the Illiniwek Indians, one of whom had murdered the Ottawa chief, Pontiac, sought safety from the avenging Ottawas atop a high sandstone butte. Surrounded by their opponents, they eventually starved to death.

The appeal of this 2,630-acre park, which stretches along the southern edge of the Illinois River, is primarily in the 18 canyons cut in the sandstone bluffs by feeder streams and in the enormous variety of plant life found here, all of which can be enjoyed from the 13 miles of well-marked hiking trails.

The Interior Canyon trails penetrate the cool, damp canyon recesses, with their rugged rock formations, impressive waterfalls, and a lush growth of ferns, mosses, and delicate flowering plants. The Bluff Trail takes you along the many slopes where oaks and sugar maples shade witch hazel, wild hydrangeas, and trilliums, and the bluff tops are crowned by oaks, cedars, white pines, and shrubs preferring a drier soil.

Along the River Trail one walks beneath a light canopy of cottonwoods and black willows and enters the forested floodplain, where the deeper soil nurtures hickories and bur oaks, blueberries, jack-in-the-pulpits, and many other nut-, fruit-, and flower-bearing plants. The River Trail also leads to Starved Rock.

The park harbors small water-loving animals, flying squirrels, deer, and many species of birds—bluebirds, indigo buntings, scarlet tanagers, chickadees, and cedar waxwings, to name a few.

If you would like to try the bridle trail, there are horses for

 Starved Rock State Park. *A waterfall is one of the pleasures encountered by hiking the cool, deep recesses of the interior canyon trails.*

rent. Fishermen may be lured to the park's streams by white bass, bullheads, channel catfish, and walleye. There is also a fishing area accessible to wheelchairs. Playgrounds, picnic sites, and campgrounds further the wide appeal. Cross-country skiing is also popular in winter.

Open year-round.
(815) 667-4726
http://dnr.state.il.us

8 Delabar State Park
Oquawka

Stretching along the Mississippi River, these 89 acres constitute a well-planned recreation area with two nature trails, a campground, and several inviting picnic areas. The park is named for the brothers who donated the land.

Most of the park is densely shaded by tall blackjack oaks, but birch trees and the stately shagbark hickory also cast their shadows. Within this limited space deer as well as smaller woodland mammals are sometimes seen, and more than 50 bird species have been counted—among them are wild canaries and white-tailed hawks.

Fishermen may launch boats at the river ramp or use the two boat docks to try for channel catfish, buffalo, walleye, and crappies, as well as large- and small-mouth bass. In the Mississippi backwaters, ice fishing and ice skating are winter possibilities.

Open daily year-round.
(309) 374-2496
http://dnr.state.il.us

9 Nauvoo Restoration
Off Rte. 96, Nauvoo

Joseph Smith, the Mormon leader, gathered his people here after they had been driven from Missouri in 1839. Buying land that was then partly swamp, he named it Nauvoo, the Hebrew word for "beautiful place." His followers were quick to make it so, building a community with stately brick homes, a school, shops, farms, and orchards, and commencing a holy temple. But in June 1844 Joseph Smith and his brother were murdered in Carthage, 24 miles away. Two years later, shortly after completion of their temple, the Mormons were again forced to move, this time under the leadership of Brigham Young.

Today, many of the original buildings have been restored to illustrate what life was like for settlers in the 1840s.

Attractions include the magnificent home of Heber Kimball, a Vermont blacksmith, with its delicate hand-carved porch railings, and the elegant Federal-style house of Wilford Woodruff. A memorial to the pioneers called "Exodus to Greatness" honors those who lost their lives trekking across the continent to the Rocky Mountains.

Displays in the large visitors center include paintings of many of the key episodes in Smith's life and a model of the temple, which was later partially destroyed by fire.

The Nauvoo Temple was recently reconstructed and stands on the original site at the corner of Mulholland and Wells streets. Near the visitors center is the monument to Women's Gardens, featuring a group of bronze statues honoring the many roles of women in society.

Open year-round.
(800) 453-0022
www.beautifulnauvoo.com

10 Chautauqua National Wildlife Refuge

Havana

In the fall and winter enormous concentrations of migrating waterfowl settle down for rest and replenishment at this 4,500-acre refuge. A major stop on the Mississippi Flyway, it comprises Lake Chautauqua and a narrow rim of timber, sandy bluffs, and marsh. More than 100,000 mallards, northern pintails, wood ducks, and other duck species stop here, and some 40,000 geese can also be expected to pay a call.

In all, nearly 300 kinds of birds frequent this area. Bald eagles claim it as a winter home. In the summer, visiting herons can be seen along the shores as they patiently wait for unsuspecting fish to come within range.

In addition to birding, wildlife enthusiasts are likely to observe deer and a wide assortment of small mammals. Badgers, muskrats, and minks, however, are elusive and rarely seen. Since the refuge includes several distinct environments, a great variety of trees, grasses, and wildflowers grow here. Along the interpretive trail near the refuge headquarters, you may find showy lady's slippers, prairie dandelions, and other endangered plants.

Boats may be launched at the recreation area. The fishing is good, especially between April and June, when water levels are kept high. Visitors are also permitted to gather nuts and mushrooms and pick the wild raspberries and blackberries.

Refuge open year-round; lake closed Oct.–Jan.
(309) 535-2290

http://midwest.fws.gov/illinoisriver

12 Lincoln Log Cabin State Historic Site. *Costumed guides stand outside a replica of the two-room log cabin where Abraham Lincoln visited his father and stepmother in the 1840s.*

11 David Davis Mansion

1000 E. Monroe Dr., Bloomington

The opulent 19-room yellow brick mansion is a Victorian gem inside and out. Designed by architect Alfred Piquenard for U.S. Supreme Court Justice David Davis and completed in 1872, it incorporates several features then unheard of in an average home, with flush toilets fed by an attic water tank, a central hot-air coal furnace, and closets with built-in drawers.

Davis actually spent little time here, leaving his wife to furnish the rooms with ornate sideboards and other fancy pieces, some of which were purchased from a furniture maker in New York.

Of the eight marble fireplaces, the one in the parlor—of dazzling white Carrara—is the most impressive. Hallway walls, seemingly covered with patterned paper, are in fact hand-painted. In the family sitting room the width of the judge's favorite rocking chair attests to his love of food, which was prepared on a cast-iron coal-burning stove.

Details of the design reflect the Victorian inclination toward an asymmetry that related to the variation found in nature. The paired windows are all different as are the iron porch and roof railings and the seven chimneys.

The visitors center, in an adjacent early 1800s horse barn, displays photos of the Davis family in settings that portray their lifestyle and their friendship with Abraham Lincoln.

Open Wed.–Sun. year-round except Thanksgiving, Christmas, and New Year's Day.
(309) 828-1084

www.state.il.us/HPA/Sites/ DavidDavis.htm

12 Lincoln Log Cabin State Historic Site

400 S. Lincoln Hwy., south of Charleston

This is a reconstruction of the two-room log cabin Abraham

Lincoln's father Thomas and stepmother Sarah Bush Lincoln moved into in 1840. At the time, the future president was a circuit-riding lawyer living in Springfield, and he often visited here while making his rounds.

Visitors are immediately immersed in the mid-19th century as period-clothed men and women assume the roles of Lincoln family members and neighbors as they go about their daily chores. They are also on hand to answer questions. If something strikes you as strange about their speech, remember that they're talking in an 1840s dialect. Such is the authentic aura imparted here. You'll also be interested to know that 18 people once shared these cramped quarters.

The 86-acre site also includes a reconstruction of an 1840s farm with a barn and smokehouse, built from hand-hewn logs, a kitchen garden, an orchard, and pastures.

Special summer programs include an 1845 Fourth of July sparked by speechifying, politicking, and flag raising while craftsmen hawk their wares. Other events of note: square dances, a bluegrass music festival, and a militia muster (with flintlock shooting competitions).

Site and buildings open daily except Thanksgiving, Christmas, and New Year's Day.
(217) 345-6489

13 Elsah and the Vadalabene Bike Trail

Elsah is a town that time forgot, leaving visitors all the richer. It courted prominence in 1883, when it was thought that railroad magnate Jay Gould might build a bridge there. He did not, and by the 1890s

Elsah had settled into its role as a sleepy Mississippi port.

The town, a small community with two parallel main streets, has changed little since the 1850s. As a charming result, limestone, frame, and brick buildings peer modestly through leafy branches and picket fences. The houses, privately owned, cannot be visited. No matter. A sidewalk stroll transports you back to mid-Victorian times with flower gardens, decorative porch railings and pillars, and the pervading sense that tomorrow here will be much like today.

Among the many places to see are the Bates-Mack house, with its carved gingerbread eaves, the 1850s brick Bradley house, and the Riverview House, a rambling clapboard that was once a hotel. The town school, circa 1857, is now the civic center. The Village Hall (1887) houses the museum with displays of local history and artists. Little wonder that the entire town of Elsah has been entered on the *National Register of Historic Places.*

A restaurant on La Salle Street has two walls and windows lined with folk art, pottery, and homemade bread. This is a good stopping point when biking the Vadalabene Bike Trail, a 25-mile macadam artery that runs from Alton to Pere Marquette State Park and offers fine views of the Mississippi, where during the winter a growing number of bald eagles are seen each year.

(618) 374-1568

www.elsah.org

For biking information:
(217) 782-7454

http://dnr.state.il.us/lands/landmgt/programs/biking/bikegde.html

14 Cahokia Mounds State Historic Site

Collinsville Rd., Collinsville
One of the first—and largest—of the hundreds of towns built by American Indians of the remarkable Mississippian culture, Cahokia once covered nearly six square miles on the now extinct meander

14 Cahokia Mounds State Historic Site. *An aerial view of 100-foot-high Monks Mound, the largest prehistoric earthwork in the Americas.*

13 Elsah and the Vadalabene Bike Trail. *A stroll through the leafy streets of the Mississippi River town of Elsah transports visitors back to Victorian times.*

channel of the Mississippi River. Like St. Louis today, it was at the crossroads of America, well located for trade as well as farming. At its peak Cahokia may have had a population of 10,000 to 20,000. It was the largest prehistoric center north of Mexico, with a "central city," suburbs, and outlying farm communities.

Of the hundred or so earthen mounds constructed here between 900 and 1250, the centerpiece is Monks Mound. Covering 14 acres of land and rising in terraces 100 feet above the plain, it dominated several plazas and avenues. On its uppermost platform loomed a stockaded building about 104 by 48 feet—the "White House"—where the ruler was ensconced.

For reasons that may never be known, Cahokia eventually went into a decline, and by 1400 it was nothing but a ghost town. Advancing white civilization has destroyed many of the mounds, but 69 are still found on this site.

Of particular interest is Mound 72. Its excavation has disclosed the grave of a chief (buried with a rich hoard of ornaments) and the remains of some 300 sacrificial victims, more than half of them young women.

Other excavations have revealed several circular arrangements of wooden posts. The most precise of these has been dubbed Woodhenge because of its similarity to England's Stonehenge; it may possibly have been a horizon calendar.

Exhibits in the museum, opened in 1989, portray life at Cahokia, including a life-size diorama, while an orientation show highlights the accomplishments of the people who built the mounds. Seasonal guided tours take you to the top of Monks Mound.

Open Wed.–Sun. except major holidays.
(618) 346-5160

www.cahokiamounds.com

15 Ingram's Pioneer Log Cabin Village

Kinmundy

If you are curious about frontier life, you'll find some answers here. A meal could set you back a nickel, while the price of a night's lodging at Jacob's Well Inn was six cents (if you had to share your bed with a stranger, the cost was shared).

Jacob's Well was formerly a stagecoach stop on the old Egyptian Trail between Terre Haute, Indiana, and St. Louis, hosting such guests as Abraham Lincoln and Jesse James.

Today, the building is one of 16 log structures in this replication of a pre–Civil War frontier village. The log cabins are furnished with period pieces. The rarest item is the immigrant's chest at the inn. Such chests were often used as coffins, and few of them have survived their owners.

During weekends in late September and mid-October, craftspeople demonstrate weaving, leather tooling, basket-making, and other old-time skills. The sounds of a country fiddler are often heard.

Open daily mid-Apr.–mid-Nov.
Admission charged.
(618) 547-7123
www.effinghamil.com/visitorsbureau/
attractfm.htm

16 McCoy Memorial Library

Rte. 142 (Washington St.),
McLeansboro

An elegant mansion built in 1884 as the residence of a local merchant now serves as the home of the McCoy Memorial Library and the Hamilton County Historical Society Museum. The original furnishings attest to the first owner's taste for gracious living. Visitors may admire among other things a handsome fireplace of African mahogany, a French *vernis Martin* cabinet, a Steinway piano, various art objects, examples of finely crafted woodwork, and a stairway of carved walnut.

A special genealogy library occupies the second floor in rooms that still preserve their original paneling of carved walnut, chestnut, and cherry, along with some handsome pieces of furniture. Objects in the museum, including photographs of street scenes and shop interiors, trace the development of this typically Midwestern county. Also featured are American Indian stone artifacts and several of the celebrated plaster groups executed by John Rogers in the 1870s. Of special interest is a huge wooden desk with hinged sides revealing mailboxes and a letter slot.

Library open Mon.–Sat, except
holidays; genealogy library open
Mon–Fri.
(618) 643-2125
www.mcleansboro.com/community/
mccoy.htm

17 Fort de Chartres

4 miles west of Prairie du
Rocher, at 1350 State Rte. 155,
or 37 miles south of Belleville

Built in the 1750s, this massive stone fort offers a glimpse into life in Illinois under the French colonial government, which ruled the land from lakes Michigan and Superior to the Ohio and Missouri rivers for about 100 years, beginning in 1673. With stone walls 15 feet high and three feet thick, and enclosing approximately four acres, the fort was the center of French control in the area. Two years after the Treaty of Paris ended the French and Indian War, the fort was surrendered to the British and eventually abandoned in 1771.

By the 1820s, visitors noted trees growing in its walls and buildings, which began to literally disappear as local residents scavenged stone and timber to serve as material for other structures. By 1900 none of the wall existed above ground level, and all of the buildings, save the powder magazine, had vanished completely.

Rescued from oblivion by the Illinois Legislature in 1913, Fort de Chartres is now partially restored and scrupulously managed by the Illinois Historic Preservation Agency. The north wall, complete with bastions and gatehouse, contains musket ports and embrasures for cannon. In the east bastion stands the rebuilt powder magazine, considered by many to be the oldest building in the state.

Other structures include the king's storehouse, now home to the Fort de Chartres Museum, where visitors can step back into life in Illinois during the colonial period, courtesy of household items and artifacts of warfare discovered during archaeological digs near the fort. The East Barracks and the Government House have been outlined by wood frames—a technique called ghosting—to provide a sense of their original size and form.

The fort also hosts many lively historic events. The annual Rendezvous at Fort de Chartres, held the first full weekend in June, re-creates a traditional French fur trapper's holiday. It features shooting competitions, military drills, traders of 18th-century-style wares, dancing, music, and food. The first weekend in October brings French and Indian War re-enactments. Other special events include Kids' Day, held the first weekend in May, with 18th-century games, contests, and crafts for children of all ages.

Open year-round except Thanksgiving,
Christmas, and New Year's Day.
Free admission.
(618) 284-7230
www.state.il.us.HPA/Sites/
FortdeChartres.htm

17 Fort de Chartres. *The partially restored Fort de Chartres shows visitors what life was like in 1750, when the area now known as Illinois was under French rule.*

Garden of the Gods Wilderness Area. *A visitor views the limestone and sandstone rock formations that overlook the Shawnee Hills mountain range and forest.*

18 Crab Orchard National Wildlife Refuge

8588 State Rte. 148, off Interstate 57, Marion

At this extensive, watery refuge (43,660 acres), a stopping place for migratory waterfowl on the Mississippi Flyway, sharecropping arrangements with local farmers specify that certain amounts of milo, corn, soybeans, and clover be left in the fields for the vast flights of Canada geese and ducks alighting here.

Common loons, green herons, turkey vultures, and yellow-crowned night herons can usually be found here as well, and the refuge is a nesting site for bald eagles and many kinds of songbirds. Two observation towers on Crab Orchard Lake offer excellent views of waterfowl and occasionally of other wildlife.

Two of the three lakes have swimming beaches, boat docks, and boat-launching sites. The refuge has nine hiking trails—don't miss the Rocky Bluff Trail with its steep bluffs, waterfalls, and numerous wildflowers. The refuge also has three campgrounds with 400 campsites.

In the southern sector of the refuge, a 4,050-acre wilderness area has been established.

Dramatic sandstone outcroppings and woodland creeks make this an exhilarating place for hiking and backpacking, but fires and camping are not permitted.

Bellwort, white trilliums, showy orchids, lady's tresses, and butterfly weed are among the many wildflowers that brighten the spring and summer scene.

Open year-round daily, 8 A.M.–5 P.M.
(618) 997-3344, Ext. 334

http://midwest.fws.gov/craborchard

19 Garden of the Gods Wilderness Area

Located in the Shawnee National Forest, off State Hwy. 145 South, Harrisburg

Illinois' most celebrated natural landmark, this truly awesome collection of rock formations was carved by ancient forces of nature. Over hundreds of millions of years, fierce wind and freezing water eroded huge slabs of limestone and sandstone to create impressive ridges and canyons thousands of feet deep. Once home to prehistoric peoples, the area now attracts photographers, bird-watchers (who hope for a peek at the resident raptors), and avid climbers.

Particularly interesting and

aptly named formations include Camel Rock, Anvil Rock, Devil's Smokestack, and Old Stone Face. Made of natural flagstone and just one-quarter mile long, the popular Observation Trail leads to areas immediately above the cliffs for outstanding views of the surrounding Shawnee Hills mountain range and nearly 3,300 acres of forest. Five additional trails lead into more of the expansive, unspoiled wilderness.

Below the bluffs, visitors can stroll among hardwood trees—maple, dogwood, oak, and pine—dotted with sandstone sculptures.

In fall the terrain turns into a tapestry of brilliant color. To maximize the view, hikers and equestrians alike can follow the River-to-River Trail, which winds across the center of the wilderness in a spacious "S" for nearly 10 miles, stretching from Battery Rock on the Ohio River to Grand Tower on the Mississippi. Along the trek, spectacular sights include Burden Falls, the tallest waterfall in Illinois; Bell Smith Springs, boasting a mighty rock bridge and the Devil's Backbone, jutting from its clear water; and Sand Cave, the largest sandstone cave in North America. From the area, hikers can also opt for a detour on the famous American Discovery Trail.

For those eager to dine or sleep with the gods, picnic sites, complete with tables and fire grills, as well as ample space for camping and overnight parking are available. Motorized vehicles, however, are strictly forbidden from entering the wilderness.

Open year-round.
(618) 287-2201

www.fs.fed.us/r9/shawnee

20 Cache River State Natural Area

Off Rte. 45, seven miles south of Vienna, west of Rte. 37

In a setting of natural wetlands, forests, and bluffs along the Cache River, this picturesque preserve provides a variety of habitats for many plants and animals not usually found this far north. The large pileated woodpecker is common, along with a host of songbirds. Occasionally river otters and bobcats are seen, as well as poisonous cottonmouth snakes that must be watched for and avoided.

Hiking trails have been marked in parts of the area's nearly 14,078 acres, and a floating boardwalk provides visitors with an intimate view of the swamp environment. The northern edge of the preserve is bordered by steep slopes and sheer rock cliffs over 50 feet high. From the high bluffs visitors are rewarded with an inspiring view across almost five miles of the forest-swamp mosaic below.

Open year-round.
(618) 634-9678

http://dnr.state.il.us/lands/landmgt/parks/r5/cachervr.htm

Cache River State Natural Area. *Cypress trees tower above the Heron Pond swamp in this picturesque natural preserve.*

Conner Prairie. *Here visitors can experience what life must have been like in the 1830s (see page 109).*

Indiana

Augmenting the gentle beauty of the land are reminders of its early settlement and the hard labor and creative energy of its pioneers.

A river that gave its euphonic name to a famous nearby battlefield now borders a peaceful park; another inviting retreat pays tribute to a heroic frontiersman whose achievements were denigrated by his contemporaries. The engaging variety of the Indiana countryside is further revealed in parks and forests and at Abraham Lincoln's boyhood home.

Restorations exemplify the life of the Amish and other pioneers who farmed here. American ingenuity is recalled in gristmills, canals, museums of steamboats, and other inventions; car fanciers will savor the collection of Cords, Auburns, and Duesenbergs, all built in Indiana and ranked among the finest automobiles ever made.

1 Bonneyville Mill
Bristol

In 1837 Edward Bonney, a local tavern keeper and entrepreneur, constructed a mill on the wooded shores of Little Elkhart River. Now known as Bonneyville Mill, it is the oldest continuously operating gristmill with a horizontal waterwheel in the state of Indiana, and as it probably has from the beginning, it produces both flour and meal. In 1976 the mill was listed on the *National Register of Historic Places.*

Rather than standing upright, the waterwheel here is installed lying on its side and is enclosed in a steel case submerged in about seven feet of water. When the 12 doors on the sides of the case are opened, water flows through and drains out the bottom. The whirlpool thus created spins the wheel, which then turns the gears that drive the mill. Visitors enter the mill through the basement, where the gear system is visible, along with a display of old milling equipment.

The main floor contains the milling area with two sets of grindstones. On this floor the flour that is produced—corn, wheat, rye, and buckwheat—is for sale.

On the second floor visitors can see a buckwheat flour sifter used to separate the flour from the hulls after it is ground. The third floor

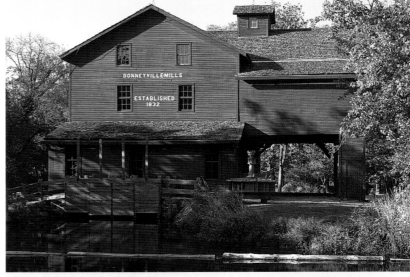

1 Bonneyville Mill. *The state's oldest continuously operating gristmill with a horizontal waterwheel still churns out flour that visitors can buy.*

houses a grain cleaner composed of a series of screens for sifting and a fan for winnowing the grain before it is milled, as well as the gears and heavy equipment that operate the mill's elevator.

On the mill grounds, which stretch along the river, shady picnic areas have been developed. Hiking trails wander through the property, and for those who like to fish, the river is stocked with trout.

Open daily May–Oct.
(574) 535-6458

www.elkhartcountyparks.org

2 Amish Acres
1600 W. Market St., Nappanee

In 1874 Christian Stahly, the first Amish settler in this area, built a farmhouse here for his son. Today the 80-acre restored farm provides not only a fascinating look at the old-fashioned ways of the German-speaking Plain People, but it also gives an overview of 19th-century American farm life.

The main house, its smokehouse and other outbuildings, and the nearby Grossdaadi Haus (Grandfather House) are visited in a group tour, which originates near the farm's main gate. The 12-room white frame farmhouse, which was greatly expanded in the 1890s, is outfitted with period furniture, cookware, wood stoves, and equipment, such as a sausage stuffer, spinning wheel, and rocker-action churn. After the tour visitors can take a hay wagon ride and are free to roam the grounds and look at the other buildings, many of which were brought here from town and from other farms.

The sweet smell of hay fills a large barn containing threshing equipment and a hay wagon. Stables and milking stalls adjoin a barnyard and pasture. A horse-drawn school bus and an Amish church-bench wagon are among the old carriages in the wagon shed.

Other buildings include a smithy, an icehouse, a sawmill, a windmill, and a small 1870s town house. The farm has a sorghum press, a mint still where aromatic oil was distilled from mint plants, and a shop where brooms are still made from broom corn. The kitchen garden includes herbs and flowers, while mulberries and other old-time favorite fruit trees grow in the orchard. The farm is least crowded in spring and fall.

Open daily Apr.–Dec.

Admission charged.

(800) 800-4942

www.amishacres.com

3 Chain o' Lakes State Park
Albion

The predominant feature in this 2,700-acre park is a series of 11 small lakes, all but three of which are strung together by natural channels of water.

The lakes, called kettle lakes, were formed at the end of the last ice age. The weight of enormous blocks of ice that were left in the

ground by a retreating glacier created the basins for the lakes. The subsequent melt-water filled the lakes and thereby carved the connecting channels.

Not surprisingly, the principal activities here are swimming, fishing, and boating. Swimming is permitted only in summer, and the only motorized crafts allowed on the lakes are low-powered electric troll boats.

Rowboats and canoes can be rented by the day, and paddle-boats can be rented by the hour. Anglers try for bluegills and bass. Winter-time activities include ice fishing, skating on the lakes, sledding, and cross-country skiing.

The park also has some interesting trails circling the lakes and meandering through woodlands and meadows.

In addition to more than 400 campsites, there is a small village of housekeeping cottages.

Park and campground open year-round, but facilities turned off Nov.–Mar. Admission charged.

(260) 636-2654

www.in.gov/dnr/parklake/parks/

chainolakes.html

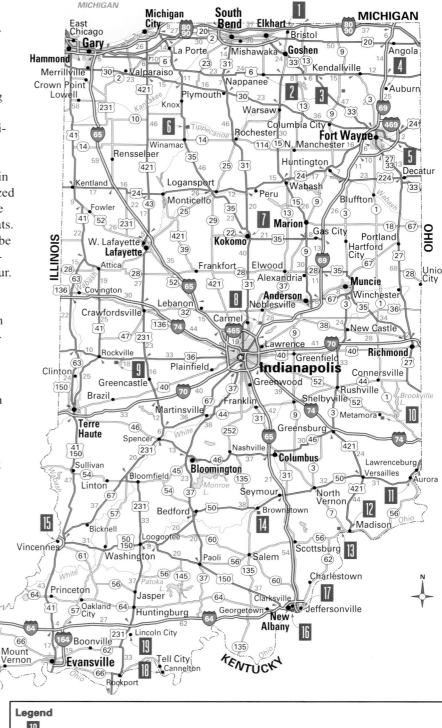

Scale:
0 — 20 — 40 Miles
0 — 20 — 40 Kilometers

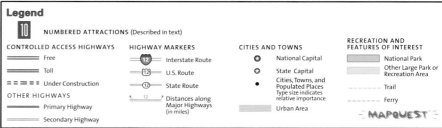

Legend

10 NUMBERED ATTRACTIONS (Described in text)

CONTROLLED ACCESS HIGHWAYS
— Free
— Toll
===== Under Construction

OTHER HIGHWAYS
— Primary Highway
— Secondary Highway

HIGHWAY MARKERS
12 Interstate Route
12 U.S. Route
12 State Route
12 Distances along Major Highways (in miles)

CITIES AND TOWNS
⊕ National Capital
⊛ State Capital
• Cities, Towns, and Populated Places Type size indicates relative importance
Urban Area

RECREATION AND FEATURES OF INTEREST
National Park
Other Large Park or Recreation Area
---- Trail
------ Ferry

MAPQUEST

INDIANA

4 Auburn Cord Duesenberg Museum

Intersection of I-69 and State Rd. 8, Auburn

Named for three noted producers of classic luxury cars, this museum is both a handsome showcase for automobiles and a celebration of the era between World War I and World War II when the luxury car was in its heyday. The sports and luxury cars of these three American makers are counted among the most beautiful automobiles ever made. The building itself is the Auburn Automobile Company's former headquarters, a spacious structure now restored to its 1930 art deco splendor. The floor is geometrically patterned in pink, green, black, and cream marble, and the high ceiling friezes, painted in relief, are enriched with complementary designs.

The main exhibit on the ground floor contains some of the best engineered and most luxuriously appointed cars ever built, including an aluminum-and-green 265-horsepower 1932 Duesenberg coupe that oil tycoon J. Paul Getty paid $15,000 for in the 1930s and a stunning 1935 Auburn Boattail Speedster that sold for $2,245. (Today it's valued at $150,000.)

The most striking automobiles here are Auburns, Cords, and Duesenbergs from the 1920s and 1930s, when those manufacturers flourished. But other makes, such as Stutz, Rolls-Royce, and Packard, are also represented. And in a gesture to the more recent past, the exhibit includes a 1952 Crosley once owned by architect Frank Lloyd Wright.

The cars exhibited on the second floor provide a more general overview of automotive history. Thematic galleries are devoted to early Auburns (1904–1924); rare cars built in the city of Auburn (McIntyre, Kiblinger, Zimmerman); uncommon makes built in Indiana (Lexington, Cole, Marmon); and cars of special interest, such as a 1933 Checker taxi cab, a 1936 Auburn hearse, and pioneer-era electric cars.

Open daily year-round except major holidays. Admission charged.

(260) 925-1444

www.acdmuseum.org

4 Auburn Cord Duesenberg Museum. *Some of the most luxuriously appointed cars ever built can be seen here.*

5 Lincoln Museum

Located at 200 Berry St., Fort Wayne

In 1931, the founders of Lincoln National Life Insurance in Fort Wayne decided to honor their company's venerable namesake with a museum. Today it stands as the world's largest museum dedicated to the life and legacy of America's most beloved president.

Stepping into "Lincoln's America," 21st-century explorers can glimpse a life-size model of Lincoln guiding a flatboat down the Mississippi River; operate an interactive fiber-optic map spanning the North, South, and expanding West; and read original documents used to buy slaves. In the "Prairie Politician to President" gallery, visitors can experience the excitement of an 1830s political meeting, including Lincoln's *House Divided* speech and his debates with Stephen Douglas.

Nearby, the Civil War gallery focuses on Lincoln's role in America's most critical years, 1861 to 1865. Along with artifacts from Lincoln's office and the words to the *Emancipation Proclamation* and the *Gettysburg Address,* visitors will find three-dimensional multimedia presentations, interactive computer activities, and touchable reproductions of Civil War military equipment.

There's also a gift shop for visitors eager to preserve a bit of Lincoln's history and memorabilia.

Open year-round, except New Year's Day, Easter, Memorial Day, Independence Day, Labor Day, Thanksgiving, and Christmas. Admission charged.

(260) 455-3864

www.thelincolnmuseum.org

6 Tippecanoe River State Park

Winamac

Farther downstream, the river that borders this park gave its name to an 1811 battle, and thus to William Henry Harrison's presidential campaign slogan, "Tippecanoe and Tyler too," in 1840. Harrison led an armed force to victory against the Shawnees on Tippecanoe Creek, and John Tyler was his running mate.

But long before that, in the 1600s and 1700s, the river was a passageway for the canoes of intrepid French voyageurs from Canada who bartered for furs with this area's Potawatomi and Miami Indians.

Although the land was once cleared and cultivated, it was marginal for farming. It has since reverted to its natural state, with terrain that ranges from oak and pine woods to marsh and sandy scrub. Returned wildlife includes wood ducks, great blue herons, sandhill cranes, beavers, muskrats, and white-tailed deer. They can sometimes be spotted along the extensive network of hiking trails. About 23 miles of the trails can also be used by riders who bring their own horses.

Tippecanoe is an American Indian word for buffalofish, a sucker that was once plentiful here. But today bass and bluegills are dominant among the catches that lure anglers. Both boaters and canoeists use the river, but it is too hazardous for swimmers. The picnic ground on the riverbank is especially pleasant, with spaciously separated tables under fine old shade trees.

Park and campground open year-round. Admission charged.

(574) 946-3213

www.in.gov/dnr/parklake/parks/ tippecanoeriver.html

7 Elwood Haynes Museum

1915 S. Webster St., Kokomo. Exit U.S. Rte. 31 at Boulevard. Go west to northwest corner of Boulevard and Webster.

Kokomo prides itself on being the City of Firsts, and the most outstanding of those firsts were the inventions of Elwood Haynes. In 1894 Haynes tested the prototype for a horseless carriage with an engine fueled by gasoline, a substance then considered of little commercial value. Four years later he put it in production, and if it was not America's first commer-

INDIANA

cially successful automobile, as Haynes advocates claim, it was certainly one of the earliest. Haynes also developed several metal alloys, most notably tungsten stainless steel and Stellite, an extra-hard blend of chromium, cobalt, and tungsten.

The museum, which is in Haynes's home, has four of his cars—the 1905 Haynes Model L, the Haynes roadster, a touring car from the early 1920s, and a 1916 Haynes. It also contains photographs and documents relating to Haynes's life and inventions.

Upstairs, local manufacturers have mounted exhibits of historic and contemporary products made in Kokomo. These range from crystal walkie-talkie radios and artillery shells to metal lifeboats, nonglare glass, pressed glass, marbles, and paperweights. Haynes's alloys are well represented. Products using them include not just rollers, bearings, and valves but also turbine blades, machine-gun barrels, and surgical instruments.

Open Tues.–Sun. except holidays.
(765) 456-7500
www.inkokomo.com/community/
elwood_haynes.html

1 Conner Prairie. *Dressed in period clothing, the "doctor" can tell visitors about medical notions popular in the 1830s.*

1 Conner Prairie. *An entire village duplicating a typical prairie settlement of the 1830s, complete with a schoolhouse, carpenter's shop, and blacksmith, greets visitors here.*

8 Conner Prairie
13400 Allisonville Rd., 6 miles north of I-465

William Conner, who was raised by American Indians, settled in this area in 1800. He lived as a trader and then as a farmer and became prominent in state politics. His Federal-style mansion of mellow red brick, built in 1823, still stands, having been restored, and an entire village duplicating a typical prairie settlement of the 1830s is also on the premises.

The village has more than five historic areas with 45 buildings. Among them are an inn, a schoolhouse, a loom house, and a barn with bins of sweet-smelling grain. The houses include those of a doctor and a weaver, and homes and shops for a carpenter, a blacksmith, a potter, and a storekeeper. The furnishings throughout include period pieces or accurate reproductions.

The buildings also have occupants in period attire, and they take their roles to heart. The carpenter, for example, hews wood and constructs items using authentic tools and materials. The doctor discourses on a then popular medical notion of the four cardinal humors that affect one's health. And a talkative widower regales visitors with tales about his exploits as riverboatman and soldier.

The Conner house itself has been furnished simply but elegantly in the manner of the period. There are built-in cupboards and bookcases in the dining and drawing rooms; in the kitchen is a beehive oven that held 15 loaves of bread; on the stairs are rag-strip loomed carpets; and the main bedroom includes a four-poster bed with an 1858 patchwork quilt.

For youngsters and the young of heart, there is also PastPort Discovery Area. Here visitors can try playing such 19th-century games as quoits and stilt-walking or crafts like candle-dipping, preparing flax for spinning, and writing with a quill pen.

Open Tues.–Sun. Closed holidays.
(800) 966-1836
www.connerprairie.org

9 Raccoon State Recreation Area
Rockville

Located in the heart of Parke County's rolling farmlands, Cecil M. Harden Lake, often referred to as Raccoon Lake, was created by a dam on Big Raccoon Creek, a branch of the Wabash River. It provides an area for water sports as well as habitats for fish and wildlife.

Parke County, once the home of the Delaware, Shawnee, and Miami Indians, is known for its wealth of sugar maples, the source of a sweetener that was enjoyed by both the Indians and the pioneers who followed them. Maple sugaring is carried on today at several local sugar camps in Parke County.

The county is also known as the Covered Bridge Capital of America. Thirty-two such structures, built between 1856 and 1921, still remain on various streams and rivers. Two of them span Big Raccoon Creek.

The lake's sandy beach is surrounded by grassy bluffs set with picnic tables. The roped-off swimming area has a bathhouse. From the beach a road leads past several more picnic grounds, shaded by groves of hardwoods, to a campground. And just beyond this area visitors will find a boat-launching ramp and a small marina for fishermen, who try for walleyes, crappies, bluegills, and catfish.

Area and campground open year-round; water provided summer only.
Admission charged.
(765) 344-1412
www.in.gov/dnr/park/lake/reservoirs/
cecil.html

10 Whitewater Canal Historic Site

Metamora

So popular was the Whitewater Valley as a thoroughfare for pioneers making their way from Ohio to Indiana that by 1830 it was the most heavily populated area in the state. In 1836, seeking a means of shipping produce from the valley to distant markets, the Indiana legislature voted to build a 76-mile canal from Lawrenceburg to Hagerstown as part of a statewide transportation improvement program.

By 1847 the four-foot-deep Whitewater Canal was completed. It was fed by the west fork of the Whitewater River, and soon several mills, using tub wheels powered by water diverted through flumes, sprang up along its banks. However, because of floods and washouts, the canal deteriorated. The cost of maintenance and competition from the expanding

10 Whitewater Canal Historic Site. *The* Ben Franklin, *a barge pulled by two draft horses, offers half-hour canal rides that cross the restored Duck Creek Aqueduct.*

10 Whitewater Canal Historic Site. *Fourteen miles of the waterway have been restored in Metamora.*

railroad system led to its demise after less than 15 years of service.

Fourteen miles of the canal have now been restored as the Whitewater Canal State Memorial, a project that includes the restoration of the Metamora Grist Mill. Built in 1845 on the bank of the canal, this two-story red brick mill, with a porch across the front and a museum on the second floor, has a waterwheel set in the spillway of one of the canal's locks.

Today the mill grinds whole-wheat cereal, white cornmeal, and grits, all for sale here. On the lower level one can see the elaborate system of slow-turning wheels and belts that power the grinding stones and sifters. A half-mile away is the restored wooden Duck Creek Aqueduct, which was built in 1843 to carry the canal 16 feet above the small stream. The *Ben Franklin,* a barge pulled by two draft horses, offers half-hour canal rides that include crossing the aqueduct.

Just below the mill a bridge crosses the canal to a picnic area with shade trees and a small bandstand. A stroll around the town of Metamora reveals some handsome old buildings.

Gristmill open Tues.–Sat. and P.M. Sun.; barge rides Tues.–Sun. in summer. Admission charged for barge rides. (765) 647-6512

www.in.gov/ism

11 Hillforest Victorian House Museum

213 Fifth St., Aurora

The Victorian mansion known as Hillforest was named Forest Hill by its builder, Thomas Gaff, a Scotsman who reached America at the age of 3. Gaff grew up in the East, and in 1837, when that area was experiencing an economic decline, he journeyed west, finally settling in Aurora in 1843. There he found water that was especially well suited to the production of whiskey and began to manufacture his own brand, Thistle Dew.

Gaff's distillery flourished, and he soon owned much of Aurora,

plus a fleet of steamboats. So enamored of his fleet was he that in 1856 he built a mansion overlooking the Ohio River with a façade reminiscent of a riverboat—broad eaves, a semicircular, two-story colonnaded porch, and a circular belvedere at the top resembling a riverboat's pilothouse.

The mansion, however, also reflects the influence of Italian Renaissance architecture so popular during that era. The main doorway, paneled with Venetian glass, opens onto an entrance hall with grain-painted Circassian walnut woodwork and parquet flooring in the Greek key design. The walls are decorated with *trompe l'oeil* painting of wood paneling and stylized lotus blossoms. Italian molds were used for the decorative plasterwork.

The suspended staircase, in steamboat style, has mahogany banisters and tiger maple spindles. Rosewood "brag" or "mortgage" buttons, traditionally installed when a house had been paid for, decorate the mahogany newel posts.

Arched walk-through windows open onto the porches, and a deliberately narrow doorway—too narrow for ladies' hoopskirts—leads from a stairway to the pilothouse, the gentlemen's retreat.

Now restored, the mansion, whose name was changed by a subsequent owner, is filled with handsome antiques—including a collection of rare blue milk glass, Meissen china, bohemian glass candleholders, and a Pennsylvania Dutch weight-driven clock.

Open Tues.–Sun. Apr.–Dec. 30. Admission charged. (812) 926-0087

www.hillforest.org

12 Historic Madison

Located on the Ohio River

Hailed as the most beautiful small town in the Midwest, Madison is known for its historic 19th-century architecture, antiques, specialty shops, distinctive restaurants, and wineries. In the mid-1800s this charming river port was a thriving center of transportation, commerce, and culture. Much of what was unique about Madison then remains the same.

Boats and barges still pass on the Ohio River, surrounded by striking limestone bluffs. Many of the grand homes and stately buildings remain in mint condition and active use.

In addition to admiring and touring the historic houses, visitors can catch a demonstration in traditional saddle-making at the Ben Schroeder Saddletree Factory, which opened for business in 1878; take a detour through authentic décor and artifacts at the Madison Railroad Station, constructed in 1895; or get a glimpse of the life and work of a frontier physician at Dr. William Hutchings's office, preserved precisely as he operated it until his death in 1903.

For outdoor enthusiasts, the scenic Riverfront Park sports a gazebo, plenty of benches, and a lighted brick walkway. At its docks, sailors can climb aboard one of the riverboats for a cruise or launch their own boat. Nearby, landlubbers can head down the Heritage Trail, a paved pathway with ample space for strolling, biking, and skating.

Open year-round.
(812) 265-2956

www.visitmadison.org/index.html

13 Clifty Falls State Park

Between State Rds. 56 and 62, Madison

The highlight of this varied woodland park is a two-mile-long gorge, cut by Clifty Creek through layers of shale and limestone 450 million years old—some of the oldest exposed bedrock in the state. Four major waterfalls, ranging in height from 60 to 82 feet, give the area a rugged grandeur reminiscent of Alpine regions.

Clifty Falls, located at the upper end of the gorge, cascades over a series of wide, shallow steps of rock jutting from the cliff before tumbling more than 70 feet into the pool below. Even in midsummer, when the flow of water is diminished, the falls are a dramatic sight. The strata of the cliff disappear into the woods on the other side of the falls like a bony shelf with a cargo of bonsai.

Ten hiking trails, of varying lengths and difficulty, run along the gorge and through surrounding woodlands. Other recreational facilities include a swimming pool, picnic areas, tennis courts, and a nature center, containing exhibits of fossils from the gorge and a bird-watching room where a one-way window enables onlookers to view the winged visitors, leaving them undisturbed. An observation tower, just a short walk from the nature center, offers a panoramic view of the Ohio River half a mile to the south.

Open year-round. Admission charged.
(812) 273-8885

www.in.gov/dnr/parklake/parks/cliftyfalls.html

14 Jackson-Washington State Forest

State Rd. 250, Brownstown

One of the most spectacular features of this primitive forest area is Skyline Drive, a five-mile auto loop running along the crest of a wooded ridge. Observation areas just off the road offer picturesque vistas of the surrounding woodlands and fertile plain, checkered with farm fields and the glinting roofs of silos and barns. Visitors are encouraged to stop at Skyline Shelter for a picnic or climb to the top of the firetower, both along Skyline Drive.

In addition, the forest is a key access point to the 60-mile Knobstone Trail for backpackers. There are also eight hiking trails of varying difficulty within the forest's boundaries, including an eight-mile loop. Two trails are available for horseback riding, although horses are not available for rent. Fishing and boat-launching facilities are provided on Knob Lake and Spurgeon Hollow Lake, where likely catches include catfish and bass. Several picnic areas and a 62-site campground make this a pleasant and convenient resting place for travelers.

Open year-round.
(812) 358-2160

www.in.gov/dnr/forestry

12 Historic Madison. *The streets of this town are filled with National Historic Landmarks, such as Lanier Mansion, completed in 1844. It was the home of James F. D. Lanier, a banker who loaned more than $1 million to the state of Indiana during a difficult period of the Civil War.*

INDIANA

15 George Rogers Clark National Historical Park. *A statue of Francis Vigo, a merchant and patriot who gave money and supplies to American troops, looks over the Wabash River in the park built on the site of Fort Sackville.*

15 George Rogers Clark National Historical Park

Vincennes

The park commemorates a soldier who in his lifetime was one of our most neglected heroes. In 1776 the 20-year-old Virginian moved to the Kentucky wilderness. A born leader, he soon turned a small group of frontiersmen into a remarkably effective group of soldiers. On February 23, 1779, Clark and some 175 of his troops crossed 180 miles of cold and flooded terrain to launch a surprise attack on the British contingent here at Fort Sackville. He had previously neutralized the British strongholds at Kaskaskia and Cahokia without firing a shot.

Clark's victories broke England's hold on the "Old Northwest" and helped secure it for the United States. The area now includes Ohio, Indiana, Illinois, Michigan, and Wisconsin. Yet this courageous leader spent most of his later life plagued by political rivals, unjustly accused of misusing funds, and on the verge of poverty. His great contribution to our nationhood was not fully appreciated until shortly before his death in 1818.

Today Clark is honored by an imposing granite rotunda built in the classical Greek style, with 16 massive columns and a skylight in the domed roof. In its limestone and marble interior are a bronze statue of Clark and seven murals depicting key episodes in his campaign. The memorial is the centerpiece of a small, graceful park built on the site of Fort Sackville, with formal lawns, steps, and a walk overlooking the Wabash River.

Other historic places in Vincennes include St. Francis Xavier Church, the territorial capitol, and Grouseland, the home of William Henry Harrison, the Indiana Territory's first governor and the ninth president of the United States. Nearby, a prehistoric American Indian mound recalls the area's most ancient civilization. An open-air bus provides a tour past many of the town's historic sites. *Memorial and visitors center open daily except Thanksgiving, Christmas, and New Year's Day.* *(812) 882-1776*

www.nps.gov/gero

16 Falls of the Ohio State Park

Located at the end of Riverside Dr., Clarksville; Exit "0" on I-65

Today no one visits Indiana for its ocean, yet 220 acres of fossilized coral provide living (or once living) proof that an ocean, indeed, flourished in the state—some 200 million years before dinosaurs existed. At this scenic site on the banks of the Ohio River, visitors can marvel over the prehistoric evidence.

Geologists, paleontologists, and curious explorers have flocked here since the 1790s. Experts date its active ocean life back to the Devonian Period, between 395 and 345 million years ago. More than 600 species of plants and animals once lived on its coral reefs—two-thirds of them "type" specimens, recorded here for the first time anywhere in the world. And five distinct fossil layers lie exposed at the park.

From August through October, when the river is at its lowest level, visitors can find the best accessibility to the fossil beds. While fossil collecting is strictly prohibited, the park staff encourages visitors to discover fossils galore from the primeval sea bottom.

Any time of year, visitors can learn all about the ancient history and wonders of the park at its state-of-the-art, 16,000-square-foot Interpretive Center.

In the lobby, a re-creation of the prehistoric Indiana island dazzles with huge wading birds and a giant, 18-foot-long Devonian fish floating overhead. Beyond the entrance, 78 exhibits take visitors back through time. The center's spacious, enclosed observation deck, situated more than 40 feet above the Ohio River and graced with 18-foot-tall windows, beckons with breathtaking views of the fossils and water below. A wildlife viewing area lets kids of all ages not only see songbirds feeding or raccoons bathing but also listen in on their tunes and chatter.

Beyond its fossils, the park offers hiking trails, grassy spots for picnicking, a boat launch ramp, and excellent opportunities for birdwatching and fishing. Biologists have recorded 265 species of birds flying through the park—herons, egrets, osprey, peregrine falcons, and an occasional bald eagle among them. More than 125 species of fish swim in this stretch of the Ohio River. Several, including the paddlefish, shovel-nosed sturgeon, and long-nosed gar, trace their ancestry to the age of dinosaurs.

As its name suggests, the park also features the falls—the Ohio River's famous cascading rapids, which cause the river to drop 26 feet in elevation over a 2 1/2-mile stretch. Seafaring visitors can take a ride through the wild waves where Lewis and Clark actually began their historic expedition. *Open daily year-round. Admission charged for Interpretive Center.* *(812) 280-9970*

www.fallsoftheohio.org

17 Howard Steamboat Museum and Mansion

Jeffersonville. Exit I-65 at exit "O." Go east to Spring St., then south on Spring to Market St. Go east (left) onto Market for 11 blocks. Mansion on left, parking in rear.

In 1834, 19-year-old James Howard borrowed $60,000 to open a shipyard. Thus began one of the greatest steamboat-building companies in America, a family enterprise that lasted over a century. At one time more than 80 percent of the steamboats docked in New Orleans were reportedly made in the Howard yards. The *J. M. White,* constructed there in the late 1870s at a cost of more than $300,000, was considered the most lavish and beautiful riverboat ever built in the Howard yards. The 1894 *City of Louisville* was the fastest in history.

Today the 22-room Howard mansion, built in the early 1890s by Howard's son, not only houses one of the country's best collections of riverboat memorabilia but is itself an intriguing architectural delight. The grand staircase is modeled on those that graced the great stern-wheelers and side-wheelers of the period, as are the 36 chandeliers and several of the hand-carved wooden archways. Many of the furnishings are original, including an ingenious shower with both overhead and chest-level nozzles, an armchair constructed from 13 pairs of perfectly matched cattlehorns, and some items purchased at the Columbian Exposition of 1893, such as a brass bed.

Several of the upstairs rooms contain a superb collection of steamboat models, including one of the giant towboat *Sprague*—longer than a football field, taller than a three-story building. There are also excellent historic photographs, tools of 19th-century shipbuilders, and relics from historic vessels, including a pilot's wheel 9.5 feet in diameter.

Open Tues.–Sun. except holidays.
Admission charged.
(888) 472-0606
www.steamboatmuseum.org

19 Lincoln Boyhood National Memorial. *A fireplace with iron pots graces the boyhood home of President Abraham Lincoln, reconstructed as it may have appeared in 1818. Behind the cabin is a smokehouse for preserving meat.*

18 Cannelton Locks and Dam
Rte. 66

Congress authorized the Corps of Engineers to start improving the navigability of the lower Ohio River in 1824. Since then improvements have constantly been made, and today shipping moves easily along this great waterway by virtue of a series of dams and locks along its length. Each dam backs up the water behind it, creating a long navigable "lake" that reaches upstream to the next dam and lock.

Overall, the Cannelton Locks and Dam create a lake extending 114 miles to Louisville, Kentucky.

The whole structure cost nearly $100 million to build in the 1960s, and ample provisions have been made for the taxpayer to get a good view of the operation from a lock-side walkway and an observation tower. From the tower the viewer sees not just the locks in operation but also the sandy banks on the Kentucky side of the river and the boiling water at the foot of the dam's massive gates. It is especially fascinating to watch a tug push a colorful thousand-foot-long convoy of barges through the main lock chamber. The whole process takes about a half-hour.

Observation deck open daily.
(888) 343-6262
www.villageprofile.com/indiana/
perrycounty/perry2.html

19 Lincoln Boyhood National Memorial
Lincoln City

Thomas Lincoln, the president's father, had moved three times in Kentucky because of land-claim disputes. When he took his family across the Ohio River into Indiana in December 1816, he was searching for a more permanent homestead site. He found it near Little Pigeon Creek on a quarter section (160 acres) of government-surveyed land, a plot he had laid claim to earlier. Here the family finally settled down and remained for 14 years.

It was at Little Pigeon Creek in 1818 that Nancy Hanks Lincoln died, succumbing to "milksick," an illness caused by milk from cattle that had eaten the poisonous snakeroot.

Today the site of the Lincoln cabin is marked by bronze castings of sill logs and a stone hearth. Just beyond this, behind a split-rail fence, is a cabin reconstruction. It contains not only the homely and convincing clutter of a log table and benches, but also a trundle bed, spinning wheels, a fireplace with iron pots, a broom, and bunches of dried herbs. In a shed behind the cabin there is a smokehouse for preserving meat.

A few horses, sheep, and chickens complete the pleasant pioneer farm scene. Interpreters in period dress are at hand to answer one's questions.

Five bas-relief panels depicting scenes from Abraham Lincoln's life decorate the visitors center, an impressive white building that contains the Abraham Lincoln and the Nancy Hanks Lincoln halls, which are used for meetings, lectures, and conferences, and a small museum of pioneer life. A walkway leads from the center to the small hill where the president's mother is buried. An exhibition of prints that record the president's assassination and its results is worthwhile.

Open daily except Thanksgiving, Christmas, and New Year's Day.
(812) 937-4541
www.nps.gov/libo

Stone City. *Some of the houses here still appear just as they did when artist Grant Wood painted them in the 1930s (see page 117).*

Iowa

The natural wonders and appealing historic and scenic places provide another perspective on the state where the tall corn grows.

One of the many state parks is enjoyable both under and above the ground; another is named for the astonishing rocks found there; and a national monument preserves the mysterious legacy of prehistoric Indians. The farm where one family lived for 100 years is now a museum and crafts center. A second Iowa family has bequeathed an amazing assortment of musical instruments, which are now on display.

A museum village recalls life at the turn of the century. Nostalgia is further reinforced in an old-time drugstore and a collection of early telephone equipment. A replica of a village street includes a bank robbed by Jesse James, while a popular American artist is remembered in a town of rural charm. Early transportation is represented in a museum of antique aircraft. And ardent birders come to Iowa to see waterfowl by the hundreds of thousands each spring and fall.

1 Plymouth County Historical Museum

335 First Ave. SW, Le Mars
This intriguing museum's split personality adds to its interest. One part of the collection is devoted to local history. Several rooms have been furnished in the style of an 1890s middle-class home, and other rooms serve as replicas of period business offices. A large one-room log cabin from the Civil War era in Plymouth County stands nearby.

The other, more surprising dimension of the museum is the Parkinson Collection of antique and exotic musical instruments. Started in 1855, the collection has now been continued for several generations by the Parkinson family, and today it includes several hundred pieces. Among the exotica are nose flutes from Fiji, Irish battle harps, two-string Asian violins with resonators made from coconut shells, a violin made from bones by Spanish pirates, and giant African prayer drums two and a half feet in diameter. The most popular pieces are late 19th-century pump organs, a handsome collection of Swiss and American music boxes, and a European military horn with the bell extending back to allow its user to face the enemy while sounding calls to the troops behind him.
Open Tues.–Sun.
(712) 546-7002

3 Old Bradford Pioneer Village. *Two log cabins built in the 1850s, along with other buildings, re-create the atmosphere of this village that thrived as a supply center on the wagon route west.*

http://plymouthcountymuseum.
homestead.com/museum.html

2 Pharmacy Museum

The Pharmacists Mutual Companies, 808 Hwy. 18W, Algona
In 1902 a druggist in Titonka was burned out of his store. Unhappy with the settlement for his loss, he established his own insurance company. That company sells primarily to pharmacists, and over the years policyholders have donated early cabinets, scales, mortars and pestles, patent medicine bottles with embossed lettering, and similar objects to this museum, which successfully recaptures the atmosphere of an early 1900s drugstore.

A container once holding heroin and terpin hydrate for coughs, plus boxes of Gastrotone, Hollister's Golden Nugget Tablets, and Mother Gray's Sweet Powders, are reminders of the days when almost any compound could be sold over the counter. A 1910 crude drug sample case once used by medical students, an optometrist's kit with lenses, and a dispensing counter with an early Oliver typewriter and handwritten prescriptions are among the rarities displayed.

A fully equipped soda fountain setting, circa 1890, brings back to life the gentle years when a root beer was often placed on the marble counter with two straws. Today, all novelties are served up by a smiling soda jerk, recalling the days of old-fashioned favorites like cherry Cokes, Zingers, and Zombies.

Open weekdays except holidays year-round.

(800) 247-5930

www.phmic.com

3 Old Bradford Pioneer Village

Hwy. 346 E., Nashua

The village of Bradford, founded in the 1840s as an American Indian trading post, was named for a Winnebago chief. It continued to thrive for many years as a supply center on the wagon route west. But in the late 1800s the village was bypassed by the railroad, and eventually it was nearly abandoned.

Today 15 buildings, many moved to the village from nearby communities, re-create the atmosphere of the Plains in the 19th and early 20th centuries. Two log cabins built in the 1850s and appropriately furnished may be seen, together with a one-room schoolhouse, a doctor's office, an 1860s blacksmith's shop, and a general store where the 1902 price list shows hamburger for seven cents a pound and a 49-pound bag of flour for a mere $1.05.

The Old Bradford Train depot, brought from Fredericksburg, is especially interesting with its pot-bellied wood stove, rack of old timetables, Western Union office, and attached baggage room.

Open daily May–Oct.

Admission charged.

(641) 435-2567

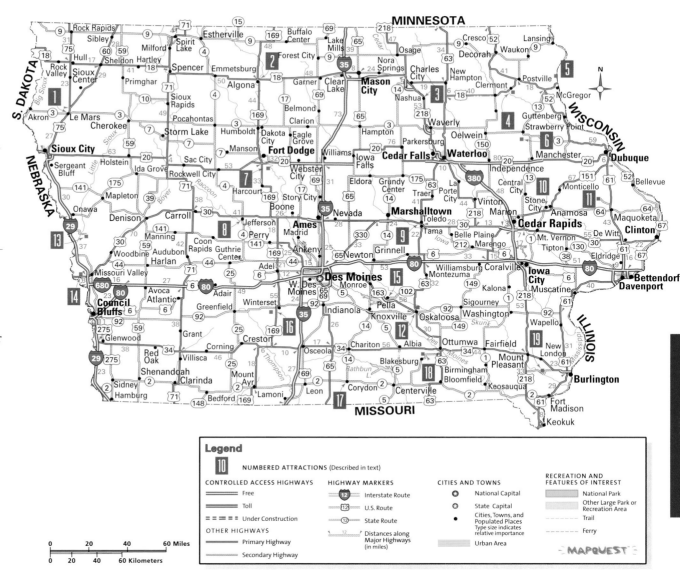

4 Montauk Historic Site

Clermont

It is odd to find a house in Iowa named for a lighthouse far away on New York's Long Island. But William Larrabee was an Easterner for whom Montauk Lighthouse was a symbol of safety, steering ships through perilous waters, and he felt that his home should serve the same function for his family. Larrabee, a wealthy miller and landowner who later became Iowa's governor, built this fine Italianate home in 1874.

The Larrabees, with their four daughters and three sons, were the only people ever to live in the house, and when daughter Anna died in 1965 at age 97, the house and everything in it was left to the state. All the furnishings, silver, china, toys, musical instruments, books, paintings, statuettes, photographs, and bric-a-brac belonged to the Larrabees.

Seldom does a house-museum so accurately reveal the taste and activities of one specific household. In any of the nine rooms

on display, one almost expects a family member to come walking in.

The outbuildings on the 80-acre estate include a laundry, creamery, well house, windmill, and workshop.

Open daily Memorial Day–Oct. 31; other times by arrangement for group tours.

Free admission.

(563) 423-7173

www.iowahistory.org

5 Effigy Mounds National Monument

3 miles north of Marquette on Hwy. 76

Dart points found locally attest to the presence of a primitive hunting people on these lands as far back as 12,000 years ago. But the fascination with this 2,526-acre national monument dates from more recent times.

Found here are 195 mounds of several types—linear, compound, conical, and effigy—and from several periods. The mounds shed light on a succession of cultures in this area from around 500 B.C. almost to historic times. The oldest (which include both linear and conical mounds) were created by American Indians of the Red Ocher culture, so called because they put their burials on a floor first sprinkled with red ocher (iron-ore dust).

Excavations of other mounds have revealed an assortment of elaborate grave goods fashioned from seashells, obsidian, and other unexpected materials obtained by far-reaching trade. The artifacts show the influence of the Hopewell culture, which centered in Ohio around 100 B.C. to about A.D. 400.

The most intriguing formations to see, however, are the 33 effigy mounds in the shapes of bears and birds in flight built by American Indians who farmed this land until about 1250. The Great Bear Mound is especially impressive, being 137 feet long, 70 feet wide from shoulder to foreleg, and more than 3 feet high.

A network of hiking trails connects the mound sites with scenic river overlooks. An abundance of birds following the Mississippi Flyway add to the pleasures of the outing. A brief orientation film is shown in the visitors center, where displays illustrate mound-building techniques and the coming of the white man. Ranger-guided tours of the mounds leave the visitors center on a regular schedule each day and take 90 minutes.

Open daily except Thanksgiving, Christmas, and New Year's Day.
(563) 873-3491
www.nps.gov/efmo

6 Backbone State Park

Dundee

A high quarter-mile "spine" of rock runs through the center of this scenic 2,000-acre state park, where some 20 miles of hiking trails offer excellent opportunities to explore caverns, climb natural rock stairways, and admire the tall white pines overhanging the cliffs. Deer, wild turkeys, raccoons, and an occasional coyote roam the land, and songbirds, including bluebirds, flit through the woods.

A lake offers swimming, and Richmond Spring at the north end of the park is stocked with trout. Paddleboats, canoes, and kayaks may be rented. Newly renovated cabins may be rented seasonally or year-round.

In winter the roads are not plowed out, and campers must either backpack in or use a snowmobile.

Open year-round. Admission charged.
(563) 924-2527
www.state.ia.us/dnr/organiza/ppd/backbone.html

7 Dolliver Memorial State Park

3.5 miles southeast of Lehigh

Creeks, ravines, forested hills, sandstone bluffs and outcroppings, and small patches of prairie make this 487-acre park a beautiful and varied place to explore. Especially intriguing is Boneyard Hollow at the park's northern end. A ravine about a quarter-mile long and 50 to 65 feet deep, it narrows down to a gash about 10 feet wide. Settlers reported finding many bones in the ravine, the remains of buffalo driven over the edge by American Indian hunters.

The sandstone bluffs, which are about 250 million years old, hold deposits of copperas, a sulfur and iron substance that was once prized by Indians for use in mixing face paint. You can get a good view of the copperas beds from the footbridge crossing Prairie Creek. The creek, which meanders through the hills to join the Des Moines River, passes beneath three Indian mounds—a linear ceremonial mound flanked by conical mounds that dates from about A.D. 1100.

Several steep hiking trails traverse the park beneath dense canopies of oak, maple, and other hardwoods. A boat ramp is provided for fishermen, who can expect to catch smallmouth bass plus channel, blue, and flathead catfish.

A campground stretches along a bluff above the river, and picnic tables are set on attractive grassy areas beside the park road. The park is named in honor of Jonathan P. Dolliver, an Iowan who served in Congress from 1888 until his death in 1910.

Open year-round. Admission charged.
(515) 359-2539
www.exploreiowaparks.com/dolliver.htm

8 Jefferson Telephone Company Museum

105 W. Harrison St., Jefferson

The imaginative precursors of the sleek, standardized telephone equipment we use today can be seen in this small museum in the basement of an independent telephone company building. Here you will see an 1880s voice box (the voice was transmitted by a string to a person not more than 100 feet away in the same building), a circa 1910 secretarial desk with a telephone mouthpiece, and a Gray Telephone Pay Station Company wall unit with slots for

5 Effigy Mounds National Monument. *The Great Bear Mound, outlined in lime for this aerial photograph, was built by American Indians who farmed this land until about 1250.*

silver dollars, half-dollars, and three other coin denominations.

Also worth seeing in Jefferson is the Greene County Courthouse, a magnificent Beaux Arts structure built in 1917 and listed on the *National Register of Historic Places*. Standing beside the courthouse is the modern 162-foot Mahanay Bell Tower, whose 32 bells play musical selections several times daily. In the summer you can take an elevator to the tower's observation deck, where the view extends for 25 miles.

Museum open weekdays.
Free admission.
(515) 386-4141
www.jeffersoniowa.com

9 Tama County Historical Museum

200 N. Broadway, Toledo
Constructed in 1869, the solid brick building now housing this museum of local history served as the county jail for 100 years before being converted to its present use. It was listed on the *National Register of Historic Places* in 1981. It is also home to the Tracers Genealogical Society.

The first floor now houses artifacts from the local Mesquakie Indians as well as a music room, rural school room, patriotic room, and school records room used by settlers. The second floor, however, preserves the mood and interior of the old jail. Four cells may be visited: two women's cells, a maximum-security cell, and one that dramatizes the chilling isolation of solitary confinement.

Displays of military uniforms, historical photographs, and memorabilia from the offices of early doctors, dentists, lawyers, and bankers are also on view. One room is devoted to the finery of

prairie life, such as china, ladies' fashions, and the prized beaver hats that men wore for dress.

The basement has two tool and machinery displays as well as an early 1900s funeral parlor display.
Open Tues.–Sat. except holidays.
(641) 484-6767
www.tamatoledonews.com/
tamacountytodayarchive

10 Stone City

Once a thriving center for limestone quarrying, as the name implies, this community started to decline around the turn of the century when cement began to replace stone as a favored construction material. But the artist Grant Wood (1892–1942) brought a brief moment of renewal when he chose the village as the site of the Stone City Colony and Art School in 1932–33. Wood was widely known for his canvases *American Gothic* and *Stone City* and other stylized renderings of rural Midwest life.

On a hill overlooking the village and the pastoral countryside stands the shell of the huge Victorian mansion that served as the colony's headquarters. Eight-week courses in sculpture, figure drawing, and other subjects were given here for $36, and dormitory lodging was provided for $1.50 a week. The mansion served as a summer camp and as a part-time residence until 1963, when the interior was gutted by fire.

Today Stone City's past is softly echoed by its handsome 19th-century stone residences. Time, in these environs, seems to slow down, and there is little to disturb the pervading calm. Tours are available through the Jones County Tourism Association.

On the second Sunday in June each year the Grant Wood Art

10 Stone City. *Artist Grant Wood painted scenes of the rolling countryside here.*

Festival attracts many artists and craftsmen who display their creations outside an 1880s stone horse barn. During the festival a collection of early photographs, tools, and other memorabilia may be viewed in an 1860s stone blacksmith's shop that is not otherwise open to the public. Nostalgia is further summoned by the replicated ice wagons parked on the hillside. Colorful vehicles such as these (reminiscent of gypsy caravans) were once used to house the art students.
Admission charged for festival.
Jones County Tourism:
(800) 383-0831
www.jonescountytourism.com

11 Maquokete Caves State Park

7 miles northwest of Maquokete on Iowa 428
A network of 13 caves runs beneath this park, and as early as 1835, explorers cut their names into the limestone walls. These chambers range from 30 feet to more than 800 feet in length. Some are lighted and have walkways, but experienced spelunkers

using flashlights may enjoy the challenge of several unlighted caves. The temperature stays at about 50°F.

For visitors more interested in aboveground activities, there are birds, wildflowers, shady forests, and scenic views to enjoy. Great horned and barred owls, red-tailed hawks, and hummingbirds can be found in the stands of oak, ash, hickory, and maple. Columbines, bloodroot, may apples, hepaticas, and the endangered monkshood share ground space with morels. Picking the mushrooms is allowed.

Hikers in all seasons can enjoy some six miles of trails in the park, leading to overlooks with views of the steep ravine that is a dominant feature here, and to a natural bridge, which stands almost 50 feet above Raccoon Creek. A trail in the western area of the park takes hikers past a restored prairie, a wildlife food plot, and an experimental savanna restoration.
Open daily year-round.
Admission charged.
(563) 652-5833
www.state.ia.us/dnr/organiza/ppd/
maqucav.html

12 Nelson Pioneer Farm

*Glendale Rd. E., off
Rte. 63 N., Oskaloosa*

The Nelson family farmed this land for 114 years. The sturdy brick house, furnished as it was in the mid-1800s, and the big barn with all its equipment are the nucleus of this memorial to 19th-century farm and community life.

A charming country store displays a typical selection of early-day merchandise. The small voting house with its curtained booth and kerosene lamps is believed to be the first built west of the Mississippi solely for voting purposes.

There's a furnished 1867 log cabin, and a post office with several names still visible on the backs of combination lockboxes. A one-room schoolhouse, furnished as it was in 1911, has a slate on every desk and a corner stool with a dunce cap awaiting the reluctant scholar.

The museum building contains early coal-mining tools, a superb 1874 round table made from 3,000 pieces of 50 different Iowa woods, vintage toy trains, and American Indian artifacts. In a plot near the museum is a touching tribute to faithful animals: the headstones marking the graves of Becky and Jenny, two mules that served in the Civil War and then came to the farm.

Open Tues.–Sat., May 1–Oct. 12.
(641) 672-2989
www.nelsonpioneer.org

13 Preparation Canyon State Park

5 miles southwest of Moorhead
Under the leadership of Charles B. Thompson in 1853, 60 Mormon families took leave of a wagon train on its way to Utah to farm this fertile hill country. Guided by Thompson, they set up the town of Preparation and began a "School of Preparation for the Life Beyond." Actually, they were preparing for a swindle by their leader, to whom they had deeded all their property. For three years Thompson grew wealthy on the labor of his followers, until finally they lost faith in his religious purity and demanded their property back. Thompson refused, was driven out, and disappeared, leaving confusion over the land titles that took 10 years to resolve. For a while the settlement thrived, but by 1900 it was dead.

The park now has 344 acres, including the site of Preparation, much of it sold to the state by descendants of the original settlers. The canyon is in a secluded part of the park, which is enclosed by a scallop of ridges. Its loess soil—a rare windblown dirt—invites nature studies along several steep hiking trails. Red foxes, deer, wild turkeys, and coyotes make their homes on the forested slopes. Red-tailed and Cooper's hawks, quails, great horned owls, and many songbirds may also be seen.

14 DeSoto National Wildlife Refuge. *Every spring and fall, snow geese are attracted to this refuge, where grasslands, woodlands, and wetlands provide them with an inviting habitat.*

Park roads open Apr.–Nov.
Use fee charged.
(712) 423-2829
**www.state.ia.us/dnr/
organiza/ppd/prepcan.html**

14 DeSoto National Wildlife Refuge

Missouri Valley
This inviting refuge flanks DeSoto Lake, actually a seven-mile-long oxbow of the Missouri River, isolated in 1960 by a levee and a new channel cut across the bend by the U.S. Army Corps of Engineers. The refuge is a popular destination for birders during spring and autumn, when more than half a million geese and ducks may stop over. Much of this former corn land has been converted to grassland, woodland, and wetland to provide diverse habitat for wildlife.

Quails, pheasants, Eastern meadowlarks, American woodcocks, and many songbirds are also drawn to this peaceful setting amid cottonwoods, prairiegrass, and lakeside vegetation.

A 12-stop auto tour of the refuge (detailed in a free interpretive folder) begins at the visitors center, where a windowed gallery on the lake offers a marvelous vantage point for viewing great numbers of migratory waterfowl.

The center also has a museum of well-preserved objects recovered in 1968-69 from the steamboat *Bertrand,* which sank in the Missouri in 1865 and became entombed in silt and sand as the river shifted course. Her 150-ton cargo included blasting fuses for the Montana goldfields, bottles of schnapps, brandy, and champagne, plus American Indian trade goods, dinnerware, glass tumblers, and even clothing.

At the last stop on this route, a short trail brings you to a platform overlooking the location where the *Bertrand* was excavated and, after the removal of her cargo, reburied.

Refuge open daily.
(712) 642-4121
http://midwest.fws.gov/desoto

15 Pella Historical Village

Located one block east of downtown Pella
Within the town of Pella, this charming and authentic area offers travelers a chance to visit the Netherlands without having to cross the Atlantic. In 1847 the Rev. Dominie Scholte led a group of immigrants out of Holland in search of religious freedom. They landed in Iowa and named their town Pella, or "refuge." Nestled in a courtyard laced with red brick walkways and beautiful gardens, 21 buildings, some more than 140 years old, preserve Pella's history and Dutch traditions.

Highlights include a traditional *werkplaats* (wooden shoe shop), a working gristmill, a Dutch bakery, a Dutch street organ, and the boyhood home of U.S. lawman Wyatt Earp. There's also an authentic Dutch windmill, built to mark the millennium. Inside the windmill an elevator carries visitors up to a platform for a wonderful view.

Open year-round except Sundays and holidays.
Admission charged.
(641) 628-4311
www.pellatuliptime.com/minivil/html

16 Pammel State Park
Madison County
Set in hilly upland country, this tranquil 350-acre park has two major features: a long limestone ridge called Devil's Backbone and Middle River, which flows north along one side of the ridge, makes a sharp turn, and then re-enters the park on the other side of the ridge, flowing in a southeasterly direction. A picturesque tunnel burrowing through the ridge once carried water to a nearby gristmill. It has since become Iowa's only road tunnel. The road leads past a pleasant picnic area at the riverside. The park has three other picnic areas as well, including one on top of the ridge.

Foot trails circle through the woods, which harbor wild turkeys, hawks, deer, foxes, coyotes, and many rabbits. Fishing, mushroom picking, and modern camping are the other attractions here.

The park is in Madison County, which has six covered bridges. The best preserved is the 1870 Donahoe Bridge in Winterset's city park. Two more of these timbered spans are nearby. All bear a striking resemblance to their counterparts in New England.

Open year-round.
(515) 462-3536
www.madisoncountyparks.org

17 Prairie Trails Museum of Wayne County
Hwy. 2, East Corydon
Although the exterior of this museum is austere, it is full of surprises.

The major attraction is the re-creation of Main Street in a typical Wayne County village of the late 19th century, with a general store, doctor's office, barbershop, jail, courtroom, dentist's office, beauty salon, and post office. There's even a replica of the Corydon bank that Jesse James robbed, including the safe actually involved in the robbery.

A highlight of the historical collection is a life-size diorama showing a Mormon family heading west in a covered wagon drawn by two oxen.

Outside, a small park contains a one-room log cabin with a loft. An exhibit of antique vehicles includes a charming horse-drawn yellow school bus.

Open daily Apr.–Oct. Admission charged.
(641) 872-2211

18 Antique Airplane Association and The Airpower Museum
Bluegrass Rd. (Hwy. 41), northeast of Blakesburg
The aircraft made before the advent of retractable landing gear, streamlining, and jet engines have a special sculptural beauty. Flying them, especially in an open cockpit, is in a class by itself, and so devoted pilots started an association here in 1953. The group's field, with its two grass landing strips and row of hangars, has become headquarters for over 22

chapters of the nationwide association, plus 11 type clubs.

The adjacent Airpower Museum presents a history of aviation and includes miniature models of combat aircraft up through World War II. In the collection of 25 operational aircraft are a 1931 Stinson Junior S. monoplane, a 1925 Anderson biplane, and a 1929 Fairchild 71 Pan Am airliner.

Open weekdays and P.M. weekends except Thanksgiving, Christmas, New Year's Day, and Labor Day.
Admission free but donations encouraged.
(641) 938-2773
www.aaa-apm.org

19 Geode State Park
6 miles north of New London
The park and 186-acre lake are named for the curious rocks formerly discovered in abundance here. Geodes are found in many places and can be purchased in most rock shops. But how amazing it must have been for the first person to break open one of these dull-looking spherical rocks and see the colorful crystalline formations inside.

The 1,640-acre park is popular with fishermen, who try for large- and small-mouth bass, bluegills, crappies, and tiger muskies up to 3 feet long. A 300-foot beach with an offshore float attracts swimmers, and there are puffy winds to challenge small-boat sailors.

Good camping facilities and nice hiking trails recommend this quiet area to anyone interested in nature. The main trail begins at the north end of the lake and follows all the way to the dam. Parts of the trail are highlighted in a printed brochure available upon request. Hickory, hornbeam, oak, American elm, and black walnut are prevalent in the woods.

In winter, cross-country skiers use the hiking trails and are often able to cross the frozen lake. Sledding, snowmobiling, and ice fishing are other cold-weather activities to be enjoyed. Crowds may be a problem on holiday weekends.

Open year-round.
(319) 392-4601
www.state.ia.us/dnr/organiza/ppd/geode.html

18 Antique Airplane Association and The Airpower Museum. *The museum houses a collection of 25 operational aircraft from the 1920s and 1930s, when flying was more an art than a science.*

Last Indian Raid Museum. *A monument stands at the site in Oberlin where displaced Northern Cheyenne Indians raided a pioneer town.*

Kansas

Among the wooded hills and rolling plains are memories of Spanish adventurers, American Indians, pioneers, and those who stayed to work the land.

The first white men in this area were the conquistadors who came seeking gold—unsuccessfully—in 1541. Their peaceful meeting with the American Indians is commemorated in a museum in Lyons. Also recalled, in other museums and through the remains of old army posts, are the inevitable conflicts between the American Indians and the pioneers heading west and those who settled here. An original Pony Express station, remnants of the Santa Fe Trail, and a vast expanse of unplowed prairie are further reminders of the early days in Kansas.

Another important highlight is the Agricultural Hall of Fame, recalling the men and machines that helped make this state the breadbasket of the nation.

1 Last Indian Raid Museum
258 S. Penn Ave., Oberlin
The "last Indian raid" in Kansas refers to the tale of some 300 displaced Northern Cheyenne Indians who wanted to return to their ancestral home.

Forcibly removed to a camp in what is now Oklahoma, they were sick, hungry, and despondent. In September 1878 some 100 warriors with their wives and children escaped and headed north through Kansas with the U.S. Army in pursuit. As they approached Sappa Creek, they recalled that three years before, 27 of their people had been slaughtered there. Between Sept. 30–Oct. 1, the Cheyennes raided the area, killed 30 people, and moved on. A number of the Cheyennes were later killed, and the survivors were sent to a reservation in Montana.

The 13-building museum contains a few relics from the raid, such as war clubs, arrowheads, and a settler's revolver. The museum also houses a variety of late 19th- and early 20th-century displays: rooms with typical period furnishings, a doctor's and dentist's office, a barbershop, and a music room with a player piano. A sod house pays tribute to pioneer life.
Open Tues.–Sat., Apr.–Nov. except holidays. Admission charged.
(785) 475-2712
www.indianraidmuseum.org

4 Pawnee Indian Village State Historic Site. *A diorama depicts the life of the Pawnee people who lived in the village, now known as the Republic, until 1830.*

2 Gallery of the Also-Rans
Mezzanine of the First State Bank in Norton
Founded in 1965, this memorial hall was established by a local banker with a passion for Americana—with a twist. Inside a working bank, trivia buffs will find photographs and colorful capsule biographies of unsuccessful candidates for president—as in president of the United States. Spanning White House history from Thomas Jefferson to George Bush, losers like Horatio Seymour and Rufus King share the walls with famous men like eventual winner Andrew Jackson (who lost to John Quincy Adams in 1824) and *New York Times* publisher Horace Greeley. In addition to his run for president, Greeley earned local notoriety for once spending the night at a bustling stagecoach station just outside Norton. A replica of this very station, Station 15, appointed with period furnishings, stands in a roadside park beside Highway 36. Legend has it that Station 15 was also a resting stop for Buffalo Bill and Billy the Kid.
Open year-round, during banking hours.
(785) 877-3341
www.firstatebank.com

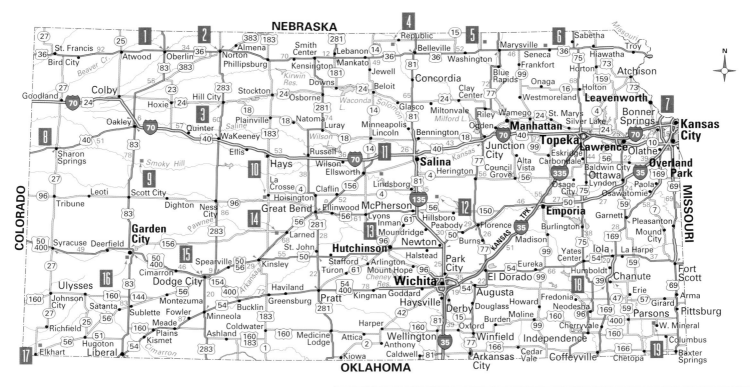

NEBRASKA

COLORADO

MISSOURI

OKLAHOMA

N

Hill City Oil Museum
Hill City

This museum, featuring items devoted to the petroleum industry, lies in the heart of the oil-producing area of Graham County, which boomed in the late 1930s and 1940s. The look of the "oil patch" is evident in the yard, where cable-tool equipment and a pumping jack are installed.

Inside, a replica of a cabletool derrick, along with other 1892 vintage equipment from Neodesha, Kansas, contrasts dramatically with the working scale model of a modern rig. Early boom days are depicted by photos of the Spindletop Field (Beaumont, Texas) and pen-and-ink drawings of other notable fields.

There are several exhibits that should not be missed: one display of a geological cross section gives an in-depth example of how wells were cored from the different rock formations, and another is a diorama

of geological history portraying oil and gas formations from the Paleozoic to the Cenozoic eras, illustrating the different procedures in oil exploration.
Open daily year-round.
Borrow key at Western Hills Motel across the street.
(785) 421-5621
www.ruraltel.net/gced/oil.htm

Pawnee Indian Village State Historic Site
Republic
Built on a grassy knoll overlooking the tree-lined Republican River, this fascinating museum encloses the site of an excavated Pawnee two-family dwelling. Of the 30 to 40 houses in a village of

some 1,000 people, this was one of the largest, with nearly 2,000 square feet of floor space.

The village was probably abandoned in 1830 when its inhabitants decided to join other Pawnees in what is now Nebraska. Ashes from the residents' last fire still remain in the hearth, and tools, weapons, and corn lie exactly as found during the excavation; in the fire-hardened earth floor, you can see the 218 holes for the posts that supported a framework of willow poles and a covering of earth and grass.

Exhibits representing various aspects of American Indian life

include artwork, bone and metal tools, and weapons and pipes. One diorama depicts a buffalo hunt—in summer and winter the Pawnees rode southwest to the High Plains in quest of these animals. Yet another describes Pawnee astronomy.

In the six-acre fenced area behind the museum, you can see 22 other lodge sites and the remains of a sod-and-timber wall that had surrounded the village.
Open Wed.–Sun. except holidays.
(785) 361-2255
www.kshs.org

0 20 40 60 Miles
0 20 40 60 Kilometers

Legend

10 NUMBERED ATTRACTIONS (Described in text)

CONTROLLED ACCESS HIGHWAYS
Free
Toll
Under Construction

OTHER HIGHWAYS
Primary Highway
Secondary Highway

HIGHWAY MARKERS
12 Interstate Route
12 U.S. Route
12 State Route
Distances along Major Highways (in miles)

CITIES AND TOWNS
National Capital
State Capital
Cities, Towns, and Populated Places Type size indicates relative importance
Urban Area

RECREATION AND FEATURES OF INTEREST
National Park
Other Large Park or Recreation Area
Trail
Ferry

5 Hollenberg Station State Historic Site

2889 23rd Rd., Hanover

During the days of the Pony Express (April 1860–October 1861), its riders galloped into the history and folklore of America.

In 1859 St. Joseph, Missouri, was the Western terminus of telegraph and railroad communication, and mail destined for the West Coast depended upon stagecoaches and mule trains. The Pony Express feat of delivering mail from St. Joseph to Sacramento, California, in 10 days (less than half the previous best time) required 120 riders, 400 horses, and a relay station every 10 to 15 miles. The operation ended when the transcontinental telegraph line was completed.

This National Historic Landmark is the only unaltered relay station still standing in its original location. Built in 1858 by rancher Gerat Hollenberg, the sturdy, weather-beaten structure served as home, general store, post office, hotel, and stagecoach stop on the Oregon-California Trail. It was also the westernmost Pony Express station in Kansas.

Here you can get the feel of the Pony Express and stagecoach businesses and see the general store with its ox shoes, bows and arrows, powder horns, kitchen utensils, and branding irons. Climbing the steep steps to the rough-planked attic, you follow the bootsteps of the Pony Express riders and stagecoach passengers who slept there. There are picnic tables and a small playground in a wooded eight-acre setting.

Open Wed.–Sun. except holidays.
(785) 337-2635
www.kshs.org

6 Fort Markley

Seneca

Approaching Fort Markley, you might think it was an old frontier ghost town, and you would not be far from wrong. The livery stable, general store, bank, and other vintage buildings have all been moved here from extinct pioneer towns. Behind their rough lumber exteriors are many intriguing artifacts.

The rustic Buffalo Café on West Highway 36 looks like an old Western saloon. It displays numerous pioneer relics and has several life-size mannequins of American Indians sitting in chairs.

The nearest Pony Express station was less than a mile away in Seneca, and the trail crossed the Fort Markley property. A short walk across the pasture takes you to the place where a creek had been dammed to create a watering spot for Pony Express horses.

A campground adjacent to the frontier buildings has sites with full electrical hookups and a small lake.

Open year-round. No admission charged for frontier buildings.
(785) 336-2285
www.ku.edu/Kansas/Seneca/tourism/attract/attract.html

7 The National Center and Agricultural Hall of Fame

630 Hall of Fame Dr., Bonner Springs

The center pays homage to the skillful, hardworking farmers who have made Americans the best-fed people in the world. The exhibits are housed in two main buildings set on 172 acres of beautiful rolling countryside.

In the center, which has one of the greatest collections of agricultural equipment in the country, visitors can see Harry Truman's plow, a 307-piece set of antique woodworking tools, and hand-operated milk-processing machines.

Hall-of-Famers include George Washington, Thomas Jefferson, Cyrus McCormick, George Washington Carver, Eli Whitney, and 30 other agriculturists.

You can also visit FarmTown, an early 1900s farming community with farmstead, one-room school, smithy, country store, train depot, and hatchery.

For a change of pace, one can climb aboard the narrow-gauge railroad that circles FarmTown or amble down a mile-long wooded nature trail.

Open Mon.–Sat. and P.M. Sun., Apr.–Nov. Admission charged.
(913) 721-1075
www.aghalloffame.com

8 Fort Wallace Memorial Museum

Wallace

Fort Wallace was one of a string of army posts established to control the Plains Indians and protect travelers along the Smoky Hill Trail. Active from 1865 to 1881, it was built for about 500 soldiers and was the busiest bastion in Kansas.

Nothing remains of the old fort except the cemetery. The museum, located about one and a half miles from the fort site, is a treasury of locally found artifacts. Here you'll see old military equipment, as well as a painted American Indian buffalo robe, a player piano, a collection of barbed wire, and cowboy equipment. Also on view is a Union Pacific depot from Weskan, complete with telegraph, switch equipment, and signal tower.

Open daily May–Oct. 1. Admission free but donations encouraged.
(785) 891-3564
www.fortwallace.org

8 Fort Wallace Memorial Museum. *A cemetery stands at the site of the fort, active from 1865 to 1881, created to protect travelers along the Smoky Hill Trail. Built for about 500 soldiers, it was the busiest bastion in Kansas.*

9 Monument Rocks

From Oakley, 20 miles south on U.S. 83, 7.5 miles south and east on Jayhawk Rd.

Rising abruptly above the treeless plain of the Smoky Hill River, the 60-foot-high "monuments" look like lonely sentinels. Sculpted over the years by wind and water erosion, many have crenellated tops like castle battlements.

The rocks graduate in color from pale gray at the bottom to gold at their peaks. They are composed of soft cretaceous chalk from the sediment of an ancient sea, and their layered formations abound with fossils.

Numbering fewer than a dozen, the towers are found in an area about a quarter-mile long and 200 yards wide. These distinctive formations served as landmarks for early wagon trains and military parties as they trekked the arduous journey westward from Kansas to Colorado along the Smoky Hill Trail. The area has now been designated as a National Natural Monument.

The plain, a semiarid prairie covered with native grasses, sage, thistle, yucca, sunflowers, and tumbleweed, is home to various animals, including antelope, jackrabbits, and small lizards, as well as a few cattle in fenced pastures.

This area also once contained fossils of shark's teeth, vertebras, and oyster shells. These unique and eclectic items can be viewed at the nearby Fick Fossil and History Museum.

(785) 672-4862
www.oakleykansas.com/fick/
monrocks.html

11 Mushroom Rock State Park. *The persistent winds that blew across the Great Plains for thousands of years carved away the soft sandstone here, sculpting it into dramatic mushroom shapes.*

10 Kansas Barbed Wire Museum and Post Rock Museum

LaCrosse

When Joseph F. Glidden patented a barbed wire "lighter than air, stronger than whiskey, and cheaper than dirt," the fate of the Great Plains was sealed. The open range was transformed into fenced farmland, and the sod-busting farmer was now able to confine his livestock and protect his homestead and crops from free-ranging cattle.

Glidden's success spurred innovative competition to create new patterns, and by 1883–40 companies were making barbed wire. The museum presents this history, together with more than 2,000 varieties of the wire. One of the most unusual exhibits in the museum's collection is an authentic raven's nest built primarily of barbed wire.

Of equal importance to frontier life were the posts used to support the wire. Wood was too scarce in 19th-century Kansas to use for fence posts. Creative settlers found a solution by making posts of soft limestone, which hardens in the sun.

Slabs of the limestone, which is abundant in Kansas, were quarried and split into stone posts averaging five to six feet long. About 40,000 miles of post-rock fence cross this section of Kansas, bestowing upon the region a distinctive character.

In the Post Rock Museum you'll see tools used to make the posts, as well as a miniature quarry showing how the limestone was stripped and cut to size.

Both museums open daily May–Sept.
(785) 222-2719 or (785) 222-9900
www.rushcounty.org

11 Mushroom Rock State Park

West of Salina.
From Rte. 141 go 2.3 miles west on gravel road.

The effects of wind erosion are widespread in the Great Plains but nowhere more apparent than at this five-acre site.

Swooping off the wheat fields and pastureland, these persistent and sometimes violently swirling winds have gradually shaved away the ground of soft sandstone, leaving small islands of resistant sandstone and gradually sculpting them into huge, dramatic mushroom shapes.

The two largest are approximately 25 feet tall, with caps about 15 feet wide. These rocks once served as meeting places and landmarks for American Indians and early pioneers, such as Kit Carson and John C. Fremont.

A gentle brook meanders through the area, shaded by oaks, cottonwoods, and elms. North of the brook you'll find some man-made art—a rock carving of a U.S. flag with 15 stripes—probably the work of pioneer travelers pausing on their westward trek.

The small park has picnic tables. A few miles to the south are the two areas of the popular Kanopolis State Park. The extensive recreational facilities in its more than 22,000 acres include swimming, boating, and fishing on Kanopolis Lake, as well as many land-based activities such as hiking and horseback riding.

Both parks open year-round.
Admission charged for Kanopolis.
For both parks: (785) 546-2565
www.kdwp.state.ks.us

12 Maxwell Wildlife Refuge and McPherson State Lake

From Canton go 6 miles north on McPherson County Rd. 304, then left 1.2 miles to refuge headquarters.
Descendants of the American buffalo are still at home on this range of rolling grassland. Indeed, they thrive so well in this habitat that their numbers are controlled, kept to about 200 by auctioning off the surplus following the annual roundup. The auction is held at the refuge corral in the middle of November, and visitors are welcome.

From the observation tower just outside the fenced territory of the buffalo, you have a good chance of seeing the animals and perhaps glimpsing some of the 40 elk that also roam these 2,800 acres.

The gravel roads provide excellent views of this rolling prairie and wooded ravines. The 46-acre lake on the refuge (made by damming Gypsum Creek) has a boat dock and a ramp; anglers are rewarded with bass, crappie, fish, pike, and bluegill. A campground is pleasantly situated on the lake's western shore.

Open year-round; tours are offered by reservation only. Admission free.
(800) 324-8022
www.cyberkraft.com/maxwell

13 Coronado-Quivira Museum

105 W. Lyon, Lyons
Lured by the lust for gold, the Spanish conquistador Don Francisco Vasquez de Coronado carried his quest for the Seven Cities of Cibola, the fabled golden cities, northward from Mexico into what is now New Mexico. He found no gold, but the native Pueblo Indians encouraged him to go on

13 Coronado-Quivira Museum. *A model of a grass hut used by Quivira-Wichita people is on display here, as well as items left behind by Spanish conquistadors.*

to the "Kingdom of Quivira." Pushing on, Coronado made his way into central Kansas in the mid-1500s to the promised kingdom and further disappointment: There was no gold at all.

This museum commemorates that expedition with exhibits of Quivira pottery, arrowheads, stone tools, and beads, as well as original chain mail, replicas of helmets, spurs, and other items left behind by Coronado's soldiers. Also shown is a model of a Quivira-Wichita American Indian grass hut.

The walls are hung with two outstanding mural-sized paintings. The *Dawn of a New Era* depicts Coronado meeting with the Quivira Indians by their grass-hut village. The other painting shows the Spanish adventurer leading his men.
Open daily year-round except major holidays.
(620) 257-3941

14 Fort Larned National Historic Site

Six miles west of Larned on State Rte. 156
As a principal guardian of the Santa Fe Trail, Fort Larned provided military escort for wagon

trains, stagecoaches, and travelers from 1859 to 1878.

The original sod and adobe structures were replaced in 1868 with nine durable sandstone-and-timber buildings enclosing the traditional parade ground. Still standing much in their original condition, they offer a realistic glimpse into military life on the Western frontier.

One of the barracks, converted into a museum and visitors center, features numerous relics, infantry and cavalry uniforms, a life-size model of a 10th Cavalry soldier leading his mount with full equipment and regalia, and some excellent American Indian artifacts and photographs of prominent chiefs as well.

An easy mile-long history trail takes you past the sites of the old barracks and other abandoned buildings, the corral, and the station that originally received the stagecoach mail.
Open daily except Thanksgiving, Christmas, and New Year's Day. Admission charged.
(620) 285-6911
www.nps.gov/fols

15 The Santa Fe Trail at Dodge City

Nine miles west of Dodge City on Hwy. 50
The best preserved section of the fabled Santa Fe Trail remains carved in the windswept, grass-covered prairie nine miles west of Dodge City.

In the mid-1800s this trail, stretching 780 miles from Franklin, Missouri, to Santa Fe, New Mexico, was the most important artery of commerce in the development of the Southwest. A single wagon train might number 400 to 500 wagons and carry more than $1 million dollars' worth of merchandise for the settlers in this part of the country and in Mexico.

Despite a century's erosion, the trail is still clearly marked. In some places here the grooves are as much as three feet deep. It is apparent that the trail was not one single lane but numerous parallel tracks, so that several ranks of traffic—freight wagons, stagecoaches, horses, soldiers, and cattle—could travel side by side for protection. More than a dozen separate pathways are evident in the 300-foot width of the trail.

Now listed on the *National Register of Historic Sites,* this area has never been plowed and probably looks much as it did when the trail was at its busiest.
Accessible year-round, weather permitting.
(800) 653-9378
www.visitdodgecity.org

16 Finney Game Refuge

785 S. Business Hwy. 83, Garden City
In what was once the heart of the great American bison range, these 3,670 acres provide shelter for a

herd of more than 120 buffalo.

These monarchs of the plains, officially designated the Kansas state animal, once numbered some 60 to 70 million. Their wanton slaughter during the 19th century reduced them to only a few hundred. This herd was established in 1924 with one bull and two cows. Thanks to similar refuges and privately owned herds in the United States and Canada, there are now more than 350,000 of these great shaggy beasts grazing in safety.

This herd usually grazes at some distance from the headquarters, on the south bank of the Arkansas River, but visitors can get a close look and take photos on a 60-minute tour.

Viewing by tour only. Accessible daily by appointment, except major holidays.
(620) 276-9400 or (888) 445-4663 with PIN No. 9400
www.gcnet.com/fofgr

17 Cimarron National Grassland
Elkhart

After the bitter lesson of dust bowls in the 1930s, the U.S. government established this and similar reserves to protect native plants and wildlife and restore badly eroded land to its natural state.

Here on 108,175 acres divided by the Cimarron River, native grasses have been seeded and new sources of water developed. More than 400 oil and gas wells coexist with some 5,000 head of cattle grazed by permit. Elk, white-tailed and mule deer, antelope, coyotes, wild turkeys, and pheasants are among the creatures at home here.

The area is also a natural habitat for the lesser prairie chicken, and on a spring morning or evening the chickens' colorful courting ritual may be seen from observation blinds.

You can see it all, including 150 windmills, on a three-hour, 50-mile self-guiding auto tour. An overlook at Point of Rocks offers views of the grassland itself and the Cimarron, which is dry most of the year. A short distance east is Middle Spring, a life-saving oasis on the Santa Fe Trail, where wagon ruts can still be seen.

Visitors are permitted to camp anywhere but are asked to avoid watering spots used by livestock in order not to disrupt them. A picnic ground on the banks of the Cimarron has drinking water and restrooms. Maps and information are available at the U.S. Forest Service office in Elkhart, just south of the reserve.

Open year-round.
(620) 697-4621
www.fs.fed.us/r2/psicc/cim

17 Cimarron National Grassland. *A 50-mile self-guiding auto tour takes visitors past 150 windmills near the Santa Fe Trail.*

18 Martin and Osa Johnson Safari Museum
Downtown Chanute

In the first half of the 20th century, Martin and Osa Johnson, an intrepid young couple from Kansas, captured the nation's imagination through their films and books of adventure in exotic, faraway lands. From 1917 through 1936, they traveled to Africa, Borneo, and the South Pacific islands documenting their experiences.

Through popular movies such as *Simba* (1928) and *Baboona* (1935), and best-selling books such as *I Married Adventure* (1940), Martin and Osa spurred widespread interest in camera safaris and African wildlife conservation.

Located in Osa's hometown of Chanute, the Safari Museum was established in 1961 with a core collection of the couple's photographs, manuscripts, and personal belongings. In 1993 the museum relocated to Chanute's renovated Santa Fe train depot as part of a $2 million project. Within its four main touring areas, visitors will find a variety of educational programs, including a 30-seat theater, an African gallery featuring masks and headdresses, an art gallery, a library with more than 10,000 volumes, and a model safari camp.

Open year-round except New Year's Day, Easter, Independence Day, Thanksgiving, and Christmas. Admission charged.
(620) 431-2730
www.safarimuseum.com

19 Big Brutus
Six miles west of junction of K7 & K10, near West Mineral.

In the heart of the Mined Land Wildlife Area, "Big Brutus" looks like a creature designed for a science fiction movie. At one time the second largest electric shovel in the world, the Bucyrus Erie model 1850B stands 16 stories tall (160 feet) and weighs a whopping 11 million pounds. Visitors come from all over for the ultimate thrill: a chance to climb to the top of its boom, which is a staggering 150 feet long, with a dipper that can fill three railroad cars. This mining monster was built in 1962 at a cost of $6.5 million and was retired in 1974 when it was no longer economically feasible to mine high-sulfur coal. Yet Big Brutus lives on through a non-profit corporation dedicated to the mining heritage of Southeast Kansas.

In addition to Big Brutus itself, visitors to the museum can see a 1920 Page dragline used by the Wilkinson Coal Company. Then there's "Little Giant," the world's smallest working replica of an early-day electric mining shovel. For those eager to stay awhile, the Big Brutus visitors center offers picnic tables and comfort facilities—complete with hot showers.

Open year-round except Thanksgiving and Christmas. Admission charged.
(620) 827-6177
www.bigbrutus.org

Pennyrile State Resort Park. *Several trails wind through this park, named for a wildflower, the pennyroyal (see page 128).*

The prehistory of this area is recalled by Mississippian Indian mounds and the bones of beasts, now extinct, that came to the salt licks, became mired in the bog, and perished there.

In the days of the pioneers, Daniel Boone explored the Appalachian Range, and evidence of his personal courage and wilderness skills still remains.

In Kentucky you can see where Abraham Lincoln was born, where a country doctor performed a famous operation, a historic log meetinghouse, the world's largest cave system, and some lovely parks. A gristmill and an iron furnace are reminders of early industry; and a tiny, remote community still stands in tribute to a hardy breed of Kentuckians.

Kentucky

The state where Daniel Boone blazed a trail to the West was also the birthplace of Abraham Lincoln.

1 Wickliffe Mounds Research Center
Rte. 51/60

Between A.D. 1100 and 1350 the bluffs at the confluence of the Ohio and Mississippi rivers were occupied by a mound-building people of the Mississippian culture. But like other mound centers of the central Mississippi Valley, it had been abandoned by the time European explorers arrived. The site here at Wickliffe, administered by Murray State University, is today an active archaeological research center and museum, offering visitors an intriguing glimpse into the way these people lived.

Of the three exhibit buildings here, each sheltering an excavation site, perhaps the most striking is the cemetery, where several of the burials have been replicated.

The Lifeways building displays an extensive collection of Mississippian pottery and stone tools. Among the exhibits are both everyday utensils and formal and ceremonial ware, including animal effigy vessels. Placards and other displays explain the prehistory of the mounds and the story of the dig.

The ceremonial mound, which is still intact, gives a view of the village site overlooking the Mississippi River. Special events and workshops are held throughout the year.

2 William Clark Market House Museum. *A must-see exhibit here is the completely restructured interior of the 1877 DuBois/List Drugstore, with its oak gingerbread woodwork, stained-glass windows, and patent medicine display.*

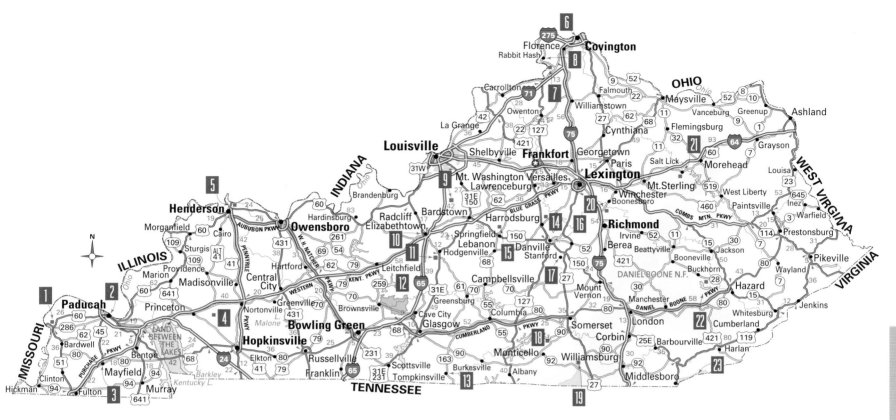

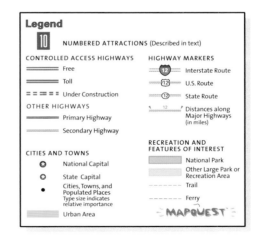

Legend

 NUMBERED ATTRACTIONS (Described in text)

CONTROLLED ACCESS HIGHWAYS

Free

Toll

Under Construction

OTHER HIGHWAYS

Primary Highway

Secondary Highway

CITIES AND TOWNS

National Capital

State Capital

Cities, Towns, and Populated Places Type size indicates relative importance

Urban Area

HIGHWAY MARKERS

Interstate Route

U.S. Route

State Route

Distances along Major Highways (in miles)

RECREATION AND FEATURES OF INTEREST

National Park

Other Large Park or Recreation Area

Trail

Ferry

MAPQUEST

0   20   40   60 Miles
0   20   40   60 Kilometers

Open daily Mar.–Nov.
Admission charged.
(270) 335-3681
http://campus.murraystate.edu/org/
wmrc/wmrc.htm

---

2 William Clark Market House Museum

Paducah

In 1827, over 20 years after returning from his westward journey with Meriwether Lewis, Gen. William Clark came to western Kentucky and purchased 37,000 acres of land for five dollars. The tract included a small village called Pekin. Clark renamed it Paducah and set aside an area near the riverfront for a marketplace. The present Market House, built in 1905, is the third to exist here.

A long, handsome structure of reddish-brown glazed brick, it is now a cultural center featuring the William Clark Market House Museum, with more than 4,800 square feet of exhibits.

One of the most intriguing is the reconstructed interior of the 1877 Dubois/List Drugstore, with its oak gingerbread woodwork, stained glass windows, and patent medicine displays. Other treasures are a life-size carving of U.S. statesman Henry Clay, which was created by a 12-year-old boy; Paducah's first motorized fire truck (1913 vintage); and the rudder wheel and brass fog bell of the USS *Paducah,* which served in the two World Wars.

In the Civil War exhibit are a quilt made by Mrs. Robert E. Lee, furniture used by the Lincolns in the White House, and a parlor used by Gen. Ulysses S. Grant when he occupied Paducah.

The block-long building also houses the Yeiser Art Center and the Market House Theatre.

Open Mon.–Sat. Closed major holidays.
Admission charged.
(270) 443-7759
www.paducah.ky.com/arts.html

3 Wooldridge Monuments

Take Hwy. 45 overpass to N. Seventh St. extension to Maplewood Cemetery.

This curious example of 19th-century eccentricity—a collection of 18 marble and sandstone figures—depicts the nearest and dearest of Henry G. Wooldridge, who as a 21-year-old moved to Kentucky in 1840. For the last 19 years of his life Wooldridge lived in Mayfield, and shortly before his death in 1899 he assembled his statuary entourage in a "strange procession which never moves."

Wooldridge, a breeder of horses who, according to Mayfield lore, lost his only true love in a riding accident, never married. His widowed mother, seven brothers and sisters, and two young nieces are represented, as well as two effigies of himself, one showing him astride his favorite horse, Fop, and the other standing at a lectern. The life-size figures surround his tomb, although only Henry G. Wooldridge himself is buried here.

The sandstone figures have now begun to erode, giving the faces of Wooldridge's entourage a bland, archaic look in sharp contrast to the more finely drawn and enduring detail of his own marble-sculpted features. The figures thus appear to distinguish between the man and his memories—or perhaps between his affections and his self-esteem.

Cemetery open daily
(270) 247-6101
http://mayfieldky.topcities.com/
cemetery/tour.htm

4 Pennyrile State Resort Park

Dawson Springs

Despite its many provisions for outdoor activities, this is a quiet, secluded resort pleasantly situated on a slope overlooking a small lake and beach. Its name comes from pennyroyal, an aromatic wildflower. The grounds of Pennyrile Lodge, which is built of native stone, are landscaped with flowering shrubs, including the delicately scented fringe tree.

With a sandy beach and a bathhouse complex, the 55-acre lake attracts many swimmers. Rowboats and pedal boats are available for rent. Lake Beshear, four miles from the park, is popular with fishermen, who try for crappies, largemouth bass, channel catfish, and bluegills.

Several trails wander through the park and the adjacent 15,000-acre forest, where white-tailed deer and wild turkeys are often seen. Bobcats also live here but rarely appear. Cardinals, wrens, and mourning doves fill the woods with their songs, particularly in spring.

The park offers an 18-hole golf course, two tennis courts, and two playgrounds. The picnic area, overlooking the lake, is equipped with tables and grills. The campsites, situated in a more remote part of the grounds, offer the luxury of water and electrical hookups.

Open daily Mar.–Oct.
(270) 797-3421
http://kystateparks.com

5 John James Audubon State Park

Rte. 41, Henderson

This is a relatively small park of some 800 acres, but it contains a full range of camping and cottage facilities, a nine-hole golf course, several miles of hiking trails, a 325-acre nature preserve, and a lake with a boat-launching area.

 John James Audubon State Park. *The museum and nature center, with its steep roofs and tower, suggesting a French château, houses a collection of original Audubon paintings, prints, and memorabilia.*

In addition, it is situated on one of the main migratory flyways and offers fine opportunities for observing many species of birds, especially the warblers that stop off here in the spring and fall.

The showpiece of the park is the John James Audubon Museum and Nature Center. The great painter of wildlife made his home in this area of Kentucky during the early 19th century, and it was here that he did much of the work from which his world-famous prints were made. The museum's superb collection of original Audubon paintings, prints, and memorabilia is remarkably comprehensive. It includes not only the familiar pictures of birds and animals but also family portraits.

The building itself, financed by the Works Progress Administration (WPA), was completed in 1938. The masonry structure, with its steep roofs and tower, suggests a French château. The Nature Center has a wildlife observatory and conducts environmental and art programs.

Park and museum open year-round except for a week at Christmas.
Admission charged for museum.
Park: (270) 826-2247
Museum: (270) 827-1893
http://kystateparks.com

6 MainStrasse Village

Covington

Toward the end of the 18th century a group of German settlers came to the southern banks of the Ohio River and established the town of Covington. Today it is a bustling, modern metropolis with a population of some 45,000. But over the years the older neighborhoods had fallen into disrepair. So in the 1970s a program was begun to restore a 30-block section of town dating from the 1830s, and the Carroll Chimes Tower was built.

Now called MainStrasse Village, with tall, narrow, closely clustered buildings reflecting the Germanic origins of its settlers, the area is filled with shops dealing in arts, crafts, and antiques. Strasse Haus, a publike café, serves traditional German and American dishes.

The Carroll Chimes Tower, a 100-foot brick structure built in traditional German medieval style with an illuminated clock on each of its four sides, stands opposite a mall with a center row of linden trees ending at a fountain decorated with a statue of a goose girl. As the carillon of 43 bells strikes the hour, animated figures step out onto a balcony and re-enact the story of the Pied Piper of Hamelin.

The village is not a museum; it is a busy, lived-in, restored area recalling the charm and appearance associated with the Old World in the 19th century.
(859) 491-0458

www.mainstrasse.org

7 Big Bone Lick State Park
Rte. 338, Union
Tens of thousands of years ago, when the glaciers of the last ice age blanketed northern Kentucky, this 525-acre park was a marshland with a sulfur spring. Prehistoric mammals, including giant mammoths, mastodons, ground sloths, tapirs, and arctic bears, driven south from their natural habitats, were attracted to the salt licks around the spring. Many became mired and perished in the bog, thus converting it into the vast prehistoric graveyard from which the park today takes its name.

7 Big Bone Lick State Park. *A model of a giant mammoth stands guard along the Discovery Trail, where real mammoths perished in the bog here tens of thousands of years ago, converting it into a prehistoric graveyard.*

A mile-long self-guiding Discovery Trail through the area of the swamp, complete with life-size models of a mammoth and a buffalo, explains the area's geological and ecological history. There is also a live buffalo herd to be seen. A small museum offers further educational displays about the history of the giant mammals.

Other enjoyable features include a 62-site campground with electrical and water hookups, a swimming pool (for campers only), a small man-made lake stocked with bluegills, bass, and catfish for anglers, a playground, and a recreation area with facilities for tennis, volleyball, and basketball. A pleasant footpath meanders around the lake.
Park open year-round.
Museum open daily Apr.–Dec.
Museum admission charged.
(859) 384-3522

http://kystateparks.com

8 Rabbit Hash General Store
Downtown Covington
Since 1831 this working general store has been doing business as usual, untouched by time or fate, in the heart of Rabbit Hash, Kentucky—a little river town whose fortunes have literally risen and fallen with the waters of the Ohio. (In fact, the town's very name is said to have originated during a flood when the abundant local rabbit population became a culinary staple.)

Over the years the store has survived many changing tides—including complete submersion during a flood in 1937 that crested at an incredible 79.9 feet. Though the store remained anchored securely to the ground,

8 Rabbit Hash General Store. *While visitors will no longer find any rabbit hash simmering, they can find lots of old-fashioned goodies like cream pull candy.*

thanks to a series of iron rods running throughout the entire structure, mud continues to linger in its attic crawl space.

Rabbit Hash General Store boasts an expansive front porch and large painted sign welcoming visitors. To meet the needs of local residents, it still sells groceries and other necessities.

Many of its eclectic wares, however, cater to tourists. It stocks an ample selection of antiques, collectible potteries, hand-woven towels and brooms, handmade soaps, wooden kitchen utensils, and the required souvenir hats, shirts, and postcards. While visitors won't find any "rabbit hash" simmering, the store also serves up lots of old-fashioned goodies, including homemade jams and cream pull candy.

Rabbit Hash also features a local history museum and shops specializing in Appalachian crafts and quilts. After shopping, visitors can take in a scenic riverboat cruise.
Open every day.
(859) 586-7744

9 Bernheim Arboretum and Research Forest

Take Exit 112 from 1-65 and follow signs to the forest. Clermont

In 1928 Isaac W. Bernheim, a German immigrant who made his fortune distilling bourbon whiskey, purchased a 14,000-acre tract "for the people of Kentucky" to be used as an arboretum and wildlife sanctuary. He also created a non-profit institution to connect people and nature.

Today Bernheim is divided into two sections—an extensive wilderness home and a parklike arboretum with 6,000 varieties of trees and shrubs.

The entrance road takes you past crab apple, maple, and beech trees, along the edge of a restored native grassland, to a unique visitors center. The center overlooks two ponds that attract hundreds of waterfowl in the spring and fall, including the elusive snow goose. From the center you can walk or drive to the Arboretum Center, with its formal gardens, which include azaleas, junipers, and witch hazels.

Nearly 35 miles of trails loop through the wilderness, including one that circles a 47-foot fire tower, which offers a superb view of the surrounding forested countryside. A self-guiding nature trail leads past a corral containing several deer and wild turkeys, and biking is also a popular activity.

The several picnic groves include tables and grills. A map of the forest is available at the visitors center.

Open year-round except Christmas and New Year's Day.
(502) 955-8512
www.bernheim.org

10 Schmidt Museum of Coca-Cola Memorabilia

I-65, Exit 94, Elizabethtown

For more than 100 years the Coca-Cola Company has been quenching the thirst of America—and that of the whole world—and reminding us just how thirsty we are with a barrage of brilliantly colored signs, coasters, dishes, glasses, ashtrays, and posters.

For most of those years the Schmidt family has been bottling Coca-Cola in Elizabethtown and collecting an astonishing assortment of Coca-Cola memorabilia. This assemblage, the private collection of Mr. and Mrs. W. B. Schmidt, said to be the largest in the world, is now on display at the Schmidt Museum.

Arranged chronologically, the exhibits show the company's ingenious approach to advertising—from the turn-of-the-century trays picturing Victorian ladies dressed as for a garden party, to cigar bands, hand axes, children's toys, and the convenient packaging of the present-day six-pack. The range of items emblazoned with the familiar logo is nothing less than overwhelming. On the case of a clock, Coca-Cola is heralded as a brain tonic and a way to relieve headaches and exhaustion.

Special exhibits throughout the year assure visitors there is always something new to see, from the 1931 Ford Coca-Cola delivery van to the Coca-Cola R2D2 robot.

Open Mon.–Fri. except major holidays, and Sat. in the summer. Admission charged.
(270) 234-1100
www.touretown.com/attractions.html

10 Schmidt Museum of Coca-Cola Memorabilia. *Serving trays from the past 100 years are just one of the Coca-Cola Company's many approaches to advertising on display here. Other items include cigar bands and children's toys.*

11 Abraham Lincoln Birthplace National Historic Site

Hodgenville

Kentucky abounds with log cabins, but none so enshrined as this. On a hill at the site of Sinking Spring Farm, a 348-acre tract bought by Nancy Hanks and Thomas Lincoln in 1808, stands a Doric-columned marble-and-granite memorial building with an impressive flight of 56 steps—one for each year of Abraham Lincoln's life. The memorial contains a simple one-room symbolic log cabin in which the 16th president of the United States was born on February 12, 1809.

Built of stout, squared, white oak beams with a wattle-and-clay chimney at one end, the cabin, unlike most dwellings of that day, has no half-loft and only one small square window, which perhaps was covered with oiled paper or an animal skin to keep out the winter cold.

Since the 1860s, as the Sinking Springs property changed hands, the cabin has been removed and later returned to the farm several times. This gave rise to a controversy as to its authenticity.

In 1905 the Lincoln Farm Association was formed by several prominent Americans, including Mark Twain and William Jennings Bryan, to preserve Lincoln's birthplace. Four years later President Theodore Roosevelt laid the cornerstone of the memorial building, and soon the cabin, if not the actual one, at least a fine facsimile, came to a permanent resting place. Original or not, it clearly captures the spirit of the time. And the contrast between the stark simplicity of the cabin and the grandeur of its protective covering seems both poignant and ironic.

 Abraham Lincoln Birthplace National Historic Site. *A Doric-columned marble-and-granite memorial building contains the simple one-room log cabin where the 16th president was born on February 12, 1809.*

The spring for which the farm was named is still there, rising from a grottolike cave at the foot of the hillside. A hiking trail winds through the fields and forests of the park, and picnic facilities are available.

Open daily except Thanksgiving, Christmas, and New Year's Day.
(270) 358-3138

www.nps.gov/abli

12 Mammoth Cave National Park

The main attraction at this 52,000-acre park is the extensive network of passageways and caverns in the cave itself. It is the world's longest cave system, and tours range from one and a half hours to a strenuous six-hour Wild Cave tour, all available by reservation.

Meanwhile, back on the surface, these hills and valleys along both sides of the Green River offer a wide range of opportunities for outdoor activities, including hiking, backpacking, camping, and horseback riding. Outings on a riverboat give views of the limestone cliffs edging Green River and occasionally of wildlife.

Seventy miles of trails and backpacking routes, some through the primitive backcountry, wind through the countryside. Camping is permitted on designated sites. Permits, available at park headquarters, are required for camping in the backcountry.

The forest is home to the Virginia white-tailed deer, raccoons, and other small mammals, as well as owls, warblers, wild turkey, pileated woodpeckers, and cardinals. Fishing and boating are permitted in the park.

Park is open year-round.
(270) 758-2328

www.nps.gov/maca/home.htm

13 Old Mulkey Meetinghouse State Historic Site

Tompkinsville

Situated in a woodland near an ancient cemetery, this simple and austere log structure was built in 1804 by the Mill Creek Baptist Congregation, whose leader was John Mulkey, the son and grandson of a Baptist preacher. Five years after the meetinghouse was completed, the congregation became divided, with one faction accepting and the other rejecting the theory of predestination.

John Mulkey, who rejected the doctrine, was followed by a majority of the members, and he continued for many years to espouse his beliefs in the area. The log building soon became known as the Mulkey Meetinghouse.

Brother Mulkey was a significant force in the religion of southern Kentucky as well as northern Tennessee. He delivered approximately 10,000 sermons and encouraged four of his six sons to become preachers.

The 30- by 50-foot building has a puncheon floor, pegleg seats, chinked walls, and clapboard shutters. It is designed with two shallow transepts, creating 12 corners to represent either the 12 apostles of Christ, or the 12 tribes of Israel; its three doors represent the Trinity. Instead of glass, the windows and doors have been fitted with rough wooden shutters. Visitors can view pictures of John Mulkey and his wife hanging on the wall beside the preacher's stall.

Hannah Pennington, Daniel Boone's sister, is buried in the nearby cemetery along with other pioneers. In addition, soldiers of the Revolutionary War and the War of 1812 are interred here.

On its 60 acres there are picnic tables and grills, a playground for children, and a shelter located under the trees, reminding visitors of the tradition of serving dinner on the meetinghouse grounds.

Open year-round.
(270) 487-8481

www.oldmulkeymeetinghouse.com

12 Mammoth Cave National Park. *Visitors can explore the world's longest cave system here, with its network of passageways and caverns, on brief 90-minute tours or six-hour treks, available by reservation.*

 Shaker Village of Pleasant Hill. *Visitors to this restored Shaker community and living museum will find simplicity in architecture and daily activities.*

14 Shaker Village of Pleasant Hill

25 miles southwest of Lexington and 7 miles east of Harrodsburg on U.S. 68

The American Shaker Movement began in 1774, when members of a religious sect with a conviction in Christ's second coming and simple living left Liverpool, England, and disembarked in New York City. By 1776 the group settled in Niskeyuna, New York, near Albany. At first the group's missionaries, who spread through New England, met with persecution, brought on by their unorthodox theology and ways of worship.

Eventually, however, the Shakers attracted many followers within and beyond New England. In 1805 believers in Kentucky began moving to a community taking shape. Pleasant Hill came into being when 44 members signed the first family covenant and purchased land on a nearby hilltop. By 1823, 491 Shakers called Pleasant Hill home.

Today Pleasant Hill claims the nation's largest and most completely restored Shaker community and living museum. A National Historic Landmark, the village offers visitors the chance to discover simplicity—in architecture, furniture, and daily activities—as intended by its founders. Thirty-four of the 270 original buildings erected by the Shakers remain. Along a self-guiding tour, visitors can meet interpreters in authentic Shaker garb.

Within the community, skilled artisans work at 19th-century trades and old-style farming. Daily demonstrations include broom making, spinning, weaving, coopering, woodworking, gardening, and domestic and farm labor. In the village, two craft stores feature Shaker reproductions, furniture, and sundry items, including hand-sewn brooms. Visitors can also board the *Dixie Belle* stern-wheeler for a trip back in time on a beautiful stretch of the historic Kentucky River.

Open year-round except Christmas Eve and Christmas Day.
(800) 734-5611
www.shakervillageky.org

15 Lincoln Homestead State Park

Springfield

This is Lincoln country, and three buildings that were important in the life of Thomas Lincoln, the president's father, have been brought together in this 275-acre park: his boyhood home, the girlhood home of his bride, Nancy Hanks, and the blacksmith and carpenter shop where he learned his trade. Of the three, only the Berry House, where Abraham's mother lived when she was courted by Thomas Lincoln, is original.

Although the 16- by 18-foot Lincoln homestead is a replica, it is constructed of 115-year-old logs and stands on the same spot as the one built by the president's grandfather (for whom he was named), who was the first of the family to settle in Kentucky. Behind the cabin is the creek that became known as Lincoln's Run shortly after the family settled here. Several of the cabin's furnishings were made by Thomas, the president's father.

The Berry House, a two-story structure built of massive yellow poplar beams and furnished in pioneer style, was moved to the park from its original site about a mile away. On display in the house is a copy of the marriage bond of Thomas Lincoln and Nancy Hanks.

A small covered bridge has been built across the creek, leading to a replica of the shop that belonged to Richard and Francis Berry, the master craftsmen who are said to have taught Thomas Lincoln his woodworking skill.

Something of an anomaly, which would have been puzzling to Thomas Lincoln, is the 18-hole golf course in the park.

Open daily May–Oct. 1.
Admission charged.
(859) 336-7461
www.state.ky.us/agencies/parks/linchome.htm

 Lincoln Homestead State Park. *The Berry House, where President Lincoln's mother lived when Thomas Lincoln courted her, was moved to the 153-acre park from its original site about a mile away.*

16 McDowell House and Apothecary

Danville, on South Second St. near Constitution Square State Shrine

The white clapboard Georgian house, dating from about 1789, was the home of Dr. Ephraim McDowell, known as the father of abdominal surgery, who lived here from 1795 until his death in 1830. It was in this house on Christmas Day, 1809, that Dr. McDowell performed the first laparotomy in America. Although the removal of the ovarian tumor was done without antisepsis or anesthetic, the patient, one Jane Todd Crawford, survived and lived on for many years.

The house and the earlier small brick structure that served as the doctor's apothecary shop and office have been restored and furnished with period pieces, many of them belonging to the McDowells. A grandfather clock scarred by an arrow, handheld fire screens (used by ladies to protect their complexions), fine handmade bedspreads, surgical instruments, candle molds, cooking utensils, and flatirons are reminders of the texture of pioneer life in this frontier town.

The apothecary-shop collection of colorful 18th- and 19th-century jars and vials, accurately labeled and filled with herbs and drug simples of the period, are neatly arranged on the shelves; a fine old brass scale stands on the counter.

The gardens, too, have been restored and are part of the tour of the house and apothecary shop.

Open Mon.–Sun. except Mon. in Nov.–Feb. Closed Thanksgiving, Christmas, Easter, and New Year's Day. Admission charged.
(859) 236-2804
www.mcdowellhouse.com

16 McDowell House and Apothecary. *It was at this house in 1809 that Dr. Ephraim McDowell performed the first abdominal surgery in America, taking out an ovarian tumor without anesthetic. The patient survived.*

17 William Whitley House State Historic Site

Rte. 150, Stanford

William Whitley, one of Kentucky's early pioneer settlers and hero of both the American Revolution and the War of 1812, completed his sturdy three-story brick dwelling in 1792. The first brick house in Kentucky, it sits on a low eminence enhanced with stately shade trees. The walls are 18.5 inches thick, and the windows are set higher than usual to give protection against attack by American Indians. A secret stairway leads from the kitchen to the second floor, providing an escape route and a hiding place.

Among the period pieces on view are Whitley's rifle and powder horn, which he engraved with his own encouraging verse: ". . . fill me with the best of power I'le make your rifle crack the lowder." These possessions were returned to Mrs. Whitley after her husband's death in 1813 at the battle of Thames in Ontario. A soldier later claimed it was Whitley who killed the great Shawnee chief Tecumseh in that encounter.

But there was more to Whitley's life here than worry about American Indians. Nearby he built a horse-racing track, one of the first in a long Kentucky tradition. Whitley's pride in his home is perhaps most evident on the exterior walls, where glazed bricks prominently form his initials in front and those of his wife in back. A costumed guide interprets the house and its history for visitors. Two picnic shelters are on the grounds.

Open daily mid-Mar.–Dec., Tues.–Sun. Closed Thanksgiving and Christmas. Admission charged.
(606) 355-2881
www.state.ky.us/agencies/ parkswmwhitly.htm

18 Mill Springs Mill

Off Rte. 90 on Hwy. 1275, 7 miles north of Monticello. The entrance, easily missed, is set back from the road.

Since the early 1800s this steep, wooded hillside has been a mill site. The present mill, which dates from 1877, has a 40-foot iron overshot waterwheel, added in 1908 and believed to be one of the largest in the world. Power for the mill comes from 13 springs, which form a stream that cascades down the hillside into a large pipe leading to the waterwheel.

The building, a large white clapboard structure with a stone foundation, overlooks Lake Cumberland. A walkway takes you under the mill for a view of the wheel and the main drive shaft. Belts run from the shaft to the upper floor, where the corn is ground, usually on Saturday and Sunday afternoons. The cornmeal is sold at the nearby gift shop.

The opening battle of the Kentucky-Tennessee campaign in the Civil War was fought at Mill Springs on January 19, 1862, a conflict that resulted in a victory for the Union forces. Still standing on the hillside above the mill is Lanier House; once the home of an early mill owner, it served as the Confederate headquarters. A fortification also remains at Mill Springs.

From the mill a path leads to Mill Spring Park on Cumberland Lake, where picnic areas and a boat dock are located. Several scenic hiking trails wind through the park.

Park open Memorial Day–Oct.; mill and gift shop open Memorial Day–Labor Day. (606) 679-6337
www.lrn.usace.army.mil/op/wol/rec/ points_of_interest.htm

19 Yahoo Falls Scenic Area

Turn west off Rte. 27 onto Rte. 700. Go 3 1/2 miles and turn north onto the gravel U.S. Forest Service road, Rte. 660. Continue 1 mile to the parking area.

As you turn onto Route 660, look for the legendary grave of Jacob Troxel. During the American Revolution, "Big Jake" Troxel was reportedly sent by George Washington's staff to live among the American Indians of Kentucky and prevent them from supporting the British. Welcomed by the Tsa-Waagan Cherokees, he lived in their village, eventually marrying the chief's daughter, Princess Corn-blossom. They had a child together whom they named Little Jake.

Today several trails are accessible at Yahoo Falls, including the 250-mile Sheltowee Trace for backpackers. The falls are reached by a signed quarter-mile path leading through the forest to the head of a steep gorge. There, from a walled observation platform, one looks down on Yahoo Creek as it plunges 113 feet from the Cumberland Plateau into the gorge below. Or hikers can take another path that leads down the cliffs for a view of the falls from the base.

On the return to the parking lot a detour leads to a spot overlooking the confluence of the creek and South Fork River as it curves beneath a sandstone crag. Surrounded by masses of mountain laurel, this is a most pleasant place to linger and picnic. For volume of water, the best seasons for viewing the falls are spring and autumn.

Open year-round.
(423) 286-7275
www.nps.gov/biso

20 Fort Boonesborough State Park

Off Hwy. 627, Richmond
The fort that stands here today, evoking the period of Kentucky's early pioneer settlement, is a detailed reconstruction of one built nearby on the banks of the Kentucky River by Daniel Boone and about 30 fellow frontiersmen in 1775. These were the first settlers sent out by Col. Richard Henderson of North Carolina to establish a colony west of the Appalachians. Despite the fact that Henderson had purchased a vast tract of land from the Cherokees for the colony, the settlers immediately found themselves at odds with the Shawnees and other local people who were being encouraged by the British to attack American settlers during the Revolutionary War. Boone's daughter and two other girls were kidnapped by American Indians. Boone and nine of his companions tracked the captors and rescued the three girls.

About two years later Boone and a group of companions were captured by the Shawnees. Boone escaped, made his way to Boonesborough, and urged improvement in its defenses. The precautions were taken, and late in the summer of 1778 the little fort withstood a 10-day siege by the Indians, thus securing the survival and growth of the Kentucky settlements.

Upon entering the fort today, a visitor is taken back to the settlers' world. Several of the cabins display furnishings typical of the period and the Spartan circumstances, and in others frontier crafts are demonstrated, including weaving, carpentry, candlemaking, soapmaking, and blacksmithing. A small museum is devoted to Boone and the life of the pioneers.

The park also offers a large campground with hookups as well as primitive tenting sites, a recreation area with facilities for various activities, an inviting sandy beach along the river for swimming, and a boat-launching ramp. Fishermen usually catch bass, perch, bream, and catfish. The park's Kentucky River Museum traces the development of commerce on the river. The park is heavily visited on holidays and summer weekends.

Campground open year-round.
Admission charged to fort.
(859) 527-3131
http://kystateparks.com

21 Clear Creek Furnace

Salt Lick. Follow signs on Rte. 211 and enter at the first picnic area.
The competition for iron ore for this smelting furnace, located on a small stream called Clear Creek, culminated in a murder and a famous trial. The structure was built in 1839 by two partners, W. S. Allen and W. S. Lane. In January 1840, during a dispute over the rights to a local iron mine between Lane and a Mr. Ewing, owner of a nearby furnace, gunfire broke out, and Ewing was killed.

Because of the prominence of the men involved, the trial drew wide attention. Conflicting opinions were formed, and rifts developed among families and friends. Mr.

20 Fort Boonesborough State Park. *This park features a detailed reconstruction of the fort built in 1775 by frontiersman Daniel Boone and 30 others.*

Lane pleaded self-defense and was acquitted.

The furnace, one of the last of its kind in this area, was fired for the last time in 1875. It is a pylonlike structure with a strong Mayan aspect and towers to some 40 feet. Massive cut stones were laid to contain the fierce 2000°F temperature required for smelting iron ore.

The ruins are in a picnic ground sheltered by pines at the northern end of the Clear Creek Recreation Area in the Daniel Boone National Forest. The recreational facility also offers campsites and several foot trails.

Open year-round.
(606) 784-6428
www.southernregion.fs.fed.us/boone/
picnichm.htm

22 Buckhorn Lake State Resort Park

Rte. 1833, Buckhorn

This quiet mountain park takes excellent advantage of the lake created in 1961 by a 162-foot dam built several miles downstream on the middle fork of the Kentucky River. Primarily designed for secluded family holidays devoted to water sports, the park offers a sandy beach, a boat-launching ramp, and a marina with 95 slips for water enthusiasts. In addition, the park has a picnic area, a playground, tennis courts, and a self-guiding nature trail that wends through the woodlands. Anglers, either in boats or on the spacious fishing pier, are likely to catch largemouth and smallmouth bass, crappies, bluegills, channel catfish, and muskies. Rental boats are available.

The quiet park roads invite

22 Buckhorn Lake State Resort Park. *The lodge at this secluded park offers guests a swimming pool with a view of the mountains.*

cyclists, and bikes may be rented. A modern 36-room lodge and three cottages are operated by the park, and a publicly operated campground is located nearby. Musical shows, square dancing, and other entertainments are offered occasionally in the lodge.
(800) 325-0058
http://kystateparks.com

23 Cumberland Gap National Historical Park

Middlesboro

It was the creek flowing north toward the Cumberland River that first showed the way through this section of the Appalachian Range. Herds of buffalo wandered along Yellow Creek; then the American Indians followed, creating the so-called Warriors Path, linking the Cherokees of the east with the Shawnees to the northwest.

Fur traders, hunters, and pioneer farmers traveled the route. In 1775 Daniel Boone and a crew of axmen blazed the Wilderness Road for some 200 miles and opened a corridor that started the first migration to the west.

In the early 1800s faster and easier westward routes were developed, and the importance of

Cumberland Gap declined. Today it is primarily interesting for its colorful history and scenery.

A road (closed to trailers and vehicles more than 20 feet long) from the park's visitors center winds precipitously up to the 2,500-foot pinnacle. A short footpath bordered with wild phlox and mountain laurel leads from the parking lot to an overlook with an astounding view of the gap and the valleys and peaks of three states.

Within the park is the Hensley Settlement, a wilderness community of 12 farmsteads established on Brush Mountain in the early 1900s by the Hensley and Gibbons families. It flourished for almost 50 years before it was abandoned in the 1950s. Visitors can hike to the area on a four-hour guided tour that leaves from the visitors center several times a day.

Now being restored, the community can be reached only by shuttle or a hike over rough terrain. Those who make the trip will gain some insight into the self-sufficient way of life that these stouthearted people chose to pursue.

Four primitive campsites, accessible only by foot, are located on the Ridge Trail, a route along the Kentucky-Virginia border. Picnic areas and hiking trails are scattered throughout the park. Maps and information are available at the visitors center in Middlesboro. Tour times change throughout the year depending on staff and weather.

Park open year-round; visitors center open daily except Christmas.
(606) 248-2817
www.nps.gov/cuga

Zemurray Gardens. *Cypress trees shade the beauty of this park, which opens to visitors each spring (see page 140).*

Louisiana

Mysterious bayous, dazzling camellias and azaleas, and stately plantation houses are here—along with some unexpected pleasures.

One of the richest archaeological sites in North America is Poverty Point, in north-central Louisiana, where prehistoric hunters built vast earthworks. Another site was once a fortress and capital of the Spanish province of Texas. A former World War II training camp is now a museum of U.S. military history.

One plantation boasts the prototypical antebellum mansion. Another, developed by a woman who was once a slave, has now become a popular center for local writers, artists, and crafts people.

Flowers, for which the South is famous, can be viewed on a hiking trail, in an arboretum, a state park, and a garden. And the 180-mile Creole Nature Trail, the Gulf South's only official National Scenic Byway, passes by the area where the pirate Jean Lafitte hid his treasure.

1 Cypress Black Bayou Recreation Area

Benton

This 340-acre piney park is perched at the junction of two large bayou-fed reservoirs. Here one can fish from several of the piers, launch a boat, swim at a sandy beach, walk for more than four miles along wood chip–paved nature trails, rent a cabin, camp with all amenities, pitch a tent, or enjoy a picnic.

The park's nature center has facilities for the study of plants and animals native to these woods. It was established with the help of the local school board and welcomes students and researchers from all parts of the country.

The park is popular with birders, who often come to observe the many kinds of songbirds and waterfowl that inhabit the towering pine forest and the quiet waterways. The park is usually crowded from July to Labor Day.

Open year-round. Admission charged.
(318) 965-0007

www.cypressblackbayou.com

2 Poverty Point State Historic Site

On La. State Hwy. 577, Epps

Just how Poverty Point got its name is not known for sure. One theory holds that repeated crop failures in the 19th century left

1 Cypress Black Bayou Recreation Area. *Two large bayou-fed reservoirs supply this piney park with plenty of water for fishing, boating, or swimming.*

the area destitute. Despite its name, however, Poverty Point remains one of America's richest archaeological sites.

The lower Mississippi Valley was inhabited from 3,500 to 2,500 years ago by American Indian tribes who developed a culture sufficiently organized and enduring to construct massive earthworks here on a bluff along Bayou Macon.

It is estimated that 5 million man-hours were required to build the complex, which consists of six semicircular rows of long, low ridges (divided into sections by aisles) and four mounds, the largest of which is bird-shaped and rises to a height of 70 feet.

These ridges and mounds were assumed to be part of the natural landscape, but when they were viewed from an airplane, it became obvious from the striking symmetry of their design that they were the work of man.

The largest of several centers of the Poverty Point people, the complex is shrouded in mystery, and scholars still ponder the purpose for which it was built. Although one of the mounds was located over a crematory, archaeologists do not interpret the place as an ancient burial site. Conjectures about the use of the concentric ridges range from building foundations to an astronomical observatory.

An observation tower provides an overview, and a guided tram tour loops through the 400-acre site. The museum in the information center displays an impressive collection of effigies, jewelry, tools, weapons, and other artifacts from the site. Some of the materials were obtained by trade with people far away.

The ingenuity of the residents of this rock-free terrain can be seen in their production of fire-hardened clay balls to use as cooking stones. They also made stone beads with perfectly cylindrical holes, a feat that has long puzzled experts. It is now believed that they used a reed at the end of a stick for a drill, with sand as an abrasive.

Open daily except Thanksgiving, Christmas, and New Year's Day. Admission charged.
(888) 926-5492
www.lastateparks.com

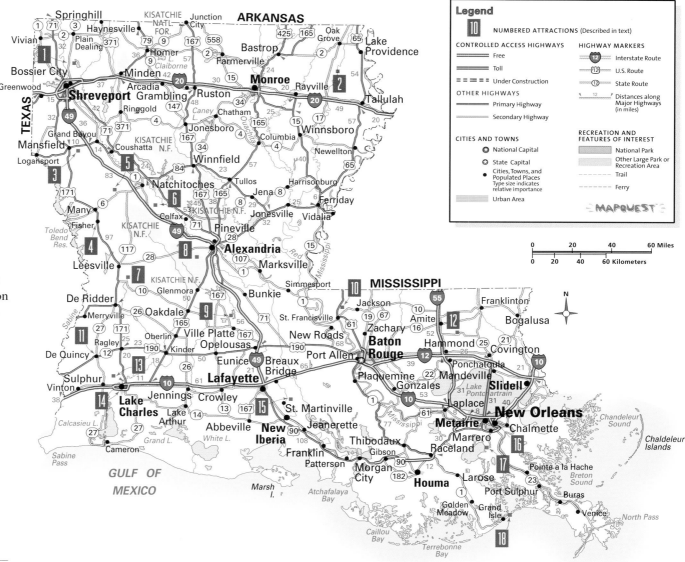

3 Mansfield State Historic Site

On State Hwy. 175, three miles South of Mansfield
Fought on April 8, 1864, the battle of Mansfield was one of the largest Civil War conflicts west of the Mississippi River and the last major Confederate victory of the Civil War. The defeat of Union forces thwarted Union Gen. Nathaniel Bank's invasion of Northwest Louisiana. Banks, who commanded 35,000 troops, was soundly defeated by the Confederate Gen. Richard Taylor, son of former President Zachary Taylor. The defeat stopped Bank's drive on Shreveport, Louisiana, the vital military headquarters for the trans-Mississippi region.

The state historic site encompasses 178 acres of the original battlefield, and it also features markers, monuments, and cannon displays, as well as a battlefield trail.

The park's interpretive center and museum feature weapon and uniform displays, battlefield artifacts, dioramas, and an introductory audio-visual program.

Monthly interpretive programs include musket and cannon firing, soldier encampments, lectures, and battlefield tours.

Nearby is the historic town of Mansfield. Some of the heaviest fighting occurred here during the Civil War, but one would never guess that today while walking down its tranquil tree-lined streets, admiring the antebellum mansions.

Open 9 A.M.–5 P.M. daily except Thanksgiving, Christmas, and New Year's Day. Admission charged.
(888) 677-6267
www.lastateparks.com

4 Fisher: Historic Sawmill Town

Off U.S. Rte. 171 six miles south of Many; turn west at blinker. Shaded by the longleaf pines that once brought wealth to its citizens, this almost completely deserted turn-of-the-century sawmill town lies at the end of a quiet road a half-mile downhill from the First Baptist Church.

As you approach the town, the long, low, white commissary faces you across a square, its porch stretching the entire width of the building. Off to one side, with a white picket fence in front, stands the old opera house, a hall that served as the center of the town's activities. Its ticket window, with a little rounded shelf, opens onto the front porch. Alongside the old railroad tracks is the railroad station, with its paneling, benches, and ticket office still intact. The interiors can be visited by appointment.

The town comes to life once a year during the third weekend in May, when the annual Sawmill Days festival is held.
(318) 256-2001 or
(318) 256-2641
www.sabineparish.com/towns/ fisher.html

5 Los Adaes State Historic Site

On Rte. 485 off Rte. 6
The fortress and mission known as Los Adaes, which under Spanish rule served as the capital of the province of Texas, was built in 1719 as a stronghold against the threat of the French. Its reign as the center of the Texas government ended a half-century later, when France gave the unprofitable Louisiana colony to Spain and the fort was closed down and deemed unnecessary.

In the 18th century, when it flourished, the town was inhabited by Spanish soldiers and Los Adaes Indians. It included a blacksmith's shop, a small chapel, and soldiers' barracks. All the buildings have disappeared, and the 58-acre site has been excavated and reconstructed.

The visitors center displays a collection of tools, weapons, and other artifacts found on the grounds. The site of the fort itself is marked by a flag.
Grounds open daily except Thanksgiving, Christmas, and New Year's Day.
(318) 472-9499
www.lastateparks.com

6 Melrose Plantation

Junction of Rtes. 493 and 119
The tales this fascinating early Louisiana property has to tell revolve around two remarkable women who held sway here a century apart. The first was a determined and enterprising slave named Marie Therese Coincoin, who in 1778 was freed along with several of her 14 children. She obtained a land grant on the Cane River from the Spanish colonial authorities and, aided by her sons, cleared the land and established a successful tobacco and indigo farm that eventually became known as Melrose Plantation.

The other woman was Mrs. Cammie Garrett Henry, known simply as Miss Cammie, who came into possession of the plantation about 1898. She carefully restored the original four-room cypress-timbered house called Yucca that Marie Therese built in 1796, as well as the imposing white clapboard Big House that Marie Therese's grandson completed in 1833, and turned

6 Melrose Plantation. *The white clapboard Big House, completed in 1833, has been restored, and the plantation, once a successful tobacco and indigo farm, turned into a center for local arts, crafts, history, and folklore.*

Melrose into a center for local arts, crafts, history, and folklore.

Miss Cammie invited artists and writers to come and work in Yucca House, and over the years the little structure probably housed more notable writers than any other in the South. The renowned hospitality of Melrose was convincingly confirmed by one writer who came for a six-week visit and stayed for 32 years.

Yet another remarkable woman came out of Melrose. In the 1940s the plantation's onetime cook, Clementine Hunter, began to paint colorful and charming primitive works; she became known as the black Grandma Moses. Some of her murals can be seen upstairs in Yucca House.

Other buildings on the grounds include the African House, the Weaving House, and the Bindery, which serves as a visitors center.
Open P.M. daily except Thanksgiving, Christmas, and New Year's Day.
Admission charged.
(318) 379-0055
www.natchitoches.net/melrose

7 Historical Holding Area

Off Rte. 171, Leesville
Named for Louisiana's famed "Fighting Bishop," Leonidas Polk, an Episcopal prelate who became a Confederate general, this post was established on the eve of World War II to support the famous Louisiana Maneuvers. Dwight D. Eisenhower, Omar Bradley, and George S. Patton, Jr., were among the key future war leaders who took part in the crucial grand-scale exercises, which tested the army's ability to use tactics, weapons, and support equipment that had been developed since World War I.

The post came alive again during the Vietnam years. At what became known as Fort Swampy, more than a million men got a foretaste of Southeast Asia in the dense, mosquito-ridden areas of junglelike growth that are part of the varied terrain here. The fort is now the home of the U.S. Army's Joint Readiness Training Center.

The museum illustrates the history of the base and the units that have served here. Its collection encompasses posters, uniforms, insignia, weapons, and other military memorabilia, some dating back to the Civil War. A 2 ½-acre park contains more than 100 military vehicles and other equipment.

Open Wed.–Sun. except Thanksgiving, Christmas, and New Year's Day.
(337) 531-7905
www.jrtc-polk.army.mil

8 Wild Azalea Trail
Kisatchie National Forest, Calcasieu District
If you enjoy walking here, you can settle for an hour or two of ambling in the woods or devote two days to hiking the full 31 miles from end to end. The trail, named for the wild azaleas that bloom in the forest in early spring, winds through great stands of hardwoods and pines, skirts a bog, and crosses open meadows and several creeks as it makes its way from Valentine Lake, west of Alexandria, to Route 165, south of the city.

Well marked with yellow blazes, the trail goes through woodlands that the U.S. Forest Service keeps in top condition by constantly clearing underbrush and thinning trees, and takes hikers through the Castor Creek Scenic Area, a part of the forest that has remained untouched for years.

At several places the trail crosses U.S. Forest Service roads, where hikers who want to walk only a part can park cars or arrange to be picked up. Tent camping is permitted along the trail.

Open year-round.
(318) 793-9427
www.r8web.com/kisatchie/

9 Louisiana State Arboretum
On La. State Hwy. 3042, Ville Platte
In this unexpectedly hilly region of Louisiana the state has established an arboretum where native plants can be studied and enjoyed. A little more than three miles of good, well-marked trails traverse woodlands and wander down into a ravine, with plants identified along the way.

Because of the variations in topography and microclimates, almost every kind of Louisiana plant life can be found here. Among the trees in the forest are American beech, flowering dogwood, hickory, and the unusual big-leaf magnolia. The animal life that flourishes here includes raccoons, white-tailed deer, opossums, wild turkeys, and great barred owls.

The interpretive center contains exhibits on the life of Caroline Dorman, a premier naturalist in Louisiana. For birders, a checklist of both migratory and native species is available at the center.

Walking and looking are the only activities that are allowed here. But adjoining Chicot State Park has full facilities; its entrance is 1½ miles to the south on Highway 3042.

Open year-round.
(888) 677-6100
www.crt.state.la.us/crt/parks/arbor/arbor2.htm

10 Greenwood Plantation
Just off Rte. 66, St. Francisville
This handsome two-story mansion is one of the loveliest antebellum plantation homes in the South. Colonnaded on all four sides, the pristine Greek Revival structure stands on a slight rise overlooking a reflecting pool edged with azaleas, willows, and moss-draped live oaks. Lavishly furnished with Victorian antiques, it is such a perfect-looking Southern mansion that it has been used as the setting for a movie and two TV miniseries.

Surprisingly, however, the building is a reconstruction. The original mansion, built by cotton and sugar-cane planter Ruffin Barrow in 1830, was completely destroyed by fire in 1960 except for the 28 columns surrounding it. The rebuilding was the dedicated undertaking of Carolyn and Richard Barnes, who also farm the plantation, now reduced in size from 12,000 acres to 278. To make it look as much like the original as possible, they used old photographs and information from Barrow's descendants for reference. Even some of the furniture and paintings are original.

Open 9 A.M.–5 P.M. daily except Thanksgiving, Christmas, and New Year's Day. Admission charged.
(225) 655-4475
www.greenwoodplantation.com *or* **www.eatel.net/~meme/louisiana.html**

11 DeQuincy Railroad Museum
DeQuincy
DeQuincy was settled in 1895 at the juncture of the Kansas City Southern and the old Missouri Pacific railroads. The imposing tile-roofed Spanish Colonial Kansas City Southern depot, which houses the museum and is on the *National Register of Historic Places,* was once the pride of DeQuincy.

On display at the museum are the tickets and timetables of the early 1900s, the old-fashioned mail pouch that the engineer of a passing express train caught with a hook, and memorabilia of the town's railroad men. The mannequin of a ticket agent, sitting in his office with his back to the door, is so real that visitors sometimes whisper for fear of disturbing him as he works at his desk, complete with antique typewriter and telegrapher's key.

On the grounds are a 1913 steam locomotive with coal car and vintage caboose attached. An annual Railroad Festival is held here the second weekend of April.

Open daily.
(337) 786-2823
www.visitlakecharles.org/dequincy.asp

10 Greenwood Plantation. *This two-story Greek Revival mansion is actually a reconstruction of the original, built in 1830 but destroyed by fire in 1960. The building has been used as the setting for a movie and two TV miniseries.*

12 Zemurray Gardens

State Hwy. 40, about 12 miles east of I-55, Loranger

Mr. and Mrs. Sam Zemurray, who purchased this property in 1928, were so impressed with its natural beauty that they decided to create a 150-acre woodland park. They repaired a dam and spillway on a stream that flows through the grounds to form tranquil 20-acre Mirror Lake. And since they were fond of spring-blooming shrubs, they planted the shoreline with camellias, redbuds, dogwoods, and especially azaleas.

The garden area around the lake is open only in the spring, when it is abloom with flowers. A trail takes visitors completely around the lake and through the landscaped grounds. It crosses a stream and passes vistas with statuary brought from Europe by the Zemurrays.

Since the exact time when the gardens are open can vary, it's best to call ahead before coming.

Gardens open daily from Mar.–mid-April. Admission charged.
(985) 878-2284
www.cr.nps.gov/nr/travel/Louisiana/zemhtml

13 Sam Houston Jones State Park

7 miles north of Lake Charles

Named originally for the hero of the Alamo, who according to legend often stayed in this area, the 1,087-acre park now carries the name of the 1940s Louisiana governor who was responsible for preserving these grounds. Here you will find some of the loveliest landscape in Louisiana—towering pines, dense woodlands, lakes, and cypress-bordered lagoons.

The quiet, scenic waters are ideal for boating, and boats are available for rent. A launch ramp and two docks are provided for those who bring their own. Fishing from a boat or along the banks can produce a catch of white perch, bream, or bass. The park has several campsites, picnic grounds, and nature trails.

During the migrating season birders come here for a tally of the species that stop to rest and feed on their way across Louisiana.

Open year-round. Admission charged.
(337) 855-2665
www.lastateparks.com

14 Creole Nature Trail

Between New Orleans and Houston off I-10

Beyond the interstate lies Louisiana's Outback—a world of natural beauty and bustling activity. This 180-mile stretch is the Gulf South's only official National Scenic Byway—a coveted designation awarded by the Federal Highway Administration that ensures a rewarding driving experience. It's in this area that the notorious pirate Jean Lafitte hid his treasure, where French explorers traded with the Attakapas Indians and created colonial Louisiana, and where Louisiana's Cajun and Creole cultures took root.

From the car, this vast expanse of prairie and marshland appears peaceful and tranquil. Yet it's teeming with life, boasting 16 species of mammals. With more than 3,000 alligator nests, it's also one of the country's largest homes to this once-hunted creature, now supported by a major alligator research center.

The Creole Nature Trail is also considered one of the nation's top 10 birding destinations. Sightings of some 250 species of birds have been recorded along this stretch of highway. Butterflies of all colors also flock here by the millions.

To better view the abundance of lovely winged creatures, drivers can stop at the Sabine National Wildlife Refuge, the Cameron Prairie National Wildlife Refuge, or the Peveto Woods Birds and Butterfly Sanctuary.

Open year-round.
(337) 436-9588 or (800) 456-7952
www.creolenaturetrail.org

15 Longfellow-Evangeline State Historic Site

Rte. 31, St. Martinsville

Like many other sites here in the heart of Cajun country, this 157-acre park, tucked behind an iron fence on St. Martinsville's main street, commemorates the original French Acadian settlers who came to the area in the mid-1700s after being expelled from Canada by the conquering British.

It also commemorates one of America's most popular and beloved poems, Longfellow's epic *Evangeline,* the tale of two star-crossed lovers separated by the expulsion. Tradition holds that the poem, which ends differently, was inspired by the story of Emmeline Labiche, who died brokenhearted after discovering her long-lost beau had married someone else. A mile down the road, a statue of Evangeline, sculpted in 1927, rests over the grave that is thought to be Emmeline's in the yard of nearby St. Martin's Church.

The main attraction in the park itself is the Maison Olivier. Built of bousillage and brick in 1780, the three-story structure is typical of French plantation architecture. It has been carefully restored and is filled with early Louisiana pieces.

The park backs onto Bayou Teche, and by a little lagoon you will find an exceptionally inviting

12 Zemurray Gardens. *An oak tree branches out over the brilliant azaleas at this park, which is open to visitors in the spring for hiking and picnicking.*

picnic area filled with trees curtained with Spanish moss.

Open daily except Thanksgiving, Christmas, and New Year's Day. Admission charged.
(888) 677-2900
www.lastateparks.com

16 The National D-Day Museum
945 Magazine St., New Orleans

Opened June 6, 2000, to commemorate the 56th anniversary of the Normandy invasion that liberated Europe, this one-of-a-kind museum celebrates the spirit of the men and women who sacrificed and persevered to win World War II. Founded by author Stephen Ambrose, who teaches history at the University of New Orleans, it is the only museum in the United States to cover all of the amphibious invasions of World War II. It is located in New Orleans because it was here that Andrew Higgins built the landing craft used by the Allies that helped win the war.

Located in the city's growing downtown arts district, the four-story museum complex, built in 1856, was formerly home to the Louisiana Brewery. The main gallery is divided into four state-of-the-art interactive exhibits. Within each, World War II buffs will find a mix of oral histories, never-before-seen film footage, frontline artifacts and photographs, and hands-on activities. Exhibits offer a realistic look at life on the home front as well as chronicle the military mobilization of Allied forces in the 17 "D-Days" around the world. Within the complex the Malcolm Forbes Theater features two exclusive films: *D-Day Remembered*

(Normandy) and *Price for Peace* (the Pacific).

Open daily year-round except Thanksgiving, Christmas, New Year's Day, and Mardi Gras. Admission charged.
(504) 527-6012
www.ddaymuseum.org/index

17 Jean Lafitte National Historic Park and Preserve
6 sites, with headquarters in New Orleans

Named after the state's famed pirate and patriot, this sweeping historic park offers six distinct locations to explore.

In the heart of New Orleans, the French Quarter Visitor Center on Decatur Street presents a lively overview of the history and cultural diversity of the Mississippi Delta. To get the big picture, visitors might want to start with a free walking tour.

Six miles southeast of New Orleans, the Chalmette Battlefield and National Cemetery commemorates the January 8, 1815, Battle of New Orleans—a decisive American victory over the British. Living history demonstrations capture details of military and civilian life.

Just outside of Marrero, the Barataria Preserve encompasses nearly 20,000 acres of hardwood forest, cypress swamp, and freshwater marsh, and it offers 9 miles of paved trails and more than 20 miles of waterways. Ranger-guided canoe treks pass through the bayous.

Finally, three sites are devoted to the distinctive traditions of the Acadian people. In Lafayette the Acadian Cultural Center traces the history and contributions of the hardworking people from Nova Scotia who emigrated here in the

16 The National D-Day Museum. *A Higgins landing craft, used by the Allies to help win World War II, is on display in New Orleans, where it was built.*

late 1700s. In Eunice, the Prairie Acadian Cultural Center reflects the heritage of Acadians shaped by grasslands, ideal for raising crops and grazing cattle. This center features live performances and radio broadcasts of traditional music in Cajun French. In Thibodaux, along Bayou Lafourche, the Wetlands Acadian Cultural Center depicts cultures closely linked with the area's swamps.

Open year-round except Christmas and Mardi Gras. No admission fee.
(504) 589-2113
www.nps.gov/jela

18 Grand Isle State Park
For those who enjoy sun, sand, and saltwater sports, this wild place of wind and waves can seem to be the very end of the world. It stretches for more than a mile along the Gulf of Mexico at the tip of a narrow eight-mile barrier island connected to the mainland by a bridge.

The 400-foot fishing pier (with a fish-cleaning station) gives visitors a chance to try their luck here, where almost 300 different species of fish are found.

Between the beach and the camping areas a wide protective levee has been built with sand dredged from just offshore. Because this created a strong undertow, swimming is allowed only at one's own risk.

Birders gather during the spring and fall to watch the migrating flocks on the flyway that crosses the island. Campsites do not have utilities, but there's running water at the boathouse. A three-day Tarpon Rodeo, one of 19 other fishing rodeos held right next to the park, is held the last weekend in July, attracting thousands of competitors.

Open year-round. Admission charged.
(888) 787-2559
www.lastateparks.com

Baxter State Park. *In this tranquil woodland setting, visitors can fish or rent a canoe (see page 144).*

Maine

The Pine Tree State is best known for its scenic rockbound coast, but the forests, lakes, and many other attractions should not be overlooked.

Maine was not an easy land to settle, and some of the hard work is memorialized in a farm museum, blacksmith shop, and logging museum that vividly recall the labor involved in living here. The parks and recreation areas, by the sea and in the remaining wilderness, reveal a little of what so much of this Northeastern area was like in times gone by. Here, too, are a couple of islands whose inhabitants exemplify the kind of rugged individualism on which state-of-Mainers still rightly pride themselves.

1 Fort Kent State Historic Site
Blockhouse Rd., Fort Kent

This area was first settled in the early 1800s by French colonists who were forced from their Canadian homes in Acadia (now the Maritime Provinces) when they refused to pledge allegiance to the conquering British.

The great stands of timber attracted lumbermen from Canada and the United States, and border disputes developed. Concerned about its interests, the state of Maine dispatched troops to the area and built a fort at a strategic juncture of the Fish and St. John rivers. Completed in 1839, the fort was named for Gov. Edward Kent. It was armed and manned, but the boundary disputes were settled in 1842, and no shots were ever fired.

The Blockhouse, which housed officers in the mid-1800s, was restored by the Boy Scouts and is maintained by the Maine Bureau of Parks and Lands and a local troop. A collection of antique hand tools is displayed inside.

Parking spaces, water taps, picnic tables, and fireplaces are available on the bank of the Fish River. True to its name, the river yields salmon and trout.
Open Memorial Day–Labor Day.
(207) 941-4014
www.state.me.us

1 Fort Kent State Historic Site. *The Fort Kent Blockhouse, built by the state in 1839, housed officers who were sent there to prevent border disputes with Canada.*

2 The Nylander Museum
657 Main St., Caribou

This museum not only serves as a window on the world for the citizens of northern Maine but as a point of interest for tourists who are merely passing through.

The museum is also a tribute to one man's lifelong curiosity about the world around him. At the young age of 10, Olof Nylander, the son of a shoemaker in a small Swedish town, sold his collection of local Stone Age and Bronze Age implements to a museum in the nearby city of Ystad.

Nylander came to America in his teens and developed a consuming interest in geology. Before his death in 1943 at age 79, he had

MAINE

2 Nylander Museum. *A likeness of scientist Olof Nylander is on display here.*

established a reputation as a tireless and innovative fieldworker and had published many articles in scientific journals. His wideranging personal collection of geological and freshwater and marine-life specimens, as well as American Indian and other artifacts, is housed in the museum.

The tidy white clapboard structure was built in 1938 by the Works Progress Administration, a federally funded organization established to provide much needed employment during the Depression.

In addition to the extensive Nylander collections and archives, the museum houses permanent displays of butterflies, artifacts made by the local Micmac and Malecite people, large taxidermy specimens from Northern Maine, and local Devonian and Silurian fossils. Special exhibits are mounted during the summer season.

Open Tue.–Sat., Memorial Day–Labor Day; winter P.M. hours, Mon., Wed., and Thurs.
(207) 493-4209

www.nylandermuseum.org

MAINE

Legend

10 NUMBERED ATTRACTIONS (Described in text)

CONTROLLED ACCESS HIGHWAYS
- Free
- Toll
- Under Construction

OTHER HIGHWAYS
- Primary Highway
- Secondary Highway

CITIES AND TOWNS
- ⊕ National Capital
- ⊛ State Capital
- • Cities, Towns, and Populated Places Type size indicates relative importance
- Urban Area

HIGHWAY MARKERS
- 12 Interstate Route
- 12 U.S. Route
- 12 State Route
- 12 Distances along Major Highways (in miles)

RECREATION AND FEATURES OF INTEREST
- National Park
- Other Large Park or Recreation Area
- Trail
- Ferry

— MAPQUEST —

0   20   40   60 Miles
0   20   40   60 Kilometers

③ Baxter State Park
Millinocket, South Branch Pond

Few governors have been more generous to their constituents than Percival P. Baxter. Between 1930 and 1962 he bought and gave to the people of the state of Maine some 200,000 acres of wilderness and set up trust funds to defray the costs of development and maintenance.

The state has kept faith with the intent of the gift, and it strictly enforces the rules that sustain the spirit of wilderness here. No pets or other domestic animals and no motorcycles, trail bikes, or other all-terrain vehicles are permitted in the park. Snowmobiles are strictly limited to specific areas. Hunting, trapping, and the use of weapons are prohibited except in certain areas during the hunting season. For anyone seeking the peace and quiet that the wilderness can offer, these are all welcome regulations.

Vehicles more than 9 feet high, 7 feet wide, and 22 feet long are not allowed in the park. Maximum length for a car and trailer is 44 feet.

At South Branch Pond, in a tranquil woodland setting, you can rent a canoe, enjoy one of the inviting picnic spots that offer fireplaces, or spend the night in a lean-to shelter or tent site (available by reservation) in a grove of white birches. Hiking trails in this area vary in length, ranging from less than half a mile to almost 10 miles.

Park open for day use and camping mid-May–mid-Oct.; winter camping Nov. 1–Mar. 31. Admission charged. Reservations suggested.
(207) 723-5140
www.baxterstateparkauthority.com

③ Baxter State Park. *A hiker stops to take in the view atop Mount Katahdin in a park that is known for its peace and quiet.*

④ Patten Lumbermen's Museum
Patten

Before the Revolution, when Britannia ruled the waves, the great stands of pine along the coastline were reserved by the Crown to be used as masts for the mighty ships of the line.

The product has changed in size, from 75-foot masts to the toothpicks now made here by the billions, but the material is the same: pine from the Pine Tree State. It is fitting that the history of lumbering is commemorated here in Patten, where the industry still survives and logging trucks continue to roar by.

Of the 4,500 artifacts on display, a goodly percentage are from the collection of the late Dr. Lore Rogers. They include tools and equipment for every imaginable lumber-camp chore.

One of the 10 buildings on the site is a reconstructed 1820 logging camp, where crew members once slept on rows of evergreen boughs. The limited space reveals how short of stature these men must have been and belies the public image of the giant lumberjack.

Photographs, dioramas, and working models illustrate how standing timber was felled and converted to lumber in the early days. A featured display is the old and rare Lombard Steam Log Hauler. As the predecessor of the continuous-tread bulldozer and the military tank, it has been declared a national historic mechanical engineering landmark.

Open Tues.–Sun., July 1– Aug. 31; Fri.–Sun. Memorial Day–June 30 and Sept. 1–Columbus Day. Admission charged.
(207) 528-2650
www.lumbermensmuseum.org

⑤ Lily Bay State Park
Greenville

This is a pleasant place to sample the appealing character of the rugged Maine woods, and with 925 acres in the park, crowding is not a problem. The moose in the area frequently favor Lazy Tom Bog. Although any moose in the wild is a memorable sight, they are at their most impressive here when autumn nights foreshadow the coming of winter and the animals begin to group together.

Also unforgettable is the haunting cry of the loon, a beautiful diving bird with a distinctive white necklace in sharp contrast to its black plumage.

Fishermen here try for lake trout, known locally as togue, brook trout, and salmon.

The views of Moosehead Lake and Big Moose Mountain to the southwest are magnificent. The park offers a pebbled swimming beach and a small field for Frisbee, volleyball, and other games.
Open May 1–Oct. 15.
(207) 695-2700
www.state.me.us

⑥ Moosehead Marine Museum
Greenville

The museum houses a small onshore collection of marine memorabilia, but the centerpiece here is a 110-foot lake steamer. The steel-hulled *Katahdin* was built in 1914 to take tourists to the luxurious Mount Kineo Resort and other destinations on Moosehead Lake. The lavishly appointed ship, with fixtures and furnishings of brass, mahogany, leather, and velvet, was queen of the Maine lake steamers for more than 20 years. When the resort failed after World War I, the *Katahdin* was reduced to the hard service of towing log rafts on the lake. Then environmental considerations put a stop to the rafting of logs, and it seemed that this historic ship (the oldest surviving steel hull built by the Bath Iron Works) was headed for the scrap heap.

She was saved, however, by a group of local enthusiasts who preserved the ship as a floating museum and put her back in service on the lake. The refurbished *Katahdin* is now available for short cruises and group charters. In addition, a number of interesting marine artifacts are displayed on board.

From the deck of the original passenger carrier here, one can see the sleek seaplanes that now serve the lakeshore and the wilderness beyond.

Open July 1–Columbus Day weekend.
Admission charged.
(207) 695-2716
www.katahdincruises.com

7 Wyman Lake
Rte. 201, Moscow
Few hydroelectric projects relate so well to their surroundings as does this one. For 16 miles along its high eastern shore, superb panoramic views of Wyman Lake and its somber background of timbered mountains await the visitor. History is remembered here, and at a scenic outlook about four miles south of Caratunk a tablet marks the place where Benedict Arnold and more than 1,000 men left the Kennebec River on an expedition to Canada in 1775. Their mission was to participate in an assault on Quebec.

Today there is excellent access to the lake to the north at the Caratunk boat landing and to the

south at the Moscow boat landing.

The views are less spectacular along the road that follows the west shore, but other attractions are found, including bathing beaches and, seven miles north of the dam, a picnic area. Of interest to birders are the bald eagles, osprey, and loons seen here.
(207) 672-4100
**http://mainetourism.com/region/
Kennebec.html**

8 The Blacksmith Shop Museum
107 Dawes Rd., Dover-Foxcroft
Before the days of mass production, mail-order parts, paved highways, and automobiles, every small community had to be largely self-sufficient, and the skills of the

ironworker were much in demand. The village smithy in earlier times was as essential to the community as the general store.

Here in a small shingled barn, where the fires of the forge went out in 1905, the tools of this demanding and disappearing craft are displayed along with some of the handmade iron objects that were used for farming, transportation, recreation, and everyday living.

A harness-repair bench, a cheese press, an ox lifter, and other old-time implements remind the visitor of a less complex time— when horsepower was provided by horses instead of machines.
Building is open daily, Memorial Day weekend–Oct.; admission is free, but donations are accepted.
(207) 564-8618
www.dover-foxcroft.org/rec.htm

7 Wyman Lake. *A hydroelectric dam created this lake, where visitors can swim, fish, go boating, or hike its perimeter.*

9 Moosehorn National Wildlife Refuge
Baring
Anyone who is interested in seeing Northeastern wildlife in its natural habitat would be well advised to spend some time here.

The refuge, one of more than 400 across the nation, is on the Atlantic Flyway and provides feeding and resting grounds for flights of migratory birds.

More than 200 species have been observed here, and most of these, including the osprey and bald eagle, are commonly seen. There are two observation decks from which birders can view the many different varieties that flock here. Visitors can even accompany wildlife biologists on certain bird-tagging expeditions. The refuge puts a major emphasis on determining and providing for the ecological needs of the American woodcock. This interesting bird has been steadily declining in number as its woodland habitat has been encroached upon.

The various tracts in the refuge total about 2,500 acres and support some 40 kinds of mammals year-round. At the Edmunds Unit, 20 miles to the south, harbor seals and Atlantic porpoises are seen offshore. The bear, moose, fox, bobcat, deer, and beaver are to be expected inhabitants in this environment, but that supposed Westerner, the coyote, is something of a surprise.

Vose Pond and Bearse Lake are recommended for fishing. Snowmobiling is also a popular sport here.
Open year-round.
(207) 454-7161
http://moosehorn.fws.gov

 Quoddy Head State Park. *Above, the Maine wilderness stretches out into the Atlantic at the easternmost point of land in the United States. Below, West Quoddy Head Light has served as a beacon to ships since 1808.*

for about two and a half miles around the head offers good views of nearby West Quoddy Head Light, where a beacon has served mariners since 1808. The sunrise can be spectacular here and often has an interesting greenish cast. In summer this is a favorite place for whale watching.

Open May 15–Oct. 15.
(207) 733-0911
www.state.me.us

Roque Bluffs State Park
6 miles off Rte. 1, Roque Bluffs
The 274 acres that make up this relatively new coastal park were acquired in 1968 and converted for recreational use a decade later. Roque Bluffs is still quiet and infrequently visited, partly because it is often enshrouded by fog. July is the best month to enjoy its half-mile crescent beach, but even then the waters of Englishman's Bay are chilly. The shore affords pleasing views of several wooded islands, one of which is Roque Island.

The park includes the 33-acre Simpson's Pond, where swimming and fishing are permitted. The most frequent catch is brown trout. The pond is also home to otters and beavers. Among the park's many species of winged residents is the bald eagle.

At several spots there are well-equipped picnic sites, one of which has a playground. The park has boardwalks but no camping facilities.

Open May 15–Sept. 30;
accessible year-round.
(207) 255-3475
www.state.me.us

Quoddy Head State Park
Lubec
A bit of the Maine wilderness can be sampled in this 532-acre park, which includes the easternmost point of land in the United States. Here in the spruce woodlands, deer and an occasional moose may be seen, but predatory bobcats and coyotes are said to be reducing their number. Porcupines and rabbits range through the park, and the usual birds of the Northeastern woods and meadows are abundant.

One of the inland trails includes a section of boardwalk beside a peat bog, with signs to identify the wildflowers that grow here in profusion. The main trail that runs

Abbe Museum
Two locations: Acadia National Park and 26 Mount Desert St., downtown Bar Harbor
American Indians have lived in Maine for more than 12,000 years. The Abbe is the only museum devoted exclusively to the state's first people, collectively known as the Wabanaki, "The People of the Dawn," who are members of the Passamaquoddy, Penobscot, Micmac, and Maliseet tribes.

A visit to the original Abbe, listed on the *National Register of Historic Places,* is a step back in time. Since 1928, it has welcomed explorers each spring through fall in a lovely wooded setting at Sieur de Monts Spring in Acadia National Park. The museum was founded by Dr. Robert Abbe, a pioneering New York surgeon and summer resident of Bar Harbor. After painstakingly assembling a collection of American Indian artifacts from the area, Dr. Abbe established a trailside museum to store and display the treasures.

Since then, the museum's collection has grown to include objects spanning 10,000 years, from kitchen utensils to contemporary crafts. Many of the oldest artifacts, such as stone and bone tools and pottery, were excavated during the Abbe's archaeology field research.

The Abbe Museum has expanded into a second site in downtown Bar Harbor, just two and a half miles from its pastoral sister. The new Abbe features a hands-on Learning Laboratory and spacious galleries for works of art and cultural exhibitions. A highlight is the Circle of the Four Directions, a unique gallery reflecting the importance of the circle in American Indian cultures. In summer and fall, a free local shuttle service eases the journey between the two Abbe locations.

Sieur de Monts Spring: Open from Memorial Day weekend—mid-October.
Downtown Bar Harbor:
Open year-round except Thanksgiving, Christmas, and the month of January.
No admission charge for American Indians and children under 6.
(207) 288-3519
www.abbemuseum.org

13 Schoodic Peninsula

The only part of Acadia National Park on the mainland, Schoodic Peninsula has fewer tourists than the larger, more diverse, and better-known Mount Desert Island. But something of the special character of Acadia is perhaps more beguiling here, where headlands of weathered rock reach down to the water, and farther out, at Schoodic Point, the ocean is tumultuous and spectacular. The heavy seas thunder headlong into great shelves of pink granite and spray high into the air.

John G. Moore acquired the peninsula to use as a wild park adjacent to a resort he was planning

to build. But he died in 1899, and the property went to his heirs. They offered it as an addition to the existing Lafayette National Park on Mount Desert Island, with the stipulation that the name of the park be changed. By an act of Congress in 1929, the peninsula was added, and the name of the park was changed to Acadia.

From Route 186 the entire rugged shoreline is paralleled by a six-mile-long stretch of well-maintained one-way road that drivers share with cyclists. At frequent turnouts splendid seascapes break through the forest wall and offer views of reed bogs, stony coves where shorebirds feed, bays dotted with lobster boats, and wooded islands in the distance. A mile-long gravel road climbs to the summit at Schoodic Head, where on clear days the coastal view is magnificent.

The Blueberry Hill parking area is the departure point for hiking trails ascending inland through stands of spruce and across open hillsides dotted with low-bush blueberries. One steep trail ascends 180 feet to a promontory called

The Anvil. One can also walk down toward the water to view marine flora and fauna. Shorebirds are abundant, and bald eagles are occasionally seen.

Open year-round, dawn to dusk.
(207) 963-7194
www.nps.gov/acad/schoodic/intro.htm

14 Stanwood Wildlife Sanctuary and Homestead

Ellsworth

This property was owned and cared for by one family for more than 100 years, and one member of that family devoted her lifetime to the careful study of nature. It is not surprising, therefore, to find here a delightful aura of tranquillity. Capt. Roswell Stanwood built his simple white frame cottage in 1850. Fifteen years later a daughter, Cordelia, the first of five children, was born in that house.

The surrounding woods, the spring, the stream, and the ponds were affectionately called "Birdsacre" by Cordelia Stanwood. Here she developed a deep appreciation of the ways of nature—especially of birds. Her inquiring mind and compelling interest in the subject led her to become an accomplished amateur ornithologist and wildlife photographer.

She lived and worked here for more than 50 years. It is fortunate indeed that others can now visit the rooms—with original furnishings, including a square piano—walk the paths, and share a legacy of peace and quiet in a place where nature was studied, respected, and preserved.

The complex includes the unpretentious house with its comfortable, lived-in quality, the nature trails and bird sanctuary, and the

Richmond Nature Center, which includes egg and nest collections and bird mounts; an art gallery featuring the work of local wildlife artists; and a gift shop.

Stanwood Wildlife Sanctuary is licensed to care for and release orphaned, sick, or injured wildlife. There are usually a number of non-releasable owls, hawks, and songbirds in residence at Birdsacre.

Buildings are open daily June 15–Oct. 15.
(207) 667-8460
www.vpa.org/museumsme.html

15 Lake St. George State Park

Maine Rte. 3, Liberty

This attractive lakeside park is a pleasant place for picnicking, swimming, and fishing. Its handsome administration buildings are reminiscent of the 19th-century architecture prevalent in the area.

Of the three main picnic areas, one is adjacent to the lake. It has bathhouses for swimmers and a camper parking area that accommodates small- to average-size vans and trailers.

About 100 yards of the pebbly shoreline serve as a swimming beach. Wood steps provide easy access to the water, and a string of buoys outlines the safe area.

Fishermen here catch mostly bass and landlocked salmon. Boat launching is permitted, and canoes and rowboats are available for rent. In addition, the park offers swings, and trails for hiking and snowmobiling.

Open for fishing Apr.– Sept.;
for camping May 15–Oct.1.
(207) 589-4255
www.campwithME.com

12 Abbe Museum. *In downtown Bar Harbor, visitors will find the expansion of the museum, devoted to the state's American Indian heritage.*

MAINE

16 Washburn-Norlands Living History Center

Off Rte. 108, Livermore
This impressive complex was built for the Washburns, a remarkable family of 19th-century political, military, and business leaders.

The Washburn house is a fine example of the Italianate style. Pure New England, however, are the farmer's cottage and the large barn attached to the house in deference to the hard winters here.

The library, built in 1883 to serve the family and the community, is a handsome granite building in the High Victorian Gothic style. Architecture of an earlier day is also exemplified by the old-time schoolhouse and the white clapboard church with tall, narrow arched windows, ornate latticed bell tower, and a steeple crowned with an old-fashioned weathervane.

A variety of hands-on living history programs, which make the past come alive, are offered year-round for groups by reservation. They range from a 90-minute "Journeys Back in Time" presentation to a 48-hour "Family Live-In" lasting two days and nights. Family members live as they might have in rural 19th-century Maine, including chores and cooking. Children attend school in a one-room schoolhouse. A 24-hour variation of this program is also offered.

Set on 445 acres of woods and farmland, the center is also open daily in the summer for drop-in tours of the historic buildings. Picnic tables are available on shady lawns.

Open daily July–Aug. Admission charged. For dates and fees for all programs and special events, call (207) 897-4366.
www.norlands.org

17 Crocker Pond Campground

Off Rte. 5, south of Bethel
This campground, near the boundary of the 3,000-acre Patte Brook Multiple Use Management Area, has seven developed sites—each of them with tent pads, picnic tables, fireplaces, water, and toilet facilities. There is also a small field where you can pitch a tent or park a trailer.

Crocker Pond and the nearby Broken Bridge Pond are stocked with brook trout. Round Pond, also good for fishing, is reached by a pleasant one-mile walk along Albany Brook. The many kinds of conifers, hardwoods, and undergrowth in the area provide shelter for deer, hares, moose, black bears, and wildfowl. About a half-mile west of Crocker Pond Road is the old Pingree Mine, where rockhounds can go to look for mica, beryllium, and other minerals.

Accessible year-round. Campground open mid-May–mid-Oct.
(207) 824-2134
www.fs.fed.us/ra/white

18 Wadsworth-Longfellow House

487 Congress St., Portland
The oldest remaining residence on the Portland peninsula and the first historic house museum in the state, this three-story brick dwelling was the childhood home of 19th-century America's most celebrated poet, Henry Wadsworth Longfellow. From his birth in 1807 until he entered Bowdoin College in 1822, Longfellow spent his early life here—much of it immersed in writing.

At the age of 13 he had his first poem published in the local Portland *Gazette*. Within this house, which he regarded as his home until his second marriage, in 1843, when he moved to Cambridge, Massachusetts, Longfellow also composed several of his best-known poems, including *The Song of Hiawatha* and *The Midnight Ride of Paul Revere*.

The Wadsworth-Longfellow House affords a fascinating glimpse of the famous poet's formative years. His father, Stephen Longfellow, was a lawyer who firmly believed in education and sent young Henry to school when he was only 3. His mother, Zilpah Wadsworth, made a daily practice of reading aloud to Henry and his siblings—with a preference for the adventures of Ossian, the legendary Gaelic hero. On his mother's side, the poet's noted ancestors included Pilgrim settlers John and Priscilla Alden, who inspired his classic *The Courtship of Miles Standish*.

Occupied by members of the Wadsworth and Longfellow families until 1901, when it was given to the Maine Historical Society and opened to the public, the house contains original furnishings and many family artifacts. Graced with New England charm, it now appears as it did during the 1850s. Behind the house the elegant Longfellow garden offers a Colonial revival oasis.

Open 10 A.M.–4 P.M. daily, June 1–Oct. 31. Admission charged.
(207) 774-1822
http://dlstewart.com/longfellow/
maine_house.htm

19 Eagle Island State Historic Site

Accessible in summer by ferry from Mackerel Cove on Bailey Island
Eagle Island, about two miles offshore, was the lifelong retreat

16 Washburn-Norlands Living History Center. *The past comes alive at this center, where visitors can experience life as it was in 19th-century Maine.*

20 Monhegan Island. *The beauty of Maine is evident here, where the ocean is calm enough to permit fishing or swimming.*

of Adm. Robert E. Peary, who discovered the North Pole on April 6, 1909. The celebration Peary expected on his return did not take place because another explorer claimed to have been there first.

Scientific evidence and a congressional inquiry later confirmed, however, that Peary's expedition was the first to raise a flag at the top of the world. Peary built the house on Eagle Island and spent most of his summers here. He left the place to his daughter and son, who donated it to the state of Maine for use as a historic museum.

The large house, with a three-sided fireplace in the living room and a big restaurant-style stove in the kitchen, has an aura of hospitality that belies the admiral's reputation as a stern authoritarian.

Peary was a taxidermist, and he prepared all of the arctic and Maine birds displayed in the house.

A small ocean beach is open to swimmers willing to brave the chill waters, and the woods offer a pleasant choice of short nature trails.

If you plan to stop over, bring food and refreshments, as none are sold on the island. Contact the Bureau of Parks and Lands for boat information to the island. *(207) 624-6080*

www.state.me.us

20 Monhegan Island

Situated 10 miles out in the Atlantic, this 650-acre isle epitomizes the beauty of windswept Maine, with its rocky coasts, rugged headlands, moors, and forests of spruce and balsam. The surrounding ocean surf is calm enough for fishing or an invigorating dip on some beaches but turbulent and unpredictable on the seaward sides. Here, also, the traditional Maine industry of lobster fishing has been refined to a science with an enforced shortened season to sustain the size and quality of the catch.

In its remoteness, Monhegan has resisted two pervasive features of modern life: electricity (there is no electric power except for privately owned generators) and automobiles, which cannot be brought to the island. The attractions are to be enjoyed on foot. Of the 17 miles of trails, some are quite rough, marked only by stacked rocks.

In the village, as dusk descends, most of the residents light up their gas or kerosene lamps to accompany the stars and moonlight. For several generations artists have summered on the island and contributed to a prodigious output of coastal landscapes and seascapes. Beginning in July, many of these works are on display in the Monhegan Museum, the Plantation Gallery, and artists' studios.

Among the most interesting of the various birds and animals seen here are the harbor seals, which are best observed at half tide at the northern end of the island. Fishing is also a favorite pastime here.

Inns, guesthouses, and cottages offer accommodations, and there are a few restaurants. There are no bars, and liquor is not sold. Camping and backpacking are not permitted. From mid-June to September, boats make daily round trips, for which advance reservations are strongly advised. *Two ferry lines go to Monhegan: Monhegan Boat Line (207) 372-8848 and Hardy Boat Cruises (207) 677-2026. Rockland-Thomaston Area Chamber of Commerce: (800) 562-2529*

www.therealmaine.com

www.briegull.com/monhegan/ mibooklet.html

20 Monhegan Island. *Artists flock here each summer to paint coastal landscapes and seascapes. Many of their works are on display in the Monhegan Museum.*

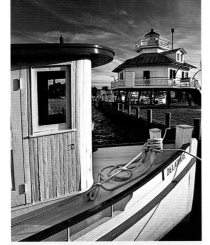

St. Michaels. *A tugboat sits in the harbor at the Chesapeake Bay Maritime Museum (see page 154).*

Maryland

From the coastal plain to the Appalachian Mountains, this state has all the natural regions that typify the eastern United States.

Endowed with a diversity of landforms—including the Piedmont, the Blue Ridge province, and the Ridge and Valley province—within its irregular borders, Maryland offers spectacular mountain scenery, lakes, streams, beaches, and a seaside cliff rich with ice age fossils. The state also supports an important refuge for waterfowl. Here on the Atlantic Flyway it is not surprising that the art of decoy carving was highly developed. Two museums are dedicated to the subject. Another attraction is a town that claims to be the seafood capital of the world.

1 Swallow Falls State Park
Maple Glade Rd., Oakland

This peaceful woodland park on the rocky banks of the swift-running Youghiogheny River contains some of Maryland's most spectacular scenery. It has been a longtime favorite with campers. A plaque marks the site where naturalist John Burroughs and inventors Thomas Edison, Harvey Firestone, and Henry Ford camped in 1918.

Today the park contains two large camping areas. Hiking trails, which cut through a stand of 300-year-old virgin hemlocks towering above verdant expanses of ferns, mountain laurel, and rhododendrons, connect to an extensive system of paths and old logging roads in adjoining Garrett State Forest.

The Canyon Trail, considered to be one of the most beautiful in the state, leads from Swallow Falls to Muddy Creek Falls. Along the rocky ledges are many plant fossils. Another hiking trail crosses a swinging bridge above sparkling Muddy Creek Falls and loops around to the pool below. The highest vertical waterfall in Maryland, with a plunge of 52 feet, it is seen to best advantage from its base. In these deep, quiet woodlands the visitor is likely to observe deer, wild turkeys, beavers, and an occasional fox. Black bears also roam the forest.

2 New Germany State Park. *This 210-acre park lies within the Savage River State Forest, where in winter a blanket of snow on Monroe Run Vista entices cross-country skiers and snowmobilers.*

The Youghiogheny River, a favorite with fishermen, is stocked with trout several times a year.

Park open year-round; camping end of Mar.–mid-Dec.
(301) 387-6938
www.dnr.state.md.us

2 New Germany State Park
New Germany Rd., Grantsville

Located on the site of several abandoned 19th-century mills in the midst of the Savage River State Forest, this 210-acre park is a favorite family recreation area.

The lake here was created in the mid-1800s, when John Swauger dammed Poplar Lick Run to provide waterpower for his sawmill and gristmill; now it is a pleasant setting for picnicking, swimming, boating, and fishing. Trout and bass are the favorite game fish, and rowboats are available for rent.

Hiking trails of varying levels of difficulty wind through the park and connect with other paths in the surrounding forest (Maryland's largest state forest), where deer, turkeys, and grouse abound. A 17-mile trail provides spectacular vistas along the crest of Big Savage Mountain. In winter many of these

trails are used for cross-country skiing or snowmobiling.

Camping facilities range from rustic but comfortably equipped log cabins and a spacious family camping area in the park to primitive sites in the more remote regions of the forest.

Both sailboating and canoeing are permitted on the 350-acre Savage River Reservoir.

Park open year-round; camping end of Mar.–beginning of Nov. Admission charged.
(301) 895-5453

www.dnr.state.md.us

3 Washington Monument State Park and Appalachian Trail Crossing

Off Rte. 40, Boonsboro
In 1827, when memories of the Revolutionary War were still fresh, several hundred townspeople from Boonsboro, including three veterans of the war, built a stone tower on top of nearby South Mountain, possibly the country's first monument to the memory of George Washington.

The tower slowly deteriorated over the years and in 1882 had to be restored. After 10 years or so a crack developed, and the tower again fell into disrepair and lay in

ruins for many years. The present 35-foot monument, built by the Civilian Conservation Corps, was dedicated on July 4, 1936, just 109 years after the patriotic citizens of Boonsboro first gathered in the town square and, to the sound of fife and drum, shouldered their pickaxes and marched up the mountainside.

The tower is reached by a fairly steep, well-surfaced trail lined with plaques highlighting George Washington's life. Inside, a winding staircase leads to the top, which affords a remarkable view of the countryside to the northwest.

The Appalachian Trail passes the tower and can be walked for a few miles within the park. The Cumberland Valley is on a major north-south flyway for migrating hawks and eagles, which can be seen from about the middle of September through November. The visitors center houses a small collection of firearms, American Indian relics, and Civil War memorabilia.

Park open year-round; visitors center Apr.–Oct.
(301) 791-4767

www.dnr.state.md.us

4 Boonsborough Museum. *Civil War relics from Antietam and Harper's Ferry can be found here.*

4 Boonsborough Museum of History & Crystal Grottoes Cavern

113 N. Main Street, Boonsboro
Founded by brothers George and William Boone, relatives of the more famous Daniel, the historic town of Boonsboro went through several name changes—Boones Berry and Margaretsville among them—before settling on its current one around 1841.

For anyone interested in the area's history, this museum houses a unique collection. In addition to Civil War relics from the battlefields of South Mountain, Antietam, and Harper's Ferry, it boasts a formidable collection of firearms, from tiny watch fob pistols to 45 cannons, some weighing several tons, as well as more than 500 weapons from around the world.

The museum features rare books, including an original copy of *Martyr's Mirror,* the largest book printed in Colonial America; a fossil collection that includes dinosaur bones and mammoth and mastodon teeth; 37 Russian icons and "relics" of famous saints; more than 150 objects from the *El Enfante,* the Spanish galleon that

sank off the Florida coast in 1733; and the reconstruction of a cabinetmaker's shop of 1860.

Boonsboro is also home to Crystal Grottoes Caverns, one of the largest caves of its kind in the country. Winding through illuminated walkways, visitors will revel at natural sculptures made of pure-white stalactites and stalagmites. Guides demystify the rare formations on a 40-minute tour.
Museum open Sundays, May– Sept. and by appointment. Admission charged. Caverns open 10 A.M.–5 P.M. daily, mid-Apr.–mid-Oct.; weekends in the winter. Admission charged.
Museum: (301) 432-6969
Caverns: (301) 432-6336
www.cyberlearningworld.com/nhhs/ atlas/boonsmus.htm
www.goodearthgraphics.com/ showcave/md/crystal.html

5 Historical Society of Carroll County's Sherman-Fisher-Shellman House

206 E. Main St., Westminster
In the days when Westminster was a trading center for grain-laden wagons bound from central Pennsylvania to the port of Baltimore, one of the finest buildings on Main Street was No. 206. The handsome Georgian town house was built in 1807 by Jacob Sherman, a German settler from Pennsylvania, as a wedding gift for his daughter.

Now called the Sherman-Fisher-Shellman House after a series of owners, the two-and-a-half-story brick mansion is now a house museum depicting life in Carroll County in the early 1800s.

Next door, in the Kimmey House (circa 1800), is the Shriver-Weybright Exhibition Gallery, which has rotating exhibits on

topics relating to Carroll County history. There are also three other historical buildings that are run by the society.
Open year-round. Closed holidays. Admission charged.
(410) 848-6494
www.carr.org/hscc

6 Rocks State Park

I-95 north to Rte. 24 exit; north on Rte. 24 to Forest Hill
Atop a 190-foot cliff overlooking the rolling hills of Deer Creek valley looms an enormous, throne-like rock formation known as the King and Queen Seat, so named, it is said, for the ceremonial meetings held here by the Susquehannock Indians.

The rock formation is only a short walk from the ridgetop parking lot; five other trails of varying length and steepness lead up the cliff from the road in the valley below. Delightful picnic spots are set along the banks of Deer Creek, a lovely little mountain stream that winds among steep-sided hills clad with mixed evergreens

and hardwoods.
Open year-round except Thanksgiving and Christmas week. Admission charged.
(410) 557-7994
www.dnr.state.md.us

7 Montpelier Mansion

Rte. 197, Laurel
This beautifully proportioned Georgian house was built for Maj. Thomas Snowden just after the Revolution. It is an elegant structure situated on a high knoll. Its English boxwood gardens, planted in the 1700s, are considered to be among the loveliest in America. Many of the rooms have been researched and furnished as they would have appeared from the end of the 18th century. The staff offers tours, re-enactments, teas, and lectures.

Major Snowden's marriage in 1774 to Ann Ridgely, a rich heiress, supplemented his already considerable estate. It also gave the vast plantation a name—Montpelier—in honor of his bride's

7 Montpelier Mansion. *George and Martha Washington enjoyed the hospitality of Maj. Thomas Snowden and his wife here, as did Abigail Adams, who praised the 18th-century Georgian house as "large, handsome, and elegant."*

7 Montpelier Mansion. *This Georgian house was built just after the Revolutionary War, and its English boxwood gardens, planted at that time, are considered to be among America's loveliest.*

birthplace in Anne Arundel County.

George and Martha Washington occasionally visited Montpelier, as did Abigail Adams, who praised the "large, handsome, elegant House" and the Snowdens' "true English hospitality."

Montpelier passed from the Snowden family to several other owners before it was acquired by Prince George's County in 1961.

Tour hours: Sun.–Thu., Mar.–Nov.; Sundays only, Dec.–Feb. Gardens open year-round. Admission charged for house tours.
(301) 953-1376
www.pgparks.com

8 Tuckahoe State Park
Rte. 404, Queen Anne
The rolling, wooded hills and open meadows of this 3,800-acre valley, traversed by quiet, lovely Tuckahoe Creek, create a remarkably attractive and varied park.

Trails of varying difficulty are here, from the Tuckahoe Valley Trail to the Lake Trail. For an even more vigorous workout, try the two-mile, 20-station exercise course and two playgrounds which are provided. Other popular pastimes at the park include kayaking and fishing. And if you have your own canoe, you can try the five-and-a-half-mile trail on

Tuckahoe Creek, or take a guided trip with a park naturalist, available throughout the year. And for nature lovers, the 500-acre Adkins Arboretum (the first to be built in Maryland) contains all the trees, shrubs, and plants indigenous to the state. A dam across Tuckahoe Creek forms Crouse Mill Lake, at the end of which is a flooded forest. A pair of bald eagles may be seen here, perched on the spectral white trunks rising from the water.

Park open year-round; camping end of Mar.–mid-Dec.
(410) 820-1668
www.dnr.state.md.us

9 Port Tobacco
As early as 1608 an Indian settlement called Potopaco was noted here on a map drawn by Capt. John Smith. In the 1630s an English community was established, and about a hundred years later the town of Port Tobacco became the seat of colonial government in Charles County. The burgeoning tobacco trade brought the planters modest prosperity, and a few handsome homes were built. Some have been

restored and can be seen today around the village.

The reconstructed courthouse, an unusual blend of late medieval and classic Georgian styles of architecture, now includes a 19th-century courtroom and a museum of American Indian artifacts, Civil War relics, and local memorabilia.

Although the canal and river that provided access to the Potomac and the sea are now filled with silt, Port Tobacco still retains the quiet charm of an 18th-century seaport village.

Courthouse and museum open P.M. Wed., Sat., Sun., Apr.–Sept. Admission charged.
(800) 766-3386
www.charlescounty.org/tourism

10 Cedarville State Forest
Brandywine
A scant 25 miles southeast of the nation's capital, this extensive forested area, once the favored winter hunting grounds of the Piscataway Indians, provides a welcome contrast to the fast pace and clamorous noise of the city. Within the 3,510 acres are 19.5 miles of

marked trails for hiking, biking, and horseback riding (but no rentals), self-guiding nature trails, picnic sites, a four-acre fishing pond stocked with bluegill, catfish, pickerel, and bass, and a historic kiln where charcoal was once made.

There's also a fish hatchery open to the public on Tuesdays and Thursdays. Legend has it that an ancient American burial ground exists in the forest, though it has yet to be discovered.

Cedarville is also the site of the headwaters of the mile-wide, 20-mile-long Zekiah Swamp, home to many plant, bird, and wildlife species. A few drainage ditches are the only remaining evidence of backbreaking efforts in colonial times to drain the swamp for cultivation. The labor was in vain, and the wooded bottomland remains largely as it was hundreds of years ago.

Park open year-round; camping end of Mar.–beginning of Dec.
(301) 888-1410
www.dnr.state.md.us

9 Port Tobacco. *Named for its prosperous tobacco farms in the 1700s, the town still retains the quiet charm of an 18th-century seaport village. Above, visitors can tour the historic one-room schoolhouse.*

11 St. Michaels

This charming colonial town on the Miles River, an inlet from Eastern Bay, is centered at St. Mary's Square, the original "green" around which the town was built. Here you will find some of the best preserved and most picturesque 18th- and 19th-century houses on the Eastern Shore.

Along the harbor nine waterfront buildings have been incorporated into the Chesapeake Bay Maritime Museum, where the fascinating lore of the tidelands is featured. These include the boatbuilder's shop with its completed watercraft on display; the historic Colchester Beach bandstand; an 18th-century corncrib, which houses small gunning boats; and the Hooper Strait Lighthouse, moved from its original site on Hooper Island.

The waterfowl building contains a splendid collection of decoys, hunting guns, and the sneakbox and sinkbox boats once used by commercial duck hunters.

Museum open daily year-round except Thanksgiving, Christmas, and New Year's Day.

(410) 745-2916

www.cbmm.org

12 Calvert Cliffs State Park
Scotland

These steep-sided, 60- to 75-foot-high cliffs, which dominate the western shoreline of Chesapeake Bay for 30 miles, are dramatic reminders that a warm, shallow sea covered this area some 15 million years ago. During the subsequent ice ages the sediments were compressed. As the ice finally receded, the land was uplifted, the sea level lowered, and the ancient seafloor was exposed to the forces of wind and water, which created

11 St. Michaels. *At the Chesapeake Bay Maritime Museum, visitors can visit the Hooper Strait Lighthouse, relocated from its original site on Hooper Island.*

the massive, precipitous cliffs.

More than 600 species of fossils have been identified here, but because of erosion, climbing on the cliffs and digging for these relics is prohibited. They can, however, be found on the beach. Sharks' teeth are the most abundant, but various kinds of fossil shells are also found. An easy two-mile trail leads to the beach.

The park also has a one-acre fishing pond, picnic tables and grills, a playground, and many hiking trails. Ranger-guided nature walks are given during the summer.

Open daily year-round; $3 per car.

(301) 872-5688

www.dnr.state.md.us

13 Solomons Island
At the confluence of the Patuxent River and Chesapeake Bay in Calvert County

Barely a mile long and fittingly fishhook-shaped, Solomons Island was named in 1870 for Isaac Solomon, the Baltimore businessman who established its first

oyster-packing plant. At one time, the island was separated from the mainland, but a 23-foot causeway now links the two.

Today visitors can stroll around the harbor and follow the riverwalk down to the main street, complete with a general store that stocks bait and tackle as a staple. This charming seaside town also offers more than 20 casual restaurants; dozens of antiques, craft, and gift shops; several lovely inns and guesthouses; and several unique attractions.

One of them is Calvert Marine Museum, which reflects the area's rich maritime history. Inside, visitors will find full-scale boats, nautical-themed woodcarvings, sea-life fossils, a "touch tank" permitting petting of crabs and turtles, aquariums teeming with jewel-bright fish, and two lively river otters.

Outdoors, exhibits include a boat basin and a re-created salt marsh. From the museum's dock, seafaring spirits can sign on for a one-hour harbor cruise aboard the *Wm. B. Tennison,* the oldest Coast Guard–licensed passenger-carry-

ing vessel on the Chesapeake, built in 1899.

For more scenic views, the adventurous can climb through the hatch of the Drum Point Lighthouse, constructed in 1883 to mark the entrance to the Patuxent River. One of just three remaining of the 45 lighthouses that served the Chesapeake Bay at the beginning of the 20th century, it is beautifully restored and appointed with period furnishings.

Also restored, and also listed on the *National Register of Historic Places,* the Joseph C. Lore and Sons Oyster House offers a taste of seafood packing, circa 1934, featuring the tools and gear used by local watermen to harvest fish, softshell clams, eels, crabs, and oysters. The vintage plant also houses a boatbuilding exhibit.

For landlubbers, the peninsula offers the idyllic Annmarie Garden on St. John, which combines sculpture with carefully cultivated flora and fauna. Throughout the year, the garden hosts cultural programs and seasonal festivities, including the Garden of Lights each holiday season.

Open year-round. Admission charged.

(410) 326-6027

http://sba.solomons.md.us/attract.htm

14 Blackwater National Wildlife Refuge
Rte. 335 to Key Wallace Dr.

This 26,000-acre preserve consists mostly of salt marsh and saltwater ponds interspersed with stands of pine and mixed woodland. It is on the Atlantic Flyway and attracts vast numbers of migratory waterfowl. Many species, including whistling swans, geese, and some 20 kinds of ducks, winter here. Found here too are great blue herons, bald eagles, peregrine falcons, and the fish-eating ospreys, for which nesting platforms are built. All told, more than 241 species have been identified on the refuge, which is an obvious destination for birders.

A five-mile auto drive traverses the best of the area. A short walking trail winds through a typical section of woodland, and a trail on a boardwalk puts you right into the marshy habitat.

Mammals here include the muskrat, otter, skunk, opossum, deer, and red fox. The Delmarva fox squirrel, a large light gray species, is on the endangered list, and its habitat here is currently being expanded.

An observation tower provides a wide view of the refuge.

Open year-round.
(410) 228-2677
http://blackwater.fws.gov

15 The Ward Museum of Wildfowl Art

909 S. Schumaker Dr., Salisbury
The Ward Foundation, named for the late Steve and Lem Ward, is the sponsor of this unusual museum dedicated to the craft and art of decoy carving. The brothers, who began carving and painting decoys in 1918, were acknowledged masters, and their work now brings high prices. The museum features a replica of the Wards' workshop at Crisfield in southern Maryland (see No. 17).

The Wards fashioned both the classic working decoys and the remarkably lifelike decorative models. Fine examples of both styles—and the work of many others—are on display.

Using decoys to attract live ducks and geese is a practice of long standing. Shown here are specimens made of rushes by American Indians about 1,000 years ago. Here too are boats and blinds, firearms, carver's tools, and a video presentation of a typical waterfowl habitat.

The foundation sponsors competitions and workshops to further the art of decoy carving and painting, and examples are available in the gift shop.
Open daily except major holidays.
Admission charged.
(410) 742-4988
www.wardmuseum.org

16 Point Lookout State Park

Point Lookout, a peninsula at the confluence of the Chesapeake Bay and Potomac River, has had a long and checkered history. It was explored by Capt. John Smith in 1612, granted by the crown to George Calvert, Lord Baltimore, in 1632, and claimed in 1634 by Calvert's son, the first governor of Maryland, as a site for the mansion he planned to build.

During the Revolution the colonists used the peninsula as a watch post for English raiding ships, and it was occasionally fired upon and plundered by the British. During the War of 1812 the British again attacked the point and in the summer of 1813 occupied the area.

In 1830 the government built a lighthouse, which still stands but is no longer used. By the time the Civil War began in 1861, Point Lookout had become a popular resort with a hotel and cottages. In 1862 the Union government leased the resort and built an army hospital. Of innovative design, the structure had ward buildings radiating out from the center like the spokes of a

wheel. Before long the Union began to use the place as a prison camp. From 1863 to the end of the war in April 1865 nearly 3,500 rebel soldiers died here as a result of exposure and disease. Two federal monuments outside the park commemorate them.

Today the point is a 1,037-acre park offering historical interest, recreational opportunities, and scenic beauty. Swimming, surf fishing, crabbing, and canoeing are all popular. The park also has rental boats, boat ramps, camping areas, playgrounds, hunting, hiking trails, and a reconstruction of an old Civil War fort and prison pen.
Open year-round. Admission charged.
(301) 872-5688
www.dnr.state.md.us

17 Crisfield

The large marina, public boat landing, wholesale and retail fish markets, and numerous crab houses and restaurants support the town's claim to be the seafood capital of the world.

Adding to the interest of this very picturesque town and the locale is the Gov. J. Millard Tawes Historical Museum, which traces the history of the Chesapeake Bay and also offers exhibits on seafood harvesting and processing. One can also take the Ward Brothers Heritage Tour and visit the workshop where the Ward brothers, famous decoy carvers, lived and worked.

For good tidewater swimming, crabbing, and fishing, the Janes Island State Park beach is accessible by ferry from Memorial Day to December. The park campground, on the mainland side, is open from March to December.

Crisfield is also the point of departure for boat trips to nearby islands. Smith Island has three quaint fishing villages and a bus service.

Tangier Island has a number of restaurants, craft shops, and guesthouses and can be toured by six-passenger beach buggies.
Chamber of Commerce: (800) 782-3913
Smith Island Cruises: (410) 425-2771
Tangier Island: (800) 863-2338.
www.crisfield.org.

17 Crisfield. *Crowds enjoy crab racing in this town, which claims to be the seafood capital of the world, offering visitors myriad crab houses, fish markets, and restaurants.*

Lowell National Historical Park. *A clock tower stands guard over the city known as the Birthplace of the American Industrial Revolution (see page 160).*

Despite a growing population, Massachusetts maintains many superb parks, preserves, and wildlife sanctuaries. It also recognizes its prominent leaders. Here you will find the home base of the remarkable Adams family and a historic house directly linked to John Alden, a signer of the Mayflower Compact. The John Greenleaf Whittier home features memorabilia of this influential poet and abolitionist. Early industry is represented by the Saugus Iron Works and the Lowell Historical Park, each of which contributed to the Industrial Revolution.

Massachusetts

Concern for its citizenry—expressed by land for public use and in memorials to its heroes—is a hallmark of the Bay State.

1 Mount Greylock State Reservation

Accessible from Rte. 2 near North Adams or from Rte. 7 near Lanesborough

If you take the road from Route 7, stop at the visitors center, which offers orientation and information on the reservation. A map available here shows campgrounds, picnic areas, and hiking trails.

As you drive the steep, winding road up the mountain from either direction, the lush hardwood forests at the lower levels give way to the low-growing, wind-sculpted evergreens at the summit, the only subalpine habitat in Massachusetts.

Greylock, at 3,491 feet, is the highest peak in Massachusetts. On the summit is a stone tower, originally designed as a lighthouse for Boston Harbor, erected here in 1933. Weather permitting, the top of the tower offers an incomparable panorama of the lovely green-clad mountains and valleys of Massachusetts, New Hampshire, Vermont, Connecticut, and New York. At the peak of Greylock is Bascom Lodge, which was built by the Civilian Conservation Corps in the late 1930s and offers food and accommodations.

Among the hiking paths in the reservation is an 11.5-mile section of the Appalachian Trail, on which you might meet some of the hardy

3 Santarella Museum & Gardens. *Sir Henry Hudson Kitson, who sculpted the Lexington Minuteman statue, designed this studio, where he worked until his death in 1947. The roof, which weighs 80 tons, was designed to simulate the swirling autumn leaves of the Berkshire Hills.*

backpackers going the full distance between Mount Katahdin in Maine and Georgia's Springer Mountain.

The weather at the summit may be quite different from that at the lower levels. Even in summer it is a good idea to take a sweater or windbreaker. The roads to the summit and campground are open from mid-May to mid-October.

Reservation open year-round; campground and lodge open mid-May–Oct. Visitors center open 9 A.M.–5 P.M. Fri.–Tues., limited hours Wed. and Thurs. (413) 499-4262

www.massparks.org

2 Pleasant Valley Wildlife Sanctuary and Canoe Meadows Wildlife Sanctuary

Take W. Dugway Rd. off Rte. 7/20 in Lenox. Canoe Meadows is located on Holmes Rd., Pittsfield.

The lifestyle of that busy builder and hydraulic engineer, the beaver, is available for all to see at Pleasant Valley, where you will get a close-up look at the gnawed stumps of the beavers' building material and the complex dams they make to control the water level in their mounded lodges.

Beavers were introduced here along Yokun Brook in 1932, and their dams have made ponds that now provide excellent habitats for

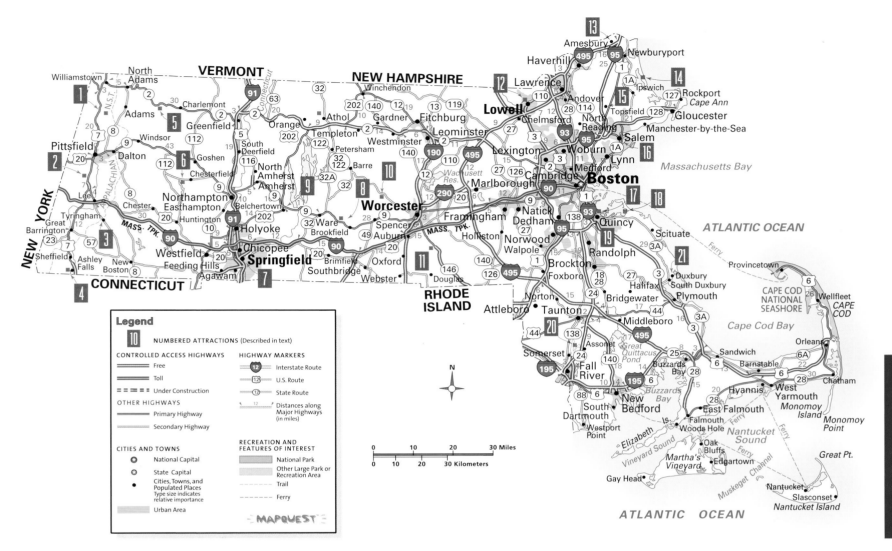

migrant waterfowl and other birds. Because the sanctuary is at a relatively high elevation, such birds as the hermit thrush, winter wren, and slate-colored junco, normally rare to this area, stay here in spring and summer instead of pushing on farther north to their usual nesting grounds.

The 1,314-acre area is laced with some seven miles of trails winding past ponds and waterways and through meadows and woods. The Trail of Ledges, which leads to a fire tower and a fine view, is steep in places and should probably not be tried by those unaccustomed to uphill hiking.

A hummingbird garden attracts numbers of these jewel-like flyers from June through August.

And if the trails and sites at Pleasant Valley have got you yearning for more, visit Canoe Meadows, located just one mile away. Established in 1975, the sanctuary consists of 262 acres of wetlands, fields, and forests along the Housatonic River, with three miles of trails and a "hidden" wildlife observation building.

Sanctuaries open year-round.
(413) 637-0320

www.massaudbon.org

3 Santarella Museum & Gardens

75 Main Rd., Tyringham
It is not surprising that this unique structure, with its undulating eaves and oddly shaped windows, set artfully behind interesting constructions of rock, was designed by a sculptor. It was the studio of Sir Henry Hudson Kitson, whose best-known works include the *Minuteman* in Lexington and the *Pilgrim Maid* in Plymouth.

While the house is reminiscent of the witch's seductive cottage in the fairy tale *Hansel and Gretel,* the attraction here is not gingerbread but modern art. After Kitson's

death in 1947, the house changed hands twice and is now a gallery dealing in sculpture, pottery, and paintings by modern artists. There is also a new museum in the old studio featuring the life and work of Kitson. Behind the house are two round silolike structures with conical roofs reinforcing the other-worldly aspect. One, attached to the house, is part of the gallery. From the back of the studio a path winds through the woods to a sculpture park with 28 statues.

Open 10 A.M.–5 P.M. daily, Memorial Day–Oct. 31. Admission charged.
(413) 243-3260

www.berkshireweb.com/santarella

4 Bartholomew's Cobble and Colonel John Ashley House

Off Rte. 7-A
Bartholomew's Cobble:
105 Weatogue Rd.
Ashley House: Cooper Hill Rd.
This site is best known for the remarkable diversity of its ferns, wildflowers, trees, shrubs, and vines and the many species of birds they attract. One need not be a naturalist to appreciate the topography of the land here, with its steep cliffs and spines of marble and quartzite.

Cobble is the New Englander's word for rocky outcrops that rise steeply, like islands of stone, from adjacent bottomlands. This one, named for George Bartholomew, who farmed the surrounding fields in the 1800s, is a natural rock garden of grand proportions.

At the small museum of natural history, you can learn more about almost everything you will see here. Walking the self-guiding Ledges Trail takes approximately 40 minutes and provides a concise, delightful experience of small-scale craggy grandeur. A somewhat longer trail leads down to the meandering Housatonic River and a classic oxbow lake.

The nearby Colonel Ashley House, built in 1735, is the oldest still standing in Berkshire County. Col. John Ashley was a member of the local committee that in 1773 drafted resolutions against British tyranny, foreshadowing the Declaration of Independence written in Philadelphia three years later. He acquired holdings of more than 3,000 acres and was among the first slave owners in Massachusetts to accept the idea of abolition.

In the house you will see handsomely finished period rooms, a

6 Chesterfield Gorge. *The force of the Westfield River cut a gorge through solid granite here, creating the setting for a perfect picnic spot.*

pottery collection, including fine examples of redware, and 18th- and 19th-century tools of many kinds.
Cobble open year-round. Natural history museum open daily Apr.1–Nov. 30. Closed Sun. and Mon., Dec.–Mar. Ashley House open weekends and Mon. holidays. Memorial Day–Columbus Day. Admission charged.
Bartholomew's Cobble: (413) 229-8600
Colonel Ashley House: (413) 298-8146
www.thetrustees.org

5 Mohawk Trail State Forest

Rte. 2 west to Charlemont
Here you will walk on paths where from time immemorial the American Indians walked, following the course of the river. The pioneers heading west through this opening named it Pioneer Valley, and they aptly called the water the Cold River.

Flowing past the picnic area and campsites, the Cold River here is swift and boulder-strewn except for a pool for swimming. To the north rises the pine-covered bulk of Mount Todd. Many paths are

available to the hiker. You can take a trail to the summit, follow the Indian Trail, which branches off to the left to a high viewpoint, or choose the one-mile trail to the south (the longest), leading to Totem Lookout.
Open year-round.
(413) 339-5504
www.state.ma.us/dem

6 Chesterfield Gorge

Rte. 143 west of Chesterfield, left on Ireland St., 0.8 mile to gorge
The dramatic power of nature is demonstrated here where the action of ancient glaciers and the erosive force of the Westfield River have cut a gorge about 100 feet deep through solid granite. The river today cascades between vertical cliffs into a deep green pool. Stunted evergreens cling precariously to crevices and ledges.

The charm of the place is its unexpected appearance. The gorge lies hardly 50 yards from a road running through farmland that

offers no clue to the powerful natural forces that created it. The ample parking and picnic facilities are a further invitation to stop off here.
Accessible year-round. Ranger on duty weekends May 1–Oct. 15. Admission charged.
(413) 684-0148
www.thetrustees.org

7 Indian Motocycle Museum & Hall of Fame

33 Hendee St., Springfield
In 1901 two bicycle enthusiasts, George M. Hendee and Oscar G. Hedstrom, opened the Indian Motocycle Manufacturing Company. (The "r" was dropped to set their product apart.)

The first motorcycles built in America were Indians, and for more than 50 years they were perhaps the world's best-known engine-driven bikes.

The permanent collection in the museum, located on a street named for one of the partners, includes one of every model of Indian Motocycle, from the 1901 Indian to the Chief, produced in 1953. Exhibits are rotated, along with other American makes of the same period.

Here, too, are other examples of early motor vehicles: the first motorcycle ever built—a Daimler manufactured in Germany in 1885—and the first of all snowmobiles, made at the request of the Canadian government for patrolling the wilderness. Adding to the early 1900s atmosphere are a nickelodeon and a hurdy-gurdy. Hundreds of pamphlets and photographs and a collection of toy motorcycles are also on display.

An Indian X-4 Dog Roadster, an automobile made in 1928, has

been restored and is on display. Few of these were produced, and a year later this enterprise was nipped in the bud by the Depression.

A motorcycle festival is held annually on the third Sunday in July. Enthusiasts come on bikes of many different makes to compete for prizes, such as for the oldest, the largest, and the farthest driven.

Open year-round except Thanksgiving, Christmas, and New Year's Day. Admission charged.
(413) 737-2624
www.sidecar.com/indian

8 Rock House Restoration
Route 9, West Brookfield
More than 10,000 years ago glaciers created the mammoth, cave-like rock shelter that inspired this reservation's name. Thanks to its southern exposure, as well as the enormity of its size, the Rock House served as an ideal winter camp for centuries of American Indians. Following the arrival of colonists from England, the surrounding forests were cleared for farming. By 1866 the Rock House was no longer a rustic haven but part of a bustling 281-acre farm owned by William Adams, whose family would tend the land for more than 125 years. In the early 20th century the Rock House was reborn as a popular tourist stop on the local electric trolley.

Today, explorers from around the country can marvel at the Rock House in its glory as the center-piece of a 75-acre nature preserve. Two miles of trails wind around the massive structure and through a young forest rich in red pine and spruce. Along the way, hikers can pass a butterfly garden and catch a glimpse of a passing blue heron, wild turkey, white-tailed deer, or even a coyote. Local reptiles, as

well as lovely wildflowers, ferns, and mosses, congregate around the Carter Pond. Man-made, spring-fed, and lovely, it was built by a descendant of farmer Adams, F. A. Carter, whose former cottage on the edge of the forest now serves as an informative trailside museum.

Open daily year-round. Free admission.
(978) 840-4446
www.westbrookfield.org/wbhc/rockhouse.htm

9 Charles L. McLaughlin State Fish Trout Hatchery
Belchertown
Trout fishing, one of the world's favorite sports, depends on well-stocked waterways. This hatchery, named for a former director of the state's Division of Fisheries and Wildlife, raises more than 300,000 trout annually just for this purpose. The fry are hatched indoors in fiberglass troughs, transferred to nursery tanks, and then, when they reach the size of fingerlings, released to develop in outdoor concrete raceways.

The most impressive of these three breeding facilities are the 200 50-foot raceways set along a shallow slope, each swarming with rainbow, brook, and brown trout. Although rainbow trout normally breed in the spring, a fall-breeding strain has now been produced.

After a year in the hatchery for some and two years for others, the fish are placed in aerated tank-trucks that take them to selected lakes and streams.

For a quarter, visitors can buy a handful of food pellets and watch the water swirl and surge as the trout rush to feed.

The water, maintained year-round at a temperature of 48°F,

comes from three gravel wells and is sometimes supplemented by a pumping station on the near-by Swift River.

Open year-round.
(413) 323-7671
www.mlin.lib.ma.us/inet_resources/science/marine.shtml

10 Moore State Park
Paxton
Long forgotten in this peaceful setting are the strident sounds of the sawmill, corn mill, and trip-hammer shop for which the water-ways here were originally built.

Turkey Hill Brook, the source of power for the mills, flows into the 25-acre Eames Pond, then down a succession of three cascades, and on through the park.

A walking trail follows the edge of the pond, where fishermen try for pickerel, perch, and bass.

The exterior of the sawmill that was first operated in 1747 by Jaazaniah Newton has been restored with siding of weathered

wood, and the remains of the old water-driven turbines can still be seen. An old schoolhouse is also being restored in the park.

In the well-tended naturalized gardens are great drifts of azalea and mountain laurel, but the star performers are the rhododendrons. The many species and hybrids produce a profusion of flowers from mid-May to mid-June.

Among the birds to be seen here are chickadees, goldfinches, nuthatches, bluebirds, cardinals, mourning doves, and scarlet tanagers. The park staff proudly calls this a botanical garden in a mill-village setting. It is certainly a serene and pleasant place to break a journey. The park is named for Maj. Willard Moore, a Paxton patriot who led the local farmers to fight the British at Bunker Hill.

Open year-round.
(508) 792-3969
www.state.ma.us/dem/parks/more.htm

8 Rock House Restoration. *A former cottage now serves as an informative trail-side museum along man-made, spring-fed Carter Pond.*

11 Purgatory Chasm State Reservation

The turnoff for the chasm is clearly marked on Rte. 146 about 10 miles south of Worcester in Sutton.
On venturing into Purgatory Chasm, one is likely to agree that it is well named. Although it is only about 50 feet wide, it reaches a depth of 70 feet or so between precipitous walls accentuated by tall Eastern hemlocks growing from seemingly solid rock.

The entrance to the chasm is across the street from the visitors center. The boulder-strewn trail descends gradually for a quarter mile. On reaching the bottom, one has the awesome feeling of having plunged suddenly into the earth's rocky body. From the bottom, trails lead along the edge of the chasm and circle back to the parking lot. The site also has a recreation area with picnic tables.

Open year-round.
(508) 234-3733
www.state.ma.us/dem/forparks.htm

12 Lowell National Historical Park

For anyone concerned with America's heritage and with community revitalization, Lowell is a place of special interest. Sometimes referred to as the Birthplace of the American Industrial Revolution, the town has a proud past as a model industrial community of the early 1800s. A further source of pride was the Lowell mill, where young farm women came to work by the thousands, operating the power looms in the textile mills and living in the strictly supervised company boarding-houses.

In the 1920s, as New England's textile industry declined, the town began its downward trend. Efforts to reverse that trend now include the establishment of the Lowell Heritage State Park and the Lowell National Historical Park, a cooperative undertaking of the city, the state, and the National Park Service.

The process of repair and renovation in the historic district is well under way, especially along the canals that were Lowell's source of power and that also served as a means of transportation in the city's heyday.

At the park's visitors center, located at Market Mills, a restored mill complex, you can arrange to take a tour by trolley, barge, and on foot that reveals the city's past. You can also visit the Boott Cotton Mills Museum, which has a re-created operating weaving room

with 88 power looms. The old mill buildings, immaculate with their spanking-new paint and clean brickwork, stand out against the rest of the urban architecture and give the curious impression of two contrasting cities—one resuscitated by a tranfusion of galleries, shops, offices, and fresh paint, the other a time-worn city.

Open year-round;
call for tour information.
(978) 970-5000
www.nps.gov/lowe

13 Whittier Home

From Rte. 95W take exit 110W into Amesbury. Turn right onto Elm St. and turn right onto Friends St.
For 56 years this was the home of John Greenleaf Whittier, an active abolitionist, a founder of the Republican Party, and one of America's best-known poets. The

11 Purgatory Chasm State Reservation. *Upon reaching the bottom of the chasm, one has the feeling of having plunged into the earth's rocky body.*

house was simply a four-room cottage when Whittier bought it in 1836. Over the years he added the portico, the upper stories, and the summer kitchen.

By the time of his death in 1892, Whittier was quite famous. Only four years later his niece (to whom he had bequeathed the property) opened his home as a museum. This continuity ensured that the Whittier memorabilia remained largely intact. It is the completeness of the personal belongings and furnishings (hats, boots, shaving brush, books, manuscripts, portraits, letters, even the original wallpaper) that gives the place its particular intimate charm. The rooms are small but comfortable, and on the walls there is ample evidence of Whittier's work as a writer and abolitionist. He wrote most of his poetry in the Garden Room, including his classic *Snow Bound.*

The house is now a registered national historic landmark. Just up the street is the Friends Meetinghouse, which Whittier, a Quaker, attended, and which served as a station of the Underground Railroad.

Open Tues.–Sat., May 1–Oct. 31.
(978) 388-1337
www.essexheritage.org

14 Parker River National Wildlife Refuge

Plum Island
This 4,662-acre refuge, which lies on the Atlantic Flyway, is a magnificent place to visit, especially during the spring and fall migrations. Most of the preserve is on Plum Island, which is eight miles long and one mile wide. A road runs its entire length. On the left, going south, are sand dunes dotted with wild roses, scrub pines, dune

 Lowell National Historical Park. *Visitors' boats now ply the canals that were at one time the city's source of power for its textile mills.*

grasses, bayberry, black cherry, and beach plum. On the right there are fresh and saltwater marshes, and beyond are the waters of Broad Sound, a long, narrow inlet. The beach, one of the finest on the Eastern Seaboard, is reached by access boardwalks tightly controlled to preserve the delicate ecology of the dunes, which act as a barrier to the sea. The beach is closed April 1 each year to provide a nesting habitat for the piping plover. It reopens mid- to late August.

Self-guiding nature trails lead to various ecological niches within the refuge. The longest is a boardwalk trail that wanders for two miles through Hellcat Swamp, where a freshwater swamp and cranberry bogs are pocketed among the dunes. At the end of the trail is an observation blind for bird-watchers. More than 300 species regularly frequent the refuge to rest and feed. Among the mammals here are deer, foxes, muskrats, minks, and weasels, but they are rarely seen during the day. In winter, harbor seals come to sun themselves on offshore rocks exposed by low tides.

The refuge is very popular in summer, but the best seasons to visit are in the early spring and in fall. Fishing permits may be obtained at the refuge gatehouse.
Open year-round; admission charged.
(978) 465-5753
http://parkerriver.fws.gov

15 Ipswich River Wildlife Sanctuary

Topsfield. From Rte. 1 turn south on Rte. 97 at the traffic light, then turn left on Perkins Row.
Occupying 2,800 acres, this is the largest of the 41 sanctuaries supervised by the Massachusetts Audubon Society. It is also the most varied, not only because of the number of wildlife habitats but also because of its extensive landscaping.

In the early 1900s the land was bought by Thomas Proctor, a wealthy Bostonian who applied himself with zeal and open-handedness to the creation of a private arboretum with an enormous rock garden—called the Rockery—as its centerpiece. In effect, the Rockery, set by a small lake, is a small man-made mountain, complete with little gorges, caves, and paths and profusely planted with exotic trees

and shrubs. Among the trees Proctor imported for his arboretum, the most notable are cork, magnolia, Korean pine, and Sawara cypress. A fine grove of pine trees stands on the hill above the Rockery.

The other notable rocky feature is a stony embankment about 20 feet high and 30 feet wide that runs for miles through the swamp. It's a natural formation, known as an esker, caused by streams flowing beneath ice age glaciers.

There are 10 miles of trails on the sanctuary and a causeway crossing a large pond to an island covered with beech trees. The woodlands are carpeted with partridge berries, starflowers, and wintergreen, while masses of blue irises grow in the marshy areas and a wildflower garden offers its special beauty. The sanctuary, which is a major courting and breeding ground for the American woodcock, has wildfowl impoundments, a special area for bird-watching, and an observation tower overlooking a freshwater marsh.
Open Tues.–Sun. year-round.
Admission charged.
(978) 887-9264
www.massaudubon.org

16 Misery Islands

Salem Bay, between Marblehead and Manchester harbors, just off West Beach in Beverly Farms
Just how the scenically delightful Great and Little Misery islands got their names is a mystery. Legend attributes the pair's christening to a shipwrecked man who spent three brutally cold December days stranded alone on the islands in the 1600s. By the

early 1900s Great Misery had overcome its unfortunate appellation to emerge as a posh summer retreat, with a nine-hole golf course and a colony of 26 cottages. But in 1926 a fire destroyed most of the buildings, and for more than 50 years the islands were abandoned. Finally, in 1997, after prolonged battles over proposals to make Great Misery the site of oil storage and sewage treatment operations, all 87 acres comprising both islands came under the ownership and protection of The Trustees for Reservations.

Today the sister islands, separated by a narrow, shallow channel, are easy to reach via a short public boat ride welcoming visitors from sunrise to sunset each day. From Great Misery's meadow hilltop, island tourists can see the bordering harbors of Marblehead and Manchester, not to mention the expanse of the Atlantic Ocean. While following three miles of woodland trails, explorers will find remnants of the island's summer resort heyday, including the stone pillars of a water tower that once served vacationers.

From Little Misery's beach it's impossible to miss the wooden remains of *The City of Rockland,* a noted wrecked steamship, poking above the waterline. Great and Little Misery also offer numerous coves for exploring, and perfectly pleasant spots for picnicking, hiking, birdwatching, and general relaxing.
Open daily year-round. Admission charged, included with passenger boat service.
(978) 741-1900
www.neadc.org/newsearch/local/ misery.html

17 Saugus Iron Works
Saugus

This national historic site is a full-scale working replica of the original ironworks founded here in the early 1640s by John Winthrop Jr., son of the governor of Massachusetts Bay Colony. Since the 1630s the small colony had been in an economic slump, suffering from a sharp decline in immigration. With fewer ships arriving from England, there was a serious scarcity of iron products—tools, nails, hinges, pots, and kettles—all of which had been imported.

To meet that need, young Winthrop sailed to England to obtain capital and a team of skilled iron-workers. Securing both, he returned home, chose a site where water-power, wood for charcoal, and iron ore were available, and built an up-to-date plant and company houses for the workers. The community was known as Hammersmith.

In the 1650s the ironworks failed because of production costs and an insufficient market for its products. But its employees trained others in their skills and thus helped to establish an iron industry in America.

The whole complex has been re-created with wonderful precision and thoroughness. A small museum showcases the history of the area with a short slide show and exhibits. From the museum a path leads to the smelting furnace and from there to the "finery." Draft for the furnace was provided by huge bellows driven by water power from the Saugus River. Water power also drove a huge hammer, used to pound the brittleness out of the cast pig iron and turn it into wrought iron. The

17 Saugus Iron Works. *This re-creation of the 17th-century plant illustrates how water power from the Saugus River helped drive the process of ironmaking here.*

machinery in the rolling and slitting mill, where sheets and rods of iron were made, also depended upon water power.

Worth visiting, too, is the blacksmith's shop. Three rooms have been restored in a "high 17th-century" style with elaborate furnishings.

In addition to the remarkable authenticity of the site, Saugus Iron Works is rewarding to visit because the processes displayed are easily understood, unlike modern high technology, and one has the feeling that with a little application one might have invented the whole business oneself.

Open year-round except Thanksgiving, Christmas, and New Year's Day.
(781) 233-0050
www.nps.gov/sair

18 World's End
At the end of Martin's Ln., off Rockland St., in Hingham

Spanning 250 acres and more than five miles of shoreline, this peerless peninsula has long been prized for its scenic vistas and dramatic topography. According to prehistoric evidence, it was a popular campsite among American Indians. The famous landscape architect Frederick Law Olmstead in the late 19th century saw it as the perfect place for developing a residential community. Although his plan (which included 179 house lots) never came to fruition, the terrain still reflects his influence. True to Olmstead's philosophy of working with nature to design places of pastoral beauty, the peninsula features lush hedgerows

bordering former farm fields, meandering gravel paths, and formal plantings of 900 trees.

One of the 30 islands of the Boston Harbor Islands national park area, World's End boasts four hills affording 360-degree views of the Boston skyline and Atlantic Ocean. Open grassy meadows lead to steep cliffs covered with red cedar and blueberry thickets, attracting birds of many feathers and a tremendous variety of butterflies.

In addition to picnicking and simply gazing at the natural splendors, the peninsula offers seven miles of trails—some for hiking, some for biking, and some for horseback riding—plus seasonal opportunities for fishing and cross-country skiing or snowshoeing. Trail maps are available at the ranger station, which also sponsors educational walks throughout the year. Each June, World's End shines as the host of an annual summer solstice celebration.

Open daily year-round.
Admission charged.
(781) 821-2977
www.realviews.com/halldocs/
infop/we.html

19 Adams National Historical Park
Visitors center, 1250 Hancock St., Quincy

Throughout four generations, one of America's most distinguished families lived on the land here, building and rebuilding to suit the changing needs of their remarkably active lives.

The family saga begins, however, about a mile south on Franklin Street (ask at the visitors center for directions), where two 18th-

MASSACHUSETTS

century houses stand side by side. John Adams, second president of the United States, was born in one house, and his son, John Quincy Adams, the sixth president, was born in the other.

The Old House, on Adams Street, was built as a country villa in the 1730s and bought by John Adams in 1787, when he and his wife, Abigail, returned from diplomatic service abroad. It is interesting to consider the contrast between the grandeur of public life enjoyed by the great and powerful in 18th-century America and the modesty of their domestic arrangements, especially compared to the estates of their counterparts in Europe. This contrast, in fact, was duly noted by Abigail Adams upon her return from the Court of St. James in London.

Among the members of the family based here were a remarkable number of accomplished statesmen, educators, historians, lawyers, and authors dedicated to demanding intellectual pursuits and compassionate service to their fellow men.

The furnishings in the Old House reflect the various tastes and interests of a widely traveled family over a period of 140 years. No other house in America offers a personal historic record of such impressive scope. The park provides a trolley bus that offers transportation between the sites. Trees planted by John Quincy Adams in the garden and behind the house have established firm roots and grown strong, as has the country that he and his family served so well.

Open daily Apr.–Nov.
(617) 770-1175
www.nps.gov/adam

20 Dighton Rock State Park
Berkley

In the picturesque woodlands of this small, inviting park is one of the most tantalizing mysteries of America's early exploration. Dighton Rock, a 40-ton boulder that was originally partially submerged in the nearby Taunton River, is engraved with ornate signs and symbols that scholars even today have been unable to decipher.

In 1963 the rock was raised from the river, and later on, a small museum was built to shelter the engravings and the exhibits explaining the four contending theories of their origin. One of the theories attributes the inscriptions to Phoenician explorers. Another suggests that they were executed by the Norse, and then there were those who claimed that the mysterious signs were American Indian symbols.

Perhaps the most popular theory attributes the engravings to a lost 16th-century Portuguese explorer who, it is claimed, ended his days among the local Wampanoag tribe. The strongest evidence for this proposal is the supposed inscription of the date 1511 and a suggested similarity between certain Portuguese words and words in the Wampanoag language.

Whatever theory is correct, the conjecture is fascinating, and the park's ample and quiet picnic grounds make this a refreshing stop any time of year.

Park and museum open daily from Memorial Day to Labor Day; in winter, park open daily, weather permitting, and museum open by appointment.
(508) 822-7537
www.state.ma.us/dem

21 Alden House Historic Site
From Rte. 3 to Alden St. to Rte. 3A, Duxbury

This shingled two-story colonial is a direct link with the first colonization of America.

John Alden, one of the voyagers on the *Mayflower,* was a signer of the Mayflower Compact, a leader of the Plymouth Colony, and the suitor of Priscilla Mullins.

The story of their romance, as recounted in Henry Wadsworth Longfellow's poem *The Courtship of Miles Standish,* may or may not be true. But they did indeed marry, and they settled first in Plymouth.

Like many of the colonists, including Captain Standish, the Aldens secured a farm plot in Duxbury and became one of the founding settlers of that town in the 1630s.

The present dwelling, which was built in the second half of the 17th century, was the second home built on the Alden property. John and Priscilla's third son, Jonathan Alden, had inherited the homestead, and his descendants lived in the house until the early 20th century.

Now owned by the Alden Kindred of America, which has held annual meetings at the homestead for more than 100 years, the house contains some handsome Early American fixtures and furnishings.

Open Mon.–Sat. and by appointment. Admission charged.
(781) 934-9092
www.alden.org

 World's End. *This peninsula in Boston Harbor Islands national park area offers seven miles of trails for hiking, biking, and horseback riding.*

Michigan

Steeped in the history of mining and lumbering, the state is also influenced by the surrounding waters on three sides.

Sleeping Bear Dunes National Lakeshore. *Stunning views of Lake Michigan are on the menu at this expansive park (see page 169).*

The beaches and lighthouses featured here are reminders that the waters of four of the five Great Lakes wash the shores of Michigan. The early iron and copper mines and the lumber camps are recalled in a variety of museums and historic towns. Adaptive use of old buildings is exemplified in one historical museum in a former church, while two well-preserved forts anchor the northern territories. Nature lovers will not be disappointed in the variety of hiking trails, rivers and waterfalls, a unique spring, and a well-appointed garden that just happens to be filled with world-class art.

1 Fort Wilkins Historic Complex and State Park
Copper Harbor

When copper was discovered in Michigan's Upper Peninsula in 1841, that wild land suddenly loomed important enough to warrant military protection. In 1844 Fort Wilkins was built, and later a lighthouse was put up as an aid to shipping on Lake Superior. Today they vividly illuminate the challenges of the age that made them.

Just outside Fort Wilkins are three log houses, once the quarters for married enlisted men. Within the stockade are 19 crisp white clapboard buildings. They include a bakery, fully equipped down to the barrels of flour and salt; a mess hall furnished with solid plank tables; the quartermaster's store, which sold both military and domestic items; and the sutler's store, where luxuries like champagne and peanuts were available.

In the company barracks, displays outline the history of the Upper Peninsula, from the discovery of copper and the United States-Chippewa Treaty of La Pointe, which opened the area to white settlement, to Fort Wilkins's eventual status as a state park.

The Copper Harbor Lighthouse can be reached by ferry from the Copper Harbor marina from May through October. The 1866 lighthouse, with its keeper's dwelling,

1 Fort Wilkins Historic Complex and State Park. *The well-preserved buildings and equipment here are a window back in time at this Upper Peninsula outpost.*

is now refurbished as a museum and home of the early 1900s.

Beyond the lighthouse is a rocky path to the tip of the point, where you can hear the sound of a bell buoy and enjoy the shore. This is an idyllic place, well worth the ferry ride in its own right. The ferry is popular, so try to book tickets in advance.

Park and fort open daily year-round; buildings open mid-May–mid-Oct. Admission charged.
(906) 289-4215

www.sos.state.mi.us/history/museum/musewil/index.html

2 Coppertown U.S.A. Mining Museum
Calumet

By the early 1900s Calumet (formerly named Red Jacket) had become the principal trading town for the copper-mining communities of the Keweenaw Peninsula.

It was rich, and part of its wealth went into its commercial and municipal buildings. Today the Old Red Jacket Downtown Historic District that is home to the museum is a fascinating, nostalgic, and slightly melancholy place, best seen on foot with the help of an excellent brochure that's available at the museum. Among the

MICHIGAN

164

highlights are the frontier gothic St. Anne's Church and the rococo Red Jacket Town Hall and Opera House.

Coppertown U.S.A. portrays the history and culture of Keweenaw Peninsula as one of the world's prime copper-producing regions. Exhibits include mining tools, heavy equipment, replicas of a mine captain's office, the 1915 Mohawk grade school, and even a surgery room. The surgery tableau shows mannequins of a nurse and patient and a collection of orthopedic devices—grim reminders of the dangerous work of miners.

Railroad memorabilia include a pump handcar and a four-man gas-driven railcar. Outside is the Russell snowplow locomotive, with a plow that is almost as high as a house. And the wooden patternshop models of cogs, valves, drive wheels, and other machine parts have a fine sculptural quality.

Open Mon.–Sat. June–mid-Oct.,
plus Sun. in July–Aug.
Admission charged.
(906) 337-4354

www.uppermichigan.com/coppertown

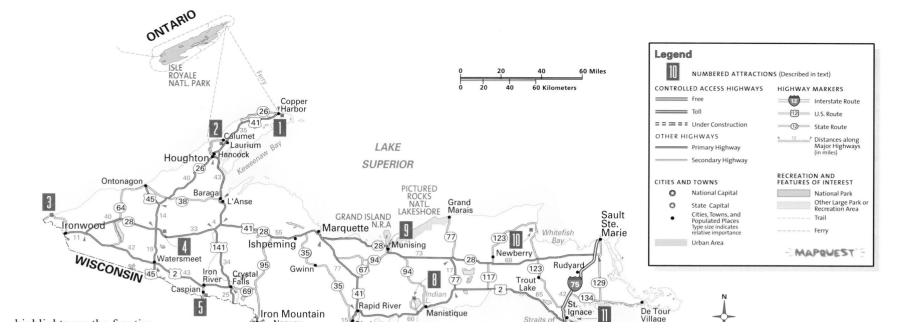

3 Little Girls Point County Park

17 miles north of Ironwood

The point is named in memory of a Chippewa girl who drowned here in the 1800s. The sandy beach is very pebbly at the waterline, and the crystal-clear water is too cold for swimming until August.

But swimming is not this park's main attraction. The beach is celebrated for the agates that can easily be found among the waterline pebbles. Look for those with a translucent quality. They are most often white but can be other colors as well. A visit to the nearby agate shop will give beginning agate hunters a good idea of their prey.

Besides agates, there are attractive pebbles of all kinds and colors here, most smoothed and symmetrically shaped by Lake Superior's constantly churning waters.

There is also great fishing here, and a large campground. And be sure to take some time to scan the skies: Bald eagles are regular residents, and you may even spot them nesting in trees near the shore.

Open May–Sept. Admission charged.
(906) 667-0411

www.gogebic.org/parks.htm

4 Agate Falls

4 miles south of Paynesville

The short trail to the falls begins in the Joseph F. Oravec Roadside Park just south of Route 28, passes under the highway, and then continues through woods above the broad middle branch of the Ontonagon River.

At a point opposite a flat-topped rock above the falls you can either rest on the massive roots of a white pine or, with a little care and agility, climb onto the rock

4 Agate Falls. *A little effort on the hiking trail pays off with a spectacular view from the bottom of these double-deck falls on the Ontonagon River.*

for a much better view of the tumbling spate of lacy water.

But the best view of the falls is attained only by way of a not-quite-sheer scramble down an earthen bank with crumbling rock "steps," slippery roots, and a few necessary handholds. This route, dangerous in wet weather, leads to a ledge from which one has a view of the first and second plunges of the falls. Care and agility are required for this part of the trail.

Open year-round but not staffed.
(906) 932-4850

www.westernup.com/waterfalls/secrets.html

5 Iron County Historical Museum

Caspian

This is an exemplary museum of mining, lumbering, and everyday life in Iron County. It occupies the former site of the Caspian Mine, whose gaunt old headframe presides over the site like a somber

guardian of times gone by.

In the onetime engine house is the Mining Hall, where intricate glass dioramas indicate different levels and convey the immense labor and skill of the old miners.

In the Lumbering Hall is the Monigal Miniature Lumber Camp, which contains more than 2,000 items, hand-carved from cedar telegraph poles by William Monigal. It's an astonishing piece of work, full of vigor, color, and information. Among other exhibits are fine photographs, including one of a 20-sled logging train carrying a 900-ton load.

The Main Exhibition Hall houses numerous other exhibits, among them the Pioneer Hall (with oilpaper maps and surveying instruments), the Athletics Hall (note the photograph of the 1911 girls basketball team), and the Pioneer Home.

The Village Green, an extensive section of the exhibition hall, contains authentic re-creations of local craft and trade shops.

MacDonell's Blacksmith's Shop, for instance, has been rebuilt with the original timbers, bricks, and tools—even the furnace ashes.

On the grounds of the museum are the Transportation, Mining, and Farm complexes, and the Logging Camp, all showing relevant tools and equipment.

Open daily mid-May–Oct.
Admission charged.
(906) 265-2617

www.ironcountymuseum.com

6 Menominee Range Historical Museum

Iron Mountain

The museum is housed in the old Carnegie Public Library, a distinguished neoclassical stone structure with a massive porch and second-floor balcony. At the entrance is a reproduction of an old general store packed with goods of the late 19th century.

There are exhibits of pioneer settlers, a diorama of Menominee Indians, and replicas of a trapper's cabin and a trading post. The cabin looks authentically uncomfortable; the trading post has whiskey and rum, bear grease, knives, snowshoes, and bolts of cloth. Among the other displays are a saddle shop and detailed exhibits of period office, banking, and brewing environments.

A watchmaker's shop is complete with workbench and tools, while the optician has an eye-test chart for nonreaders. The barbershop is endowed with a chair that looks as if it might easily be converted for electrocutions. And the Morely Folding Bath Tub (1885) provided a convenience for cramped quarters at home.

Open daily Memorial Day–Labor Day; call for occasional off-season hours.
(906) 774-4276

7 Menominee County Historical Museum

Menominee

The museum celebrates the spectrum of life in Menominee County, from the earliest periods of American Indian settlement to World War II, with emphasis on the mid-19th and early 20th centuries. The collections are housed in a former church, built in 1921 and notable for its stained-glass windows.

Menominee is named for a tribe of American Indians whose name means "wild rice," and the county's Indian heritage is displayed in stone and copper weapons, beadwork, and two dugout canoes believed to be more than 800 years old. There is also a fine collection of arrowheads among the many other artifacts.

Menominee is in lumber country, and the museum has good photographs of logging camps, river drives, and timber trains, as well as a variety of lumbering tools.

There are also re-creations of a law office, photographer's studio, cobbler's workshop, music store, railroad ticket office, and dentist's office. Law and order are represented by leg-irons, handcuffs, a ball and chain, and early types of police radar.

Early-day home decor is also on display; note the lampshade made from a mandarin's coat, sent by a young woman then living in Shanghai to her mother in Menominee—and the notice of its reception in the local newspaper. In such details the museum gives local history a human face.

The church was rebuilt in 1921 on the site of the original place of worship. Its bell tower still holds the original bell, which dates to 1871. The church itself is a piece of history: It's on the *National Register of Historic Places.*

Mon.–Sat. Memorial Day–Labor Day. (906) 863-9000

www.fmmarinette.com/ river8.htm#menominee

 Iron County Historical Museum. *Occupying the former site of the Caspian Mine, this is an exemplary museum of mining, lumbering, and everyday life in Iron County.*

8 The Big Spring at Palms Book State Park

Manistique

Here is a wide pool of eerily clear green water, 40 feet deep, fed by a cluster of springs flowing at a rate of 10,000 gallons per minute. The flow is such that the water never has time to freeze in winter or warm up in summer—it's always a steady 45°F.

To view the Big Spring, visitors climb into rafts that run round-trip along a cable. The sides of the pool are steep and white, delicately streaked with drifts of darker clay and sand. Bleached logs lie under the water like massive bones, and the springs belch plumes of white silt resembling miniature volcanoes.

Large, slow brown trout cruise the pond, hemlock and arborvitae surround it, and ducks and seagulls paddle its periphery. The outflow of the mighty spring is a shallow, bubbling river.

The spring is closed from mid-October to mid-May, but Palms Book offers the hearty cross-country skier some excellent trails.

Open year-round. Admission charged. (906) 341-2355

www.michigandnr.com/parksandtrails/ parklist.asp

9 Pictured Rocks National Lakeshore

Munising

The park is 42 spectacular miles long and no more than 5 miles at its widest. The Lakeshore Trail runs from the visitor center at Munising north to Sable Falls.

Miners Castle Overlook, reached via Miners Castle Road, gives stunning views of a smoothly curved inlet of white cliffs above a submarine outcrop of yellow sandstone; the offshore water of Lake Superior is intensely blue, but above the yellow lake bed it becomes a rim of vivid green, and the shorescape is banded with white and yellow cliffs and green and blue water.

At the northern tip of the inlet is Miners Castle, a double crag of cliff carved by erosion into the semblance of a medieval castle. A side road from Miners Castle Road goes to Miners Falls, a high and narrow plummet between two massive cliffs; at their base are swirl holes, and the face of the nearer wall has been scooped out by erosion.

The park is a camper's delight. Three campgrounds in the park are accessible by car: Little Beaver Lake, Twelvemile Beach, and Hurricane River.

From Little Beaver Lake it's a short walk to Beaver Lake and the Lakeshore Trail. The campground at Twelvemile Beach provides access to an unbroken stretch of white sand.

From Hurricane River one can walk $1\frac{1}{2}$ miles to the 1874 lighthouse at Au Sable Point, and beyond that to a 500-foot wooden log slide and the Grand Sable Banks and Dunes area.

There are also 13 backcountry campgrounds along the Lakeshore Trail. Scuba divers are catered to along the shore by the Alger Underwater Diving Preserve. Late summer provides magnificent weather, but the park is also beautiful in winter when snowshoeing is a favored pastime.

Open year-round. Fees for camping. (906) 387-2607

www.nps.gov/piro

10 Tahquamenon Falls State Park
Paradise

This nearly 40,000-acre park has three developed sections: the Upper Falls, the Lower Falls, and the Tahquamenon River mouth.

The Upper Falls are among the largest east of the Mississippi and are most easily approached by way of the Brink stairs, an elaborate series of observation decks that wind down to river level.

The 200-foot-wide lip of the falls, about 50 feet high, is a shallow S-curve of ancient sandstone over which the soft brown water, stained by its passage through cedar and hemlock swamps, pours at a rate of up to 50,000 gallons per second. The Gorge stairs downstream are steeper and longer but allow more complete views.

The Lower Falls, actually a series of falls, lie on either side of an island (reached by renting a rowboat) and are seen either from there or from an easily walked half-mile trail that offers close-up views of the water boiling and fuming over the shallow falls. There are strong currents, undertows, whirlpools, and floating debris here, and understandably, swimming is forbidden. A modern campsite is also available here.

The river mouth section offers two campgrounds, swimming facilities, and boat access to Lake Superior's Whitefish Bay. A number of trails thread through the thick forest and touch the river at several points. The Tahquamenon, which means "Marsh of the Blueberries," plays a part in Hiawatha lore.

Open year-round. Admission charged.
(906) 492-3415

www.exploringthenorth.com/
tahqua/tahqua.html

11 Mackinac Island State Park
Mackinac Island

Fort Mackinac occupies the crest of a hill overlooking the harbor and the charming old town. Within its stockade the original buildings re-create with the greatest fidelity the history of the fort and island.

In the commissary, dioramas portray episodes in the War of 1812: the capture of the island by the British and their 350 Huron allies, the subsequent blockade by two American ships, and their capture by British boarding parties.

The British connection is no coincidence: The fort was built by the British in 1780 during the Revolutionary War to protect fur trading interests in the region.

The island's nonmilitary history is recorded, too, including the curious story of Dr. Samuel Beaumont's pioneering experiments on the human digestive system. Also recalled are the lives of such sturdy Mackinac women as Madeleine La Framboise, who ran a trading post at Grand River, and Bertha Palmer, "the undisputed queen of Chicago society," who graced the opening of the Grand Hotel and was a social fixture during the island's most glamorous years as a top resort.

No motorized vehicles are allowed on the island, so if you want to travel extensively you walk, bicycle, take a guided tour in a horse-drawn carriage, or rent your own saddle horse at the Chambers Riding Stable on Market Street. The park also has hiking trails in the woodlands.

Park open year-round. Fort open early May–mid-Oct. Other buildings open early June–Labor Day. Admission charged for fort includes admission to several nearby historic sites.
(906) 847-3328

www.mackinacparks.com/statepark/

12 Wilderness State Park
Carp Lake

In general, this 8,000-acre park lives up to its name: The woods are too thick for casual sightseeing, the beaches too pebbly, the lake water too cold for comfortable beach lounging or swimming, and much of the open terrain is too swampy for walking.

The good news is that those who enjoy nature in its unmodified state will find this a rewarding stop. The park lies on a peninsula of thick woodlands, marsh, and beaches.

A dirt road leads from the campground and visitors center through woods toward the end of the peninsula; side roads lead from this central axis to beach and swamp areas on Sturgeon Bay and along the southern side of the Straits of Mackinac.

The beaches are a mixture of sand and pebbles. The pebbles predominate at the waterline, and the lake-surge makes them rumble like distant thunder. The vegetation is patchy and dunelike near the water, and marshy with reedbeds near the inland woods. At its furthest point the road reaches a marshy meadow with a view of Sturgeon Bay to the south and woods to the north and west. There is no way to cross the marsh except by boat or by plunging across wearing waders.

No dogs are allowed from May 1 to August 31 lest they disturb the endangered piping plovers that nest here in that season. Wood ducks, pintails, great horned owls, and pileated woodpeckers are often seen here.

Campers can choose from 250 modern sites in two locations: deep in the woods or tucked along the lakeshore.

Open year-round.
(231) 436-5381

www.michigandnr.com/parksandtrails/
parklist.asp

10 Tahquamenon Falls State Park. *This calm, misty-morning pond is a quiet respite from the rushing, many-tiered falls that feed the Tahquamenon River.*

13 Old Presque Isle Lighthouse and Museum

Presque Isle

One hundred and fifty years ago, Presque Isle had the finest harbor in the Great Lakes, a cove protected from Lake Huron's fierce weather by headlands to the north and south. A busy port grew up there, and $5,000 was appropriated in 1838 from federal funds to build a lighthouse. In 1840 the light was lit, and for the next 30 years it served as a beacon to mariners up and down the coast.

In 1870 a taller lighthouse began service just a mile north, and the old light was left to weather the storms of time as best it might. Its four-foot-thick walls of hand-cut stone proved durable, and so did the keeper's small cottage. In the early 1900s the property passed into private hands and was steadily restored by a series of owners. In 1995 the property passed to the local township, which continues its upkeep.

Today the cottage houses a museum crammed with curios, as a place on a trade route should be: a wine cabinet with hand-blown bottles, a crab-shaped incense burner, and a saucy Indian statuette. Best of all, one is urged to handle things, whether it's the torpedo-boat binnacle or the elephant trainer's hooked stick.

At the foot of the lighthouse is a bronze bell from Lansing city hall's old clock tower. It weighs 3,425 pounds, more than 1 1/2 times than of the Liberty Bell, and visitors can make it ring out over the bay by pulling the bell hammer.

Open daily May 15–Oct. 15.
Admission charged.
(517) 595-2787

15 Sleeping Bear Dunes National Lakeshore. *Visitors flock to the dunes' many scenic overlooks, which afford spectacular views of Lake Michigan.*

14 Hartwick Pines State Park

Grayling

When the first loggers came to Michigan, they found white pines of amazing size in the virgin woods. Legend has it that there were trees more than twice as high as those you'll see in Hartwick Pines State Park now.

But the present-day giants are remarkable in their own right. They tower more than 150 feet above the forest floor, each green pinnacle seeming to sway to its own rhythm. It's cool, shady, and easy to walk the forest, as the canopy of foliage shields the sun and limits the undergrowth.

On the north end of the park is the Hartwick Pines Logging Museum. Nineteenth-century logging life is reflected here in exhibits that tell the story of the fast-paced and freewheeling industry that carved up much of the surrounding white pine forest.

The state of Michigan's Forest Visitor Center is also here. It, too, features exhibits on the colorful logging past, but its focus is on preserving the forest. The stunning 49-acre Old Growth Pines area is strong testament to that effort.

Park open year-round. Visitors center open daily Memorial Day–Labor Day; Tues.–Sun. Labor Day–Memorial Day. Museum open daily May 1–late Oct. Admission charged.
(517) 348-7068
www.michigandnr.com/parksandtrails/ parklist.asp

15 Sleeping Bear Dunes National Lakeshore

Empire

The most spectacular feature of this beautiful 71,000-acre park on the Lake Michigan shoreline is the Sleeping Bear Dunes area, readily seen from the 7.6-mile Pierce Stocking Scenic Drive, which overlooks South and North Manitou islands. The lake views from here at sunset can be surreal, and the inland views to the east of ridges, valleys, and lakes are no less beautiful.

A nine-mile trail also crosses the dunes; it's easy to get lost here, and no drinking water is available.

At Glen Lake, just west of the dunes, there are swimming and picnicking facilities. The nearby village of Glen Haven hosts the Coast Guard Station/Maritime Museum.

The park also includes the Platte Bay and Pyramid Point sections to the north and south, and North and South Manitou islands. Canoe rentals are available at the Platte River campground, and there are foot trails.

In the Pyramid Point section there is a hiking trail, beach access, and picnicking at Good Harbor Bay. Both South Manitou Island and the primitive wilderness of North Manitou Island can be reached mid-spring to mid-fall by a ferry from Leland.

Park open year-round. Pierce Stocking Scenic Drive open May–Nov., road conditions permitting.
(231) 326-5134
www.nps.gov/slbe

15 Sleeping Bear Dunes National Lakeshore. *An aerial view of the dunes along Lake Michigan.*

16 Historic White Pine Village. *An old-fashioned Civil War troop muster gets a decidedly newfangled taste during one of the town's historical re-enactments.*

16 Historic White Pine Village
Ludington

An extensive reconstruction of a small Michigan town in the late 1800s, this village's buildings are set in carefully tended grounds and are all authentically furnished.

The Abe Nelson Blacksmith Shop, for example, has a working smithy, and Cole's General Store has an intriguing stock of goods, a countertop extended to accommodate hoopskirts and an exotic green pagoda-like tea chest.

Dwellings include the Quevillon trapper's cabin, built before 1850, where a hand-colored photograph of a severe-looking Catherine Quevillon presides over a single bed strewn with animal skins. The Burns farmhouse, built around 1880, is one of the most detailed reconstructions. In the kitchen is an elaborate flour and spice cabinet, in the dining room a portable home altar, and in the drawing room a 100-year-old Regina Music Machine that plays perforated metal discs and still produces a tuneful, mellow sound.

In the Abe Nelson Lumbering Museum are mementos of the old lumber camps, including excellent models of ox- and horse-drawn lumber wagons and good collections of lumbering tools, cowbells, and railroad lamps.

The Mason County Courthouse was built in 1849 from loose lumber pulled from the lake and still sits on its original site.
Open Tues.–Sat. late April–mid-Oct.; winter hours Tues.–Fri.
Admission charged.
(231) 843-4808
www.historicwhitepinevillage.org

17 Dow Gardens
Midland

The gardens were developed in 1899 by Herbert Dow, founder of the Dow Chemical Company. They include massed plantings of annuals and perennials, a necklace of ponds, and collections of flowering crab apples, roses, rhododendrons, junipers, and herbs.

Plantings are changed regularly. One can always expect to find the circular herb garden, for example, set with an intriguing variety of such plants as salad burnet, comfrey, scented geraniums, and nasturtiums. This and the three beds nearby, with candytuft, statice, heliotrope, strawflowers, carnations, and stock, are the sweetest-smelling part of the gardens—

along with the rosebeds, with their superb show of prize-winners.

Other attractions include the formal gardens, several magnificent old willow trees, the conservatory, a display of Staffordshire pottery, a maze, and the rockery of dwarf evergreens near the entrance.
Open year-round except holidays.
Admission charged.
(800) 362-4874
www.dowgardens.org

18 Huron City Museums
Port Austin

Huron City was founded in the 1850s by lumberman Langdon Hubbard. It prospered, suffered two major fires, and finally declined when its wells went dry. Today it's a museum town that reconstructs life here in the latter part of the 19th century.

Dogcarts, sleighs, and coaches are displayed in the carriage house. In Hubbard's barn is a collection of farm equipment that includes a forerunner of the forklift.

17 Dow Gardens. *Take in 110 acres of colorful, varied plantings here.*

The ground floor of the Community House Inn (1877) is furnished in the busy style of the Victorian period, and the general store is provisioned with goods from toys to tea chests.

One of the most interesting buildings is the Point Aux Barques Life Saving Station, built in 1876 and moved here from its original site. Its lifeboat, which once saved 200 lives in a single mission, is on display in the Wreck Room.

Also worth seeing is the large, airy Huron City Church, where as many as 1,000 used to gather to hear the sermons of William Lyon Phelps, a Yale professor and one of the notable literary figures of his day. The Phelps family's House of Seven Gables contains his desk (made from a grand piano), a display of Staffordshire pottery, calling cards, and other memorabilia.
Open daily July 1–Labor Day.
Admission charged.
(989) 428-4123
www.tour-michigan.com/~hcmus

19 Frederik Meijer Gardens and Sculpture Park
Grand Rapids

This unique botanical garden features colorful flowers, exquisite topiary, and world-class works of art. Thirty of the gardens 125 acres comprise an open-air museum showcasing the work of more than 25 renowned sculptors in a variety of natural settings.

Complementing the sculpture park is an indoor gallery that also highlights celebrated pieces from the late 19th century to the present. Along the meandering garden paths nature and art lovers alike will delight in animal imagery. Visitors are invited to explore nature trails and discover expertly crafted works, including the famed, imposing

Leonardo da Vinci's *Horse*.

The trails wind through about one mile of Michigan woodlands and wetlands. Visitors are able to see a variety of both native and indigenous plants, as well as many types of birds and other wildlife. Inside, conservatories and greenhouses highlight plants galore, both the beautiful and the bizarre. A popular stop with kids, "Little Greenhouse of Horrors" presents an up-close and riveting look at bug-devouring plants.

The gardens specialize in seasonal events, and so there is *something* going on here 363 days (closed New Year's Day and Christmas) a year.

Open year-round.
Admission charged.
(888) 957-1580
www.meijergardens.org

20 Kalamazoo Nature Center
Kalamazoo

This imaginative, attractive site includes an interpretive center, an arboretum and botanical garden, a farm, a period homestead, and nature trails. It's a great place to take children.

The Tropical Sun-Rain Room in the interpretive center stretches from the basement to the glass roof and re-creates the environment of many exotic plants, with 600 tons of rock serving as the thermal mass in the naturalistic landscape. A walkway spirals past this jungle to the basement, where there are displays of living snakes, fish, turtles, toads, a crow, and a screech owl.

The Glen Vista Room has a picture window on a tract of woodlands, with microphones bringing in the sounds of the wild. Outside

the center are cages for predatory birds and access to the 11 different hiking trails.

The young trees in the 11-acre arboretum are spaciously set in a large meadow, which also includes the botanical garden, featuring rhododendrons, junipers, and plants adapted to arid conditions. Nearby is the Family Farm, with pettable horses, cows, pigs, goats, and sheep.
Open year-round, except holidays.
Admission charged.
(269) 381-1574
www.naturecenter.org

21 Waterloo Farm Museum
Waterloo

This is a small but attractive and well-maintained mid-19th-century farm outside the peaceful village of Waterloo. The brick farmhouse was built in 1846-47 with decorative panels of fieldstone in the fashion then popular with German-American builders.

The kitchen pantry has an ingenious cabinet that forms a dividing wall with drawers

accessible from the dining room. The dining room itself has an aura of period charm with rag rugs, wood stove, tea-leaf-pattern china, and a lamp with a painted glass shade.

The parlor was kept for special occasions and used to display prized possessions: a horsehair settee, an arrangement of dried fruit in a big black oval frame, and tables hung with heavy fringed cloths.

Upstairs are a children's toy room with clothing and toys of the period, a bedroom with a trundle bed, and a device for tightening the ropes supporting the mattress so that one could "sleep tight."

The outbuildings include a granary, blacksmith's shop, barn, log cabin, windmill, and bakehouse. The blacksmith's shop has a full complement of tools. On Pioneer Day (the second Sunday in October) cookies are baked in a brick oven, and old-time crafts like blacksmithing are practiced.
Open Wed.–Sun. June–Sept.; call for occasional off-season hours.
Admission charged.
(517) 596-2254

19 Frederik Meijer Gardens and Sculpture Park. *Arnaldo Pomodoro's* Disk in the Form of a Desert Rose *is one of the many impressive works on the grounds.*

22 Walker Tavern
Brooklyn

In the mid-1800s, a trip from Detroit to Chicago meant a traveler endured an arduous five-day trek by horse-drawn stagecoach, which is why this tavern became a favorite stopover. Located near a major junction and two premier ports, it was also popular for local gatherings.

No longer serving ale or offering rooms for rent, and scrupulously run by the state, the tavern now stands as the centerpiece of a historic site devoted to Michigan's frontier settlement and stagecoach heyday. Along with a vintage barroom, the tavern includes a kitchen, fully equipped with the tools of its day, and a dining room and parlor decked out in 1840s style.

After a tour of the tavern, anyone thirsty for a taste of local history can head next door to the visitors center. Exhibits celebrate pioneering people who traveled these historic crossroads, as well as the man who owned and ran the popular tavern at its peak, Sylvester Walker. He was also an accomplished farmer, and also on display are his tools of that trade, from a scythe for harvesting buckwheat to a flail to separate the grain from the chaff.

In addition, the tavern complex features a reproduction of a New England-style barn similar to the one the Walkers actually used. The barn was an essential building for both the farm and the tavern. It housed animals, feed for livestock, and—when the tavern was full— even the extra visitors.
Open Wed.–Sun. Memorial Day– Labor Day. Admission charged.
(517) 467-4401
www.sos.state.mi.us/history/ museum/musewalk

Jay Cooke State Park. *The waterfall in St. Louis River gorge is one of the many sites along the 50 miles of trails here (see page 176).*

Minnesota

The ice age glaciers left a magnificent legacy of lakes, streams, valleys, hills, and rolling plains, an ideal land for touring and camping.

The exploits of Minnesota's American Indians, French voyageurs, and fur trappers are recalled in scenic and historic places and in place-names throughout the state.

In the mining area one can descend almost half a mile underground to experience the unique world of the workers there. And at Pipestone National Monument one can visit the quarries of catlinite reserved for use by American Indians in fashioning their traditional ceremonial pipes. Museums feature distinctive architecture; collections of tools, utensils, and equipment used by pioneers; and artifacts reaching far back into our past.

1 Zippel Bay State Park
Williams

These 3,000 acres of wilderness parklands are situated along the shores of Lake of the Woods, a 950,000-acre body of water that forms part of the border between Minnesota and Canada. As early as 1700 the voyageurs—those French fur traders who plied the waters of the Northwest—traveled along this great waterway.

Zippel Bay, a reedy inlet running almost at right angles from the lake, borders the park on the west. It is a pleasant, quiet stretch of water with a small marina, a boat ramp, and a fish-cleaning station.

Along the lakeshore, reached from the park entrance by a straight gravel road, is the swimming beach—three miles of sand considered to be the finest in the state. The nearby picnic area, with tables and a shelter, is set in a mown meadow surrounded by woodlands. Sixty primitive campsites are available, located in remote areas of the park. Trails through woodlands of white birches are excellent for skiing and snowshoeing in winter.

Many visitors come just to pick blueberries in midsummer, when a plentiful wild crop borders the roadways, or for the excellent fishing. For others, the anticipation of seeing a moose or black bear, which roam the park freely, or the

3 Grand Portage National Monument. *Visitors can get a sense of how difficult life was for early traders and trappers here.*

likelihood of hearing the forlorn call of the timber wolf, is the appeal. Other attractions are the white pelicans, which nest around the lake, the sandhill cranes, and the common loon, the state bird, whose haunting cry often breaks the stillness of the woods.

Open year-round. Admission charged. (218) 783-6252

www.dnr.state.mn.us

2 Voyageurs National Park
Off State Hwy. 53, International Falls

The trappers and traders who canoed the waters of this scenic wilderness in the 1700s would be surprised to know that their legacy is not in furs or dollars but in a 217,000-acre park named in their memory. Within the bounds of the park are countless streams and ponds and more than 30 lakes, interspersed by islands of bog, marsh, water meadow, and forest, forming many hundreds of miles of waterways. The only way to see the entire area up close is by boat, or by snowmobile after January 1, when roadways are plowed on the frozen waters. Forty miles of hiking trails are maintained, of which $12^1/_2$ miles are accessible only by water. There are also more than 120 campsites, 75 houseboat sites, and many day-use sites available.

Wildlife abounds here. Black bears are common, and in winter the park is home to about 40 timber wolves. Beavers and white-tailed deer are also plentiful, and moose are sometimes seen. Among the birds that nest here are the osprey, eagle, and great blue heron.

From both Rainy Lake and Kabetogama Lake visitors centers, park naturalists lead guided canoe trips, providing canoes, life jackets, and instructions. Less strenuous boating is also available on both lakes. Fishing is allowed throughout the park, and catches include black crappies, lake trout, muskellunge, northern pike, rock bass, and walleye. Several fine beaches offer excellent swimming.

During the winter, snowmobiling, ice fishing, cross-country skiing, and snowshoeing are popular.

Open year-round. Fee charged for trips and cruises. Free overnight-use permits are required for overnight camping.
(888) 381-2873
www.nps.gov/voya

3 Grand Portage National Monument

Grand Portage

Long before Europeans arrived, American Indians had been bypassing an unnavigable stretch of the Pigeon River by an overland route they called Great Carrying Place. French voyageurs, translating the title literally, named it Grand Portage. In 1778 the North West Company, formed by a group of Canadian traders, established its headquarters at the start of the trail on the shore of Lake Superior. At the time this was a crossroads for hundreds of fur trappers and traders. The headquarters was

abandoned in 1803 and fell into disrepair. The general area became an Indian reservation in 1854.

In 1958 the Grand Portage Band of Minnesota Chippewa Indians donated the site of the Grand Portage National Monument to the U.S. government. The monument now features a carefully re-created complex of North West Company buildings. The principal structure

is the Great Hall, an impressive log-and-post structure originally chinked with river clay and bear grease—and now with concrete. Also on the grounds are a kitchen fully equipped with period utensils, a fur press for packing furs into bundles, a warehouse with birch-bark canoes, and a cabin built in 1900 that is now a gift shop. Part of the complex is enclosed in a stockade built to create a sense of order during the Rendezvous, the trappers' hectic annual meeting.

The site also has two trails: the original 8 1/2-mile Grand Portage Trail, which cuts through the reservation to Fort Charlotte, where you will find primitive backpacking campsites, and the half-mile Mount Rose Trail, which offers a view of Lake Superior.

Open May–Oct.; call for exact dates.
Admission charged.
(218) 387-2788
www.nps.gov/grpo

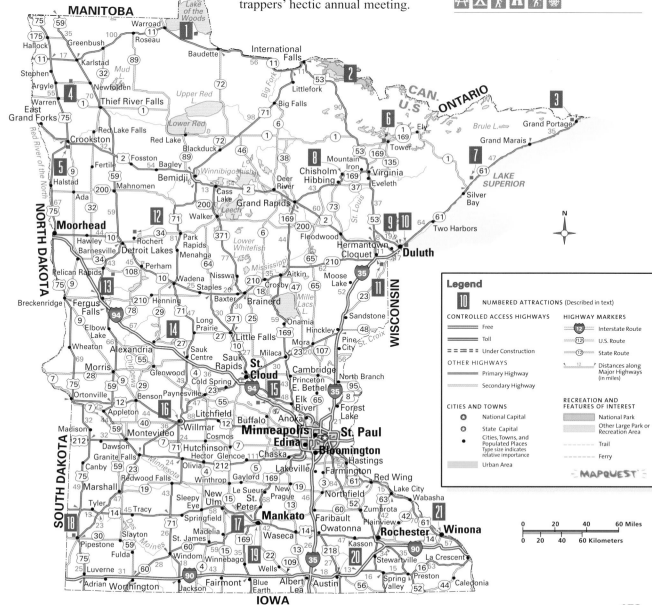

MINNESOTA

Legend

10 NUMBERED ATTRACTIONS (Described in text)

CONTROLLED ACCESS HIGHWAYS
Free
Toll
Under Construction

OTHER HIGHWAYS
Primary Highway
Secondary Highway

CITIES AND TOWNS
⊙ National Capital
⊚ State Capital
• Cities, Towns, and Populated Places Type size indicates relative importance
Urban Area

HIGHWAY MARKERS
Interstate Route
U.S. Route
State Route
Distances along Major Highways (in miles)

RECREATION AND FEATURES OF INTEREST
National Park
Other Large Park or Recreation Area
Trail
Ferry

MAPQUEST

173

4 Old Mill State Park

13 miles east of Argyle

As you cross the seemingly endless open acres of the Red River valley's well-kept cropland, it is difficult to believe that the homesteaders who settled this region just over a century ago encountered prairies and riverine forests much like the ones found in this 287-acre park today.

Beavers, raccoons, deer, and an occasional moose may be seen here, along with many of the area's native plants. Inviting paths, including a three-quarter-mile self-guiding nature trail, weave across the varied terrain. Many of these trails are groomed for snowmobiling and cross-country skiing in the winter. In addition, the park offers picnic and camping sites, a swimming pond, and winter ice-skating and sledding areas. Fishermen try for pike and bullheads.

The park's centerpiece, as the name suggests, is an old mill. Built in 1889, it is powered by an eight-horsepower steam engine, and grinding demonstrations are given once a year on the last Sunday of August. A restored one-room log cabin, evoking the rugged life of the area's early homesteaders, may be seen nearby.

Open year-round. Admission charged.
(218) 437-8174
www.dnr.state.mn.us

5 Polk County Museum

Crookston

Many intriguing aspects of the 19th and early 20th century seem alive and well in this excellent museum, which is run by the Polk County Historical Society and a well-informed curatorial staff. The buildings and hundreds of artifacts

5 Polk County Museum. *The 19th and early 20th centuries come alive in this museum, which contains hundreds of vintage artifacts.*

are well displayed. Engaging in their variety, they represent all aspects of life in this region.

The buildings include an 1890 schoolhouse that was used until the 1930s, a log cabin built in 1872 by a Norwegian settler, and a reconstruction of a blacksmith's shop. Several early automobiles, a five-foot Minnesota binder, a thresher, a tractor, an 1898 fire engine, a one-horse sleigh, and a variety of small farm implements are displayed in a pole barn.

The main building, a large, modern structure, contains well-furnished period rooms and a general store, doctor's office, barbershop, editor's office, a 60-year-old model electric train, and a carousel layout with horses that "gallop." Here too are a square piano made in Boston and an amusing assortment of ladies' hats.

The museum grounds hold the world's largest ox cart. It is an exact replica of the type used to move goods from Fort Garry to St. Paul, complete right down to the wooden pegs used in construction. An authentic ox cart can be found inside the museum.

The local people who acquired the objects on display here are

shown with their farms, their animals, their industries, and their countryside in an excellent collection of photographs.

Open daily May–Sept. Admission charged.
(218) 281-1038
www.ohwy.com

6 Soudan Underground Mine State Park

U.S. Hwy. 169, Soudan

The unusual centerpiece of this splendid park is 2,400 feet underground and is reached by a three-minute elevator descent, a three-quarter-mile subterranean train ride, and a climb up a short flight of stairs. Visitors don hard hats and enter a "cage" for the descent into the mine. This is the 27th and lowest level of the Soudan Iron Mine, sometimes called "the Cadillac of mines" because of its outstanding methods of operation and safety record during its 80-year history.

The rock here is ancient and stable, relatively dry, and does not produce toxic or explosive gases. The fine red dust that clings to some of the machinery and structure is a silent reminder of the ore crusher, whose voice was a constant assurance that all was well when the

mine was operating. The tunnel, part of some 55 miles of underground access, is spacious, well lit, and a steady 50 degrees year-round. Fresh air circulates naturally down from the surface, and knowledgeable guides make one's visit enjoyable and informative. Sturdy shoes and a sweater or jacket are recommended.

The park visitors center offers exhibits explaining the geology of the area and the mining process. In addition, various pieces of specialized mining machinery may be seen, including the hoist, the giant ore crusher, and the 500 horsepower air compressor used to operate the drilling equipment. It was last worked in the early 1960s.

Visitors can also take an hour-and-a-half tour of a high-energy physics laboratory that is also located on the lowest level of the mine.

The 1,200-acre park offers five miles of surface trails for hikers and about 50 miles of trails for cross-country skiing and snowmobiling. A wildlife habitat, the park is home to timber wolves, deer, hawks, and other creatures.

Tours offered daily Memorial Day weekend–Sept. 30. Additional group tours can be arranged off-season.
Admission charged.
(218) 753-2245
www.dnr.state.mn.us

7 George H. Crosby-Manitou State Park

Silver Bay

Dramatically highlighting the wild beauty of the rugged Manitou River valley is the rocky gorge shaped by ancient volcanic and glacial action and the river itself, tumbling through the forested landscape to Lake Superior.

At the cascades the river moves down through a series of branching waterfalls to a peat-dark pool. Along the edge, boulders, some convenient for sitting, show high-water marks, indicating the water level during the spring melt. But even in August there is a quick, substantial flow between the conifer-shaded banks.

Twenty-three miles of wilderness trails follow the river and wind through the park's stands of birch, aspen, and hemlock. Some of the trails are difficult, but an easy quarter-mile path leads from the parking area to a picnic site beside Benson Lake in the center of the 3,400-acre park. The topographic trail map shows the relative steepness of the routes.

Along the river and by the lake 21 primitive campsites have been cleared for backpackers. Water must be carried in or boiled, and fire rings are provided.

Moose come here to browse on the fast-growing conifers, black bears are common, and timber wolves prey on the large population of white-tailed deer. Hikers often see the ruffed and spruce grouse. If you can get close enough, you can tell them apart by their markings.

The tail of the spruce is dark, with a single band at the edge; that of the ruffed is striped white, brown, and black. Trout fishing is permitted in both stream and lake. Snow frequently stays from November through April, and although the trails are rough, the campsites are open. Experienced skiers can enjoy 11 miles of cross-country trails.

Open year-round.
(218) 226-6365
www.dnr.state.mn.us

8 Minnesota Museum of Mining
Chisholm

When Minnesotans speak of "the range," they aren't referring to a string of mountains or to vast grasslands; they are talking about the Mesabi, Vermilion, and Cuyuna–some of the richest iron-ore ranges in the United States. Located in the heart of this area is a sprawling museum that rewards visitors with a vivid sense of the sheer magnitude and ruggedness of iron mining.

Fascinating exhibits of antique miners equipment, old photographs, and models of ore-processing operations are just the beginning.

On the museum grounds visitors can tour a variety of heavy mining machines, some of truly astounding size. One of these is a piercing machine that uses a high-velocity 5000-degree flame to drill through rock. Dominating the area like some great mechanical dinosaur is a 1910 Atlantic steam shovel weighing 110 tons. But perhaps the awesome scale of iron mining is made clearest in a simple exhibit of ore truck tires, some 10 feet in diameter and weighing nearly three tons, each more costly than today's average automobile.

The most moving display is a life-size underground replica of a 150-foot turn-of-the-century mine drift. Visitors descend a short stairway to enter the miners daily world, where well-worn picks and drills, electric pit-mule carts, water pumps, columns of carefully placed support timbers, and wire-covered rescue stretchers make it easy to imagine the courage and determination of these early diggers of ore.

New to the museum is a diorama of railroading by world-famous naturalist and artist Francis Lee Jaques.

Open daily early May–Sept.
Admission charged.
(218) 254-5543
www.exploreminnesota.com

9 Superior National Forest
Stretching 150 miles along the U.S.-Canadian border, north of Duluth

Established in 1909, this 3.85-million-acre forest is an impressive natural resource. Rich in pine, spruce, aspen, birch, cedar, and tamarack, it harbors bald eagles and ospreys, moose and deer, black bear and red fox.

Most notably, the forest is home to a large, stable population of about 400 gray wolves. Within the

8 Minnesota Museum of Mining. *Visitors gain a sense of the ruggedness and magnitude of mining through the museum's fascinating display of mining equipment.*

dense woodland, explorers will also find evidence of sweeping sheets of ice dating back hundreds of millions of years. Over the eons, glacial quarrying formed the forest's distinctive character, marked by huge boulders, polished bedrock outcroppings, deep eskers, and hundreds of lake basins. In addition, the forest contains more than 2,000 miles of lakes and streams, both cold and warm water. Walleye, pike, bass, and trout swim in profusion.

Canoeing, fishing, and wildlife viewing are the most popular pastimes here, but visitors do come to swim, bicycle ride, and rock hunt as well. Winters are ideal for cross-country skiing, sledding, and ice fishing. The forest hosts thousands of campsites.

Open year-round. Fees charged for developed campgrounds and overnight use in the wilderness.
(218) 626-4300
www.fs.fed.us/r9/superior

1 George H. Crosby-Manitou State Park. *Through a series of branching waterfalls, canoers paddle down the Manitou River.*

10 Glensheen

3300 London Rd., Duluth

Among the welcome by-products of Minnesota's prosperous iron industry in the early 1900s are the stately homes built in the Duluth area. One such sumptuous manor house is Glensheen, the 39-room Jacobean-style home of millionaire attorney and iron-mine owner Chester Congdon, built from 1905–08 on the shore of Lake Superior. Named for the soft shimmer of the sun on a brook flowing through a small glen, the 7 1/2-acre estate includes a carriage house, boathouse, bowling green, and well-tended gardens.

Glensheen is noted for its hand-carved woodwork, elaborate ceiling plasterwork, and stained-glass windows. The entrance hall, oak-paneled in a 16th-century English pattern, is lighted by brass chandeliers incorporating the motif of the British lion. A red marble fireplace sets the color scheme of the mahogany-paneled drawing room, which is considered to be the most beautiful room in the house. The living room, which has a brick fireplace, burlap wallpaper, and a canvas ceiling, contains "the Little Museum," where mementos of the family's travels are displayed.

The reception room features a ceiling of gold leaf, and the billiard room has walls paneled of oak and "Japanese leather" (made of paper). For all the elegance and fine materials, an inviting sense of human scale is sustained throughout. A series of terraces with balustrades and a small pond lead from the house to the lakeshore.

Visitors are guided through the mansion but may tour the gardens and outbuildings on their own.

Open daily Apr.–Oct; Fri.–Sun. from Nov.–Mar. Closed Easter, *Thanksgiving, Christmas Eve and Day, and New Year's Day. Admission charged.*
(888) 454-4536
www.glensheen.org

11 Jay Cooke State Park

Hwy. 210, near Carlton

The importance of railroads in the 19th century is easy to forget in this era of superhighways and jet planes. A reminder is the fact that this 8,715-acre park is named for Jay Cooke, who was instrumental in establishing Duluth as the eastern terminus of the Central Pacific Railroad's route to the West Coast. The park comprises the rugged countryside flanking both sides of the St. Louis River as it flows through massive rock formations toward Lake Superior. The hills, forested with hardwoods, harbor 46 species of animals, including timber wolves, black bears, and coyotes.

Fifty miles of trails wander through the woodlands and along the river. There are some easy hikes in the park, but the Lost Lake and Silver Creek trails, traversing swamps, steep hills, and ridges, are best left to the well-conditioned. Trout fishing is popular in Silver Creek.

The Grand Portage Trail, part of which lies within the park, was used by travelers 300 years ago to avoid an impassable section of the St. Louis River cutting through this area. Several trails are shared by hikers and horseback riders, and some lead to overlooks with fine views of the river valley. The Carlton Trail begins near the park nature center and crosses the river by means of a swinging bridge.

Modern campsites and group camps are located within walking distance to the river; backpacking sites are found in wilderness areas. Two picnic grounds, one by the river and the other on Oldenburg Point, are invitingly set among birch trees. In the springtime one should ask about the superb display of trilliums and other wildflowers.

In winter the park is popular with cross-country skiers as well as snowshoers.

Open year-round. Admission charged.
(218) 384-4610
www.dnr.state.mn.us

11 Jay Cooke State Park. *Tilted slate bedrock punctuates the St. Louis River in this 8,175-acre park that boasts trails ranging from beginner to those best left to the well-conditioned.*

12 Tamarac National Wildlife Refuge

Headquarters at junction of Rtes. 26 and 29, Rochert

Crisscrossed with quiet roads and gently sloping hiking trails, just shy of 43,000 acres, these woodlands and wetlands offer the solitude of unspoiled nature. More than 20 lakes dot the refuge, their shores providing nesting sites favored by loons, herons, Canada geese, wood ducks, mallards, and teals. Bald eagles also nest here, and golden eagles sometimes may be seen during their fall migration. In all, more than 200 bird species have been observed within the refuge, along with deer, black bears, beavers, and moose.

Berry picking and mushrooming are allowed in the lower third of the refuge, where in a good season chokecherries, pin cherries, raspberries, and morel mushrooms are abundant. Fishermen are likely to catch northern pike, walleye, bluegills, and yellow perch, and boat-launching areas are provided on several of the lakes. Nearly eight miles of trails are groomed for skiing in the winter.

Two of the most popular ways to enjoy the preserve are the Blackbird Auto Tour and the Old Indian Hiking Trail. The auto tour makes a 10-mile loop along refuge roads and passes many areas of geological and ecological interest. A printed guide to the tour is available at the visitors center. The hiking trail, about a one-mile loop, leaves Route 29 at the shore of Tamarac Lake and leads past an ancient Sioux burial ground to a camp area used as late as the 1930s by American Indians gathering wild rice and sap for maple sugar. Harvesting the wild rice today is allowed only by special permit.

Open daily year-round.
(218) 847-2641

www.detroitlakes.com/tamaracrefuge

13 Maplewood State Park
Pelican Rapids

This exceptionally beautiful park—some 9,500 acres of hills, valleys, woodlands, and small lakes—lies between Minnesota's eastern forests and western prairies, and it has plants and animals native to each of the ecological zones. Archaeological evidence indicates that the area was inhabited by American Indians at least 6,000 years ago.

Lida, the largest of the lakes, features a swimming beach and a picnic area nearby. Family campgrounds overlook Grass Lake, and smaller ponds in remote areas have primitive campsites. Miles of trails for hiking, horseback riding, skiing, and snowmobiling wander

14 Runestone Museum. *Among the museum's various exhibits is its most coveted: the Kensington Runestone, dated 1362.*

through the parklands; many lead to overlooks with superb views of the surrounding hills and valleys.

Two ramps are provided for boaters—one at South Lake Lida and one at Beers Lake. Fishing is excellent at both lakes, with walleye, northern pike, and panfish the likely catches.

Forty acres have been set aside as a demonstration woodland. Trees here are labeled with botanical notes and information as to their usefulness to man. Basswood, for instance, is good for beekeepers and cabinet- and toymakers. Paper birch, black cherry, sugar maple, and ironwood (including the largest such tree in Minnesota) are included. Experiments here show that shrubs and trees increase dramatically in size, number, and variety when deer and rabbits are excluded from the area.

Open year-round.
(218) 863-8383

www.dnr.state.mn.us

14 Runestone Museum
206 Broadway, Alexandria

Visitors at this comprehensive museum of local history are rewarded with an intriguing glimpse of Minnesota's Scandinavian heritage and a look at pioneer life in west-central Minnesota. Harnesses and sleighs, ladies' fashions, razors, mustache cups, American Indian artifacts, and stuffed animals (including a bear and timber wolves) are but a few of the countless wonders here. Also visit the beautiful 40-foot-long replica of the Viking ship *Snorri*.

The museum's prize, however, is the runestone itself. Discovered in the nearby town of Kensington by a Swedish farmer in 1898, the three-foot-high stone bears an inscription in the runic alphabet used in Medieval Scandanavia. Some investigators claim it was carved in 1362 by Norsemen exploring the interior of the continent, placing them in the Americas more than 100 years before Columbus. The arcane debate over the stone's authenticity is eloquently depicted in various displays.

On the museum grounds is a replica of the original 1862 Fort Alexandria, which includes a blacksmith's shop, general store, church, and schoolhouse. There is also another large exhibit featuring antique boats, farm equipment, and a large steam engine.

Open daily mid-May to mid-Oct.;
Mon.–Sat. mid-Oct. to
mid–May. Admission charged.
(320) 763-3160

www.runestonemuseum.org

15 Lake Maria State Park
8 miles west of Monticello

This hilly, forested land, with two lakes and numerous marshes

and ponds, is a surviving 1,580-acre fragment of the Big Woods, a mighty primeval forest that originally covered 3,000 square miles of south-central Minnesota. Glaciers advanced and receded here three times. The last incursion, during the Wisconsin ice age, which ended 10,000 years ago, deposited boulders and rocky debris along with till and loam from the Lake Superior and Red River valley regions.

The landscape is a superb habitat for wildlife. Popular with birders, it harbors more than 200 species, including goldfinches, meadowlarks, gulls, bald eagles, Cooper's hawks, and several species of owls—screech, great-horned, snowy, and short-eared. Blandings turtles, one of Minnesota's threatened species, also make their home here. They are easy to locate because of the bright yellow spots on their shells.

Lake Maria, fringed with tall reeds and water lilies and encircled by dense woods of maple, birch, and red oak, brings fishermen, who try for walleye, perch, sunfish, carp, bullhead, and bass. A boat ramp is provided.

A large, primitive group campground has a parking lot; several other primitive campsites must be reached by foot. Opposite a small wooded island in Lake Maria is a shady picnic ground.

The park has six miles of horseback riding trails, and 14 miles of hiking and ski trails. Nature walks are conducted by the park's naturalist.

Open year-round.
Admission charged.
(763) 878-2325

www.dnr.state.mn.us

Pipestone National Monument. *Established in 1937, this 283-acre park is known for its quarries of soft red stone, once used to make ceremonial pipes. Several of the pits are still quarried today.*

16 Kandiyohi County Historical Society and Museum

610 Hwy. 71 NE, Willmar
Here is an enticing little museum with the eclectic charm of grandmother's attic. Its well-organized displays feature everything from American Indian artifacts and a Red River oxcart, used by early settlers on Minnesota's western frontier, to old cars and antique dental and printing equipment.

Other buildings on the grounds add to the vivid sense of a varied and lively local history. The Dakota Sioux and the history of their conflict with settlers are included. In the restored Sperry House, built in 1893, the pump organ and cylinder phonograph in the parlor, the curling irons heated by a kerosene lamp, the carved oak woodwork, stained-glass windows, and period furnishings create with remarkable authenticity the atmosphere of a prosperous turn-of-the-century farmer's home.

A fully equipped 1880 schoolhouse stands nearby, with an 1895 riddle scrawled on the blackboard. The agriculture building has an extensive collection of antique farm tools. Many professions, trades, and industries, including transportation, are interestingly presented. You can climb into the cab of a steam locomotive, put your hand on the throttle, and wish the great whistle would really work.

Open daily Memorial Day–Labor Day; the rest of the year, Mon.–Fri.
(320) 235-1881
www.seeyouinwillmar.com

17 New Ulm

90 miles southwest of the Twin Cities
In 1854, a group of German immigrants landed in the heart of the scenic Minnesota River Valley and found the perfect spot for their new home. Named after the premier city in the settlers' homeland province, New Ulm continues to celebrate its German heritage.

Twelve blocks from downtown, the 102-foot tall Hermann Monument stands as a glowing tribute to an ancient Teutonic hero who liberated Germany from Rome in A.D. 9. For $1, visitors can step inside and climb up to a railed, outside lookout for stunning views of the valley from any one of its 10 windows. Nearby, the New Ulm Glockenspiel plays like clockwork at noon, 3 P.M., and 5 P.M. daily. During the holiday season, a nativity scene replaces the clock's regular cast of diminutive moving characters.

Other sites of interest include the mansion that was home to John Lind, the first Swedish-born American to be elected to Congress, built in 1887 at a cost of $5,000 and placed on the *National Register of Historic Homes* nearly a century later; the childhood home of Wanda Gag, author of the classic children's book *Millions of Cats,* built in 1894; and Schell's Brewery.

Throughout the year, New Ulm hosts a number of festivals rich in German tradition. Oktoberfest, held the first and second weekends in October, serves up German fare, libations, and music in two locations, along with a craft show and horse-drawn trolley rides past the city's historic homes.

Many historic attractions are open year-round, free of charge.
(888) 463-9856
www.newulm.com

18 Pipestone National Monument

Southwest Minnesota
For centuries tribal groups traveled to the quarries here to obtain the soft red stone, also known as catlinite, to make their ceremonial pipe bowls. Legend holds that when the different tribes were at war with each other, the Great Spirit called them together here and fashioned a pipe from the stone. As he smoked the pipe, he told the tribes that this place belonged to them all, that they must make their ceremonial pipes of the stone, and that they must meet in this honored place as friends.

But in the 19th century the Yankton Dakota Indians took over the quarries and made other tribes trade to obtain the pipestone. The U.S. government seized the site in 1893 and in 1937 established the Pipestone National Monument (a 283-acre park) by an act of Congress, which once again gives all American Indians the right to quarry pipestone.

A short loop trail leads from the visitors center past the quarries

Pipestone National Monument. *Guides are on hand to explain the various plants that adorn the short trail that leads from the park's visitors center to the quarries.*

through a tract of prairie where plants are identified and their use by the American Indians explained.

At the historic area you can see an exposed quartzite cliff and several pits that are still quarried, and near the visitors center you can enter a pit in which the floor and lower wall are pipestone.

The visitors center has displays of pipes and various smoking equipment, as well as a gift shop and eight-minute slide show. A nearby cultural center, where craftsmen can be seen at work, sells mementos, pipes, and other carved articles.

Open daily except Christmas and New Year's Day.
(507) 825-5464
www.nps.gov/pipe

19 Hubbard House
Mankato

Rensselaer D. Hubbard, founder of the Hubbard Milling Company, built this elegant white brick two-story house in 1871, only 19 years after the town was first settled. Its handsome proportions, pillared porches, mansard roof patterned with different colors of slate, and stained-glass windows set the style for local mansions yet to come. In 1890 he added a splendid carriage house next door. The buildings are now on the *National Register of Historic Places.*

· The restored house has a notably rich interior, with carved cherry and oak woodwork and three unusual fireplaces (one of Brazilian white onyx and Italian black marble, another of Spanish marble, and a third of Georgia marble). Displayed in the rooms are 19th- and early 20th-century furniture, kitchen equipment, and other memorabilia from the early days of Mankato. Among the

vehicles in the carriage house are a real Concord stagecoach and an 1895 Haynes-Apperson auto in perfect running condition.

Open weekends May–mid-Sept., group tours available year-round by prior arrangement. Admission charged.
(507) 345-5566
www.internet-connections.net/ reg9/bechs

20 The Spam Museum
1937 Spam Blvd. in Austin, about 90 minutes south of Minneapolis

Since 1937, Spam, a mixture of fully cooked pork and ham, has sold a total of nearly 6 billion cans. Next to its "father" plant, Hormel Foods, this 16,500-square-foot complex presents a nostalgic tribute to the all-American luncheon meat.

A treat for trivia buffs, it features 19 permanent exhibits, serving up facts of Spam history and mania. Upon walking through the entrance, you see a towering wall of Spam. Composed of 3,390 cans of Spam, it rises to the lobby's ceiling. A video, "Spam Exam," hosted by comedian Al Franken, challenges connoisseurs to test their product knowledge. Promotions include Spam spoofs (including the infamous Monty Python sketch) and recent corporate efforts to distinguish Spam from the disparaging term for junk e-mail.

There's also a Spam Cyber-Diner, a working radio station (dubbed K-SPAM), and a replica of a Hormel production line, where visitors can pack and label their own can of Spam (fake, of course). For those hungry for Spam memorabilia, the eclectic gift shop offers official Spam playing cards, salt shakers, bobble-head dolls, dog leashes, and earrings.

Visitors can take a quick drive

21 Julius C. Wilkie Steamboat Center. *Housing a trove of riverboat memorabilia from America's age of steam is a reconstruction of the stern-wheeler* Julius C. Wilkie, *which comprises a grand salon and museum.*

to the eastern side of town, on 21st Street NE, for a stroll through the Jay C. Hormel Nature Center. This 279-acre expanse offers 10-plus miles of walking trails past restored and remnant prairie, hardwood forest, and wetlands. In addition, visitors can stop by the informative interpretive center, which features a touch-and-see exhibit and a live beehive.

Open Mon.–Sat. year-round except major holidays. Admission is free for both attractions.
Museum: (507) 437-5100 or (800) 588-7726
www.spam.com
Nature Center: (507) 437-7519
www.austin-mn.com

21 Julius C. Wilkie Steamboat Center
Levee Park, end of Main St., Winona

The riverboat ranks with the locomotive as a reminder of the glorious age of steam in America. The housing for this trove of riverboat memorabilia is a

true-to-life reconstruction of the stern-wheeler *Julius C. Wilkie* (which burned in 1981), its essence vividly created through the sumptuous atmosphere of such rooms as the grand salon, decorated in pink, white, and burgundy, with gilt chairs from Spain, plush curtains, chandeliers, and a floral carpet.

The lower "deck" is a museum containing manuscripts by paddle-boat inventor Robert Fulton, a "doctor" pump (used to prevent the ship's boiler from running dry and exploding), and the Wilkies carbon filament spotlight, capable of throwing a 500-foot beam— a crucial piece of equipment for travel at night along the ever-changing river channels.

There are also a number of riverboat models, such as the *War Eagle,* which carried Civil War troops, and the stern-wheeler *Buckeye.*

Open Wed.–Sun. Admission charged.
(507) 454-1254
www.exploreminnesota.com

Florewood State Park. *This antebellum-style mansion sits amid a 100-acre cotton plantation near the Yazoo River (see page 182).*

The memorial plantations and the tributes to the Delta blues singers and to Jimmie Rodgers, the seminal country-and-western singer, are not unexpected. Although Casey Jones was not a singer, he is the well-remembered hero of a ballad about his train wreck near Vaughan.

Some of the less well-known features include artifacts from Mississippi's considerable American Indian heritage and an impressive petrified forest.

The arts are splendidly represented. Holly Springs has a fine collection of paintings by a local artist, and a museum in Laurel features works of Sargent, Whistler, and other American masters, as well as a remarkable collection of Georgian silver. Literature is represented in the home of a famous local author and winner of the Pulitzer Prize.

Mississippi

A culture influenced by generations of farming the rich soil of this gentle land is reflected in myriad ways.

1 Kate Freeman Clark Art Gallery
300 East College Ave., Holly Springs

In the 1890s Kate Freeman Clark, a talented 16-year-old who grew up in Holly Springs, was taken to New York by her mother to study painting. During the next 30 or so years she produced more than 1,000 works, which she signed "Freeman Clark" to conceal the fact that she was a woman. Her paintings were widely shown, but she sold only a few of them. Following her mother's death in 1923, Clark returned home, immersed herself in social activity, and abandoned her brushes. When she died in 1957 at age 81, she left her paintings and funds to the town for a gallery.

Today a modern single-story building houses her work: portraits, landscapes, and still lifes, which range from an academic treatment to a brighter, more contemporary style. One painting of a woman wearing a white dress in an impressionistic meadow seems to prefigure the advent of photorealism. Most of the works are pleasing, and so is the small museum.

Anyone interested in antebellum architecture will enjoy exploring the streets of Holly Springs. A tour map is available at the Chamber of Commerce.

Museum open weekdays; contact the

2 Rowan Oak. *Surrounded by lush magnolia and cypress trees, the home of writer William Faulkner is remarkable for its simplistic interior.*

First State Bank at (800) 206-6252 or the Chamber of Commerce at (662) 252-2943
www.visithollysprings.org

2 Rowan Oak
Take University Dr. exit from Rte. 7; turn left on Lamar, then right to Old Taylor Rd., Oxford.
This was the home of the famous writer William Faulkner (1897–1962). The scion of two old Southern families, he incorporated into his novels and short stories the myths, traditions, and memories of his locale. He was awarded the 1949 Nobel Prize for Literature and two Pulitzer prizes.

A stately antebellum house with a columned portico, Rowan Oak is remarkable for its interior simplicity and for the sense it conveys of having been furnished by happenstance: Faulkner's work, not his home, was his object and his legacy.

To the left of the entrance is the library, in which the writer worked prior to 1952. His portrait as a young man hangs above two

Chinese vases; copies of *Field and Stream* and a book about Switzerland lie on a small table beside a piece of abstract sculpture. To the right of the hall is a plain sitting room. The most interesting room is the one at the back, where he worked the last few years—on one wall is the outline of a short novel written in his hand. Upstairs are four sparsely furnished bedrooms. The grounds, by contrast, are lush with magnolia and cypress trees and climbing rose vines.

Open Tue.–Sun. except major holidays.
(662) 234-3284

www.touroxfordms.com

3 Tupelo Buffalo Park
2272 North Coley Road, Tupelo

This is the ideal place to get to know the mighty buffalo. Home to the largest herd east of the Mississippi River, this park boasts more than 200 of the majestic creatures. If you're lucky, you'll spot the rare white buffalo.

On the exciting Monster Bison Bus Tour, visitors ride right beside these gigantic beasts. The tour, which lasts about 35 minutes, also provides striking views of Texas longhorn cattle.

After the tour, visitors can stop at a petting and play area. Here, you can meet a pair of baby buffalo, Elvis and Priscilla. Or you can simply stay and watch the antics of the park's other residents, including a monkey named Oliver. Before leaving the land of the buffalo, visitors might want to stop in the gift shop for a souvenir —or even a package of dried buffalo meat.

Open year-round. Admission charged.
(866) 272-4766

www.tupelobuffalopark.com

4 Great River Road State Park
Rosedale

Set between the Mississippi River and the levee, this pleasant and scenic park of some 200 acres centers around Perry Martin Lake, an oxbow of the great river. Fishing and boating are popular on the lake, but swimming is not allowed. The park has 61 concrete pads with water and electrical hookups for campers, as well as a primitive camping area.

From a 75-foot four-level stockadelike observation tower there are splendid views of the Mississippi, its extensive sandbars, and the scrubland and cottonwoods that lie between the picnic area and the river.

The Deer Meadow Nature Trail winds through a woodland of pecan and mulberry trees and Virginia creeper. It's an easy trail to follow, although it is unsigned and its various forks and branches do not seem to coincide with the map provided. The path ends in a scrubby pastureland where deer are likely to be seen.

From the parking lot a narrow "fisherman's footpath" gives views of the lake, picturesque with dense stands of reed and the stark white trunks of dead trees. In early June the path is bordered by thickets of blackberry cane. The park has a boat launch and canoe and paddleboat rentals. The park has 61 camping sites.

Open daily year-round.
(662) 759-6762

www.wildernet.com

Legend

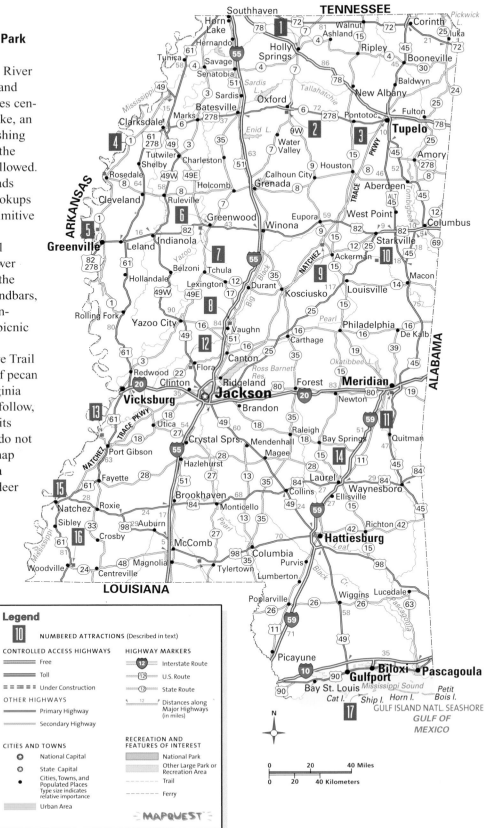

10 NUMBERED ATTRACTIONS (Described in text)

CONTROLLED ACCESS HIGHWAYS
━━━ Free
━━━ Toll
═══ Under Construction

OTHER HIGHWAYS
Primary Highway
Secondary Highway

CITIES AND TOWNS
◉ National Capital
⊛ State Capital
• Cities, Towns, and Populated Places Type size indicates relative importance
Urban Area

HIGHWAY MARKERS
12 Interstate Route
12 U.S. Route
12 State Route
12 Distances along Major Highways (in miles)

RECREATION AND FEATURES OF INTEREST
National Park
Other Large Park or Recreation Area
Trail
Ferry

MAPQUEST

5 Winterville Mounds State Park

On Hwy. 1, 6 miles north of the intersection of Hwys. 82 and 1 in Greenville.

This is one of the ceremonial mound complexes built in prehistoric America by American Indians of the Mississippian culture. Although not as spectacular as the one at Etowah, Georgia, it is nevertheless an impressive example of this strange way of life. Built about 1,000 years ago by an agricultural people who were the predecessors of the Choctaw, Chickasaw, and Tunica tribes, it was probably occupied for some 600 years before its populace was completely decimated by disease, drought, war, or famine.

The 40-acre park is said to contain 12 mounds, but only eight are readily discerned. A flight of stairs leads to the top of the largest mound (about 55 feet high), where there is a roofless, windowless structure. The view is of pancake-flat Delta farmland, with a 360-degree horizon of woodland. One can see the pattern of other mounds, and to the east is an open space called the Sacred Plaza, where dances and other ceremonies were held.

A museum in the visitors center contains American Indian artifacts, including arrowheads, celts, adzes, chunky stones and ball sticks, clay pipes, shell beads, and pots. A wall-length mural depicts American Indians hunting and gathering food. The park has a picnic ground with tables and grills.

Grounds open daily. Museum open Mon.–Sat. and P.M. Sun.
(662) 334-4684
www.mdah.state.ms.us

6 Cottonlandia Museum

Hwy. 82 West, Greenwood

Despite its name, this is far from being a one-crop museum. Cottonlandia offers a fascinating overview of the archaeological, natural, economic, and social heritage of the Delta.

The museum's extensive collection of American Indian artifacts includes some of the earliest arrow and spear points made on this continent; a few are of the type used about 10,000 B.C. to kill mastodons. (On view are the locally unearthed bones of a mastodon that may have been killed in a hunt.) You can also see examples of the earliest ceramics produced in the New World: small, fire-hardened clay balls made and used as a source of heat for cooking food by the people of the Poverty Point culture, which thrived in the lower Mississippi Valley some 3,000 years ago.

One of the most valuable—and exquisite—displays is the group of multicolored pottery effigy vessels, which depict a bobcat, deer, fish, opossum, and other creatures in a very naturalistic manner. The vessels date from sometime after A.D. 700.

The enormous and colorful collection of beads alone makes a visit to this museum worthwhile. Various methods of manufacturing beads are described, along with fashions in beads from prehistoric times. Included are some 17th-century European beads of the kind that Peter Minuit used in trading for the island of Manhattan.

Relics of King Cotton include a miniature Improved Eagle cotton gin, a John Deere tractor of the sort that retired mules from the cotton fields, an 1850 wooden harrow with hand-forged points made by slaves, and a boll weevil catcher. One case displays the various grades of cotton from "good middling" to "middling tinged" and "strict good ordinary."

A hands-on, natural science room and life-sized diorama of a Mississippi swamp interest both children and adults and offer a break from the usual "no touch" rules of most museums.

Cottonlandia also features

7 Florewood State Park. *One of the distinctive features of this reconstructed 1850s cotton plantation is its vintage farm equipment.*

artifacts from the Malmaison, the home of Greenwood Laflore, the last Choctaw chief before their removal to Oklahoma in the 1800s.

A large collection of Mississippi artwork graphically displays the range of styles of native artists, from photography to abstract sculpture, watercolor to ceramics, and all things in between.

Open weekdays and P.M. weekends except major holidays.
(662) 453-0925
www.gcvb.com/cl.html

7 Florewood State Park

Greenwood

This outstanding reconstruction of an 1850s Mississippi cotton plantation is sited on 100 acres of land near the Yazoo River, just outside the town that describes itself as the cotton capital of the world.

The museum in the visitors center gives a vivid picture of the 19th-century cotton business. Two outstanding exhibits are the Whitney gin and the rare, shiny, red-and-yellow Lane and Bodley side-crank box-bed steamboat engine.

The mansion and other buildings are in parklike grounds attractively planted with Southern wax myrtle, Japanese boxwood, crape myrtle, live oak, peach, Callery pear, and dwarf plum trees. Costumed guides give tours of the mansion, which is decorated in strikingly elegant antebellum style. The period furnishings include the indispensable wig-dresser in the master bedroom and a "petticoat table" with a floor-level mirror, so a lady could make sure her ankles were decently covered.

Among the many outbuildings are the potter's and candlemaker's shops, where scheduled demonstrations are given and costumed interpreters describe 19th-century life. The use of the land on a Delta cotton plantation of the period is also well represented, with a vegetable garden and fields of cotton, corn, sorghum, and peas. In the fall you may help pick the cotton balls. Mules and horses graze in one pasture, goats in another.

Plantation open Tues.–Sat. and P.M. Sun., Mar.–Nov.; admission charged. Museum open Tues.–Sat. and P.M. Sun. year-round. Entire park closed Thanksgiving, Christmas, and New Year's Day.
(662) 455-3821
www.ohwy.com

8 Casey Jones Railroad Museum State Park

Vaughan
The famous train wreck in 1900 that sent the brave engineer Casey Jones on a one-way "trip to the promised land," as the ballad goes, occurred at Vaughan not far from this museum. The building is a turn-of-the-century train station brought from the nearby town of Pickens.

The exhibits include rail station telephones and telegraphs, trainmen's uniforms, track maintenance tools, flagmen's signal kits, scale models of trains, and an Illinois Central engine bell to which 20 silver dollars were reportedly added to produce its distinctive tone.

Among the exhibits devoted to Jones are commemorative depictions of the wreck and the bell from engine No. 382 of the Cannonball Express that Casey drove that fatal night.

Open Mon.–Sat. year-round. Admission charged.
(662) 673-9864
www.trainweb.org/caseyjones

9 Jeff Busby Campground

Natchez Trace Pkwy.
This small, pleasant recreation area offers an agreeable place to camp and the opportunity to drive up Little Mountain, at 605 feet the highest point on the Natchez Trace. The view of forest all around, dotted with pockets of cultivated land and even fewer habitations, provides a refreshing sense of wilderness.

An exhibit in the shelter at the top of the hill is concerned with the past glory, recent tribulations, and current partial recovery of the great Eastern hardwood forest (once the greatest hardwood forest in the world), of which it was said that "a squirrel could have gone from Maine to Texas without touching ground." But to the white settlers the forest was an enemy to be beaten back. Today the salutary effects of proper land management can be seen along the Natchez Trace.

From the top of Little Mountain a short trail descends the hill in wide, easy loops.

Open year-round.
(800) 305-7417
www.nps.gov/natr

10 Noxubee National Wildlife Refuge

Reached from either Rte. 25 or Alt. 45; watch for signs. 15 miles south of Starkville.
Surprisingly, only 3,000 of the more than 48,000 acres in the refuge are designated as a sanctuary. Anglers enjoy Loakfoma Lake and Bluff Lake and take good catches of largemouth bass, bluegills, and crappies from their waters.

For birders the best place is Canada Goose Overlook, an elevated walkway and viewing platform

10 Noxubee National Wildlife Refuge. *Hikers, anglers, and birders alike enjoy the plethora of wildlife that exists in this 48,000-acre refuge—from the American alligator to largemouth bass to tens of thousands of waterfowl.*

that juts out high above Bluff Lake. It's well worthwhile to bring binoculars. From November through January tens of thousands of waterfowl, primarily wood ducks, green-winged teals, Canada geese, and American widgeons, visit the refuge. In late winter and early spring a variety of songbirds add their grace notes. Wood storks and wild turkeys may be seen, and occasionally the endangered red-cockaded woodpecker and the bald eagle. From this elevation one can see other wildlife as well, like white-tailed deer feeding in grassy meadows or the American alligator crawling about.

The refuge is crisscrossed with narrow gravel roads and seven hiking trails; a map may be obtained at refuge headquarters. Visitors entering the woods during the gun-hunting season in November and December are required to wear hunter orange.

Open year-round.
(662) 323-5548
http://noxubee.fws.gov

11 Jimmie Rodgers Museum

Off 39th Ave., Meridian
Jimmie Rodgers, "The Singing Brakeman," is honored here as the 1920s progenitor of country music.

Rodgers, who died in 1933, was indeed a brakeman, as well as a baggageman and switchman, during the era of the steam engine. The museum building resembles a train station, complete with an engine and caboose outside.

Rodgers's popularity is demonstrated by fan mail from as far away as Japan, honorary citizenship papers from the city of New Orleans, and first-day covers of the postage stamp acclaiming him as the Father of Country Music. Original recordings and sheet music of his songs are displayed, as well as his denim jacket and other belongings. In early May, Meridian sponsors a Jimmie Rodgers Memorial Festival.

Open Mon.–Sat. and P.M. Sun. year-round. Closed Thanksgiving, Christmas, and New Year's Day. Admission charged.
(601) 485-1808
www.jimmierodgers.com

12 Mississippi Petrified Forest
Flora

Considering the comparatively short span of time allotted the human record, the scope of the geological record here is almost impossible to comprehend. The fossilized logs in this small forest (the only petrified forest east of the Rockies) are some 36 million years old. The remains of living denizens of primeval forests, they were deposited here as driftwood and buried in and preserved by the sand and silt. A smooth path traverses the site, a lush woodland of loblolly pines, sweet gums, elms, wild plums, and occasional clumps of yucca and pear cactus.

The most striking feature found here is a curiously anomalous section of deeply eroded red and pink cliffs, studded with extruding petrified logs, that resembles a miniature badlands. These exposed cliff walls are a fascinating cross section of natural history. The red sands in their lower parts were the river deposit in which the petrifaction process originally began.

Markers along the path are keyed to a descriptive leaflet available at the entrance to the site. The 40-minute walk terminates at a small but interesting museum devoted to petrified wood. The displays also include some vertebrate fossils and an array of gems and minerals.

Open daily except Christmas.
Admission charged.
(601) 879-8189
www.mspetrifiedforest.com

12 Mississippi Petrified Forest. *In the only petrified forest found east of the Rockies, visitors are free to touch the fossilized logs while traversing a path profuse with loblollies and sweet gums.*

13 Grand Gulf Military Park
Port Gibson

The restored buildings here are reminders that this was once a thriving river port nurtured by the cotton boom and so prosperous that it was a candidate to become the state capital. But in 1843 a yellow fever epidemic struck. Ten years later many who survived the epidemic were killed by a major tornado. Then in 1855 the Mississippi River began to shift its course, and in the next five years it destroyed 55 city blocks, including the entire business area. In April 1863 Union naval forces attacked Grand Gulf and later outflanked Confederate troops established here and forced them to abandon Grand Gulf. Nothing remains of Fort Wade and Fort Cobun but some remnants of earthworks.

Today the park commemorates both the battle and Grand Gulf's heyday. The museum here has a detailed map of that battle and photos of the Union ironclads that were involved, along with swords, rifles, muskets, cannonballs, flags, and war-related documents.

On the handsome park grounds are a few hand-hewn log houses, a lovely Carpenter Gothic chapel, and an atmospheric graveyard overhung with Spanish moss. Probably unique in the world is the homemade submarine, powered by a Model-T Ford engine, which was used to run whiskey during Prohibition. A paved road leads to the edge of the river, and a hilltop observation tower provides an overview of this instrument of Grand Gulf's rise and fall.

Open year-round.
(601) 437-5911
www.grandgulfpark.state.ms.us

14 Lauren Rogers Museum of Art
Fifth Ave. at Seventh St., Laurel

The emphasis here is on 19th- and 20th-century painting, and indisputably this distinguished museum houses one of the most outstanding collections in the South. Seven elegant galleries invite one to linger with masterpieces by James McNeill Whistler, John Singer Sargent, Winslow Homer, and Mary Cassatt, among other notable artists. There is a rich collection of landscape paintings, from dramatic renderings of the American wilderness by Albert Bierstadt to Thomas Moran's grandiose sunset scene and the moody impressionism of George Inness's later works.

In addition, the museum contains an excellent exhibit of Georgian silver. Highlights include a classic 1785 George III teapot by Hester Bateman, one of the few female silversmiths of her time; William Plummer's celebrated cake baskets; and plates by Paul Lamerie, acclaimed in the early 1700s as the finest of England's craftsmen in silver and gold.

Another of the museum's displays provides a fascinating insight into the subtle relationship between art and archeology. The Catherine Marshall Gardiner Basket Collection features the superb work of American Indians. The craftsmanship in one set of miniature baskets is so fine that it is displayed under a magnifying glass.

Also on display is an impressive Japanese collection of *Ukiyo-e* woodblock prints from the 8th century.

The Georgian Revival building, with its handsome brick exterior, golden oak hallways, and elaborate ironwork, is itself an elegant tribute to the admirable architecture of the Old South.

Open Tues.–Sat. and P.M. Sun. year-round.
Closed major holidays.
(601) 649-6374
www.lrma.org

15 Historic Natchez
At the intersection of U.S. Highways 61, 84, and 98, on the Mississippi River

Perched on the highest promontory north of the Gulf of Mexico, Natchez is the oldest civilized community on the Mississippi River. Originally settled by the Natchez Indians, it was claimed by the French in 1716, the British in 1763, the Spanish in 1779, and finally the Americans in 1798. In 1817, it was named the first capital of the new state of Mississippi.

During the early 19th century, the city boomed as cotton was exported by steamboat. Today, Natchez is known for its rustic beauty, sense of history, and Southern hospitality. Visitors can stroll scenic trails, try their luck at riverboat gambling, or take a nostalgic tour via trolley or horse-drawn carriage. The town has an Antiques Row, with nearly 20 shops.

Natchez is also home to the Old South Winery and several historic houses. One of the most impressive, Rosalie mansion, reflects the classic Federal style, enhanced by wide galleries and Doric columns. Its lovely garden borders a four-acre riverside park, which hosts the Great Mississippi River Balloon Race festival every October.

Nearby, Lansdowne Plantation invites travelers to step back in time and experience the gracious lifestyle of an elite antebellum home, surrounded by more than a hundred wooded acres. Built in 1853 and meticulously preserved—in fact, it has never been restored—Lansdowne includes original furnishings and décor, down to the hand-blocked Zuber wallpaper.

From the plantation, visitors can head off on the Natchez Trace Parkway. Over 440 miles long, this sweeping stretch commemorates the Old Natchez Trace, which evolved from a Natchez Indian trail into a post road and pioneer highway. Designated as a National Scenic Byway, it encompasses historic sites such as Emerald Mound, the second largest American Indian ceremonial site in the United States. Winding across Mississippi, it tells the story of celebrated leaders, like Meriwether Lewis and Andrew Jackson, and notorious outlaws, like John Murrell and Samuel Mason. Along the way, the roadside features plenty of informative exhibits, interpretive markers, and self-guiding nature trails.

Open year-round.
(800) 647-6724;
Natchez Trace Parkway:
(800) 305-7417
www.natchezms.com

Rosemont Plantation
Woodville

Jefferson Davis grew up on this gracious plantation, reached from the highway by a long, shady lane. Though best known as the president of the Confederate States of America during the Civil War, Jefferson Davis had already made his mark as a soldier, congressman, senator, a founder of the Smithsonian Institution, and a U.S. Secretary of War.

The pastures and gardens of the plantation are bordered by hand-split rail fences, and the roses that gave the plantation its name still grow in profusion. Even in summer the grounds can be surprisingly cool, shaded by evergreen magnolias and immense live oaks festooned with Spanish moss. One can readily believe the roadside sign that reads: "Quiet, you are entering the early 19th century."

The inviting white manor house, built in 1810 by Jefferson Davis's father in the Federal "planter's cottage" style, has been well preserved. A porch with square pillars runs the width of the building, and a roof of multiple peaks rises high above the first story. Dormer windows and white latticework add their appeal. At the end of the porch the lattice supports a bush of tiny magenta roses. Among the furnishings of the Davis family are a whale-oil chandelier and a spinning wheel that belonged to Davis's mother.

Near the house are former slave quarters, an office, and a kitchen.

Open Mon.–Fri., Mar.–Dec. 15.
Admission charged.
(601) 888-6809
http://members-tripod.com/woodville4/
rosemont.htm

17 Ship Island
Biloxi

From a pier just beside the Marine Life Oceanarium located at the Gulfport Small Harbor, the Ship Island Excursion ferry sets out on its 1-hour, 12-nautical-mile trip through the Mississippi Sound to Ship Island, part of the Gulf Islands

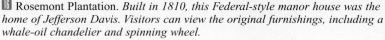
16 Rosemont Plantation. *Built in 1810, this Federal-style manor house was the home of Jefferson Davis. Visitors can view the original furnishings, including a whale-oil chandelier and spinning wheel.*

National Seashore. For most of the voyage the shore is out of sight, and one has the sense of being truly at sea. Only leaping dolphins and an occasional fleet of shrimp boats, their nets outstretched like wings, break the flat expanse of blue.

The ferry lands at a pier to the left of which stands Fort Massachusetts, a grand and elegant red brick structure with rows of arched doorways and waves of vault-ceilinged chambers that give one the impression of walking through a Renaissance painting. Designed by the French engineer Simone Bernard, the fort was begun in 1859 as part of a coastal defense system. It was first occupied by the Confederates, and then by Union forces in the Civil War and named for the Union ship *Massachusetts,* which was involved in a minor engagement here. Free tours of the fort are conducted twice a day.

A boardwalk bisects the island, leading to a long white beach staffed by lifeguards and dotted with grass-roofed cabanas and bright beach umbrellas. Body- and windsurfing are popular. Along the boardwalk are bathhouses, picnic pavilions, and a snack bar. The walkway's purpose is expressed in a sign: "For want of grass the sand is lost, for want of sand the dune is lost, for want of dune the island is lost, for want of the island the harbor is lost." Best in spring and fall to avoid fierce heat.

Open year-round. Excursions run from Mar.–Oct. Fare charged for boat.
Gulf Islands National Seashore:
(228) 875-9057
Ship Island Excursions:
(228) 864-1014
http://msshipisland.com

Wilson's Creek National Battlefield. *The calm waters at this national park belie the fierce 1861 Civil War battle along the creek in which more than 2,500 men died (see page 192).*

Missouri

The two great waterways that border and divide this state brought early explorers and settlers whose influences can still be appreciated.

The most dramatic evidence of early settlement is the town of Ste. Genevieve, established on the Mississippi River more than 250 years ago when France claimed this area. An attractive legacy is the French-Creole architecture that evolved. Another charming river town is Arrow Rock on the Missouri. Settled in 1815, it reflects the character of the frontier. The influence of early 19th-century German immigrants is apparent in the village of Hermann.

Two water-driven mills are reminders of the time when every farmer's daily bread was made from grain that he grew himself. Among the eight recreation and wildlife areas included here is one that preserves a magnificent section of the "sea of grass" that seemed so endless to the pioneers headed west. Some impressively famous people are honored in Missouri. They include such diverse personalities as a universally celebrated writer, a great scientist who was born a slave, and an unforgettable British prime minister.

1 Squaw Creek National Wildlife Refuge

Mound City
This is the kind of spacious landscape that encourages one to linger and look. The sizable refuge—an expanse of 7,350 acres of marsh, pond, meadow, and wooded bluffs—provides a year-round haven for birds of many kinds.

Pheasants and hawks are best seen in January and February; a variety of waterfowl stop off in spring; May is the month for warblers; and in late summer the avocets and other shorebirds arrive. Come October legions of snow geese and ducks descend. In the winter months one of the largest concentrations of bald eagles in America—as many as 3,000 at peak—makes this refuge a temporary home. Great-horned owls are also around.

Squaw Creek also shelters white-tailed deer, minks, foxes, Southern lemmings, and mule deer (a few stragglers from the West). And along the refuge roads early in the morning, the wary coyote is often seen.

The extensive gravel roads and a number of trails offer visitors a choice of driving, bicycling, or hiking through the refuge. The Bluff Trail, starting behind the visitors center, gives panoramic views of the ponds and marshes. In spring the area blushes with wild-

 Watkins Woolen Mill State Historic Site. *Visitors step back in time during a tour of the 20-room Watkins family home. The nearby woolen mill is the only one remaining in the country with its original machinery still intact.*

flowers, and the end of July finds the American lotus in flower.
Open year-round.
(660) 442-3187
midwest.fsw.gov/squawcreek

2 St. Joseph Museum
1100 Charles St., St. Joseph
Known as the city "where Southern hospitality meets Western democracy," St. Joseph played a vital role in 19th-century westward expansion as a key stop for railroads and steamboats.

The town became quite prosperous in the post-Civil War decades. Homes constructed in that period include this museum building, an impressive 43-room Gothic-style mansion erected in 1879 and decorated by Tiffany of New York for its second owner, Kate Tootle.

MISSOURI

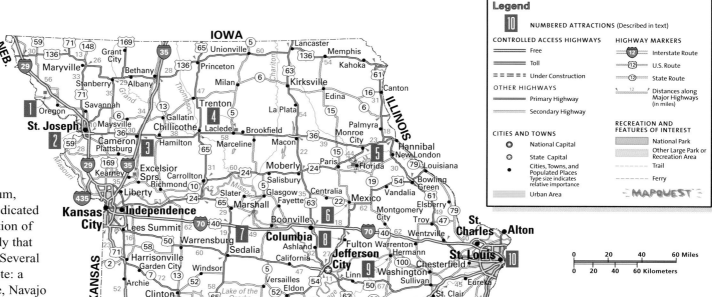

The St. Joseph Museum, established in 1927, is dedicated primarily to the preservation of diverse cultures, especially that of the American Indian. Several items are of particular note: a beautiful birchbark canoe, Navajo baskets, colorful Pomo basketry, Iroquois masks, and Seminole costumes. In the Eskimo collection you'll see clothing, domestic and hunting utensils, masks, and exquisite walrus carving.

Various mounted animals haunt the natural history section, while local history devotes one room to Jesse James, who was shot and killed in St. Joseph on April 3, 1882. Other exhibits in this potpourri of a museum include Tiffany windows, military equipment, 19th-century women's fashions, dolls and dollhouses, and mannequins.

A Pioneer Wall honors the past by listing all the people who jumped off at St. Joseph to head west to seek fertile land or a fortune in the gold mines.

Open Tues.–Sat. Jan.–Mar.; Tues.–Sun. Apr.–Dec. Admission charged.

(800) 530-8866

www.stjosephmuseum.org

3 Watkins Woolen Mill State Historic Site

Lawson
This interesting and attractive 19th-century complex includes the woolen mill and family home of Waltus Watkins and his wife, Mary Ann. Begun in 1850 and completed four years later, the house has a simple but elegant brick façade and 20 rooms, which accommodated the family of 11 children.

Watkins's first venture was a cotton mill, which was unsuccessful, but he had a flair for farming and expanded a holding of 80 acres into a property of 3,600— the Bethany Plantation. In 1860 Watkins turned again to the textile business and began to build his woolen mill. Like the house the mill was made from his own timber and bricks. Deer tracks made on the bricks before they dried can be seen in the floor of the storage shed. More than 50 textile machines were shipped in by railroad and steamboat and hauled the final 20 miles by oxen. Eventually the Bethany Plantation became a self-sustaining community.

The three-story woolen mill is the only one remaining in the country with its original machinery. The various hankers, pickers, twisters, and looms stand lean and elegant in silent tribute to a prosperous business that finally succumbed to new techniques of mass production at the turn of the century.

Adjacent to the historic site is the Watkins Mill State Park, which features a 100-acre lake, campsites with hookups, and trails.

Open year-round except holidays. Admission charged.

(816) 580-3387

www.mostateparks.com/wwmill

4 Gen. John J. Pershing Boyhood Home State Historic Site

Laclede

Graduated from West Point in 1886, Pershing underwent his baptism by fire against Geronimo's Apache Indians and completed his career as commander in chief of American forces in World War I.

Pershing's boyhood home is an unpretentious but attractive two-story white clapboard with restrained Gothic trim. While the furnishings are not those of his family, they are of the period, and there are Pershing memorabilia throughout. An upstairs room serves specifically as a small museum for Pershing's many medals, among them the Silver Star for gallantry. Also on view are photos of some of his early campaigns and the bejeweled sword given him by the city of London in 1919.

From an audio tape that outlines his life, you'll learn that Pershing favored Gary Cooper for the leading role in a planned movie about his life, and that his nickname, "Black Jack," was a reference to his onetime command of the 19th (black) Cavalry.

Relocated on the site is the small school where Pershing taught for $35 a month before heading to West Point. A bronze statue of Pershing also stands on the grounds before a Wall of Honor inscribed with the names of several hundred war veterans.

Open year-round. Admission charged.
(660) 963-2525

www.mostateparks.com/pershingsite.htm

5 Mark Twain Birthplace State Historic Site and State Park

Florida

Samuel Clemens was born November 30, 1835, in what he later described as "the almost invisible village of Florida, Monroe County, Missouri." On another occasion he noted: "Recently someone in Missouri sent me a picture of the house I was born in. Heretofore I always stated that it was a palace, but I shall be more guarded now." The small two-room plank cabin is

5 Mark Twain Birthplace State Historic Site. *The Mark Twain Museum's main exhibit: the "palace" where Twain was born in 1835.*

modest, to say the least.

Moved to its present site in 1930, the house is now enclosed by the striking Mark Twain Museum. Here you will see first editions of his books and a manuscript copy of *The Adventures of Tom Sawyer*. Other displays offer a colorful view of Twain's adventurous life as a steamboat pilot, printer's apprentice, soldier, gold and silver prospector, laborer, newspaper reporter, and one of America's best-loved writers.

Just north of the birthplace site is Mark Twain State Park, a 2,775-acre expanse anchored by the sprawling Mark Twain Lake. Fishing, boating, and swimming are permitted. From the oak-shaded picnic area you can take a short, rugged path to the observation platforms on the sheer cliffs of Buzzard's Roost for excellent views of the surroundings.

Birthplace and museum open year-round except holidays; admission charged.
Park open year-round.
Birthplace: (573) 565-3449
Park: (573) 565-3440

www.mostateparks.com/twainsite.htm

6 Audrain County Historical Society

Mexico

Located within the 11-acre Robert S. Green Park, the historical society features two museums, a country school and church, and stables. Graceland Museum, an imposing mansion built in 1857, was bought in 1868 by Colby T. Quisenberry, who introduced Kentucky saddlebreds to the area, begetting Mexico's title as the "Saddlebred Capital of the World."

The American Saddlebred Horse Museum adjoins Graceland and features trophies and other mementos of memorable horse Rex McDonald and famous trainer and equestrian Thomas Bass. Rex, a black stallion, was considered the "champion of champions and sire of champions." Other exhibits include riding habits, the saddles of famous riders, and paintings of saddle horses by George Ford Morris.

The country church was reconstructed on the society's grounds in 1998 from the original 1889 structure. The one-room country school dates to 1903 and includes a slate blackboard and original desks and books.

Open year-round except holidays.
Admission charged.
(573) 581-3910

www.audrain.org

7 Arrow Rock State Historic Site

Arrow Rock

Arrow Rock was first settled in 1815 and was established as a town in 1829. It was an important stop on the Santa Fe Trail, and in the 1860s its population peaked at more than 1,000. Then the railroads bypassed the town, and Arrow Rock began a decline to its current level of about 80 full-time residents.

5 Mark Twain Birthplace State Historic Site. *The two-room plank cabin in which the then Samuel Clemens was born is now housed in the Mark Twain Museum.*

The most interesting buildings can be seen on a guided walking tour that starts at the visitors center on Main Street. Among them is the restored house of the portrait painter George Caleb Bingham, a two-room log cabin built by the artist himself in 1837 on land that he bought for $50. The furnishings are of the period, but the only piece that belonged to Bingham is his easel.

Another famous resident was Dr. John Sappington, who brought quinine to Arrow Rock to combat outbreaks of malaria. The museum in his name contains first editions of his medical book and memorabilia of his practice.

The John Sites Gun Shop (1844), with its bullet molds and powder horns, and the medicinal herb garden of the Country Doctor Museum illustrate various aspects of 19th-century self-preservation. And the town centerpiece, then as today, is the Old Tavern, built in 1834 and still serving meals. After touring the historic village, you can spend the night in the site's modern campground.

Open year-round.
(660) 837-3330
www.mostateparks.com/arrowrock.htm

8 Winston Churchill Memorial and Library
Westminster College, Fulton
In 1946 Britain's former prime minister, Winston Churchill, accepted an invitation from his Missouri-born friend President Harry Truman to speak at Westminster College.

In that historic address Churchill described the Soviet grip on Eastern Europe: "From Stettin in the Baltic to Trieste in the

8 Winston Churchill Memorial and Library. *The church of St. Mary, the Virgin, Aldermanbury, reconstructed at Westminster College in honor of Winston Churchill.*

Adriatic, an iron curtain has descended across the continent."

In the early 1960s the college decided to honor the great British leader by reconstructing on its grounds a London landmark destroyed in World War II. The structure was the church of St. Mary, the Virgin, Aldermanbury, a 12th-century London church demolished by the great fire of London in 1666 and rebuilt by Christopher Wren in 1677. The church was knocked to the ground by German bombs in 1940.

Dismantling began in 1965. Seven thousand stones weighing a total of 700 tons were cleaned, numbered, and shipped to Fulton, with new stones hand cut as necessary. Wood carvings, plasterwork, windows, and brass chandeliers were all re-created from Wren's designs. A new organ was built in London, five new bronze bells were cast in Holland, windows were copied by a glass company in West Virginia, and a London wood carver matched the original pulpit.

Dedicated in 1969, the white church radiates an elegant simplicity. The interior is light and spacious, the decor rich but unobtrusive.

A library and a museum in the undercroft relate the life and long public service of the prime minister.
Open year-round except holidays.
Admission charged.
(573) 592-5232
www.westminster-mo.edu/cm

9 Historic Hermann Museum
Hermann
The German school building with its clock tower recalls an era when German immigrants established a number of Midwestern towns like Hermann, founded in 1837. The school was built in 1870 and functioned as such until 1955. It now houses town offices and a museum.

The Kinder Room, with its German readers, dolls and dollhouses, and toy carousel, reminds one of the origin of kindergarten. In the German Heritage Room you'll see a collection of long-stemmed Dresden pipes. Wine labels attest to Hermann's once flourishing, then moribund, and now revived wine industry. Redware pottery, old German newspapers, Bibles, and language primers document the roots of the settlement.

The River Room, with its steamboat memorabilia and old

photos of riverboat personalities, emphasizes Hermann's location on the Missouri River.
Open daily except Thurs.
Admission charged.
(573) 486-2017
www.hermannmo.com

10 Chain of Rocks Bridge
St. Louis County
Opened to traffic in 1929, this marvel crosses one of the most historic and scenic sections of the Mississippi River, connecting Missouri to Illinois.

Once part of the fabled Route 66, the bridge is famed for a unique 22-degree turn at its midpoint. The bridge was closed in 1968 when a new structure was built to serve I-270. It sat abandoned and decaying until 1999, when it was restored and reopened thanks to a preservation group.

Today the Old Chain of Rocks Bridge has a new life as a nature and recreation trail. At 24 feet wide and just more than a mile in length, it lays claim to being the longest pedestrian and bicycle bridge in the world. You'll see panoramic views of the St. Louis skyline, and the river views reveal the inspiration for the bridge's name: a collection of rocky shoals just to the south that create a waterfall-like effect at low water levels.

When cold weather comes, these rapids attract one of the largest concentrations of bald eagles in the entire continent. Visitors can watch the eagles hunt fish, ride ice floes, roost in trees along the shore, or soar majestically overhead.
Open year-round.
(314) 416-9930
home.att.net/~old.chain.of.rocks.bridge

⑪ Lake of the Ozarks State Park. *Great swimming beaches are among the many options here, where recreation runs the gamut from nature hikes to cave tours.*

⑪ Lake of the Ozarks State Park
Kaiser

Created in the 1930s by the damming of the Osage River, the Lake of the Ozarks is the largest state park in Missouri. The park's 17,441 acres embrace the Grand Glaize arm of the lake and the surrounding Osage River Hills. The landscape includes dense oak and hickory forests, stretches of prairie-like savannas, caves, bluffs eroded by the Grand Glaize Creek, and open, rocky areas with temperature extremes, known locally as glades.

In addition to the pleasures of the lakeshore, the park offers 10 trails of varying lengths for horseback riders (horses can be rented at a stable on Rte. 134 near the campground), hikers, and backpackers. The Trail of Four Winds features a scenic overlook of the valley, while the Woodland Trail offers the peacefulness of Patterson Hollow Wild Area, an untouched wilderness of old meadows and oak and sassafras woodland. Spring wildflowers are best observed along the Lake View and Rocky Top trails.

Missouri claims more caves than any other state, some 4,000 in all. The Ozark Caverns' main attractions: the stalactite formations and Angel's Showers, a waterfall descending from apparently solid rock. A guided one-hour tour covers 1 1/2 miles, where you will see sleeping bats, bear claw marks, and the same speleological wonders the first explorers did.
Open year-round.
Admission charged for cave tours.
(573) 348-2694
www.mostateparks.com/lakeozark.htm

⑫ Dillard Mill State Historic Site
Davisville

Situated by Huzzah Creek and surrounded by grassy bluffs, Dillard Mill is unusually picturesque and beautifully restored.

During the heyday of water power in the late 1800s, Dillard was one of 20 mills within a 40-mile radius. At full summer-time capacity, it produced 25 196-pound barrels of flour a day in a 24-hour shift. At the height of the season, farmers camped as many as four days to get their harvest of grain converted to flour.

The mill closed for business in 1956, but the equipment is fully operational for daily tours. The roller mills, grain elevators, sifting machines, and original leather drive belts are still impressive. The main drive wheel inside the mill has teeth of hard maple so that if anything goes wrong, the teeth break, not the wheel or belts. And the 24.2 horsepower Leffel turbine, which sits under water in the flume, runs on wooden bearings to avoid rust. The skills of the old millwrights and engineers are clearly in evidence.

The 132-acre site offers trails, picnic areas, and fishing in the clear Ozark creek. Spring and fall offer the best weather.
Open daily year-round except holidays.
Admission charged for mill.
(573) 244-3120
www.mostateparks.com/dillardmill.htm

⑬ St. Francois State Park
Bonne Terre

Moonshiners and outlaws once made this wilderness in the Pike Run Hills their own. Today it is a natural escape of 2,735 acres of meadow and hill, creek, bluff, glade, forest, and lush bottomland, plus a well-tended camping area, picnic sites, and several trails.

Beginners and families can canoe the meandering Big River. Anglers favor the stream for its bass and catfish. Both horseback riders and overnight backpackers use the 11-mile Pike Run, which starts in a meadow dotted with juniper (and in June and July bright with yarrow and black-eyed Susans) and then enters woodlands, crossing creek beds as it follows an old logging road through some of the wildest parts of the park.

The Mooner's Hollow Trail, which is for hikers only, makes a 2.7-mile loop in the Coonville Creek Wild Area, once a favorite haunt of illicit whiskey-makers who used the clear, cold creek water to make moonshine. This path runs through some idyllically attractive countryside, mostly beside or within earshot of the bubbling creek.

The park is a camper's paradise, with 110 sites (including more

⑫ Dillard Mill State Historic Site. *The signature red mill is nestled along Huzzah Creek and features hiking trails, picnic areas, and tours of its machinery.*

than 60 electric campsites) and more than 160 picnic spots.

Open year-round. No water at campsite in winter.
(573) 358-2173
www.mostateparks.com/stfrancois.htm

14 Ste. Genevieve

The oldest town west of the Mississippi, this charming community was settled by the French more than 250 years ago, when the area was still part of French-claimed Upper Louisiana. A walk through the streets reveals a rich architectural heritage, heavily accented by many old French-Creole buildings with walls constructed by logs set vertically, not horizontally.

Tours from the visitors center take in a number of historic buildings. One of the more prominent is the Guibourd-Valle House, built around 1784. In the attic take note of the handsomely pegged oak beams and fine Norman trusswork. Another is the Bolduc House Museum, a strong example of the vertical log construction, first built in 1770 and reassembled in 1784 after a flood.

Along the south side of the town square runs the Old Plank Road. Originally surfaced with logs, it was 42 miles long and connected the town with iron and lead mines.

Visitors center open year-round.
Charge for tours.
(800) 773-7007
www.ste-genevieve.com

15 Bollinger Mill State Historic Site

Burfordville
A picturesque scene from America's past is captured here. The four-story mill stands by a wide millpond

and weir along the Whitewater River, and just beyond is one of Missouri's four covered bridges.

The present-day structure dates from 1867 and was built by Solomon Burford. Powered by a turbine, it is beautifully restored and in working order. During the tour a wheel is turned to open the turbine louvers; the drive shaft and belts begin to turn, the elevators move, and the massive buhrstones begin to grind. The staff is enthusiastic and well-informed.

The 140-foot-long Howe-truss bridge, originally built of yellow poplar, was begun in 1859, but completion was delayed by the Civil War. The bridge was restored in 1998 and is open to pedestrians only, except for one weekend in April when vehicles are allowed.

Mill open year-round Tues.-Sat. except holidays. Admission charged.
(573) 243-4591
www.mostateparks.com/bollinger.htm

16 Sam A. Baker State Park

Patterson
Geologically interesting and scenically wild, this 5,000-plus-acre park in the St. Francois Mountains, with its many domes of igneous rock, contains some of the oldest exposed formations in North America.

The highest of these is Mudlick Mountain. At 1,313 feet, its summit is battered by high winds, ice storms, and lightning, which have gradually bent, stunted, and shaped the trees here into a variety of fascinating forms. You can reach the fire tower at the summit by foot or horseback on Mudlick Trail.

You can also hike the 1½-mile Shut-Ins Trail, which drops to the base of Mudlick Mountain as it

follows Big Creek Valley. Past the sharp outcrops of rock jutting through the trees, you reach the Shut-Ins area, where the creek has swung wide of an imposing granite cliff, creating a large pool. You can swim here in a setting that is a natural sun trap.

From this trail you can scramble to the top of the ridge to connect with Mudlick Trail. Along the way the view over the valley to the distant hills is spectacular, and there are three convenient stone shelters for resting or picnicking. The remaining climb to the ridge is a real challenge. Take it if you're in good shape and not daunted by steep slopes.

You can canoe and fish both Big Creek and the St. Francois River, and the latter stream is better in summer for the flow of water. The park also counts a unique equestrian campsite, riding and cycling trails, rental cabins, and a nature center among its many amenities.

Open year-round.
(573) 856-4411
www.mostateparks.com/baker.htm

17 Elephant Rocks State Park

Pilot Knob
Elephants in the Ozarks? Ancient granite incarnations of the huge creatures abound at this geologic marvel. Giant boulders of red granite, dating back 1.5 billion years, populate the park with massive formations.

And this "population" is constantly—if gradually—changing, as the forces of nature continue to wear away existing rock forms while exposing new ones. The granite animals have been meticulously documented, with the park's

17 Elephant Rocks State Park. *The massive red granite rocks at this geologic playground began forming 1.5 billion years ago.*

patriarch, Dumbo, at 27 feet tall, 35 feet long, and 17 feet wide, and tipping the scales at an estimated 680 tons.

The Braille Trail offers a quick and accessible route to the mammoth rocks. Featuring interpretive signage, this one-mile paved pathway is specially designed for those with visual or physical disabilities. The trail leads to the top of the granite outcrop, where explorers can wander through the maze of giant rocks at their leisure, or take a break at one of 30 picnic sites conveniently situated amid the red boulders.

Just outside the park is the state's oldest known commercial granite quarry, opened in 1869. The nearby town of Graniteville, once dominated by quarry life, still boasts original granite buildings, such as an impressive stone schoolhouse.

Open year-round.
(573) 546-3454
www.mostateparks.com/elephantrock.htm

18 Mingo National Wildlife Refuge

Puxico

The vast area of marsh, dike, and river (21,676 acres) in the southeast corner of the state supports large numbers of wildlife but is maintained primarily as a feeding ground for migratory waterfowl on the Mississippi Flyway.

A gravel loop road skirting most of the refuge allows leisurely walking, horseback riding, and driving. The diked waterways and the Mingo River itself are open to canoeing, an ideal way to see this region. Motorboats are not allowed.

The Flat Banks Road offers access to the river and an 8,000-acre wilderness preserve that runs through verdant marsh meadows and woodland. The Mingo River is lovely, with ghostly cypress stumps and flat, lightly wooded banks.

The mile-long Boardwalk Nature Trail loops through the woodland swamp, hung with vines and rich with sycamores, sweet gums, pin oaks, sugar maples, and some water tupelos and bald cypresses. The Bluff Overlook Trail, starting at the visitors center, is enchanting when spring wildflowers bloom and affords splendid views across the marsh.

From September 30 to March 15, visitors are asked to stop at the center before venturing into the refuge. Limited picnic facilities are available.

Refuge open daily year-round; admission charged. Visitors center is free and open weekdays and most weekends year-round.
(573) 222-3589
midwest.fws.gov/mingo

19 Big Oak Tree State Park

East Prairie

This 1,029-acre preserve is part of the virgin forest and swampland that once covered much of Missouri's Bootheel region.

The park, noted for state and national champion trees of dramatic size, was named for a bur oak that dated to about 1620. Felled in 1954 after it died, it was 143 feet tall with a spread of 114 feet. Its sawn-off trunk stands at the head of a quarter-mile boardwalk that runs to a grassy swamp and passes some of the most magnificent trees in the forest.

The swamp was created by a series of earthquakes in 1811, and parts of it look like a giant bowling green planted with dead trees. The "green" is actually duckweed, and among the trees are some living bald cypresses. The loud plops you hear along the boardwalk may be slider turtles dropping into the

19 Big Oak Tree State Park. *Hiking trails wind through bur oaks and bald cypresses, among the largest trees of their species in the country.*

water, or perhaps a jumping buffalofish, which can weigh as much as 20 pounds. The swamp is also home to the ruddy duck, the hooded merganser, and the harmless banded water snake.

The park is anchored by the 22-acre Big Oak Lake, which offers boating and fishing in waters stocked with catfish, bass, and bluegill.

Open year-round.
(573) 649-3149
www.mostateparks.com/bigoak.htm

20 Laura Ingalls Wilder-Rose Wilder Lane Home and Museum

Mansfield

This is a required visit for dedicated admirers of *The Little House on the Prairie* series. It was here that author Laura Ingalls Wilder penned her beloved books of rural America, published in some 40 languages.

Museum displays include foreign and domestic editions of her various books, press clippings, and worldwide fan mail, much of it from children. Among personal belongings are the 1889 lap desk Laura brought here by covered wagon from her home in De Smet, South Dakota, along with her sewing machine, samples of her needlework, her father Charles's famous fiddle, and several handwritten manuscripts.

Half of the museum is devoted to the mementos of her daughter, Rose Wilder Lane, a noted author as well.

Laura and her husband, Almanzo, moved to Mansfield in 1894 and into their house in 1897. Laura thought it best "to be happy with simple pleasures," and the

small house—shown by guided tour only—is next door to the main museum.

Note the Currier and Ives prints and a Western Cottage organ in the drawing room, some throw pillows made by Laura, and several tables crafted by Almanzo, a carpenter. His workshop contains the tools of his trade as well as some leather and lasts, for he also made his own shoes.

Open year-round. Admission charged.
(417) 924-3626
www.lauraingallswilderhome.com

21 Wilson's Creek National Battlefield

Republic

The battle fought here on August 10, 1861, largely determined the side Missouri would be on for the ensuing years of the Civil War. Many Missourians favored neutrality, but some, including the governor, championed the South.

After pro-Union forces seized the state capitol at Jefferson City, installing their own government, Confederate efforts to gain control led to the bloody confrontation at Wilson's Creek. Though the Confederates drove the Union forces from the field, they were unable to follow up and recapture the capitol, and Missouri remained in Union hands.

The visitors center has excellent displays whose very titles provide a mini-history of events, such as "Missouri's Dilemma: Union or Confederate?" and "Why Wilson's Creek?"

The highlight, however, is the topographic battlefield model in the small theater: Computer-controlled points of light reconstruct troop movements and artillery fire, with commentary and realistic effects on the sound track.

 Wilson's Creek National Battlefield. *After camping along the creek the previous night, Union and Confederate forces clashed in a bloody battle on August 10, 1861.*

Other places of interest are the Ray House, used as a Confederate field hospital, and Bloody Hill, the site of the fiercest fighting. A marker honors "the hundreds of brave men, North and South, who, on this field, died for the right as God gave them to see right."

Open daily except holidays.

(417) 732-2662

www.nps.gov/wicr

22 Ralph Foster Museum

On the campus of the College of the Ozarks (near Branson)

Ralph Foster, a pioneering radio broadcaster, was also a philanthropist whose donation of American Indian artifacts to the history museum at this liberal arts college accounts for its name.

"Everything under the sun" aptly describes the thousands of items displayed here. A single glance may take in antique furniture, oyster plates, clocks, watches, international dolls, and a potpourri of other artifacts and improbable novelties. Take, for example, the

original truck used on *The Beverly Hillbillies* television series, a gift from the show's producer.

The museum's first floor houses the Edwards Art Gallery, the Si Siman Country Music Room, and a kewpie doll exhibit from local artist Rose O'Neill. The second floor is dominated by an exhibit on firearms, while the third floor lightens things up with a nine-foot polar bear, a moose, and colorful birds, rocks, and minerals.

The third floor is also home to the museum's impressive galleries and displays devoted to the history of life in the Ozarks.

Open Mon.-Sat. from Feb.-Dec. except holidays.

www.rfostermuseum.com

23 George Washington Carver National Monument

Diamond

Educator, scientist, and humanitarian, George Washington Carver was born a slave in 1864 on the Moses Carver farm, located here. Shortly afterward he and his mother were kidnapped by Confederate bushwhackers and taken to

Arkansas. The young child was later returned to the Carvers, who reared him as their own. Though George left when he was about 12, the love of nature he gained on this site stood the future botanist in good stead.

On view in the museum are many tributes paid this remarkable man: a model of the submarine named for him, stamps issued in his honor, a commemorative half-dollar, and a letter from Albert Einstein referring to him as "the great scientist."

Collections of his publications, together with scientific exhibits, dramatize his impact on agricultural methods. He derived more than 300 products from the peanut, 100 from the sweet potato (including ersatz coffee, shoeblacking, and ink), and scores of products from Alabama clay.

The 210-acre site includes the Carver birthplace cabin, Moses Carver's 1881 dwelling, and a one-mile loop trail that runs through woods and over streams to the family cemetery and back to the visitors center.

Open year-round except holidays.

(417) 325-4151

www.nps.gov/gwca

24 Prairie State Park

Liberal

Two hundred years ago, one-third of Missouri—some 13 million acres—was prairie, a level or rolling expanse of tall grasses, wildflowers, and few trees. With settlement and farming, there are now fewer than 65,000 acres of prairie in Missouri. This 4,000-acre-plus park is the state's largest remaining preserve of tallgrass prairie landscape.

A number of interlinked trails traverse the open prairie and stream valley. You'll be struck by the spaciousness of the land and skyscape and the endless horizon with the sealike expanse of grass melting into the blue of the sky. It is easy to understand why the pioneers called their wagons prairie schooners. Striding freely along the mown path in the sweet-scented air, you'll also notice how this vast tableau is balanced by minute natural detail—petal, leaf, grass blade, and seedpod—calling for close scrutiny.

Bison and elk roam in some areas. For safety, stay in your car until you have learned from the park office where the animals are located on a given day. The visitors center has a variety of exhibits, and naturalists conduct interpretive programs year-round.

Open year-round.

(417) 843-6711

www.mostateparks.com/prairie.htm

 Prairie State Park. *Wildlife like this bison are not uncommon sights in the vast expanses of tallgrass prairie protected at this wide-open shrine.*

193

Lewis and Clark Caverns State Park. *Wander among fantastic, still-evolving formations (see page 198).*

Montana

The Old West of song and story is recalled here in a variety of ways, as are some admirable works of man and nature.

A superb museum is dedicated to the American Indians who once dominated the plains, and a refuge protects a herd of bison descended from the millions that once thundered across this land. Here, too, is the battlefield where the Sioux and Cheyenne won a victory that led to their ultimate defeat.

Another side of life on the plains is revealed in a historic site where one can savor the good life of a successful rancher. There's also the home, the studio, and the works of an artist who captured the spirit of the Old West.

The early days of mining are remembered in a preserved ghost town and two others restored to life. Nature's stunning beauty is on display at a massive "gate" to the West and a forest frozen in time. And nature's unpredictable forces are exemplified in an underground fantasyland, a devastating landslide, and some marvelous sandstone formations carved by wind and water in a prehistoric riverbed.

1 Museum of the Plains Indian
Browning

The Museum of the Plains Indian, managed by the U.S. Department of the Interior, contains superb collections of costumes, accessories, and dioramas that detail the lifestyles of 11 tribes of the northern plains before the arrival of white settlers in the 1800s.

Weapons, beadwork, ceremonial objects, toys, and other crafts are shown. The associated craft center also displays contemporary American Indian work. Carved wood panels by Blackfoot sculptor John Clarke can be enjoyed, as well as murals by artist Victor Pepion. During the summer there is a display of painted tepees.
Open daily June–Sept.; Mon.–Fri. Oct–May. Admission charged.
(406) 338-2230
www.doi.gov/iacb/museum/ museum_plains.html

2 Fort Peck Dam
Fort Peck

Among the world's largest earthfill dams, Fort Peck Dam is a major prototype for virtually all such dams now in existence. Begun in 1933 for flood control, improved navigation along the Missouri River, irrigation, and the creation of hydroelectric power, it was finished seven years later and is an astonishing colossus: 250.5 feet high, 3.96 miles long, and .96

3 National Bison Range. *The estimated 350 to 450 bison here share the land with black bears, coyotes, and bald eagles, to name just some of their neighbors.*

of a mile wide at the base. The cutoff wall is 2 miles long and consists of 17,000 tons of steel sunk to a maximum depth of 163 feet.

During dam construction many fossils were excavated. At the museum in the dam's powerhouse you can examine more than 400 fossils, including the horn core of a 63-million-year-old triceratops dinosaur. And don't miss the guided tour of the powerhouse itself.

Fossil hunting is a popular activity in this area, which has remained virtually unchanged for some 65 million years, but to find fossils requires some experience, and you must obtain a permit.

Walled up behind the dam are the gleaming waters of Fort Peck Lake: 134 miles long and up to 16 miles wide. Its astounding 1,520-mile shoreline is surrounded by the million-acre, buffalo-grazed Charles M. Russell National Wildlife Range. Fishing, boating, and swimming are allowed in the lake, and several public recreation areas offer boat-launch ramps, campgrounds, and picnic facilities.
Powerhouse tours offered daily Memorial Day–Labor Day.
(406) 526-3431
visitmt.com

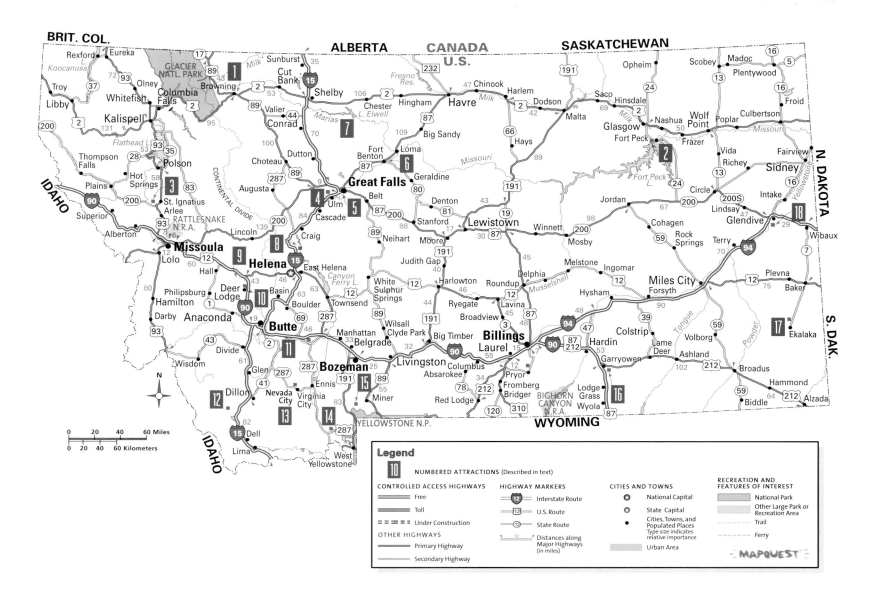

Legend

NUMBERED ATTRACTIONS (Described in text)

CONTROLLED ACCESS HIGHWAYS

Free
Toll
Under Construction

OTHER HIGHWAYS

Primary Highway
Secondary Highway

HIGHWAY MARKERS

Interstate Route
U.S. Route
State Route
Distances along
Major Highways
(in miles)

CITIES AND TOWNS

National Capital
State Capital
Cities, Towns, and
Populated Places
Type size indicates
relative importance
Urban Area

RECREATION AND
FEATURES OF INTEREST

National Park
Other Large Park or
Recreation Area
Trail
Ferry

National Bison Range
Moiese

An estimated 50 million bison (the scientifically correct term for the American buffalo) once roamed the American prairies, but hunters so reduced their numbers that by 1900 fewer than 100 were known to exist in the wild.

In 1908 at the instigation of the American Bison Society and with President Theodore Roosevelt's help, the range was born: some 18,500 fenced acres of high prairie, forest, and bottomlands in the Flathead Valley.

The first group of bison on the range totaled 37. The majority of these were purchased from the Charles Conrad herd out of Kalispell with money raised by the American Bison Society.

Today there are about 350 to 450 bison, an average herd. Elk, deer, black bears, and more than 200 species of birds are just some of the wide variety of wildlife that share the land here.

Two self-guiding auto tours provide a safe and leisurely way to see this untamed country, which is colorful with wildflowers and

flowering shrubs in late spring and rich with animal and bird life at all seasons. The shorter auto tour, the Buffalo Prairie Drive, takes only about 20 minutes.

The two-hour, 19-mile Red Sleep Mountain Scenic Drive (open mid-May into October) is in some places steep and winding, but its views range from mountains clad with ponderosa pine and Douglas fir to high, rolling grasslands and stream sides thick with alder, birch, and willow.

Golden eagles soar at the higher elevations, where mule deer,

mountain goats, and bighorn sheep range; pronghorn antelopes wander the high grasslands, and white-tailed deer and water birds frequent the marshy spots. Mission Creek, north of the range, is favored by migrating waterfowl in fall.

Fishing is allowed along stretches of the creek, and there are some scattered picnic spots.

Open year-round. Admission charged. (406) 644-2211

http://visitmt.com

4 Ulm Pishkun State Park
Ulm

Centuries before the invention of rifles or the arrival of horses, the Plains Indians devised an efficient way to provide for their needs.

Taking advantage of steep cliffs in this area, the wily hunters herded bison toward the precipice and then stampeded them over the edge to a bison kill area, known as a pishkun. Families working below gathered and butchered the bison for their livelihood: meat for food, hides for clothing and tepees, skins for blankets, and horns for tools and utensils.

This scenic park is home to perhaps the largest such bison kill site. Experts date its use back to the year 900. The park's 6,000-square-foot visitor center documents the area's archaeological digs and rich natural history.

Visitors might also catch a hunting demonstration, peruse ancient stone cairns (thought to be the remains of drive lines set up eons ago), hike the surrounding trails, stop for a picnic, or simply gaze at the spectacular cliffs and panoramas of Big Sky Country.

Open year-round. Admission charged.
(406) 866-2217
fwp.state.mt.us

5 C.M. Russell Museum
Great Falls

Charles M. "Charlie" Russell, "the cowboy artist" who came to Montana from Missouri in 1880 when he was 16, is honored at this authentic Western museum. Working as a rider and wrangler during the era of the great ranches, Russell made his first sketches to entertain his fellow cowboys. His first nationally famous paint-

ing was *Last of the Five Thousand*, showing a starving cow in the dreadful winter of 1886-87. In 1914 an exhibition of his work was shown in London, and one of his last paintings sold for $30,000 after his death in 1926.

The museum stands next to Russell's log-cabin home and studio, built in 1903. In the museum are some of Russell's most famous paintings and sculptures, including *Jerk Line* and *Buffalo Hunt*, which recall a legendary period in the American West. Among the personal memorabilia shown are Russell's letters and sketches.

Open daily May–Sept.; Tues.–Sun. Oct.–Apr. Admission charged.
(406) 727-8787
www.cmrussell.org

6 Fort Benton

On the wooded banks of the uppermost navigable point of the Missouri River, this historic town was born more than 40 years before Montana became a state.

Fort Benton began as a fur and buffalo robe trading post in 1846. Spanning over 150 feet square, the actual fort was built in quadrangle, with portholes in its bastion wall for both riflemen and cannons. After the decline of fur trading and prior to the arrival of the railroad, Fort Benton bustled as the travel hub for Western adventurers. Lewis and Clark, Jim Bridges, Kit Carson, and John Colter all explored its shores.

During the gold rush, 50 steamboats a season docked along its levee, unloading supplies and stocking up on precious metal. Gradually the plains were claimed by ranchers and farmers, and Fort Benton settled down as a premier wheat-producing area.

Today Fort Benton retains much of its "steamboat days" character, especially within its National Historic Landmark District along the river.

The steamboat levee is now a lovely park with great views of the Missouri. You'll see the carefully preserved remains of the old fort—still standing as the state's oldest building. In addition to its vista, the park features a memorial to Lewis and Clark, a museum devoted to the area's history, and interpretive signs throughout.

In the Museum of the Northern Plains and Montana Agricultural Center complex, you'll get a chance to explore a typical 1900s rural community. Most of the buildings have been moved onto the site and have been accurately restored and furnished. A small country church, bank, and drugstore are just some of the buildings that you will see.

Fort Benton is also home to the Grand Union Hotel, Montana's oldest, opened in 1882 at the height of the town's steamboat-era prosperity. Restored to its original splendor in 1999, the hotel combines old-world charm with modern amenities.

Open year-round.
(406) 622-5316
www.fortbenton.com

7 Upper Missouri River Breaks National Monument
Near Fort Benton

Declared a national monument by executive order of President Bill Clinton in January 2001, this awe-inspiring site is comprised of majestic cliffs of white sandstone overlooking the famous Upper Missouri River Breaks.

Its impressive form was sculpted through the force of thousands of years of glaciers, volcanic activity, and erosion. The 377,346 pristine acres here contain rich geological and historic resources, remarkable wildlife populations, and rare opportunities for solitude.

The area is home to huge herds of elk and bighorn sheep, who share the terrain with sage grouse, prairie dogs, and antelope. The cliff faces serve as popular perches for sparrow hawks, peregrine falcons, and golden eagles.

7 Upper Missouri River Breaks National Monument. *The sparkling white sand stone cliffs line the waters of the Missouri in this virtually untouched area.*

Grant-Kohrs Ranch National Historic Site. *The north gate offers a peek into the sprawling complex that hearkens back to the heyday of the rancher baron.*

The centerpiece is the Upper Missouri National Wild and Scenic River. A trip down the river is a trip back in time, passing by the vistas Lewis and Clark described as "scenes of visionary enchantment" on their 1805 expedition. The waterway spans 149 miles, starting upstream at historic Fort Benton and culminating at the Charles M. Russell Wildlife Range.

On a breathtaking voyage down the river by passenger boat or canoe, 21st-century explorers will see remnants of American Fur Company forts and other landmarks evoking the Western frontier, the lives and labors of American Indians, and the dreams of early homesteaders.

Back on land discover the Lewis and Clark National Historic Trail, the Nez Perce National Historic Trail, the Missouri Breaks National Back Country Byway, the Cow Creek Area of Critical Environmental Concern, and six wilderness study areas.

Open year-round.
(406)538-7461
www.mt.blm.gov/ldo/um

Gates of the Mountains

About 16 miles north of Helena
Some 300 million years in the making, Meriwether Canyon, through which the Missouri flows, is spectacular to see. Limestone cliffs, intricately folded and studded with fossil remains from the ancient Mississippian Sea, rise sheer above the river to 1,200 feet.

The "singular appearance" at first stunned Meriwether Lewis and William Clark on their passage through here in 1805; it appeared the river had ended, until Lewis noted in his journal that the rocks opened up like "the Gateway to the Rocky Mountains."

The site can only be accessed by trail or boat. Cruises of the nearly six miles of gorge are available from Gates of the Mountains Landing. From the boat you can see ancient American Indian pictographs and perhaps bighorn sheep, goats, and bald eagles. The boat stops at the Lewis and Clark campsite before its return run.

Cruises and canoe trips Memorial Day–Sept. Fare charged.
(406) 458-5241

Grant-Kohrs Ranch National Historic Site

Deer Lodge
In the 1850s a Canadian fur trapper named Johnny Grant abandoned his traplines and started raising cattle in Montana. By 1866, when he sold his ranch to Conrad Kohrs, he had 2,000 cattle and the finest house in the state.

Kohrs became one of the great cattle barons of the American West. His wife, Augusta, whom he brought to Montana when she was 19, made her frontier home a model of 19th-century elegance, importing the best furnishings from St. Louis and Chicago.

Although the ranch land has been reduced from its original 25,000 acres to only 1,500, the main house and its original furnishings are preserved intact, along with the bunkhouse, stables, barns, sheds, and workshops dating as far back as the 1860s. Park rangers conduct tours of the main house; the 13 outbuildings are on a self-guiding tour. A former barn for thoroughbreds now houses a collection of horse-drawn vehicles.

Open year-round except holidays.
(406) 846-3388
www.nps.gov/grko

Powell County Museum

Deer Lodge
Deer Lodge is home to more museums than any other town in the Northwest. It boasts 22 acres of history and nostalgia in and around an imposing complex that once was the Old Montana Territorial Prison.

Listed on the *National Register of Historic Places,* the towering structures alone are worth the trip. The Powell County Museum features vintage photos of the area as it was, complemented by a collection of classic photo equipment, antique slot machines, and jukeboxes. Also on display are authentic mastodon bones, uncovered in a gravel quarry near town.

Nearby the Frontier Montana Museum continues the journey through the authentic American West. Fans will find eclectic items actually used by cowboys, ranchers, and pioneering men and women—including more than 300 handguns and rifles. American Indian artifacts also abound.

Also close by is Desert John's Saloon, which treats travelers to the most extensive collection of whiskey memorabilia in the United States. The saloon shelves are filled with whiskey bottles, shot glasses, and decanters, reflecting the names of popular bygone brands, like Old McBrayer and Samaritan Rye. Early brands are also colorfully promoted in the signs, trays, posters, and calendars plastering the walls all the way up to the real tin ceiling.

Yesterday's Playthings houses the foremost collection of antique and collectible dolls in the state, while the Montana Auto Museum has 120 classic cars on display, all in mint condition.

Finally, a tour of this rehabilitated prison wouldn't be complete without a stop at the Montana Law Enforcement Museum. In addition to displays of official uniforms, badges, patches, and weapons, it features historic accounts of feats of peace-keeping and a memorial to law enforcement officers throughout Montana who have died in the line of duty since 1863.

Main complex open year-round; most museums open year-round, but call to confirm hours. Admission charged.
(406) 846-3111
www.powellpost.com/museums.htm

11 Lewis and Clark Caverns State Park

19 miles west of Three Forks
Although the caverns were not discovered until 1892, they are named for the explorers Lewis and Clark, who passed this way in the first decade of the 19th century.

The caverns, a series of corridors and chambers, reach 326 feet below the entrance. A long flight of steps descends to the Spiral Staircase Room, graced by perfectly formed fluted pillars—opaque stalactites and stalagmites. Continue to the Cathedral Room, from whose floor stalagmites rise to a domed ceiling.

Corridors filigreed and draped with mineral deposits lead to the Garden of Gods, which has stalactites, stalagmites, and helictites resembling twisted roots coming out of the walls. The long chamber also contains the Crystal Pool, tinted green by the oxidation of pennies tossed by tourists. The last stop on the two-hour walk is the Paradise Room, where you can see active cavern formations.

Open year-round, but tours May–Sept.
Admission charged.
(406) 287-3541
visitmt.com

12 Bannack State Park

26 miles southwest of Dillon
On July 28, 1862, gold was found in Grasshopper Creek, and the town of Bannack was born. Population surged to 3,000 in 1864, when Bannack became the Montana Territory's first capital.

Today Old Bannack is a ghost town, preserved as a state park but not restored. Along its dusty streets is a fascinating collection of weathered and decaying buildings,

all in their own way more descriptive of the frontier than perfect restorations would be.

There is also a replica of the gallows where Henry Plummer, sheriff of Bannack, and his henchmen were hanged in 1864. He and his "road agents," who murdered more than 100 travelers, had for their secret identification a special cut of the beard, a particular knot in the necktie, and the password "I am innocent."

The vigilantes who tracked them down also had a code, the mysterious numbers 3-7-77, which are worn today on the shoulder patches of the Montana highway patrol. At Bannack reminders of the past are especially vivid.

Adjoining the town is a well equipped campground in a grove of cottonwoods frequented by magpies. The creek is fished for trout.

Open year-round.
(406) 834-3413
visitmt.com

13 Nevada City and Virginia City

In 1863 the biggest gold strike in Montana's history took place at Alder Gulch. Within three years the deposits yielded some $30 million in gold, and Montana was declared a territory. Virginia City, a brand-new mining town at the hub of an area where population boomed to more than 10,000, became territorial capital in 1865.

Today Virginia City and nearby Nevada City, another frontier mining town, are owned by the state of Montana and are restored to look as they did in their heyday in the late 1800s. Along Nevada City's five streets are shops, a Chinese neighborhood, a music hall containing a notable collection

of mechanical "music machines," and a hotel offering today's guests both airy Victorian rooms and restored miners' cabins.

A narrow-gauge railway line carries passengers along the 1 1/2-mile route between Nevada City and Virginia City. Along the tree-lined boardwalks of the latter are authentically furnished stores—an assay office, a jeweler's shop, and Montana's first newspaper office. The Fairweather Hotel is striking for its Victoriana.

Open year-round. Nevada City guided walking tours Apr.–Sept.; fee charged.
(406) 841-4014
www.edheritage.org

14 Madison Canyon Earthquake Area and Visitors Center

27 miles from West Yellowstone
This unusual site is a monument to a recent natural disaster, one that happened suddenly the night of August 17, 1959. In but 30 seconds, 40 million cubic yards of rock and earth, an entire mountainside, broke loose from

the south side of Madison River Canyon and, traveling at a speed of about 100 miles per hour, piled up 400 feet high against the canyon's northern wall.

The mile-long landslide was caused by an earthquake measuring 7.5 on the Richter scale. The earth had cracked open, dropping Hebgen Lake 100 feet and causing huge waves for hours. Behind the landslide a new lake, called Quake Lake, was formed. Twenty-eight people died, but 250 others, campers in the canyon, miraculously survived on the ridge now known as Refuge Point.

You can see the results of the quake from several sites and follow a hiking trail to a dolomite boulder that floated across the canyon. The visitors center explains the event with a slide show.

Open Memorial Day–mid-Sept.
Admission charged.
(406) 646-7369
visitmt.com

15 Gallatin Petrified Forest. *This amazing collection of trees forever frozen in time covers nearly 26,000 acres of the Gallatin National Forest.*

Gallatin Petrified Forest

17 miles north of Gardiner

Part of the Gallatin National Forest, the petrified forest here is overwhelming in its grandeur: 40 square miles of ancient stone trees buried millions of years ago by volcanic ash. More than 100 species of trees and shrubs have been identified in the remains of 27 successive forests, each in turn destroyed by volcanic eruptions.

This petrified forest is unique because many of the trees were frozen in an upright position. Most other petrified forests contain trees that were petrified after being transported by mud and lava flows, which leaves the majority of trees in a horizontal position.

The U.S. Forest Service operates an interpretive trail that enables visitors to identify specimens in the forest. The trail begins approximately 1,000 feet from the Tom Miner parking area and climbs upward at a roughly 13 percent grade past numerous rock cliffs embedded with petrified wood specimens.

Petrified wood cannot be taken from the trail, but you may collect up to 20 cubic inches elsewhere in the forest with a free permit obtained at the Ranger office.

Open year-round, but the snow season will limit viewing.
(406) 848-7375
www.fs.fed.us/r1/gallatin

16 Little Bighorn Battlefield National Monument

2 miles south of the Crow Agency

Few American military engagements are as infamous as the Battle of Little Bighorn.

During June 25–26, 1876, Col. George Armstrong Custer,

18 Makoshika State Park. *The Montana badlands in all of their contrasting beauty and severity are apparent in the harsh, imposing, rocky landscape.*

hero of the Civil War and Plains Indians campaigns, and more than 200 of his troops were killed by Sioux and Cheyenne warriors under the command of Chief Crazy Horse and Chief Gall. News of Custer's disaster shocked the nation, and within months a strongly reinforced army destroyed the last remnants of the Indian resistance in the Black Hills.

There are actually two battlefields here. The larger, which contains the Custer National Cemetery, includes the site of Custer's "last stand." Small white marble markers indicate where the dead may have fallen. The other battlefield is the Reno-Benteen area, where troops led by Maj. Marcus Reno and Capt. Frederick Benteen were surrounded.

A 4 1/2- mile self-guiding tour trail connects the battlefields. At the visitor center is a scale model of the engagement and other excellent interpretive materials. The entire area is contained within the Crow Indian Reservation.

Open year-round.
(406) 638-2621
www.nps.gov/libi

17 Medicine Rocks State Park

14 miles north of Ekalaka

Here is one of the strangest landscapes in Montana: The sandstone of a prehistoric riverbed has been eroded by wind and water into an amazing gallery of surreal formations, some rising 80 feet above the plain.

You will be dazzled by the arches, columns, caves, pinnacles, and flat-topped mountains up to 200 feet wide, pocked with holes and crannies. Tan colored by day, the bizarre formations are silvery and eerie in moonlight. Fossils of mammals that roamed this area 50 million years ago have been found, and there is evidence of human habitation dating back more than 11,000 years.

Theodore Roosevelt thought the Medicine Rocks "as fantastically beautiful a place as I have ever seen" and is said to have inscribed his initials on the soft stone. The rocks take their name from the Indian medicine men who performed ritual dances here before hunting expeditions.

The park has 12 primitive campgrounds, a six-mile guided nature trail, and a steep half-mile walk down to the badlands.

Elevations here approach 3,500 feet, and the 320-acre expanse is home to mule deer, antelope, and sharp-tailed grouse.

Open year-round, but may be inaccessible by car in winter.
(406) 232-0900
www.fwp.state.mt.us

18 Makoshika State Park

Glendive

The Montana badlands are dramatically beautiful, especially at sunset, dawn, or after a light snowfall. They are also severely inhospitable.

In Makoshika State Park the land has been stripped to the bone, its 8,000 acres gnawed by the elements into gulches and steep-walled valleys, spires, pinnacles, and table-topped buttes.

A maintained road brings visitors to a trailer campground 1 1/2 miles within the park. From there a 12-mile self-guiding drive (closed in winter) leads to several panoramic lookouts. Many fossils have been found here, including the skull of a triceratops dinosaur on display at the visitors center.

This parched and rocky terrain is tinted with every bold and delicate hue in the palette of earth colors. The region is windswept, baked, and frozen by endless weather extremes.

Hiking trails and the scenic drive are used for cross-country skiing and snowmobiling in winter. In the hot summer, shaded picnic areas atop its buttes are cooled by refreshing breezes.

Open year-round but water is turned off Oct.–Apr.
(406) 365-6256
www.fwp.state.mt.us

MONTANA

Bessey Ranger District, Nebraska National Forest. *The planted woodlands here are a welcome patch of green on the plains (see page 203).*

Nebraska

American Indians, pioneers, and some wondrous animals—now extinct—have left their mark on the broad plains and sculptured landscapes here.

A state park reveals a rock shelter where American Indians lived for some 3,000 years, and a historic site discloses the remains of incredible animals long vanished from the earth; elsewhere are images incised on stone by prehistoric artists. Fort Hartsuff, built to protect settlers, is a reminder of more recent history.

More heartening is a national monument's tribute to legislation that spurred westward settlement, and an impressive reproduction of the American Indian's spiritual sacred hoop treasured by an enlightened white poet.

Visitors can travel a section of the Oregon Trail and see some of nature's mighty sculptures that beguiled pioneers on their westward course. A restored pioneer village, a community made famous by a Pulitzer Prize-winning author, and a great old mansion invite inspection. The days of water power are splendidly represented by two historic mills. Here, too, are some beautiful and refreshing recreation areas.

1 Toadstool Geological Park
20 miles northwest of Crawford

Toadstool Park is noted for unusual geological formations and valuable fossil deposits. It also contains the longest known mammal trackway of the Oligocene epoch. This one-mile trail is featured in an interpretive kiosk and a self-guiding trail brochure.

Historically called Little Badlands, this remote, unstaffed area is one of the most spectacular settings outside of Badlands National Park. Dramatic cliffs and gullies plunge among domes of clay some 100 feet high, creating the illusion that you are standing amid a toy model of a vast mountain range. Even more intriguing are the rock toadstools that give the park its name. Hard, rocky material was left balanced on slender columns when the soft clay beneath eroded more quickly.

These clay beds were deposited here by ancient rivers as many as 40 million years ago. The erosion that sculpted them has been going on for nearly a million years.

A sod house stands near the picnic area, and a mile-long hiking trail—showcasing eroded clay and sandstone formations— leads across the Badlands, where you have a good chance of seeing elk and hawks. The ground is loose and steep in places, so sturdy

3 Scotts Bluff National Monument. *A view of Eagle Rock, one of the many striking formations that served as a navigation point for travelers.*

shoes are recommended. You can camp here, but be warned: It's rough and has few amenities.
Open year-round but may be inaccessible in wet weather. Honor admission charged Memorial Day-Labor Day.
(308) 432-4475
www.fs.fed.us/r2/nebraska/units/prrd/ toadstooltemp.html

2 Chadron State Park
Chadron

Nebraska's oldest park is a mixture of prairie, broken ridges, sandstone buttes, stands of ponderosa pine, and occasional small streams.

The scenery in the Pine Ridge region has a variety and beauty unlike any other part of Nebraska. At an altitude of 4,000 feet the relatively low temperature and humidity are also pleasantly atypical, particularly in summer.

The approach to the park, a divided road passing through a gate flanked with serpentine brick walls, suggests an environment much too formal to be off the beaten path. The literature handed out at the gate furthers the impression, listing activities that include paddleboating, horseback riding, film programs, archery and tomahawk-throwing lessons, craft classes,

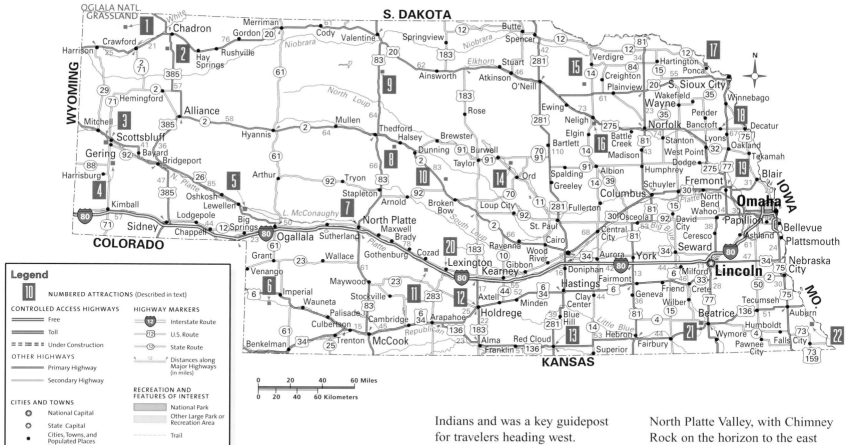

"trapper's stew" campfire cookouts, swimming in a large, man-made pool, and cross-country skiing in winter. Demonstrations of old-time fur trader life add to the richness of the offerings here.

But this park is indeed far from well-traveled highways, and the only part that receives heavy use is the campground area in midsummer. Otherwise, solitude is always a short walk away in the 974 acres here. A hiking trail winds through the park and extends for some nine miles into the surrounding national forest. The park also has five miles of scenic roads with picnic areas sited on overlooks.

The varied topography in the area contributes to an unusual diversity of plant and animal life as Eastern and Western species mingle. A handout lists some 70 varieties of plants, 24 kinds of mammals, and 60 species of birds. *Open year-round. Admission charged. (308) 432-6167*

www.ngpc.state.ne.us/parks

3 Scotts Bluff National Monument
Gering
This bluff takes its name from a trapper who met his end here around 1828. But long before that the prominent, 800-foot-high landmark was known as "the hill that is hard to go around" by the Plains Indians and was a key guidepost for travelers heading west.

Much of the history here centers around Mitchell Pass, which proved to be the best way through these steep, eroded bluffs and became part of the Oregon Trail. Thousands of westward-bound families came through here, and the ruts made by their wagons can still be seen.

At the visitors center, photographs, artifacts, slide presentations, and living-history demonstrations help to dramatize the westward passage through this forbidding land. A unique collection of watercolors by frontier photographer and artist William Henry Jackson is also showcased here.

The bluff's summit is accessible by road or a steep hiking trail that should be walked with great care; climbing is for the experienced only here. From the north overlook there's a spectacular view of the North Platte Valley, with Chimney Rock on the horizon to the east and Laramie Peak to the west. Part of the legendary Oregon Trail can be seen from the south overlook.

Even more compelling than the view is the stark evidence of the power of erosion. By standing on the bluff's highest point and extending an imaginary line to the tops of the surrounding hills, you can establish the level of the original mile-high grassy plains that were once here.

Everything from where you stand down to the rugged land below has been ground down and washed away to distant deltas, seas, and shorelines. To consider the passage of time in this context can be a humbling experience. *Open year-round. Admission charged. (308) 436-4340*

www.nps.gov/scbl

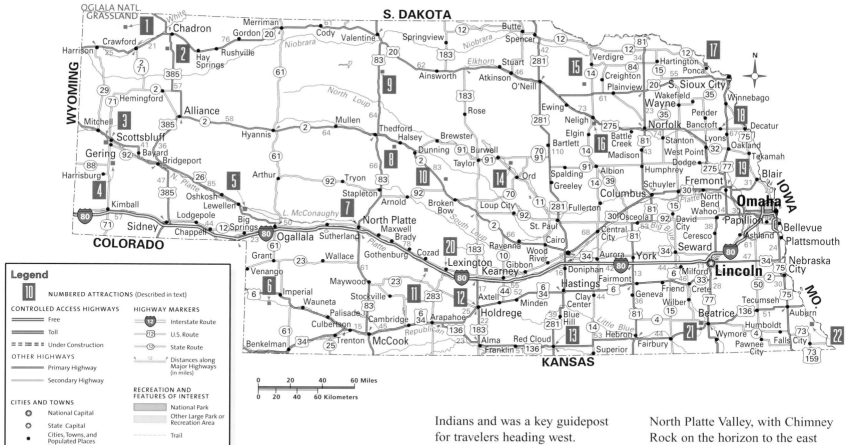

Legend

10 NUMBERED ATTRACTIONS (Described in text)

CONTROLLED ACCESS HIGHWAYS
— Free
— Toll
= = = = Under Construction

OTHER HIGHWAYS
— Primary Highway
— Secondary Highway

CITIES AND TOWNS
⊛ National Capital
⊛ State Capital
• Cities, Towns, and Populated Places Type size indicates relative importance
Urban Area

HIGHWAY MARKERS
12 Interstate Route
12 U.S. Route
12 State Route
12 Distances along Major Highways (in miles)

RECREATION AND FEATURES OF INTEREST
National Park
Other Large Park or Recreation Area
Trail
Ferry

MAPQUEST

4 Wildcat Hills State Recreation Area

Gering

The stealthy bobcats for which the area is named are seldom seen and are now few in number. But you will probably spot some elk and buffalo venturing near the fence in the enclosed game preserve. Wild turkeys are sometimes seen; falcons, eagles, and vultures often wheel overhead.

Although the area is just off Route 71, it is not heavily used, probably because there are no lakes and streams. This makes it an excellent choice for those seeking solitude and natural beauty.

In the recreation area there are several steep-walled canyons laced with about three miles of hiking trails. The trails cross two footbridges and lead to three shelters built of native stone in the early 1930s by the Civilian Conservation Corps.

Particularly inviting is the group shelter, with large picnic tables, two fireplaces, and a spectacular view down a canyon to the plain with the great monolith of Scotts Bluff far in the distance. Scatterings of ponderosa pine bring accents of green to the brown, arid ridges and canyon walls. Here, too, are mountain mahogany trees, rare in Nebraska, along with yucca, cactus, grasses, and wildflowers.

The Nature Center's split-level design takes advantage of the hilltop location, and the building's windows are deeply tinted so visitors can closely observe birds and other wildlife coming from the forest to use the feeders. A dramatic 27-foot-tall artificial ponderosa pine tree extends from the lower level through an opening in the ceiling.

5 Ash Hollow State Historical Park. *These rolling plains are rich in history, from a shelter dating back thousands of years to a water spot for the Overland Trail.*

If you're pulling a trailer, leave it in the parking lot, at least until you explore the area. The roads are rough, and several are dead-end with little or no room to turn a trailer around. Sledding and snow-tubing are popular here in winter.

Open year-round. Admission charged.
(308) 436-3777
www.ngpc.state.ne.us/parks/
wildcat.html

5 Ash Hollow State Historical Park

Lewellen

Archaeological evidence indicates that the freshwater springs in this canyon have attracted visitors for some 8,000 years, including Plains Indians who used a rock shelter here for about 3,000 years. Even earlier, skeletal remains show, prehistoric mastodons and other mammals roamed these plains.

More precise are the records of the pioneers who sought this well-watered oasis with shady groves of ash trees as a place to rest, refresh their livestock, and repair their wagons and other trail-worn gear. The visitors center features exhibits describing prehistoric animals, early man, and Plains Indians.

A restored schoolhouse, a trading post site, and a nature trail are also located here. A short walk takes you to the rock shelter, and a steep paved path leads down to Ash Hollow Springs itself, reputed to have the best water on all the Overland Trail.

Wagon trains entered the hollow from Windlass Hill, about two miles to the south, and their tracks can still be seen. Another exhibition center there provides historic background on the challenge of the hill, and a covered wagon shows the size and weight of the equipment that had to be handled on this steep grade.

Apart from the historical interest of the site, the 1,000-acres-plus of upland prairie here are brightened by wildflowers in season. From late November until March, bald and golden eagles winter at nearby Lake McConaughy and frequently use the updrafts at Ash Hollow to reach their cruising altitude.

Grounds open year-round;
visitors center open
Memorial Day–Labor Day.
Admission charged.
(308) 778-5651
www.ngpc.state.ne.us/parks/

6 Champion Mill State Historical Park

Champion

This mill, rebuilt in 1892 after a fire damaged the original, stands today as the last functional water-powered mill in Nebraska.

The three-story white clapboard structure, the 10-acre millpond, and seven acres of land were taken over by the state in 1969, the year after the mill stopped commercial operation. Some of the original machinery has been removed, but the penstock and turbine are in place, and if the pond's water level is high enough, the mill can still function.

When the operator turns a control that resembles a ship's wheel to tighten the main drive belt, the whole complex of belts, shafts, and pulleys starts moving, and the ingenuity involved in putting one power source to many uses is clearly evident.

A small milling machine has been installed and is run by the turbine. Milling demonstrations can be given on request, and bags of whole-wheat flour are for sale.

From the beginning the millpond has been used for recreation. It was at its most popular in the 1920s, when a new boathouse and diving tower drew crowds from miles around. Today the facilities are less elaborate, but the pond can be used for fishing, swimming, boating, and skating, and there are camping and picnic areas alongshore. The site attracts waterfowl and other birds.

Mill open Memorial Day–Labor Day;
grounds open year-round.
Admission charged.
(308) 394-5118
www.ngpc.state.ne.us/parks/

7 Lincoln County Historical Museum

North Platte

To contemplate the small collection of restored frontier-era buildings on the museum grounds here is to sense the feeling of isolation and interdependence that the early settlers must have had.

And here, too, is the urge to grow. The founders of the museum have continued in their quest to re-create a complete frontier town, just as their forebears worked to provide more amenities for their growing communities. Preserved structures include a depot, Pony Express building, army headquarters, log homestead, pioneer house, church, and schoolhouse.

In the museum building itself the displays recall many aspects of pioneer life on the plains. Weapons, Indian artifacts, tools, and barbed wire attest to the more demanding tasks, while gentler pursuits are represented by fashions, jewelry, musical instruments, and room settings. There are also replicas of a post office, doctor's office, barber and beauty shop, and telephone switchboard. The most unique re-creation is a World War II-era canteen that provided hospitality and entertainment for the men on passing troop trains.

Most of the objects were donated by local residents, which accounts for the aura of informal charm. The museum is likely to be crowded during Nebraskaland Days, the third week in June.

Open Memorial Day weekend–last Sun. in Sept. Admission free but donations accepted.
(308) 534-5640

http://npcanteen.tripod.com/canteen/lchm.html

8 Bessey Ranger District, Nebraska National Forest

2 miles west of Halsey

Even native Nebraskans find it strange to come upon a huge, sprawling forest in the middle of the otherwise bleak Sandhills prairie; and indeed, these woods are unusual and have their own special beauty, for they were put here by humans.

The Nebraska National Forest was established by presidential proclamation in 1902 at the urging of Charles Bessey, a professor of botany at the University of Nebraska, who believed that forests could survive on the plains. In April 1903, 85 acres were planted with ponderosa pine, eastern red cedar, and jack pine. Today more than 20,000 acres of planted woodlands flourish on the 90,000 acres of this splendid national forest property.

At the inviting, spacious Bessey Arboretum, which was established to demonstrate the wide variety of plants that can survive in the Sandhills area, more than 100 species are identified for visitors.

The road through the arboretum continues on to a high bluff and the Scott Lookout Tower, a fire-watch station offering splendid views of the rolling countryside. When there's a ranger on duty, the tower can be climbed. But even the view from the base is well worth the drive.

The Bessey Recreation Complex offers campgrounds, a picnic area, canoeing in the Middle Loup River, and a swimming pool. A three-mile hiking trail leads from the campground area to the lookout tower. Backpack camping is generally allowed, and in winter the area is open for snowmobiling and cross-country skiing.

Arboretum and recreation area open year-round; tower open Mon.–Tues. and Fri.–Sun. Memorial Day-Labor Day.
(308) 533-2257

www.fs.fed.us/r2/nebraska/units/brd/brd.html

9 Valentine National Wildlife Refuge

20 miles south of Valentine

The rolling dunes that give the entire Sandhills region of north-central Nebraska its name were created by deposits of windblown sand from an ancient seabed to the west. Native grasses invaded the dunes, the water table rose, marshes and lakes were formed, and the grass became even more abundant.

The unusual environment was threatened by settlers who drained the marshes to obtain more cropland. But in 1935 this refuge of more than 70,000 acres was established to preserve a part of the Sandhills. In 1976 it was designated a national natural landmark.

Since the refuge was created primarily for the preservation of wildlife, anyone with an interest in nature will find it a fascinating place to visit. Trails for hiking or horseback riding lead to the more remote areas and to some of the lakes, nine of which are open to anglers. Among the animals occasionally seen are pronghorn antelope, white-tailed and mule deer, coyotes, and badgers.

The most compelling attractions are the great flights of waterfowl that regularly take refuge here. In fall and spring, up to 300,000 migrating ducks may inhabit the refuge. Most prevalent are teals, mallards, pintails, shovelers, and gadwalls; but many other species can be seen, including the trumpeter swan, once nearly extinct. Flocks of wild turkeys also may be spotted, and shorebirds are abundant.

Open year-round. Admission charged.
(402) 376-3789

http://mountain-prairie.fws.gov/refuges/valentin/valentin.htm

8 Bessey Ranger District, Nebraska National Forest. *The Bessey Arboretum has proved that more than 100 species of plant life can survive in the Sandhills.*

10 Victoria Springs State Recreation Area

7 miles east of Anselmo

The history of this picturesque 70-acre park capsulizes the rapid social change on the plains in the late 19th and early 20th centuries. Settlers first came in the early 1870s, an era represented here by two rough-hewn log cabins; one served as the first post office in Custer County.

The pioneers endured devastating grasshopper infestations, Sioux Indian uprisings, and a range war with cattlemen. But the next generation lived quite a different life. A flourishing health resort grew up around the small lake and natural mineral springs here, with a plant that bottled not only the "medicinal" waters but also champagne and soda pop.

Today the remnants of this commercial era are gone, and the area has returned to its natural beauty. Fishing is allowed in the lake and in Victoria Springs Pond, where bass and catfish are common. Paddleboats can be rented, but swimming is prohibited. Herons can be observed from the shady lakeside picnic area.

Another treasure is a one-room schoolhouse in use from 1889 until the 1960s, complete with wall maps, books, and folded flag.

Open year-round. Admission charged.
(308) 749-2235
www.ngpc.state.ne.us/parks/

11 Gallagher Canyon State Recreation Area

8 miles south of Cozad

This secluded camping and picnic area on a small lake is truly far off the beaten path. It is reached only by a labyrinthine but well-marked journey down winding backcountry roads, including one that cuts through a cornfield.

Once you get there you'll be on your own; the 400-acre park is unstaffed. The rustic facilities include shady picnic sites, a dirt boat-launching ramp, a swimming area, and a large, grassy campground. Fishing is permitted in the lake, which is part of the area's water supply. Catfish, white bass, and walleye are likely catches.

Many kinds of birds are attracted to the area by the abundance of wild berries and grapes. Orioles, cardinals, finches, blue jays, magpies, and others may be seen flitting through the cover of cedar, ash, cottonwood, and Russian olive trees.

Open year-round.
(308) 785-2685
www.ngpc.state.ne.us/parks/

12 Nebraska Prairie Museum

Holdrege

From American Indian artifacts to the tools of homesteaders to unique World War II memorabilia, this expansive museum celebrates the vibrant history of the community and the state. Extensive collections of arrowheads, quilts, glassware, household items, and vintage clothing, along with rooms decorated in period style, recall life as it was on the prairie.

A series of exhibits evokes a typical bygone town square, complete with a print shop, blacksmith, and general store. Visitors can walk around pioneering agricultural equipment and antique automobiles while contemplating the impact of technology on farmers and townsfolk. Other points of interest outside the main museum include a one-room schoolhouse, a classic farm house, a windmill, and an early Lutheran church.

In addition to its extensive prairie heritage, the museum stands out for its tribute to Camp Atlanta, a World War II POW camp for German prisoners, originally just five miles from the museum's present site. For years after their release, German prisoners told stories of their exceptional treatment at the camp, and many forged lifelong friendships with their former guards.

An authentic scale replica of the tower that stood at Camp Atlanta now serves as an interpretive center, with items donated by U.S. military officers who worked at the prison, German soldiers confined there, and local people who got to know the POWs. Video interviews with former POWs and guards, as well as several books on the subject, are sold at the museum store.

Open daily year-round.
(308) 995-5015
www.nebraskaprairie.org

13 Willa Cather Pioneer Memorial

Red Cloud

The Pulitzer Prize-winning author lived in Red Cloud only from 1884 to 1890, when she left to attend the University of Nebraska. But she returned regularly to visit her parents and sometimes spend the summers.

The people and places in this town appeared in six of her novels, including *One of Ours*, the 1923 Pulitzer Prize winner.

How specifically and accurately she wrote about the places she knew is demonstrated in the house rented by the Cathers from 1884 to 1904. Passages from her books are narrated while you view the rooms she described. The house itself, she wrote, had "everything a little on the slant."

Here also is the wallpaper that Willa took as pay for working in Dr. Cook's drugstore and installed herself. The drugstore building still stands and is included in a pamphlet listing more than a score of houses, streets, business and municipal buildings, monuments,

13 Willa Cather Pioneer Memorial. *The Cather family Bible, with a lock of Willa's hair, in the family house with "everything a little on the slant."*

and churches that have appeared under one guise or another in Cather's books.

There is also a self-guiding tour of Cather landmarks in the surrounding countryside. Pamphlets are available at the historical center headquarters, where tours of the Cather home originate.
Open year-round except Sundays in winter and holidays.
Admission charged for some tours.
(402) 746-2653
www.willacather.org

14 Fort Hartsuff State Historical Park

4 miles from Ord
The frontier army post was established in 1874 to protect settlers and friendly Pawnees from hostile Sioux. Nine of the original main buildings still stand, stationed around a spacious parade ground.

With gravel and lime more readily available than lumber, most of the buildings were made of grout—which was scribed to give it the more fitting appearance of stone. Such symbolism was important; the soldiers organized an expedition to Long Pine Creek, some 70 miles to the north, to cut a 97-foot pine for a flagpole.

Times were hard when the fort was built, and the settlers were thankful for the construction work. Close ties with civilians continued, and the fort became the social center of the Loup Valley.

The garrison had only one major encounter, a battle in 1876 in which the Sioux were handily defeated. As more settlers moved in and the Sioux's power waned, so did the need for the fort. It was abandoned in 1881, and the grounds eventually became farmland; the ever-solid buildings were left in place.

14 Fort Hartsuff State Historical Park. *This onetime frontier outpost comes alive with re-enactments of a military routine on its painstakingly preserved grounds.*

Now, after considerable restoration, the barracks, officers' quarters, and the other buildings look much as they did more than a century ago. It's especially convincing when living-history demonstrations are given, weekends from Memorial Day to Labor Day.
Open year-round. Admission charged.
(308) 346-4715
www.ngpc.state.ne.us/parks/

15 Ashfall State Historical Park

8 miles from Royal
In the spring of 1971, heavy rains eroded part of a rural Nebraska cornfield. The farmer's bad luck proved to be a windfall for paleontologists: The exposed gully yielded the skull of a baby rhinoceros, preserved for some 10 million years beneath volcanic ash.

Since then, skeletons of hundreds of rhinos and other animals—including camels, cranes, turtles, and three-toed horses—have been uncovered. The onetime cornfield is now a 360-acre working excavation site that is open to curious observers.

Within the 2,000-square-foot "Rhino Barn," visitors can watch paleontologists as they carefully brush away ash from the skulls of prehistoric rhinos and piece together puzzles of scattered bones. The visitors center offers a fossil-preparatory laboratory where visitors will see what makes this excavation site so rare: the recovery of complete, intact skeletons that represent an entire rhino community.

On the grounds, several short, easily accessible trails grant a closer look at the striking local geology. The park also offers opportunities for serious hiking, bird-watching, and picnicking. Explorers might catch a glimpse of the area's living creatures, including white-tailed deer, wild turkeys, and prairie chickens. Canoeing is available at the nearby Grove Lake State Recreation Area.
Open daily Memorial Day–Labor Day; closed Mon. and some Sundays off-season. Admission charged.
(402) 893-2000
www.museum.unl.edu/ashfall

16 Neligh Mill Historical Site
Neligh
Of some 550 mills that have served Nebraska farmers over the years, this three-story brick mill, with branching annexes added at different times, is one of the few that remains with all of its machinery intact.

Construction on the building was started in 1873 by John D. Neligh, the town's founder. But it was another local luminary, W.C. Gallaway, who brought the mill to completion in 1874. In 1886 the original millstones were replaced with steel rollers.

The mill operated successfully with water power through World War I, but in 1920 a flood broke the millpond dam, and electricity had to be generated to keep the plant running.

Unlike many other local mills, this one survived the Great Depression and continued in the flour business until 1959. It was sufficiently automated to produce 500 barrels of flour a day with a crew of 12 to 14 people per each 12-hour shift.

Although flour has not been ground here for a long time, one is reminded of the persistence of dust by the little piles of white stuff still visible in various places under the machines—tangible ghosts of a more prosperous past.

The warehouse and power-plant additions have exhibits relating to the mill's history. The old office, with its original furnishings, serves as a visitors center and bookstore, where you can buy your own copy of *The Neligh Mill Cookbook*.
Open daily Memorial Day–Labor Day; Mon.–Fri. off-season.
Admission charged.
(402) 887-4303
www.nebraskahistory.org/sites/mill

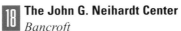

17 Ponca State Park
Ponca

Anyone who thinks of Nebraska as a vast expanse of flatness is in for a pleasant surprise here on the shores of the mighty Missouri River amid the hills where the Ponca tribe once roamed.

The hills rising directly from the river tend to give the roads a roller-coaster effect, and from some favored places provide superb views. At Three State Overlook, for example, visitors can see parts of Nebraska, South Dakota, and Iowa.

Rocky outcrops and an extensive hardwood forest add to the park's appeal. The forest boasts a magnificent oak more than 350 years old. Winding through some 1,400 acres are about 20 miles of hiking trails, and in winter cross-country skiing is popular. Many small picnic sites are scattered through the woods and along the bank of river.

The wrangler-led horseback rides traverse some of the most scenic areas of the park. Hikers and riders watch for white-tailed deer, raccoons, wild turkeys, eagles, and other wildlife.

The Missouri beckons anglers, and there's a boat ramp, but the swift current precludes swimming in the river. The park has a modern pool, however. Both are likely to be crowded on weekends in good weather. The 100-site campground offers full facilities, and there are 14 housekeeping cabins as well.

Open year-round.
Campground open Apr.–Nov., weather permitting.
Admission charged.
(402) 755-2284
www.ngpc.state.ne.us/parks/ponca.html

18 The John G. Neihardt Center
Bancroft

The Nebraska poet, teacher, writer, and historian John G. Neihardt was posthumously designated the state's Poet Laureate in Perpetuity in 1982. This center, in his memory, has a research library largely dedicated to his life and works, illuminated by tape and slide presentations.

A major theme here relates less to the man himself than to his lifelong interest in the American Indians and his deep respect for their beliefs, best reflected in the Sacred Hoop Prayer Garden.

The hoop, prominent in American Indian beliefs, is traditionally inscribed in the soil and represents the world. The world is divided by two roads. The east-west line marks the road of life experience, while the north-south line is the road of the spirit. From the center, where they cross, grows the tree of life, and each quarter of the circle has further symbolic meaning.

This concept is elegantly memorialized with a large prayer circle formed in the tiered brick floor of the circular exhibition gallery. The garden is also fashioned into a prayer circle and has signs explaining the symbolism.

Other displays in the center illustrate highlights from Neihardt's remarkably productive writing career. First published at the age of 19, he wrote, lectured, and taught continually, compiling a very impressive list of honors, including a special place of honor with the Lakota Indians. He was working on the second volume of his autobiography when he died in 1973 at age 92.

In striking contrast to the modern center with its curved, windowless

20 Heartland Museum of Military Vehicles. *A U.S. Army Bradley Fighting Vehicle is one of the machines on display at this unique site.*

brick walls is the humble, one-room frame building where Dr. Neihardt worked; it was brought here from his Bancroft home and restored under his supervision.

An old typewriter, kerosene lamp, potbellied stove, and comfortable rocker evoke thoughts of a homely, unhurried era that contrasts dramatically with the age of the word processor.

Open daily Mar.–Dec., and Mon.–Fri. Jan.–Feb. Donations accepted.
(402) 648-3388
www.nde.state.ne.us/SS/markers/207.html

19 Louis E. May Museum
Fremont

When in 1874 Theron Nye, the first mayor of Fremont, chose the Italianate Revival style for his new house, he was obviously out to make an impression.

Upon his death the big red brick house was left to his son, Ray Nye, who chose to remodel, expand, and make it even more grand and imposing. Young Nye's taste ran to the classical, and he added a portico of two-story fluted white columns with Ionic capitals.

The structure—a 25 room mansion—itself is an architectural museum piece, and today it appropriately serves the Dodge County Historical Society as its headquarters.

The museum, named for the benefactor who made its purchase possible, features changing displays of antiques, decorative arts, and historic photographs reflecting life from the late 19th and early 20th centuries.

The museum also includes a general store display, a one-room schoolhouse, a formal rose garden, and a Victorian garden with brick-lined paths. Outstanding details in the house itself include carved oak and mahogany paneling, art glass windows, decorative mantels, and some remarkable tile work in the master bathroom.

Open Wed.–Sat. and most Sundays from Apr.–Dec.
Admission charged.
(402) 721-4515
www.connectfremont.org/club/dchs_may.htm

20 Heartland Museum of Military Vehicles

Lexington

Conceived in 1986 by four friends with a shared passion for historic military vehicles—and who thrilled at driving their own vintage models in parades—this museum has developed into a place to honor America's other veterans of the battlefront.

It boasts a collection of more than 60 meticulously restored fighting machines, ready to roll at a moment's notice. Most vehicles have been acquired within a 150-mile radius of the museum. When tractors were in short supply in the 1940s and early 1950s, local farmers often relied on retired warriors—rugged jeeps, trucks, and half-tracks—to work their land.

The Heartland's dedicated staff has rescued many from rust and oblivion, returning them to mint condition. Beyond local treasures, the museum's collection features military ambulances, an M-60 tank, a U.S. Army Bradley Fighting Vehicle, and the rare Downed Airman Retriever, one of the few remaining in the world. Since military vehicles command-ed the skies as well as the road, the museum is also home to a "Huey" helicopter and a 1942 twin-engine Beechcraft C-45.

Visitors can touch and even sit in the formidable, fully operational vehicles. The museum's interpre-tive exhibits and its extensive reference library demonstrate how the collected machines were built, how they were used, and why those who wielded these weapons hope they will never have to be used again.

Open year-round. Admission charged.
(308) 324-6329
www.heartlandmuseum.com

21 Homestead National Monument of America

Beatrice

On May 20, 1862, President Abraham Lincoln signed the Homestead Act, enabling people to become land owners by paying an $18 filing fee and living on the land for five years.

This 160-acre park—the same amount of land granted under the act—pays tribute to what many consider the most important piece of legislation in U.S. history. The gritty endurance of thousands of ruggedly determined Americans, as well as countless European immigrants, spurred the westward spread of the country. Displays in the large visitors center illustrate their hardships and joys.

The park itself is located on the former homestead of Daniel Freeman, one of the first settlers to file a claim under the provisions of the act. A well-maintained path loops through woods and an exten-sive stretch of restored tall-grass prairie that gives a good sense of the terrain the early pioneers faced. A tiny log cabin built in 1867 vividly evokes the character of daily life.

A guide to the wildlife you may see along the path is available at the visitors center. A quarter-mile away stands a furnished, one-room schoolhouse. Built in 1872, it served the community as both an educational and a social focal point for nearly a century. Check at the visitors center for informa-tion about seeing the school.

Open year-round except holidays.
(402) 223-3514
www.nps.gov/home/home.htm

22 Indian Cave State Park
Shubert

This magnificent area—3,000 acres of oak-clad hills and bluffs along the Missouri River—takes its name from a deep overhang of rock that provided American

21 Homestead National Monument of America. *The Palmer-Epard Cabin, which was originally built a few miles away, has been preserved at the Homestead site.*

Indians with a natural shelter.

At the cave are large rocks incised with images of the hunt and the surroundings. Local residents call this area the Little Ozarks and come to see the lovely displays of redbud flowering in spring and the blazing colors of the hardwood forest in the fall. In fact, October tends to be the park's busiest month.

A scenic road and some 20 miles of trails for day walks and backpacking provide panoramic views. Horseback trail rides are also available. From the Missouri anglers catch bass, catfish, bull-head, carp, and the occasional sturgeon. In winter 16 miles of trails are marked for cross-country skiing, and some steep hills pro-vide excellent sledding. There are 225 campsites.

Also within the park are a reconstructed schoolhouse and general store, and the two grave-yards that remain from the town of St. Deroin. The store and school are the site of living history demonstrations given daily in summer and on weekends in fall.

The unusual community of St. Deroin is a story unto itself. It was established in the mid-1800s on land set aside for the homeless offspring of white traders and trappers who had married Indian women and then moved on.

The town was named for Joseph Deroin, who ran a trading post. The "Saint"—which he purportedly was not—was added to the name of the town in a vain attempt to attract more settlers to the new settlement.

Open year-round. Admission charged.
(402) 883-2575
www.ngpc.state.ne.us/parks

Nevada

In the land whose geologic wonders and scenic beauty now reign supreme, the ghost towns remind us of the transience of the frantic quest for wealth.

Red Rock Canyon. *The cliffs soar to 8,000 feet and are full of unique rock formations (see page 213).*

Some mining camps and towns have been spruced up, while others, gone to seed, have nearly disappeared. They are, however, the unique legacy of an era, and represent the reality of dust, mud, privation, high jinks, and random violence bred by gold fever in cramped quarters where the stakes were high.

It is unlikely that many miners took time to lay down their picks and shovels long enough to contemplate the greater wealth of the magnificent mountains, valleys, deserts, and volcanic landscapes here. As visitors soon find, there's much more to see than atmospheric ghost towns. There are otherworldly landscapes—including a cave still in the process of forming—as well as wildlife areas where hikers, horseback riders, fishermen, and swimmers come for rejuvenation.

1 Tuscarora

Tuscarora is a sleepy scattering of tumbledown buildings left over from the mining town's 19th-century heyday. The dusty structures are interspersed with the shiny campers and trailers in which many of the present-day residents (about 20 old-timers) prefer to live.

A visitor's first stop might be the Tuscarora Tavern, housed in the former Masonic and Oddfellows Hall, where in hunting season the once-bustling corner of Weed and Main comes alive again. Still standing as well is the Tuscarora "brewery," a low building that supplied refreshments for the dozen saloons.

Tuscarora was founded a couple of years after the Civil War but didn't hit its stride until the big silver strike of 1876. Population soared to a peak of 5,000 in 1877, including one of the largest concentrations of Chinese people outside of San Francisco. Estimates on the final take from its mines run as high as $10 million.

By World War I silver and gold mining in Tuscarora was mostly a memory, although there have been some controversial efforts to renew mining around the area in the last 20 years. For now, it remains a place of dusty charm.

www.ghosttowns.com/states/nv/tuscarora.html

1 Tuscarora. *Some of the remaining buildings in this ghost town are now just dusty reminders of the gold and silver boom that yielded as much as $10 million.*

2 Unionville

Perhaps 20 people still live along the main street of Unionville, which winds nearly three miles deep into Buena Vista Canyon. The road is flanked with ruined walls and foundations that recall earlier days of hope and, in the 1860s, a measure of prosperity.

The camp was settled in 1861 by silver miners of divided loyalties. Southern sympathizers named it Dixie, but when the Northern faction gained the upper hand, they changed it to Unionville. Mark Twain came to do some prospecting here, but he got involved in buying up shares in dozens of other mining operations and left after a week or two.

A fire in 1872 destroyed a number of buildings, and the mines were also slowing considerably by then. By 1880 Unionville was in a rapid decline.

There are a number of very well-preserved structures here, most notably a covered bridge and a schoolhouse built on a hill. And the Old Pioneer Garden Country Inn—built in 1861, meticulously restored and operated today as a bed-and-breakfast—is a lodging oasis for travelers.

www.ghosttowns.com/states/nv/unionville.html

3 Grimes Point and Hidden Cave

Fallon

Abundant echoes of the daily lives of ancient tribes of American Indians are at the core of these linked archaeological treasures.

Prehistoric carvings and line drawings engraved on the stone surfaces of the self-guiding, interpretive Grimes Petroglyph Trail form a timeline of development, from simple patterns begun at least 7,000 years ago to later, more pictorial images, such as lizards and deer.

The mile-long Grimes trail leads to Hidden Cave, which was first discovered in the 1920s by four schoolboys and is so named because of its well-concealed entrance.

Dust kicked up from centuries of bat droppings (guano) that littered the cave made exploration difficult at first, but by the late 1970s caches of artifacts as well as stratified deposits from the ice-age Lake Lahontan, now the Carson Desert, were unearthed. Basketry, unused dart shafts with points of shiny stone, and seeds and nuts perhaps reserved for future meals indicate that the cave was used for storage.

Fallon's Churchill County Museum on Maine Street offers guided tours of the cave the second and fourth Saturday of every month. Prehistoric Nevada is also highlighted at Carson City's Nevada State Museum.

Open year-round.

Museum: (775) 423-3677

www.ccmuseum.org/programs/

hiddencavetour.htm

www.nv.blm.gov/carson/recreation/

2_grimespoint.htm

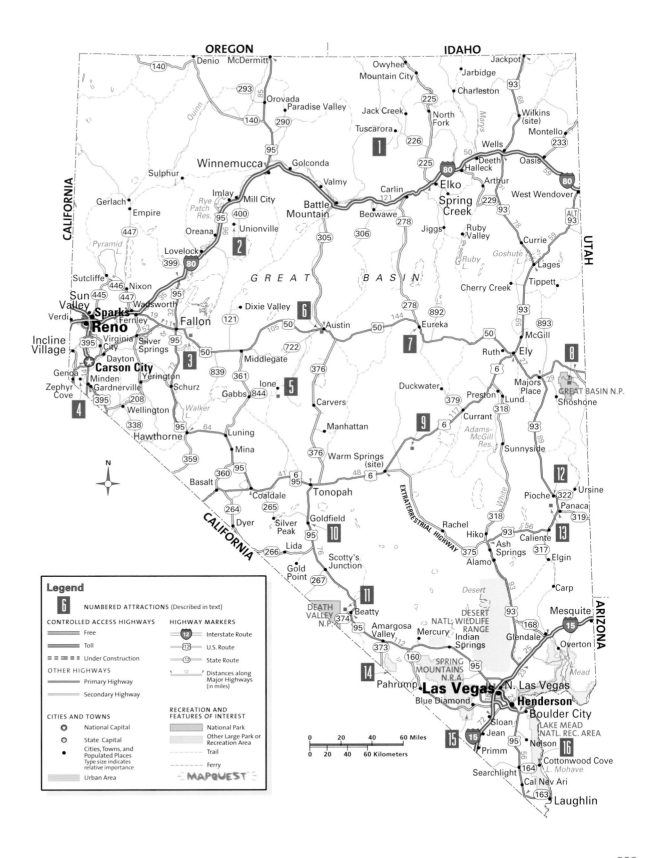

 Genoa. *The Genoa Bar, Nevada's oldest saloon, is one of the highlights here, along with detailed exhibits at the Courthouse Museum and Mormon Station.*

4 Genoa

This attractive town has the charm of what in Nevada passes for antiquity: It was founded as a trading post and wagon-supply station in 1851 and contains the state's oldest saloon, the Genoa Bar, with its collection of electrified gas and kerosene chandeliers.

Two other buildings are worth a detour. The first is the Genoa Courthouse Museum, an elegant, two-story brick building dating from 1865 (like the Genoa Bar, it is said to be the oldest building of its kind in Nevada). Washo Indian artifacts and other exhibits are on display, and you can wander through the old courtroom, the original jail cells, a period kitchen, and a blacksmith's shop.

Across the street is the Mormon Station Historic State Monument, which looks like a Wild West fort but is actually a reconstruction of the 1851 log-cabin trading post and its compound. The original burned in 1910; this replica (which houses a small museum

devoted to pioneer life and Nevada history) was built in 1947. You can picnic here.

Museum open daily May–Oct.; admission charged. Mormon Station open daily May–Oct.
Museum: (775) 782-4325
www.carsonvalleymuseums.com/Pages/ genoa.html

🏕

5 Berlin-Ichthyosaur State Park

23 miles east of Gabbs
The company town of Berlin, established in 1897, is now a classic ghost town. The wood shacks and the remains of the mill and gold mine look much as they did in 1910, when the town was virtually abandoned.

Some of the buildings have new roofs, but otherwise they show the effects of standing for some 90 years on the open hillside. Inside, a few remnants of furniture and utensils and an old bathtub reinforce the reality that

the miners essentially just picked up and moved on.

The park ranger leads tours of the town on summer weekends. If he's not there, take a self-guiding tour, following the signs that identify such sites as a miner's cabin, a boardinghouse, the stamp mill, an assay office, and a stage station.

The ichthyosaur fossils are in Union Canyon in the heart of the Shoshone Mountains, a two-mile drive from Berlin. In the fossil shelter the remains of 11 of these huge "fish-lizards" (which became extinct 70 million years ago) are shown just as they were found.

Despite their resemblance to today's whales and porpoises, these predators were the largest animals of their time, ranging up to 50 feet in length. Their remains have turned up all over the world, but the ichthyosaurs here are among the largest ever excavated. If the shelter is closed, you can see these fossils through an observation window. Picnic tables are nearby, and a nature trail leads to a campground.

Both sites open year-round, but call for weather conditions in the winter. Tours of Berlin and fossil area Memorial Day–Labor Day; call for occasional off-season tours. Admission charged.
(775) 964-2440
www.state.nv.us/stparks/bi.htm

🏕

6 Stokes Castle

Austin
Legend has it that this striking tower, built in 1897, was modeled on an ancient Roman castle. It stands on a promontory midway up the western flank of the Toiyabe Mountains, overlooking the Reese River valley and the far-off Shoshone Mountains.

The three-story "castle," a touching reminder of brave beginnings and lost dreams, was built at the behest of Anson Phelps Stokes, an owner of the 92-mile Nevada Central Railroad, which went defunct in 1938. Stokes intended the structure as a summer retreat for his family, but they spent only a single season there.

The walls are hand-hewn granite, and the floor joists are lengths of steel rail that extend to support now-vanished balconies. Now floorless and stairless, the house is closed to visitors, but even from ground level it's easy to imagine the incomparable view.

The half-mile entrance road from Austin is open year-round but can be difficult in the snow. But there is an RV campground in Austin, and within a 12-mile radius, a couple of U.S. Forest Service campsites. Other camping, hiking, riding, and fishing facilities are available along the area's creeks and canyons.

Open year-round
(775) 964-2200
www.austinnevada.com

🏕

🏰 Stokes Castle. *You can't explore the interior, but the strategic perch of this structure offers great views of the Reese River valley.*

 NEVADA

7 Eureka

Of the many Nevada mining towns whose fortunes have waxed and waned over the years, Eureka is a well-preserved gem with a statewide reputation.

It didn't suffer the usual cycle of boom-and-bust because almost all the profits from its lead mines went to its English owners. There wasn't enough left over to build the flamboyant Victorian structures so prominent in Virginia City and elsewhere. There was always money to keep the town going, but never enough to justify tearing down and building anew.

Today Eureka is a small, quiet place. The people are friendly, and you can sense in them a pride in the restoration work they have lavished on buildings like the courthouse and the Jackson House.

At the courthouse, the finest building in town, you can pick up a guide map to Eureka's attractions. A major one is the Sentinel Museum, located in what is possibly the oldest existing newspaper building in the state. On the ground floor you will find a complete press room from the 1800s, with posters that were printed by the *Eureka Sentinel* and plastered on the press room walls.

Over at the Eureka Opera House you'll see the social center of the old town almost as it was when the structure was built in the 1880s. The elegantly appointed building was completely restored in 1993 and is busy today hosting conventions, business meetings, and even the occasional performance.

Sentinel Museum open daily Apr.–Oct.;
Tue–Sat. Nov.–Mar.
(775) 237-5010.
Opera House open Mon.–Fri. year-round.
(775) 237-6006
www.co.eureka.nv.us

8 Great Basin National Park
Baker

Designated a national park in 1986, the main attraction here is the amazing Lehman Caves, full of elongated formations that look as though dripping water had been frozen into solid stone.

In a sense, that's essentially what happened, of course, and deposits carried by calcite-laden water seepage are still hardening into stone formations along the caves' 1 1/2-mile system of tunnels and rooms.

Cave tours are offered in 30-minute increments, with the longest and best being the 90-minute, half-mile journey that winds past formations ranging from the expected stalactites and stalagmites to elegant, rippling drapery and the rare pallets—disc-shaped formations with streamers of flowstone.

One of these, known as the Parachute because of its balanced shape, has become a symbol of the cave. Lacy, frostlike crystals of aragonite and nodules of calcite and cave coral enhance the beauty. The tour provides an eerie, inspiring experience—and a chilly one, too; bring a jacket.

Back above ground, there's a picnic area, cafe, and gift shop near the cave entrance and visitors center, and a quarter-mile nature trail. The visitors center supplies information about the wealth of hiking, riding, and camping opportunities based around the adjacent 13,000-foot Wheeler Peak.

Open year-round except holidays.
Cave tours run mid-June–mid-Aug.;
admission charged.
(775) 234-7331
www.nps.gov/grba

9 Lunar Crater Volcanic Field
75 miles east of Tonopah

As close to a moonscape as most of us will ever get, Lunar Crater and the adjacent 100 square miles of volcanic terrain are similar to features found on the moon. Indeed, before the 1969 moon shot, the area was used to test lunar-expedition equipment.

Thanks to the stable, dry climate at this national landmark, there's been little change since the volcanic activity that began some 2 million years ago ended only a few millennia back—in geologic terms, relatively recently.

It's a fascinatingly desolate place, dotted with saltbush and greasewood. But in the years when rainfall exceeds the four- to six-inch annual average, the wildflower displays after the rainy season (about mid-May to early July) can be magnificent, particularly when globe mallow slashes the desert with scarlet.

Lunar Crater sets the scale for the field's formations. It's nearly three-quarters of a mile across and 400 feet deep. From the crater's rim you can see more than 20 extinct volcanoes in the nearby hills. The smaller Easy Chair Crater, four miles to the north, gets its name from its situation on the edge of a tall cinder cone—together the two formations look like an over-stuffed chair.

Other features in the area include The Wall, a steep face of fused volcanic ash; Lunar Lake, a shallow lake in the midst of alkali mud flats; and Black Rock Lava Flow, a 1,900-acre basalt plateau.

There are no trails, but hiking is not difficult. Be on the alert for rattlesnakes and avoid hazards like abandoned mine shafts and unstable crater slopes. And remember to bring plenty of food and water and have enough gas for the trip. This is unforgiving land, and you are truly off the beaten path here.

Open year-round.
(775) 482-7800
www.nv.blm.gov/bmountain/misc/
recareas.htm

9 Lunar Crater Volcanic Field. *Named for its resemblance to the lunar landscape, this severe terrain was shaped by volcanic activity 2 million years ago.*

10 Goldfield

When Goldfield was going strong, the streets indeed seemed paved with gold. From its founding in 1902 until 1910, it was one of the most celebrated boomtowns in the country and the largest community in Nevada.

A lot of people got rich quick. Goldfield boasted banks, breweries, hospitals, newspapers, and the fanciest hotel in the West. Built in 1908, the Goldfield Hotel had a 22-karat gilt ceiling in the mahogany-paneled lobby, brass beds, and an electric elevator. But the gold began to run out after 1910, and a 1923 fire ravaged much of what was left of the town.

A monument on U.S. Hwy. 45 commemorates one of Goldfield's big claims to fame: A legendary 1906 title fight between Joe Gans and Oscar Nelson, won by Gans when Nelson was disqualified for a low blow—in the 42nd round. The fight is thought by many to be the longest in history.

Today the remnants of past glories are not so obvious, but with some patience and imagination you can get a sense of what Goldfield used to be. Besides the hotel there is the courthouse, built in 1907 and still well maintained. You can also belly up to the bar at the Santa Fe Saloon. Walking maps and other brochures can be obtained at the chamber of commerce.
Open year-round.
(775) 485-9987

11 Rhyolite and the Bottle House

When Rhyolite, one of Nevada's last great gold rush towns, was founded in 1905, earlier Nevada mines were closing at a regular pace, and thousands of prospectors headed here for another fling with lady luck.

During the boom years the town, with a floating population of about 16,000, had its own stock exchange, the railroad depot was the finest in the state, and the main street bustled with business and twinkled with electric lights. By 1911, however, it became evident that the quality and quantity of ore was less than expected. The miners and speculators began to leave as quickly as they had arrived.

The wishfully named Golden Street is now lined with the foundations and broken walls of once-proud stone buildings, although the train depot has been restored.

One of the favorite stops is the Tom Kelly bottle house with walls made of as many as 50,000 bottles set in clay. Most are Adolphus-Busch beer (known today as Budweiser) bottles, although there are also medicine bottles for good measure. When it was built in 1905, these no-deposit bottles provided a cheap alternative to lumber. Restored in 1925 for a movie setting, it is now maintained as a historic site. The interior is a hodgepodge of curios, memorabilia, and odds and ends; call the chamber of commerce for information on occasional tours.
Open year-round.
(775) 553-2424
www.governet.net/nv/as/bea/ rhyolite.htm

12 Pioche

Silver was found near Pioche as early as 1863, and after the mines opened in 1869, the settlement boomed. It also gained notoriety as a trigger-happy, lawless town, the toughest in the West. Local legend has it that not one of the first 70 entrants in its cemetery died of natural causes.

But this is no bust town. Pioche bills itself today as a "living ghost town," and it's a vibrant community that takes enormous pride in its past. Three annual heritage celebrations (June, July, and Labor Day weekend) draw large crowds.

History is all around here, starting with the "Million Dollar Courthouse," so named for its costly (some say corrupt) 60-year debt repayment on the initial 1871 construction costs of $26,400. Other reminders of days gone by are the Masonic Hall (1872), Thompson's Opera House (1873), and the exhibits in the Lincoln County Museum.

The town's shaded, gently winding streets afford such amenities as shops, cafes, and overnight accommodations. Nearby Eagle Valley Dam, Echo Dam, and Cathedral Gorge offer picnicking, camping, fishing, and boating.
Courthouse open daily mid-May–Oct.
Museum open year-round.
(775) 962-5544
www.piochenevada.com

13 Cathedral Gorge

Panaca

The buff-colored, roughly hewn spires reaching heavenward from the Meadow Valley inspired the name of this state park.

The gorge is part of the Panaca Formation, created when the freshwater lake that had covered the land receded, and erosion carved the bentonite clay into jagged pillars, gullies, and caves.

Nomadic tribes of Fremont, Anasazi, and Southern Paiute passed through from 10,000 B.C., hunting and gathering plants. Mormons founded the town of Panaca in 1864 after discovering water. Nearby Bullionville sprang up in 1869 when silver ore was found. In the 1920s open-air plays were performed against the otherworldly backdrop.

11 Rhyolite. *The shell of Cook's Bank is among the half-crumbled structures that line the once-thriving streets here in Nevada's last gold rush town.*

At an elevation of 4,800 feet, the park is home to a great variety of wildlife—like coyote, gophers, roadrunners, blackbirds, and non-poisonous lizards and snakes. In the summer, however, the Great Basin rattlesnake stops for a visit.

At the north end, where the park tapers sharply, Miller Point provides a panoramic view and can be reached by a road just north of the information center.

Open year-round. Admission charged.
(775) 728-4460

www.state.nv.us/stparks/cg.htm

14 Ash Meadows National Wildlife Refuge

22 miles west of Pahrump
The transparent, one-inch-long Devil's Hole pupfish, an endangered species, spawns on a rock ledge in only one place.

You'll find that place here in a deep spring on a federally protected refuge in the Amargosa Valley of southern Nye County.

Each of Ash Meadows' half-dozen geothermal pools claims its own variety of pupfish, and Point of Rocks is the best pupfish-viewing site. At least 24 species of animals and plants concentrated in these spring-fed wetlands and alkaline desert uplands are found nowhere else in the world.

Thousand-year-old "fossil" water comes to the surface in springs, providing rich and disparate environments. Carson Slough, an area of historic wetlands in the north and west, is in the midst of an ongoing restoration to help bring more wildlife here.

Desert oases, now very uncommon in other parts of the Southwest, can be found among the sagebrush and mesquite of this 24,000-acre

13 Cathedral Gorge. *Stunning views are the norm here along trails that offer a number of scenic overlooks at an elevation of 4,800 feet.*

former alfalfa, and later, cattle ranch. Sandy dunes populate the center.

Swimming is allowed only in the man-made Crystal Reservoir in order to protect the rest of the delicate ecosystem. Sport hunting is permitted for certain species, such as geese, quail, and jackrabbits.

Open year-round.
(775) 372-5435

desertcomplex.fws.gov/ashmeadows

15 Red Rock Canyon

10 miles west of Las Vegas
With the glitter of Las Vegas in the distance, 8,000-foot cliffs rise out of Red Rock Canyon in the Mojave Desert.

The Spring Mountain Range and Aztec sandstone formations frame a scene of serenity that is home to 197,000 acres of unique geologic outcroppings, wild animals, and desert plants.

The passage of millennia can be seen in the petrified sand dunes and the canyon's most notable geologic feature, the Keystone

Thrust Fault. Broad layers of gray limestone and red sandstone are visible where two of the earth's plates collided with great force an estimated 65 million years ago.

Visitors will find waterfalls that tumble into the canyons, sheltered ravines, scenic overlooks, and trails for both experienced and novice climbers. All of the areas at Red Rock are accessible from the highway. Late summer weather can be extremely hot.

Wild burros, whose ancestors were brought to the Southwest by gold and silver miners in the 1800s, roam freely in this National Conservation Area. They are best seen from a distance, as they have been known to kick and bite. The endangered desert tortoise is on view in its own habitat in the visitors center, and red-tailed hawks float on air currents over the Calico Basin.

Open year-round. Admission charged.
(702) 515-5050

www.redrockcanyon.blm.gov

16 Cottonwood Cove

10 miles east of Searchlight
In the southern offshoot of the massive Lake Mead National Recreation Area you'll find Lake Mohave, a watery respite on the dry domain of the Mojave Desert near the Nevada-Arizona border. The lake was created by Davis Dam on the Colorado River.

This is a haven for swimmers, boaters, anglers, backcountry explorers, and other desert fanciers. Rockhounds searching for agate and turquoise find this a popular spot as well.

The road in cuts through a forest of cholla cactus, and at the visitors center these and other local cactus species are identified. On a nature trail you will be introduced to a number of other plants native to the desert.

There are some 100 miles of back roads to be explored in the area; maps are available at the visitors center. Along the roads keep an eye out for wild burros, jackrabbits, and coyotes. The birds most often observed are roadrunners, quail, owls, and hummingbirds. The trees that grace this desert landscape include cottonwoods, olives, palms, and the lovely paloverde.

Fish here include striped and largemouth bass, crappie, rainbow and cutthroat trout, and channel catfish. Boat rentals, including houseboats, are available at the marina. From the water you sometimes see bighorn sheep on the red bluffs of Black Canyon, north of Cottonwood Cove, or Pyramid Canyon to the south.

Open year-round. Admission charged.
Lake Mead information:
(702) 293-8907

www.nps.gov/lame/lakemohave.html

Lake Francis State Park. *Moose are regular residents of this remote park in the Great North Woods.*

New Hampshire

With its stretch of seashore, vast national forest, and hundreds of lakes and ponds, this is truly a state for all seasons.

Where there's such a wealth of waterways, a great forest, and a seashore, scenic beauty is expected. But there are also some man-made attractions. These include an archaeological mystery—still unsolved—and a castle built by a man who dreamed of beauty on every side, and made the dream come true. Beauty and grace were the concerns of a renowned sculptor whose studio and home are now on public view. President Franklin Pierce's homestead is here, as is the birthplace of Daniel Webster, the great orator and champion of national unity. And nature is all around, with majestic parks full of year-round pleasures, from great fishing to peerless cross-country ski trails.

1 Lake Francis State Park
Pittsburg

The park is situated on an inlet of Lake Francis in the Connecticut Lakes region of the Great North Woods. From the park you can view the rapids of the Connecticut River—a juvenile stream here that belies the wide expanse it becomes on its seaward course.

And yet the young river gathers itself in Lake Francis into a tranquil, expansive body of water, stretching beyond the horizon as if to preview what it will become a few hundred miles downstream.

Wildlife is a major attraction here: More than 100 different species of birds have been sighted, including bald eagles, loons, and endangered woodpeckers. Deer and moose are frequent visitors, and bears are occasionally seen.

The old logging roads that wind in and around the park are enjoyed by both hikers and bicyclists. For hikers there are several possibilities, starting with an easy trail that runs through the woods along the Connecticut River and leads from a campground to a covered bridge 1 1/2 miles away.

Another trail provides a three-mile hike up Magalloway Mountain. Although the last mile is quite steep, the spectacular view from the top makes the effort worthwhile. On a clear day you can see Maine, Vermont, and Canada.

1 Lake Francis State Park. *The cold, pristine waters of this 2,000-acre lake offer great fishing, especially for brown, lake, and rainbow trout.*

Fishing is good, and you can rent a boat or canoe nearby; the park has a public boat launch. Within a mile or so of the park are a swimming beach, a stable that rents horses, and riding trails.
Open year-round. Camping mid-May–mid-Dec.; no water after mid-Oct.
(603) 538-6965
**www.nhparks.state.nh.us/parkspages/
lakefrancis/lakefrancis.html**

2 Coleman State Park
Stewartstown

This small, remote park is in a beautiful, alpine-like setting on the shore of Little Diamond Pond, high in the White Mountains. From it there is a beautiful view across the wooded slopes of Dixville Notch.

The park is sufficiently isolated that bear and moose may be seen; sometimes moose come down to the pond in the evening to feed.

Loons settle on the pond, and eagles and ospreys are occasionally spotted overhead.

The camping area here is the definition of basic: a large, grassy field with a scattering of fragrant balsam trees and hardwoods. There are no hookups for trailers, but each campsite has a fireplace with a grill, and during the camping season water is piped in from a spring.

If you are lured by the prospect of catching rainbow trout or squaretail brook trout to grill over your campfire, you may want to bring a boat, which you can launch at the small beach. Boats can also be rented from a privately owned outfit a short way down the main road.

Fishing can be strong here, especially if you hit the right season. Rainbow trout and lake trout are plentiful in the much deeper Big Diamond Pond, with spring and fall the best times. Little Diamond Pond is best in the spring, and rainbow trout are common here as well.

From Little Diamond Pond the road continues on to Big Diamond Pond a mile away, providing an enjoyable walk and a good chance for seeing deer. For a more rigorous outing you can hike the fairly steep, roughly half-mile trail from the campground up Sugar Hill. The park is the northern end of the 55-mile Androscoggin Trail.

In winter the park is an ideal place for cross-country skiing, snowshoeing, and snowmobiling.

Open year-round. Camping mid-May–mid-Dec.; no water after mid-Oct.

(608) 538-6965

www.nhparks.state.nh.us/parkspages/ coleman/coleman.html

3 Shelburne Birches Memorial Forest

Shelburne

Flanking the highway for nearly one-fifth of a mile at Shelburne is a dense stand of paper birches, dazzlingly graceful throughout the year in their white bark, and especially ravishing in spring or autumn, when their leaves are in the first delicate flush of green or the last glory of gold and yellow.

This is the kind of tree from which the American Indians made their birch-bark canoes, and some of the trees growing here are giants—among the largest to be found in the eastern United States. This forest—a rare sight along the well-traveled highway—is a commemoration of Shelburne citizens who served in World War II, and was established shortly after the war's conclusion.

Open year-round

Town offices:

(603) 466-2262

www.shelburnenh.com/attract.html

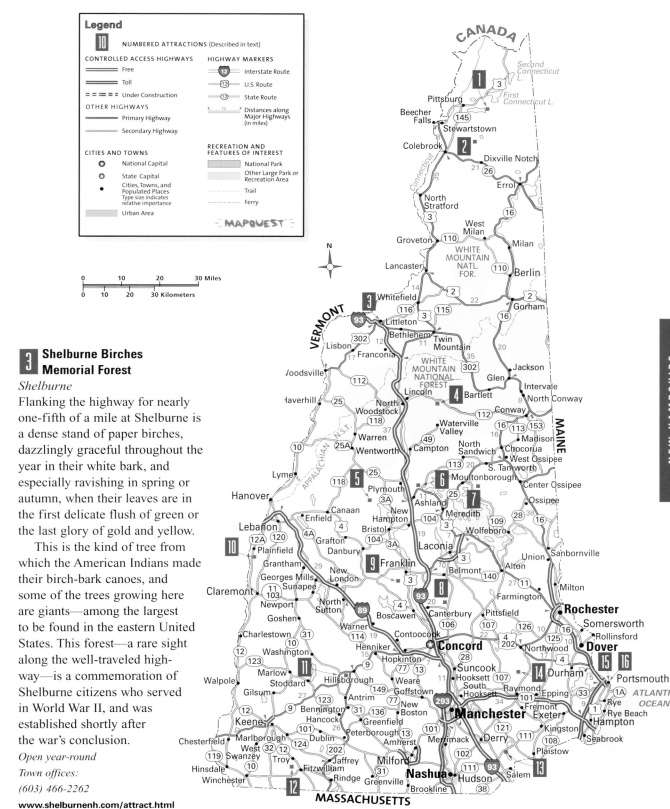

8 Canterbury Shaker Village. *The 1792 Meeting House is one of the original buildings still standing at this historic remembrance of the utopian community.*

4 **Greeley Ponds**
Lincoln

There are two ways to access the excellent trails here. One entrance is off Livermore Road, about two miles north of Rte. 49. The second entrance is off the Kancamagus Highway (Rte. 112), about nine miles east of I-93.

The two intersecting trails here run 2.1 miles and 5.4 miles. The shorter trail passes only one pond, although the second pond is just another half-mile more. It's fairly easy walking, with no extreme gradients. Log bridges span streams and swampy places, and the trails are clearly marked.

The only obstacles are the knotted tree roots that crisscross the path almost every step of the way. The forest here is a mixture of conifers and deciduous trees.

In winter these trails are a cross-country skiing paradise. The paths are well maintained, and routes are set up for novice and advanced skiers alike.

The Restricted Use Scenic Area (where fires and camping are not allowed) is more open than the rest of the forest, and as you enter it you begin to glimpse the cliffs towering above you and realize that you have been walking up a wide valley. Near the first pond a steep trail leads to a peak on one of these ridges, Mount Osceola.

The ponds themselves are dark green and calm. As you approach the first, look for the mature hemlock growing atop a seven-foot-high boulder. The roots reach down the rock to the earth like muscular boa constrictors.

Open year-round.
(603) 536-1310
www.hikenh.com

5 **Sculptured Rocks**
Groton

At this intriguing stretch of the Cockermouth River, the stream has worn a chasm some 100 feet long and 30 feet deep. Its granite walls, striated in pale colors, have been carved and polished by the water into a fantasy of bowls, beaks, curves, and swirls. Adding to the scenery are ferns that have somehow established a precarious foothold in the rock.

The best viewing is from a bridge spanning the river. If you face downstream and look directly below, you can see the shape of a lion's head in the rock, with its nose at the stream and a round hole for the gape of the mouth.

Elsewhere you can see what appear to be toad and lizard heads, shell creatures with bulging eyes, and whatever else your imagination and the water level permit. The water is clean, pure, and very, very cold. The brave souls who can tolerate the water temperature can jump from the cliffs, and there is even a small underwater tunnel to explore. The gorge is estimated to be about a million years old.

Open year-round.
**www.pemibaker.com/outdoors/swim/
sculprocks.html**

6 **Squam Lakes Natural Science Center**
Holderness

A lovingly tended place, the center's purpose is to introduce the visitor to a variety of natural environments and the creatures that live in them.

An exhibit trail, which is open from May 1 to November 1, leads from the visitors center across rocky meadowland through which a small stream flows. The stream

drains another ecological zone, an area of marsh, and finally flows into a trout pond. The attractive expanse of water, with white granite boulders at its edge, mirrors venerable white pines and paper birches on its dark surface.

Nearby are enclosures for bears, deer, owls, river otters, and bobcats. In July and August live animals are displayed during talks given by naturalists about the local wildlife. The center also has special programs for school groups.
Open May 1–Nov. 1.
Admission charged.
(603) 968-7194
www.nhnature.org

7 **Castle in the Clouds**
Moultonborough

This lovely place in the Ossipee Mountains edging Lake Winnipesaukee is the dramatic expression of a desire easy to understand and all but impossible to fulfill.

The castle was the dream of Thomas Gustave Plant, a multimillionaire whose objective was to have an environment in which he could behold nothing but beauty.

Purchasing 6,000 acres of woodland and sparing no expense, Plant built his mansion on a promontory with views of the island-studded lake below and the White Mountains in the distance. To achieve the perfection he required, Plant utilized the skills of vast numbers of European artists and craftsmen. The estate, completed in 1913 at a cost of $7 million, was named Lucknow after a castle in Scotland.

Miles of carriage roads and riding trails wind through quiet woods fragrant with pine to waterfalls, ponds, streams, and hilltops with breathtaking views of the surrounding countryside. There are garden walks and tours of the mansion, where the stained-glass windows depict some of the scenery here. The best time to visit is from mid-September to mid-October, when the autumn foliage is brilliant and the crowds have dwindled a bit.
Open weekends starting in mid-May, daily June–mid-Oct. Admission charged.
(800) 729-2468
www.castlesprings.com

NEW HAMPSHIRE

8 Canterbury Shaker Village
Canterbury

"Put your hands to work and hearts to God" was the essence of the "Shaking Quakers" way of life for 200 years, and the results of that philosophy are on display at this preserved community about a 20-minute drive north of Concord.

Visitors can take tours through 24 of the original 100 wood-frame buildings. The structures sit in austere relief on a hilltop surrounded by open fields and ponds. Nature trails through the rolling countryside lead to remains of old mills and dam sites.

Founded in the 1780s, the community had 300 people at its peak in 1860, living, working, and practicing celibacy and equality of the sexes. Shakers relinquished private property for the welfare of all, and in their utopian view of heaven on earth, they worshiped, farmed, manufactured medicines, and created spare but finely made furniture and crafts.

Women came to the Sisters Shop for confessions and counsel. That is also where they perfected their needlecraft, called fancy work and much in demand in the outside world.

The community creamery produced ice cream and butter for the village from its Guernsey cattle, and today there is a restaurant on site that serves the traditional food. Skilled craftspeople offer demonstrations in such arts as oval box making, broom making, and spinning and weaving.

Open daily May–Oct., weekends only in April, Nov., and Dec. Admission charged. (603) 783-9511

www.shakerworkshops.com/csv.htm

9 Daniel Webster's Birthplace Historic Site
Franklin

Daniel Webster was born here on January 18, 1782. The son of a poor farmer, he became one of America's preeminent statesmen.

Throughout his long career as lawyer, legislator, Cabinet member, and presidential aspirant, he was renowned for his oratorical eloquence, powerful presence, and championship of national unity. For 40 years he was New England's most respected and influential spokesman, serving first as a representative for New Hampshire and then as a senator for Massachusetts. Webster, who died in 1852, was elected to the Senate Hall of Fame in 1957.

His birthplace, a small, single-story building of dark gray clapboard with cedar shingles, is an essay in simplicity. The two-room interior is simple in the extreme, with wide-board floors, a brick fireplace, a bench, and a table. The house, in its modesty, is in telling contrast to the eminence that Daniel Webster later achieved.

Although the Webster family moved from the home in 1785, it is significant today not just as a famous birthplace, but also as a snapshot of frontier life in the 1780s and the early years of the growing nation that Webster would one day serve.

Open weekends and holidays Mother's Day–Labor Day. Admission charged, but free for seniors and under 18. (603) 934-5057

www.nhparks.state.nh.us/parkspages/ danwebster/danielwebster.html

10 Saint-Gaudens National Historic Site
Cornish

This fine house—a large, elaborate structure set on high ground with distant views of the Vermont hills—was once the home of one of America's most distinguished sculptors, Augustus Saint-Gaudens.

Originally a coach inn on the old stage road between Windsor and Meriden, it was bought by Saint-Gaudens in 1885 for a summer place, but from 1900 until his death in 1907 the estate served as his permanent home.

10 Saint-Gaudens National Historic Site. *The garden here comes alive with many of the artist's works.*

Here he combined his interests in gardening and the styles of the classical Greek and Roman periods to create a fairyland of porticoes, wide vistas, colonnades, and formal gardens. On the property are two studios, the Gallery and the Temple; the artist is buried in the latter. Many of Saint-Gaudens's most famous works are on display all around here.

Saint-Gaudens's father, an immigrant shoemaker, had encouraged his son's artistic interests; remembering this, the sculptor named the estate Aspet, after his father's birthplace in France.

Saint-Gaudens was an inspirational teacher, and many young artists studied with him at Aspet. He encouraged students and apprentices to follow his personal inclination "to develop technique, and then to hide it."

Park open year-round. Tours of Aspet offered late May–Oct. Admission charged. (603) 675-2175

www.sgnhs.org

www.nps.gov/saga

10 Saint-Gaudens National Historic Site. *The main residence of Aspet, where sculptor Augustus Saint-Gaudens lived and worked for the last years of his life.*

11 Franklin Pierce Homestead
Hillsborough

This white clapboard Georgian-style mansion was completed in 1804 by Benjamin Pierce, a prosperous politician. That same year saw the birth of a son, Franklin, who later became the 14th president of the United States.

The Pierces were a sociable family, and many great men of the time, including Daniel Webster, visited them during Franklin's youth. Handsome, intelligent, and well liked, Franklin rose quickly in politics and left home in 1833 to serve as a Democratic congressman in Washington, D.C.; 20 years later he was inaugurated president.

Pierce's presidency was not a terribly memorable one; indeed, he is remembered today as the "Forgotten President." Unable to deal effectively with the issue of slavery, he lost his party's support and retired from politics in 1857.

The interior of the homestead at Hillsborough has been largely restored to its original appearance. Of special interest is the elegant ballroom on the second floor, with hand-stenciled walls. Among the antique items in the barn is Franklin Pierce's fine old horse-drawn sleigh, decorated with painted flowers. The homestead is managed by the Hillsborough Historical Society.

Open daily July–Aug.;
open weekends June and Sept.
Admission charged.
(603) 478-3165
www.franklinpierce.ws

12 Rhododendron State Park
Fitzwilliam

In the 2,700 rolling acres of this park is a 16-acre stand of *Rhododendron catawbiense* and *Rhododendron maximum*. The stand of *R. maximum* is the largest

12 Rhododendron State Park. *The flowering plants here cover 16 acres and grow as high as 15 feet.*

to be found at such a northerly latitude. The shrubs, blooming in July, create a flowering canopy that runs as high as 15 feet.

The park's genesis dates to 1902, when Mary Lee Ware bought the land to preserve the rhododendrons from the damage that would ensue from a proposed lumbering operation. The next year she gave the land to the Appalachian Mountain Club, which donated it in turn to the state in 1946.

The rhododendron trail is easily walked in about an hour, and even when the shrubs are not in flower it is a very pleasant excursion. The woodland is fairly open, and the higher parts of the trail offer an excellent overview of the carpet of rhododendrons.

Just off the path leading to the picnic area is the Wildflower Trail, where an interesting selection of wild plants has been planted and labeled. The Little Monadnock Mountain Trail also branches off this park; its one-mile hike offers a view of Mount Monadnock.

Open early May–Labor Day.
Admission charged.
(603) 239-8153
www.nhparks.state.nh.us/parkspages/
rhododendron/rhododendron.html

13 America's Stonehenge
Salem

Scattered across about 20 acres on this lightly wooded hilltop are several curiously placed stone slabs and tumbled stone walls that form higgledy-piggledy avenues. For visitors, perhaps the greatest interest in this place is the mystery and prolonged debate it has provoked.

According to some investigators, this is the most significant pre-Columbian site in North America, clear evidence of a great civilization that flourished here, perhaps in the Bronze Age. Those who support this view call the place America's Stonehenge, comparing it to England's famous monument from prehistoric times.

According to the others—the majority of academic archaeologists—the complex dates from the colonial period and no earlier, the work, perhaps, of an eccentric and imaginative farmer. If such a person's purpose was to mystify, he certainly succeeded.

Among the intriguing formations: The Oracle Chamber, an intricately built rock shelter that is testament at least to a high degree of planning by *someone;* and the Sacrificial Table, a large rock slab that may well be nothing more than . . . a large rock slab.

At the visitors center, evidence for both schools of thought is displayed in museum cases containing finds from this and other "pre-Columbian" sites, including what some claim are inscriptions in Runic, Punic, and other ancient Old World scripts. Tour maps explain the various features found along the path looping the area.

Open daily year-round.
Admission charged.
(603) 893-8300
www.stonehengeusa.com

12 Rhododendron State Park. *July and August are the peak months for viewing the dazzling rhododendron groves that give this park its name.*

14 Pawtuckaway State Park
Nottingham

A rolling road through this varied park—5,500 acres of unspoiled nature—takes you to picnic grounds and campsites on a promontory above Lake Pawtuckaway.

On the way you pass two large swamps, picturesque with sedge and cattails, and a beaver pond where the skeletons of drowned trees rise starkly from the water. At the boundary of the park (and visually a part of it) is Mount Pawtuckaway, imposing with its granite cliffs.

The woodland here, primarily composed of oak, white pine, and birch, is especially interesting for the many large glacially deposited boulders that are scattered throughout the area. The shores of the lake are also strewn with boulders.

Fishermen come for the bass and pickerel, while birders look for the blue herons, eagles, and Canada geese that frequent the area. In winter the park is opened only when there is snow; the parking area is plowed to give access to trails for cross-country skiing and snowmobiling.

Open mid-June–Labor Day, and accessible for some winter activities; camping available early May–mid-Oct. Admission charged.
(603) 895-3031
www.nhparks.state.nh.us/parkspages/
pawtuckaway/pawtuckaway.html

15 Strawbery Banke Museum
Portsmouth

Sailing up the Piscataqua River in 1630, Capt. Walter Neal and his band of Englishmen spotted the wild strawberries ablaze on the western bank, and decided it worthy enough to call home.

 Strawbery Banke Museum. *Along with the museum's exhibits, the streets of Portsmouth in the waterfront area are a living history of this historic settlement.*

A London company had sent the men to develop a colony for trade and, with the wives' arrival, the community began to prosper. The name was changed from Strawbery Banke to Portsmouth because, it was said, "We are at the river's mouth, and our port is as good as any in the land."

Walk through almost four centuries of this seaside city's evolution in the restored homes and exhibit buildings of the waterfront neighborhood's historical museum, helped along by role players and regular activities.

Once a bustling port with sleek clipper ships built in its shipyards, the city has a rich history populated by sea captains, rich merchants, shopkeepers, revolutionaries, and waves of European immigrants. The unknown children of the Puddle Dock, playing their games of Jacob's ladder and ring toss, are revealed, as are people like Paul Revere and Daniel Webster.

Jefferson Street's Herb Garden displays a useful assortment of remedies used before 1800: angelica and flax, always dependable when warding off a witch; borage for courage; basil to repel flies; and johnny jump up, a one-time staple in love potions.

Open daily May–Oct.; Thurs.–Sun. Nov.– April (but closed Jan.). Admission charged.
(603) 433-1106
www.strawberybanke.org

16 The Wentworth-Coolidge Mansion Historic Site
Portsmouth

Back in colonial times this handsome, green-shuttered frame house, sprawling over a knoll facing Little Harbor, was the hub of the state's social and political activity.

As the residence of Benning Wentworth, a native of Portsmouth who became New Hampshire's first royal governor, it was the colony's seat of government from 1741 to 1767. Wentworth granted large parcels of land, signed charters incorporating new towns, and arranged trade alliances, all of which had an immense impact on the colony's development.

Governor Wentworth also gave a great deal of attention to the development of his mansion. He employed the best artisans he could find to embellish the interior with elaborate woodwork, a beautifully carved pine mantelpiece, and other architectural grace notes. The results attest to the skills of 18th-century craftsmen.

Since 1816 the Wentworth estate has been owned in turn by the Cushings of Massachusetts and then by impressionist painter J. Templeman Coolidge and his heirs, who presented the property to the state of New Hampshire in 1954. The entire area is now maintained by the state's parks and recreation department.

The house has remained almost intact. Some of the rooms have been refurbished to appear as they did when the Wentworths lived here, while others reflect the times of the Cushings and the Coolidges, thus providing a fascinating view of changing lifestyles over a period of more than 260 years. An adjacent gallery presents Coolidge paintings and a selection of contemporary regional art.

You can take a tour of the mansion, enjoy a picnic on the 10-acre estate, with its rolling lawns and profusion of lilacs (in early May), and amble down to the dock to view the harbor.

Open Wed.–Sun. early June–Labor Day weekend; call for occasional autumn weekend hours. Admission charged.
(603) 436-6607
www.nhparks.state.nh.us/parkspages/
wentworthcoolidge/wentcoolhom.html

Island Beach State Park. *Nature's fury separated this island paradise from the mainland (see page 226).*

New Jersey

If you are one of those to whom "Jersey" means turnpike, it's time to seek out some of the delights to be found off that beaten path.

The Great Swamp, the Pine Barrens, and Sandy Hook are celebrated New Jersey landforms, but even so, sections of each are not unduly crowded. Also closely identified with the state is a celebrated general and his many pivotal exploits during the American Revolution.

It was here that George Washington experienced a dramatic escape from the British, had a frustrating near-victory at the Monmouth Battlefield, enjoyed a pleasant sojourn at the Wallace house, and saw his troops endure a bitter winter near Morristown.

New Jersey's natural resources and numerous waterways made it an early leader in industry, as evidenced by the ironworks at Allaire, Batsto, and Ringwood, and the Delaware and Raritan Canal. Spacious parks and preserves for wildlife add further scope to the state's appeal.

1 High Point State Park
4 miles south of Port Jervis

In the late 1800s this magnificent tract of land on the crest of the Kittatinny Ridge was part of an elegant private resort. A carriage road wound up the forested slopes to High Point Inn.

A short walk then led to New Jersey's highest peak (1,803 feet), where guests enjoyed cool breezes and panoramic views of the New Jersey, New York, and Pennsylvania countryside. Years later the inn was partially dismantled and converted to a smaller lodge; the property was given to the state and opened to the public in 1923.

The most prominent feature in the 14,000-acre park is the granite-faced obelisk that soars 220 feet from the top of High Point.

With its forests, lakes, creeks, glens, swamp, and old farm fields, the park is a haven for wildlife, especially for white-tailed deer, which often dart across park roads. A few black bears roam some areas, steering clear of people, and once in a great while a bobcat is sighted. Several species of hawks and other raptors wheel about, and bluebirds and wild turkeys are regularly seen.

The park has 11 hiking trails of varying lengths and ease, each with its own rewards. Trail guides are available at the visitors center near the entrance.

High Point State Park. *The appropriately named High Point Monument rises 220 feet from atop the state's highest mountain to offer some unsurpassed views.*

The Old Trail, for example, utilizes a former horse-and-buggy road through a pleasantly open forest for half a mile, and is easy to walk. The more arduous and scenic Monument Trail leads into Cedar Swamp, where you can find pitcher plants and sundews—carnivorous plants that are uncommon in this region. And don't miss the famous Appalachian Trail, which runs through the park.

The park's day-use area includes spring-fed Lake Marcia (with a beach for swimmers) and tree-shaded picnic tables. Sawmill Lake provides a retreat for campers only. There are other camping spots as well, and even some furnished rental cabins, available by reservation only. The lake is stocked with trout, bass, and pickerel, and on winter weekends many come here for ice fishing.

Open year-round. Admission charged. (973) 875-4800

www.state.nj.us/dep/forestry/parks/ high.htm

Wawayanda State Park
Hewitt

Spaciousness and excellent upkeep are the immediate impressions of this fine park, partly because of the manicured entrance grounds and the two miles of excellent road rolling from the park headquarters to the parking lot on Lake Wawayanda.

The 250,000-acre lake offers several islands, a swimming area with a sandy beach, and a shoreline edged with forests, coves, and cliffs. Picnic tables are located in the wooded areas nearby.

A short walk from the beach is a marina where canoes, rowboats, and live bait are available. Several species of trout and bass are caught in the lake. Ice fishing is a popular sport in winter.

More than 40 miles of hiking trails lead to small ponds, a swamp, and scenic overlooks. The park is an excellent place for riding, and horses are available from stables nearby. Bird-watching is another favorite recreation; warblers are frequently seen, as well as hawks and other raptors, including an occasional eagle. Lucky visitors might also glimpse the endangered red-shouldered hawk.

A wide variety topography is the signature here, from mountains to ravines to swamps to forests. Twenty miles of the Appalachian Trail traverses many of those settings. Camping (but no water) is available at three sites. The park gates are sometimes closed to prevent overcrowding during busy times, so get there early.

Open year-round. Admission charged. (973) 853-4462

www.state.nj.us/dep/forestry/parks/ waway.htm

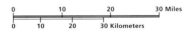

NEW JERSEY

3 Ringwood State Park
Ringwood

On a gentle slope in the Ramapo Mountains stands a rambling, white stucco manor house whose history is intertwined with America's first large-scale iron industry.

In 1740 the Ringwood Company acquired several rich mines in this vicinity and established an ironworks here on the present manor grounds. During the American Revolution the company supplied the army with ordnance, hardware, and camp stoves. The ironmaster at that time, Robert Erskine, was also a topographical engineer and prepared military maps for Gen. George Washington.

The original house, where Washington sometimes stayed, was replaced in 1810 by the ironmaster Martin Ryerson, who built a fine 10-room house in the Federal style. In 1853 Ringwood was purchased by Peter Cooper (the founder of Cooper Union Institute), who turned the property over to his son-in-law, Abram Hewitt, one of the great ironmasters of that time. Making Ringwood their residence, the Hewitts gradually added 41 rooms. The house today is a charming mix of styles. The exterior unabashedly combines gables, Ionic columns, and Victorian filigree, and the antique-filled interior is equally intriguing.

In front of the house spacious lawns sweep down to a small brook and lake picturesque with water lilies and resident geese and ducks. The park also features the State Botanical Garden—96 acres of immaculately tailored grounds.

Everywhere are reminders of the past, including the blacksmith shop where Washington's horses were shod. The 5,237-acre park offers hiking trails, a playground, and dozens of picnic tables spaced along a woodland stream. Boating, fishing, hiking trails, and winter activities are among this gem's many other offerings.

Open year-round; house open for tours Wed.–Sun. year-round.
Admission charged.
(973) 962-7031
www.state.nj.us/dep/forestry/parks/ringwod.htm

4 Steuben House
River Edge

Located on the bank of the Hackensack River, the golden sandstone house and the adjacent acreage form an oasis of quiet amid a heavily populated area.

In the late 18th century, however, this was the site of a small but busy inland port and a strategic point for both sides in the ebb and flow in this region during the American Revolution. A few yards from the house are the old wharf and an iron swing bridge built in 1888 to replace a wooden span called New Bridge, which was built in 1744.

It was across this bridge that Gen. George Washington led his Continental Army in November 1776 on a dramatic escape from the British at Fort Lee, and the structure became known as "the bridge that saved a nation."

In 1777 the owner of the house, Jan Zabriskie, was accused of passing military intelligence to the British. His property was subsequently confiscated and presented in 1783 to the Prussian officer Baron von Steuben as a reward for his services to the Continental Army; he sold the estate back to the Zabriskie family in 1788.

Acquired by the state in 1928 as a historic shrine, part of the two-story, 12-room house is now a museum for artifacts of local manufacture, charmingly displayed. The Bergen County Historical Society houses its collection here.

All around there are fine examples of matchstick furniture, pottery, textiles, antique dolls, folk art, and a well-stocked medicine cabinet. Near the hearth in the keeping room stands an oak settee with an unusually high back that forms a cabinet in which hams were cured.

Open Wed.–Sat. year-round.
(201) 487-1739
www.state.nj.us/dep/forestry/histsite.htm

5 Delaware Water Gap National Recreation Area. *The tree-lined Delaware River separates New Jersey and Pennsylvania in this idyllic shelter off I-80.*

5 Delaware Water Gap National Recreation Area
Exit 1 on I-80

Winding through a deep, narrow rent in the Kittatinny Mountains, the Delaware River creates a vista that draws thousands of tourists annually. But just north of the water gap lies a seldom visited recreation area of unspoiled beauty.

Flanking the Delaware River for some 35 miles as it flows between the Kittatinny Ridge in New Jersey and the Pocono Mountains in Pennsylvania, the largely wooded hills and vales around the Kittatinny Point visitors center include ponds, brooks, gorges, waterfalls, swimming beaches, and a variety of wildlife.

You access the Kittatinny Point area of the park from an entrance just off the last exit on I-80 in New Jersey. A blacktop road traverses the length of the recreation area on the New Jersey side, overlooking the river for part of its length. Heading north the narrow lane threads through the fern-carpeted Worthington State Forest. The rural peace and quiet and lack of traffic hearken to earlier times.

The roadside trails lead to cool glens, swift brooks, and scenic points along the Delaware River, where on summer weekends several hundred canoes may be seen gliding downstream.

An ideal and well-marked picnic spot is found at Watergate, where the trees open on a large, rolling meadow bordered on one side by a pond and on the other side by a brook shaded by trees. In summer the air is heady with the scent of mown grass drying in the sun; birds sing, and the brook ripples musically. It's so blissful here that, for the time at least, all seems right with the world.

Picnic tables are widely spaced beneath shade trees. Maps and trail guides are available at the Kittatinny Point center.

Park open year-round; Kittatinny Point visitors center open mid-Apr.–mid-Oct. and most winter weekends.
Admission charged.
(908) 496-4458
www.nps.gov/dewa

6 Morristown National Historical Park

Morristown
With the approach of winter in 1779, Gen. George Washington needed an encampment for the Continental Army from which he could keep close watch on the British in New York City.

Morristown was a strategic location, and Mrs. Jacob Ford, whose husband had died during one of the early campaigns, offered the use of her home and surrounding land.

The elegant, Georgian-style frame mansion is furnished approximately as it was when it served as Washington's headquarters. Walking through the rooms, you can visualize the activity here, with George Washington and wife Martha, Mrs. Ford and her four children, many servants and officers, and visitors such as the Marquis de Lafayette.

Leaflets for tours of the house are available at the headquarters museum. There's also a film that

attempts to capture the brutal conditions at the Jockey Hollow camp, where 10,000 ill-clad, starving soldiers endured one of the worst winters of the century.

Although it was an hour's ride by horse from headquarters, Jockey Hollow was chosen for the encampment because it had sufficient timber for firewood and the construction of nearly 1,200 huts. Today it is a serene 1,800-acre park populated with woodlands, brooks, and meadows.

From the entrance a pleasant road passes several reconstructed cabins and the parade ground. The park's 27 miles of trails are used for hiking, horseback riding, and cross-country skiing. Behind the Jockey Hollow visitors center are open fields, an old apple orchard, a re-creation of an 18th-century garden, and the sturdy Wick farmhouse, where Washington aide Gen. Arthur St. Clair was headquartered to watch over the camp.

Along with the self-guiding

6 Morristown National Historical Park. *A section of Jockey Hollow, where troops of the Continental Army spent the horrific winter of 1779-1780.*

tours and information available from the visitors centers, there are frequent special events and seminars that focus on the enormous history here. The park is often heavily visited on spring and fall weekends and on Washington's birthday in late February.

Open year-round except for holidays.
Admission charged.
(973) 539-2085
www.nps.gov/morr

7 Great Swamp National Wildlife Refuge

Basking Ridge
Established in 1960, the refuge has 7,500 acres of cattail marshes, grassland, and swamp woodlands; most of it has been designated a wilderness area. It is also frequented by more than 200 species of birds, both migratory and resident.

The headquarters of the refuge supplies trail maps and brochures that list the wildflowers, mammals,

7 Great Swamp National Wildlife Refuge. *Sunrise is an ideal time to enjoy the swamp's magical calm.*

birds, and reptiles found here season by season. Don't miss the Wildlife Observation Center, where a boardwalk crosses a small swamp to two wildlife observation blinds.

The swamp, marvelously beautiful, is covered by bright duckweed sprinkled in May with tiny yellow flowers and clumps of delicate purple iris. Here and there are open spots where turtles can be seen napping in the murky water. Peepholes in the blind offer an overlook of a larger swamp filled with pond lilies. The croaks and peeps of frogs and calls of birds are the only sounds in this mysterious and fascinating place.

The best viewing times are early morning and late afternoon. Visitors should cover their arms and legs completely to protect them from this favorite habitat of mosquitoes and ticks.

Open year-round.
(973) 425-1222
northeast.fws.gov/nj/grs.htm

8 The Red Mill Museum Village
Clinton

The buildings comprising this picturesque 10-acre site are remindful of the life, work, and customs in the area from the early 1800s to the early 1900s.

The centerpiece is the old Red Mill on Spruce Run. Local enterprises such as this were indispensable in the days when transportation was slow and uncertain. Mills would grind whatever might be profitable at the time. The Red Mill, which dates to about 1810, is a prime example of this versatility. The structure started as a woolen mill, and over the years ground flaxseed (to make linseed oil), grains, plaster, and graphite. It even produced electricity and pumped water for the town.

Today it serves as a museum. On the top floor is a working model of a typical mill. The other three floors are devoted to room settings of tools and equipment, fixtures and furnishings, toys, and decorative objects illustrating the early-day life in this area.

Other attractions along Spruce Run are an old schoolhouse, a blacksmith shop, a general store and post office, a log cabin, and the stone-crusher and kilns used to process limestone quarried from the cliffs that parallel the river. Weekends, when special events are frequently held, are more crowded than weekdays.
Open Tues.–Sun. Apr.–Oct.
Admission charged.
(908) 735-4101
www.theredmill.org

9 Wallace House
Somerville

The months Gen. George Washington spent in this house, from December 1778 to June 1779, must have been among the most pleasant in his years of service to the Continental Army.

He had endured the hardships and frustrations of the previous winter with his ill-equipped army at Valley Forge. Then at the Battle of Monmouth in June 1778, his troops had successfully harried the British as they retreated from Philadelphia (see site No. 12 for more). Now with the enemy engaged to the north and in the south, and his own troops well established in the nearby Watchung Mountains, Washington was able to savor the mild winter weather and enjoy the chance to entertain in the finest house in the vicinity.

The eight-room house was built in the Georgian style for John Wallace, a Philadelphia merchant, but shortly after the Wallaces took residence, arrangements were made for its use as Washington's headquarters. On June 3, 1779, the army moved northward to the Hudson River, and life returned to normal for the Wallaces; the house stayed in their family until 1801.

In 1897 the Revolutionary Memorial Society bought the place, and in 1946 gave it to the state. The house has remained almost unchanged since the 18th century. It is furnished in a manner appropriate for a wealthy family of the era. The guided tours of the house provide an insight into the life and style of the times.
Open Wed.–Sun. year-round.
(908) 925-1015
www.state.nj.us/dep/forestry/
histsite.htm

10 Delaware and Raritan Canal State Park
Somerset

As early as 1676 William Penn is said to have considered building an inland waterway across the narrow "waist" of New Jersey to expedite the trip from Philadelphia to New York. More than 150 years were to pass, however, before work began on a canal connecting the Delaware River north of Bordentown and the Raritan River at New Brunswick.

This 44-mile waterway (7 feet deep and 75 feet wide) required 14 locks to complete its course. The water came from a feeder canal 22 miles farther up the Delaware. Largely dug by hand by Irish immigrants, these giant trenches extracted a high price: construction costs soared past $2.8 million, and scores of workers housed in crowded labor camps died of cholera.

By way of the canal, which opened in the spring of 1834, the trip from Bordentown to New Brunswick took the better part of two days. The waterway remained in operation for nearly 100 years.

Since 1974 large sections of the canal have been set aside as a unique state park, whose character varies with its changing surroundings as it wanders through central New Jersey. With its 19-cent bridges, bridge-tender houses, cobblestone spillways and stone-arched culverts, the canal is a mecca for history lovers. Its trails are enjoyed by hikers, cyclists, and horseback riders, and there's cross-country skiing in the winter.

Canoes can be rented near Bull's Island, where a campground is maintained, and at several towns along the canal, including Titusville, Kingston, and Griggstown. Sections of the canal are stocked with trout, and anglers are also likely to catch bluegill, perch, pickerel, and largemouth bass.
Open year-round. Admission charged.
(732) 873-3050
www.state.nj.us/dep/forestry/parks

8 The Red Mill Museum Village. *After 200 years, the versatile mill still remains the centerpiece of life in the historic town of Clinton.*

Sandy Hook Lighthouse. *Protected by the British in the Revolution, the lighthouse is now part of the Gateway National Recreation Area.*

11 Sandy Hook Unit, Gateway National Recreation Area

Monmouth County

For more than 200 years this sandspit in lower New York Bay has been identified with military defense and the saving of lives at sea. In colonial times the shallows here were known as a graveyard for ships, and in 1764 a lighthouse was constructed to aid navigation in this thriving channel.

During the American Revolution the lighthouse was a crucial navigation tool for the British, who protected it from numerous attacks by the Continental rebels. Today the lighthouse, which was renovated in 2000, is part of the Sandy Hook Unit of the Gateway National Recreation Area, a unique park that covers three New York City boroughs and this section of land in northern New Jersey.

Now maintained by the Coast Guard, this is now the oldest working lighthouse in the country. Because ocean currents have deposited sand at the end of the peninsula, the octagonal structure

is today about 1 1/2 miles back from the edge of the point.

Another witness to the perils of the seas is the 1878 U.S. Lifesaving Service Station that now serves as the visitors center. In fact, Sandy Point was home to one of the nation's first such stations, built around 1849.

Of the many military defense systems that have been installed on the peninsula, the most colorful is Fort Hancock, which was built in the late 1800s and kept in use until the 1970s, when the last of the Nike missiles poised here were removed. You can explore the officers' houses and other buildings of this old army town. Also worth seeing are the 20-inch Rodman gun (1869) and the massive concrete mortar battery (1894).

But Sandy Hook has much more to offer. Its miles of ocean beach, dunes, and salt marsh invite exploration by pleasure seekers and nature lovers. Trails lead through the dunes and to a unique holly forest on the bay side. The best times to visit are summer weekdays and the off-season months, when crowds are small.

Open year-round. Admission charged.
(732) 872-5970
www.nps.gov/gate

11 Sandy Hook Unit, Gateway National Recreation Area. *Fort Hancock's first power plant (left) and Battery Potter are among the buildings on display here.*

12 Monmouth Battlefield State Park

Manalapan

The battle here on June 28, 1778, enhanced the morale of the Continental Army: for the first time the colonials engaged the British in open-field combat and stood them off.

Historians, however, consider the Battle of Monmouth a missed opportunity for a stunning American victory. At a critical point in the conflict Gen. Charles Lee retreated instead of attacking as ordered, infuriating his commander, Gen. George Washington. The British, after a day of fighting, were able to retreat under cover of darkness and safely make their way north. Lee was court-martialed and found guilty of disobedience and misbehavior.

A diorama in the visitors center shows the sequence of the battle hour by hour. The center also provides information on the historic Craig House, which can be reached by car or trails in the park.

If you walk you'll see the land much as it was on that historic day in 1778. John Craig, a paymaster for the local militia, was involved in the battle; his house on the battlefield has been restored. Built in 1710, it has seven rooms, three fireplaces, and a cold cellar.

A re-enactment of the battle takes place each year on the weekend closest to its anniversary. And if you can't make it for the summer fun, the park also offers winter activities.

Open year-round. Admission charged.
(732) 462-9616
www.state.nj.us/dep/forestry/parks/ monbat.htm

13 Turkey Swamp Park

Georgia

Long ago the nearby town of Adelphia was called Turkey, and the thickly forested, swampy lands and bogs surrounding it were known as Turkey Swamp. The name was adopted by this now roughly 1,200-acre park.

Several self-guiding nature trails around the 17-acre lake and bogs lead through the woodlands of oak and pitch pine, with their undergrowth of blueberry and pepperbush. The Fit-Trail, with 20 exercise stops along the 1 1/4-mile route, circles the entire park.

The park features a shelter—open in summer and enclosed and heated in winter—with a fireplace, picnic tables, and a kitchen. Family campgrounds are located in the woodlands; wilderness campgrounds in a remote section may be reserved by groups.

Canoes, rowboats, and paddleboats are available for rent, and there are playgrounds, picnic groves with grills, and fields for soccer and other sports.

Open year-round; fees for camping and special facilities.
(732) 462-7286
www.monmouthcountyparks.com/parks/ turk_swamp.html

14 Allaire State Park
Farmingdale

The park, with more than 3,000 acres laced with roads and trails, watered by two rivers, and with campgrounds and a golf course, is a major attraction. And here, too, is the restoration of an early 19th-century company town.

In 1812 the first furnace was built here to extract ore from local deposits of bog iron. The industry expanded, and by the mid-1830s this was a busy community of about 60 buildings and 400 people employed by the Allaire Works. But great improvements in smelting were being made elsewhere, and the Allaire furnace could not compete after a while.

Were it not for the generosity of Mrs. Arthur Brisbane, widow of the famous journalist, who deeded the village and surrounding land to the state, and the active interest of local Boy Scouts and service clubs, Allaire would simply have disappeared, as did so many similar communities in New Jersey.

The serenity of the tree-shaded grounds and well-tended 19th-century buildings belie the din, smoke, and hard, grimy labor involved in turning bog iron into the pots, kettles, pipe, hand irons, and other products made here. A sawmill, gristmill, and blacksmith shop contributed to the din. The smelter roared night and day, and the scores of charcoal pits making fuel for the furnace added a pall of pungent, acrid smoke.

As another reminder of earlier days, you'll hear the distinctive sound of a real steam whistle as the narrow-gauge Pine Creek Railroad runs past the village—no mere coincidence, since the New Jersey Museum of Transportation is located within the park.

16 Island Beach State Park. *This barrier beach became an island in 1750 when turbulent waters broke through the spit of land connecting it to the mainland.*

The park office provides lists of the species of wildflowers, birds, mammals, reptiles, turtles, and fish that inhabit the park. The nature center displays fossils and mounted animals from the area. For the half-mile nature trail there are cassettes and pamphlets. Canoes are available for rent nearby, and some of the trails are suitable for cross-country skiing.

Open year-round. Admission charged.
(732) 938-2371
www.state.nj.us/dep/forestry/parks/
allaire.htm

15 Double Trouble State Park
Bayville

This wilderness of woods and marsh in the Pine Barrens is a nature lover's delight at all times of the year, and on a gray day it has a misty, almost other-worldly aura that is especially appealing.

The park's history goes back to the late 18th century, when a sawmill was built and a dam constructed for water power. According to local lore, muskrats repeatedly gnawed through the dam, causing leaks that were announced with a cry of "here's trouble" and quickly repaired. One day the owner found two gaps in the dam and shouted to his men: "Here's double trouble!" And so a park name, at least, was born.

Faced with a dwindling supply of timber around the end of the 19th century, people began to grow cranberries to augment their incomes. The land was sold to the state in 1965, but the sawmill and the cranberry operation are still open for demonstrations.

Within the park's more than 5,000 acres are a general store, cranberry packing house, one-room schoolhouse, migrants' cottage, and other early-day buildings, some of which are periodically being restored.

From the cranberry processing plant a self-guiding nature trail about $1^{1}/4$ miles long crosses Cedar Creek, winds around the bogs, and ends at the sawmill. The red tint in the creek is caused by cedar bark and iron deposits. The air is aromatic with cedar, and in season

rhododendrons, mountain laurel, sweet bay, and fragrant honeysuckle bloom beneath sassafras trees, pitch pines, and red maples. Plant-lovers might also find in this moist environment the insect-eating sundew.

Great blue herons, egrets, red-tailed hawks, and quails are seen here. Fishermen can expect pickerel and catfish. Cedar Creek is very popular with canoeists, and canoes can be rented nearby. The park is especially enjoyable in springtime and in autumn. Be sure to bring insect repellent in the summer.

Open year-round.
(732) 341-6662
www.state.nj.us/dep/forestry/parks/
double.htm

16 Island Beach State Park
Seaside Park

On leaving New Jersey's heavily developed coast, you will find Island Beach State Park a pleasant surprise, with its seven miles of undeveloped seashore.

The southern end of a long barrier beach, this area became an island in 1750, when raging seas broke through the narrow bar of land at Seaside Heights. The inlet was open until 1812, when another storm closed it.

In the 1950s, to preserve the fragile environment of dunes and grasses found here, the state purchased 2,694 acres for a park with a botanical preserve, a recreation zone, and a wildlife sanctuary; today the park boasts more than 3,000 acres. The nature center at the north end of the park offers guided walks and has exhibits of the shells, butterflies, and primitive maritime vegetation found all around the island.

A paved road lined with dunes and beach heather leads from the park entrance to the recreation zone (a marvelous stretch of white, sandy beach on the ocean) and continues to the wildlife sanctuary, which is also open to visitors. At the end of the road the Barnegat Lighthouse can be seen 1½ miles in the distance. A beach buggy is required to reach the Barnegat Inlet.

The park is especially lovely in autumn, and the good weather can extend until Thanksgiving. The water stays warm, the beaches are empty of people but filled with shells, swarms of monarch butterflies cling to the branches of goldenrod, and the southbound birds are on the wing.

Open year-round. Admission charged.
(732) 793-0506
www.state.nj.us/dep/forestry/parks/
island.htm

17 Wharton State Forest
Hammonton
In this large forest are the Batsto and Mullica rivers, Atsion Lake, several streams, nature trails, a long hiking trail, and a number of campgrounds.

The combination of iron ore from the local bogs and fuel from the dense forests led to the establishment of many small iron-producing centers in southern New Jersey in the 18th century. Local forges made water pipes, stoves, firebacks, kettles, and other homely necessities; and during the American Revolution and the War of 1812, they supplied firearms and ammunition.

When coal from the Pennsylvania mines became available, the wood-burning forges could not compete. Glass factories were built here in

the mid-1800s, but they eventually failed as well. Batsto would have disappeared, as did similar villages in the area, had it not been for Joseph Wharton of Philadelphia, who bought the property and started redevelopment in 1876.

The more than 30 buildings preserved there today include the ironmaster's handsome mansion, the general store, post office, sawmill, smithy, barns, and iron-workers' houses. An ore boat, the charcoal kiln, and the furnace site are silent reminders of the hot and noisy work that once dominated the sights and sounds of life here.

The forest is composed mostly of pines, with some cedar and mixed hardwoods. A nature area adjoins the village, and a section of the 50-mile Batona Wilderness Trail runs through here. The Atsion Lake area, about a 20-minute drive from Batsto, has a playground, picnic area, and swimming beach. The forest offers shelter for many

birds and other wildlife. Fishing is good, mainly for pike, pickerel, and perch.

Miles of sandy roads in the forest are open for hiking, horseback riding, four-wheel-drive vehicles, and snowmobiles in season.

Atsion Lake is likely to be crowded on summer weekends.

Open year-round. Parking fee charged
Memorial Day–Labor Day on weekends
at the village and daily at the lake.
(609) 561-0024
www.state.nj.us/dep/forestry/parks/
wharton.htm

18 Edwin B. Forsythe National Wildlife Refuge
Oceanville
Among the most effective conservationists are those who serve in Congress—where environmental concerns can be translated into law. It's fitting that one man who served that cause is remembered here.

17 Wharton State Forest. *A view off the piggery at Batsto Village, with a mansion in the background, some of the 30-plus historic structures here.*

The late Congressman Edwin B. Forsythe worked diligently to protect the natural environment, and in 1984 the already established Brigantine and Barnegat Wildlife refuges were united and renamed in his honor.

The area now includes more than 43,000 acres of bays, channels, salt marshes, barrier beaches, dunes, upland fields, woodlands, and abundant wildlife.

Birds are one of the main draws, as the refuge is a major stop on the Atlantic Flyway. The peak of northbound migration is mid-March to mid-April. During the summer warblers, shorebirds, and wading birds are abundant.

The southbound migration is from mid-October to mid-December, with spectacular concentrations of ducks, geese, and brant in early November. During the winter as many as 150,000 birds stay in the area.

At the visitors center you can get a list of the roughly 300 species observed here. Leaflets are also available for an eight-mile, self-guiding auto tour; the suggested stops along the way include observation towers, a pool covered with water lilies, a nesting area where 600 Canada geese are hatched every year, and other areas where bald eagles, ospreys, and wood ducks may be seen.

For hikers, the self-guiding People's Trail leads through a typical coastal woodland, while the Leeds Eco-Trail penetrates an estuarine environment where incoming tides mix with freshwater streams flowing seaward.

Open year-round.
(609) 652-1665
forsythe.fws.gov/index.htm

19 Fort Mott State Park
Pennsville

The strategic importance of the Delaware River was recognized as early as 1838, when the federal government purchased land here at Finns Point.

The first guns were installed in 1878. In 1895 strong American sympathy for the Cuban revolt against Spain led to the likelihood of a U.S. war with Spain. As a precaution, naval defense guns were placed here and Fort Mott was constructed. The fort never saw any action, as the brief conflict with Spain was confined to Cuba.

The garrison was gradually reduced and the guns removed; in 1951 the abandoned fort became a state park, where the plotting rooms, the ammunition and powder magazines, and the range-finder towers can still be seen.

But the attraction today is the peaceful setting in which one can savor the expanse of sky and see the ocean-going ships sailing the waters of the Delaware. In midstream on Pea Patch Island is Fort Delaware, the site of a Civil War prison camp. In the national cemetery adjacent to the park is a memorial to Confederate soldiers and, in particular, to those prisoners who died at Fort Delaware. Another monument is dedicated to Union soldiers buried here.

A (literal) highlight in the area is Finns Point Lighthouse. The 115-foot wrought-iron tower was built in 1876. You can climb to the top on selected Sundays for a spectacular view.
Open year-round.
(609) 935-3218
**www.state.nj.us/dep/forestry/parks/
fortmot.htm**

20 Hancock House
Hancock's Bridge

The Hancock House was built in 1734 by Judge William Hancock on land that had been in his family since 1675. The house was one of a number of handsome brick homes built around this time, a symbol of growing prosperity in the area. Judge Hancock's home was attached to a simple structure erected a few years earlier.

The Hancock name has always been prominent here; the town of Hancock's Bridge was named for John Hancock, who helped the development of the community by constructing a bridge across Aloes (now Alloway) Creek in 1908.

The exterior of the two-story house is a fine example of the ornamental brickwork favored in this region. Colored brick was combined with standard red clay brick in various patterns. The corners of the Hancock house feature a striped zigzag pattern in blue and red, with a checkerboard effect in front. The interior is furnished with pieces typical of their time.

20 Hancock House. *The interior of the house is today filled with furnishings that reflected the growing prosperity of the area in the mid-1700s.*

During the Revolutionary War a tragic incident occurred in the house. About 30 Quakers, assigned to defend the drawbridge, were garrisoned here. The British, who were foraging in the area, had lost a battle at Quinton's Bridge on March 18, and were seeking revenge and a victory over the local militia.

Just before dawn three days later, a force of 300 British troops and local loyalists surprised the two sentries on duty at Hancock's Bridge and, without firing a shot, used their bayonets to massacre the guards and small garrison asleep in the house.
Open Wed.–Sun. year-round.
(856) 935-4373
**www.state.nj.us/dep/forestry/
histsite.htm**

21 Parvin State Park
Pittsgrove

In this quiet retreat it is hard to imagine that this was once the site of a busy gristmill and sawmill. The Parvin family operated the mills, and the original millpond—created by damming Muddy Run—was given their name.

Although Parvin Lake and the smaller Thundergust Lake are major attractions, the eight miles of trails winding through the swamps, groves, thickets, and forest in this 1,309-acre preserve are of special interest to nature lovers. The woods include some 40 kinds of trees, 60 different shrubs, more than 200 flowering plants, and many ferns and mosses. Birders have spotted 123 species in the park, and deer, raccoons, squirrels, and other wildlife are all around.

The inviting picnic grounds and play areas on Thundergust Lake are sensibly separated. In summer a lifeguard is on duty at the swim-

20 Hancock House. *The ornamental, zigzag brickwork is still readily visible on the house (pictured here from the back), originally built in 1734.*

ming beach on Parvin Lake, boats and canoes are available for rent, and the fishing is considered to be good. This is a camper's delight as well, with 56 campsites and 15 cabins around the park.

Open year-round.
(856) 358-8616
www.state.nj.us/dep/forestry/parks/parvin.htm

22 Wheaton Village
Millville

The first successful glassworks in America was started here in southern New Jersey in 1739 by Caspar Wistar. A rapidly growing population soon created a good market for bottles and window glass.

Southern New Jersey, with its abundant silica sand, plentiful wood for the furnaces, and excellent waterways, became a major center for glassmaking. In the late 1800s some 70 glassworks were flourishing here, including the T. C. Wheaton Company.

Theodore C. Wheaton, a physician, pharmacist, and drugstore owner, recognized the growing importance of glass containers, and in 1888 he bought an existing glassworks in Millville. As the T. C. Wheaton Company, the business prospered from the start, and today Wheaton Industries is the largest family-held glass producer in the world.

The centerpiece of Wheaton Village, established in 1968, is a working replica of the original factory. Glassblowers (gaffers) are at work here using the old tools and equipment.

The Museum of American Glass, on the village grounds, has some 7,000 pieces displayed in cases and in period settings of a kitchen and a pharmacy that effectively show their function.

Although glassmaking is the focus of the village, the 19th-century architecture, the tinsmith's and potter's shops, a schoolhouse, a general store, a half-scale railroad, and a live medicine show help create the ambience of an earlier era.

Open daily Apr.–Dec.; Fri.–Sun. Jan.–Feb.; Wed.–Sun. in Mar. Call for holiday availability. Admission charged.
(800) 998-4552
www.wheatonvillage.org

23 New Jersey Coastal Heritage Trail Route
From Perth Amboy south to Cape May and west along Delaware Bay to Delaware Memorial Bridge

Going to the shore takes on new meaning when you immerse yourself not just in surf, sun, and sand, but in the natural and cultural heritage of the five coastal regions of New Jersey: Sandy Hook, Barnegat, Absecon, Cape May, and Delsea share ocean-related topography, industry, and wildlife.

The nearly 300-mile Trail Route is meant for vehicular tourism, with markers along roadways that indicate points of interest. Trail literature is available at local centers and the regions' welcome centers.

You can find lighthouses, fishing villages and cranberry bogs, or learn about glassmaking. Eagles, ospreys, whales, and dolphins use the Jersey shore as a stopping-off point, as do other species for whom it is a seasonal refuge. Barrier islands, wetlands, tidal salt marshes, and dense maritime forests invite closer inspection.

Visit the Nature Conservancy's Cape May Migratory Bird Refuge, or explore the Pine Barrens at Double Trouble State Park in the Barnegat Bay region. When you know what you're looking at, it makes the drive to the beach an event in itself.

Open year-round.
(609) 292-2470
www.nps.gov/neje/home.htm

22 Wheaton Village. *History is side by side with 21st-century commerce here, as Wheaton Industries is still an active glass producer.*

24 The Wetlands Institute
Stone Harbor

The narrow strip of coastal wetlands that separates land from sea on southern New Jersey's Cape May Peninsula is a delight for bird-watchers and naturalists.

This people-friendly research center welcomes scientists, teachers, children, and families, and it is committed to preserving and encouraging understanding of the resources of the Atlantic Coast.

Species like the Louisiana heron and yellow-crowned and black-crowned night egrets find protection at the heronry, which is part of the 21-acre Stone Harbor Bird Sanctuary. A mini-cam transmits live pictures of nesting osprey onto a television monitor in Marshview Hall for all to see.

The terrapin release program has won national attention: terrapin babies, raised from eggs of mothers that have met an untimely death on the road, are re-introduced to the salt marsh. Horseshoe crabs, in residence here even before the dinosaurs, continue to lay billions of eggs, giving the migrating ruddy turnstones and red knots a solid meal before takeoff.

Three-hour kayaking tours of the coastal marsh ecosystem, salt marsh safaris, and Sunday morning bird walks can take you into a world in which you might be surprised by a laughing gull from the world's largest colony, or chance upon a glossy ibis picking its way out of the water on elegant, spindly legs.

Open daily May 15–Oct. 15, Tues.–Sat. Oct. 16–May 14. Admission charged.
(609) 368-1211
www.wetlandsinstitute.org

Living Desert State Park. *A kit fox is among the many native animals in its natural habitat here (see page 237).*

New Mexico

From its prehistory to the atomic age, ice caves to lava flows, arid deserts to snowcapped mountains—this is a land of incredible contrast.

In settings of superlative scenery is dramatic evidence of an ancient people who built intricate complexes, created communities connected by an extensive network of roads, and practiced sophisticated methods of agriculture.

Recent accomplishments, with untold implications for the future, are celebrated in museums dedicated to the atomic age and space exploration. The 19th century is recalled in a famous landform where pioneers literally left their mark, a historic Army fort, a town that time forgot, and the mansion of a lucky miner.

Great sand dunes, sculpted monoliths, hiking trails and nature walks, a wildlife refuge, a treasure field for rockhounds, a magnificent folk museum, and a miniature world of carved wood further contribute to the contrast here.

1 Aztec Ruins National Monument

Aztec

The ruins here were discovered in the 1870s and mistakenly named for the Aztec Indians. The 450-room structure, built in the early 1100s by the Anasazis—the ancestors of the Pueblo—was one of many outlying communities linked to Chaco Canyon by a network of excellent roads.

Eventually the Anasazis abandoned the site, and by the early 1200s it was occupied by tribes of the Mesa Verde from the north. Differences in masonry techniques and architectural styles distinguish their additions and modifications from the original construction.

An easy half-mile self-guiding trail leads through part of the ruins, allowing you to study the masonry and the interiors of the rooms. The ceilings here are original, and the green sandstone band running the length of the west wall is unique to this structure. The visitors center exhibits weaving, basketry, some fine pottery, and a 25-minute video with more background. The area was named a World Heritage Site in 1987.

Open daily year-round except holidays.
Admission charged.
(505) 334-6174
www.nps.gov/azru

1 Aztec Ruins National Monument. *The trail winding through the West Ruin offers visitors the best view of this intricate stone structure dating to the 1100s.*

2 Red River

For an off-season stay in the majestic Sangre de Cristo Mountains, try this small alpine resort village nestled in a narrow valley at an altitude of 8,750 feet. The village bulges with vacationers during the summer, and is also a popular winter and early spring ski spot. But it's great any time of the year, especially when the crowds are gone.

Late spring and early autumn are perfect times to explore the trails and narrow dirt roads twisting up the mountainsides, green and fragrant with ponderosa pines, Douglas firs, cedars, and hemlocks.

In summer the slopes are bright with primroses, mountain orchids, bluebells, and columbines. Elk, black bears, mountain lions, bobcats, and coyotes roam the forest, and at the higher altitudes marmots and mountain pikas are seen.

Red River is surrounded by the massive Kit Carson National Forest, and from mid-May through October you can arrange a pack trip to camp at a high mountain lake and fish for trout. For the less ambitious, another campground along the highway just a mile west of the village provides an idyllic picnic spot on the banks of the Red River.

Or drive to the Rio Grande Wild and Scenic River Recreation Area about 13 miles away, where you can view the mighty river far below as it thunders through a sheer-walled canyon.

(800) 348-6444

www.redrivernewmexico.com

---

3 Chaco Culture National Historical Park

Nageezi

For anyone interested in architectural design or the history of American Indians, Chaco Canyon is a place to stimulate and reward the imagination. The standing evidence of a sophisticated culture existing here about 800 to 1,100 years ago is overwhelming.

On a dozen major sites in the park, where several thousand ancestral Pueblo once lived and farmed, are the remains of their multistoried structures, believed built as early as 850 and vacated by 1300. The largest and most remarkable is Pueblo Bonito ("the beautiful village"), a stone edifice covering nearly three acres. Its 660 or so rooms rise like steps to four or five stories and curve around two great stone-paved plazas.

A looping nine-mile road winds through the canyon with stops at each of the five major sites here, and each site in turn offers its own trail. The Casa Rinconada and Tsin Kletsin sites offer a magnificent view of the valley.

The campground lacks water, so stock up at the visitors center.

Open year-round.

Admission charged.

(505) 786-7014

www.nps.gov/chcu

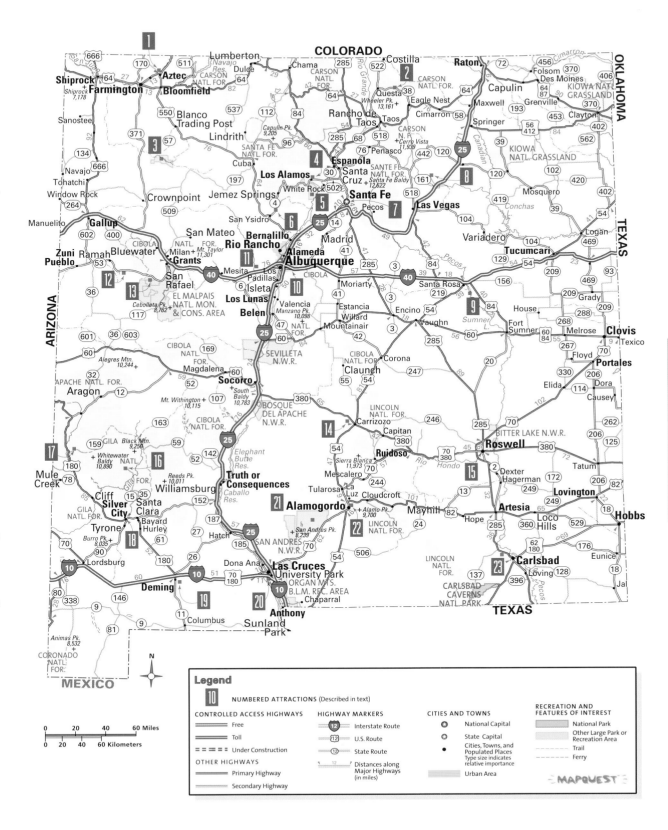

Legend

10 NUMBERED ATTRACTIONS (Described in text)

CONTROLLED ACCESS HIGHWAYS
- Free
- Toll
- Under Construction

OTHER HIGHWAYS
- Primary Highway
- Secondary Highway

HIGHWAY MARKERS
- **12** Interstate Route
- **12** U.S. Route
- **12** State Route
- 12 Distances along Major Highways (in miles)

CITIES AND TOWNS
- National Capital
- State Capital
- Cities, Towns, and Populated Places Type size indicates relative importance
- Urban Area

RECREATION AND FEATURES OF INTEREST
- National Park
- Other Large Park or Recreation Area
- Trail
- Ferry

MAPQUEST

0 20 40 60 Miles
0 20 40 60 Kilometers

4 Bradbury Science Museum
Los Alamos

The Los Alamos National Laboratory was built to support the Manhattan Project, which was responsible for designing and building the atomic bomb. The project's director, J. Robert Oppenheimer, chose the site for secrecy and scientific considerations, but also because he thought the ruggedly scenic country would appeal to his team of scientists.

The museum—named in honor of Norris E. Bradbury, the lab's long-serving second director—moved to its current location in downtown Los Alamos in 1993. Exhibits are divided into three main halls: History, Technology, and National Security. In the museum theater are regular films on scientific subjects.

Among the memorabilia on display is the 1939 letter from Albert Einstein to President Franklin D. Roosevelt suggesting the potential power of atomic fission and urging authorization for development. For the present day-minded, dozens of hands-on exhibits include computer and video interaction.

Most of the museum is devoted to contemporary energy research and use. There are displays on geotechnology, solar energy, nuclear reactor technology, and America's energy future. Various aspects of weapon design, testing, and deployment are also shown.

Open year-round except holidays.
(505) 667-4444
www.lanl.gov/worldview/museum

5 Bandelier National Monument
Los Alamos

The road to Bandelier takes you through some of the most spectacular country in New Mexico, offering enormous vistas of mountains, mesas, cliffs, and canyons. The monument itself covers nearly 50 square miles, almost all of it undisturbed wilderness.

Some 70 miles of maintained hiking trails lead in and out of steep-walled canyons, bringing you to pueblo ruins, cave rooms hewn from rock cliffs, petroglyphs and pictographs, waterfalls, and scenic overlooks.

An easy self-guiding walk described in a pamphlet leads from the visitors center along the floor of Frijoles Canyon to the ancestral pueblo where Anasazi Indians once farmed. A somewhat steep fork in the trail takes you to cave rooms and dramatic rock formations. From here one has a magnificent view of the valley and a stream lined with cottonwoods and box elder maples that turn a brilliant yellow in the autumn.

A popular summer activity is a bat walk, a tour of the bat cave at Long House, led by a park ranger. The Mexican freetail bats, seamlessly navigating the dark, are a unique, unexpected beauty. Also in the summer are one-hour night walks—silent, pitch-black journeys through the archaeological sites behind the visitors center.

A much longer, more demanding trail takes you down-canyon to two beautiful waterfalls and eventually to the Rio Grande as it courses through White Rock Canyon. The great variety of trees, shrubs, and flowering plants adds to the appeal of Bandelier. The monument is at an altitude of 6,500 feet, and the terrain is fairly rugged, so take it slow.

Permits are required (free at the visitors center) for backcountry hiking, horseback riding (bring your own steed), and cross-country skiing. Be advised, though, that there are strict no-fire regulations in the backcountry, and during peak fire season in the summer access may be limited.

Open year-round except holidays.
Admission charged.
(505) 672-3861, Ext. 517
www.nps.gov/band

5 Bandelier National Monument. *The 70 miles of hiking trails here—many steep but all worth the climb—wind through an array of pueblo ruins.*

6 Pueblo of Jemez
Jemez Pueblo

The people of the Pueblo of Jemez have lived on the high mountain mesas and canyons of north central New Mexico for a thousand years. They invite you to visit their ancestral tribal lands and experience their proud and rich culture, preserved throughout the centuries.

This is the last village of the Towa-speaking Pueblos, one of the mightiest of the Pueblo cultures when the Europeans arrived in 1851. "Hemish" ("the people") is their original name, reconfigured by the Spanish into "Jemez." The Pueblo of Jemez is "Walatowa," or "this is the place" in Towa.

Today this area, about an hour north of Albuquerque, is a window to the past as well as a living Pueblo town.

A reconstructed traditional stone fieldhouse, once used as a hunting and farming base camp, is the cornerstone of the visitors center, which also offers photo exhibits, crafts, and oral histories. Feast days and ceremonial dances are held throughout the year; guests are asked to treat them with respect.

This is also the gateway to the Jemez Mountain Trail that meanders through the Santa Fe National Forest and the Valles Caldera National Preserve.

Fishing streams, hot springs, and excellent trails are interwoven through the magical geologic formations. The national forest area is managed through a unique partnership between the U.S. Forest Service and the people of Jemez.

Open year-round.
(505) 834-7235
www.jemezpueblo.org

7 Museum of International Folk Art

Santa Fe

This fine collection, a part of the Museum of New Mexico, contains more than 130,000 objects from both hemispheres, making it the world's largest folk art treasury.

Ceramics, furniture, toys, jewelry and amulets, textiles, folk costumes, and religious and ceremonial objects are included, with such diverse artifacts as Bhutanese and Indonesian textiles, several pieces of Palestinian costume jewelry, and a collection of American weather vanes and whirligigs.

Some of the most remarkable displays are the strikingly realistic dioramas of street scenes, marketplaces, and theaters from around the world. A highlight is the miniature bull ring, rendered in perfect detail and populated by hundreds of tiny costumed figures.

One is captivated by the ingenuity and playfulness demonstrated throughout, even in sober historical scenes and religious pieces. It was the goal of the founder, Florence Dibell Bartlett, to promote world peace and understanding through the study of material culture, especially the joyful medium of folk art. This superb museum justifies her optimism.

Open Tues.–Sun. year-round except holidays. Admission charged.
(505) 476-1200
www.moifa.org

8 Fort Union National Monument

Watrous

Fort Union has had three incarnations. The first fort, built in 1851, was a key station on the Santa Fe Trail. After the outbreak of the Civil War a star-shaped earthen fortification was constructed in

8 Fort Union National Monument. *The ruins are on a grand scale at this fort, once the largest in the Southwest and a key outpost along the Santa Fe Trail.*

anticipation of a Confederate attack, which never came. The third and last installation was the largest in the Southwest upon its completion in 1869.

Troops stationed here waged several campaigns against the Indians of the southern plains, finally defeating them in 1875. In 1879 the railroad replaced the Santa Fe Trail, and in 1891 the fort was finally abandoned.

Enough remains of the third fort to indicate how very extensive it once was. From the visitors center at the parking lot, a 1.6-mile interpretive walk leads through its two units: the Post, where the troops and their officers were garrisoned, and the Depot, where those responsible for supplies, commissary, transportation, and equipment were stationed.

Along the trail are photographs showing the fort when it was in use and recorded re-enactments of what dialogue among the men might have been like 150 years ago. The self-guiding trail also visits the site of the second fort. Exhibits in the visitors center relate to life at the fort and conflicts with the Indians.

Open year-round except holidays.
Admission charged.
(505) 425-8025
www.nps.gov/foun

9 Rock Lake State Fish Hatchery

Santa Rosa

This innovative hatchery is best known lately for its test-tube walleye program, part of a 20-year effort to prove the walleye can survive in New Mexico's waters.

There's natural breeding here as well, and in total about 40 million walleye eggs are hatched and nurtured here each year. The stock is annually dispersed to waters all over the state.

Silvery minnows and rainbow trout are also on the premises. The rainbows are brought here as finger-

lings and reared to a length of 8 to 10 inches, which takes about 10 months. As they grow they are moved from one tank to another. Aerated flowing water allows the fish to live in incredible density. They are packed in so tightly that sardines come to mind.

The trout feed themselves by pushing a feeder wire. Some 140,000 rainbows per year are raised here for release around New Mexico.

Open year-round.
(505) 472-3690
www.gmfsh.state.nm.us

10 National Atomic Museum

Albuquerque

A visit to this modest museum on the Kirkland Air Force Base is fascinating, terrifying, and unforgettable. Here one is brought face to face with the ultimate weapon.

The Energy Horizons Room is devoted to the peaceful uses of energy. There are explanations of the various ways that fossil fuels, solar energy, nuclear fission, and the wind and tide are used for power. There's also a library and a theater that shows films related to the development and use of energy. The 53-minute feature is a documentary on the secret Manhattan Project, which led to the production of the first atomic bomb.

On display in a separate section of the museum are aerodynamic containers in which atomic and nuclear warheads can be delivered— by land, sea, and air. Outside the museum are rockets, missiles, and a B-52 aircraft that was used for testing nuclear weapons in the atmosphere.

Open year-round except holidays.
Admission charged.
(505) 284-3243
www.atomicmuseum.com

11 Tinkertown Museum
Sandia Park

Ross Ward's intricate wood-carved world in miniature is a decidedly unexpected roadside attraction along New Mexico's Turquoise Trail National Scenic Byway. "I did all this while you were watching TV," is one of the adages hanging up in the 22-room museum.

Some 50,000 glass bottles and bits of kooky Western memorabilia are mortared together to form the walls and exterior of this former traveling country fair exhibit.

Acting like a lovably dotty collection of knickknacks, Ward's animated characters come to life: teeny-tiny circus aerialists balance on the high wire, while a Navajo silversmith plies his trade in a town of the Old West. Brightly colored stagecoaches drop off passengers in front of a cross section of rooms at the Monarch Hotel.

Some of the exhibits are from the museum's eccentric collection of Americana—like Otto's automatic one-man band that plays joyful music, and Esmerelda, who will tell your fortune for a quarter.

A surprise of a different sort is across a ramp outside the museum: a 35-foot wooden cutter (definitely not a miniature), sailed on a 10-year trip around the world by Ward's brother-in-law.

Open daily April–Nov. 1.
Admission charged.
(505) 281-5233
www.tinkertown.com

12 El Morro National Monument
Ramah

El Morro, or the "Inscription Rock," is the massive point of a sandstone mesa rising some 200 feet above the valley floor. A waterhole fed by rain and snowmelt at the base of the bluff has long attracted travelers passing through the desert.

Members of three civilizations—Zuni Indians, Spanish soldiers and priests, and American settlers, soldiers, and adventurers—have left hundreds of inscriptions, from crude scratchings to elegant script, in the soft yellow stone. Indeed, El Morro is one of the great historical graffiti walls in America. The first inscription by an American is dated 1849.

A trail leads from the monument headquarters up the side of the mesa, passing many inscriptions. Along the way are markers keyed to a self-guiding booklet, which identifies petroglyphs and translates Spanish inscriptions, including an eight-line poem elegantly incised in 1629.

Many inscriptions, however, are of the "Kilroy was here" variety, like the message (pictured below) of a passing official from the Santa Fe region, roughly translated as: "On the 25th of the month of June of this year 1709, passed by here on the way to Zuni—Ramon Garcia Jurado."

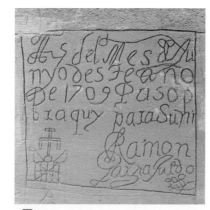
12 El Morro National Monument. *This 1709 travelogue chronicles Ramon Garcia Jurado's visit here.*

12 El Morro National Monument. *The trail up these sandstone towers is filled with the site's famous inscriptions, but don't miss the large ruins at the top.*

A steep climb continues to the windswept top, where there are two large American Indian ruins and expansive views of the valley and the Zuni Mountain Range. And in case you're wondering: No, you cannot leave your mark here.

Open year-round except holidays.
Admission charged.
(505) 783-4226
www.nps.gov/elmo

13 El Malpais National Monument
28 miles southwest of Grants

The main attraction of El Malpais ("the badlands") is the stunning display of nature's extremes at the Bandera crater and ice caves.

The phenomena were promoted for nearly 100 years by the Candelaria family, but in 1987 most of this area was absorbed into the newly created El Malpais National Monument, managed by the U.S. Park Service and the Bureau of Land Management. However, the family continued to run its famous tours from its private ranch.

At a half-mile long and rising 150 feet, the dormant Bandera Volcano crater is a sight to behold. A trail runs the length of the crater and rises along with it. You're already at an altitude of 8,000 feet, so be sure to take it easy. At the end of the trail up here you are on the Continental Divide.

When the volcano erupted some 5,000 years ago, molten rock coursed down the mountainside and created many lava tubes as it cooled. Sections of tubes collapsed by an earthquake have formed small caves; with a temperature that never exceeds 31°F, ice has slowly accumulated in them. You can reach one of the ice caves by a short, level trail across a lava field that still shows its flow.

Oddly enough, this strange, moonlike area draws an abundance of hummingbirds, best seen in July, when flowers are in bloom.

Open year-round except holidays.
Admission charged.
(505) 285-4641
www.nps.gov/elma

14 Valley of Fires State Park
Carrizozo

Here you can see one of the youngest lava beds in the United States, the Carrizozo Malpais.

An estimated 1,500 years ago red-hot lava flowed for 44 miles from Little Black Peak, visible to the northeast, covering 125 square miles of valley floor, in some places to a depth of more than 150 feet. As it flowed it began to cool and solidify, forming a ropy, corrugated crust.

The Malpais Trail leads into the park, a rugged 463-acre field of fissured black lava. Thick-soled shoes are recommended. A brochure describing the highlights on the trail is usually available near the trailhead. Along the loop trail, a very pleasant, easy, and dramatic walk, one sees a remarkable variety of shapes and textures—whorls, eddies, and bubbles—created by the cooling, moving lava, and, where domes formed by escaping gases have collapsed, gaping black pits.

For all the forbidding aspects of this landscape, many plants have established themselves in the soil that has blown into the cavities and depressions in the lava crust. It is remarkable to see yucca, juniper, hackberry, prickly pear, beargrass, and squawbush, to name a few, growing out of this seemingly impermeable substance.

A number of animals—mice, snakes, and lizards—have also found the lava field a viable environment. Some have developed abnormally dark coloration, called melanism, for camouflage on the dark lava—perhaps to ward off the great horned owls that nest here. The Sierra Blanca Mountains to the south and east provide a superb backdrop for this landscape.

Hiking trails, interpretive displays, and camping sites are among the amenities. For best weather go in spring or summer, but the area is seldom crowded just about any time of year.

Open year-round. Admission charged.
(505) 648-2241
www.americansouthwest.net/new_mexico/
valley_of_fires/recreation_area.html

15 Roswell Museum and Art Center
Roswell

Devoted to art, science, and history, the eclectic collection in this museum provides a fascinating view of Southwestern culture.

Colorfully outfitted mannequins in the history section portray the full range of people significant in the region's development: conquistadors armed with maces and battle-axes, warriors from local Indian tribes, cowboys, hunters, and soldiers. Among the cowboy displays is a surprisingly large collection of chaps.

The science area features the works of Robert Goddard, the "Father of Modern Rocketry," who lived near Roswell in the 1930s and did many of his pioneering experiments in this area.

The earliest devices look as though they had been made by a surrealist plumber, and it's very difficult to believe that less than 40 years after these early models were built, their successors carried man to the moon. The Goddard planetarium, New Mexico's largest, changes its high-tech shows monthly.

The art collection, which focuses on Southwestern painters, has a canvas by Georgia O'Keeffe and an entire room devoted to works by Peter Hurd, whose portrait of President Lyndon B. Johnson won special attention. There are also small bronzes depicting life in the Southwest, a collection of kachina dolls, and some splendid examples of Pueblo pottery.

Open year-round except holidays.
(505) 624-6744
www.roswellmuseum.org

16 Gila Cliff Dwellings National Monument. *The Mogollon Indians lived in this cave between the 13th and 14th centuries.*

16 Gila Cliff Dwellings National Monument
42 miles north of Silver City

Five natural caves high in the face of a cliff contain the ruins of dwellings built and occupied by the Mogollon Indians between the 13th and 14th centuries. A diligent farming people, they were also skillful weavers and artistic potters.

One of the ruins can be reached by a trail that climbs some 180 feet in its mile-long loop. A short flight of steps reaches up to the cave, which is very large, with an arched ceiling. Gazing out from its cool, dark recesses and seeing the West Fork of the Gila River as it flows past fields where crops once grew, one has a sense of having entered another era. Wandering through the rooms, one finds structural timbers dating back to the 1280s, as well as the remains of food stored centuries ago.

This is a popular site, but it is usually uncrowded from March to mid-May and in September and October. The visitors center offers relevant information, exhibits, and an audiovisual presentation; guide booklets may be purchased. The Gila River Recreation Area has picnic sites and campgrounds about a quarter-mile away. Be sure to carry water with you, and be advised: The trails are steep.

Because the Hwy. 15 approach out of Silver City is a severely winding road, cars with large trailers—or squeamish passengers—should take the Hwy. 35 alternate route, which is 25 miles longer but about the same driving time.

Open year-round. Admission charged.
(505) 388-8201
www.nps.gov/gicl

17 The Catwalk and Mogollon
5 miles east of Glenwood

At separate times both Geronimo and Butch Cassidy used the hard-to-navigate, boulder-strewn White-water Canyon as a hideout, but today its main attraction for visitors is the Catwalk.

The narrow metal walkway is firmly bolted into the canyon's steep walls. At the end of the trail, a vertiginous suspension bridge sways over the rushing waters of the Whitewater Creek.

The catwalk follows the route of a pipeline that was built to carry water to the gold-mining town of Graham in the 1890s. The town is gone, but the catwalk—with its dizzying views—remains.

The Catwalk was rebuilt in the 1930s as a recreation area for the Gila National Forest, and strengthened again in the 1960s by the U.S. Forest Service. Expert climbers can continue up a dirt trail to a ridge 10,000 feet up in the Mogollon Mountains.

You can also drive or motorcycle to the town of Mogollon, once a gold rush–era boomtown that surged for about 20 years and now has a population of 5,000 hardy souls. Almost deserted for most of the last century, it now has two small museums, some shops, and a bed-and-breakfast.

The road here is a breathtaking seven-mile ascent with no guard rails on the switchbacks. In the winter it is often impassable. Gouged out of the mountains, the old mines are easy to see, as are the deer, elk, and bison that live there.

Open year-round
(505) 539-2481

www.fs.fed.us/r3/gila/rec/catwalk.htm

18 Silver City Museum
Silver City

The eclectic charm of this little museum aptly recalls Silver City's rich and varied history.

The handsome Victorian house with its square tower and mansard roof was once the home of Henry B. Ailman, a young prospector who struck it rich in the 1870s. The building, listed on the *National Register of Historic Places,* is filled with furniture, clothing, household goods, musical instruments, and decorative objects typical of the era.

One room in particular evokes the heyday of the area's mining boom, with stylish mannequins in period attire and historic photographs that vividly recall impressions of the enormous profits and considerable dangers that surrounded silver mining.

The area's ranching heritage is represented by a fine display of cowpuncher's clothing and gear. Artifacts from Southwestern American Indian tribes are also displayed, including an excellent collection of Casas Grandes pottery.

Open Tues.–Sun. year-round.
(505) 538-5921

www.silvercitymuseum.org

19 Rockhound State Park
14 miles southeast of Deming

The park is dedicated to the genus rockhound, that special breed that savors the dusty challenge of the search and the thrill of discovery.

The parkland, on a mountain-side formed of volcanic rhyolite, is rich in semiprecious stones, primarily jasper, opal, blue agate, and psilomelane. Visitors can dig their own stones here and take away up to 15 pounds per visit.

You must bring your own equipment, but you can count on the park staff to provide helpful tips on methods and places for digging. A small exhibit in the visitors center displays many of the minerals found here. Summer is quite hot; the most comfortable season for digging is winter.

The 250-acre park is perched on a slope of the Little Florida Mountains, and it's a worthwhile destination just for the scenery. The campground and picnic area offer sweeping views of Deming and the valley below.

Open daily year-round. Admission charged weekends, April–Labor Day.
(505) 546-618

www.nmparks.com

20 Mesilla

For scores of early Western towns, it was a disaster when the railroad laid its tracks elsewhere. For Mesilla, it was nearby Las Cruces the railroad chose in 1881.

20 Mesilla. *The town's rich history ranges from a Civil War clash to an infamous outlaw's murder trial.*

But today this is considered by many to be a blessing, for the bypassed town has retained its tranquil charm and historic interest, unmarred by the rush of progress the trains brought to much of the rest of the country.

The first settlers arrived by wagon train in about 1847, during the U.S.-Mexican War, when Mexican troops were stationed here. In 1854 the American flag was raised in Mesilla Plaza, and four years later the Butterfield Stage put the community on the map, despite continuing threats from the Apache.

Captured by Texans during the Civil War, Mesilla served briefly as the capital of the Confederate Territory of Arizona. The Union quickly regained its foothold, and its forts dominated town life.

Famous and infamous visitors included Mexican revolutionary Francisco "Pancho" Villa and Wiliam Bonney, better known as Billy the Kid, who was once tried, convicted, and jailed here before being transferred to another town's jail (from which he escaped).

Mesilla, or "little tableland," was declared a state monument in 1957. The visitors center is equipped with videos, brochures, menus, and photos dating to the late 1800s to help acquaint you with the area.

Around the plaza and elsewhere in the town are some fine old adobe buildings, many dating from the mid-19th century. Don't-miss highlights here are the twin-towered church of San Albino, where the Angelus is rung three times daily; the Gadsden Museum, with displays of historic items from the area; and Mesilla Plaza.

(505) 647-9698

www.oldmesilla.org

White Sands National Monument

15 miles southwest of Alamogordo

Ever changing and always beautiful, these vast, brilliantly white dunes trace their existence to the layers of gypsum in the surrounding mountains. Seasonal rains and snow dissolve the gypsum and carry it to Lake Lucero, southwest of the dunes.

When the lake bed is dry, the prevailing southwest wind grinds the gypsum crystals into tiny grains and deposits them in these undulating waves of sand. The dunes shift slowly to the northeast, some by more than 20 feet per year, and new dunes are formed behind them.

From the park entrance a gypsum roadway leads for some eight miles into the sands. Numbered signs along the way are keyed to a pamphlet, available at the visitors center, which describes the area's remarkable geology, flora, and fauna. The outer dunes are covered with such desert plants as four-wing saltbush and iodine bush.

Hiking options range from a one-mile self-guiding nature trail to a 4.6-mile (round-trip) backcountry trail that crosses the heart of the dune field.

Hiking and sand surfing are popular in the dunes. Picnic sites are provided near the end of the roadway, but water is available only at the visitors center, eight miles away. The park advises visitors to call ahead, as testing at the nearby White Sands Missile Range occasionally closes roads in the area for short periods.

Open year-round except Christmas.
Admission charged.
(505) 479-6124
www.nps.gov/whsa

21 White Sands National Monument. *The park's flowing, constantly shifting dunes offer excellent opportunities for sand surfers and hikers alike.*

New Mexico Museum of Space History

Alamogordo

Much of the development of rocketry in America took place in the New Mexico desert. Appropriately, this seemingly lunar landscape is the setting for a modern museum dedicated to those who introduced the space age.

Within the museum is the International Space Hall of Fame, where more than 130 key players from around the world are honored.

Inductees include Johannes Winkler, a German rocket pioneer; Robert Goddard, "the Father of Modern Rocketry"; test pilot Chuck Yeager, the first man to fly faster than the speed of sound; American and Soviet astronauts such as Neil Armstrong and Yuri Gagarin; Britain's William Congreve, who introduced a solid-propellant artillery rocket in 1805; and even newsman Walter Cronkite, an expert on space history.

Among the exhibits are satellites and capsules, lunar vehicles, and a great variety of rocket engines and guidance systems.

Detailed history is the theme, with an emphasis on the long evolution of our understanding of the skies above us. Take, for example, the story of Clyde Tombaugh, who discovered Pluto in 1930.

Other favorite attractions include a "physics playground," where visitors can explore the laws of aerodynamics; an IMAX theater that features a wide variety of informative shows; and a sophisticated planetarium.

And the Challenger Memorial Garden on the grounds honors the seven astronauts killed in the 1986 shuttle explosion, with chilling control-room photos that capture that frozen moment in time.

Open year-round. Admission charged.
(505) 437-2840
www.spacefame.org

Living Desert Zoo and Gardens State Park

Carlsbad

Set on a rise above the town, this park is a showcase for the native plants and animals of the Chihuahuan desert.

Paths bordered with hundreds of desert plants, all clearly marked, lead to the various buildings and enclosures. Cacti in an amazing variety of shapes and sizes grow in a large greenhouse, and in the spring many burst forth with brilliant flowers.

Enclosures flanking the park contain larger animals, including Mexican pronghorn, bison, mule deer, wolves, and elk. There is also a prairie dog town, a bear den, a reptile house, and a nocturnal house. Their denizen include fish, aquatic turtles, nocturnal reptiles, badgers, and ringtail cats.

An aviary provides a close look at hawks, owls, roadrunners, and other desert birds. And at the far end of the park is a small lake for waterfowl and mammals that prefer wet places.

As you walk the trails, keep an eye out above for bobcats and mountain lions, part of an exhibit that showcases these animals in their natural habitat.

While on the 1.3-mile self-guided tour, visitors will discover sand dunes and mountainous areas where pinyon and juniper trees contrast with the desert floor below. During the summer season here—from April to September—it is more comfortable to visit in the cool of morning or evening.

Open year-round except Christmas.
Admission charged.
(505) 887-5516
www.livingdesertfriends.org

Iroquois National Wildlife Refuge. *Autumn is the best time of year to spot a wood duck.*

New York

The ocean, the lakes, and the rivers that border the state offer watery retreats to complement the attractions of the interior.

Populous though it is, the Empire State has a surprising number of getaway places that offer a wide variety of choices for relaxation and recreation. There are beaches on the Atlantic and on lakes Ontario and Erie, islands in the St. Lawrence River, and some inviting small towns on the banks of the Hudson. Scattered across New York are hundreds of sizable lakes. The vast wilderness areas in the Catskills and Adirondacks are laced with streams, waterfalls, and hiking trails. Thoughtful perusal of the map and some exploration of the smaller back roads can reveal places to supplement the numbered highlights on the following pages.

1 Iroquois National Wildlife Refuge

Alabama

These 10,818 acres of marsh, swamp, wet meadow, forest, and pasture are set aside to offer food, rest, and protection for more than 200 species of birds, especially during the spring and fall migrations. In early to mid-April, the peak of the spring season, as many as 40,000 Canada geese may be seen feeding at a single time. And flights of great blue herons, which nest here, are a common sight.

Although fewer numbers of migrating birds pass this way in autumn, it is the best time for observing ducks, especially wood ducks, mallards, and blue-winged teal. At any time of the year birders can expect to see a number of permanent residents, including great horned owls and downy woodpeckers.

The refuge is a place for a peaceful, leisurely visit, with many trails and overlooks to explore.
Except for roads and designated trails, the refuge is closed to visitors from March 1 to July 15, the nesting and brood season. Headquarters open Mon.–Fri. except holidays; weekends mid-Mar.–May.
(585) 948-5445
www.gorp.com

1 Iroquois National Wildlife Refuge. *The sun lowers itself on the horizon, adding even more tranquility to an already peaceful setting.*

2 Elbert Hubbard-Roycroft Museum & Millard Fillmore House

Roycroft Museum at 363 Oakwood Ave., Fillmore House at 24 Shearer Ave., East Aurora, southeast of Buffalo

When Elbert Hubbard met William Morris on a walking tour of England, the idea for the Roycroft Community was born. The successful soap salesman and sometime writer was inspired by Morris, a guiding light of the Arts and Crafts movement, to start a printing press and publish his own work. The business grew from one printing shop to a self-

sufficient, handicraft community, employing more than 500 artisans at its height in 1910.

The museum, near the main 14-building Roycroft Campus, is housed in a craftsman-style bungalow that had been the home of George Scheide Mantel, a director of leather bookbinding.

In 1915, Hubbard and his wife died on the *Lusitania*. By 1938 American tastes had shifted and the Roycroft era was over.

Just off Main Street, the tidy frame house behind the picket fence was built by our 13th president, Millard Fillmore. His wife, Abigail, had her own library, and

NEW YORK

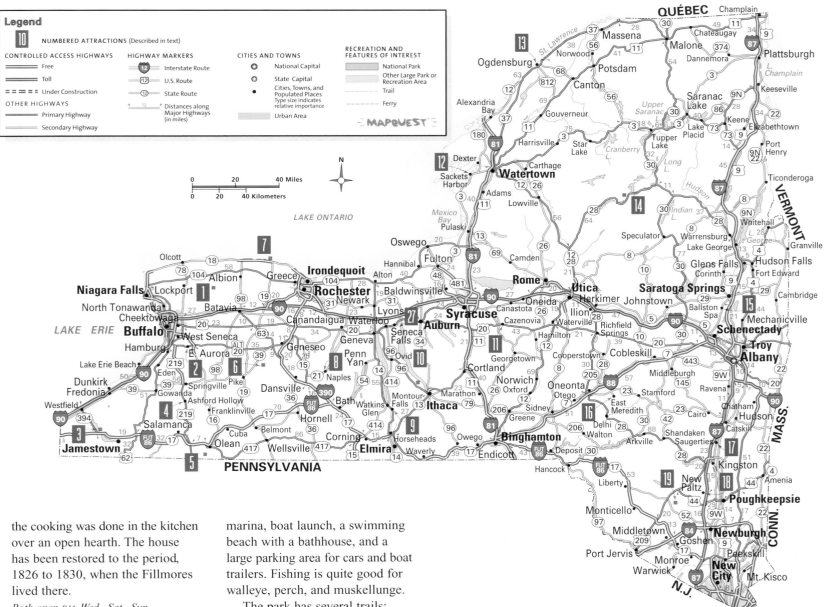

Legend

10 NUMBERED ATTRACTIONS (Described in text)

CONTROLLED ACCESS HIGHWAYS
Free
Toll
Under Construction

OTHER HIGHWAYS
Primary Highway
Secondary Highway

HIGHWAY MARKERS
12 Interstate Route
12 U.S. Route
12 State Route
12 Distances along Major Highways (in miles)

CITIES AND TOWNS
◉ National Capital
⊛ State Capital
• Cities, Towns, and Populated Places Type size indicates relative importance
Urban Area

RECREATION AND FEATURES OF INTEREST
National Park
Other Large Park or Recreation Area
Trail
Ferry

MAPQUEST

the cooking was done in the kitchen over an open hearth. The house has been restored to the period, 1826 to 1830, when the Fillmores lived there.

Both open P.M. Wed., Sat., Sun., June–Oct. 15. Admission charged.
Roycroft Museum:
(716) 652-4735

www.roycrofter.com/museum.htm

Fillmore House:
(716) 652-8875

www.millardfillmorehouse.org

3 Long Point on Lake Chautauqua State Park

Bemus Point

This pleasant day-use park is water-oriented, with an extensive

marina, boat launch, a swimming beach with a bathhouse, and a large parking area for cars and boat trailers. Fishing is quite good for walleye, perch, and muskellunge.

The park has several trails: some follow the scenic lakeshore, and one, flanked by fine old oak trees, goes out to the end of a long, narrow point projecting about a quarter-mile into the lake.

Open year-round. Admission charged daily in summer, and on weekends and holidays May–late June and Labor Day–Columbus Day.
(716) 386-2722

www.nysparks.state.ny.us

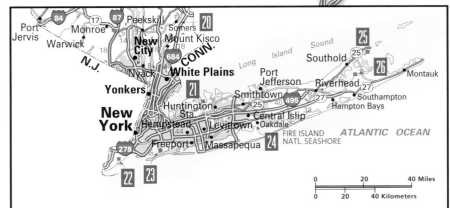

NEW YORK

 Griffis Sculpture Park. *These oversized Aluminum Bathers by Larry Griffis Jr. seem to be cavorting about the pond, enjoying the beautiful scenery.*

4 Griffis Sculpture Park

Ashford Hollow. Reached by Ahrens Rd. off Rte. 219. Towering sculptures at either side of the road mark the entrance.
Delightfully displayed in a sylvan setting is a collection of 200 objective and nonobjective sculptures fashioned of aluminum, bronze, steel, cast iron, and wood, the creations of several different artists. Trails crisscross the park's 400 acres of meadows, ponds, and lightly wooded slopes. As you walk along, abstract forms and surreal figures come boldly into view or lurk to astonish you among the trees.

Particularly striking are the sculptures of a giant woman striding across a field and a bishop confronting a king and queen. Farther on you come upon a flight of giant geese, a life-size giraffe browsing for twigs at the edge of a woods, and a huge, silvery crab with a gigantic, rust-colored mantis and a king cobra for companions. At a pond you see glistening aluminum bathers.

The creation of the Ashford Hollow Foundation for the Visual and Performing Arts, the park is altogether unique and charming. A map-board in the parking lot to the right of the entrance provides a detailed guide to the exhibits; trail maps are also available.
Open daily May–Oct.; all other times by private tour only. Admission charged, children under 12 free.
(716) 667-2808
www.griffispark.org

5 Rock City Park

Olean
Upon reaching this outlook high in the Allegheny Mountains (elevation 2,350 feet), one is at first riveted by the panoramic views. But the gigantic boulders of dramatic shapes and formations found here are the featured attraction.

Estimated to be 500 million years old, the rocks, known as pudding stone, are a quartz conglomerate formed at the bottom of a prehistoric sea. During the uplifting of this mountain system, the rocks were exposed to the surface. When the shale beneath the pudding stone began to erode, the rocks toppled, creating the unusual forms seen today.

The trail, winding through Rock City, starts and ends near Signal Rock, once used by American Indians for their signal fires. Walking single file, you squeeze through narrow passageways, pass beneath great overhanging boulders, and descend into crevasses carved out by extinct waterfalls. On the last leg of the trail you climb a stone stairway said to have been built by the Indians for easier access to the top, which served as a fortress. (The trip takes about 45 minutes.)

In June, pink and white mountain laurel bloom in profusion, and many other plants flower beneath the maples, hemlocks, pines, and oaks on the hillsides.
Open daily May–Oct. Admission charged.
(716) 372-7790
www.enchantedmountains.org/
outdoor/parks.shtml

6 Letchworth State Park

35 miles south of Rochester
Rich in history and scenic beauty, this 14,350-acre park stretches along 17 miles of one of the most spectacular gorges in the eastern United States. Three waterfalls accent the twisting Genesee River as it cascades through valleys and canyons where the cliffs at some places tower nearly 600 feet. This awesome setting, together with the area's Iroquois and pioneer heritage, has helped to make the 1907 gift of land from Buffalo businessman William Pryor Letchworth a diverse park with year-round recreational opportunities.

The roadway wandering through the center of the park provides easy access to scenic vistas. The park offers highly developed recreation areas (including two swimming pools), an extensive system of 20 hiking trails, a fishing pond stocked with trout, and the Pioneer and Indian Museum, which highlights the culture of the region's original inhabitants, the Senecas, and the lifestyle of the early pioneers.

On a bluff near the museum a statue marks the grave of Mary Jemison, known as "the White Woman of the Genesee." Captured as a young girl by the Senecas during the French and Indian War, Mary adopted tribal ways, married, and bore eight children to two Seneca husbands.

Accommodations in the park range from the Glen Iris Inn, originally Mr. Letchworth's home, to rustic cabins and campsites. One of the many picnic areas in the park is on the site of a "ghost town" abandoned in the mid-1800s with the failure of the Genesee Valley Canal. Remains of the canal can be seen in the park.

For the truly adventurous, one can arrange both white-water rafting and hot-air balloon trips during the spring, summer, and fall. There is also a winter recreation area maintained for crosscountry skiing, skating, snowmobiling, and tube-sledding.
Open year-round. Admission charged.
Museum open mid-May–Oct.
(585) 493-3600
www.nysparks.state.ny.us

7 Hamlin Beach State Park

Camp Rd., Hamlin

Stretching for three miles along the breeze-swept shore of Lake Ontario, this park is especially appealing in summertime. It has a mile of sandy beach, picnic tables, a ball field, walkways along the water's edge, campsites with electrical hookups, and a launching area for car-top boats. Fishermen here are likely to catch trout, bullheads, bass, and salmon.

The park's most unusual and interesting feature, however, is the Yanty Creek Nature Trail, which is being designed for use by both sighted and blind visitors and, for part of its length, for wheelchairs. The trail, nearly a mile long, leads through various ecological environments: deciduous woods, marshland, a coniferous woodlot, an old field returning to scrub and wood, and a pond. At frequent intervals the path will be posted with signs, in both braille and print, describing what you can—or are likely to—see, hear, touch, and even smell.

There are four elevated platforms that overlook the Yanty Creek, where one can watch for wildlife and birds. An information hut on the trail posts a list of the 74 species of birds sighted in the park, among them the bald eagle. In the springtime the pleasure of the walk is enhanced by the wild roses and dogwood blossoming beneath the oaks and white pines.

Accessible year-round; picnic area open mid Apr.–mid-Oct.; campground open May–Columbus Day. Camping is available year-round in B Loop. Admission charged Apr.–Thanksgiving for day use.
(585) 964-2462
www.nysparks.state.ny.us

8 Naples Valley

Off the southern tip of Canandaigua Lake

If you wander around the village of Naples in the Finger Lakes region of western New York, you'll notice a particular fondness for grapes and the color purple. Here, the fire hydrants are painted purple. The police cars are painted purple—and they even have grapes painted on the doors.

This is a place where 70,000 grape pies are sold every year, where a GrapeFest is held each September, and where two wineries open their doors to the public for tastings and tours. The Seneca Nation of the of the Iroquois tribe named the spot where the village and lake are located Kanandarque, or "the chosen spot."

The village itself is a picturesque throwback to the 1950s, with a single Main Street and offshoots fanning up into the glacier-created Bristol Hills. Surrounded by the Hi-Tor Wildlife Management Area, with its turkey, deer, and the occasional bear, the spot where Naples is set is so beautiful, even longtime residents take the two-hour paddleboat tour around the lake to enjoy the fall foliage.

Wizard of Clay Pottery, north on Route 20A, spirits away fallen leaves from the hills and incorporates them into its Bristol-leaf pottery glazes. Fifteen studios offer an array of creations, from wildlife sculptures to glass works to pottery, as well as traditional art on canvas.

Hiking trails in Ontario County Park at Gannett Hill connect to the extensive Finger Lakes Trail System, and Grimes Glen's 60-foot waterfall in the village is a restorative sight. The Bristol Mountain Winter Resort, not too far north on Route 64, helps make the area an all-season wonderland.

Open year-round.
(877)386-4669
www.naplesvalleyny.com

9 Montour Falls

West Main St., village of Montour Falls

Almost as high as Niagara, these beautiful falls descend in three tiers to form a dramatic all-seasons backdrop for the village, spectacular

6 Letchworth State Park. *This gorge, located entirely within the state park, sweeps on for a stunning 17 miles.*

in summer and sparkling with sheets of ice in winter.

The falls were named Chequaga (Tumbling Waters) by the band of Seneca Indians who came here from Pennsylvania in the 1760s with their matriarch, Catharine Montour. Catharine, of French and Indian descent, was chosen to be the leader of their small group following the death of her husband, a Seneca chief. Intelligent and progressive, she traveled extensively as a representative of her people and was popular in society.

The group chose to move north during the American Revolution. Catharine returned to this beloved spot after the war to live out her life. She died in 1804 at the age of 94. A marker in her honor is found in Cook Cemetery in the village of Montour Falls.

The village's historic district is known for its handsome Greek Revival buildings. Several of these are on the *National Register of Historic Places.* They include the public library, built in 1864 in the form of a Greek cross with a porch supported by Doric columns, and the 19th-century county clerk's office, a porticoed building of mellow red brick that is now used as a private law office.

At Havana Glen, a two-mile-long ravine on the edge of the village, a series of low waterfalls cascades through the woods, forming an occasional quiet pool. Its tranquil beauty has made it a favorite place with nature lovers. An inviting picnic and camping area is located at the lower end of the ravine.

Open daily May–Oct.
(800) 607-4552
www.schuylerny.com

10 Taughannock Falls State Park. *The view of the falls changes with each new season.*

10 Taughannock Falls State Park
Rte. 89, 8 miles north of Ithaca

Before the Continental Army marched through this area of the Finger Lakes in 1779, the Cayuga people, who lived in a village at Taughannock Falls, and who were in the area for hundreds of years, decided to flee.

During the 19th century settlers harnessed the power of Taughannock Creek to power mills and a gun factory, and in the 1870s a resort was developed in the area. As tourism here declined at the end of the century, the resort failed, and in 1925, on a tract of 64 acres, the state park was established. Today it includes almost 800 acres.

The falls, 33 feet higher than Niagara, plunge 215 feet into a natural amphitheater created by thousands of years of erosion

and the effects of seasonal melting and freezing. They are named, according to legend, in memory of Chief Taughannock of the Lenape Indians who was thrown over the cascade to his death after a disastrous battle with the Cayugas. Hiking trails lead along the north and south rims of the gorge and to the foot of the falls.

Taughannock Creek empties into Cayuga Lake, where a delta formed by the stream provides a site for picnic grounds, a boat launch, and a swimming beach.

The park has campsites, cabins, a bathhouse, and a marina, and in winter offers ice skating.
Park open year-round; campsites open Apr.–mid-Oct. Admission charged. (607) 387-6739
www.nysparks.state.ny.us

11 Lorenzo
Cazenovia

Sent to America in 1790 by Dutch investors to find land for development, John Lincklaen reached the rolling hills at the tip of Lake Cazenovia and stopped. "Situation superb, fine land," he wrote back. Authorized to proceed, he purchased 120,000 acres, laid out the village of Cazenovia (named for his company's manager), built roads and mills, and promoted the development of the region.

On a knoll overlooking the lake, Lincklaen built a magnificent Federal-style mansion in 1807 and named it Lorenzo, apparently after Lorenzo de' Medici. Formal and gracious, with a severe brick façade highlighted by delicately proportioned blind arches, the house provided an appropriate setting for entertaining the notables of his time.

The property, occupied by the Lincklaen/Ledyard families for 160 years, was purchased in 1968 by the state of New York as a historic site. Now a museum, it is furnished with family possessions. On the surrounding grounds are formal gardens, groves of trees, walks, and a carriage house containing a wonderful collection of 19th-century horse-drawn vehicles.

Allow time for a tour of Cazenovia. One of the most beautiful villages in the Northeast, it has a charming main street and hundreds of fine old houses, mostly Victorian and carefully maintained. *Open Wed.–Sun., May–Oct.; special hours in Dec. Grounds open year-round.* (315) 655-3200

12 Sackets Harbor

This small lakeside village with its calm, relaxed air was not always so. During the War of 1812 the settlement, situated beside a bluff commanding access to the St. Lawrence River and blessed with a fine harbor, became an important naval base for the United States, which hoped to take Canada and expel the British. Soldiers, sailors, marines, and shipbuilders arrived here by the thousands; timber was cut, barracks flung up, a shipyard established, and a fleet built. Twice the British attacked, each time unsuccessfully, but the second assault, in May 1813, left Sackets Harbor almost demolished.

With the approach of winter in 1814, nearly 3,000 workers were engaged in constructing two vessels that would each carry 1,000 men. News of peace arrived before the ships were completed, and the young nation's largest shipbuilding venture was halted. Sackets Harbor, however, remained an active naval yard until the late 1800s.

The battlefield, a state historic

12 Sackets Harbor. *An 1892 water tower looms over the 1816 stone officers' quarters at the Madison Barracks in this historic village.*

site, is now a waterfront park offering views of Lake Ontario and a few reminders of the past. Nearby are officers' quarters built in 1847 and the 1817 Union Hotel, now called the Seaway Trail Discovery Center, with exhibits that give a view of life here during the War of 1812. Among the displays are the colorful tunics, breeches, smocks, pantaloons, and feathered hats worn then— a startling contrast to the drab practicality of uniforms today.

Grounds open year-round.
Visitors center open Memorial Day through Labor Day, and by appt.
(315) 646-2321
www.sacketsharborny.com

13 Frederic Remington Art Museum

303 Washington St., Ogdensburg
Housed in an 1809 white mansion, the home of George Hall, a boyhood friend of Remington's, the museum contains a most comprehensive collection of the artist's work.

Known as the foremost artist of the Old West, Frederic Remington was born in Canton, New York, in 1861 and spent most of his youth here in Ogdensburg, a town that claims him today as a native son. At 17 he left home to attend Yale University, where he studied art. With the exception of a brief stint at New York City's Art Students League, these classes were the only formal training he ever had—he was much more interested in boxing and football than in school. He soon headed west, where he began to work as an illustrator and artist.

The museum's collection of 70 Remington oils includes *The Charge of the Rough Riders,* which stirringly depicts the famous battle in Cuba during the Spanish-American War, when Remington was a war correspondent for the Hearst newspapers. Fourteen bronzes (among them *The Bronco Buster*), 140 watercolors, and many pen and ink sketches are also on display. You will see many of his personal belongings in the museum, including his rifles, Indian weapons, and a stuffed buffalo head.

Another collection which should not be missed is that of Remington's close friend, Sally James Farnham. Especially compelling are her bas-relief of Theodore Roosevelt, and her bronze sculpture of a cowboy and his horse, which was in Remington's personal collection.

Remington died in 1909 in Ridgefield, Connecticut.

Open year-round except major holidays.
(315) 393-2425
www.fredericremington.org

14 Eighth Lake Public Campground

Off Rte. 28
Adirondack Park is such an enormous wilderness, with 2,800 lakes and ponds, 31,000 miles of rivers and streams, and 42 mountains above 4,000 feet, that singling out a place from which to enjoy it can be a challenge. One delightful place is the Eighth Lake Public Campground, which extends from Seventh Lake to Eighth Lake, the easternmost of a series of lakes connected by the streams that form the Fulton Chain.

The campground has 121 sites, most of which can accommodate trailers up to 35 feet in length. The sites, some close to the water, are inviting alcoves in the forest offering privacy, cooking facilities, and picnic tables, but no hookups. Campers and day users will also find picnic areas, swimming beaches, and boat launches here.

Surrounded by quiet forests, the Fulton Chain offers beautiful, unspoiled waters for canoeing and a sense of remoteness, which is often heightened by the accompaniment of ducks or an occasional deer at the shore. Fishing is quite good, especially in the Seventh and Eighth lakes, which are cold enough for lake trout. Also caught here are smallmouth bass and occasionally landlocked salmon. Among the many trails in the area is one to Black Bear Mountain, two or three miles away, a suitable place for mountain climbing. Campsites may be crowded on weekends.

Open daily two weeks before Memorial Day–Columbus Day.
(315) 354-4120;
Reservations: (800) 456-2267.
www.reserveamerica.com

15 National Bottle Museum

76 Milton Ave., Ballston Spa
This museum preserves the history of bottle-making, which was one

15 National Bottle Museum. *A selection of 19th-century bottles shows an amazing variety of shapes, sizes, colors, and uses.*

of our nation's first industries in the early 1800s. There was an incredible demand for all types of glassware, from mineral water containers to whiskey flasks sought after by hard-working, lonely men settling the Western frontier.

Collectors, potential collectors —and even visitors with a more casual interest—will be intrigued by the examples on display here. The pieces, mostly organized by kind, range from milk bottles and fruit jars to bitters bottles and soda bottles.

One exhibit is a reconstructed pharmacy with bottles large and small, quaint and colorful, created for a remarkable variety of nostrums both herbal and alcoholic. Glassblowing tools and equipment are also shown.

All phases of the bottle-collecting hobby are covered in the books, articles, and other research materials in the library.

Open daily June–Sept. 30;
Mon.–Fri., Oct.1–May 31.
Admission charged.
(518) 885-7589
http://family.knick.net/nbm

16 Hanford Mills Museum
*County Rtes. 10 and 12,
East Meredith*

Seventeen historic buildings preserved and restored here offer a vivid insight into the development of rural American industry and technology in the late 19th and early 20th centuries. The original water-powered mill, built on the banks of Kortright Creek in the 1840s, was first used to saw lumber. Later a gristmill was added.

Then in 1860 David Josiah Hanford purchased the property and created a multifaceted business, adding a supply store and a woodworking shop that produced everything from architectural trim to milk boxes and buggy parts. Around the turn of the century Hanford's sons were among the first to harness the flow of water to generate power for rural electrification.

Today this rich heritage can be appreciated in a fine collection of over 200 antique milling machines, including the 12-foot-wide, 10-foot-diameter, 1926 Fitz waterwheel, shingle mills, barrel-top shapers, handhole cutters, and the eight-kilowatt dynamo that was used to produce electricity. A collection of early photographs provides a unique view of the social history of a rural area typical of the Northeast.

Special events are organized on many summer weekends, including an old-fashioned Fourth of July celebration, and a traditional ice harvest in February.
*Open daily May 1–Oct 30
Admission charged.*
(800) 295-4992
www.hanfordmills.org

17 Opus 40 and The Quarryman's Museum
Fite Road, Saugerties

One man's vision of paradise led to the monumental environmental structure and sculpture garden known as Opus 40 on the western shore of the Hudson River in Ulster County, 100 miles north of Manhattan. Harvey Fite took his inspiration from Mayan Ruins in Honduras, and spent almost 40 years of his life turning an abandoned bluestone quarry into a harmonious interplay of art, nature and light in the shadow of the Catskill Mountains.

Flame Woman, with her arms stretching to the clouds, is one of the sculptures tucked into the six-plus acre landscape. The center-piece is a whorl of fitted stone whose terraces twist around fountains, pools and trees, leading to a nine-ton monolith at the foot of Overlook Mountain. The sculptures can also be seen as a tribute to the industry that once thrived here, quarrying the bluestone and shipping it throughout the world.

Fite built the adjacent museum to house the traditional quarryman's tools he used in creating his magnum opus.
*Open Memorial Day–Columbus Day,
Fri.–Sun., plus holiday Mondays
Admission charged.*
(845) 246-3400
www.opus40.org

18 Huguenot Street
New Paltz

Even before King Louis XIV banned their religion (in 1685), many French Protestants, known as Huguenots, had exiled themselves, finding refuge in neighboring countries. From 1660-1675 several Huguenot families from die Pfalz (the Rhine-Palatinate) arrived in the Hudson Valley. They bought land from the American Indians, built log huts, and named their settlement after their previous home. In the 1680s they replaced the huts with steep-roofed stone houses.

Six of these quaint, medieval-looking dwellings remain on Huguenot Street, designated a National Historic Landmark with the claim of being "the oldest street in America with its original houses."

These were originally one-room structures, and the large family kitchens with enormous fireplaces and cupboards displaying pottery and old pewter are especially appealing. Also on Huguenot Street are the stone church, which was completely reconstructed in 1972 and rebuilt from its original 1717 plans, and the DuBois Fort (1705), used formerly as a home and meeting place and now as a visitors center.

Huguenot Street is heavily visited during the Colonial Street Festival the second Saturday in August, and is often visited by school groups on weekdays in May, June, September, and October.
*Open Tues.–Sun., May–Oct.
Admission charged.*
(845) 255-1660
www.hhs-newpaltz.org

19 Sam's Point Preserve
*Off Rte. 52 in Ulster County,
Cragsmoor*

Sam's Point Preserve, a 5,000 acre preserve owned by the Open Space Institute and managed by the Nature Conservancy, contains one of the best examples of a ridgetop dwarf pine barrens in the world. It is also part of the 90,000-acre Northern Shawangunk Mountains, whose cliffs, summits, and plateaus form a unique landscape of extraordinary ecological significance. Home to nearly 40 rare

17 Opus 40 and The Quarryman's Museum. *One man's dream turned a six-acre abandoned bluestone quarry into a sculpture garden.*

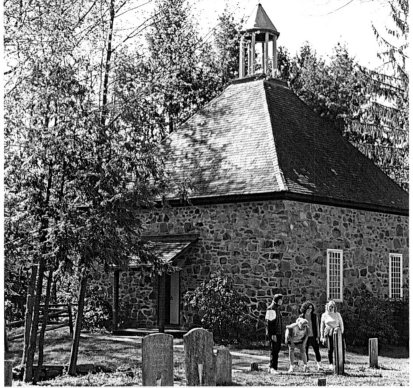

18 Huguenot Street. *This church was completely reconstructed from its original plans, which were drawn up in 1717.*

plants and animal species and three rare natural communities, the Northern Shawangunks represent one of the highest priorities for conservation in the Northeastern United States.

The preserve offers expansive views and hiking trails in a wilderness setting. Trails lead to Sam's Point, Verkeerderkill Falls, High Point, Indian Rock, and the Ice Caves. Sam's Point, a scenic overlook, provides views of the Shawangunk Ridge stretching for miles to the southwest and northeast. On a clear day, High Point Monument, the highest point in New Jersey, can be viewed. The Ice Caves, a favorite destination for hikers, were formed along fractures in the bedrock and in a jumble of boulders or talus blocks that fell from the face of the cliff. Snow and ice enter the caves through openings at the top and can't escape. This refrigerated environment often preserves snow and ice into the summer.

Visitors should wear comfortable hiking boots and carry plenty of drinking water. The preserve is open year round from dawn to dusk. The Ice Caves are open seasonally, from late spring to late fall.
(845) 647-7989
www.nature.org

20 Muscoot Farm and Elephant Hotel
Farm on Rte. 100, off Rte. 35; Hotel at junction of Rtes. 100 and 202, Somers
It's worth delving into the luxuriant greenery of northern Westchester County's countryside to find this living history farm, originally owned by the inventor of "Mother Sill's Seasick Remedy." The elixir's success helped build Ferdinand T. Hopkins's fortune, and enabled his family to live on Muscoot Farm for three generations.

"Muscoot" means "by the swamp" in a local American Indian dialect. A red maple swamp, seven miles of woodland trails, and butterflies-in-residence are part of the farm's charm. The country gentleman's farming life, circa 1880 to 1950, is depicted in the original buildings. Barnyard animals, and events such as a "Victorian faerie" woodland walk and seasonal hayrides, appeal to young children.

The Federal-style Elephant Hotel houses the Somers Historical Society and Museum of the Early American Circus. It celebrates America's second elephant, Old Bet, brought here in 1804 by native son Hachaliah Bailey. The hotel was built by Bailey and later used as a meeting place for fellow menagerie owners. There is a wealth of circus information here, as well as local history. And make sure not to miss the display of Tom Thumb's suit. A special circus library is also on the premises, but appointments must be made in advance.

Although many residents commute to New York City, Somers' rural roads are heavily wooded, so it's easy to lose your way if you don't pay attention to the route numbers.
Muscoot Farm:
Open 10–4 daily year-round.
(914) 232-7118
www.westchestergov.com
Elephant Hotel:
Open Thurs., and on the 2nd and 4th Suns. of the month.
Donations accepted.
(914) 277-4977
www.westchesterny.com

21 Sagamore Hill National Historic Site
20 Sagamore Hill Rd., Oyster Bay
Sagamore Hill was built in 1884 for Theodore Roosevelt, who in 1901 was to become the 26th president of the United States. The large, rambling house and its surrounding 90 acres served as an idyllic setting for Roosevelt's large family and, for the years of his presidency, as the summer White House.

The future president's specifications for the 23-room house included a big piazza (or porch) facing west to view the sunset, a drawing room across the entire west end, and a library with a bay window facing south.

The piazza, overlooking Oyster Bay Cove and Long Island Sound, was the scene of many historic events, including the day in 1904 when Roosevelt, having served as president for three years after McKinley's assassination, learned he had been nominated to serve his country again.

On the library mantel the "ting-tang clock," so named by the Roosevelt children because of its unique sound, still ticks off the hours. Most imposing is the North Room, a 30- by 40-foot hall added in 1905, which became the center of family activity. Paneled in black walnut, swamp cypress, hazel, and mahogany, it contains Roosevelt's many hunting trophies, paintings, books, presidential memorabilia, and other treasures.
Open daily Memorial Day weekend through Labor Day weekend; the rest of the year, closed Mon. and Tues. Admission charged; children under 16 free.
(516) 922-4788
www.nps.gov/sahi

22 Jacques Marchais Museum of Tibetan Art

338 Lighthouse Ave., Staten Island
Two stone buildings, designed to resemble a Tibetan Buddhist gompa, or monastery, are sited on a terraced hillside, with stone-paved garden walks, planted patios, a lotus pond, and a magnificent view of New York City's Lower Bay. These buildings house the only museum in the United States that concentrates on Tibetan and Buddhist art.

The museum, opened in 1947, was the vision of Jacqueline Norman Klauber, who used the professional name Jacques Marchais. She designed the buildings and assembled the collection, including an extensive library on Oriental art, philosophy, and history. The serenity here has impressed even visitors from Tibet.

The main museum building, a replica of a Tibetan temple, features a large tiered platform with ritual figurines and objects arranged like a Tibetan altar.

22 Jacques Marchais Museum of Tibetan Art. *Buddha watches over the gardens in tranquility.*

22 Jacques Marchais Museum of Tibetan Art. *Visitors can appreciate the beauty of this exotic Tibetan altar on display here.*

Colorful tankas (temple paintings on cloth) depicting Buddhas, bodhisattvas, and other deities decorate the walls. Among other highlights in the museum are a jewel-encrusted Nepalese shrine, Tibetan musical instruments, and a group of silver objects that once belonged to the Panchen Lama and are used in the Buddhist fire ritual ceremony. The center sponsors various public programs on weekends. Parking may be a problem.
Open Wed.–Sun. Admission charged.
(718) 987-3500
www.tibetanmuseum.com

23 Jamaica Bay National Wildlife Refuge

Brood Channel
Perhaps the most singular feature of this watery wilderness is its contrast to the surrounding cityscape. In spring and fall thousands of birds swoop down to these wetlands for shelter and food, unfazed by the millions of people rumbling by in cars and the jets roaring overhead. In proximity, humans and birds follow their own rhythms.

For city people, the 9,155-acre refuge (which has seven miles of paths) offers easy access to the natural world. Most visitors come during the migratory seasons, when herons, egrets, hooded mergansers, warblers, hawks, and roughly 150 other feathered species are seen here.

But the summer and winter are also rewarding times to visit the refuge, not only for birding but for enjoying the scenery, the relative peace, and the pleasant illusion of being nowhere—but still within the sight of Manhattan's skyline.

The refuge is particularly lovely in wintertime, when crystals of ice form on the trees and grasses and the sense of solitude is heightened.
Open daily except Christmas and New Year's Day.
(718) 318-4340
www.nps.gov/gate

24 Bayard Cutting Arboretum

Off Rte. 27A. Take the Southern State Parkway to Exit 45 East, Great River.
In the mid-1700s, English gardening was revolutionized by the informal, parklike landscape designed by Lancelot ("Capability") Brown. One of his admirers a hundred years later was Frederick Law Olmsted, the landscape architect best known as the creator of New York City's Central Park.

When William Bayard Cutting established his arboretum in 1887, he employed Olmsted's firm to design it. The garden, much in the style of Capability Brown, is a magnificent 690-acre park of trees, rhododendrons, azaleas, wildflower plantings, small ponds, and wide lawns that sweep down to the Connetquot River.

The names of the five trails through the grounds indicate the special characteristics of each: Pinetum, Wildflower, Rhododendron, Bird Watchers, and Swamp Cypress. All are detailed on a map available at the arboretum center.

The estate, donated to the Long Island State Park and Recreation Commission by Mrs. William Bayard Cutting and her daughter, Mrs. Olivia James, includes the former Cutting home, which now serves as a center for the arboretum. The interior is noted for the ornate oak paneling, stained glass windows, and handsome antique fireplaces. On display are collections of mounted birds, American Indian artifacts, and interesting plants. Near the entry is a spectacular specimen of a weeping European beech.

Rooms in both the mansion and the carriage house are reserved for concerts, classes, and horticultural exhibits.

Open Tues.–Sun. and legal holidays.
Admission charged early-Apr.–late Oct.
(631) 581-1002
www.nysparks.state.ny.us

25 Orient Beach State Park
Long Island Expressway (Rte. 495) east to end, then Rte. 25 east to Orient

That a state park exists here is due to the foresight of local farmers some 60 years ago. At that time the land was owned by the Male Taxpayers of Orient, a farmers organization with an interest in preserving this marshy peninsula as a barrier protecting their farms from the sea. In 1929 the organization donated the land to the state, hoping that the government would take over the burden of maintenance. The farmers plan worked, and in the early 1930s the park was established.

Today this 357-acre park is an inviting place for a family day trip. The five-mile-long peninsula in quiet Gardiner's Bay provides 10 miles of sand-and-pebble beach, a small portion of which is reserved for swimming. The lifeguards on duty and the gentle waters here make it suitable for children. The large picnic area is shaded by a grove of cedars. Fishing is allowed from the shore, but boats may not be launched. Flounder and snapper are the likely catch.

Open daily year-round except Christmas.
(631) 323-2440
www.nysparks.state.ny.us

26 Morton National Wildlife Refuge
Noyack Rd., Sag Harbor

Long before the 17th century, when Europeans invaded eastern Long Island, this narrow strip of land between Little Peconic and Noyack bays was the home of the Montauk and Shinnecock Indians, who farmed and fished and traded with the Corchaugs, their relatives on the North Shore. The property was deeded in 1679 to John Jessup, who had come here from Massachusetts some 40 years earlier. Known as Jessup's Neck, the peninsula has 187 acres of woodlands, salt marshes, sandy shores, and a freshwater pond.

After almost 200 years of private ownership and use as farmland, the property was given by Mrs. Elizabeth Morton to the U.S. Fish and Wildlife Service in 1954; the land is now slowly reverting to its natural state.

The refuge is an important resting and feeding stop for birds on their seasonal migrations. Since 1956, when the refuge was established, more than 200 species of waterfowl, songbirds, hawks, and waders have been observed. Black ducks, goldeneyes, and scaups are among those staying in the area all winter. An observation blind on the bank of the small pond is a great boon to bird-watchers.

The refuge also harbors white-tailed deer, foxes, raccoons, and opossums, and the tidal waters abound with bluefish, weakfish, clams, scallops, and oysters.

A one-mile self-guiding nature trail leads through woods of oak, sumac, and juniper, and past quiet ponds and marshes to the beach. Guided tours and educational programs are available on request.
Open year-round.
(631) 286-0485
http://northeast.fws.gov/ny/lirc.htm

27 Women's Rights National Historical Park & National Women's Hall of Fame
Seneca Falls

The same kind of rebellious zeal that motivated America's founding fathers to envision the Declaration of Independence also fired the passions of the 19th-century women who, chafing at their limited opportunities, went on to lead the women's rights movement. Thomas Jefferson's document was their model.

"We hold these truths to be self-evident, that all men and women are created equal" is a line from their Declaration of Sentiments, presented at the first Women's Rights Convention in July 1848 in this small mill town between Syracuse and Rochester. The 19th Amendment to the Constitution was not ratified until 1920, when women were granted basic rights —voting and property ownership among them—that we take for granted today.

The historical park focuses on sites in and around Seneca Falls, like the home of movement organizer Elizabeth Cady Stanton, and the Wesleyan Methodist Chapel, where the convention took place. There is a modern visitors center, and a 100-foot-long waterwall engraved with the Declaration of Sentiments and its signers' names. The park includes the M'Clintock House on East Williams Street in neighboring Waterloo, where the declaration was drafted.

Stanton delivered her famous speech calling for women's suffrage not far from the building that now houses the National Women's Hall of Fame, conceived in 1969. Anthropologist Margaret Mead and astronaut Sally Ride are examples of the women whose lives are honored here with interactive displays and biographical information.
Historical Park:
Open year-round except federal holidays in fall and winter. Admission charged.
(315) 568-2991
www.nps.gov/wori
Hall of Fame:
Open Mon.–Sun., May through Sept.;
Wed.–Sun., Oct. through Apr.;
Gallery closed in Jan.
Admission charged.
(315) 568-8060
www.greatwomen.org

26 Morton National Wildlife Refuge. *This is a true birders paradise: Here, one can enjoy studying a colony of terns without disturbing them.*

Nantahala Gorge. *The gorge's Nantahala River has a number of interesting offshoots, including the cascading waters of Big Laurel Falls.*

North Carolina

The remarkable diversity of its out-of-the-way places is a cordial invitation to explore the byways of this pleasant state.

The deep, dramatic gorge that attracts river-runners, hikers, and fishermen contrasts sharply with the serenity of the farm where Carl Sandburg, the "people's poet," spent his last years.

In two state-owned settings are colorful displays of native wildflowers and flowering trees. Museums here are dedicated to such subjects as 12,000 years of American Indian cultures, a pre-Revolutionary battle, two Civil War forts, gold mining, the good works of country doctors and a progressive governor, and a village that time almost forgot. And stop to enjoy a famous Revolution-era town and discover why one British general surely must have wished he had never left.

1 Nantahala Gorge
12 miles southwest of Bryson City

Carved by the Nantahala River, this eight-mile gorge takes its name from a Cherokee word meaning "land of the noonday sun." Indeed, the canyon here is so deep and narrow that only when the sun is directly overhead can its rays reach the bottom of the gorge.

The gorge burrows down some 1,800 feet at its deepest and is less than 100 yards wide at its narrowest. It is the centerpiece of the Nantahala National Forest, with easy access to the Appalachian Trail, which crosses the eastern end of the gorge.

The river offers a variety of recreational opportunities. Water released from the Duke Power dam several miles upriver rushes down the gorge for about 12 hours on most days, creating an ideal run for whitewater rafting.

Rafts, canoes, and kayaks may be rented in the area, and the trip, while exhilarating, is not overly challenging for novices. Picnic areas are maintained, and the river is stocked with trout; fishing is better in the calm evening waters than in the daytime torrents.

Open year-round.
(800) 867-9246
www.greatsmokies.com

1 Nantahala Gorge. *The rushing waters of the Nantahala River cut a deep, narrow path through the gorge and create ideal whitewater rafting conditions.*

2 Land of the Waterfalls
Brevard

Up in the Pisgah National Forest, at an elevation of 2,230 feet, you could be forgiven for thinking you've veered off the Blue Ridge Parkway into an outdoor lover's dream world.

Start with crystal clear streams full of trout; lakes offering up bream, bass, and crappie; and rivers crying out for swimming and tubing. Add outdoor sports and activities of all description, easily available during the more than 200 clear days per year here. And of course, audible around seemingly every bend of the road are the signature splashes of countless waterfalls.

It certainly seems like all the heaven and nature visitors could ever want, but there is another dimension to Transylvania County: its scenic loveliness, courtesy of the Blue Ridge Mountains, is also a mecca for artists. The county's name is from the Latin "across the woods." Brevard, its main city, hosts annual arts and music festivals, and many cultural offerings are on the program at Brevard College's Paul Porter Performing Arts Center.

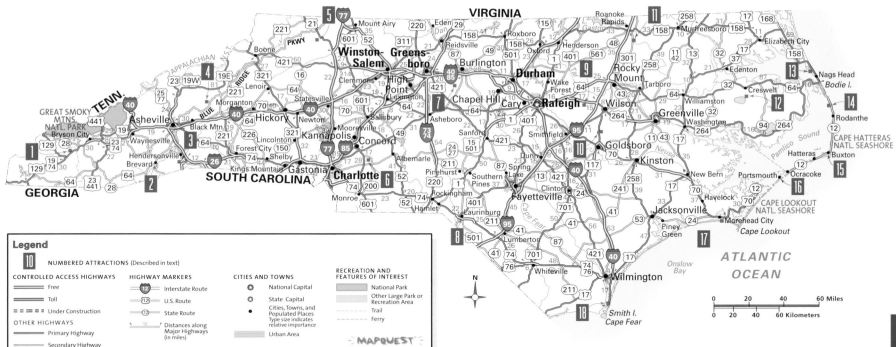

Take the 77-mile Forest Heritage National Scenic Byway and enjoy a palette of burnished autumn colors. Glide your canoe down the French Broad River, where timber floated to market.

And then there are the falls, more than two dozen around the area that are open to visitors. Whether you stop at Looking Glass, Slippery Witch, Turtleback, Pounding Mill, or the impressive 411-foot Whitewater Falls, always keep in mind the precautions of the U.S. Forest Service rangers: Stay away from the falls' spray area, never climb on rocks around waterfalls, and do not walk in the river above any waterfall.

Open year-round. In winter, portions of Blue Ridge Parkway may be closed for cross-country skiing.
(800) 648-4523
www.visitwaterfalls.com

3 Carl Sandburg Home National Historic Site

Flat Rock
Named Connemara by previous owners, who likened its view of the distant Blue Ridge Mountains to that of a mountainous region in western Ireland, this was Carl Sandburg's last home. Though perhaps best known as a son of the Midwest, the poet and two-time Pulitzer Prize–winner lived here for 22 years until his death in 1967.

Large but unpretentious, the 1830s clapboard structure stands as a memorial to the man and his work, and its interior reflects his life at the height of his career. In the living room his guitar leans against a favorite easy chair, and magazines from the 1940s lie in untidy stacks on tables and across the floor. Over the fireplace is a framed photograph of Sandburg and his wife taken by his brother-in-law, Edward Steichen.

3 Carl Sandburg Home National Historic Site. *The main house at Connemara, where Carl Sandburg lived from 1945 until his death in 1967 at age 89.*

A large office contains a typewriter surrounded by piles of books and cardboard boxes filled with research material and notes. On his desk, giving the impression that he has left only momentarily, lies one of the green eyeshades he invariably used.

A self-guiding walk leads to the farm area, and trails cross the pastures and woodlands of the 260-acre park, leading up Big Glassy Mountain (about 2 1/2 miles round-trip), where bluebirds vie for attention with the wildflowers. A small, wooded picnic area is near the visitors center. Expect crowds in late spring and foliage season.

Open year-round except Christmas.
Admission charged.
(828) 693-4178
www.nps.gov/carl

 Stone Mountain State Park. *The imposing granite dome of Stone Mountain dominates the scenery at this park, while fishing and hiking dominate the fun.*

4 Crabtree Meadows Recreation Area

About 10 miles north of Celo
Named for the cloudlike pink blossoms of the flowering trees that highlight the meadows in May, this is a most appealing 253-acre picnic and camping stop on the Blue Ridge Parkway.

Columbines, crested dwarf irises, lady's slippers, and showy orchids also signal the spring season here, along with many songbirds. Raccoons, opossums, and white-tailed deer roam the meadows and adjacent forest. Also in residence are a few bobcats and black bears.

The picnic grounds are located in an area called "the loggy patch," a name it was given in the early 1800s by local farmers. At that time trees were killed by girdling so that crops could be grown underneath; the dead trunks were usually cut down later. In the loggy patch, however, the dead timber were left standing until they fell of their own accord, making the land more suitable to cattle raising than farming. Also dating from the early days are "the rye patch" and "the wheat patch."

A little hiking will reward you with some great views of Crabtree Meadows Falls, the other main attraction here. The three-mile trail from the picnic grounds is shaded by birches and hemlocks and includes four different overlooks of the falls and the surrounding Catawba Valley.

The park offers naturalist programs, nature walks, hiking trails, and tent and trailer campgrounds.
Open May–Oct.
(888) 233-6111
www.mcdowellnc.org/parks.htm

5 Stone Mountain State Park

7 miles southwest of Roaring Gap
Plunging waterfalls, granite outcroppings, narrow dirt roads, and trails twisting through catawba rhododendrons and mountain laurel populate this park's more than 14,000 acres.

Creeks stocked with trout—rainbows, browns, and "brookies"—make this a fisherman's paradise. In Bullhead Creek (a "Fish for Fun" stream where fly-fishermen may practice their techniques but must toss back their catch) rainbows as long as 26 inches have been hooked.

Trails lead to the 2,300-foot summit of rugged Stone Mountain, and you'll also find paths to Stone Mountain Falls, Cedar Rock, and Wolf Rock. Mountain climbers can choose from 13 different ascent routes, many of which are difficult and not recommended for beginners.

Throughout this densely forested area, lady's slippers, trilliums, bluets, and other wildflowers and ferns are often seen in settings that also frequently include feathered populations of red-tailed hawks, ruffed grouse, black vultures, wild turkeys, and owls. White-tailed deer, beavers, otters, minks, and foxes are occasionally glimpsed. Bears have also been reported but are extremely rare.
Open year-round except Christmas.
Fee for fishing.
(336) 957-8185
ils.unc.edu/parkproject/visit/stmo/ home.html

6 Reed Gold Mine State Historic Site

Stanfield
In 1799 the young son of German immigrant John Reed found a shiny rock in Little Meadow Creek near his father's farm. Unable to

6 Reed Gold Mine State Historic Site. *Learn the art of placer mining at this famous lode, where you can pan for gold in the creek—and keep what you find.*

identify its composition, the elder Reed used it as a doorstop until a jeweler offered him $3.50 for it in 1802; Reed sold it.

The shiny rock was a 17-pound chunk of gold—the first authenticated gold find in the young United States. Reed soon established a mining company, and in 1831 he expanded the operation from placer mining (creek panning) to underground mining, an operation that continued under several ownerships until 1912.

Guided tours of the site today take you through a maze of mine shafts, restored to memorialize the nation's first gold rush.

A large building near the mine contains a restored 1895 stamp mill, used today to demonstrate how, with several crushing blows, gold can be extracted from quartz. At the panning area, visitors are shown how to separate gold from soil. Lucky panners may keep their strikes. Gold objects serving monetary and other purposes are displayed in old bank and office safes at the visitors center.

A self-guiding nature trail winds through the fields and forests of this 822-acre historic site. A picnic area is across the road from the main entrance.

Open Tues.–Sun. year-round, but panning site open Apr.–Oct. Fee for panning.
(704) 721-4653

www.ah.dcr.state.nc.us/sections/hs/ reed/reed.htm

---

7 Alamance Battleground State Historic Site

Burlington
On May 16, 1771, more than two years before the Boston Tea Party, a brief revolt here ended in defeat for about 2,000 of the then-colony's

7 Alamance Battleground State Historic Site. *The annual celebration here during Colonial Living Week in October brings the 18th century to life.*

independent western frontiersmen, who stood in armed rebellion against the royal governor and the colonial militia.

Known as "Regulators," these men and their families had been voicing increasing dissatisfaction with the corruption of British rule for years. They began acting on their frustration early in 1771 by refusing to pay taxes. After warnings from the governor, a royal militia was sent to challenge the upstart Regulators.

For all their justifiable anger, the poorly trained and ineffectively led frontiersmen were unable to prevail against the Crown. Their efforts, however, were not in vain. Their bold use of armed resistance became well known around the colonies and set the stage for the coming battle for independence.

Flags on the battlefield show where each side stood, and a

bronze map explains the events that took place. A granite monument dedicated in 1880 commemorates the battle.

Another attraction on the grounds is the 1780 Allen House, an oak and ash log dwelling typical of those built by settlers of the era on this frontier. A clock with wooden gears, a walnut desk, and other original furnishings evoke the homespun comforts of the past. The visitors center displays weapons and uniforms and presents a brief audiovisual show.

Expect crowds for the many special events that take place here during Colonial Living Week in mid-October.

Open Mon.–Fri. year-round.
(336) 227-4785

www.burlington-area-nc.org/ attrc-alamancebattleground.htm

---

8 Indian Museum of the Carolinas

Laurinburg
The museum's emphasis is on the early American Indians of the Carolinas, a region that was enriched by more than 45 different Indian cultures. The history of the tribes here dates back more than 12,000 years.

Their present-day descendants include Cherokees, Coharies, Tuscaroras, Waccamaw-Siouans, Catawbas, and Lumbee. North Carolina, in fact, has the largest Indian population in the eastern United States.

The museum's mission is to compare the lives of these groups with other cultures, and so its exhibits include American Indian artifacts and examples of tribal customs from all around the United States and South America.

The permanent collection contains more than 200,000 artifacts, some more than 10,000 years old. In the 40 different exhibits are examples of pottery, stone tools and weapons, jewelry, and dugouts. Contemporary paintings add further dimension to the rich displays here.

Tours of the museum and slide presentations are conducted by a staff archaeologist. The excellent research library and the museum's collection are available to students and scholars.

Evolving exhibits include one that focuses on the various plants cultivated by the Indians of the Carolinas, and how the plants were used for foods, fibers, dyes, and medicine.

Open Wed., Thurs., and Sun. year-round.
(910) 276-5880

9 The Country Doctor Museum
Bailey

In the rough and tumble environment of rural America's yesteryear, country doctors had to set bones, deliver babies, combat disease, and even prepare their own prescriptions. This museum demonstrates their multiple talents with a fine display of instruments, medical books, handwritten notes, and office equipment.

The collection is housed in a pair of connected 19th-century buildings once used by two North Carolina country doctors: Dr. Howard Franklin Freeman's office dates to 1857, and Dr. Cornelius Henry Brantley's to 1887. In the front room is a vast wooden cabinet displaying apothecary jars and a large rolltop desk with cubbyholes for prescriptions and bills.

Civil War surgeons' amputation kits, a hinged leather artificial leg, turn-of-the-century obstetric instruments, and a model of a doctor's horse and buggy help to illustrate the history of medicine in the United States from about 1800 to the early 1900s.

One interesting exhibit shows the tools used to amputate the left arm of Confederate Gen. Thomas "Stonewall" Jackson in 1863. Ironically, Jackson, who was shot accidentally by his own men, died eight days later, a devastating loss for the Confederates.

Walk across a small garden of medicinal plants to the Art of Nursing exhibit, showcasing uniforms and equipment of the trade spanning the last 200 years.

Open Tues.–Sun. year-round.
Admission charged.
(252) 235-4165

10 Governor Charles B. Aycock Birthplace

2 miles south of Fremont
As governor of North Carolina from 1901–05, Charles B. Aycock improved the state's public education system; over 1,000 schools were built during his tenure.

10 Governor Charles B. Aycock Birthplace. *The simple, original buildings here reflect the humble beginnings of the man known as the "Education Governor."*

The youngest of 10 children, Aycock was born in 1859 in the simple, unpainted frame house that is now the main attraction at this 19th-century farm complex. Among family furnishings on display are a pine chest, side table, and an assortment of frames. Two shed rooms flanking the front porch were used occasionally by travelers in need of lodging.

A restored kitchen in a separate building contains a large fireplace with many early pots and pans, along with a dining room. The original smokehouse, pantry, stable, and corn barn are still standing. An 1893 one-room schoolhouse was moved to the site and furnished with desks and blackboards, bringing to life rural education in the state at the turn of the 20th century.

Guided tours originate at the visitors center, where a small exhibit area displays Aycock's gold-headed cane, law books, and replicas of his law office and the parlor of his home in Raleigh.

An audiovisual program describes Aycock's life and significant contributions to education.

Special events are scheduled throughout the year, and living-history demonstrations include candle dipping, spinning, and other home crafts.

Open Mon.–Sat. Apr.–Oct., and Tues.–Sat. Nov.–Mar.
(919) 242-5581
www.ah.dcr.state.nc.us/sections/hs/ aycock/aycock.htm

11 Historic Halifax State Historic Site

The British general Lord Cornwallis briefly occupied Halifax in 1781 with his massive army, which comprised the bulk of the Crown's forces in the colonies.

As visitors here do today, Cornwallis should have considered staying longer and enjoying all this historic town has to offer; instead, he and his army continued

9 The Country Doctor Museum. *This collection illustrates the history of medicine in the 19th century, including more than 2,000 medical books from the era.*

their fateful march north to Yorktown and the humiliating defeat that essentially ended the American Revolution.

Even at the time of Cornwallis's visit, this was a busy commercial and social center; its restored area continues to reflect the aura of prosperity enjoyed here from 1760 through the late 1830s, when the railroad left the town behind and its commerce and political influence soon waned.

The area's colorful past is dramatized in an audiovisual show at the visitors center. Additional displays in an adjacent museum depict the early local tobacco and fur trade, along with the elegant lifestyle of the Roanoke Valley's planter gentry.

Guided tours include the Constitution–Burgess House, which, according to one tradition, is where the first constitution of North Carolina was framed. (It later became the property of Thomas Burgess, a local lawyer.)

Also shown are two tavern-hotels, an early jail and town clerk's office, and typical homes of the area's merchants and planters. Tours start at the visitors center.

Special events run throughout the year to honor the town's past and its important role as a recruiting center and weapons depot during the Revolution. An annual celebration in April remembers the Halifax Resolves of 1776, the colony's bold call for independence from England—considered the first such by any colony.

Open year-round.
(252) 583-7191

**www.ah.dcr.state.nc.us/sections/hs/
halifax/halifax.htm**

12 Somerset Place State Historic Site and Pettigrew State Park
Creswell
History and recreation blend nicely in this 17,873-acre park, part of which was once a coastal plantation named for the home county of its English owner, Josiah Collins.

His grandson built a handsome clapboard mansion on his ancestral land around 1830. The mansion's distinguishing features include

12 Somerset Place State Historic Site. *A walk through the elegant mansion and its well-appointed grounds brings the plantation era to life.*

marble fireplaces, wood-grain painted doors, and wide porches. A rare 1850 Wilson sewing machine and a toy stagecoach with beeswax horses are further reminders of the past. Close by are the kitchen, dairy, icehouse, and other clapboard outbuildings, and a formal garden adds to the gentrified feel here.

The park is named for Confederate Gen. James Pettigrew, who led the famous and deadly charge on Cemetery Ridge at the Battle

of Gettysburg on July 3, 1863—a turning point in the Civil War.

Nine miles of trails penetrate the park's virgin forest of huge oaks, bald cypresses, poplars, and sweetgums, which shelter pileated woodpeckers, big-eared bats, and black bears. A major attraction is Phelps Lake, second largest in the state and famous for the largemouth bass that entice anglers from near and far. Many ducks and geese can be seen on the lake in winter. The park has a picnic area, trailer and tent campsites, bicycle trails, scenic overlooks, a fishing pier, and a boat ramp.

Park open year-round;
Somerset Place open daily Apr.–Oct.,
Tues.–Sun. Nov.–Mar.
Pettigrew Park: (252) 797-4475
Somerset Place: (252) 797-4560

**ils.unc.edu/parkproject/visit/pett/
home.html**

13 Nags Head Woods Ecological Preserve
Kill Devil Hills
An outstanding example of a mid-Atlantic maritime forest, this 1,400-acre preserve was created in 1978 through the cooperation of local citizens and the Nature Conservancy.

More than 60 different biotic communities are supported in the diverse environments here, from the wind-sculpted sands of Jockey's Ridge and Run Hill—the two largest dunes on America's East Coast—to the more than 40 small woodland ponds containing duckweed and rare water violets.

This rich ecological variety results from the protection the high dunes give delicate habitats from ocean wind and salt spray and from the often harsh climatic effects generated by the converging of the southern Gulf Stream and the northern Labrador Current just offshore.

An unusual ecological mosaic has been created here on the western shore, where freshwater marshes—formed by water draining from the island ridges—adjoin saltwater marshes among the offshore hammocks.

This is an ideal habitat for deer and river otters, as well as herons, egrets, geese, swans, and ducks. Some other feathered creatures seen along the nature trails are pileated woodpeckers, ospreys, and red-shouldered hawks. There are more than five miles of self-guiding trails.

Open Mon.–Fri. year-round;
Sat. in the summer.
(252) 441-2525

**nature.org/wherewework/northamerica/
states/northcarolina/preserves**

14 Pea Island National Wildlife Refuge

10 miles south of Nags Head
Each spring and fall, geese, ducks, and other migratory birds use the Atlantic Flyway for the same reason that travelers use the interstate highways—to get where they're going by the fastest route.

This sliver of an island—almost 13 miles long and no more than a mile across at its widest—is one of the eastern seaboard's finest vantage points to observe the migration. And beach lovers, fishermen, hikers, and photographers will also find much to enjoy here.

This complex of salt marshes and freshwater ponds supports otters, muskrats, nutrias, diamondback terrapins, and loggerhead, sea, and snapping turtles. Ring-necked pheasants abound, while egrets, herons, and ibises are among the waterfowl and shorebirds that nest here. Peregrine falcons are often seen during spring and fall migrations, and more than 250 other bird species are occasionally observed.

A number of strategically placed observation platforms facilitate sightings of all varieties, while freshwater ponds supporting ducks, geese, and swans are easily observed from the car.

Five access points to Atlantic beaches and one to Pamlico Sound along the western shore attract bathers. Anglers can cast for sea trout, channel bass, pompano, and bluefish. The island is heavily visited in spring and fall.
Open year-round.
(252) 473-1131
peaisland.fws.gov

15 Buxton Woods Coastal Reserve

Hatteras Island
Forests are rare on the Outer Banks, where wind and salt spray reign. But at Buxton, the island broadens to nearly four miles, and the distance from the ocean and higher elevations combine to create a fascinating example of ecological interdependence.

Here in the 825-acre forest, stunted trees form a protective canopy over the more fragile undergrowth, and this low foliage in turn stabilizes the soil that the trees need for their roots.

The three-quarter-mile loop of the pleasant self-guiding Buxton Woods Nature Trail offers an enlightening introduction to this symbiotic environment and its various inhabitants, many seldom found elsewhere on the islands.

Woodland songbirds and wetland egrets, herons, and grebes make the forest and adjoining marsh their home. Ospreys may be seen overhead, and in spring and fall the area is visited by migratory birds. Mammals, generally rare on the Outer Banks, live here too, including raccoons, otters, minks, nutrias, and white-tailed deer.
Open year-round.
(252) 473-2138
ncnerr.org/pubsiteinfo/siteinfo/buxton/ buxton.html

16 Portsmouth Village

For an adventure that's definitely off the beaten path, try this isolated island village, a 250-acre historic preserve administered by the National Park Service.

In the 1850s and 1860s the village prospered as a port in which cargo was transferred from seagoing ships to smaller boats for the journey inland. But shoaling of the inlet ended this enterprise, and by the 1890s most of the inhabitants had moved away.

Today some 20 old buildings stand as weather-beaten reminders of the struggle between men and the sea on the Outer Banks. Many of the buildings in this picturesque village have been restored and are open to the public. They include a Methodist church, lifesaving station, schoolhouse, post office, and the Salter-Dixon House, which now doubles as the visitors center.

The easiest access to Portsmouth Village is by a small passenger ferry from Ocracoke. You can also get there by taking a car ferry

from the town of Atlantic, which crosses to the southern end of the North Core Banks, some 20 miles south of the village.

If you leave from Atlantic, keep in mind that only four-wheel, over-sand vehicles can make the trip. For a list of all the ferry operators in the area and other information, call park headquarters.

And however you plan to get there, be sure to check the forecast in advance: The village is closed during inclement weather.

Open year-round, weather permitting.
Fee for ferry to island.
(252) 728-2250
www.nps.gov/calo/pv.htm

17 Fort Macon State Park
Atlantic Beach

Since the early 1700s, when the pirate Blackbeard used Beaufort Inlet as a hideout, its strategic importance has been well recognized. After several unsuccessful attempts to fortify the island, the construction of Fort Macon was begun in 1826 and completed eight years later.

But in the course of succeeding wars, the only action at this five-sided brick fort was on April 25, 1862, when it was shelled by Union forces after a long standoff and captured the next morning.

The fort, named for Nathaniel Macon, a North Carolina senator, is encircled by a moat that could be flooded with the tidewaters of Bogue Sound. From its impressive ramparts, which once overlooked the inlet, there are commanding views of the Beaufort region.

Circling the fort's inner grounds are quarters for the garrison, storerooms, and a kitchen. The commandant's quarters also have

18 Fort Fisher State Historic Site. *A diver in the Cape Fear Shoals saltwater marine exhibit—which houses sharks, barracudas, groupers, and loggerhead turtles—is part of the New North Carolina Aquarium at Fort Fisher.*

been restored, and there is a small museum.

In addition to the fort, the park offers a protected ocean swimming area, a sheltered picnic grounds with grills, and hiking. Fishermen will enjoy surf-casting from the park's shores.

Open year-round except Christmas.
(252) 726-3775
www.ils.unc.edu/parkproject/visit/foma/home.html

18 Fort Fisher State Historic Site
Kure Beach

Late in the Civil War the Union blockade of Southern ports prevented the South from receiving war supplies. To counter this, Confederate blockade runners made daring trips through fog and moonless nights to get precious cargoes.

Fort Fisher was built to provide cover for the Confederate seamen entering Cape Fear River on their way to the Confederacy's major port in Wilmington. Extending for one mile along the Atlantic Coast and across a sand peninsula, this series of redoubts was the South's largest earthen seacoast fort. With a complement of 47 guns, it provided a mile of defense seaward and one-third mile inland.

Only a few mounds remain, carefully preserved from the eroding action of wind and rain. Exhibits in a small museum detail events that took place here from December 1864 to January 1865, when the fort finally fell to a determined Union action that employed some 58 warships and 8,000 infantrymen.

A quarter-mile tour trail surrounds what remains of the fort

today. Features along the route include wayside exhibits, a reconstructed palisade fence, and a partially restored gun emplacement.

The visitors center offers audio-visual programs and a permanent exhibit hall that displays an extensive collection of artifacts from the blockaders and the blockade runners. Also here is a large and impressive fiber-optic–powered map that shows the final battle for the fort in 1865.

For a more peaceful theme, explore the New North Carolina Aquarium at Fort Fisher, a 22-acre beachfront complex that fronts the Atlantic Ocean. A wide variety of sea life is on display here.

Fort and aquarium open year-round, except holidays; admission for aquarium.
Fort: (910) 458-5538
Aquarium: (910) 458-8257
www.ah.dcr.state.nc.us/sections/hs/fisher/fisher.htm

18 Fort Fisher State Historic Site. *A conservatory at the New North Carolina Aquarium houses frogs, snakes, turtles, bass, catfish, and perch in this tree-filled atrium.*

Danish Mill. *The 18-foot-long vanes of the mill were covered with canvas sails and revolved about 100 times a minute.*

North Dakota

Here in the geographical center of North America are some fabulous landforms and bittersweet recollections of pioneer times.

Dramatic sections of badlands terrain can be seen in different parks, and the pioneer era is memorialized by a fine old wind-driven gristmill, a museum of impressive early-day farm machinery, and a reconstructed pioneer village with an extensive collection of memorabilia. The history of the inevitable and tragic conflict between the American Indians, whose land this was, and the settlers, who claimed it as their own, is recalled in the forts and Indian villages.

On a peaceful note are an international garden, sanctuaries for game and waterfowl, and a couple of good places to fish.

1 Writing Rock State Historic Site

12 miles northeast of Grenora

No one knows who etched the mysterious maplike network of lines, circles, and dots on the five-foot-high gray granite rock found at this site by Gen. Alfred Sully in 1864. And although the imaginative viewer can discern a bird in flight and other possible figures, no one is really sure what the ancient pictographs represent. Scholars speculate that the markings are the handiwork of a prehistoric people who were later driven away by repeated droughts.

The Plains Indians who settled in this region some 700 years ago held the markings in awe, and one of their many legends about the symbols contended that they changed from time to time to foretell the future. Some Indians continued to make pilgrimages here even after being resettled in other states.

Today the rock, together with a smaller, similarly etched specimen found about a mile away, is in a simple fieldstone building for protection from erosion by the harsh North Dakota weather. Here they stand as reminders of an ancient urge to communicate.

Open year-round.
(701) 328-2666
www.state.nd.us/hist

3 International Peace Garden. *This serene setting symbolizes the peaceful relationship that the United States and Canada share.*

2 Danish Mill

Kenmare

The two 1,800-pound grinding stones in this three-story windmill are the only originals in any of the six similar mills surviving in the United States. Built in 1902 by Christian Jensen, a Danish immigrant, the picturesque red-shingled mill ground up to 200 sacks of grain per day at its original site 11 miles to the north. It ceased operation in 1918 and is now a respected fixture in Kenmare's town square.

Visitors willing to climb the cramped stairway can inspect the heart of the great machine—hand-hewn maple gears. The speed of the gears, and thus of the grinding, was regulated by turning and trimming the four canvas sails that powered the mill.

Open year-round.
(701) 385-4857
www.kenmarend.com

3 International Peace Garden

Hwy. 281, north of Dunseith

This 2,300-acre wooded garden commemorates the heartening fact that the boundary between the United States and Canada is the longest undefended international

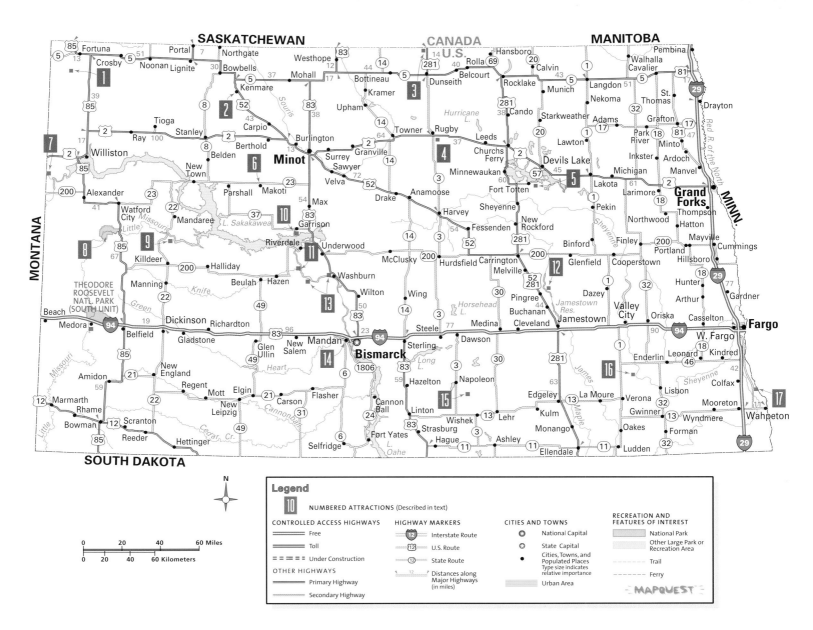

border in the world. On a monument marking the line the two nations pledge that ". . . as long as men shall live, we will not take up arms against one another."

The garden, on land donated by North Dakota and the Canadian province of Manitoba and dedicated in 1932, was the inspiration of Henry Moore, a Canadian horticulturist who believed that those who love flowers, trees, and the outdoors could be a powerful force for peace between nations.

Moore's dream of a garden symbolizing the human yearning for peace is beautifully realized here on the rolling foothills of the Turtle Mountains.

Two automobile tours—one in the Canadian half and the other in the United States—are each 3½ miles long and have several stopping places for sightseeing and picnicking. The Canadian Natural Drive winds past Lake Stormon through groves of birches, maples, and oaks. At the start of the United

States Cultural Drive is an 18-foot floral clock, which is one of the park's most photographed features. This drive also leads to the park's campground, International Music Camp, CCC lodge, and the Legion Sports Camp.

To enjoy the natural beauty more closely, one can take the 1½-mile Lake View Hiking Trail, where beavers may be seen at work. Another walk of the same length goes through the well-tended formal gardens marking

the nations' boundary line in the center of the park. It continues on past several reflecting pools and cascades to the 120-foot Peace Tower. Also to be found on this walk is a Peace Memorial in remembrance of the events of September 11, 2001.

Open daily year-round.
Admission charged.
(888) 432-6733

www.peacegarden.com

4 Geographical Center Prairie Village and Museum

Rte. 2, Rugby

When you visit this 20-acre park, you are halfway "from sea to shining sea." Nearby is a cairn marking the exact geographical center of the North American continent. The Atlantic, Pacific, and Arctic oceans and the Gulf of Mexico are all about 1,500 miles away.

The village consists of some 30 authentic North Dakota frontier homes, offices, a general store, livery stable, saloon, church, home-operated telephone exchange, and the stately windmill—that lonely sentinel of the prairie farmstead before the advent of modern power. Most were donated, moved to the site, restored, and furnished by local people and businesses.

Walking down the town's main street, you are transported back to the region's tempestuous past as part of the Dakota Territory. In the extensive collections of frontier memorabilia are reminders of the conflicts between the American Indians and the first settlers, who included many Scandinavians, Germans, and Russians.

A fascinating railroad exhibit features an 1886 Great Northern Railroad depot and, on the other side of the tracks, a hobo jungle.

The museum houses a colorful array of frontier artifacts that include feathered Indian head-dresses, a fine beaded vest once worn by a Chippewa medicine man, and old photographs and postcards showing how towns in the area looked in the early days. Among other collections are old clocks, lamps, firearms, and mounted specimens of native birds and animals. The museum also has records of a local youth reputed to be the world's tallest man.

Open Mon.–Sat. and P.M. Sun., May–Sept. Admission charged.
(701) 776-6414
http://rugbynorthdakota.com/ attractions.htm

5 Fort Totten State Historic Site and Sullys Hill National Game Preserve

Hwy. 20/57 S, Spirit Lake

In the summer of 1876 troopers of the U.S. 7th Cavalry rode from the fort into the pages of history. They were assigned to join another cavalry unit commanded by the flamboyant Lt. Col. George A.Custer in a punitive expedition against American Indians led by chiefs Sitting Bull and Crazy Horse. The confrontation at the Little Bighorn region of Montana is recalled today as Custer's last stand.

Fort Totten is the best preserved of all forts west of the Mississippi built during the turbulent days of the Plains Indian wars, and Infantry Post looks much as it did on that fateful day more than a century ago. Restored officers' and enlisted men's quarters, the commanding officer's house, and other buildings still look out onto the broad square. A display of photos at the visitors center in the old commissary traces the history of the fort, first as a military outpost. Then, as part of the surrounding Fort Totten Sioux Indian Reservation, it became a school, a tuberculosis sanatorium, and from 1940 to 1959 a community school. In the former hospital are displays of Indian and pioneer clothing.

Almost next door is the Sullys Hill National Game Preserve, a 1,674-acre home for grazing herds of buffalo, elk, and white-tailed deer, a well-populated community of animated black-tailed prairie dogs, birds, and waterfowl that seek out the two lakes. A four-mile auto tour leads to a scenic overlook and to Sullys Hill, where there is an observation tower and three Indian burial mounds. A short hiking trail and a 1 1/2-mile ski trail are other attractions.

Historic site open year-round. Fort Totten visitors center open daily mid-May–mid-Sept; off-season by appt. only. An auto tour is available May–Oct., weather permitting.
(701) 766-4441
www.devilslakend.com/home/home.html
Sullys Hill open May–Oct.
(701) 766-4272
http://mountain-prairie.fws.gov/ refuges/sullys

6 Makoti Threshers Museum

Makoti

The era when four-footed horse-power was first being replaced by four-wheeled machines has not been forgotten in the small agricultural community of Makoti. The Threshers Association boasts a remarkable museum of antique and classic threshers, farm tractors, and stationary engines. Housed in six buildings, this impressive collection includes a number of very rare pieces of farm equipment. Most of the machines are operational, and some are lovingly restored.

You don't have to be a tractor buff to be fascinated by a 1909 Hart Parr, a 1917 Plow Boy, a 1920 Titain, and a wood-body thresher made by International Harvester in 1920. One prize exhibit is the massive 110-horse-power Case steam traction engine built in the early 1900s—about 14 feet high with iron rear wheels 7 feet in diameter.

The first weekend in October is the highlight of the year. That's when crowds of enthusiasts arrive for the annual Makoti Threshing Show, and the steam and gas tractors, antique cars, and trucks are paraded at the town's showgrounds by their owners. Also featured are a flea market and the John Deere Two-Cylinder Slow Race.

5 Sullys Hill National Game Preserve. *Gazing out upon the vastness of this unspoiled land, visitors will feel the same sense of awe that the earliest settlers must have experienced.*

Luncheon is served from the so-called cook cars that were hauled into the fields to feed farmhands. *Open year-round by appointment. Admission free but donations encouraged.* *(701) 726-5693 or* *(701) 726-5649 (weekends)* **www.makoti.net**

7 Fort Union Trading Post National Historic Site
Williston
On a typical busy day some 150 years ago, this fortified trading post on the banks of the upper Missouri River would have been surrounded by American Indians grouped according to tribe, all eager to trade beaver and buffalo hides for guns, powder, beads, and blankets.

Fort Union was built by John Jacob Astor's American Fur Company in 1828 to buy and ship beaver pelts to the Eastern market. When silk top hats became more fashionable than ones made from beaver, the trade declined, and was supplanted by the demand for buffalo robes.

As one of the most remote and luxurious large Western outposts of the period, the fort was visited by many prominent travelers and adventurers, including the artists John James Audubon, Karl Bodmer, and George Catlin, who traveled by steamboat 1,800 miles from St. Louis.

The fort was largely dismantled in 1867. The National Park Service acquired the site in 1966 and began the excavations that are now open to visitors. Outlines of foundations are visible, and signs identify the various building sites. The staff of the visitors center, dressed as trappers and traders, will explain the displays of Indian clubs, military buttons, and other relics.

B Theodore Roosevelt National Park, North Unit. *These badlands honor the president who first had the vision of creating a nationwide park service, and this site is dedicated to him.*

Open year-round, weather permitting. *(701) 572-9083* **www.nps.gov/fous**

8 Theodore Roosevelt National Park, North Unit
Watford City
In 1883 a young politician from New York came to the North Dakota badlands to hunt buffalo and was inspired by the beauty of the place. A few months after his return to New York, his wife and his mother died, both on the same day, whereupon he returned to this haunting wilderness for comfort and solace. Later, as president, Theodore Roosevelt championed the idea of a National Park Service, and this, the only national park honoring an individual, is dedicated to his memory.

The badlands' configurations tell the history of this part of the continent. Some 60 million years ago, runoff from the Rocky Mountains deposited the debris that forms the badlands' distinctive multicolored layers. Ash from volcanoes in the west added the layers of blue.

Bolts of lightning ignited seams of soft coal, baking the sand and clay and adding red hues. In time swift-running streams cut through the layers, sculpting the terrain.

This moonlike landscape can be enjoyed along a 13-mile scenic drive or experienced on foot or horseback along several well-marked trails that include 11-mile routes through the rugged backcountry as well as a half-mile nature walk. Either way, the chances are good you will see some of the park's abundant wildlife, such as coyotes, golden eagles, buffalo, mule deer, and prairie dogs. There is good canoeing when the water is high in the Little Missouri after the ice melts in early April.

Open year-round; part of scenic drive closed Dec.–Mar. Admission charged. *(701) 623-4466* **www.nps.gov/thro**

9 Little Missouri State Park
Off Rte. 22 north of Killdeer
Few places in North Dakota offer visitors a better opportunity for a firsthand experience of the bad-

lands wilderness than this remote 4,600-acre park. Some 25 miles of trails for hiking and riding offer unexcelled views of the dramatically eroded landscape and Little Missouri Bay in the distance. There are corrals where you can keep a horse, and a concession that offers guided rides from May 1 through October 31.
Open year-round. *(701) 764-5256* **www.ndparks.com**

10 Fort Stevenson State Park
Garrison
Fort Stevenson, a frontier post, was built in 1867 and named for Union Brig. Gen. Thomas G. Stevenson, who died in the Civil War. It was abandoned in 1883 after the Sioux surrendered and now lies beneath the waters of man-made Lake Sakakawea. But the wooded 549-acre park offers many attractions. Fishing for walleye, northern pike, bass, and crappies is excellent.

The campground offers beautiful views from the bluffs overlooking the lake. Near one of the park's two boat ramps a busy prairie dog town will charm children. A jogging trail and a quarter-mile nature trail offer opportunities to see great horned owls, pheasants, migrating eagles, and songbirds.

Paddleboats, canoes, and fishing boats are available for rent at the park's full-service marina.
Open year-round; water and electricity shut off Oct.–mid-May. Admission charged. *(701) 337-5576* **www.ndparks.com**

11 Knife River Indian Villages National Historic Site

Stanton

Centuries before Lewis and Clark wintered nearby in 1804–05, Hidatsa, Arikara, and Mandan American Indians established themselves productively along the Missouri River in this area of prairies and rich bottomland. They lived in round earthen lodges supported by wood frames. Excellent gardeners, they grew corn, squash, tobacco, beans, and sunflowers, and they hunted buffalo, deer, and elk.

Hundreds of years ago, the villagers established an extensive trade network based on agricultural goods and Knife River flint. They traded with other American Indian peoples such as the Crow, Cheyenne, Arapaho, Cree, and Sioux. When European traders arrived, they quickly tied into this established system. Trade and prosperity increased until 1837, when a smallpox epidemic devastated the people living in the area.

In the present 1,765-acre park, the remains of three Hidatsa villages can be explored. A walking path from the visitors center leads to two of the villages. A separate path leads to the third. A 15-minute video is offered in the visitors center along with displays and artifacts that describe life in the villages. Summertime programs include hourly tours of the earthlodge each day and other Ranger programs on weekends. Cross-country skiing is popular in winter.

Open year-round except Thanksgiving, Christmas, and New Year's Day. For canoe tour reservations call (701) 745-3300.

www.nps.gov/knri

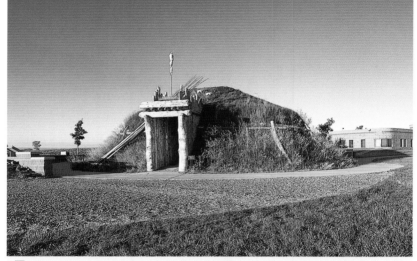

11 Knife River Indian Villages National Historic Site. *Centuries ago, the Hidatsa, Arikara, and Mandan American Indians lived in round earthen lodges.*

12 Arrowwood National Wildlife Refuge

Pingree

During the dawn of life in this region, glaciers scoured out the potholes and shaped the gentle slopes that now provide a remarkably beneficial environment for a variety of wildlife—a mixture of watery marshes, wooded ravines, cropland, and extensive grassland.

Encompassing almost 16,000 acres on which 266 species of birds have been observed, this serene, uncrowded refuge also harbors a herd of about 300 deer. These shy and graceful animals are often seen along the 5 1/2-mile self-guiding Auto Tour Route. Colonies of inquisitive prairie dogs inhabit this route, as do mourning doves, minks, and raccoons.

In spring there are outings to a blind from which the intricate and artistic mating dances of male sharp-tailed grouse may be seen at close range. The 16-mile-long James River valley is an excellent site for observing white pelicans, Canada geese, and many duck species, including shovelers, canvasbacks, redheads, and coots. Boating and canoeing are permitted on selected waterways. Other popular activities are picking chokecherries and Juneberries and picnicking. In winter this peaceful place is ideal for cross-country skiing and ice fishing.

Open daily. For grouse-blind reservations call (701) 285-3341, mid-Mar.–mid-May only. (701) 285-3341

http://mountain-prairie.fws.gov/ arrowwood/arwframes.html

13 North Dakota Lewis & Clark Interpretive Center

Intersection of U.S. Hwy. 83 and N.D. Hwy. 200A on McLean County Hwy. 17 in Washburn, north of Bismarck

In 1804 Captains Meriwether Lewis and William Clark settled into the long winter on the wild shores of the Upper Missouri River. For five frigid months until the spring thaw, as they prepared for their journey west to the Pacific Ocean, they mapped vast areas of uncharted territory, recorded plants with curative powers, and sketched animals they were seeing for the first time. Fort Mandan was the log compound they fashioned for shelter.

The interpretive center illuminates the explorers, expedition, and their relationships with the Americans Indians of the Hidatsa and Mandan villages. A guest can try on a buffalo robe, or wear a cradle board like the one probably used by the Shoshone guide and interpreter, Sakakawea, to carry her infant. A complete collection of watercolorist Karl Bodmer's prints gives a reliable account of Upper Midwest American Indian cultures of that era.

There is a small trading post at Fort Mandan, which has been rebuilt a mile and a half west of the interpretive center. Its original location is open to question since it burnt down long ago, and its grounds have been eroded by the waters of the Missouri.

Open year-round. Admission charged. (877) 462-8535

www.fortmandan.com/lewisclark.html

14 Fort Abraham Lincoln State Park

Hwy. 1806, Mandan

Tucked between the Heart and Missouri rivers, this wonderfully scenic, 1,000-plus acre park is rich in history. First called Fort McKeen, the park was officially renamed for President Abraham Lincoln in 1872. But its grounds evoke another legendary figure: Gen. George Custer. From Fort Lincoln, Custer rode out with the Seventh Cavalry to take on the Sioux Indians in the Battle of Little Bighorn. Several buildings from Custer's infantry post, including the house he called home before his "Last Stand," have been meticulously reconstructed.

The park also honors American Indians—particularly the area's true pioneers, the Mandans. Complete with earth lodges, the On-A-Slant Indian Village captures the daily life and labors of the Mandan people, who claimed the area as their home in the late 1500s. History buffs can learn more about the park's past in the visitors center museum.

From the park, avid walkers can pick up the Lewis and Clark Trail, named for the explorers who reached this area in 1804, and choose among the many inviting trails for hiking, biking, and horseback riding. During the summer, visitors might catch a performance by local thespians at the Granary in Cavalry Square or participate in a quill-working or hide-tanning workshop at On-A-Slant Village. The park also offers shoreline fishing, a playground for children, picnic areas, campsites, cabins, and breathtaking river views.

Open daily year-round. Entrance fee.
(701) 663-9571
www.state.nd.us/ndparks/Parks/FLSP.htm

13 North Dakota Lewis & Clark Interpretive Center. *A replica of Fort Mandan, which Captains Lewis and Clark built to shelter themselves from the frigid winter of 1804-1805, welcomes visitors.*

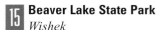
15 Beaver Lake State Park
Wishek

This 290-acre park on the west bank of Beaver Lake preserves a fragment of the landscape as it must have looked since time immemorial—a setting of water fringed by box elder, chokecherry, and Juneberry giving way to prairie uplands.

The park, created with the help of a Works Progress Administration workforce during the arduous times of the Depression in the 1930s, has over the years developed into an attractive secluded site.

Apart from providing opportunities for general outdoor activities, Beaver Lake Park is an excellent place to observe a surprisingly large variety of birds—whistling swans, pelicans, grebes, and cormorants can be seen here, as well as throngs of warblers, finches, and migratory waterfowl. Other wildlife and geological features are indicated along a nature trail.

There are 25 trailer campsites with water and electricity situated around an oval that used to be a popular local racetrack, and six primitive sites as well. For anglers there are pike and carp to be had in the lake, and an area is set aside for swimmers. On summer weekends campfire programs are held in the evening in a natural amphitheater overlooking the water. But holiday weekends are best avoided. The winter sports are ice fishing, cross-country skiing, and snowmobiling.

Open year-round; campground open mid-May–Labor Day.
Admission charged.
(701) 452-2752
www.state.nd.us/ndparks

16 Fort Ransom State Park
Abercrombie

American Indians and Norwegian settlers once fought bitterly for control of this region of hilly grassland and wooded slopes. Today a 900-acre park that sits along the Sheyenne River preserves much of the scenic beauty that was noted by the area's first farmers.

A road leads to a centrally located vantage point with a fine view of the park and surrounding farmland. For further explorations there are facilities for horseback riding and hiking. Wildlife is plentiful. Bird-watching, with more than 140 species to see, is exceptionally rewarding. The river is lined with American elm, bur oak, and green ash, and there is an ongoing project in the northwestern part of the park to re-establish the native prairie grasses.

The park offers a wide range of camping options including primitive camping, corrals for campers' horses, and modern sites with electrical hookups. A comfort station with hot showers and flush toilets is also available for use. In winter there are 50 miles of groomed snowmobile trails.

Open year-round. Admission charged.
(701) 973-4331
www.state.nd.us/ndparks

17 Fort Abercrombie State Historic Site
On Rte. 81

Established in 1858 at the approximate head of navigation on the Red River of the North, this outpost served to protect the northwestern frontier and guard the Montana gold fields. In 1862 its soldiers and more than 150 homesteaders withstood a six-week siege by Sioux Indians. Afterward the post was strengthened with log blockhouses and palisades. As the American Indians were pushed farther west the fort's importance diminished, and it was abandoned in 1877.

The only surviving original building is a guardhouse. But three new blockhouses and a palisade have been reconstructed on the site, and signs indicate where officers' quarters, storehouses, traders' posts, and other structures once stood.

A small museum nearby displays objects of local significance, and the violence of frontier life is also represented by stone tomahawks, arrowheads, padlocks, and pistols found at the site. Ceremonial ornaments, a buffalo robe, and a leather mail pouch used by Pony Express riders round off the collection.

Open mid-May–mid-Sept.
Admission charged.
(701) 553-8513
www.state.nd.us/hist/sites/
sitelist.htm#aber

Ohio

The thousands of years represented by the attractions here are supplemented by the intriguing diversity of the subject matter.

Hopewell Culture National Historical Park. *Visitors can examine artifacts that were excavated from these ancient burial mounds in southcentral Ohio (see page 268).*

(see page 268).

OHIO

The evidence of their art, pottery, mounds, and elaborate burial rituals confirms that advanced peoples lived here some 2,000 years ago. How incredulous those Indians would be to know that near their tribal lands would be born a man who would walk on the moon.

More believable, but nevertheless exciting in its time, was the iron horse and a local museum that exemplifies the caring relationship between a town and its railroad. The past is also recalled in the glassworks, potteries, and museums of Midwestern America and the homes of two U.S. presidents. A special treat features the amazing handiwork of a fabulous woodcarver, who was a true American genius.

1 Kelleys Island

Take the ferry from Marblehead
It is not known how long Kelleys Island was inhabited by people of the Erie or Cat nation before they were destroyed by the Iroquois in the late 1600s. But these first settlers are credited with leaving an enigmatic memorial: Inscription Rock, a large, flat-topped slab of limestone covered with Indian pictographs—of humanlike creatures, birds and animals, and smoking pipes—that have never been deciphered. The inscriptions, which are now nearly obliterated by the elements, were copied by U.S. Army Capt. Seth Eastman in 1850; a reproduction of his work is placed at the site.

Kelleys Island was resettled in the early 1800s. By 1910 it had a population of more than 1,000 and a thriving economy based on limestone quarrying, agriculture, winemaking, and fishing. Today, only about 200 people inhabit the island year-round. Eco-tourism is the major industry, and fishing, boating, swimming, and dining facilities are plentiful.

Visitors can ferry their cars over from Marblehead but may prefer to rent bicycles or golf carts on the island to get about and see the sights. About a 10-minute bike ride from the center of town is the 2-acre site of Glacial Grooves. The limestone, scored to a depth of

1 Kelleys Island. *A view of the Glacial Grooves, which were formed by the retreat of a huge glacier 10,000 years ago.*

several inches by the irresistible force of a moving glacier, gives the appearance of smoothly rounded gray waves. One trough, some 400 feet long, 35 feet wide, and 10 to 15 feet deep, is thought to be the world's most spectacular example of glacial grooving. The glacier was part of the great ice sheet that covered part of North America and inched southward for 5,000 years to reach this point. It melted about 10,000 years ago. Best times to visit are spring through late fall.
Accessible year-round.
(419) 746-2360
www.kelleysislandchamber.com

2 Inland Seas Maritime Museum

480 Main St., Vermilion
The Inland Seas Maritime Museum is operated by the Great Lakes Historical Society and overlooks Lake Erie from the shoreline of picturesque Vermilion. It is home to one of the nation's finest collections of Great Lakes maritime art. Original oil paintings, pen and ink drawings, watercolors, and mixed media are used to document the history of the Great Lakes, from passenger steamers to freighters to lighthouses and tugboats. The museum also maintains a fine collection of ship models and nautical artifacts including ships' wheels, binnacle compasses, antique steam engines, and shipwright's tools

that help explain the history of America's Inland Seas. Of particular interest to many visitors are the original timbers from Commodore Perry's USS *Niagara*, a life ring and sounding board from the USS *Edmund Fitzgerald*, and the one-of-a-kind Second Order Fresnel Lighthouse Lens from Spectacle Reef in Lake Huron. Also available to the visitor is the actual pilothouse from the SS *Canopus*, with working whistles, bells, and ship-to-ship communications systems.

In 2001, the museum added a series of computer-based interactive exhibits that visitors of all ages can enjoy: One can dive to eight various Great Lakes' shipwrecks using digitized video on a 42-inch plasma screen monitor or try to steer a freighter up the "crooked" Cuyahoga River. Children can build their own scale model of a 1,000-foot freighter or operate an engine room telegraph. The youngest visitors can make an effort at spelling their names using nautical signal flags or operating a schooner bilge pump to save their ship from sinking.

Open daily except Thanksgiving, Christmas, New Year's and Easter. Admission charged.

(800) 893-1485

www.inlandseas.org

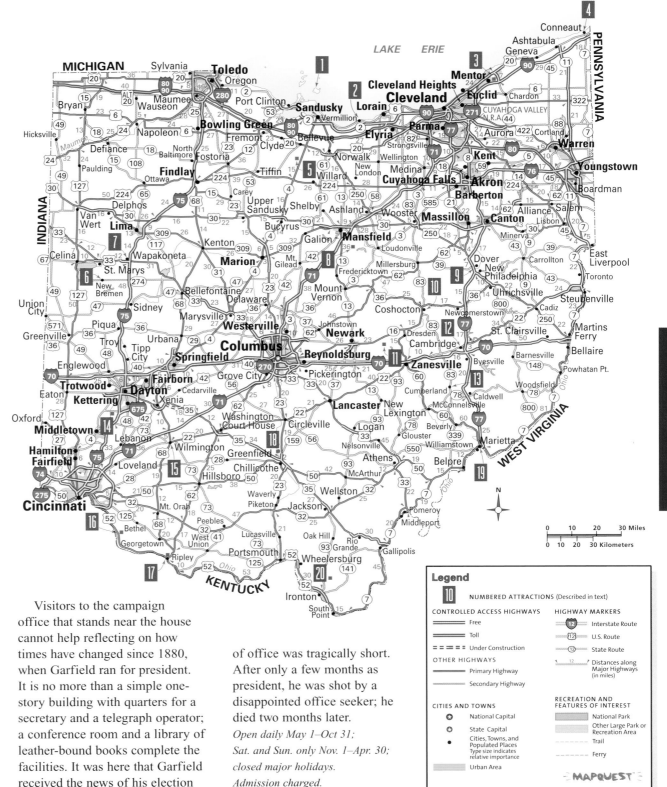

3 James A. Garfield National Historic Site

Mentor

Lawnfield, the home of President James A. Garfield, is a large white clapboard structure with a gambrel roof, brick chimney, large porch, and a porte cochere. The 9-room farmhouse built in 1832 was modified and expanded in the 1870s and 1880s into a rambling 29-room mansion with 12 fireplaces.

Visitors to the campaign office that stands near the house cannot help reflecting on how times have changed since 1880, when Garfield ran for president. It is no more than a simple one-story building with quarters for a secretary and a telegraph operator; a conference room and a library of leather-bound books complete the facilities. It was here that Garfield received the news of his election on the very telegraph equipment that stands on a table. His term

of office was tragically short. After only a few months as president, he was shot by a disappointed office seeker; he died two months later.

Open daily May 1–Oct 31; Sat. and Sun. only Nov. 1–Apr. 30; closed major holidays. Admission charged.

(440) 255-8722

www.wrhs.org

Legend

| | NUMBERED ATTRACTIONS (Described in text) |

CONTROLLED ACCESS HIGHWAYS
- Free
- Toll
- Under Construction

OTHER HIGHWAYS
- Primary Highway
- Secondary Highway

CITIES AND TOWNS
- National Capital
- State Capital
- Cities, Towns, and Populated Places Type size indicates relative importance
- Urban Area

HIGHWAY MARKERS
- Interstate Route
- U.S. Route
- State Route
- Distances along Major Highways (in miles)

RECREATION AND FEATURES OF INTEREST
- National Park
- Other Large Park or Recreation Area
- Trail
- Ferry

MAPQUEST

Conneaut Railroad Historical Museum

Watch for signs from I-90, Conneaut

Trains have long been powerful symbols of freedom, high adventure, and expansion; and since the 1880s the economy of Conneaut has been linked to the Nickel Plate Road, connecting Buffalo to Chicago with 513 miles of track. The railroad employed much of Conneaut's labor force, contributed substantially to the town's revenue, opened it to development, and became part of its folklore. That the bond between the railroad and the townspeople goes beyond economic factors is proved by the prodigious contributions of volunteer labor and donated money that went into the creation of this excellent museum.

Housed in the old New York Central Railroad depot, the museum overflows with railroad memorabilia. One eye-catcher is a 19th-century advertisement showing a train in mother-of-pearl inlay, with mountains painted in watercolors in the background. There are also timetables, a chart of hobo codes, railway bonds, and travel permits, including that of Abraham Lincoln, signed by his own hand in 1857 when he was chief attorney for the Illinois Central Railroad.

Workaday exhibits include carmakers' and inspectors' tools, telegraph equipment, a fully equipped ticket office, and a working model of a boiler. There are also model trains, including an original cast-iron Lionel. Outside the depot children and buffs will enjoy climbing into the cab of a handsome 100-foot-long Berkshire steam locomotive built in 1944. A hopper car and a 1913 caboose complete with stove, washstand, and instructions for operating the air brakes are also intriguing.

Open P.M. daily Memorial Day–Labor Day. Admission free but donations encouraged.
(440) 599-7878
www.nrhs.com/chapters/conneaut.htm

5 Seneca Caverns
Bellevue

In 1872 two boys were out hunting when their dog chased a rabbit into a brush-filled pit. When the dog did not return, the boys began searching through the brush. Toward the bottom of the pit, they discovered a small hole with cool air streaming through it, and they could hear their dog barking below. As they dug to widen the opening, the limestone supporting them collapsed, and they tumbled some 10 or 12 feet down to the opening of a cave. The three companions climbed back out, and the caverns came to public notice.

Unlike most caves, the Seneca Caverns were not formed by the dissolution of the bedrock, but rather by the collapse of the limestone into a subsurface void. The resulting fracture is Seneca Caverns. Its physical aspect differs accordingly from the norm: Here one sees the bones of the earth—the tumbled strata of Columbus limestone—in their raw condition, not smoothed by the flow of water or the action of ancient seas.

The path through the cave is not an easy walk, and the tour has been called a vigorous though not overly difficult one. The largest chamber is some 250 feet long and 10 or 12 feet high. At one end is Pie Rock, so called because it resembles a huge wedge of pie. Beyond it one descends to Ole Mist'ry River, whose waters are so clear that they seem almost not to exist, but merely to be a light mist at the bottom of the cavern. The river's source is unknown, but it has been found that it slowly flows into Blue Hole Spring at Castalia, a few miles away.

The river's water level (which depends upon rainwater seeping down) determines how far one can descend into the cave. Twelve cave levels have been explored. The one-hour guided tour through seven rooms, or levels, ends on the seventh level 110 feet below the surface. On the return route one squeezes through the Needle's Eye and passes the Lock Stone, which is said to hold the jumbled and fractured strata in place; it's 150 feet long, 45 feet deep, and 60 feet wide and is estimated to weigh several hundred tons.

Emerging into the light again, one thinks of the underground landscape and the great monolith that holds the rocks in place, and with them the trees and peaceful Ohio fields.

Open daily Memorial Day–Labor Day; weekends only May, Sept., mid-Oct. Admission charged.
(419) 483-6711
www.senecacavernsohio.com

6 The Bicycle Museum of America
7 W. Monroe St., New Bremen

High-wheelers, boneshakers, velocipedes, tandems, and more bits of bicycle esoterica than you knew existed are in this collection that was previously located in Chicago. Jim Dicke, whose grandfather worked at the Dayton Bicycle Company at the turn of the century, brought the group of multi-wheeled wonders to Ohio.

When Leonardo da Vinci sketched the bicycle drive chain in the late 15th century, he couldn't have anticipated the infinite variety of vehicles that would ensue. There was the 1898 Chilion ladies' model, a wooden bike that didn't rust but did tend to splinter at inopportune moments. The Schwinn Sting-Ray Orange Krate, circa late 1960s,

6 The Bicycle Museum of America. *Donald Duck's eyes flashed and the electric horn quacked on this classic 1949 model.*

was ready to burn rubber on the drag strip in one's mind with its stick-shift lever and chrome-plated fenders. (One sold at auction in the late 1990s for over $16,000.) Some of the bicycles on display here were dedicated to popular entertainers: Crooner Cowboy Gene Autry, for example, had a Western model made in his honor in 1950, with a rodeo-brown finish, jeweled fenders, and a pony-head adornment. The Shelby Cycle Company produced a Donald Duck model in 1949 that intrigued many a baby in the boomer generation with its Donald eyes that flashed and a horn that squeaked "quack-quack."

Open year-round. Closed Sun.
Admission charged.
(419) 629-9249

www.bicyclemuseum.com

7 Neil Armstrong Air and Space Museum

500 S. Apollo Drive Wapakoneta
"One small step for man, one giant leap for mankind": thus spoke the first man to set foot on the moon, astronaut Neil Armstrong. Armstrong's own first steps were taken in Wapakoneta, his childhood home, where this museum was established in his honor.

The museum building is a domed structure, half buried in a grassy mound, with two wings for galleries. The upper floor contains the Infinity Room and the Planetarium. In the Infinity Room, an 18-foot cube, one walks between ingeniously positioned rows of mirrors that reflect each other, oneself, and moving lights in numerous planes. In the Planetarium, pinpoints of revolving lights are thrown against the roof and walls to the accompaniment

7 Neil Armstrong Air and Space Museum. *This building, with its half-dome, was designed to resemble a futuristic moon base.*

of electronic music. Both rooms seek to create a sense of being in infinite space.

One of the most fascinating items found here is a genuine *Gemini VIII* spacecraft, with a panel cut away to reveal the interior: This was the world's first docking satellite, flown by Armstrong and Maj. David Scott in March 1966. Also displayed are the many honors bestowed upon the astronauts, including the Presidential Medal of Freedom.

Open year-round.
Admission charged.
(419) 738-8811

www.ohiohistory.org/places/armstron

8 Malabar Farm

Rte. 1, Lucas
In 1939 the Pulitzer-prize-winning author Louis Bromfield bought four neglected farms, built a large, comfortable, and elegant home around one of the old farmhouses,

and began to restore the fertility of his farmland. Since most of the money for the project came from the proceeds of a novel set on the Malabar Coast in India, he called the property Malabar Farm.

The "big house" is exceptionally attractive. The furnishings are predominantly French rural antiques highlighted by such striking objects as an Italian marble fireplace surmounted by ceramic Chinese horses set against a huge mirrored wall in the living room, a Steinway grand piano beside the floating double staircase in the hallway, and in the Red Room, paintings by Grandma Moses. An enormous curved desk with 28 drawers dominates the author's library despite the fact that it was too high for Bromfield to use comfortably.

Nine bedrooms upstairs include one where Humphrey Bogart and Lauren Bacall, who were friends of the author, stayed on their honeymoon.

The farm still supports a herd of beef cattle, and the self-guiding tour of the barns, stables, meadows, and flower gardens allows visitors to see the farm animals and touch those in the petting barn.

About half of the acreage here is under cultivation; the rest is woodland, where there are hiking trails and a campsite for horse riders. A final appealing touch is the spring, supposedly once used by Johnny Appleseed, that wells up in its own enclosure at the edge of the property.

Weekends only, Jan.–Apr.; Tues.–Sun. May–Dec. Closed holidays.
Admission charged.
(419) 892-2784

www.malabarfarm.org

7 Neil Armstrong Air and Space Museum. *A moon rock collected during the* Apollo 11 *mission in 1969 still thrills visitors.*

⑨ Warthers. *This walnut and ivory working model of a real factory, including depictions of people who worked there, is incredible for its detail.*

OHIO

⑨ Warthers

331 Karl Ave., Dover
Ernest Warther was quite different from other artists. Although his wood carvings of trains, locomotives, and an old steel mill were immensely valued during his lifetime (the Smithsonian called his oeuvre "priceless"), Warther never sold a single piece of his work because, he said, "Our roof don't leak, we ain't hungry, and we don't owe anybody."

"Warthers" refers to the home the artist and his wife built in 1912, which now houses his remarkable collection of carvings in wood, bone, and ivory.

Inside is a working model of the American Sheet and Tinplate Company, where Warther worked between 1899 and 1923. It is made of walnut and ivory and re-creates in detail the floor of the factory—not only the machines but his friends there. His best friend, for instance, is shown eating rhubarb pie and a piece of Swiss cheese complete with holes. The model was done from memory nearly 30 years after he left the factory.

He recorded the history of steam locomotion from 250 B.C. to the 20th century in a series of 64 accurately scaled, detailed working models.

Many of the carvings are large. The eight-foot-long model of the Empire State Express is shown crossing a bridge, which is made of 4,000 individually cut ebony bricks, with strips of ivory for the mortar. Warther's favorite was the Lincoln funeral train. A keyhole in the funeral coach has an ivory key that fits it, and the body in its draped coffin can be seen through a window.

The gardens are pleasant, and a small picnic area is provided.
Open daily except major holidays.
(330) 343-7513
www.warthers.com

⑩ Johnson-Humrickhouse Museum

300 N. Whitewoman St., Coshocton
The museum is located in Roscoe Village, a restoration of an 1800s canal town. Most of its collections relate to Ohio's pioneering past, with exhibits of cornhusk dolls, domestic and farm implements, lamps and lanterns, early-day interior settings, and 19th-century weaponry, including Colt and Remington revolvers and the first rifle used by the U.S. military, the 1860 Spencer repeating carbine.

In addition, the museum has a high-quality collection of American Indian art and artifacts. Haida masks, Acoma pottery, Chippewa cradleboards, Eskimo animal effigies, a Crow headdress, distinctively patterned Apache basketry, and a Pomo mortuary basket are among the exhibits that exemplify Indian life.

Still another gallery features Oriental treasures. Inro and netsuke, 19th-century Japanese porcelain, vases and boxes of carved cinnabar lacquer, samurai swords and cases, antique stoneware bottles, and many other exquisite pieces are shown.

The museum also contains a large assortment of the personal memorabilia of the Johnson and Humrickhouse families. One can further delight in a unique exhibit of French, Irish, Flemish, and American lace. All of these collections are well lit and spaciously displayed.

Roscoe Village, a picturesque historic site, gives you an opportunity to become acquainted with the canal era. In addition to exploring the small village with its attractive shops, you can walk along the towpath and take rides on a trolley and a canal boat.
Museum open daily May–Oct., closed Mon. Nov.–Apr.
Admission charged.
(740) 622-8710
www.jhm.lib.oh.us.com

⑪ Blackhand Gorge State Nature Preserve

Newark. Watch for signs on Rte. 146 near junction of Rte. 16
About 10,000 years ago, the runoff of melting glaciers carved a gorge here in the sandstone bedrock known as Blackhand conglomerate. The preserve follows the course of the Licking River through this gorge, and a number of trails and a paved bicycle path invite exploration of the terrain.

The bike path passes a buttonbush swamp and then enters a woodland of sycamore, maple, sumac, and yellow poplar. In July the route is awash in wild phlox flowers and bergamot.

Along the bike path one enjoys dramatic views of cliffs towering above the woods, with ferns, massive tree trunks, and roots delineating the weathered strata and fault lines. Across the gorge stands Blackhand Rock, a concave rock face above a bend and a wide pool in the river. Beyond this the path passes narrowly between two cliffs and then reenters the woodland, where one has intermittent views of the river and its dry-season sandpits and exposed boulders.

The bike path that follows the old railroad bed was originally used by the railroad to carry sand from an adjacent quarry to the glassworks of Newark, the nearest sizable town. One footpath traverses the rim of the old quarry; a second footpath ascends to higher woodlands looping through ferny hemlock woods and then returning to the bicycle path.
Open year-round.
(740) 763-4411
www.dnr.state.oh.us

12 The Degenhart Paperweight and Glass Museum

From I-77 take Rte. 22 west at Exit 47 and look for the museum on your right, Cambridge.

This part of Ohio was once a center of the art glass industry, in which John Degenhart, founder in 1947 of the Crystal Art Glass Company of Cambridge, was an eminent figure. The museum gives an excellent general account of commercial glassmaking in the Ohio Valley and of John Degenhart's work, in particular his craftsmanship and artistry as a maker of paperweights. The son of a glassmaker, Degenhart became a glassmaker himself at the age of nine.

As an introduction to the exhibits, the museum offers a short videotape on glassmaking. The first displays give a broad survey of the major glassmakers of the region. This introduces you to a comprehensive display of pressed glass that shows the major trends and the wealth of patterns developed. In the 1870s most patterns were adapted from nature, while in the 1880s complex imitations of cut glass were in vogue. In 1900 there was a return to the plainer earlier styles.

Another exhibit shows collectors how to distinguish copies of old pressed glass from the originals. Technicolor arrays of glass owls, puppies, and dolls demonstrate the great variety of colors produced in glass by the addition of chemicals. The paperweight section of the museum shows the parts and steps in the making of a "five lily" weight and some of the major types of paperweights. Also shown are paperweights in the forms of lamps, doorstops, and even grave markers; these last are a tradition that is peculiar to the Guernsey County area of Ohio. Most of the glass was collected by Degenhart's wife, Elizabeth. One exhibit shows her dining room packed floor to ceiling with pieces from her collection.

Open Mon.–Sat. and P.M. Sun. Apr.–Dec.; Mon.–Fri. only Jan.–Mar. Closed major holidays.
Admission charged.
(740) 432-2626
www.degenhartmuseum.com

13 The Wilds

International Road, Cumberland

A pastoral sight unfolds at twilight across the panorama of the wide-open range. The Southern white rhino grazes peacefully on the veldt. A sable antelope bounds across the savanna. Bactrian camel lope by, and a small herd of North American bison munches on prairie grasses. The animals are actually sharing almost 10,000 acres of land on a wildlife preserve in Ohio. Endangered and threatened species from Asia, Africa and North America have been brought together to live and prosper on this soil that has been reclaimed from strip mining.

Since the early 1970s, the strip mining industry has replaced topsoil and replenished grasslands where the mining for coal took place. It is a "human-induced prairie" that affords these species a place to roam in their natural habitat. Wetlands are also being brought back to health so that the balance of interlocking ecological systems is restored.

The Columbus Zoo helps manage the Wilds, where visitors can savor the natural world via guided safaris. Conservation research and educational programs are key elements here, and work is ongoing in areas such as reproductive biology and animal husbandry.

Open daily May 1 through Oct. 31.
Admission charged.
(740) 638-5030
www.thewilds.org

11 Blackhand Gorge State Nature Preserve. *An ancient petroglyph of a large black-colored human hand adds a sense of mystery here.*

14 Miamisburg Mound State Memorial

900 Mound Ave., Miamisburg

This is the largest conical burial mound in Ohio, and like Grave Creek Mound in West Virginia (see page 354), it is attributed to the Adena Indians, who lived here probably between 1000 B.C. and A.D. 400. The Ohio Valley was the heartland of the Adena culture, but its influence spread into Indiana, Kentucky, and as far east as New York and Delaware. The Adena settled in small communities, practiced a limited horticulture, and buried their dead in conical earthen mounds. Within their orbit of influence, there may be as many as 300 to 500 mound sites.

The Miamisburg Mound, which was built on a bluff, rises to a height of less than 70 feet from a base of one-and-a-half acres. But originally, before excavations, it was more than 70 feet high and may have been the largest in the eastern United States. Eight feet from the top of the mound, archaeologists discovered a bark-covered skeleton; 31 feet below that they found an empty vault surrounded by logs. Layers of ash and stone indicate that the mound had been built in stages over a period of time.

The slopes of the mound are shaggy with trees and vegetation. A flight of 116 stone steps leads to a paved circle on top, from which one can view the environs. A notice on the site gives some particulars of the excavations. The surrounding park has picnic tables and a playground.

Open year-round.
(937) 866-4532
www.ohiohistory.org/places/miamisbur

15 The Clinton County Historical Society and Museum

Rombach Place, 149 E. Locust St., Wilmington

This most pleasant and unpredictable museum of local history is located in Rombach Place, an elegant town house built in 1835 by Gen. James William Denver, commissioner of Indian affairs under President Buchanan, governor of the Kansas Territory in the 1850s, and the man for whom the city of Denver, Colorado, was named. The house is listed on the *National Register of Historic Places* and is furnished throughout with handsome antiques.

To the right of the entrance hall is the Denver library, which contains the general's collection of Indian relics, his beaver top hat, the sand shaker used to dry the ink on his letters, and other memorabilia.

Beyond this elegant room is a sitting room containing a handsome horsehair settee and an oil painting by Eli Harvey, a local Quaker famous for his animal bronzes. A number of these, including a sleek, recumbent greyhound, a "nervous puma," a stag, and an enraged elephant, may be seen in the Eli Harvey Room. A second sitting room is furnished with three pianos, violins by a local maker, and a wonderfully elaborate mirror. Porcelain dishes, toby jugs, and pewter sconces are displayed in the dining room.

Upstairs one finds a roomful of children's toys, a re-creation of an early 20th century dentist's office with false teeth of that time, a collection of antique clothing, and a sewing room containing quilts. One of the most interesting items is a bathtub (with a built-in water heater) that folds up against the wall. In the barn behind the house are antique farm equipment, a storm buggy, and a very fine fire engine, circa 1876.

Open P.M. Wed.–Fri. Admission free but donations encouraged.
(937) 382-4684
www.clintoncountyhistory.org

16 Grant's Birthplace

Intersection of Rtes. 232 and 52 south of New Richmond

The first home of Ulysses S. Grant, general of the Union Army during the Civil War and later president of the United States, is a typical small pioneer house: a white clapboard structure resting on a stone sill, with a brick chimney. Grant was born here in 1822, and the following year his family moved to Georgetown, where he spent his boyhood years.

From 1895 to 1936 the house stood as a historical exhibit in Columbus, Ohio, but in 1936 it was returned here to its original site beside Big Indian Creek and facing the Ohio River. Simply furnished in the tradition of his time, the house contains Grant's cradle, the trunk he took to West Point, his Bible, and his cigar case.

Outside the house is a covered well of dressed sandstone. A cannon, set in concrete and bearing Grant's name and birth date on a plaque, points toward the river. Majestic chestnut trees grace the spacious lawn, which stretches down to the road, and behind the house is the Grant Memorial Church, an imposing structure with Ionic columns.

Open weekends and holidays May–Labor Day. Admission charged.
(513) 553-4911
www.ohiohistory.org/places/grantbir

17 Rankin House & Parker House

Ripley

A candle in the window of a house on a hill once signaled the all-clear to more than 2,000 runaway slaves looking for help from the Underground Railroad. The last leg on this part of the route to freedom was an arduous climb up 100 steps of an outside staircase that took people from the Ohio River to the home of Presbyterian minister John Rankin and his wife, Jean. As many as 12 people at one time could be hidden on this property in southern Ohio. Fugitive slaves were delivered to conductors like Rankin, who would help them get to the next depot in the network of stops. His home, with a commanding view of the river and a reconstructed staircase, contains memorabilia of his activities as an abolitionist.

John P. Parker, born into slavery in 1827, was able to buy his freedom at the age of 18 and went on to prosper in the iron molding foundry business. He was among a small number of African Americans who became patent holders in the 19th century.

Parker returned to slave territory, risking his life, to lead people to shelter in Ripley, often to the Rankin home. The Parker House, on Front Street, is where many escapes from the borderlands of Kentucky were planned. Both houses are National Historic Landmarks and are very worthwhile for anyone interested in this country's history.

Rankin House: Open Wed.–Sun., Memorial Day–Labor Day; after Labor Day, open weekends only through Oct. 31. Admission charged.
(937) 392-1627
Parker House: Call for hours.
(937) 392-4188
www.ripleyohio.org

18 Hopewell Culture National Historical Park

Chillicothe

The bountiful river valleys of southcentral Ohio were home to a flourishing center of the Hopewell culture about 2,000 years ago. Known for their large geometric

16 Grant's Birthplace. *The famous general and president was born in this typical pioneer white clapboard house in 1822.*

OHIO

earthworks and elaborate artifacts crafted from exotic materials, the Hopewellian people prospered from 200 B.C. to A.D. 500.

Their mound construction was particularly extensive in the Scioto River-Paint Creek area. Five archaeological sites in this area are now preserved by the National Park Service.

Overlooking the banks of the Scioto River is one of the most important sites of the Hopewell culture, Mound City. The people built structures here that housed their political, economic, and social activities, including burial ceremonies. After a period of time, they razed each structure and constructed a mound over the location.

Today, the park's visitors center, located at this site, establishes what is known of the Hopewell lifestyle and displays some of the artifacts found in excavations of these mounds. In some cases, the quantity and types of objects, in particular the burial mounds, indicate the status and possibly the occupation of the deceased. Artifacts include shell beads, bear and shark teeth, pottery, ear spools of copper and silver, and a series of effigy pipes bearing the likenesses of animals and birds. The original pipes are now in the British Museum in London; replicas are on display here.

Beyond these parklike grounds the Scioto River flows, smooth, brown, and rapid. An interesting one-mile trail follows its banks, passing yet another earthwork. Along the way plaques identify plants and shrubs once important to the Hopewell and other American Indian populations.

Grounds open daily from dawn to dusk; Visitors Center open daily P.M.

🖼 Hopewell Culture National Historical Park. *An artist's rendering of what a Hopewell cremation ceremony might have looked like 2,000 years ago.*

except Thanksgiving, Christmas, and New Year's Day.
(740) 774-1126
www.nps.gov/hocu

🔟 Campus Martius Museum
Marietta. Intersection of Washington and Second Sts.
In April 1788, 48 New England men led by Gen. Rufus Putnam arrived here in the Northwest Territory to settle a tiny portion of the 1.8 million acres granted by Congress to the Ohio Company of Associates. On a bluff overlooking the confluence of the Ohio and Muskingum rivers, they built a fort, which they named Campus Martius (literally, "field of Mars"). On the plains below they laid out their village, leaving undisturbed the strange prehistoric mounds they had discovered.

Today Campus Martius is a museum that explains the history of settlement and migration in Ohio, and it contains many relics of the early days. It includes the last standing portion of the fort, as well as General Putnam's five-room house, which has been restored and partially furnished. Many of the pieces on display belonged to the Putnam family.

Other exhibits in the museum include early surveying instruments and an extensive collection of frontier rifles, many of them made by J. Vincent, a local gunsmith. A collection of Masonic memorabilia includes a ritual Masonic apron worn by George Washington. Behind the museum is the first office building in Ohio, the original log and clapboard headquarters of the Ohio Company of Associates.

Marietta's later development is represented by exhibits as diverse as 18th-century furniture in the Hepplewhite and Chippendale styles and 19th-century farming equipment.
Open year-round Wed.–Sun.
Admission charged.
(800) 860-0145
www.ohiohistory.org/places/campus

🔟 Lake Vesuvius Recreation Area
Set among the rolling hills and scenic woodlands of the Wayne National Forest, this is a place of tranquil beauty.

The recreation area takes its name from the Vesuvius Furnace, located in one of the picnic spots. This truncated giant, built in 1833, was one of the first iron blast furnaces in the region, and it was one of the last to close, holding out against the prevailing economic winds until 1906. The structure has been partially restored by the U.S. Corps of Engineers. Though it lacks some of the ancillary buildings faithfully re-created at Buckeye Furnace, Vesuvius has the poignancy of a fallen hero.

Several loop trails, ranging from a half-mile walk to a 16-mile path for backpackers, skirt Lake Vesuvius and cross a varied terrain. The facility also offers a 28-mile horse trail, campsites, picnic grounds, a boat dock, and rental boats and canoes.

Lake Vesuvius is ideal for canoeing and boating, and the sandy beach at Big Bend is inviting for swimmers. The fishing is also good for bass and catfish.
Open year-round.
(740) 534-6500
www.fs.fed.us/r9/wayne

Woolaroc. *The Native American Heritage Center here features displays of Navajo and Plains Indian culture (see page 272).*

Oklahoma

Highlights relate to the American Indian and pioneer heritage, preservation of endangered species, and a variety of inviting parks and trails.

The earliest foragers on these grassy plains are documented by dinosaur footprints and fossilized remains of the mastodon and mammoth. Under the same roof is the legacy of the Plains Indians and the five flags that have flown over this land. Elsewhere, ancient American Indian mounds can be seen, a famous Wild West show is recalled, and ancient alphabet characters can be viewed. The Trail of Tears is remembered, and there's a memorial to Sequoyah, inventor of the Cherokee alphabet.

There are parks featuring a mesa, a cavern, waterfalls, and boulders as well as hiking and nature trails. Buffalo, elk, and longhorns are safe in their preserves, and the Chisholm Trail is immortalized.

1 Black Mesa and Black Mesa State Park

27 miles west of Boise City on Hwy. 325

A dark, brooding countenance dominates the arid countryside of the extreme northwestern Oklahoma Panhandle. Rising some 700 feet in relief above a stark plain, Black Mesa extends for about 45 miles from Oklahoma into Colorado and New Mexico. Its highest point above sea level in Oklahoma, 4,973 feet, is marked by a granite slab. At its western edges, in Colorado, the mesa reaches an altitude of 6,600 feet.

Geologists believe the mesa was formed by basaltic lava flows originating at what is today Piney Mountain, Colorado, five miles from the Oklahoma border. There are marked trails and the slopes are gentle enough for hiking to the top.

Black Mesa State Park, about 15 miles southeast of the mesa, offers a splendid base for exploring the area. The 349-acre park is also noteworthy in its own right for its huge rock pinnacles suggesting human profiles and figures, and for the flora and fauna thriving in its rugged landscape. A small lake offers boating and fishing.

Open year-round.
(580) 426-2222
www.oklahomaparks.com

1 Black Mesa and Black Mesa State Park. *Hikers can take marked trails to the summit of the mesa, which was formed by basaltic lava flows.*

2 No Man's Land Historical Museum

Sewell St. and North E St., Goodwell, off Hwy. 54

Oklahoma's Panhandle, a 34- by 168-mile strip, was for many years unclaimed by any state or territory. In 1850, Texas, a proslave state, agreed not to extend its border north of latitude 36°30'. In 1854 the boundary of Kansas had been set at the 37th parallel, and thus the long, narrow area that remained became known as No Man's Land. The settlers here asked that Congress name it the Cimarron Territory. But Congress refused to do so and in 1890 designated the area as part of the Oklahoma Territory.

The museum, on the campus of Panhandle State University, has outstanding exhibits depicting the history of this region from prehistoric times to the tragic Dust Bowl days of the 1930s. The paleontology displays include mastodon and mammoth bones and teeth, a dinosaur track, and intriguing fossil freshwater fish.

The William E. Baker Archaeological Collections, housed in the museum, contain artifacts of the Basket Maker Indians, early occupants of these lands, the Plains Indians, who formerly roamed the region, and white pioneers. Over the main entrance to

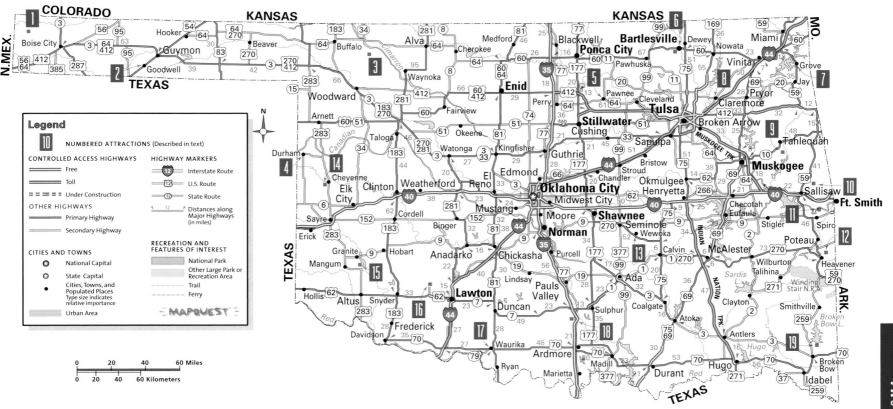

the museum are the flags of Spain, France, Mexico, Texas, and the United States, all of which have flown over the territory.

Open Tues.–Sat. except holidays.
(580) 349-2670

www.opsu.edu

---

3 Alabaster Caverns State Park
Freedom

The feature here is a 2,300-foot-long cavern sectioned into chambers by spectacular formations of alabaster and glittering selenite crystals. (Alabaster is a fine, translucent gypsum.) Its formation began some 200 million years ago when a great inland sea receded, leaving huge deposits of gypsum. Underground streams slowly tunneled the rock, creating the series of chambers. Today a murmuring stream continues the

ancient process of erosion.

The entrance to the cavern is in rugged Cedar Canyon. Short tours take visitors into chambers given such descriptive names as Gun Barrel Tunnel, Devil's Bathtub, Echo Dome, and Encampment Room. Bring comfortable walking shoes and a light jacket. For years the cavern was known as Bat Cave for the host of winged mammals that still reside here, hanging harmlessly from the rock ceiling by day, leaving by night to feed upon insects.

Campsites and picnic grounds are available.

Open year-round.
Admission charged.
(580) 621-3381

www.oklahomaparks.com

---

4 Metcalfe Museum
Rte. 1, northwest of Cheyenne, near Durham

Branding calves, riding horses, and doing household chores in the Oklahoma Territory didn't leave Augusta Corson Metcalfe much time for herself. She relaxed at night by recording the day's events in paintings and sketches. Metcalfe was a pioneer woman who ran her farm and raised her son by herself in the sagebrush-strewn red hills of the Upper Washita Valley in the late 19th century, when the Cheyenne and Arapaho lands were opened up to settlers.

Howard Metcalfe, her son, donated their home for this museum, which stands on the Break O' Day Farm. Life on the high plains, from the rugged early frontier days to the Dust Bowl hardships of the 1930s,

is depicted in several buildings and in a newly constructed gallery.

Besides Augusta's paintings, which gained her renown as the Sagebrush Artist and entry into the National Cowgirl Hall of Fame, you can look at items like the cook box her homesteading family brought across the plains in their wagon, a spinning wheel, and antique furniture and farming tools. There is even a horse-drawn sorghum mill, used in the making of syrup.

A pioneer-era general store has been re-created, and the Blue Goose Saloon is a remnant transported here from the territorial town of Hamburg that is no more.

Open Tues.–Sat., Mar.–Nov.
(580) 655-4467

www.plainsfolk.com/metcalfemuseum

5 Pawnee Bill Ranch
Pawnee

Gordon William Lillie, pioneer rancher, Wild West showman, and successful businessman, chose Blue Hawk Peak, a hill in Pawnee Indian country, for the site of this handsome sandstone mansion. The sprawling, two-story structure, built in 1910 of locally quarried stone, is maintained by the Oklahoma Historical Society.

Lillie had lived among the Pawnee, working as a teacher on the Pawnee agency. With his wife, May, an expert rider and sharpshooter, he formed the Pawnee Bill Wild West Show in 1888. For a quarter of a century he toured the United States and many foreign countries—part of the time with the famous Buffalo Bill Cody. When his show finally closed in 1913, Lillie indulged his interests in the American bison and enlarged his herd to assure the preservation of these already endangered species.

His mansion today contains the original furnishings and treasures from his travels. The museum contains memorabilia of the family and prominent guests, a miniature replica of the Pawnee Bill Wild West Show, and a collection of American Indian artifacts. A pleasant picnic area is located on the grounds, as well as a drive-through exhibit pasture where buffalo, longhorn cattle, and draft horses can be seen.

Open Tues.–Sun. Closed Tues. Nov.–Mar.
(918) 762-2513
www.ok-history.mus.ok.us

6 Woolaroc
On State Hwy. 123, Bartlesville
This lovely 3,500-acre property in the rugged Osage hill country was

 Woolaroc. *Wapiti, also known as American elk, can be seen at this wildlife preserve in the rugged Osage hill country.*

acquired in the 1920s by Frank Phillips, co-founder of Phillips Petroleum Company, for a wildlife preserve and a family retreat. Now owned and managed by a foundation created by Phillips, Woolaroc (woods, lakes, and rocks) is open to the public. On the grounds are a world-renowned museum established by Phillips, the Native American Heritage Center, and the rustic but spacious lodge where the Phillipses entertained the nation's leaders and celebrities.

The museum is reached by a road that curves from the grounds' entrance and picnic area through the preserve, a forest of blackjack oaks, post oaks, and sycamores, where buffalo, deer, elk, and longhorn cattle graze. For safety, visitors must stay in their cars.

The museum, which portrays the story of man in the New World, contains 55,000 items from prehistoric times through the middle of the 20th century. Its displays of American Indian blankets and Navajo and Plains Indian jewelry are outstanding. A permanent exhibit of Western art (one of the

world's finest) includes works of Frank Tenney Johnson, Charles M. Russell, and Frederic Remington.

Next to the museum is the Native American Heritage Center, a longhouse with exhibits illustrating American Indian culture and achievements. From the center the Enchanted Walkway leads to the 1 1/2-mile-long Thunderbird Canyon Nature Trail.

Open daily Memorial Day–Labor Day; closed Mondays Sept.–May.
Admission charged.
(918) 336-0307
www.woolaroc.org

7 Grand Lake O' the Cherokees
I-44, Afton or Grand Lake exit
Flying in tight formation with Air Force-worthy precision, flocks of American white pelicans head annually to South America from Canada. But they know a good thing when they see it and always spend a six-week layover at Grand Lake in September. The gigantic reservoir was formed in 1940 by the building of the Pensacola Dam,

the longest multiple-arch dam in the world, on the Grand River. There are 46,500 surface acres of water and 1,300 miles of shoreline here.

It's a migratory waterfowl haven, the mudflat areas having been seeded with Japanese millet in an effort to provide a food source for many types of birds, including buffleheads, shovelers, and cormorants. The dense vegetation also gives protective covering for young fish. Bald eagles winter here, and it's best to see them in the early morning, near water below the dam.

The lake wanders through 66 miles of the foothills of the Ozarks called "Green Country." It's tucked into the corner where four states meet: Oklahoma, Kansas, Missouri and Arkansas. Although fairs, flea markets, festivals, and rodeos occur throughout the seasons, people are often content to just look at the water here. Bass fishing is always popular, and sailboat enthusiasts can pick up prevailing winds for a pleasant ride across the lake.

Open year-round.
(866) 588-4726
www.grandlakefun.com

8 Will Rogers Memorial Museum
Off State Hwy. 88, Claremore
"I never met a man I didn't like" is the saying usually associated with humorist and philosopher Will Rogers. Born in 1879, the man of Cherokee Indian descent once remarked, "My forefathers didn't come over on the Mayflower, but they met the boat." Rogers had a remarkably varied and successful career. He was a trick roper, Ziegfield Follies and vaudeville performer, and radio commentator. His witty, homespun remarks were

published daily in 350 newspapers.

Rogers' movie star career catapulted him to fame. The archives and nine galleries in this museum contain 15,000 photographs and 2,000 books about this man of the West and the world, whose larger-than-life spirit still permeates this part of northeastern Oklahoma. There are manuscripts, motion pictures, home movies, and a saddle collection. A sunken garden frames the Rogers family tomb. The museum is built on 20 acres Rogers had purchased in 1911 for his hoped-for retirement, but in 1935 he was killed in a plane crash with a fellow Oklahoman, pilot Wiley Post, over the Alaskan territory.

To get to Rogers's birthplace, take Route 88 out of Claremore to Dog Iron Ranch in Oologah, where newsreels run about Rogers's life and times.

Visitors might want to take Route 66 north to the town of Foyil, which has a colorful Totem Pole Park, and then to the town of Vinita. The Will Rogers Rodeo has been held there every August for more than 60 years.

Open year-round. Donations accepted.
(800) 324-9455
www.willrogers.com

9 Murrell Home and Nature Trail

Tahlequah; drive 2 miles south on Rte. 82 and follow signs.
Vintage Americana and a state government's first attempt to provide self-guiding nature explorations for the handicapped combine at this unusual setting. The quiet, elegant atmosphere of the antebellum South pervades a mansion built around 1845 by George Murrell at Park Hill, the cultural center of the

Cherokee Nation after being displaced from Georgia in 1838–39.

Murrell, a longtime friend of the Cherokees, married a niece of the great chief John Ross in Tennessee in 1834, and after her death, her sister. He himself died in New Orleans in 1894.

Hunter's Home, so named because of Murrell's fondness for hunting, has high-ceilinged rooms, each with a fireplace. It is impressively furnished in antebellum style and displays portraits of Murrell and his Cherokee wives. Outbuildings on the 38-acre grounds include a springhouse, log cabin, and smokehouse. The three-quarter-mile nature trail, paved to accommodate the handicapped, winds through dense stands of sycamore, Osage orange, willow, and hickory. Birders come especially for the flycatchers and vireos.

Open Wed.–Sun., Mar.–Oct.;
weekends Nov.–Apr.
(918) 456-2751
www.ok-history.mus.ok.us

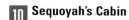

10 Sequoyah's Cabin

3 miles north of Sallisaw on U.S. 59, then 7 miles east on U.S. 101
In 1829, George Guess, better known as Sequoyah, came to present-day Oklahoma and built a log cabin in what is now Sequoyah County.

Today the restored cabin, which is enclosed in a museum, is an intriguing historical attraction.

Sequoyah is best remembered for his invention of the Cherokee alphabet—a syllabary of 86 characters. After it was adopted by the Cherokee Nation in 1821, it enabled the people to become literate in less than two years.

Another cabin built of logs believed to have been hewn by Sequoyah houses an information center where his syllabary is demonstrated. Both cabins display artifacts of Cherokee life in 1800 Indian Territory.

Other displays include a Trail of Tears exhibit depicting the removal of the Cherokee Nation in 1838-39 from Georgia, North

Carolina, and Tennessee.

Open Tues.–Fri. and P.M. Sat. and Sun.
except state holidays.
(918) 775-2413
www.ok-history.mus.ok.us

11 Spiro Mounds Archaeological Center

From Rte. 271 go north 4 miles on Lock and Dam Rd., Spiro.
One of the four greatest centers of the Mississippian Indian culture—and the most mysterious of them all—flourished here at this wide bend in the Arkansas River from the ninth to the 15th century. The park includes 140 acres and 12 mounds.

In the 1930s the great Craig Mound, which contained more than 1,000 burials and a charnel house, was ruthlessly excavated and looted. Since then archaeologists have worked to salvage and restore the mound.

Among the rich grave goods taken from it were stone effigies, copper breastplates, textiles, pottery, wooden figurines, wooden masks with shell inlays, and delicate shell cups. Some of the artifacts were engraved with skulls, body parts, falcons, and the plumed serpent, the deity of earth and sky. Because of the strange symbolism of the mortuary art, some believe that for a time Spiro was a religious center where elaborate funerary practices were observed.

Many of the artifacts are displayed at the interpretive center. A 1 1/2-mile-long trail winds among the mounds and passes a replica of a thatched-roof dwelling.

Open Wed.–Sat. and P.M. Sun.
except state holidays.
(918) 962-2062
www.ok-history.mus.ok.us

11 Spiro Mounds Archaeological Center. *The ancient mounds at this site hold clues to the mysterious Mississippian Indian culture that thrived here for centuries.*

12 Heavener Runestone State Park

3 miles north of Heavener

By a small mountain creek in a tree-shaded glen halfway up Poteau Mountain stands the Heavener Runestone, a 12-foot-high slab with eight Nordic runes (alphabet characters) representing a boundary marker for "Glome Valley." Although there is no absolute proof, some scholars believe that the runestones were left by Viking explorers almost 500 years before Columbus arrived in the New World.

The Vikings' route to the location may have been from the Gulf of Mexico to the Mississippi River, up the Arkansas and Poteau rivers, and into nearby Morris Creek. The Heavener stone is protected with plastic and is housed indoors.

A hilly one-mile nature trail meanders through the 50-acre park. Hickory, dogwood, redbud, oak, cedar, and pine trees provide cover for raccoons, beavers, armadillos, and deer, and the woods and sky resound with the cries and wing beats of hawks, blue jays, quail, and brown thrashers. A picnic area, community building, and playground are easily accessible.

Open year-round.
(918) 653-2241
www.oklahomaparks.com

13 Seminole Nation Museum

524 S. Wewoka Ave., corner of Sixth St., Wewoka.

"I fought in the Civil War and have seen men shot to pieces and slaughtered by the thousands," wrote a Georgia militia veteran, "but the Cherokee removal was the cruelest work I ever knew."

For the Seminole Indians, this tragic journey in the 1830s led from the farms of Florida's Everglades to Wewoka on the Oklahoma prairie, the new capital of the Seminole Nation.

The museum here chronicles the transition of the tribe from its southeastern roots to life in a new region. Displays range from a replica of a chuko—the traditional Seminole Everglades dwelling built of logs, palm leaves, and hides—to the reconstructed façade of the Wewoka Trading Post, the enterprise from which the new Indian capital grew. Historic photographs recall daily life in the 19th-century Indian Territory and the oil boom of the 1920s. Also shown are examples of the patchwork clothing for which the Seminoles are still famous. An annual Sorghum Day festival, held the last Saturday in October, features demonstrations in how the plant is ground and cooked into a sweet syrup. Flint-knapping, to make arrowheads, finger-weaving, to make straps and belts, and hide-tanning are also demonstrated.

Open daily, Feb.–Dec.
Donations accepted.
(405) 257-5580
www.wewoka.com

14 Black Kettle Museum

Intersection of Rtes. 283 and 47, Cheyenne

In the cold morning twilight of November 27, 1868, Lt. Col. George Armstrong Custer led his 7th Cavalry in a surprise attack on a sleeping Cheyenne Indian village on the shore of the Washita River. The chief of the village was Black Kettle, an outstanding Indian statesman who just days before had gone to Fort Cobb attempting to negotiate the safety of his people. Figures vary concerning the number of Cheyennes slaughtered, but many women and children died. Black Kettle and his wife were killed while attempting to escape on their pony.

Black Kettle Museum displays artifacts from the battle and from pioneer and Indian cultures of the period 1860–80. Poignant exhibits recount the antagonists' sad history of misunderstanding. The actual battle site is accessible two miles west of Cheyenne on Route 47A.

Open daily.
(580) 497-3929
www.ok-history.mus.ok.us

15 Quartz Mountain Nature Park

State Hwy. 44A, Lone Wolf

Set in the lee of the rugged Quartz Mountains, whose enormous red granite boulders seem to be tumbling down the hillsides, this park was once the winter campground of Kiowa and Comanche Indians. Today its 4,284 acres lure vacationers with a fine resort lodge, cabins, campsites, and picnic grounds along the shore of Lake Altus-Lugert, a large reservoir formed by a dam across the North Fork of the Red River. Fished for its bass, crappie, walleye, and catfish, the lake also offers excellent boating, canoeing, and swimming.

A nature center displays wildlife, plants, and items of local history. Native birds include vultures, hawks, kingbirds, cardinals, bluebirds, and scissor-tailed flycatchers. The half-mile New Horizon hiking trail scales the park's highest peak through live oak, yucca, prickly pear cactus, and stands of cedars. Swimming pools, a golf course, and a rugged backcountry area for off-road vehicles are additional attractions.

Open year-round.
(580) 563-2238
www.quartzmountainresort.com

16 Wichita Mountains Wildlife Refuge

Indiahoma, reached from Rte. 49

Comanche Indians, Spanish conquistadors, outlaws, and prospectors have prowled the boulder-strewn hills and surrounding grasslands of this 59,000-acre wildlife sanctuary.

16 Wichita Mountains Wildlife Refuge. *Created in 1901 to protect endangered prairie animals, this refuge is roamed by buffalo, longhorn cattle, and elk.*

Created in 1901 to protect endangered prairie animals, the refuge is roamed by a buffalo herd maintained at around 400 head. Other protected species include longhorn cattle, elk, and wild turkeys. A prairie dog town may be seen east of the refuge headquarters.

Portions of the refuge are fenced off for the protection of wildlife and visitors, but much of it can be explored by car or on foot. The public use area (which totals about 22,400 acres) offers fine fishing for bass and catfish, boating, camping, picnicking, and hiking. Mount Scott rises 1,000 feet to the summit from its base, and the drive is worth it for the views. Fifteen miles of hiking trails lead into remote regions, including the Charons Garden Wilderness, where backpack camping is allowed by permit. The challenging 900-foot ascent of Elk Mountain brings the hiker to a labyrinthine plateau pocked with passageways and small caves among huge boulders.

Open year-round.
(580) 429-3222

http://wichitamountains.fws.gov

17 Chisholm Trail Historical Museum

1 mile east of Waurika near junction of Hwys. 70 and 81
The trail through the center of the old Indian Territory, from Texas north to Kansas, was named for Jesse Chisholm, a part-Cherokee trader who opened up the famous route just after the Civil War. With good grazing and plenty of water along the way, it was ideal for the great herds of Texas longhorns that were driven to a Kansas rail terminal for shipment east. The Chisholm Trail was used for about 20 years, from 1867 until the end of the 1880s, when the railroads reached Texas. Near Monument Hill, about six miles north of Waurika, you can see a wide depression in the landscape, thought to be a remnant of the old route.

At the museum entrance a mural portrays cowboys herding half-wild longhorns. Exhibits include saddles, hats, guns, lariats, guitars, playing cards, branding irons, a stained glass window mapping the trail, railroad exhibits, Indian artifacts, an antique clock collection, and a number of pioneer farm implements. A 15-minute film presentation dramatizes the trail's history.

Open Sat. and Sun. except major holidays. Closed first Sun. of month.
(580) 228-2166

www.travelok.com

18 Turner Falls Park

Davis, off Rte. 77
Cascading over Honey Creek's 77-foot-high limestone rocks into

18 Turner Falls Park. *Honey Creek flows over 77-foot-high limestone rocks into a wide, natural plunge pool. Swimmers can enjoy the water at the base of the falls.*

a wide, natural plunge pool, these falls (named for Mazzepa Turner, who was a rancher and state representative of the early 1900s) are the centerpiece of a 6,000-acre park in the heart of the Arbuckle Mountains. The upward thrust of the terrain exposes many rock formations in nearly vertical positions so dramatically that the area is renowned as a geological window on the past. In spring the slopes and fields along the roadways turn a brilliant yellow as myriad black-eyed Susans begin to bloom.

A short walking trail to the bottom of the falls winds through Honey Creek Canyon, shaded by oak, poplar, cottonwood, locust, and walnut trees. The area is the habitat of deer, raccoons, and opossums and is frequented by many common and gregarious birds. Miles of more difficult hiking trails are also available, as are camping sites, cabins, and picnic grounds. Three natural caves are available to be explored. From an overview on a rocky bluff off Route 77, visitors can see the falls and the forested canyon.

Open year-round. Day admission fee.
(580) 369-2917

www.turnerfallspark.com

19 Beavers Bend Resort

8 miles north of Broken Bow on Hwy. 259A
Named for John Beavers, who once owned much of the land, this park borders the meandering Mountain Fork River deep in the Ouachita Mountains. Forested with pine and hardwood, accented by mistletoe, dogwoods, and bald cypresses along the riverbanks, the park is home to deer, small mammals, quail, wild turkeys, and many species of birds.

Forest Heritage Center, a rustic circular building, contains dioramas and other exhibits, including a slice of trunk from a 340-year-old bald cypress. A group of live Southern flying squirrels can be seen in the nature center.

The David L. Boren Hiking Trail extends for 26 miles through the forest to nearby Hochatown State Park, with two backpacking campsites along the way. Beavers Bend has four nature trails threading its 3,482 acres, and the river and Broken Bow Lake are stocked with trout, catfish, bass, crappie, and perch. Activities include swimming, boating, waterskiing, and horseback riding; scattered in the woods are cabins, campsites, and picnic grounds.

Open year-round.
(580) 494-6300

www.beaversbend.com

Historic Columbia River Highway State Trail. *Hikers enjoy the view along America's first scenic highway (see page 279).*

Oregon

Created largely by volcanic action, with a western edge sculpted by the raging sea, the varied and dramatic landscape is inevitable.

Along the coast of the Pacific Ocean are the justly famous sea stacks, promontories, dunes, beaches, and driftwood, as well as formal gardens, birds, and fields of wildflowers.

Oregon's fiery geologic past is revealed in a bleak and forbidding lava bed, a butte of black volcanic glass, a lava tube that swallows a river, and a fabulous lake in the caldera of a collapsed volcano.

There is old-time logging equipment to examine and a goldfield steam train to ride; in another mining area, there's a fascinating collection of Oriental artifacts. Other museums feature cowboy, American Indian, and pioneer memorabilia. You'll find some truly rugged scenery to explore, incredible numbers of waterfowl, and places you can catch salmon, trout, and largemouth bass.

1 Columbia River Maritime Museum

Marine Dr., Astoria

For five miles its foghorn could cut through the heavy mist, heralding the way home for bone-tired sailors. The bright beacon of the lightship *Columbia* was a comforting sight for seamen approaching the mouth of the Columbia River, known for its danger to ships. The first lightship on the Pacific Coast began its tour of duty in 1892. The last *Columbia* lightship to be in active service was replaced in 1979 by an unmanned navigational buoy of heroic proportions, measuring 40 feet wide by 86 feet high. Both floating aids are now on display here.

Two hundred years of Pacific Northwest maritime history are explored here, with the powerful waterway visible through the large windows of the wavelike structure. Interactive exhibits allow people to see what it's like to pilot a tug boat, engage in a Coast Guard rescue on the river bar, or go salmon fishing in Astoria. You can even clamber up to the bridge of a World War II naval destroyer, the USS *Knapp*.

Open year-round; closed Thanksgiving and Christmas. Admission charged.

(503) 325-2323

www.crmm.org

2 Cape Meares State Park and Cape Meares National Wildlife Refuge. *Driftwood, a piece of nature's sculpture, rests in this haven on the ocean.*

2 Cape Meares State Park and Cape Meares National Wildlife Refuge

Tillamook, off Three Capes Scenic Dr.

In 1788 Capt. John Meares, exploring the coast, came upon this imposing headland and named it Cape Lookout. When the coast was surveyed in 1850, a point 10 miles to the south was erroneously designated Cape Lookout, and by 1857 the name had become so well known that the original site was renamed Cape Meares. The 40-foot octagonal lighthouse, perhaps built here by mistake, operated from 1890 to 1964.

The park and lighthouse sit atop Cape Meares, a 217-foot-high bluff with sheer cliffs dropping straight to the sea. A sturdy fence along the 250-yard path to the lighthouse protects visitors from a possibly fatal tumble.

Some $2^1/_2$-miles of trail cross the 232-acre park. From the trail on the south side of the cape, you can view the Three Arches Wildlife Refuge, three islands of rock about $2^1/_2$ miles to the south. With binoculars you may catch a glimpse of the sea lions inhabiting the marine refuge.

To find the Cape Meares Wildlife Refuge, take the Oregon Coast Trail east from the parking lot. The trail leads through the refuge and down to the beach. On the way you'll pass the Octopus Tree, a Sitka spruce that is striking for its enormous size and candelabra branching. Its six limbs extend horizontally from the trunk for 30 feet before turning upward. From early February through July, trilliums, skunk cabbage, lilies of the valley, and other wildflowers add color to the landscape. Tufted puffins and pelagic cormorants are among the numerous seabirds nesting on the 139-acre refuge, where black-tailed deer are also seen.

The Three Capes Scenic Drive, about 35 miles long, offers spectacular views of coast, dunes, and picturesque villages.

Park open year-round; lighthouse open Thurs.–Mon., June–Sept.

(503) 842-4981

www.oregonstateparks.org

3 Sea Lion Caves
Florence

Both California sea lions, which are black and have a sharp bark, and Steller's sea lions, brown with a deep roar, are found here. During fall and winter as many as 400 gather in the cave, their only permanent year-round home on the American mainland. In spring and summer they often bask on the rocky cliffs.

Entrance to the cave (despite the official name, there is only one) is by an elevator that descends 208 feet from the visitors center to the observation window. The 300-foot-wide cavern, about two acres in size with a dome 125 feet high, is believed to be the world's largest sea cave and a rookery for Brandt's cormorants, which usually arrive in April and stay until the middle of August. As many as 2,500 nests have been found on the cliffs. The view from the visitors center makes this a popular place for whale watching.

Open year-round except Christmas. Admission charged.

(541) 547-3111

www.sealioncaves.com

4 Jessie M. Honeyman Memorial State Park

3 miles south of Florence
Sand dunes, ocean beaches, two freshwater lakes, and a forest of Douglas fir, spruce, hemlock, and cedar await visitors to this splendid 522-acre park.

The dunes, mere infants by geologic reckoning, were formed during the last 10,000 to 15,000 years by the erosive power of the sea. Cleawox Lake, with dunes to the west and woodlands to the east, has a sandy swimming beach and a picnic area. Freshwater swimming is also available at Woahink Lake, east of Route 101.

Other summertime activities include boating, waterskiing, canoeing, and fishing for bluegill, bass, and trout. In fall the park attracts mushroom hunters. Winter brings storm watchers, flocks of geese and other birds, and rock-hounds hunting for agates; during March visitors climb the dunes for whale watching.

The park, named in honor of Mrs. Jessie M. Honeyman, an early supporter of Oregon's conservation movement, has several picnic grounds, 350 camping sites, 10 yurts (tentlike domes that sleep up to five), and a boat-launching ramp. Hiking trails range from short walks through the forest to longer treks over the dunes to the ocean.

Open year-round, including the camp-ground. Day-use fee charged per vehicle.
(800) 551-6949
www.oregonstateparks.org

5 Golden and Silver Falls State Park

24 miles northeast of Coos Bay
The two falls, located at opposite ends of the 157-acre park, are about three-quarters of a mile apart. Golden Falls (named in honor of an early visitor) drops over a rounded ledge of lava; Silver Falls (named to complement its "sister") cascades from a basalt amphithe-ater over a series of boulders and divides into two streams that become Silver Creek.

A parking lot and picnic ground are halfway between the two falls. To reach Golden Falls, follow a half-mile path along the canyon through stands of evergreens; the trail offers a pleasant view of Glenn Creek. Silver Falls is reached by a quarter-mile path along the canyon floor among

5 Golden and Silver Falls State Park.
A quarter-mile path along a canyon floor leads visitors to Silver Falls.

ferns and moss-draped trees.

The park, which has been left in its natural state, is notable for its grove of myrtles—rare and beautiful hardwood trees that flourish in southern Oregon. Chip-munks, porcupines, and black bears are found here, with elk and deer coming to forage in winter. Trout fishing in both Glenn and Silver creeks is excellent in early summer. Picnic tables and grills are provided.

Open year-round.
(800) 551-6949
www.oregonstateparks.org

6 Sunset Bay State Park

3 1/2 miles southwest of Charleston
When trapper Jedediah Smith arrived at Sunset Bay in 1828, he

found it inhabited by American Indians who fished its waters and gathered shellfish from the inter-tidal zone. People still come to Sunset Bay to fish, particularly for sea perch, rockfish, and sea trout. Swimming is popular too in the calm, warm, cliff-encircled bay. A fish-cleaning station, a pine-sheltered campground, eight yurts (tentlike domes that sleep up to five), and a boat-launching ramp are provided.

You can enjoy lunch beside a small creek, on a grassy point overlooking the beach, or even under a roofed pagoda. Picnic tables and grills are scattered throughout the rest of the park.

Afterward you can walk along the beach or hike through a wood-land inhabited by deer, raccoons, and seldom-seen bobcats. If you really wish to explore the shore-line, take the Oregon Coast Trail, which begins at Sunset Bay's park-ing lot, winds for 3 1/2 miles along the shore, and continues through the Shore Acres gardens to Cape Arago's beaches.

For an outstanding view of the bay's rugged sandstone cliffs, drive about a mile south on the Cape Arago highway to a stairway that crosses the guardrail and leads to a lookout at the edge of a cliff.

Park and camping open year-round.
(800) 551-6949
www.oregonstateparks.org

7 Indian Mary Park and Hellgate Canyon

11 miles north of Merlin on Merlin Galice Rd.
Indian Mary Park and Hellgate Canyon are side by side on Oregon's Rogue River. Novelist Zane Grey, who owned a cabin on the river,

wrote of Hellgate in several of his stories. A portion of Indian Mary Park was once the smallest American Indian reservation (40 acres) in the United States, granted by the government in 1855 to Umqua Joe, Mary's father, for warning white settlers of an impending massacre. The reserva-tion is now a 65-acre park with exotic trees and shrubs planted among native ponderosa pine and Douglas fir. Spring brings extra touches of beauty, when the trees and shrubs, complemented by azaleas, lupines, and yellow mon-key flowers, burst into bloom. In autumn the foliage is brilliant.

The park has shaded picnic grounds, playgrounds, and camp-sites with hookups. The river, wide and calm near the park, is popular with swimmers and fishermen. The Indian Joe Trail, a steep 3 1/2-mile route, leads to a lookout from which you can see the forested hills and grasslands of the Rogue River valley.

Hellgate Canyon, a jumble of sheer cliffs and overhanging rocks, is a favorite with rafters, kayakers, and tubers. An excursion boat, which departs from Hog Creek a mile above the canyon, also weaves through the chasm. Sandbars here attract gold panners as well as picnickers.

Open year-round.
Admission charged.
Indian Mary Park:
(541) 474-5285
www.rogueweb.com/indianmary
Hellgate Canyon:
(503) 479-3735
www.southernoregon.com/
merlin-galice/index.html
www.co.josesphine.or.us/parks/
index.htm

8 Kerbyville Museum and History Center

Kerby
Following the discovery of gold on the banks of Josephine Creek in 1851, several towns, including Kerbyville (since shortened to Kerby) mushroomed. Few of these towns remain, but the heirlooms, tools, and mementos of many of the people who once lived in them have been donated to the Kerbyville Museum.

In the main museum building you'll see a colorful facsimile of an old-time country store interior, American Indian handiwork, a new military display featuring artifacts from the Civil War to the Vietnam War, and a collection of women's clothing illustrating that the apparel of a well-dressed lady could weigh as much as 100 pounds.

The complex also includes a quaint one-room log schoolhouse, a barn-sized blacksmith's shop, farm equipment, and the 1871 Stith-Naucke House. A life-size replica of a Takelma Indian pit house is also on display. The two-story building is charmingly furnished with Victoriana and other antiques that belonged to early Josephine County families. Both creek and county were named for the daughter of an early prospector.
Open daily; call for winter hours. Admission charged.
(541) 592-5252
www.kerbyvillemuseum.com

9 Natural Bridge, Rogue River National Forest

55 miles north of Medford off Rte. 62
Natural Bridge is visible during summertime periods of low water; it's also a spectacular sight at other times, when the Rogue submerges it in swift whitewater rapids. The bridge is a large, intact lava tube that channels the river underground for about 200 feet before the waters resurface.

Its origins date back to the eruption of Mount Mazama, which formed Crater Lake nearly 7,000 years ago and sent lava flows raging across the surrounding countryside. As their surfaces cooled and hardened, tunnels, or tubes, formed underneath.

Natural Bridge campground has sites for tents and small trailers, each with a picnic table and grill. There are several hiking trails, one to Woodruff Bridge, a favorite spot for catching rainbow trout, and another to Big Bend.

Avoid wading near the opening of Natural Bridge and walking on its slippery-smooth surface. Tales are told of people and pets being dragged into the rushing waters and never seen again.
Open Memorial Day–Labor Day.
(541) 858-2200 or (541) 560-3400
www.fs.fed.us/r6/rogue

10 McKenzie Pass Lava Beds

Off Hwy. 242 between McKenzie Bridge and Sisters
Stretching for some 75 square miles on both sides of McKenzie Pass Road are the jumbled lava beds that resulted from thousands of years of eruptions along the High Cascade volcanic chain. Markers along the half-mile Lava River Trail, which starts at the summit of the pass, explain lava gutters, pressure ridges, cooling cracks, crevasses, and other formations, and identify the fascinating dwarf trees—among them mountain hemlock, lodgepole pine, and Pacific silver fir.

Except for the Belknap Crater flows, which are rolling, graceful rivers of rock, the lava is a broken, jumbled mass of rocks, like ice breaking up on a river, the result of its surface cooling over molten turbulence. A 1.5 mile loop trail on the west end of Hwy. 242 leads to Proxy Falls. A 3.8-mile trail on the east end, quite steep in places, takes you from the highway at Windy Point to Black Crater.

10 **McKenzie Pass Lava Beds.** *Mountain hemlock trees manage to cling to the jumbled lava beds here as the Cascade peaks rise in the background.*

The Dee Wright Observatory, at the crest between Proxy Falls and Black Crater, offers spectacular views of several Cascade peaks. Built from lava rock during the Great Depression and completed in 1935, it remains one of the most popular attractions at the lava beds.
Open July–mid-Oct.
(541) 822-3381
www.fs.fed.us/r6/willamette

11 Historic Columbia River Highway State Trail

East of Portland, between Troutdale and The Dalles
They call it the king of roads, this expansive thoroughfare that travels east-west through the Columbia River Gorge. America's first scenic highway, built between 1913 and 1922, was also the first modern highway in the Pacific Northwest. Running alongside the south side of the Columbia River, it was designed to be in harmony with nature. Since the mid-1980s more than 10 miles of abandoned highway have been restored as pedestrian and bicycle paths known as the Historic Columbia River Highway State Trail. You pass between two climate zones in the Twin Tunnels portion of the trail, between Hood River and Mosier. Leaving the car allows you to take a more leisurely look at the Ponderosa pine, moss-covered rocks, ferns, and wildflowers. The gorge itself is among the most awe-inspiring sights in the United States.
Open year-round. Day-use admission charged per vehicle.
(800) 551-6949
www.oregonstateparks.org

12 Smith Rock State Park

3 1/2 miles east of Terrebonne
Smith Rock is known as one of the world's most popular rock-climbing destinations. The keynote here is color: 623 acres of spectacular sandstone formations—boulders, cliffs, crags, and pinnacles—in magnificent pale yellows, burnt reds, rich greens, and purples that change with the shifting sunlight. The Crooked River, a ribbon of blue, twists among them. The park was named for its discoverer, John Smith, a Kentuckian who came to Oregon in the 1850s and rose to political prominence.

Picnic sites are scattered throughout the park. Several paved pathways lead from the parking lot to the river's edge and across a footbridge, where a network of trails spreads out among the formations.
Open year-round. Day-use admission charged per vehicle.
(800) 551-6949
www.oregonstateparks.org

13 The High Desert Museum

3 miles south of Bend on U.S. 97
Both indoor and outdoor exhibits as well as a series of educational programs bring the natural and cultural history of this high desert region alive.

Birds of prey, like the golden eagle, can be seen up close in their natural habitats at the museum, as well as a life-size diorama of an 1800s Western settlement. Visitors can also explore a 1950s reservation home and schoolhouse.

The Wind, Earth, and Fire trail educates visitors on the region's fire history as well as the effects of modern-day forest management.

Continuing on the trail, you'll see otters frolicking in the stream that runs through it, as well as porcupines relaxing in the sun.
Open year-round except Thanksgiving, Christmas, and New Year's Day.
Admission charged.
(541) 382-4754
www.highdesertmuseum.org

12 Smith Rock State Park. *The Crooked River twists through one of the most popular rock-climbing destinations in the world.*

14 Crater Lake National Park

57 miles north of Klamath Falls, off Rte. 62
Crater Lake is particularly beautiful in winter, and despite an annual snowfall of 533 inches, easy to visit. The road is kept clear, and a 30-mile ski trail circles the crater rim. On weekends from Thanksgiving to April, you can join snowshoe hikes led by a park ranger.

Crater Lake is the deepest (1,943 feet) and probably the bluest lake in the United States, set like a sapphire in the bowl-shaped caldera of old Mount Mazama, a volcano that erupted and collapsed nearly 7,000 years ago.

Traces of past volcanic activity can be seen at The Pinnacles, reached by Sand Creek Highway, a seven-mile paved road passable from late summer until heavy snow. These pumice and scoria formations, 75 to 100 feet tall, rise like an army of obelisks from a 200-foot-deep canyon. Some 30 trails (ranging from less than a mile to 35 miles) crisscross the park.

Hikes up Watchman Peak (0.7 mile) and Mount Scott (2.5 miles) provide the best views of the lake. There are two campgrounds, at Mazama and at Lost Creek, both accessible by road from Rim Drive. And with a permit you can camp in the backcountry.
Park open year-round; main visitors center also open year-round.
(541) 594-3000
www.nps.gov/crla

15 Collier Memorial State Park

30 miles north of Klamath Falls, near Chiloquin
The 650-acre park's main attraction is a logging museum founded by Alfred and Andrew Collier, who donated most of the acreage to the state in 1945 as a memorial to their parents.

Two years later the brothers began to round up the museum exhibits, many of them drawn from a time and technology that no longer exist. Equipment on display ranges from ox yokes and horse-drawn wagons to a modern generating plant capable of supplying enough power for an entire sawmill. A wood-burning locomotive, 19th-century steam tractors, chain-saws, and a wealth of other logging and pioneering artifacts are housed in the museum buildings, which include a turn-of-the-century logger's homestead, a blacksmith's shed, and a group of authentic pioneer cabins.

A spacious day-use area is set among pine and aspen where the Williamson River and Spring Creek come together. A second, more secluded picnic area is located on the creek's west shore. The river is also a superb spot for trout fishing. The camping area has 68 sites, 50 with full hookups.
Museum and day-use areas open year-round. Campground open mid-Apr–Oct.
(800) 551-6949
www.oregonstateparks.org

16 Upper Klamath National Wildlife Refuge

Rocky Point, off of Hwy. 140 west
There is only one way to tour this vast wetlands preserve: by boat. More than 14,000 acres of marsh and open water here provide food and nesting sites for some 250 species of birds. The small village of Rocky Point on the western edge of the refuge at Pelican Bay offers access to the marshes and

 Crater Lake National Park. *The deepest and probably the bluest lake in the United States, Crater Lake is set like a sapphire in the bowl-shaped caldera of old Mount Mazama, a volcano that erupted and collapsed.*

a fine viewing spot on the shore.

From here you can follow a 9 1/2-mile self-guiding canoe trail through the marshlands, a trip that provides a unique opportunity for watching bird life, particularly the pelicans, egrets, herons, and Canada geese. The best time for viewing these birds (and perhaps raccoons, deer, otters, and minks) is at sunrise. Bald eagles and ospreys nest nearby and can occasionally be seen fishing the waters.

Both hunting and fishing are permitted in season on 5,700 acres of the refuge territory. Trout average four or five pounds. Yellow perch is another likely catch. Hunting is limited to geese, ducks, coots, and snipe.

The Forest Service maintains campgrounds near Rocky Point, and from April into November a few sportsmen's resorts in the area offer marina facilities, cabins, and motorboat and canoe rentals.

Refuge open year-round; campgrounds open year-round, depending on snow access.
(530)-667-2231
www.klamathnwr.org

17 Glass Butte Recreational Rockhound Area

Off U.S. Rte. 20; at milepost 77, turn south
Serious rockhounds come from near and far to dig at Glass Butte. The Bureau of Land Management allows rock collecting for personal use only, and you can collect up to 250 pounds of rock per year.

Formed by a volcanic eruption nearly 5 million years ago, the 6,400-foot mountain has some of the world's largest outcrops of obsidian—a black volcanic glass that forms when lava with a high silica content cools quickly.

American Indians prized the brittle, easily chipped obsidian and turned this area into a virtual factory for axes, scrapers, chisels, and weapon points.

While ordinary jet black obsidian is appealing and makes attractive jewelry, the material can also be streaked with gold, silver, and other colors, or have an iridescent sheen. Even the rare fire obsidian is found here. Some 23,000 acres have been set aside for rock-hounding, and in the valley chunks can be kicked up with a boot or found lying loose in the roadbed. Anyone seeking the more valuable varieties, however, should bring shovels, picks, and rock hammers. No mechanical equipment is allowed.

The road to the site is rutted and rough and best traversed with four-wheel drive. The area is primitive, with no facilities, although overnight camping is permitted. Camping or not, visitors should bring food and water.

Open year-round. No admission charge.
(541) 416-6700
www.sova.org/desert.htm

18 Sheep Rock Unit, John Day Fossil Beds National Monument

Intersection of Rtes. 19 and 26, Kimberly
Thirty million years ago, saber-toothed cats pursued sheep-sized horses amid vast forests here, while piglike entelodonts and rhinoceroses grazed the lush under-brush. You can see fossil evidence of these and other prehistoric plants and animals discovered in volcanic and sedimentary layers of a colorful, near-desert landscape.

The place to closely examine hundreds of fossils is the Thomas Condon Paleontology Center, where you will find a working fossil laboratory and exhibits showcasing current research.

Hiking trails, most fairly easy, lead through spectacular "bad-lands" scenery where fossils are still being found. (Collecting is prohibited without research permits.) The John Day River crosses the area and provides good fishing, mostly steelhead and smallmouth bass.

Open daily year-round; Paleontology Center to be open daily.
(541) 987-2333
www.nps.gov/joda

 John Day Fossil Beds National Monument. *Evidence of prehistoric plants and animals can be found in the volcanic and sedimentary layers of rock in this colorful landscape.*

OREGON

19 McKay Creek National Wildlife Refuge

From Pendleton, drive 5 miles south on U.S. Hwy. 395.
Established as a refuge and breeding ground for wildfowl, this preserve is almost completely inundated with visitors much of the year. In spring and early summer, the reservoir is a serene, mirror-smooth lake covering more than two-thirds of the 1,800-acre refuge—the only dry land a rim of shoreline. During these seasons it attracts boaters, fishermen, and water-skiers and serves as the major source of water for nearby cropland. By August, however, it shrinks to less than one-fifth its former size, exposing mud flats that sprout vegetation, providing food for wildlife.

Birds found here include great blue herons, American coots, long-billed curlews, ring-billed gulls, and red-winged blackbirds. Spring and fall bring an increase of waterfowl—mallards and Canada geese, with some American widgeons, green-winged teals, and pintails. Their population peaks at 30,000 in winter.

Refuge open Mar.–Sept.;
600 acres remain open during state
waterfowl hunting season, Oct.–Jan.
(509) 545-8588
http://midcolumbiariver.fws.gov

20 Hat Point Overlook, Hells Canyon National Recreation Area

24 miles southeast of Imnaha via one-lane dirt road
Hat Point Overlook is really only for those with four-wheel-drive vehicles. The trip, however, is extremely rewarding, because of the views of Hells Canyon—the

20 Hat Point Overlook, Hells Canyon National Recreation Area. *The view from the summit shows the Snake River, more than a mile below, and the Seven Devils Mountains, above.*

deepest river gorge on the North American continent.

The 24-mile trip on a one-lane dirt road from Imnaha takes $1^{1}/_{2}$ hours, not counting stops, and goes from an altitude of approximately 1,700 feet to 6,982 feet. At Five Mile Viewpoint the road levels out and goes through pine forests and wildflower-filled meadows inhabited by a variety of wildlife.

Besides Hells Canyon, the view from the summit includes the Snake River, more than a mile below, and across the canyon in Idaho, the craggy peaks of the Seven Devils Mountains. For an even more panoramic vista visitors can climb the 100-foot tower, which is manned in summer. A hiking trail begins in the picnic area and winds through meadows and down the cliff to the canyon far below.

Campgrounds are provided for tents and light campers. No running water is available.
Road open July–Nov.
(541) 426-5546
www.fs.fed.us/r6/w-w

21 Oxbow Dam, Hells Canyon National Recreation Area

70 miles east of Baker at junction of Oregon Rte. 86 and Idaho Rte. 71
When Hells Canyon Power Development Complex was completed in 1968, three dams spanned the Snake River Canyon—Oxbow, Brownlee, and Hells Canyon—their backwaters forming three man-made lakes and a recreation area 90 miles long. Oxbow is the center of the complex and the smallest of the three.

Oxbow also has a fish hatchery, where steelheads can be seen from September through the end of April.

All three dam areas are popular with power-boaters, water-skiers, swimmers, and fishermen, who try for trout, bass, catfish, steelheads, and crappies. Here, too, are large populations of deer, elk, and bighorn sheep, as well as chukars, quails, Hungarian partridges, bald and golden eagles, cranes, geese, grouse, swans, and a variety of ducks and songbirds.

A scenic highlight of the entire recreation area is the 22-mile

Hells Canyon Drive, which begins at Oxbow. Several miles of hiking trails and picnic areas are available.
Park open year-round; hatchery open daily.
(541) 426-4978
www.fs.fed.us/r6/w-w/hcnra.htm

22 Sumpter Valley Railway

Off I-84, 22 miles from Baker City
Travel back to the glory of eastern Oregon's turn-of-the-century lumber and mining industry aboard the open-air cars and original caboose of this restored narrow-gauge railway, driven by an authentic wood-burning Heisler locomotive.

The Sumpter Valley Railway Company, started in 1890 by lumber magnate David Eccles, was a highly prosperous operation by the time its tracks were extended to the Sumpter gold mines in 1896. During the 1930s, however, business declined, and in 1947 the railroad, known as the Stump Dodger, ceased operation.

Since 1970 local volunteers have been restoring the track bed and offering rides through the picturesque countryside. Occasionally a run is attacked by "bandits," provided by volunteers, who add to the colorful illusion of the Old West. While you're waiting for the trip to begin, browse through the historic photographs and railroad memorabilia in the depot's museum, or visit the engine cab, where the crew is happy to explain how the steam locomotive works.

Open weekends Memorial Day–Sept.
Admission charged.
(541) 894-2268
www.svry.com

23 Kam Wah Chung & Company Museum

Northwest Canton St., John Day

Here's a reminder of the days when Chinese laborers outnumbered white miners and ranchers nearly three to one in eastern Oregon. Kam Wah Chung & Company, built in the 1860s as a trading post, was bought in 1887 by two young immigrants, Lung On, a merchant, and Ing Hay, an herbalist. They lived and worked there until the 1940s, having grasped the "Golden Flower of Opportunity" implied by the store's name.

Kam Wah Chung & Company became a center for the Chinese community: a general store, doctor's office, pharmacy, temple, gambling and opium den, and speakeasy. Today the tiny herbal dispensary is jammed with boxes, tins, and jars full of traditional remedies. The building's shrines are still hung with effigies, paper cutouts, and peacock feathers. Joss sticks and fortune sticks survive along with shriveled offerings of a variety of fruit.

And there's more: bootleg-whiskey bottles, fireworks, playing cards and dominoes, gold-mining pans and scales. There are also pieces of handmade furniture built in traditional style by members of the local Chinese community.

A visit to this well-preserved place of multifarious business evokes the history of Chinatowns in the West. It's a worthwhile cultural and historical experience.

Open Mon.–Sat. and P.M. Sun., May–Oct. Admission charged.
(541) 575-0028
www.oregonstateparks.org

22 Sumpter Valley Railway. *Passengers on this locomotive can experience what it was like to travel by train through gold and timber country a century ago.*

24 Lake Owyhee State Park

33 miles southwest of Nyssa

You can boat the 53-mile length of Lake Owyhee and never be more than a half-mile from its shoreline's spectacular scenery. The lake is really a reservoir backed up behind Owyhee Dam (completed in 1935). Its 310 miles of shoreline are the steep sides of the rocky gorge through which the Owyhee River runs; its name comes from a 19th-century spelling for Hawaii (the story goes that two Hawaiians died here at the hands of American Indians in 1819).

You cruise past stone pinnacles and spires, multicolored layers of bent and broken strata, soaring red-rock outcrops. Some visitors may prefer to concentrate on fishing what has been called the most overstocked and underfished lake in Oregon. Tournaments meet here to take the renowned largemouth bass, and there is plenty of black crappie and catfish—as well as a smaller population of rainbow trout.

Wildlife abound here, and one can see bighorn sheep, pronghorn antelope, wild horses, and golden eagles.

About two miles above the dam, you'll find a picnic area and two campgrounds. The rest of the shoreline is virtually inaccessible, although there are a few trails leading from the campground, and 70 miles of dirt roads (four-wheel drive only) twist through the terrain. Boaters and water-skiers should keep to the center of the lake to avoid offshore boulders.

Park open year-round; camping mid-Apr.–late Oct.
(800) 551-6949
www.oregonstateparks.org

25 Malheur National Wildlife Refuge

Off Rte. 205, 32 miles south of Burns in Princeton

This 187,000-acre wetlands preserve, situated in desert uplands covered with sagebrush and juniper, encompasses two large, shallow lakes (Harney and Malheur) and a number of ponds, ditches, dikes, and canals. The refuge's permanent bulrush marshes and seasonally flooded meadows provide ideal habitats for both nesting and migrating birds. The best way to see it all is by car, starting at refuge headquarters. Here the George M. Benson Museum offers an impressive array of mounted birds, from common flickers to cranes and eagles, as well as tip sheets on current bird-watching hot spots.

Spring brings pintail ducks, sandhill cranes, tundra swans, and snow and Canada geese, and fall draws mallards and warblers as well. May and August are the prime months for songbirds. Ducks, geese, and trumpeter swans are winter stay-overs. Birds of prey spotted here include great horned owls and golden and bald eagles. Beavers and muskrats in the marshes and mule deer in the uplands are among the 58 mammal species seen.

Cross-country hiking is only allowed on designated trails. Flooding in the refuge's northern lowlands can limit access and may require detours. It's best to call first.

Refuge and museum open year-round; some roads may be impassable in spring and winter.
Headquarters open weekdays year-round, plus weekends spring, summer, and fall.
(541) 493-2612
www.r1.fws.gov/malheur

Brandywine River Museum.
A century-old gristmill now serves
as a spacious spot to display paint-
ings and sculpture (see page 293).

Pennsylvanians' interest in preserving the natural scene is confirmed by its more than 100 state parks. Reclamation is also of primary concern, as you will see at a tree nursery and a fish hatchery that support this purpose. In one state park are a restored glacial lake and a beautiful landscape once scarred by strip mining and oil drilling. Museums in the state fulfill a diversity of interests—such as toy trains, dolls, watches, antique tools and implements, and Little League baseball. A valued cultural contribution is the showplace created for the works of a family of renowned American artists. Many were inspired by the beauty of the Pennsylvania countryside.

Pennsylvania

For 300 miles, from east to west, the state spans a fascinating range of history, culture, industry, agriculture, and landforms.

1 Presque Isle State Park
Erie

Seven miles of pristine beach can be enjoyed in this 3,200-acre park on a peninsula jutting into Lake Erie. Fifteen miles of paved trail provide a great place for walking, biking, or in-line skating.

In addition to the swimming beaches, reached by a loop road, the park has about 20 miles of hiking trails, some leading around inland ponds and a lagoon. Spring anglers bring in bass, walleye, salmon, and perch. Rental boats and boat launches are available, as well as a 498-boat marina.

In addition, birders come from all over the world for spring and fall migration.

In winter, Presque Isle is a wonderland, with trees and ground mantled by sparkling white snow. Cross-country ski trails abound, and ice fishing attracts hundreds of enthusiasts. Visitors will be thrilled by the incredible ice dunes that form. From the inland side of the peninsula, which hooks back toward the mainland to form Erie Harbor, the city of Erie serrates the horizon when the weather is clear.

Open year-round.
Free admission.
(814) 833-7424
www.dcnr.state.pa.us

2 Baldwin-Reynolds House Museum. *A U.S. Supreme Court justice based the design of this three-story 19th-century home on a Southern mansion.*

2 Baldwin-Reynolds House Museum

639 Terrace St., Meadville
Henry Baldwin, a U.S. Supreme Court justice from 1830 to 1844, based the design of his stately three-story home on a Southern mansion. It sits on a gentle rise in the midst of landscaped grounds with a commanding view of French Creek, once the major trading route in the area. The pre-Civil War Southern culture and lifestyle are represented in this elegant frame structure.

After Baldwin's death in 1844, the house was bought by a relative, William Reynolds. Members of his family lived here until 1963.

The 19th-century kitchen and servants' lodgings are tucked away on the ground floor and in the basement. Massive, high-ceilinged rooms with arched doorways, parquet floors, Italian marble fireplaces, doors with satin glass floral designs, and incredibly delicate cherry, ash, and walnut woodwork combine to give each room its own delightful character.

The total effect is one of an opulence in which every conceivable personal whim is fulfilled. There are secret compartments in the library where important papers could be hidden, and specially designed false pillars that can be removed to reveal a small proscenium-style arch for family entertainment and performances.

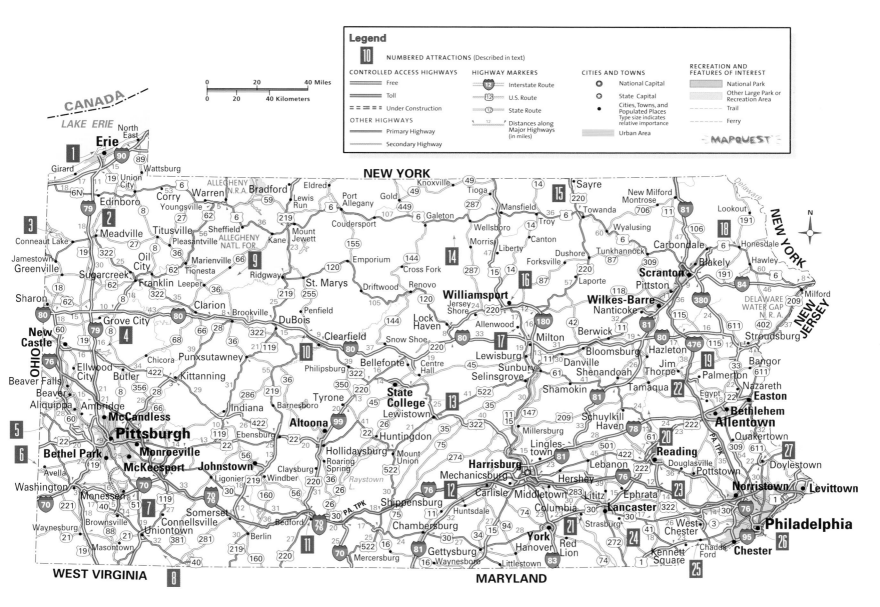

Legend

NUMBERED ATTRACTIONS (Described in text)

CONTROLLED ACCESS HIGHWAYS
- Free
- Toll
- Under Construction

OTHER HIGHWAYS
- Primary Highway
- Secondary Highway

HIGHWAY MARKERS
- Interstate Route
- U.S. Route
- State Route
- Distances along Major Highways (in miles)

CITIES AND TOWNS
- National Capital
- State Capital
- Cities, Towns, and Populated Places Type size indicates relative importance
- Urban Area

RECREATION AND FEATURES OF INTEREST
- National Park
- Other Large Park or Recreation Area
- Trail
- Ferry

The museum also contains a number of historical and antique displays, including a large collection of paperweights.

Next door to the Baldwin-Reynolds house is the Dr. J. Russell Mosier office, which was left intact after his death in 1938. It contains a pharmacy, medical skeleton, and even the unopened mail received the day Dr. Mosier died.

Open Wed., Sat., Sun., Memorial Day–Labor Day. Admission charged.
(814) 724-6080

www.visitcrawford.org/hosted/brhouse

3 Pymatuning Reservoir

Accessible via U.S. Routes 6 or 322, north of Jamestown

Once a great swamp, the reservoir was created when the Pymatuning dam was completed in 1934. It was intended to conserve water going into the swamp, impound flood-waters, and regulate the flow of water into the Beaver and Shenango rivers. The name Pymatuning came from the Iroquois and means "the crooked mouthed man's dwelling place," referring to someone's deceit.

The swamp that had trapped stray cattle in its marshy depths and provided familiar hunting grounds for bear and mountain lion became a peaceful, golden lake.

The lake teems with activity in the summer, when warm-weather fishing is bountiful. The annual Winter Fun Days offer a whole range of winter sports, from ice fishing to cross-country skiing. Most of Pymatuning is in north-western Pennsylvania, but one-quarter of it rests in Ashtabula County, Ohio.

The spillway near Linesville is known as the place "where the ducks walk on the fish." So many carp congregate to catch stale bread thrown by visitors that the ducks have no room to swim, and it looks as though they're walking over the fish.

Open year-round.
(724) 932-3142

www.dcnr.state.pa.us/stateparks/parks/pyma.htm

4 Moraine State Park
Portersville

Through the marvels of environmental engineering, what was once an ugly, man-made hole in the ground has been transformed into a serene recreational park. Moraine State Park is located upon land used for coal mining, strip mining, and gas and oil drilling. The reclamation was accomplished by sealing off the abandoned mines, plugging the wells, and dramatically altering the physical landscape.

A glacial lake that existed 10,000 years ago was re-created by damming existing streams. Lake Arthur covers more than 3,000 acres, has 40 miles of shoreline, and is well stocked with bass, walleye, muskellunge, and channel catfish. The lake's seven-mile length makes it ideal for canoes, kayaks, rowboats, and sailboats. Motorpowered boats up to 18 horsepower are also permitted here.

Although the lake is the centerpiece, creeks, swamps, marshes, hardwood forests, and mud flats add variety to the natural environment here. More than 150 different species of birds, including osprey, bald eagles, hawks, loons, owls, blue jays, and herons, can be spotted at the park, many of them year-round.

Marked hiking trails extend throughout the park. The relatively short Hilltop Nature Trail takes hikers through land cleared for farming that is slowly reverting to its natural state.

More ambitious hikers can tackle the seven-mile-long Glacier Ridge Trail, a segment of the projected North Country National Scenic Trail, a 3,200-mile hiking route from Crown Point, New York, to Lake Sakakawea, North Dakota.

Open year-round.
(724) 368-8811
www.dcnr.state.pa.us/stateparks/parks/morain.htm

5 Raccoon Creek State Park
Hookstown

Although most of the land surrounding man-made Raccoon Lake is landscaped, much of the remaining 7,300-acre area is in its heavily forested natural state. In the fall the foliage of 42 different kinds of trees turns color in a spectacularly vivid display of nature's diversity. Forty-one miles of trails await hikers, bicyclists, horseback riders, and cross-country skiers. The trail system includes a 20-mile loop for backpackers.

Hikers can follow the five miles of trail crisscrossing a 314-acre wildflower reserve where more than 500 species of flowering plants can be found. The peak blooming seasons are mid-April to mid-May and August through October. One of the other hiking trails includes a tour of the Frankfort Mineral Springs. During the 19th century the mineral water here was reputed to possess healing powers, and the springs were quite famous. The annual winter freeze forms tremendous ice sculptures that stand immobile until they melt in the spring thaw.

The lake yields bluegills, sunfish, bullheads, brook and rainbow trout, walleye, crappies, large-mouth and smallmouth bass, and yellow perch.

For visitors not solely concerned with recreational activities, the Wildflower Reserve Interpretive Center offers a wide variety of educational programs, including scheduled walks for bird-watchers, night hikes, snowshoe hikes, four self-guiding nature trails, and a Christmas bird count.

Open year-round; camping mid-Apr.-mid-Dec; modern cabins available year-round.
(888) 727-2757
www.dcnr.state.pa.us/stateparks/parks/racc.htm

5 Raccoon Creek State Park. *Fishermen take in the vivid colors of fall as they wait patiently to catch brook and rainbow trout on man-made Raccoon Lake.*

6 Meadowcroft Museum of Rural Life
Avella

Fifteen thousand years ago, western Pennsylvania was a land where man hunted to survive. At this museum, visitors can find out how archaeologists uncovered the earliest evidence of people living in North America and can check out a tool of their trade—a spear-thrower called an atlatl (at-LAT-tul).

Explore the re-created 19th-century village, complete with demonstrations of a woman spinning wool and a blacksmith forging red-hot iron. Visitors can attend class in the one-room schoolhouse or stroll across the covered bridge.

Other displays include the contents of a turn-of-the-century general store and a collection of horse-drawn vehicles and agricultural implements. Racing fans will be interested in the Delvin Miller harness racing exhibit.

Open Wed.–Sun. Memorial Day weekend to Labor Day weekend. Admission charged.
(724) 587-3412
www.meadowcroftmuseum.org

7 Nemacolin Castle. *This red brick Tudor-style castle with a crenellated octagonal tower and 22 rooms started out as a simple trading post on the site of old Fort Burd, which guarded an east-west trade route.*

7 Nemacolin Castle

Front St., Brownsville

Named for the American Indian leader Nemacolin, who established the first English trading route between Ohio and Maryland, Nemacolin Castle is an imposing brick edifice set on a hill with a commanding view of the Monongahela River. The early trading route connected with the river at present-day Brownsville. In 1806 it became part of Route 40, the country's first east-west national highway.

What is now the castle started as a simple trading post on the site of old Fort Burd, which guarded the trade route. As the post prospered, its owner, Jacob Bowman, gradually added onto the original stone structure, turning it into a red brick Tudor-style castle with a crenellated octagonal tower and 22 rooms. The tower bedroom is especially memorable; an immense Victorian carved walnut bed is swallowed up by the room's sheer size. Next door, the balcony gives

a wonderful view of the entire town.

Most of the rooms contain original 19th-century furnishings. In the "bishop's bedroom" are a massive Victorian mahogany bed and a flawless mirror made in 1850. Marble fireplaces and delicate mahogany woodwork add to the air of 19th-century opulence.

Visitors are invited to picnic on the grounds outside the castle and contemplate the steady flow of the Monongahela River.

Open Tues.–Sun. June–Aug.; weekends Sept.–May. Admission charged.

(724) 785-6882

www.nemacolincastle.org

8 Fort Necessity National Battlefield

Rte. 40, Farmington

A replica of the hastily constructed Fort Necessity marks the site of the opening battle of what would become the French and Indian War. The original fort was built by Virginia militiamen under the

command of George Washington, then a 22-year-old lieutenant colonel, to bolster a tenuous defensive position against an attack by a superior French force. Although Washington's first command ended in the only surrender of his career, this battle and Washington's previous skirmish at Jumonville Glen started the future Revolutionary War commander on his distinguished military career.

Fort Necessity, a small, palisaded log structure, has been reconstructed on its original site. There is a half-mile walking tour, which details the progress of the battle. A series of informational exhibits along the way guide visitors from the construction of the fort, through the battle, to the surrender.

Overlooking the battlefield is the Mount Washington Tavern, which was built in the 19th century as a stagecoach stop on the old National Road. The tavern served as a restaurant and hotel and provided a much-needed respite for weary travelers. It was named for George Washington, who bought land where his first major battle was fought. The Mount Washington Tavern Museum has a number of period rooms and an authentic Conestoga wagon in the front yard.

A new Fort Necessity/National Road Interpretive and Education Center is set for construction. It will feature multimedia exhibits that explore the clash of cultures leading up to the French and Indian War, as well as more about the National Road and the westward expansion of the new nation.

Open year-round except winter holidays. Entrance fee.

(724) 329-5512

www.nps.gov/fone

9 Buzzard Swamp Wildlife Area, Allegheny National Forest

Warren

This is an excellent place to see wildlife in its natural environment. Motorized vehicles are not allowed to enter this huge, quiet, and undisturbed marsh, which is maintained as a migratory waterfowl propagation area.

Owing to the massive beaver dams, most of the water in the swamp lies still and unmoving. Birders can see white herons, whistling swans, sandhill cranes, and hawks. Although there is a resident population of Pennsylvania songbirds, most of the species are migratory. Early spring and early fall are the best times to visit.

The park provides a well-marked 1 1/2-mile interpretive hiking trail called the Songbird Sojourn.

Open year-round.

(814) 723-5150

www.fs.fed.us/r9/allegheny

9 Buzzard Swamp Wildlife Area, Allegheny National Forest. *Waterfowl flock to this huge, undisturbed marsh each spring and fall.*

10 S.B. Elliott State Park
Penfield

Formerly a climax forest of huge pines and hemlocks, this area was devastated by the logging industry by the turn of the century. In 1911, when the timber was gone and most of the land was deserted by the lumber companies, the conservationist Simon B. Elliott prompted the Pennsylvania legislature to establish a tree nursery here. During the Great Depression in the 1930s the Civilian Conservation Corps built six log cabins (which can be rented) and a picnic area adjacent to the nursery.

In today's thickly forested park there are eight well-marked and well-maintained hiking trails. They range from strolls over rolling terrain to tough hikes through heavy foliage and underbrush. They are not long, however, and all eight could be walked in one day.

Most of the large trees in the park are hardwoods, principally red oak, white oak, and sugar maple; there are also some fine stands of pine. Trailer sites are situated among the trees.

The primitive, natural state maintained here is attractive to such wildlife as beavers, turkeys, foxes, squirrels, deer, and black bears. Many of the mountain streams surrounding the park are stocked with trout.

Open year-round;
campground open mid-Apr.–late Dec.
(814) 765-0630

www.dcnr.state.pa.us/stateparks/parks

11 Gravity Hill and Bedford Covered Bridges

Hill south of New Paris; bridges on roads throughout the county
Gravity Hill in Bedford County

12 Huntsdale Fish Cultural Station. *This baby trout is one of more than a million fish produced here each year for lakes and streams in Pennsylvania state parks.*

would make Sir Isaac Newton's hair stand on end. The laws of gravity seem not to apply here.

To find this unusual spot, take Route 96 one-half mile south of New Paris, cross a small metal bridge, and turn west onto Bethel Hollow Road. Drive six-tenths of a mile and bear left at the "Y" in the road, staying on the main road. After one and one-half miles, bear right at the stop sign, drive two-tenths of a mile and look for the letters "GH" spray-painted onto the road. Go about one-tenth of a mile and stop before the second "GH." Put the car in neutral and take your foot off the brake. You should now be rolling up the hill. If you need another thrill, proceed one-tenth of a mile past the second "GH." Look for the telephone pole painted "69." Stop beside the pole, and you'll defy gravity once more.

Some people speculate that what is occurring is no more than an optical illusion. Others insist

that a gravity warp in the earth causes what they're experiencing. Whatever the cause, it's definitely a natural funhouse.

Finally, if your head isn't spinning, you can drive through some of the county's 14 covered bridges, all built about 100 years ago. The romantic spans range from the 56-foot Palo Alto Bridge to the 136-foot Herline Bridge. A free booklet from the visitors bureau lists the locations of all the bridges and another traces a 90-minute route through six bridges, a bison farm, and Gravity Hill.

Open year-round.
(800) 765-3331

www.bedfordcounty.net

12 Huntsdale Fish Cultural Station

195 Lebo Rd., Huntsdale
If you have ever wondered where fish used to stock streams and lakes come from, a visit to this facility

will answer your questions. The spawning, fertilization, incubation, and maturation of freshwater fish all take place in the 160-acre Huntsdale hatchery. This is one of the largest fish-culture facilities in the country. Here more than a million fish are produced annually for lakes and streams in Pennsylvania state parks. Most of the fish are trout and striped bass fingerlings, although other warm-water species, such as walleye, tiger muskies, and purebred muskellunge fingerlings, are sometimes raised.

A brochure available at the reception area explains the breeding and fingerling procedures step by step. Most impressive here are the 24 raceways, each of which may contain as many as 35,000 fish. You will see the greatest number of large trout in the early spring, when the fish are approaching full size and stocking season has not yet begun.

The entrance to Kings Gap Environmental Education and Training Center, a half-mile drive on Pine Road, is a fastidiously maintained nature study area in a natural forest preserve. More than 15 miles of hiking trails circling up a mountain provide a clear picture of indigenous plant and animal life.

Wildlife abounds. Deer, wild turkeys, ruffed grouse, raccoons, and gray squirrels may often be seen on a day's hike. At the top of the mountain a stone mansion housing the Education Center offers a commanding view of the Cumberland Valley.

Both facilities open year-round. For guided tours, call two weeks in advance.
(717) 486-3419

www.fieldtrip.com/pa

13 Penn Roosevelt State Park

Huntingdon. Heading east on Rte. 322, turn right about 18 miles from State College, just before passing a huge reservoir on the left. Take the road for a quarter-mile, turn right and follow the signs. Featured here are picnic spots and primitive camping grounds centered around a small, spring-fed lake with a dam in a peaceful, isolated mountain setting. Although the place is only five miles from the highway, the constant, gentle splash of water over the dam into the mountain stream is the only sound that penetrates the stillness of the surrounding forest.

Penn Roosevelt Lake is not stocked, so any trout caught here are native to the lake and stream. A hiking trail leads deep into the forest, where rhododendrons and laurel grow in profusion. Deer, turkeys, grouse, and raccoons prosper, and black bears are sometimes seen. One caution: keep an eye out for the occasional copperhead snake or timber rattler.

Open year-round, but no winter road maintenance; camping mid-Apr.–mid-Dec.
(814) 667-1800

www.dcnr.state.pa.us/stateparks/parks

14 Leonard Harrison State Park and Colton Point State Park

Wellsboro
Occupying mountains on opposite sides of Pine Creek Gorge, each park offers breathtaking views of the Grand Canyon of Pennsylvania and the course of Pine Creek as it snakes its way between heavily forested ridges. In the distance mountain ranges seemingly stretch to infinity.

Although family camping facilities are available, both parks are largely in their natural state. Rhododendrons, azaleas, and wild laurel, which usually bloom in mid-June, abound. Both parks offer a variety of hiking trails. Those at Colton Point are somewhat more challenging.

The popular new Pine Creek Trail cuts through the floor of the canyon where a railroad once ran. The tracks were removed in 1988 to make way for a smooth, flat 42-mile biking and hiking trail that starts in Ansonia and runs to Waterville and parallels beautiful Pine Creek the entire way. Cross-country skiers may enjoy it during the winter. An additional 20 miles of trail are expected to be completed in the future.

The great stands of pine for which the creek was named were logged off in the 19th century. Today's second-growth forest includes black cherry, aspen, red oak, black birch, beech, white ash, shagbark hickory, sassafras, and sycamore. In autumn this diversity creates a broad palette of colors that dominate the landscape as far as the eye can see, making it a photographer's haven.

Mountain streams and creeks are stocked with trout and other freshwater fish. The best angling begins after mid-June, when the creek begins to dry up. Rafting should be enjoyed earlier. Both supervised and unsupervised whitewater raft trips down Pine Creek are arranged by a local concessionaire.

Open year-round but winter access is limited; camping mid-Apr.–mid-Oct.
(570) 724-3061

www.dcnr.state.pa.us/stateparks/parks

14 Leonard Harrison State Park and Colton Point State Park. *On opposite sides of Pine Creek Gorge, these two parks offer breathtaking views of the Grand Canyon of Pennsylvania and the course of Pine Creek. A flat, smooth trail allows bikers and hikers to enjoy the view from the bottom.*

15 Mount Pisgah State Park

Troy. Watch for signs on Rte. 6. The 75-acre Stephen Foster Lake, named for the Pennsylvanian who wrote "Camptown Races," "Oh! Susanna," and other popular songs about the Old South, is the central feature of this 1,300-acre park. Stocked with bass, perch, crappie, bluegill, and bullhead, the lake offers good fishing, particularly in spring. Boats and canoes are for rent in the summer or visitors can launch their own. The lake is restricted to electric motors only. In winter the frozen lake is popular for ice fishing and skating.

Ten miles of trails pass through wooded acres, open farmland, and marshes. Since much of this countryside was once under cultivation, the effects of farming, such as fieldstone and stump fence rows, can be seen throughout the park.

The park sponsors demonstrations of maple syrup making in the spring. Visitors can see how sap is collected, boiled, and reboiled. Then everyone gets a free sample of warm, fresh maple syrup.

Open year-round.
(570) 297-2734

www.dcnr.state.pa.us/stateparks/parks

16 Peter J. McGovern Little League Baseball Museum

Williamsport
Opened in 1982, the museum chronicles the development of Little League baseball from the first eight-team league that started here in Williamsport in 1939 to the present-day organization with 7,000 teams in 24 countries. The man for whom the museum is named served from 1952 until his death in 1984 as the first full-time president of the Little Leagues.

Incorporating the latest in design, exhibit, and display techniques, the Little League Baseball Museum was created for fans of all ages. The hands-on displays include light-box questionnaires on Little League rules; 10-foot-tall track-mounted sliding panels with special baseball tips; and pitching and batting cages where prospective hurlers and hitters can study their styles with the aid of 90-second videotapes of themselves in action.

Inside the "play-it-safe room" are life-sized murals demonstrating 10 important warm-up exercises for young athletes. Here too are exhibits showing the evolution of Little League safety equipment, such as batting helmets, shin guards, and chest protectors. One exhibit includes mementos of current major league players who began as Little Leaguers. Any young player is likely to be inspired by the sight of his idol as a youngster wearing a Little League uniform.

Both children and adults alike will surely savor the opportunity to do their own play-by-play commentary on a World Series game.

Highlights of championship games in the past are shown on videotape. Team pictures of the winners dating back to 1947 are also on display.

Behind the museum is the stadium where the annual Little League World Series is played. For ballplayers young and old, the sight of the empty baseball diamond can conjure up stirring visions of what might have been—or what might yet come to pass.

Open daily Memorial Day–Sept. 30; closed Tues.–Wed. Oct 1–Memorial Day. Admission charged.
(570) 326-3607
www.littleleague.org/museum

17 Clyde Peeling's Reptiland

U.S. Route 15 near Allenwood
The reptile is often feared or misunderstood. Reptiland owner Clyde Peeling dispels myths and increases understanding of reptiles and their amphibian cousins in an atmosphere that is both fun and educational. His specialized zoo, accredited by the American Zoo and Aquarium Association, offers five live shows each day. There are interactive games like "Lizard Wizard" and "Turtle Trivia" and daily feedings where you can observe natural behavior. Visitors are invited to touch harmless species. Snakes, turtles, frogs, lizards, and alligators populate the displays.

Special events during the year include October's "Flashlight Safari," a Halloween alternative where guests can observe the zoo's inhabitants at their most active. Unusual rainforest denizens are in the spotlight during April's "Tropical Rainforest—Nature's Hothouse" program, which also demonstrates the use of the blowgun.

A multimedia show introduces these beautiful but potentially deadly creatures to visitors. Just in case you're planning to venture out into the jungle again, remember: The Gaboon viper has two-inch fangs. A king cobra carries enough venom to slay an elephant. And if you're tempted to touch that beautiful, shimmering dart-poison frog from South America–don't. One of its species is the most poisonous on earth, more than any snake or spider. Even touching its skin is not a good idea.

Open year-round. Admission charged.
(800) 737-8452
www.reptiland.com

18 Wayne County Historical Society Museum

810 Main St., Honesdale
In a superb 150-year-old brick building that was once the office of the Delaware and Hudson Canal Company, the Wayne County Historical Society Museum recalls the rich economic, geographical, and cultural history of the area.

When the eastern Pennsylvania anthracite mining industry started to prosper in the early 19th century, Honesdale became a focal point of commercial transport. Mined anthracite coal was taken to the town of Carbondale and then hauled to Honesdale by the Gravity Railroad, in 1829 the first commercial American locomotive to run on this track. From Honesdale the coal was shipped by boat through the 108 locks on the Delaware and Hudson Canal to the markets in New York.

The museum has an exhibit showing how the canal linked the county to New York City and beyond. The old photographs of bridge construction, relay designs, factories, and burgeoning towns show how challenging engineering problems were solved back then, and how the canals influenced the development of new communities.

The major industries of Wayne County are also explored. One room displays rotating exhibits, such as the work of craftsmen in the glass-cutting factories that once dotted the vicinity. Here too is a glassblower's typical work station, complete with all the tools required to blow and shape glass.

Connected to the museum by a glass hallway is the recently restored 19th-century Torrey Land Office that served Honesdale. On the streets of Honesdale one can still find many splendid early 19th-century buildings. Inquire at the museum about walking tours of the town.

Museum open Wed.–Sat. Mar.–Dec.; Sat. Jan.–Feb. Call for summer and fall Sunday hours. Admission charged.
(570) 253-3240
www.waynehistorypa.org

17 Clyde Peeling's Reptiland. *An American green alligator seems to be smiling at a boy at this zoo that features many other slithering creatures.*

19 Jim Thorpe
80 miles northwest of Philadelphia

At about the time the legendary American Indian athlete, Jim Thorpe, died in 1953, the Pennsylvania towns of Mauch Chunk, East Mauch Chunk, and Upper Mauch Chunk were seeking a solution to their economic decline. It was suggested by Mr. Thorpe's widow that a consolidated town named for her husband would be a fitting tribute as well as an aid to tourism. The idea was accepted, a memorial was built, and in 1954 the towns combined under the name Jim Thorpe. The community bearing his name became Jim Thorpe's final resting place. Fifty years later, the major attractions here are the old buildings and the beauty of the surrounding mountains, particularly in the fall.

The Mauch Chunk Historical District still exudes a quiet elegance. Millionaires Row is a series of lavishly appointed brick town houses built for the most prominent families. Just two blocks away is Stone Row, with modest, three-story stone row houses built by Asa Packer, president of the Lehigh Valley Railroad, for the line's foremen and engineers.

Many of the public and commercial buildings are handsome examples of 19th-century architecture. Inside the Carbon County Courthouse is an oak-paneled courtroom with an elaborate spindled backdrop and a stained-glass skylight. The Dimmick Memorial Library has attractive terra cotta panels and a plush two-story reading room.

The Asa Packer mansion, perched on a steep hill overlooking the town, was the home of a local self-made millionaire and

20 Hawk Mountain Sanctuary. *Hikers take in the view atop North Lookout, the prime observation point to see the fall migration of thousands of birds of prey.*

entrepreneur. The rambling, three-story Italianate mansion, a frame structure, has been maintained in its original state since the death of its owner in 1879.

The 20-room interior contains intricately hand-carved Honduras mahogany wood paneling and beautifully crafted rosewood furniture. The building and the well-groomed surrounding grounds all have an air of 19th-century elegance.
Mansion open Tues.–Sun., Memorial Day–Oct. Admission charged.
(570) 325-2644
www.jimthorpecamping.com

20 Hawk Mountain Sanctuary
Kempton

One of the few sanctuaries in the world set aside for migrating birds of prey, Hawk Mountain is a favorite site for birders. From this 1,500-foot ridge one can watch for more than 200 species of birds that frequent the area, as well as 16 species of raptors—including eagles, ospreys, hawks, and falcons—on their flights to their winter or summer ranges.

Hawk Mountain is named for the 18,000 raptors or so that soar past its lookouts between mid-

August and mid-December each year. An eight-mile trail system leads visitors to many observation points, including the one-mile trek to North Lookout—the prime observation point for the fall migration. South Lookout is an easily-accessible 100-yard stroll from the visitors center.

Hunting is not permitted, and deer, chipmunks, squirrels, and raccoons are plentiful here. After the mountain laurel blooms in early summer, nesting warblers and other songbirds take up residence on the tranquil mountain and fill the air with their gentle calls.

To enhance your appreciation of this unique environment, stop at the visitors center, featuring a bookstore, the Wings of Wonder raptor gallery, and interpretive displays.
Open year-round. Trail fee.
(610) 756-6000
www.hawkmountain.org

21 Watch and Clock Museum
Poplar St., Columbia

When you first walk in, you're appropriately greeted by chiming

bells as you walk through a Time Tunnel. The National Association of Watch and Clock Collectors manages the museum, which traces the history of time measurement—from a reproduction of the incredible non-mechanical Rhodes Antikytheron clock, circa 79 B.C., to the most sophisticated modern atomic clock.

Among the musical clocks played here are a 1770 Glune glass bell clock, an 1840 organ clock, and a one-of-a-kind animated monumental clock. The massive inner works of large tower clocks are contrasted with the delicate mechanisms of small pocket watches. On display also are clocks with Japanese characters, mantel clocks of various styles, mirror clocks, master-and-slave clocks, banjo clocks, a lantern clock, a Swiss water clock, and all sorts of novelty timepieces.

Many items are exhibited in glass cases so that the inner movements of wood, iron, and brass may be studied from all sides. Most of the clocks are originals.

Nearly all of the clocks and watches are in working condition. The museum is so filled with the various pitches and rhythms created by the precise mechanical measure of time that one is acutely aware of the passing of each second. If you are in the museum at noon, you will hear the cacophony of chimes, rings, and gongs announcing the hour of 12. A 10-minute video presentation on the history of timekeeping in the new theater is well worth your time.
Open Tues.–Sun. Apr.–Dec.
except major holidays. Open Tues.–Sat.
Jan–Mar.
Admission charged.
(717) 684-8261
www.nawcc.org

 Mary Merritt Doll Museum. *Thousands of dolls, dating from 1725 to 1900, are on display here, along with dollhouses and furnishings from all over the world.*

22 Troxell-Steckel House and Barn

Egypt

During the 18th and 19th centuries the Lehigh Valley was settled primarily by farmers from Germany. In 1756 the son of one of these immigrants, John Peter Troxell, built a medieval-style German farmhouse near what is now the town of Egypt. Fifteen years later the house and surrounding property were sold to Peter Steckel—thus the name.

The fieldstone farmhouse has been restored and furnished to suggest the lifestyle of the German settlers in the area. The austerity of the home reflects the simple and rigorous lives of its inhabitants; a telling feature is a box built into a wall for the reverent storage of the family Bible.

The 18-acre property includes a small stream, an idyllic meadow, and a field that is still farmed. Beside the stream is a springhouse where dairy products were stored in the old days.

In the Swiss-style bank barn, built in 1875, each stall has its own exterior door; the animals were fed from a wooden platform above the stalls. An earthen ramp against the rear side of the barn provides wagon access to the upper storage area. Farming equipment, hand tools, and a collection of horse-drawn carriages and sleighs are displayed inside the barn.

Open P.M. Sat.–Sun., June–Oct. and by appointment.
(610) 435-4664
www.voicenet.com/~/chs

23 Mary Merritt Doll Museum

Douglasville

The more than 2,500 examples here, dating mostly from 1725 to 1900, are good evidence of the widespread appeal of toys made in the human image. Along the walls are eight-foot-tall glass cases filled with dolls, dollhouses, and doll accessories and furnishings from all over the world—collected by Mrs. Mary Merritt, a lifelong doll enthusiast.

The dolls and settings shown, mostly made during the 19th century, represent a variety of cultures and lifestyles. The simple Mennonite bedroom in one dollhouse, for example, contrasts dramatically with the decor of the lavish Victorian parlor in another miniature setting.

The huge collection includes a replica of a real Georgian-style house, authentically furnished with miniature pieces, a number of superb wax baby dolls, an 8th-century Egyptian doll, Queen Anne dolls, French fashion dolls, china dolls, mechanical dolls, and dolls with two faces (one smiling and one crying).

Many 19th-century dolls were made at home by doting parents, using whatever material was handy—cornstalks, dried apples, beeswax, and rags, to name a few. The admission fee includes a visit to the Merritt Museum of Childhood next door. The museum, which evokes a nostalgic sense of an early 20th-century toy store, also displays a fascinating miscellany that includes old cavalry rifles, pottery, baskets, antique pewter, and china goods.

Open daily except Tues.
Admission charged.
(610) 385-3809
www.merritts.com/

24 Strasburg Rail Road, the Railroad Museum of Pennsylvania, and the National Toy Train Museum

Strasburg

The Strasburg Rail Road is the oldest continuously operating railroad in the United States. The steam-powered train runs through beautiful Pennsylvania Dutch farmland as it travels between Strasburg and Paradise, where it connects with Amtrak's main line between Philadelphia and Harrisburg.

The train features a parlor car, a lounge car, and a dining car, where you can have lunch or dinner. All cars are restored to look like they did in 1915. For railway enthusiasts especially, this is a bit of the real thing.

Across the street, at the Railroad Museum of Pennsylvania, more than 100 historic locomotives and railroad cars are on display. Visitors can sit in the engineer's seat of a mammoth engine, board a real caboose, or check out the interactive education center.

Nearby, the National Toy Train Museum will appeal to anyone nostalgic for or curious about the era of the great steam locomotives and the wonderful toys they inspired.

The historical section of the Toy Train Museum has examples of all types of trains from 1880 to the present. Each era of development, including the standard-gauge classic period, is represented. Five complex operating layouts have push-button controls with which visitors can activate the trains and accessories.

Strasburg Rail Road open daily Mar.–Dec. Admission charged.
(717) 687-7522
www.strasburgrailroad.com
Railroad Museum of Pennsylvania open daily Apr.–Oct.; closed Mondays Nov.–Mar. Admission charged.
(717) 687-8628
www.rrmuseumpa.org
National Toy Train Museum open daily May–Oct.; weekends Apr., Nov., Dec. Admission charged.
(717) 687-8976
www.traincollectors.org/toytrain.html

25 Brandywine River Museum
Chadds Ford

A century-old gristmill overlooking the Brandywine River has been handsomely renovated with a circular wing to make a spacious and airy three-story museum with informal galleries for the display of paintings and sculptures.

Major works of art from three generations of the Wyeth family are featured, including paintings by N.C. Wyeth, his son Andrew, and his grandson Jamie. The renowned commercial illustrations of N.C. Wyeth and Howard Pyle, the father of modern American illustration, and works by Pyle's students are also shown.

Much of the museum is devoted to the art of the Brandywine region, and to the still life and landscape painters and sculptors associated with the "Brandywine Tradition." The collected works represent more than 100 years of activity, and the tradition continues.

Part of each floor serves as a lobby where visitors can rest and enjoy the enchanting views of the Brandywine countryside through floor-to-ceiling windows. Sunshine washes through a skylight, warmly bathing these areas with light. The effect helps provide an understanding of the source of inspiration for this celebrated school of painting, with its emphasis on natural light.

The Brandywine River Museum is named for the adjacent river. Visitors are encouraged to picnic on its banks, enjoy the wildflower gardens and nature trail, and discover for themselves the beguiling character of a place that has influenced so many artists.

Open daily except Christmas.
Admission charged.
(610) 388-2700

www.brandywinemuseum.org

🎨 Brandywine River Museum. *Artist N.C. Wyeth's studio displays a painting of George Washington that Wyeth was working on when he died in 1945. Tours of the studio are available from the museum.*

26 The Mütter Museum of the College of Physicians
South 22nd Street, Philadelphia

If you're interested in medical anomalies and how doctors practiced medicine more than 100 years ago, this is the place to go.

Thomas Dent Mütter, a professor of surgery, founded the museum in 1858 to display pathological anatomy. It now has 3,000 human specimens and a sampling of medical instruments from the 19th century to the present. An elegant two-level gallery houses most of the exhibits, which are displayed in period wooden cases.

Among the exhibits is the Hyrtal Skull Collection, which presents 139 skulls from Central and Eastern Europe. The connected livers of conjoined twins Chang and Eng (the original Siamese twins, 1811-1874) are shown along with a plaster cast of their torsos and a chair made for their use. A high point is the Dr. Chevalier Jackson collection of 2,000 objects swallowed or inhaled and then safely removed. They range from bones and safety pins to dental material.

Some of the other fascinating-depending-on-your-point-of-view displays are slices of the head, including the brain; skeletons of a giant and a dwarf; and what is believed to be the thorax of Lincoln assassin John Wilkes Booth. Make sure to visit the President Health Exhibit, where you'll find the tumor of President Grover Cleveland—taken from his jaw in a secret operation in 1893.

Open year-round. Admission charged.
(215) 563-3737

www.collphyphil.org

27 The Mercer Museum
Pine St., Doylestown

Henry Chapman Mercer, a pioneering archaeologist and anthropologist born in 1856, saw that the essence of American culture was to be found in its tools and equipment, so he collected more than 40,000 artifacts from the 18th and 19th centuries.

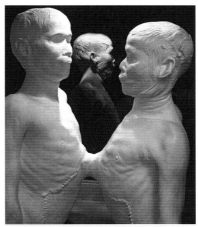
🏛 The Mütter Museum of the College of Physicians. *A plaster cast of the conjoined twins Chang and Eng, the original Siamese twins, is on display here.*

Mercer then designed and supervised the construction of a museum to accommodate the vast accumulation. The medieval-looking edifice was finished in 1916 according to specifications he carried in his head, without benefit of blueprints.

The exhibition hall is a gigantic, barnlike room. Each of the six levels has a balconylike corridor and small exhibit rooms. Each room contains tools and objects representing some 60 crafts and trades, or facets of early American life, with incredible completeness.

The place is packed with everything imaginable. Many items—stagecoaches, sleighs, Conestoga wagons, a whaleboat, iron stoves—are suspended from the walls and ceiling by iron rods set in the concrete, to be seen from all angles.

The museum is a national historic landmark.

Open daily. Admission charged.
(215) 345-0210

www.mercermuseum.org

Green Animals Topiary Garden. *A giant cat holds up its paws to welcome visitors (see page 296).*

Rhode Island

Although dominated by busy Narragansett Bay and the seashore, our smallest state offers some rewarding inland discoveries.

This is one of our most densely populated states, but consistent with its traditional independence, it takes a strong stand regarding the importance of nature and wildlife—as evidenced by the bird sanctuaries and a fish hatchery. A related interest is expressed in a superb topiary garden where plants are artfully trimmed to geometric and animal forms. The changing seasons here are celebrated by a succession of harvest festivals sponsored by an American Indian museum, and its pioneer heritage is represented by a 17th-century farmstead.

1 George Washington Management Area

Rte. 44, West Glocester
Land for the camping area in this 4,400-acre park was donated to the state in 1933 to honor the bicentennial of our first president's birth, which was observed the previous year.

There are 75 camping sites near the tip of Bowdish Lake, where a sandy beach invites swimmers; fishermen are most likely to catch largemouth bass, yellow perch, and pickerel. A launching ramp may be used by boats with motors under 10 horsepower. The picnic ground on Peck Pond, at the other side of the management area, also has a sandy beach and a supervised swimming area. This pond is stocked with trout.

Access to the more remote regions of the forest is provided by the Walkabout Trail, an easy eight-mile loop with several cutoffs allowing shorter hikes. The trail, built in 1965 with the help of Australian sailors, takes its name from the traditional wanderings of Australian aborigines.

Winter is one of the best seasons here. Many snow-covered gravel roads, accessible from the campground, are open for snowmobiling; in the area around Peck Pond four trails ranging from three-quarters of a mile to more than four miles in length are

1 George Washington Management Area. *Fishermen are likely to catch largemouth bass, yellow perch, and pickerel at scenic Bowdish Lake.*

groomed for cross-country skiing. A warming house is maintained for relief from the winter's cold.
Open year-round. Camping May–Sept. Use fee charged.
(401) 568-2013
www.huntri.com/georgewa.shtml

2 The Museum of Work and Culture

42 S. Main St. (Market Square), Woonsocket
In the heart of Woonsocket's historic Market Square, an interactive museum celebrates New England's French-Canadian immigrants. Maintained by the Rhode Island Historical Society, it tells the story of men and women who left their farms for the new world of factories—a story of hardship and resilience echoed by immigrants nationwide.

Housed in a converted textile mill, the museum traces a dramatic labor story—the rise of the Independent Textile Union—while opening a window on the everyday life of a close-knit ethnic community determined to preserve its language, customs, and faith.

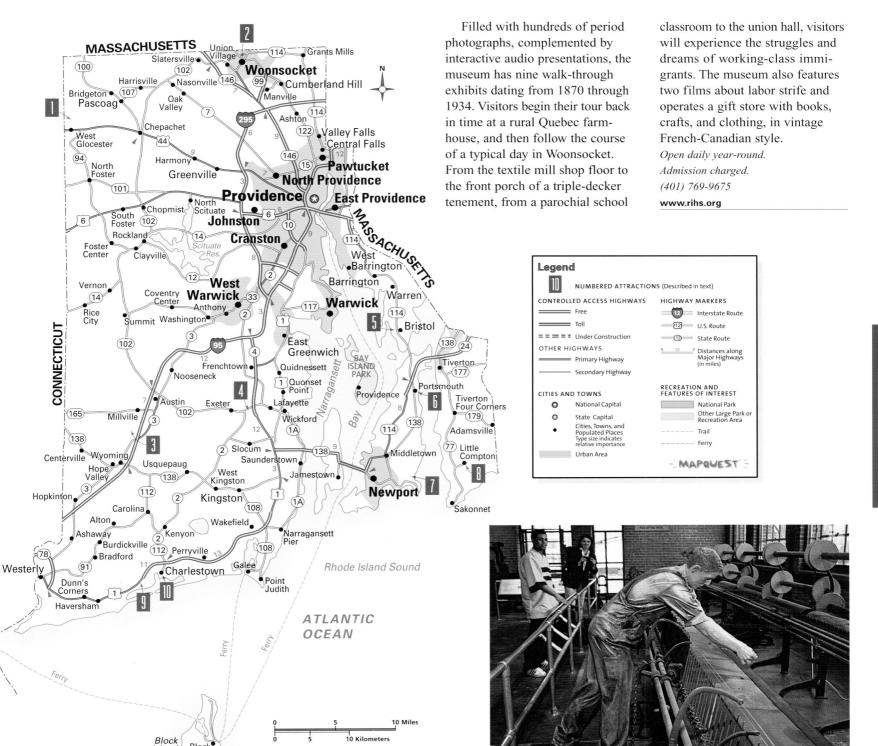

Filled with hundreds of period photographs, complemented by interactive audio presentations, the museum has nine walk-through exhibits dating from 1870 through 1934. Visitors begin their tour back in time at a rural Quebec farmhouse, and then follow the course of a typical day in Woonsocket. From the textile mill shop floor to the front porch of a triple-decker tenement, from a parochial school classroom to the union hall, visitors will experience the struggles and dreams of working-class immigrants. The museum also features two films about labor strife and operates a gift store with books, crafts, and clothing, in vintage French-Canadian style.

Open daily year-round.

Admission charged.

(401) 769-9675

www.rihs.org

2 The Museum of Work and Culture. *A model of a 1920s textile mill worker can be seen at this unique museum in Woonsocket.*

3 Tomaquag Indian Memorial Museum

Arcadia, Summit Rd., Exeter
Situated amid the Arcadia Management Area, this large white house contains several cabinets containing American Indian artifacts from various North American tribes, with a focus on those of the Northeast. In addition to stone tools and leather strapwork by Plains Indians, weavings by Navajos, and baskets by northwestern tribes, the collection features ash splint basketwork of the Mohegans, Scaticooks, and local Narragansetts. *Tomaquag* is the Narragansett word for beaver.

The museum serves as a focal point for four annual festivals of thanksgiving associated with the harvesting of important crops: maple sugar in March, strawberries in June, string beans in July, and cranberries in October. In addition, the Nickomo Festival is celebrated in early December with an exchange of gifts.

These gatherings offer feasting on seasonal foods and Indian dances, led by local Narragansetts, in which visitors are encouraged to participate.
Open seasonally and by appointment.
Donation requested.
(401) 539-7213

4 Lafayette State Trout Hatchery

Hatchery Road, off Rte. 4, south of Lafayette
Also known as Goose Nest Spring Hatchery, this complex, founded in 1922, is one of the oldest hatcheries in the country. It consists of about 20 raceways, each about 100 feet long, and buildings in which tanks containing fingerling trout may be seen. The hatchery's capacity of about a million trout helps to stock Rhode Island's

6 Green Animals Topiary Garden. *A camel made of California privet stands among 80 topiary forms in these Portsmouth gardens.*

streams for the enjoyment of an estimated 40,000 fishermen. The place, charming in appearance, is fascinating to see.

Since the fish are accustomed to being fed by humans, they rise to the surface as one approaches the edge of the cement raceways. To discourage depredation by herons, the raceways are covered with chain-link fencing. Each section of the raceway contains thousands of trout—approximately the same size in order to minimize their cannibalistic behavior.
Open year-round. Free admission.
(401) 294-4662
www.state.ri.us

5 The Audubon Society of Rhode Island's Environmental Education Center

Rte. 114, on the town line between Bristol and Warren
Founded in 1897 by about 30 men and women determined to put a stop to the slaughter of wild birds for their feathers, the Audubon Society of Rhode Island has grown to several thousand members and has expanded its mission.

Surrounded by a 28-acre wildlife

refuge on the scenic Narragansett Bay, the society's 10,300-square-foot, state-of-the-art Environmental Education Center is home to the state's largest aquarium. For hands-on experiences, it features tide pool touch tanks teeming with marine life. The center's show-piece is an authentically detailed, life-sized, 35-foot model of a typical 3,200-pound North Atlantic right whale. Step inside its body for up-close views of a whale's heart, tongue, ribs, spine, baleen, and blubber. Back on the outside, visitors can meander through exhibits reflecting the diversity of Rhode Island's native habitat. Dioramas and assorted displays capture wetlands, woodlands, salt marshes, the shoreline, and even a cornfield at night. A boardwalk leads visitors through freshwater wetlands and a salt marsh to the shore of Narragansett Bay, where you can see frogs, turtles, shore-birds, ducks, and maybe even a seal or two in the winter.
Open daily year-round.
Admission charged.
(401) 245-7500
www.asri.org

6 Green Animals Topiary Garden

Cory's Lane, off Rte. 114, Portsmouth
Thomas E. Brayton, a Massachusetts manufacturer, purchased this seven-acre estate in 1872 and summered here until his death in 1939.

Exquisite evidence of Brayton's interest in topiary (the ancient art of training and pruning plants into geometric designs or animal shapes) may be seen today as one wanders through the gardens. But it was his daughter, the late Alice Brayton, an amateur horticulturist, who helped bring these 80 forms to their present perfection, putting them in a class with the nation's best examples of topiary.

Among the animal shapes are a cat, a camel, a giraffe, a horse and rider, and a mountain goat. A fat bear is especially appealing. The animals are all fashioned from California privet, yew, and English boxwood; the geometric designs are made of sheared boxwood.

Elsewhere, perennial, biennial, and annual flower beds, as well as plantings of ferns, shrubs, and fruit trees, create a subtle blend of scent and sight.

From the clapboard main house there is a lovely view of Narragansett Bay. Inside, a small toy collection is displayed, including an impressive exhibit of toy soldiers.
Open daily May–Oct.
Admission charged.
(401) 847-1000
www.newportmansions.org/
connoisseurs/greenanimals.html

7 Norman Bird Sanctuary

Third Beach Rd., Middletown
George Norman was a late 19th-century Newport merchant who made a fortune in waterworks and

utilities. His daughter donated the land for this sanctuary in 1949. Eleven trails, from one-tenth of a mile to 1.3 miles in length, lead through the 300-acre site, where birders can look for many common and some unusual species. This is an interesting landscape because it includes virtually every type of terrain found in New England, from lofty crag to meadow, woodland, dense thicket, freshwater swamp, and pond.

Each trail has its own appeal, which may include sightings of woodcocks, green herons, great blue herons, snowy owls, and other less common birds. Red foxes are known to lurk within the sanctuary and often may be seen.

Legend maintains that veins of quartz in the rocks along Indian Rock Trail were a source of stone for Narragansett arrowheads. A popular hike leads to Hanging Rock, beside a large pond. It is believed by some that criminals were once hanged here. The curious conglomerate structure, with its overhang, rises 70 feet above sea level and provides fine views.

The sanctuary has a shop where birdfeeding supplies and environmental gifts are sold. In the nearby outbuildings, birds brought in to recover from injuries are cared for and may often be observed.
Open year-round.
(401) 846-2577
www.normanbirdsanctuary.org

8 Wilbor House Museum
Little Compton
Wilbor House, the Little Compton Historical Society's headquarters, stands on land purchased from the Sakonnet Indians in 1673. Built by Samuel Wilbor in the 1680s, the

original house consisted of only two rooms and was typical of 17th-century New England.

Today the Wilbor House spans four centuries and contains rooms representative of each. Eight generations of Wilbors continuously occupied it until the 1920s. Restoration of the Wilbor House began in 1955 when the society purchased the home and opened it to the public. Visitors can also tour the society's seven outbuildings, including a one-room schoolhouse and a carriage house that holds antique vehicles. There is also a permanent exhibit commemorating the cultural contributions and traditions of the Azoreans who came to Little Compton during the late 1800s.
Open mid-June to mid-October; call for hours.
Admission charged.
(401) 635-4035
www.littlecompton.org

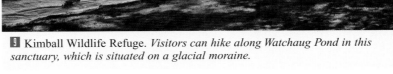

9 Kimball Wildlife Refuge. *Visitors can hike along Watchaug Pond in this sanctuary, which is situated on a glacial moraine.*

9 Kimball Wildlife Refuge
Charlestown. Exit from Rte. 1 south, taking a right onto Prosser Trail. Take first left onto Montauk Rd. and then turn left again at the pond.
The land for this 29-acre woodland sanctuary was bequeathed by William Hammond Kimball, a summer resident of the area, to the Audubon Society of Rhode Island in 1924. Two years later Everett and Mary Southwick became the caretakers. Today's well-tended trails and the garden memorializing past benefactors reflect this naturalist couple's lifelong devotion to the development of the refuge.

Situated on a glacial moraine deposited some 12,000 years ago, the sanctuary invites contemplation of a glacier's irresistible force. One trail leads past several bowl-shaped kettle holes carved as the giant ice sheets receded. Indeed, Toupoyesett Pond here is really a

large kettle hole deep enough to reveal the water table. In May and June, starflowers, Canada mayflowers, and pink lady's slippers are in bloom along the quiet trails, and the memorial garden is occasionally visited by ruby-throated hummingbirds. Adjacent to Burlingame State Park, the refuge hosts migrating warblers and a variety of resident songbirds. The refuge offers a number of nature programs throughout the year.
Open year-round.
(401) 949-5454 or (401) 874-6664
www.asri.org

10 The Fantastic Umbrella Factory
Charlestown
The Fantastic Umbrella Factory is not really an umbrella factory at all. It's an offbeat assemblage of stores that sell everything from blown glass to natural foods to Halloween costumes. There are umbrellas for sale, too, but they're not the main focus here.

What is the main attraction at this place, founded in 1968, is a farmstead that dates from at least the 19th century. Out in back, a menagerie includes guinea hens, sheep, emus, and chickens. There's a main store and international bazaar, with trinkets galore.

The Umbrella Factory Gardens are known for their moss baskets. While they custom-plant your basket, you can drink a smoothie, check out the art gallery, find some antiques or even incense at one of the many stores there.
Open year-round.
(401) 364-6616

Santee National Wildlife Refuge. *Fishermen will find a haven here (see page 302).*

(see page 302).

H ere you'll see contrasting aspects of Southern enterprise: the thread of cotton that is woven through two centuries of Southern life, and antebellum mansions built with profits from the cotton trade. The 19th century is further represented by a working gristmill and a hand-dug canal.

An abiding interest in nature is confirmed in vast preserves set aside for local wildlife, and in another context, by an amazing collection of mounted African animals. The tragedy of war in the South is remembered in battlefields of both the Revolution and the Civil War.

South Carolina

The romance of the Old South blends with memories of the Confederacy and 19th-century enterprise—and the promise of the space age.

1 Hagood Mill
Pickens

Benjamin Hagood was an enterprising miller who sought to capitalize on the traffic generated by the gristmill he built in 1825. On the same site he also operated a tannery and a general store. Rebuilt in 1845, the mill stands as good evidence of the workmanship that went into the two-story clapboard structure, with its heavy beams held in place by wooden pegs. The mill was active for more than 100 years; old-timers in the area recall that as late as the 1930s, crowds of farmers still gathered here to have their corn ground.

A descendant of Ben Hagood's donated the mill to Pickens County in 1972, and it was completely restored. Situated beside a narrow creek spanned by a wooden footbridge, in a quiet setting of oaks and mountain laurel, the mill is very photogenic. The huge wheel is still turned by water brought down from a mountain spring in a wooden sluice. On special occasions the sluice is opened, the wheel begins to turn, and with a great, rumbling racket of wooden cogs and gears, the mill again confirms the ingenuity of its builders.

Open the third Sat. of every month. Group tours by arrangement.
(864) 898-5963
http://bbayles.home.mindspring.com/ pickens/hagood.htm

1 Hagood Mill. *This water-powered gristmill, rebuilt in 1845 and still in working condition, was once a local hub of commerce.*

2 Museum of York County
4621 Mount Gallant Rd., northwest of Rock Hill

Here in the northern reaches of South Carolina it is a pleasant surprise to come upon this fine museum of natural history, technology, and the arts, which so imaginatively presents aspects of the larger world and the universe.

On display in the Stans African Halls is the Southeast's largest collection of more than 200 full-mounted African animals; the North American Hall features large animals; and the Hometown Habitats exhibit shows plants and animals special to the Carolina Piedmont.

Among several galleries of changing exhibitions in history, science, natural history, and art, the museum is also home to the Vernon Grant Gallery, which is devoted to the creator of the Rice Krispies' characters Snap! Crackle! and Pop!

On weekends, explore the cosmos in the state-of-the-art Settlemyre Planetarium. Afterward take a stroll on the 0.7 mile nature

SOUTH CAROLINA

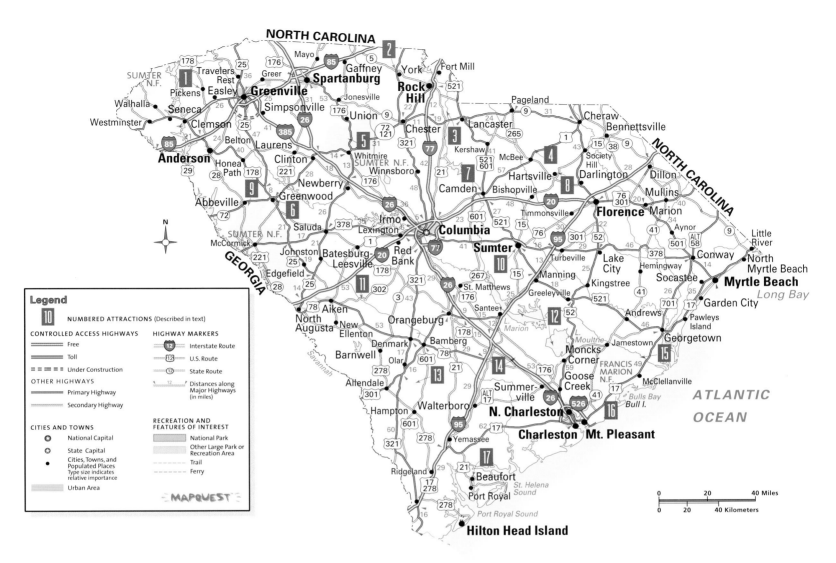

Legend

NUMBERED ATTRACTIONS (Described in text)

CONTROLLED ACCESS HIGHWAYS

Free

Toll

Under Construction

OTHER HIGHWAYS

Primary Highway

Secondary Highway

HIGHWAY MARKERS

Interstate Route

U.S. Route

State Route

Distances along Major Highways (in miles)

CITIES AND TOWNS

National Capital

State Capital

Cities, Towns, and Populated Places Type size indicates relative importance

Urban Area

RECREATION AND FEATURES OF INTEREST

National Park

Other Large Park or Recreation Area

Trail

Ferry

MAPQUEST

SOUTH CAROLINA

---

trail and explore the native trees, shrubs and wildflowers.

Open Mon.–Sat., P.M. Sun.

Admission charged.

(803) 329-2121

www.yorkcounty.org

3 Landsford Canal State Park
Catawba

Had the 19th-century canal promoters known how quickly the railroads would develop, many of them would probably never have started the laborious process of digging. By hindsight, the Landsford Canal could be an example. The

Irish laborers started the job in 1820, working with picks and shovels, and took three years to create a two-mile stretch of navigable water. The canal was used primarily to bring cotton from the backcountry to the market at Charleston. After a few years the railroad put the canal out of business.

Landsford is the best preserved complete canal in the state and its remarkably well-preserved 200-foot section of locks built of cut stone blocks is an example of fine masonry work required for the early-day canals. Note in particular the precise stonework

on the arched bridge at the end of the locks.

The original lockkeeper's house, which holds the museum's displays, was moved here from Dearborn Island. A peaceful, pine-shaded area with tables and grills beside the Catawba River provides a pleasant place to picnic, and the 1½-mile towpath suggests an after-lunch stroll. Native birds can be identified along a nature trail.

Open Thurs.–Mon.

Admission charged.

(803) 789-5800

www.wildernet.com

4 Carolina Sandhills National Wildlife Refuge

Off Rte. 1, between McBee and Patrick

With American wildlife habitats steadily being destroyed by human encroachment, the 400 national wildlife preserves in the country have become key elements in sustaining the natural scene. The Carolina Sandhills Refuge is of particular interest because of its long history.

Fifty-five million years ago the Atlantic Ocean's incessant pounding of the shores created the dunes that stand there today. Within a short span of time, settlers, in their struggle to survive, cut the timber and overworked the land in this area. Eventually the soil was depleted and the farms were abandoned. In 1939 the federal government purchased 46,000 acres and established a wildlife refuge.

Now restored to its natural state, with forests of longleaf pines, pond pines, mockernut hickories, and persimmons, the land once again supports its original inhabitants. Beavers, deer, bobcats, rare woodpeckers, owls, and wild turkeys are among the 42 species of mammals and 190 species of birds observed here.

A nine-mile drive, hiking trails, observation towers and platforms, spring wildflower displays, and a photo blind provide extensive access to the wildlife. Several picnic tables with stone fireplaces are found at the Lake Bee Recreation Area. Fishing is allowed in designated lakes and creeks.

Open year-round.
(843) 335-8401
carolinasandhills.fws.gov

5 Rose Hill State Historic Site
Off Rte. 176, 7 miles north of Whitmire
Visitors to this magnificent stucco mansion, built between 1828 and 1832, will see evidence of the gracious and elegant life enjoyed by those who lived in antebellum plantations. The owner of Rose Hill was Gov. William Henry Gist. Known as the Secession Governor, Gist was elected in 1858; since South Carolina had no official governor's residence at that time, he lived and worked here.

Furnished in authentic period style, the house contains several fine pieces that had belonged to the governor. An 1832 pianoforte

5 Rose Hill State Historic Site. *This elegant antebellum plantation was home to William Henry Gist, who was known as the Secession Governor.*

and an 81-key piano stand in the second floor ballroom, which also features two fireplaces. Gist's own bedroom contains his wardrobe and four-poster bed, which has three hinged steps with a chamber pot concealed in one of them.

A fine example of the Federal style, the mansion has graceful front and rear porches built in 1860, and a handsome front door flanked by sidelights and a fanlight. On the grounds, enclosed by the original black wrought-iron fence, are boxwoods arranged in decorative patterns and several stately magnolias. Dogwoods line the entrance drive, and the garden features several antique varieties of roses, though they are not the original roses for which the plantation was named. Picnic tables and a pleasant quarter-mile nature trail complete the amenities of this 44-acre park.

Park open year-round; mansion open Thurs.–Mon. Admission charged for mansion tours.
(864) 427-5966
www.wildernet.com

6 Emerald Farm
409 Emerald Farm Rd. on the edge of Greenwood
Spanning nearly 75 pristine acres, this unique dairy farm is a treat for novelty as well as nature enthusiasts. Fans of lush, green pasture will find it here in abundance, along with hay barns, smokehouses, fruit trees, herb gardens, and an array of animals—sheep, cows, horses, chicken, and productive honey bees, along with Saanen dairy goats.

But they won't find a nibble of cheese. This working farm puts its goats milk to work to create exquisite soaps. All natural, each bar of soap is made completely by hand in the on-site soap factory. In addition to its signature skin-softening soap, combining goats milk and olive oil, the farm offers fragrant novelty soaps, with names like "Beach" and "Wildlife," assorted sachets and lotions, and even a shaving set for men. Along with homemade soap and hand-crafted beeswax candles, the farm serves up homemade food. The emphasis is on healthy, satisfying

fare for people with special nutritional needs and challenges, from lactose intolerance to diabetes.

Beyond its eclectic homemade products, Emerald Farm boasts its own train station and airplane hanger—in miniature forms. The main depot features a large and meticulously detailed railroad layout, with miles of tracks and fast-moving, whistling trains. Hobbyists who prefer airborne adventures will find an extensive selection of model plane kits and remote control airplanes.

Visitors can arrange for guided tours of the dairy farm and soap factory. For those eager to rest awhile after exploring and shopping, the grounds offer grassy spots for picnicking, a pavilion overlooking a pond, and plenty of meandering paths.

Open Mon.–Sat. year-round.
864-223-2247
www.emeraldfarm.com

7 Historic Camden Revolutionary War Site
Exit 98/I-20, Camden
More than 200 years ago Camden, the backcountry supply headquarters of Lord Cornwallis, was a hub of British activity, and owing to its strategic location, the focal point of two major Revolutionary War battles. Today the original buildings, restored and in some cases relocated, re-create the aura of the period.

Visitors can take a short self-guiding tour that includes the Drakeford House, an old log structure serving as a small museum of Revolutionary War artifacts excavated at the site. On a slightly longer loop, which can be walked or driven, information plaques explain several reconstructed points of interest, most notably the 1780 Kershaw-Cornwallis House, two British outer defense redoubts, and a 1777 powder magazine.

A hiking trail leads to unspoiled natural scenery observed by the region's first settlers. Camden's downtown national registered district includes 63 houses and buildings that predate 1865.

Open daily; guided tours given Tues.–Sat. Admission charged.
(803) 432-9841
www.historic-camden.org

8 South Carolina Cotton Trail

Stretching from Bishopville, off I-20, to Bennettsville, off I-95
Much more than the premier crop, cotton shaped the fabric of Southern culture and life for hundreds of years. Spanning five towns rich in history and character, this sweeping trail traces its thread of influence.

The trail begins at Bishopville, home to the South Carolina Cotton Museum. Capturing the toil and spirit of tenant farmers, it features a life-sized replica of a farmhouse, with original furnishing and artifacts from "shotgun houses." Nearby, trail-blazers can see a working cotton gin in action.

The second stop, Hartsville, features beautifully restored houses, including one seized by the Yankees during the Civil War. Transformed into enemy head-quarters for two days, the Jacob Kelly House now hosts living history demonstrations.

Next on the trail, the charming Society Hill claims the state's only working commercial rice planta-tion: the Carolina Plantation. It is also home to pioneering lending libraries, built in 1822.

The fourth town is one of South Carolina's oldest and loveliest, Cheraw, named for the Cheraw Indians. Its attractions include Old St. David's Anglican Church, built in 1770—and the last "state" church decreed by King George III. In its cemetery stands the very first monument erected in memory of Confederate soldiers.

The final town, Bennettsville, was once famed for its rich, fertile soil. Along with a local history museum and stunning antebellum homes, it boasts a unique church. Founded in 1867 by African Americans recently freed from slavery, the Evans Metropolitan AME Zion Church served the devout of three denominations—Zion, Methodist, and Baptist.

Call for hours; some admission fees.
(888) 427-8720
www.sccottontrail.org

9 Parsons Mountain Lake Recreation Area

Edgefield. From Abbeville go south on Rte. 28 for 2.1 miles. Turn left on Rte. SI-251, drive 1.5 miles to entrance on right.
A quiet lake is the centerpiece of this fine wooded tract devoted to tent and trailer camping, picnick-ing, hiking, riding, and fishing. A large picnic grove flanks a supervised swimming area on the lakeshore, and a boat ramp invites fishermen to try for crappie, catfish, bass, and other species common to the region.

From the top of a nearby 80-foot tower one has a panoramic view of the mixed pine and hard-wood forests of the Carolina pied-mont. In the woods are deer and small mammals and a variety of birds to watch for. Indian paint-brush and lady's slipper are among the wildflowers that brighten the woodland trails.

Open Apr. 1–Dec. 31; Admission charged.
(803) 637-5396
www.fs.fed.us/r8/fms/rec/parsons.htm

10 Sumter County Museum

122 N. Washington St., Sumter
The Sumter County Museum is based on the classic concept that the more we know of the past, the better we know ourselves. The past is represented by structures rang-ing in time from a one-room cabin built in 1812 to the new Heritage Center. Relocated from the Pine-wood area, the Weeks Cabin was lived in for more than 150 years by several families, including slaves, freedmen, and tenant farmers.

Other structures include exhibits on farming life, the rail-roads, and transportation. The 1920s garage holds several carriages and a classic surrey, complete with fringe on top. A pole barn contains an array of farm equipment used when mules were the primary mode of power in the South.

The handsomely furnished Williams-Brice House (1916) included period rooms, an exhibit on Gen. Thomas Sumter featuring the portrait by Rembrandt Peale, the "Always Coca-Cola" exhibit with several examples of Coke memorabilia, and rotating exhibits on topics ranging from World War II to quilts. The gardens surround-ing the Williams-Brice House are beautiful year-round.

Along with the Carolina Back-country Exhibit that portrays life as it was on a farm from 1750 to 1850, it's worth seeing the mus-eum archives in the old Carnegie Library (1916), and the brand-new 10,500-square-foot Heritage Education Center that features the Witherspoons of Coldstream Plantation Collection.

Open Tues.–Fri. and P.M. Sun.
(803) 775-0908
www.sumtercountymuseum.com

10 Sumter County Museum. *Every March, May, October, and December, the Carolina Backcountry Homestead comes alive with costumed guides demon-strating skills used on a farm in 1800.*

11 Aiken State Natural Area
Windsor

When places are named in honor of worthy citizens, the names are remembered, but their good works are often forgotten. This park and the county were named for William Aiken Sr., president of the Charleston-Hamburg Railroad, which in the 1830s was the longest line in the world and a considerable engineering accomplishment. It deserves to be remembered.

The pleasant, hilly terrain of the 1,067-acre park provides lake and stream fishing, a spring-fed pond with a swimming area, canoe rentals, campsites, and a picnic ground, as well as a playground, softball field, and game areas.

A jungle nature trail about three miles long has markers identifying such native trees as red maple, water oak, persimmon, sweet gum, and sweet bay. Conducted walks in spring familiarize the visitor with the profusion of wildflowers that flourish here. The park, where more than 160 feathered species have been observed, is a favorite destination for birders in the spring and fall.

The four fishing ponds surrender bass and bluegill. Anglers also favor the south fork of the Edisto River, which borders (and enters) the park. The area is apt to be crowded during the summer months, especially on weekends.
Open year-round.
(803) 649-2857
www.southcarolinaparks.com

12 Santee National Wildlife Refuge
Summerton

Four separate units, all flanked by Lake Marion, make up this

11 Aiken State Natural Area.
Popular with anglers, the south fork of the Edisto River and the area's four ponds are teeming with bass and bluegill.

15,095-acre tract where a vast array of bird, mammal, fish, reptile, and amphibian species thrive in a protected environment. The visitors center, on a cove called Scott's Lake, has a diorama, an aquarium, and other displays that help to acquaint nature lovers with some of the wildlife indigenous to the reserve, including American bald eagles, ospreys, river otters, striped bass, and alligators.

Across Scott's Lake is the site of Fort Watson, which was recaptured from the British in 1781 by Gen. Francis ("The Swamp Fox") Marion. It stands on the site of a Santee Indian ceremonial and burial ground.

This general area is ideal for hiking, bicycling, and fishing—Lake Marion is known for its Atlantic sturgeon, freshwater eels, chain pickerel, and bluegills. Each unit in the refuge has its own boat ramp. Birders can obtain a free printed checklist of the 293 species observed here. Among

the permanent residents are pied-billed grebes, little blue herons, painted buntings, bluewinged teals, and Cooper's hawks. The many winged visitors include American woodcocks, barred owls, and rock doves. There is also a significant wood duck population.
Open year-round.
(803) 478-2217
www.fws.gov

13 Rivers Bridge Historic Site
Ehrhardt

This is one of the many delightful recreation areas in the South that owe their existence to the tragedy of war.

It was here in February 1865 that a force of Confederate artillery, cavalry, and infantry under Gen. Lafayette McLaws fought in vain to stop Gen. William T. Sherman on his devastating march from Savannah north to Virginia. Outnumbered and out-flanked, the Confederates were only able to delay Sherman for two days before he went on to burn McPhersonville and Columbia.

Years later the bodies of the Confederate soldiers who died then were brought here for reburial and a monument was erected. Donations and purchases of land adjoining this hallowed ground brought the total acreage to 390, and in 1945 it was acquired by the state for a park.

Facilities now include campsites, picnic areas, and a wading pool for children. A mile-long interpretive trail, following the progression of the battle—beneath pines and live oaks draped with Spanish moss—is aglow in early April with the colorful blossoms of wisteria, dogwoods, and native

azaleas. Observant hikers may see pileated woodpeckers, which are among the more unusual birds in this area. Fishing along the river and on a creek yields crappies, catfish, gar, and largemouth bass.
Park open year-round.
(803) 267-3675

14 The Francis Beidler Forest in Four Holes Swamp
Harleyville

Ancient groves of bald cypresses taller than a 10-story building and up to 1,000 years old; virgin stands of loblolly pine and tupelo gum trees; alligators, cottonmouths, and fish-eating spiders hiding in a maze of swamp waters—all these contribute to the somber and mysterious majesty of this primeval sanctuary.

The forest preserve within the swamp was named for Francis Beidler, a remarkable lumberman and conservationist who allowed much of his timberland to stand untouched. In 1960 the National Audubon Society acquired 3,415 acres from the Beidler family for a sanctuary. Today it encompasses more than 11,000 acres.

The swamp is a flooded forest and by its nature difficult to penetrate. Some sense of the inner character of this ecosystem is provided by the 1 3/4-mile-long boardwalk with its 31 informative signs along the way. In season, experienced canoeists can take a half-day trip with a naturalist guide to reach the interior of the swamp.

Exhibits, photographs, and a video show in the visitors center help one to understand and appreciate the swamp and the mammals, birds, and reptiles that abound here.

Open Tues.–Sun. year-round.
Admission charged. (843) 462-2150
www.beidlerforest.com

15 Hampton Plantation State Historic Site

McClellanville
In this wilderness dominated by loblolly pines and stands of other native trees, it is hard to visualize the orderly plantations of rice and cotton that thrived here from the early 1700s until 1860.

The sole reminder of those prosperous times is the plantation house, built in the mid-1700s. After slavery was abolished, the plantation system became unprofitable, and Hampton was farmed by sharecroppers, as were many other places.

The house was eventually left to Archibald Rutledge, a Hampton descendant and the state's first poet-laureate. In 1937 he undertook its restoration, a process he chronicled in the book *Home by the River*. Years later in 1971, he sold the place to the state of South Carolina.

The 15-room house, which had evolved over the years, now has a Georgian façade and two-story columns. It is left unfurnished to let its design speak for itself. In some areas a section of wall has been removed to show some of the architectural and structural details of the past.

Grounds open year-round;
House open daily Memorial Day–
Labor Day; Thurs.–Mon. P.M.
Labor Day–Memorial Day.
Admission charged.
(843) 546-9361
www.southcarolinaparks.com

16 Cape Romain National Wildlife Refuge

Awendaw
Except for changes brought about by erosion—acres of forest destroyed and the shoreline and islands rearranged—this area is virtually as it was in the days of the Sewee Indians, who fished and hunted here, and the pirates who found the maze of waterways to their occasional liking.

Most of the refuge's 20-mile stretch of coast, barrier reef, salt marshes, and open water are inaccessible by land. Its remoteness makes this a most likely environment for the preservation of such endangered species as loggerhead turtles that nest here. The bird list available at the Seewee Visitor and Environmental Education Center includes 262 species, plus 76 that are considered rare. The greatest population here is during the spring and fall migrations and in the winter, although there are summer residents as well.

White-tailed deer are frequently seen. Southern fox squirrels are plentiful, and raccoons, though nocturnal, may be seen during the day. If you are lucky, you may spot a playful family of river otters or dolphins cruising the creeks and bays. Alligators are common and should be given a wide berth. Also keep an eye out for cottonmouths and copperheads, the poisonous snakes in the area.

Bull Island (named for an early settler) is the focal point for visitors. A two-mile trail, with informative plaques, leads through a lush forest of live oaks, magnolias, and loblolly pines, with such shrubs as cabbage palmetto, wax myrtle, and holly. A fine beach and excellent birding are other attractions on the island. Fishing is allowed in designated areas. Surf fishermen try for channel bass. Access to Bull Island is by ferry from Gams Landing.

Refuge open year-round.
(843) 928-3368
www.seeweevisitorcenter.fws.gov

17 The Sheldon Church Ruins and Historic Beaufort

Between Yemassee and Gardens Corner
In 1745, a majestic church with massive arches was erected for the bayside community of Prince William Parish. Today, that community has been reborn as the city of Beaufort. All that remains of one of the most beautiful churches ever to grace the South are its ruins, now listed on the *National Register of Historic Places*. A tragic casualty of two major wars—Revolutionary and Civil—Sheldon Church was first burned by the British Army in 1779. In 1826, it was rebuilt in all its original glory. It was burned again by Sherman's Army in 1865.

Like Sheldon Church, the city of Beaufort has a proud and turbulent history. Beckoning with its large natural harbor, the area attracted settlers long before it was officially discovered by the Spanish in 1514. French explorers followed, which led to fierce wars with the tribes of American Indian inhabitants. During the Revolutionary War, Beaufort was often under siege; South Carolina hosted more battles and claimed more casualties than any other colony. On the cusp of the Civil War, Beaufort again came under fire as a focal point of secessionist action.

Today's Beaufort is a place of quaint Southern charm and natural beauty. Horse-drawn carriage rides depart from the downtown historic district, past celebrated landmarks and sites where major movies, including *Forrest Gump*, have been filmed. Port Royal, the city's noted boardwalk, offers spectacular views of the sound. Beaufort also serves as a gateway to dozens of islands—from Parris Island, for a guided tour of the U.S. Marine Corps Depot, to Hilton Head, for a deluxe day at the beach.

(843) 785-5924
www.beaufortsc.org

17 The Sheldon Church Ruins. *The church was built in 1745, burned by the British in 1779, rebuilt, and burned by General Sherman in 1865.*

Badlands National Park. *Rich in fossil beds dating back 35 million years, the dramatic landscape spans nearly a quarter million acres (see page 308).*

South Dakota

Inviting parks and forbidding badlands merge here with memories of trappers, traders, homesteaders, and the indomitable Sioux.

The many parks include shady retreats, lakes, and a variety of hiking trails. A vast wildlife refuge offers prairies, marshlands, streams, and ponds where the birding is unexcelled.

In the badlands, wind, water, and time have created some 244,000 acres of colorful buttes, pinnacles, plateaus, valleys, and ridges; the distant geological past is further recalled in a petrified forest and two ancient caves. More recent human history is represented by artifacts of the American Indians whose territory this was, and the buildings, tools, utensils, and weapons of the soldiers, traders, and homesteaders who ultimately prevailed on the prairie.

1 Petrified Wood Park and Museum

500 Main Ave., Lemmon
Long ago tropical swamps covered the region around Lemmon. Gradual climatic and chemical changes and the passage of time turned the remnants of that distant era—trees, grasses, plants, and marine and animal life—into stone. In the 1930s O.S. Quammen, an amateur geologist, collected some of the best specimens of the petrified material for an unusual but artistic outdoor display.

The small park is studded with 100 cone-shaped pyramids ranging up to 32 feet in height and piles of "cannonballs" in graduated sizes. A turreted fairy-tale castle, built with more than 300 tons of petrified material, including tree trunks more than 30 feet tall, is especially intriguing.

Teeth marks, petrified snakes, and fossilized marine life are eerily recognizable in many surfaces. The castle contains the fossils of enormous animals, while a circular museum built of petrified logs and slabs of petrified grass houses pioneer artifacts. The multiplicity of forms and the incredible range of colors make this a fascinating place to see.

Park open year-round; museum open mid-May–mid-Sept.
(605) 374-3964
www.lemmonsd.com

1 Petrified Wood Park and Museum. *The "castle," as this building is known, was the vision of amateur geologist O. S. Quammen. It was constructed in the early 1930s using more than 300 tons of petrified wood.*

2 Klein Museum

West of Mobridge on Rte. 12
This museum, with its excellent collection of artifacts from the area's pioneer days, was the inspiration of Jake Klein, an early South Dakota homesteader. One of the more colorful features is the trapper's shack, complete with a skillet and coffeepot on a wood-burning stove and a life-size model of a bundled-up trapper standing as if to greet you. You can also explore the old-time offices of a dentist and a doctor, and Jake's Room, which displays items from Klein's own homesteading days.

In addition the museum has a good assortment of pioneer tools and an exhibit of American Indian artifacts, including headdresses and beaded bags. Vintage vehicles and heavy machinery are on view in another building, and a one-room schoolhouse is open for inspection.

Just west of Mobridge, on Highway 20, you'll find the grave of Sitting Bull, marked by a huge

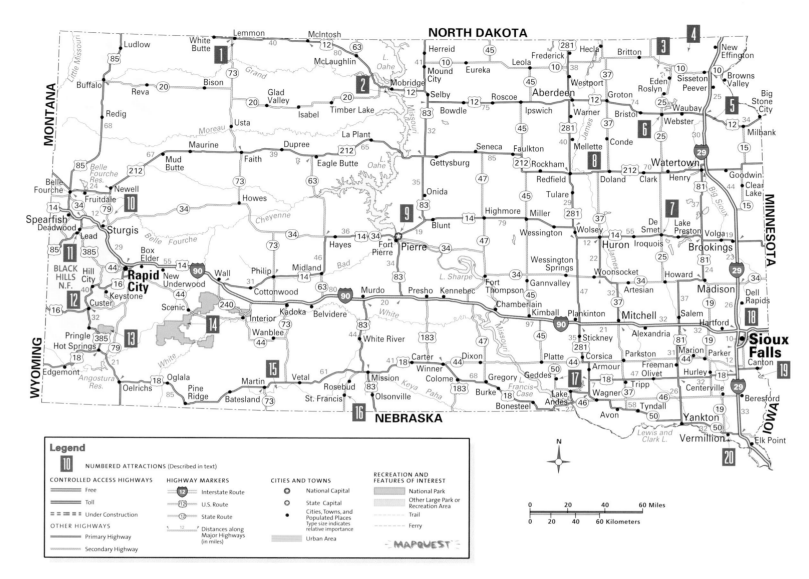

stone sculpture of this Sioux medicine man and leader. Nearby, overlooking Lake Oahe, is a monument to Sacajawea, the young Shoshone woman who in 1804–06 served as a guide and interpreter for Lewis and Clark on their expedition to the Pacific Coast.

Museum open Mon., Wed.–Fri. and P.M. weekends. Admission charged.

(605) 845-7243

www.mobridge.org

3 Fort Sisseton State Park
Lake City

The establishment of Fort Sisseton in 1864 followed the Sioux rebellion against broken treaties and the influx of settlers on their lands. In service for 25 years, the fort was finally closed in June 1889, just months before South Dakota became a state.

On the spacious, grassy grounds dotted with shade trees are 15 buildings, including officers' quarters, a stable, and a library-schoolhouse. The visitors center and a museum are housed in the North Barracks, designed as living quarters for 200 soldiers. Picnic areas and camping facilities are provided.

Park open year-round; visitors center open daily, Memorial Day–Labor Day.
Admission charged.
(605) 448-5701

www.state.sd.us/gfp

4 Sica Hollow State Park
Lake City

This peaceful park, located in what the French explorer Nicollet called the Coteau des Prairie, or Hills of the Prairie, is in a deep winding hollow almost invisible from the surrounding hills. Despite the abundant, free-flowing streams that provided drinking water to people and animals, the Sisseton Indians believed there was something sinister about the place, and they named it Sica, or evil. Reports of people being swallowed by the bogs gave rise to various spirit legends. Sica Hollow was selected for designation as a National Natural Landmark in 1967. Today visitors can hike the Trail of the Spirits or any of the 15 miles of hiking, horseback, or mountain biking trails.

Open year-round.
(605) 448-5701

www.state.sd.us/gfp

5 Blue Cloud Abbey

12 miles west of Milbank off Rte. 12, Marvin

The doors are never locked at this quiet, peaceful abbey, a Benedictine monastery founded in 1950. Guests are welcome to come here for rest and contemplation and, with reservations, may stay the night or longer. The monks have vowed to live by the rule of St. Benedict, written by the saint in the 6th century and emphasizing the importance of prayer and work.

The monks labored for 17 years in building the abbey. Today they are involved in making candles, keeping bees (honey is sold at the abbey), and tending the gardens that provide much of their food. In a workshop open to visitors, they create ornate and colorful vestments for churches of many different denominations throughout the world.

On the outside wall of the monastery is an excellent mosaic of the Virgin Mary. Contemporary stained glass enhances the church's sanctuary, and current artwork hangs in the lower lounge. A room has been adapted as a chapel for Protestants; however, everyone is welcome in the abbey church.

The abbey also houses the American Indian Culture Research Center, created by members of 14 Midwestern reservations to preserve the heritage and beliefs of the first Americans. Researchers are welcome to use the facilities here, but must make an appointment in advance.

The home cooking and caring atmosphere provided here make even a short visit a pleasant and memorable one.

Open year-round.
(605) 398-9200
www.bluecloud.org

6 Museum of Wildlife, Science, & Industry

W. Hwy. 12, Webster

One thing you might not expect to find, should you be looking for it on the plains of South Dakota, is an extremely large replica of the shoe of Mother Goose. The Shoe House is one of 24 structures, 12 of which are historic, that comprise this museum intended to preserve both heritage and culture of the northeastern part of the state.

The big shoe contains over 9,000 shoes that Mildred Fiksdal O'Neill began accumulating in high school, from her father's snowshoes to moccasins used to carry messages during World War II.

Another interesting item here is the one-cell Grenville Jail, notable for not being bolted to the floor, which was moved here in 1988. Men held for minor infractions would lift the cell but never managed to walk it out of the building.

Two other buildings that were moved here to add interest to the museum were the Kozy Korner Café and the general store, both originally located in Butler, circa 1940.

Another building, dedicated to pioneer women, contains a Norwegian-style bedroom and a loom. American Indian stone tools, a sleigh and buggy, vintage farming vehicles, and early printing presses also give a flavor of what life was once like here.

Wildlife is also represented here by a group of animals, including mounted water buffalo and zebra, which were donated by one of the original benefactors, who was a hunter and world traveler.

Open May 1–Nov. 1. Donations accepted.
(605) 345-4751

www.sdmuseum.org

9 South Dakota Cultural Heritage Center. *"Kitty," also known as the Medora-Deadwood Stagecoach, was used to take travelers between the towns of Medora and Deadwood. The trip, which covered 215 miles, took 36 hours.*

7 De Smet

This is the Little Town on the Prairie made famous by Laura Ingalls Wilder in the Little House books describing her childhood here in the 1880s. For a self-guiding map of the town locating the places she wrote about, go to the Laura Ingalls Wilder Memorial Society, which is headquartered next door to the Surveyor's House (at the corner of First Street and Olivet Avenue).

The map leads you to 16 restored places and sites, including the Loftus store, the church that "Pa helped build," the home where Laura and Almanzo Ingalls lived in 1894, and the family homestead site right outside of town.

The society gives guided tours of the Surveyor's House, where the family lived for the first winter on the Dakota prairie, and the Ingalls House, which was built by Laura's father in 1887 after she married. The Ingalls House is furnished with many original pieces, and displays family memorabilia.

Open year-round. Tours daily Jun.–Aug. Admission charged.
(605) 854-3383
www.liwms.com

8 Fisher Grove State Park

Redfield

Along the banks of the winding James River, this pleasant grove is a welcome oasis in the midst of the seemingly endless prairies, its cottonwoods, willows, and box elders fringing the riverbanks and sheltering the picnic and camping grounds.

The 360-acre park honors Frank I. Fisher, an early settler who in 1878 purchased 80 acres of land here along the James for 40 cents an acre with the intention of establishing a settlement. Shortly

SOUTH DAKOTA

afterward, however, the railroad bypassed the area, and the few buildings that had been constructed were torn down and used for firewood. A three-quarter-mile nature trail winds through the park and leads to the location of the original settlement. An 1884 schoolhouse, fully restored, serves as the visitors center. A boat ramp is provided for canoeists.

Open year-round. Admission charged.
(605) 472-1212
www.state.sd.us/gfp

9 South Dakota Cultural Heritage Center

900 Governors Dr., Pierre
South Dakota history, from the time of its early American Indian cultures up through World War II, comes alive in this splendid underground museum. Among the displays are those of a Sioux Indian, a walk-through tepee, and a magnificent streamlined wooden stick carving of a galloping horse (circa 1875). The carving was included in an American Indian art show sent to England in 1976.

An exhibit of special historic interest is the Verendrye Plate, a lead plate that was placed on a bluff overlooking the Missouri River by a French expedition in 1743, claiming this area for France, and found in 1913.

Other displays show how the lives of South Dakota's people have been affected by such change as the fur trade, the gold rush, the coming of the railroad, and military service.

Open daily year-round; P.M. weekends. Closed Thanksgiving, Christmas, and New Year's Day. Admission charged.
(605) 773-3458
www.sdhistory.org

10 Bear Butte State Park
Sturgis

The centerpiece of this park is a solitary, cone-shaped mountain that rises 1,200 feet above the plains. Named Bear Mountain by the Sioux, it was regarded as a holy place by both the Sioux and the Cheyennes. Red Cloud, Sitting Bull, and other Indian leaders paid visits here, and an Indian conference was held at Bear Butte in 1857 to discuss the encroachment of white settlers and gold prospectors in the region.

For more than a century the mountain has also drawn scientists from far and wide. Among geologists it is a famous example of a laccolith. Formed millions of years ago by a great upheaval of molten rock, it is a volcano that never erupted.

For ambitious hikers, a national recreation trail leads from the parking lot to the summit. You can see a few buffalo grazing in a pasture near the base. Camping and boating facilities are found at Bear Butte Lake just across the highway.

Open May–mid-Sept.
(605) 347-5240
www.state.sd.us/gfp

11 George S. Mickelson Trail
Deadwood to Edgemont

Calamity Jane and Wild Bill Hickok. Badlands. Steam trains chugging through the landscape of dense spruce and pine forests. Desperadoes lurking up in the cliffs. Our notions of the Black Hills of South Dakota have long been tinged with Western myth and legend.

Now a friendly 114-mile trail that traverses the whole length of the Black Hills has been designed for the pleasure of bicycle riders, hikers, and people on horseback.

Following the tracks of the defunct Burlington Northern Railroad, this "jewel" of the state park system takes you from Deadwood to Dumont, the highest point, on a steady incline of 19 miles. Some portions of the trail are considered to be strenuous, but the grade is never more than 4 percent. The crushed limestone surface and wide paths offer comfortable travel across 100 converted railroad bridges and through four hard-rock tunnels.

Other mountain bike trails that vary in difficulty can be reached from this one, named for Gov. George S. Mickelson, who passed away in 1993.

11 George S. Mickelson Trail. *Set in the heart of the Black Hills, this well-groomed, 114-mile trail, with its numerous access points and gentle grade, is a haven for cyclists and hikers.*

Open year-round. Small use fees.
(605) 584-3896
www.mickelsontrail.com

12 Jewel Cave National Monument
Custer

The dazzlingly beautiful cave filled with jewel-like calcite crystals is the star attraction in this 1,275-acre park. Located in Hell Canyon, it was discovered in 1900 and declared a national monument in 1908. Exploration has proved it to be the nation's second-largest cave system: more than 125 miles of passageways have been mapped so far.

Visitors to the cave have a choice of three tours. The popular 80-minute-long Scenic Tour follows a paved half-mile route, with aluminum stairways and handrails, and is specially illuminated to show the diverse cave formations. The more difficult Candlelight Tour is unpaved, with ladder-like steps and no lighting (visitors carry lanterns), and takes almost two hours. Reservations are required for the Spelunking Tour, part of which is covered on hands and knees. But it is carefully supervised, and no previous caving experience is needed. To avoid long waits, arrive first thing in the morning or visit early or late in the season. Wear low-heeled walking shoes and a sweater, because it's chilly.

Monument and visitors center open daily year-round. Scenic Tours year-round, Candlelight and Spelunking Tours summer only; admission charged for cave.
(605) 673-2288
www.nps.gov/jeca

13 Wind Cave National Park
Hot Springs

The cave here, named for the strong barometric winds found at the entrance, contains more than 100 miles of chambers and passageways. It is famous for the excellent examples of boxwork, a strange, honeycomb-like formation of calcite, and for other decorative deposits such as frostwork, flowstone, popcorn, and delicate helictite bushes.

Cave tours of varying difficulty and length are offered throughout the year. Wear good walking shoes and a jacket. Reservations are recommended for the special Candlelight Tour, which ventures through unpaved and unlighted parts of the cave, and they are required for the strenuous four-hour spelunking tour.

The 28,000-acre park is a wildlife refuge, with great stretches of open prairie grassland interspersed with mixed hardwood and ponderosa pine forests. One might see buffalo, elk, pronghorn antelope, coyotes, mule deer, badgers, and prairie dogs. Birds that find refuge

13 Wind Cave National Park. *Calcite formations, known as "popcorn," line the walls of the underground passageways here.*

here include owls, grouse, magpies, and golden eagles.

The park has a campground and amphitheater, three self-guiding nature trails, a backcountry camping area, and a picnic area. Bicycles are permitted on the roadways.

Park open year-round. No cave tours on Thanksgiving and Christmas; admission charged for tours.
(605) 745-4600
www.nps.gov/wica

14 Badlands National Park
Interior

One can imagine the dismay with which pioneers eyed this 50-mile stretch of seeming moonscape that appears so abruptly on the grassy plain. The cliffs, gorges, soaring spires, knife-edged ridges, flat-topped mesas, and fossil-filled canyons, carved and etched by millions of years of rain, wind, and frost, stand as a classic example of the effects of erosion.

Most visitors to the Badlands simply drive the scenic 30-mile loop along Highway 240. But for those willing to venture off this well-worn path there are many little-known spots to enjoy. The park encompasses nearly a quarter-million acres, and some 64,000 acres of the most spectacular landscape are a roadless wilderness area open only to hikers, backpackers, and horseback riders.

Bighorn sheep, buffalo, pronghorn antelope, and mule deer roam the Badlands. White-throated swifts and cliff swallows nest in the cliff faces, and golden eagles build on the buttes. Junipers, cottonwoods, and wildflowers manage to survive the extremes of weather.

During the summer, the Ben Reifel Visitor Center, at the eastern

end of the park, schedules several ranger-guided nature walks, evening slide lectures, and stargazing programs. The White River Visitor Center is located in the South Unit of the park, which includes part of the Pine Ridge Indian Reservation. There are two campgrounds with limited facilities; water is available at only one of them.

Park open year-round; Ben Reifel Visitor center open daily except Thanksgiving, Christmas and New Year's Day; White River Visitor Center open mid-June–late August. Admission charged.
(605) 433-5361
www.nps.gov/badl

15 Lacreek National Wildlife Refuge
Off Rte. 73, Martin

This 16,250-acre refuge, a mixture of sand-covered dunes, marshland, streams, and ponds, offers protection to some 281 species of birds, many of them migrating and nesting waterfowl, and more than 50 kinds of mammals. Its name was derived from Lake Creek, the spring-fed stream that provides much of the water for the refuge.

Trumpeter swans, white pelicans, cormorants, Canada geese, and many kinds of ducks nest here annually, along with sandpipers, pied-billed grebes, coots, and long-billed curlews. From early March to the end of May, migrating birds gather here by the thousands, and again from late August until the middle of November.

Visitors can drive through the refuge on the gravel roadway. There is also a short bird walk. Mosquitoes are numerous in summer, so bring along insect repellent. Adjacent to

the refuge is the White River Recreation Area, which offers fishing, boating, swimming, camping, and picnicking facilities. Fishing is also permitted within the refuge at Pools 7 and 10 and Cedar Creek Pond.

Open year-round.
(605) 685-6508
http://lacreek.fws.gov

16 Buechel Memorial Lakota Museum
350 S. Oak St., St. Francis

The small but fascinating museum is part of St. Francis Mission on the Rosebud Indian Reservation. The museum was established as a memorial to Father Eugene Buechel, a Jesuit missionary who spent a great deal of his life among the Lakota, or Sioux, and died in 1954. In addition to collecting and preserving the artifacts of their culture, he helped to preserve their language, writing three books and compiling 30,000 entries of Dakota words that formed the basis for a dictionary.

The museum's collection includes elaborate tribal robes, headdresses, jewelry, tools, hunting knives, bows and arrows and other weapons, musical instruments, horse gear, and games. Some of the pieces date back to the 1850s.

Father Buechel left two other valuable legacies: 2,300 photographs that he took during his years among the Lakota and a collection of Plains plant specimens that he gathered, mounted, and cataloged, noting the Lakota's use of them.

Open daily Memorial Day– Labor Day.
(605) 747-2745
www.littlesioux.org

14 Badlands National Park. *The harsh beauty of the Badlands by moonlight is particularly striking. Frank Lloyd Wright was said to have remarked, "I was totally unprepared for that revelation called the Dakota Bad Lands."*

17 Papineau Trading Post
Geddes

The trading post, a 20- by 30-foot log cabin, was built in 1857 by Cuthbert Ducharme, a French-Canadian fur trader, on the bank of the Missouri River a few miles from Geddes. It was relocated at this small turn-of-the-century railroad town when the first site was flooded by the construction of a dam. The room now serving as a lobby was a later addition.

Soldiers, cowboys, boatmen, and westward-bound travelers stopped at the post for supplies, including liquor. Legend has it that Ducharme, who was nicknamed Papineau (meaning pap water, or whiskey), poured the whiskey into a dishpan and tied a tin cup to it, allowing his customers to help themselves— a full cup for 25 cents. Ducharme was also known for his skill at handling a gun, and the records of the U. S. Army Corps of Engineers state that the original Ducharme cemetery contained 27 graves,

14 of which were unidentified. Several of the tombstones have been removed to the trading post in Geddes; they are considered fine examples of 19th-century mortuary art.

The original log structure contains the accoutrements of a fur trader's life in the second half of the 19th century: traps, knives, guns, a kerosene lamp, dishes, pots and pans, a table, some rawhide chairs, and a liquor barrel, plus American Indian relics.

Open daily May–Sept. Admission free but donations encouraged.
(605) 337-2501
www.geddessd.org/historicalvillage.html

18 Palisades State Park
Garretson

This strikingly beautiful park of gorges, vertical cliffs, and dramatic rock formations borders both sides of Split Rock Creek. According to American Indian legend, the sheer-walled canyon through which the stream flows was created when a

god from the spirit world threw a tomahawk to earth.

The massive layers of quartzite in the cliffs, formed some millions of years ago, are interspersed with beds of pipestone, or catlinite, a soft red stone held sacred by the Indians.

The creek, which has several rapids and quiet pools, provides excellent swimming, fishing, and canoeing. The 111-acre park has a tree-shaded campground and two picnic areas overlooking the picturesque stream. Hiking trails follow its course, wandering along 80-foot-high cliffs, which are very popular with rock climbers. During the summer a park naturalist offers a junior ranger program for youngsters, outdoor cooking classes, nature walks, and evening hikes.

Open year-round.
Admission charged.
(605) 594-3824
www.state.sd.us/gfp

19 Newton Hills State Park
Canton

Newton Hills is the southern end of a chain of hills named Coteau des Prairies by early French explorers. Stretching for some 200 miles and rising more than 2,000 feet above sea level, the ridge was formed by glacial deposits.

The park, in a beautiful wooded setting, has a bridle trail and several hiking trails, some with swinging bridges spanning small ravines. Many of the trees and shrubs are identified along the Coteau and Woodland trails.

More than 200 species of birds have been observed in the park, whose 1,050 acres also harbor white-tailed deer, marmots, and other wildlings. Pine-shaded

campgrounds, picnic shelters, and handbuilt stone fireplaces are provided, as well as game courts. Man-made Lake Lakota, at the southeast border of the park, has a sandy swimming beach, a boat ramp, and an adjacent picnic ground.

Open year-round.
Admission charged.
(605) 987-2263
www.state.sd.us/gfp

20 The National Music Museum
On the University of South Dakota campus, Vermillion

Professor Arne B. Larson has gathered more than 2,500 musical instruments from around the world and donated them to the university. They include instruments of all kinds—American, European, and also non-Western—thoughtfully grouped and handsomely displayed.

There are also some marvelous oddities, such as a zither in the shape of a crocodile, a trombone whose bell is a dragon's head, and an ancient harp so elegantly arched that one wonders how it could be plucked. These instruments, both ancient and modern, are valued not only for documenting the history of music in various cultures of the world, but also for revealing the imagination and superb craftsmanship of those who created them.

Today the collection numbers some 10,000 pieces, including a Stradivari guitar and violin, and is rivaled only by collections in Europe.

Open Mon.–Sat. and P.M. Sun. except major holidays. Admission free but donations requested.
(605) 677-5306
www.usd.edu/smm

Fort Donelson National Battlefield. *The Confederate Monument here honors Southern soldiers who died in battle (see page 312).*

The varied communities to see include a treasure of Victorian architecture, a hamlet that recalls the stark realities of 19th-century life in the Tennessee hills, a charmingly naive experiment in gentlemanly colonization, and the oldest town west of the Appalachians. Here too is a reconstruction of an American Indian village abandoned about 500 years ago.

The Tennessee Valley Railroad is memorialized, as are the home, the locomotive, and the immortal story of Casey Jones. There are fine log structures to visit, a water-driven mill, a famous whiskey distillery (where they provide an excellent drink of lemonade), and a million-dollar collection of unusual teapots.

Tennessee

The superb state parks and the variety of other attractions might be predictable. The dedication to preserving historic towns is a lovely surprise.

1 Chucalissa Museum

Memphis. From I-55 take the Third St. South exit (Rte. 61) to Mitchell Rd. Go west on Mitchell Rd. about 5 miles to the entrance. In the Choctaw language *Chucalissa* means "abandoned house." Here at the edge of T. O. Fuller State Park, not far from the Mississippi River, lies the site of an American Indian village that seems to have been abandoned in the 1500s, probably before the arrival in the area of the Spanish conquistador Hernando de Soto. De Soto may have visited the place in 1541, but his accounts are vague as to his exact location. It wasn't until the late 1930s, when excavation was under way for a swimming pool in T.O. Fuller State Park, that the modern world discovered the remains of the prehistoric village.

A full-time staff of archaeologists and Choctaw Indians now maintains a reconstructed village and museum on the site.

The reconstructed houses, set on a roughly circular plaza with a platform mound to the north, are rectangular, with conical thatched roofs resting on five-foot-high pole-and-mud walls. On the platform mound sits a much larger house, presumably that of the chief. Inside the houses are depictions of daily life in the village: women preparing meals; a shaman,

1 Chucalissa Museum. *Choctaw women in traditional native dress form a circle for a social dance during August festivals.*

or medicine man, performing a ceremony to cure a sick child; and the chief receiving a messenger from a neighboring tribe.

The half-mile-long Chickasaw Bluff Interpretive Trail takes visitors through ravines that offered protection from other tribes and from the Mississippi River when it flooded. You can see medicinal plants like willow bark (aspirin) and golden rod, used to treat sore throats.

T. O. Fuller State Park, which encompasses 1,138 acres, offers equipped campsites (which are an easy half-

mile walk from Chucalissa), picnic grounds, game fields, and trails that wend through woods inhabited by deer and wild turkeys. The park is heavily visited in summer.

Chucalissa open Tues.–Sun. except major holidays. Admission charged.
Park open year-round.
(901) 785-3160

www.chucalissa.org

2 Reelfoot Lake State Resort Park

Tiptonville

A cataclysmic earthquake on February 7, 1812—perhaps the most violent ever to strike the continental United States—caused an enormous area of land to sink as much as 10 feet. Water from the Mississippi River entered this depression, creating a 14-mile-long lake. Much of the lake's charm and strangeness is imparted by the venerable bald cypress trees that fringe its margins. They rise tall and ghostly from the dark water, and in spring and summer canopy the shoreline with delicate, fresh green foliage.

The shallow 15,000 acres of water are dotted with islands. The park includes a narrow strip around most of the shore, where campgrounds, picnic and day-use areas, and boat launches are available. From May 1 through September 30 a cruise boat leaves from a jetty near the visitors center every morning for a three-hour cruise, stopping at Caney Island, where visitors can walk a nature trail and see American Indian mounds. In mid-summer the American lotus blooms abundantly in parts of the lake; when that happens the cruise boat stops to let people pick the flowers.

A sanctuary for wildlife, Reelfoot Lake is a resting place for a large number of migrating waterfowl and therefore a favorite with birders. As many as 200 bald eagles have been observed wintering here before returning north.

Between January 2 and the first weekend in March the park conducts daily bus tours to look for these majestic birds. The tours depart from the Reelfoot Lake State Airpark Inn in the morning and take about two hours. Reservations are required. Known as the "Turtle Capital of the World," the lake features thousands of sliders, stinkpots, and mud-and-map turtles. The visitors center, in Tiptonville, has a small museum of natural and local history. Among the exhibits are American Indian artifacts and stuffed birds and animals.

Park open year-round.
Fee charged for tours and cruises.
For bald eagle tour information call (731) 253-7756

www.tnstateparks.com

Legend

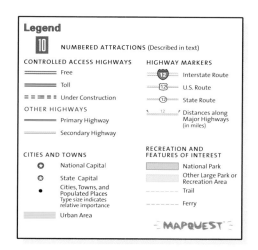

TENNESSEE

311

3 Teapot Museum

South College Street, Trenton

Although known locally as the Teapot Museum, this exhibition's official title is "The World's Largest Collection of Rare Porcelain Veilleuses." A *veilleuse-théière* is hardly an ordinary teapot: it is also a night-light. The earliest *veilleuses* were food warmers, with a vessel in which a candle or oil was burned with a bowl above, on a stand. Eventually a teapot replaced the bowl. In 19th-century Europe these simple utensils for brewing tea and providing a night-light became works of art.

This 19th-century collection—now valued at more than $1 million—was donated to Trenton by Dr. Frederick C. Freed, a local citizen. The town gave it a home in the local municipal hall. Housed in glass-fronted cases, the 525 teapots—several from Napoleon's own collection—are decorated in varying degrees of sophistication and charming naiveté with palm trees, Romeos and Juliets, birds, dogs, horses, flowers, vines, mermaids, cathedrals, and castles.

Seeing these ornamental objects, you can easily envision one glowing and flickering on a bedside table, offering comfort in an era before electricity.

Open Mon.–Fri. year-round.
(731) 855-2013
www.teapotcollection.com

4 Casey Jones Home and Railroad Museum

Jackson

The legendary railroad engineer and hero of the song "The Ballad of Casey Jones" died in the wreck of the *Cannonball Express* the night of April 30, 1900, in Vaughan, Mississippi. His speeding train had rounded a bend and come upon a freight train; Casey heroically stayed at the throttle in order to save the lives of his passengers.

His house is as it was at the time of his death: a simple white one-story clapboard with green shutters and wraparound porch. Two rooms are devoted to memorabilia and railroad history, including a model of the fatal accident scene complete with miniature trains. The watch Casey wore, marking the time of the accident at 3:52 A.M., is on display. There are tributes to two men: Wallace Saunders, the engine wiper who wrote the song, and Jim Webb, Casey's friend, who kept the legend alive.

In the rest of the house there are also some lovely period touches—a lead tub, a marble sink, a straight-edge razor and strap, and a bottle of Nash's Laxative Syrup in the bathroom; a coal stove, a churn and dasher, and old green mason jars in the kitchen. Expanded exhibits will be featured in an 8,000-square-foot train station, set to open in the future.

Outside the house is a replica of Illinois Central Railroad engine No. 382, the train in which Jones died. You can climb into the cab, handle the massive coal rake, and lean out of the window.

Open daily. Admission charged.
(731) 668-1223
www.caseyjonesvillage.com

5 Fort Donelson National Battlefield

U.S. Hwy. 79, Dover

Early during the Civil War the Confederacy seemed to be invincible. But a Union reconnaissance in January 1862 indicated that the South's western line of defense was vulnerable at Fort Henry on the Tennessee River and Fort Donelson on the Cumberland. The North's expedition against the two forts was led by an obscure brigadier general, Ulysses S. Grant, whose strategy involved the first use of the Union's ironclad gunboats. Fort Henry quickly submitted, but the battle at Fort Donelson raged for three days.

Gen. Simon Buckner was forced to surrender unconditionally to Grant on February 16, 1862, at the nearby Dover Hotel. It marked the North's first major victory in the Civil War and the emergence of a new hero, "Unconditional Surrender" Grant.

The visitors center has rotating displays of relics of the battle, such as sabers, muskets, pistols, canteens, military maps, and likenesses of the commanders.

An auto tour of the battlefield passes earthworks, trenches, and two reconstructed Confederate huts, as well as the Confederate Monument, honoring the Southern dead who were not interred in the nearby national cemetery.

Perhaps the most interesting features of the park are the two gun batteries overlooking a sweep of the Cumberland River. Near the lower battery are the barrels of eight 32-pound guns as well as a columbiad, a cannon capable of firing a 10-inch cannonball.

Park visitors should be alert for ticks and poisonous snakes, and should be cautious when approaching the Cumberland River, which is deep and swift.

Open year-round except Christmas.
(931) 232-5706
www.nps.gov/fodo

6 Shiloh National Military Park

Shiloh, south of Savannah

The Civil War battlefield of Shiloh lies along the western bank of the Tennessee River. Here, on April 6, 1862, the Union forces under Gen. Ulysses S. Grant held their ground against a surprise assault under the command of the Confederate Gen. Albert S. Johnston. The battle began at about 5:00 A.M. just as

5 Fort Donelson National Battlefield. *Log huts of the type used as winter quarters for the Confederate army have been reconstructed here. The more than 400 originally built were destroyed after a measles epidemic in the early 1860s.*

the Northern troops were settling down to Sunday breakfast. At first, Johnston's men appeared to be winning, but by nightfall Grant was able to regroup. During the night, the Army of the Ohio reinforced Grant's troops with 17,000 men. The next day, he attacked, and the defeated Confederates retreated some 20 miles to their base at Corinth, Mississippi.

Shiloh was a bloody battle, fought mainly by raw, untrained recruits. Nearly 24,000 men died or were wounded or missing— almost one-quarter of the initial fighting force. Grant's victory led to the eventual defeat of the western Confederate states.

A 25-minute movie of the battle is shown at the visitors center, and talks are given on everything from Civil War medicine to soldiers' uniforms. You can tour the 3,872-acre park in your car. The bookstore will supply you with a cassette that explains in detail the course of battle. Allow a couple of hours for this drive.

Open year-round except Christmas Day. Admission charged.
(731) 689-5696
www.nps.gov/shil

7 Franklin
South of Nashville

The town of Franklin is a treasure of Victorian architecture surrounded by neatly trimmed lawns and sheltered by the venerable maples lining its quiet streets. A 15-block section of the downtown area is listed on the *National Register of Historic Places.*

Most of the homes are privately owned, but the exteriors can be enjoyed from the car or on a leisurely stroll. One of the few

open to the public—and also one of the best—is the Carter House, built in 1830 by Fountain Branch Carter and subsequently inhabited by three generations of his family.

His son, Capt. Tod Carter, was mortally wounded in the fierce battle that was waged on the grounds and is now commemorated in a museum and tour. The rooms are appointed with family heirlooms and furnishings. Outbuildings of the same era include a smokehouse, tool shed, family kitchen, and slave cabin. The farm office, with 207 bullet holes, is the most gunshot-riddled building of the Civil War.

The Historic Carnton Plantation, which is outside the historic district, is also open to the public. Completed in 1826, it is a fine example of the palatial homes built by wealthy Southern planters.

Information for self-guiding walking tours of the historic district is available at the Franklin Chamber of Commerce in the City Hall building on the town square.

Admission charged for house tours.
(615) 794-1225
www.williamsoncvb.org

8 Wynnewood State Historic Area
State Hwy. 25, east of Nashville, Castalian Springs

Built in 1828 as a stagecoach inn and a mineral springs resort, this is the largest log structure in Tennessee and probably the largest ever built in the state. It next served as a resort, then as a working farm, and remained in the Wynne family until 1971, when the state acquired it.

Scrupulously maintained, Wynnewood has qualities that make it a pleasure to visit. You enter the house for a guided tour by way of a dogtrot, the local term for a hallway running through the building from front to back.

The room above the dogtrot functions as a small museum of diverse family souvenirs, mementos, and trophies. Adjacent rooms include a simply furnished "ladies' sleeping room" and two "sleeping rooms for gentlemen," one of which houses a loom, a cotton gin, and a weasel (used to wind yarn).

Outside you'll find a well-tended old garden and a one-room log building. Formerly a doctor's office, it houses a collection of 19th-century medical equipment.

Open Mon.–Sun. Apr.–Dec.; closed all major holidays. Admission charged.
(615) 452-5463
www.srlab.net/bledsoe

9 Jack Daniel's Distillery
Lynchburg

Here's your chance for a spirited tour of one of America's most famous distilleries. From the moment you enter, the air is permeated by the pungent aroma of Tennessee sour mash whiskey.

A brief introductory slide show explains the reasons for the distillery's location: the ready availability of good spring water, high-quality grain, and ample supplies of maple, from which the charcoal for filtering is made. This all-important material gives the whiskey its unique flavor.

You'll pass through a warehouse, one of almost 70, where the whiskey is aged in white oak barrels, made locally and used but once. Each warehouse holds 20,160 of the 55-gallon barrels (worth about $500 million in U.S. taxes alone). In turn you'll see all the operations required for the production of this heady concoction.

Along the way you'll visit the original company offices, which serve as a museum, and see the safe that led to the demise of Jack Daniel. Unable to open the safe, he kicked it in a fit of rage, broke a toe, and developed a fatal case of gangrene.

On a happier note: at the end of the one-hour tour, complimentary coffee and lemonade are served.

Open daily except major holidays.
(931) 759-6180
www.jackdaniels.com

9 Jack Daniel's Distillery. *Whiskey is still bottled in Lynchburg, where you can tour the operations required to make this heady concoction.*

Falls Mill

Rte. 64, west of Belvidere

A good mill site must have a dependable flow of water for the raceway, a solid streamside foundation for the building, and easy road access to a nearby trading area. When these conditions are met, the turning wheels can be adapted to serve a variety of needs, as has been demonstrated here.

Beginning operation in 1873, Falls Mill produced cotton thread and wool for home spinning. In 1906 it became a cotton gin, and after World War II the structure served as a woodworking shop. In 1969 the mill was restored and, with equipment purchased from nearby mills that had closed, converted to a gristmill; it serves as such today. The 32-foot overshot wheel is said to be one of the largest in the country still in productive service.

The first floor of the building is given over to exhibits of tools and equipment related to power and industry. The second floor accommodates the working mill itself and a replicated old country store.

The mill is attractively situated at the head of a wooded riverside dell. A short path brings you to a picnic area in a beautiful cove. You may find yourself in the company of deer and wild turkeys.

Open daily except Wed. and major holidays. Admission charged.
(931) 469-7161
www.fallsmill.com

Cumberland Caverns
McMinnville

Rarely is nature's sculptural art more dramatically revealed than in these remarkable caverns. Three hundred feet below the surface

---

of the ground, they were formed some 500 million years ago by the erosive action of a sea now known as the Gulf of Mexico, which then extended this far north.

A stream flows through the entrance gallery into a crystal-clear pool swarming with blind white crayfish. From the center of this pool rises a 4-million-year-old flowstone (formed by a conjunction of a stalactite and a stalagmite) named Moby Dick. Covering the ceilings is a wide and leaflike stalactite mass referred to as curtains. When lightly tapped they produce the bell-like tone of a pipe organ.

Equally mysterious caverns follow: the Graveyard, the Popcorn Bowl, and the largest of the tour, the truly cavernous Hall of the Mountain King, 600 feet long, 140 feet high, and enhanced with curious formations called the Pagodas and the Chessmen. As you proceed through this enormous space—the largest cave in Tennessee—the sensation of being at the bottom of the Grand Canyon gives way to the impression of climbing through an archaic Italian hill town.

Open daily May–Oct. Admission charged.
(931) 668-4396
www.cumberlandcaverns.com

Historic Falcon Manor
Faulkner Springs Road, McMinnville

Southern gentleman and clever entrepreneur Clay Faulkner sweet-talked his wife, Mary, into letting him build her "the finest mansion in the region" in 1896. The only stipulation was that it had to be next to his woolen mill, 2 1/2 miles outside of town. The promise of electric lights, central heating, and

---

indoor plumbing convinced his wife that living next to the factory wasn't such a bad idea after all, and the Victorian dream of the man whose mill made Gorilla Pants ("so strong even a gorilla couldn't tear them apart") became a reality.

The home, a 10,000-square-foot, all-brick tribute to the elegance of the era, has a sweeping staircase, meticulous woodwork, and gracious rooms filled with regal colors, antiques, statuary, music boxes, and all the appointments befitting a rich mercantile family of the Gay '90s.

After a period in which the large house was turned into a hospital, an enterprising couple bought Falcon Manor at auction. The McGlothins' renovation was so adept, it received an award from the National Trust for Historic Preservation in 1997. Today, the well-loved home that reigns as Tennessee's "premier

---

Victorian mansion," halfway between Nashville and Chattanooga, offers guided tours and a Victorian Tea Room for lunch. The faint chuckle that lingers in the air might even belong to Clay Faulkner's ghost, who occasionally visits for old times' sake.

Open year-round. Admission charged.
(931) 668-4444
www.falconmanor.com

Pickett State Rustic Park
Jamestown

Rolling hills and deep valleys, sparkling waterfalls, and natural bridges and caves are but some of the discoveries to be made in this 17,372-acre wilderness nestled in the upper Cumberland Mountains. The park also includes some excellent runs for white-water canoeing.

The sinuous shoreline of a dark green lake, the centerpiece of Pickett, rewards boaters and hikers alike with an ever-changing view. The road to the lake sweeps past

Historic Falcon Manor. *In one of the bedrooms here, visitors will find an oak and chestnut "half-teaster" canopy bed, typical of antiques in the mansion.*

lightly wooded bluffs and dales set discreetly with cabins and campsites. The park is laced by a network of nine marked hiking trails. One of the most pleasing and accessible is the Lake View Trail, which is true to its name. Reaching this trail is a delight—first by a swinging bridge (which really swings), then a path winding above the laurel, dogwoods, and magnolias fringing the lake.

Another scenic excursion is the Natural Bridge Trail. For a distance of about 1 1/2 miles the path wends upward through a forest of evergreens and hardwoods to higher altitudes and panoramic views before descending toward its terminus at Natural Bridge.
Open year-round.
(877) 260-0010
www.tnstateparks.com

14 Rugby

The 19th century bred a number of attempts at utopian living. Rugby, one of the more curious and colorful, was an English colony founded by Thomas Hughes, a social reformer, writer, and the author of *Tom Brown's Schooldays*.

In the model community he hoped to provide the younger sons of the English upper classes an opportunity to lead useful lives in areas of employment considered beneath them in England, where the law of primogeniture denied inheritance to all but the eldest son.

Named after the school Hughes had attended in England, Rugby was plagued by problems from its very beginnings in 1880. Its members were remarkably ill-equipped to wrest a living from the wilderness of the Cumberland Plateau. They took less to plowing than

14 Rugby. *Old-fashioned English country dancing is featured at the town's Festival of English and Appalachian Culture, held every May.*

to tennis, croquet, the Dramatic Club, and putting out the newspaper, *The Rugbeian*. Although Hughes's colony was fraying at the edges by 1893, it attracted attention in America and Europe.

Today the village, with its charming Victorian air and architecture, comes as a surprise in the rural countryside. Sixteen of the town's almost 70 original buildings have been preserved, and others have been reconstructed.

Three of the most important of the original structures are open for guided tours. These include a 7,000-volume library of Victorian literature; Christ Church, built in the Carpenter Gothic style; and the Kingstone Lisle House, which contains many of Hughes's own belongings. Other houses are open during the Rugby Pilgrimage, usually on the first full weekend in August. Self-guiding maps are available at the visitors center.

A number of trails, some of them are steep and rocky in places, have been preserved here. They lead to the Clear Fork River and what used to be the Gentlemen's Swimming Hole.
Open year-round except major holidays.

Admission charged.
(888) 214-3400
www.historicrugby.org

15 Frozen Head State Park and Natural Area
East of Wartburg
This is an out-and-out backcountry wilderness area for hikers and serious backpackers, with development confined to the trail system and one picnic area.

The region is crisscrossed by 10 blazed trails of varying difficulty, some of which are described on a trail map available at the headquarters. It is a 3 1/2-mile hike to the Frozen Head fire tower at an elevation of 3,324 feet. From the tower there's a fabulous view of the Cumberland Plateau and the Tennessee River valley.

The area is renowned for its wildflowers and flowering trees, and is especially popular in April, when they begin to bloom. August is the time for the Folk Life Festival with its dancing, arts, and crafts. There are over 50 miles of foot trails that meander throughout the natural area, passing by water-

falls, rock shelters, and giant mountain-top cap rocks.
Open year-round.
(423) 346-3318
www.tnstateparks.com

16 Tennessee Valley Railroad and Museum
Grand Junction Station, 4119 Cromwell Rd.
This fine preservation of our colorful railroad history includes steam and diesel locomotives, Pullman cars, day coaches, mail cars, and all the other rolling stock that once made train travel such an exciting adventure.

In Office Car 98, the Eden Isle, you'll discover how executives traveled in the heyday of the steam trains. Built in 1917 for the president of the Baltimore & Ohio Railroad, it contains the original mahogany paneling, a sitting room, three bedrooms, a dining room with elegant glass-fronted cabinets, and a kitchen. A museum car contains such intriguing items as semaphore signals, pressure gauges, and lanterns.

One of the museum's major attractions is a six-mile round-trip departing from Grand Junction Station six times daily. On arrival at East Chattanooga Station you'll find yourself in an exact copy of an old small-town Southern railroad station.

The Polar Express runs from the Chattanooga Choo Choo Hotel to Grand Junction, evenings in November and December.
Museum open daily Apr.–Oct.; weekends in Nov. Admission charged.
(800) 397-5544
www.tvrail.com

17 Ducktown

Copperhill. In Ducktown, follow signs to the Burra Burra Mine and the adjacent museum

Picture this: from the edge of the museum parking lot you look down upon a desert-like area of red earth, undulating and rifted, with scant and scrubby vegetation that extends into the distance. In the foreground of this landscape, far below you, is a chasm filled by a deep green lake.

The colors in this stark landscape, from soft pastels to glowing reds and copper tones, constantly change with the seasons and time of day. The barren beauty of the 56-square-mile area has prompted comparison with the Dakota Badlands. But this is Tennessee's Copper Basin, and the vista is man-made.

Full-time copper mining began in 1851, and the early settlement grew into Ducktown, named for Chief Duck, a Cherokee Indian. Over the years a number of mines have flourished, and the creation of this surreal scene may be claimed jointly by timber stripping, erosion, sulphur dioxide fumes, and subterranean blasting done 20 years ago to crumple the network of exhausted mines. The green lake is said to be 4,100 feet deep.

The Ducktown Basin Museum is located on the historic Burra Burra mine site where 300 acres of land have been set aside as a memorial to the devastation of the Copper Basin. After you finish your visit to the museum, you can drive a short distance to inspect the massive machinery used for mining, and you can also collect garnets and massive pieces of pyrite. You must bring your own tools, however. The museum proper displays items of local history.

Site and museum open year-round.
Admission charged for museum.
(877) 790-2157

www.ocoeetn.org

18 Lost Sea

Sweetwater

Although not exactly a sea, the underground lake in this cave system is said to be America's largest. The lake itself was not discovered until 1905, but the caverns were known in pioneer times as a source of red clay, which when mixed with buttermilk produced a durable red paint. During the Civil War the Confederates mined the saltpeter for gunpowder. Some of their mining tools are on display, as well as moonshine equipment.

Descending to the lake, on the "Commercial Tour," you pass through a number of surreal chambers. There is the 600-foot-long Keel Room where they made the paint. The Baby Grand Canyon is so rifted it resembles a miniature canyon. The Sand Room was used by settlers to store food. (The cave has a steady temperature of 58°F and is largely free of insects.) If you take the longer "Wild Tour," you'll also visit the Cat Chamber, where the remains of a Pleistocene jaguar were found.

There are glass-bottom boat trips on the lake, which occupies 4 1/2 acres. So perfectly do the still, clear waters reflect the ceiling that at first glance there seems to be no lake at all.

The lake has been stocked with trout. Regularly fed in an environment free of predators (and fishermen), many reach old age and great size. The largest to be recorded was a whopping 47 inches long and weighed 21 pounds.

19 Museum of Appalachia. *Outdoor country music lends authenticity to the atmosphere of this museum.*

Beyond this lake is another that is more than twice as large, but it can be reached only by expert divers with scuba gear. The regular tour lasts about an hour. To take the three- to five-hour Wild Tour, arrangements must be made at least two weeks in advance.

Open daily except Christmas.
Admission charged.
(423) 337-6616

www.thelostsea.com

19 Museum of Appalachia

Norris, 16 miles north of Knoxville, one mile off I-75 at the Norris/Clinton exit

If through some time warp one could wander into an early 19th-century Appalachian village, it might well resemble this remarkable museum.

John Rice Irwin, the owner-operator-curator-restorer, has assembled a fascinating collection of almost 40 buildings on 65 acres of land. Log cabins, a log church, a schoolhouse, a smokehouse, a corn mill and cribs, an underground dairy, a loom house, a smithy—these and similar structures were all acquired locally, moved to this 70-acre site, and when necessary, restored. They are all authentic for their time and function down to the smallest wooden hinge.

The main display barn also houses a comprehensive collection of frontier items: axes, boots, saddles and bits, a dog-powered treadmill, rifling machines and bullet molds, fishhooks, ox yokes, cowbells, looms, corn grinders, and animal traps.

Dulcimers, banjos, and other instruments are in the Hall of Fame, along with displays recognizing people who share a common heritage, from World War I hero Alvin C. York, to President Franklin D. Roosevelt's Secretary of State Cordell Hull, to a mountain man. All this is but a small sampling of the more than 150,000 old-time articles to be seen here.

Dresses hang from the wall of a cabin. A wheel awaits completion in the wheelwright's shop. Someone has left an ax stuck in a stump, plates of dried beans and peppers on a table. It looks like the people might have gone to pick some vegetables for lunch, or gone down to the spring to fetch some water.

Open daily except Christmas.
Admission charged.
(865) 494-0514

www.museumofappalachia.com

20 Abraham Lincoln Library and Museum

Lincoln Memorial University, Harrogate

In 1863 President Abraham Lincoln expressed to Gen. Oliver Otis Howard (founder of Howard University) the hope that after the Civil War Howard would "do something for these people who have been shut out from the world all these years." He referred to the loyal mountain youth of East Tennessee.

Howard carried through, founding Lincoln Memorial University in 1897. The museum, opened in 1977, is now among the top five devoted to the great president. It houses more than 30,000 objects, over 6,000 rare books, including regimental histories, and 2,000 pamphlets and is still growing. The museum is remarkable in melding the dark and light sides of Lincoln's life and the period of history he helped to shape.

Arranged thematically, the exhibits trace the various periods and undertakings of Lincoln's life, from his days as a rail splitter to the fateful night in Ford's Theatre. Among the many personal objects to be seen are a photograph of Lincoln's father, Thomas; the carriage belonging to Lincoln's Secretary of State, William H. Seward; and the silver-topped cane Lincoln carried the night he was shot.

Those years are even further documented by tableaux and holographs. Displays focusing on the Civil War period include uniforms, weaponry, and an ambulance. Also on view are the original model of the Lincoln Memorial by Daniel Chester French and the bronze bust of the president by Gutzon Borglum.

Open daily. Admission charged.
(800) 325-0900, Ext. 6235
www.lmunetedu/museum

21 Rocky Mount Living History Museum

On Rte. 11E, just north of Johnson City

Rocky Mount, a handsome two-story house of hand-hewn, notched white oak logs, is one of the oldest territorial capitals in the United States standing on its original site. It was built circa 1770 and served "as the capital of the territory of the United States south of the river Ohio" from 1790 to 1792, when Territorial Governor William Blount used the building as his office. He was a guest in the house of William and Barsheba Cobb. Since 1959 it has been a state historic site.

The house and outbuildings stand on a pleasant rocky bluff overlooking rolling farmland.

Restored to its original appearance, the house is authentically furnished with a pre-1740 grandfather clock, a huntboard (a sideboard on which food was put for men returning from a hunt), old crockery, an ingenious swiveling cradle, and other quaintly colorful items.

A museum located in the visitors center houses historical exhibits, manuscripts, and memorabilia.

Costumed interpreters portray original family members and invite visitors to step back into the year 1791.

Open Mar.–Dec. Call for winter hours.
Admission charged.
(423) 538-7396
http://pages.preferred.com/~rmm

22 Jonesborough Historic District

Jonesborough

The oldest American town west of the Appalachians, Jonesborough

22 Jonesborough Historic District. *The oldest American town west of the Appalachians became the portal to the Southwest before the Louisiana Purchase.*

was established in 1779 and became the portal to the Southwest prior to the Louisiana Purchase in 1803. The picturesque community, the first town listed on the *National Register of Historic Places,* is intent on preserving its 200-year-old legacy of history and architecture.

Daily guided tours of historic Jonesborough, the central part of the town, begin in the visitors center at the History Museum, where the community's development is charted by displays featuring pioneer tools and building techniques, early trades, commerce, transportation, religion, education, and recreation.

One can enjoy the rich variety of architectural styles, with Victorian homes predominating on and near Main Street. Among other highlights are the Chester Inn, the town's oldest commercial building (1797), and the Christopher Taylor House, a two-story log cabin where President Andrew Jackson once lived as a young lawyer. You'll pass the Mail Pouch building, formerly a saloon, and the Salt House, where salt was rationed to the townspeople during the Civil War. Also to be seen are some very fine pre-Civil War churches. Homemade ice cream is featured in an inviting turn-of-the-century ice-cream parlor.

The town also preserves the Appalachian storytelling heritage with its International Storytelling Center, built to blend in with the historic Main Street architecture.

Museum open year-round.
Admission charged.
(877) 913-1612
www.historicjonesborough.com

Aransas National Wildlife Refuge. *The preserve's waterscape and distant grassy islands are a haven for animals (see page 327).*

Texas

The long and colorful history of the Lone Star State is well represented, as are its varied scenery and natural resources.

(see page 327)

Some of the oldest evidence of technology in North America can be seen in a flint quarry here. A number of museums feature the many facets of Texas history, including prehistoric Indians, conquistadors, conflicts with Mexico, American Indian wars, cattle ranching, the railroads, the oil boom, and turn-of-the-century nostalgia.

Several cavalry forts serve to recall the Plains Indians' determined resistance to the settlement of the land; and a petroleum museum, silver-mining ghost town, and a plantation are reminders of nature's bounty here in the Southwest.

There's a presidential museum, the home of a renowned congressman, and the restored courtroom-saloon of a legendary judge. The state's parks reveal the beauty of the natural scenery from the hill country to the shores of the Gulf of Mexico.

1 Alibates Flint Quarries National Monument

On Hwy. 136, about 6 miles south of Fritch. Watch for signs to Bates Canyon and the quarries.

To walk along the bluff here is to walk in the footsteps of the prehistoric people who first came to this place some 12,000 years ago in search of stone that was hard enough to kill the mammoths and buffalo upon which their subsistence depended. The Paleo-Indians, who discovered Alibates flint, used it for spear points, arrowheads, knives and scrapers, axes and awls, and other necessities. It was the only wealth they knew.

Flint is usually a solid color, but here it is rainbow-hued in infinite variations and patterns. The craftsmanship shown in the ancient articles made of this material is usually so superior to that of objects made of ordinary flint that the early artisans must have been responding to its beauty.

The quarries are shallow pits in the ground from 5 to 25 feet across, not much to see—except that they are the source of some of the oldest evidence we have of human technology in the continental United States. The only access to the site is by a two-hour guided walking tour from the information station at spectacular Bates Canyon on Lake Meredith. Tours are by reservation only. You'll need sturdy

Carson County Square House Museum. *The Eclipse windmill helped produce the water here in the 1880s.*

shoes and a hat for protection from the hot sun. There's no water, so a canteen is a good idea.

Open year-round except holidays.
(806) 857-3151
www.nps.gov/alfl

2 Carson County Square House Museum

Rte. 207 at 5th St., Panhandle

The heart of this 10-structure historic complex is indeed a square house. Of a distinctive colonial stick style and measuring 24 by 24 feet, it was built on the N Bar N Ranch in the mid-1880s. The white pine for its construction was brought by oxcart from the nearest railroad terminal, which was then at Dodge City, Kansas. Because it is the oldest house in town, it has been the residence of several prominent citizens.

The museum's dugout dwelling, with its limited space, is typical of housing in early Texas days, when lumber and building stone were in short supply and there was barely enough water to make good adobe. Water was produced by windmills—the Eclipse windmill here is a fine example of this important technological advance.

In one building are dioramas

TEXAS

of native wildlife; another features antique farm and ranch equipment. Another spotlights a pioneer space suit, pictures of early settlers, quilts, kitchen essentials, artists, writers, American Indian wars, and Indian artifacts. A commercial exhibit illustrates a bank, circa 1927 (with a display of cattle brands), a depot, a blacksmith's shop, a dentist's office, and a country store. Two art galleries offer a variety of changing exhibits.

Open Mon.–Sat. and P.M. Sun. year-round except holidays.

(806) 537-3524

www.squarehousemuseum.org

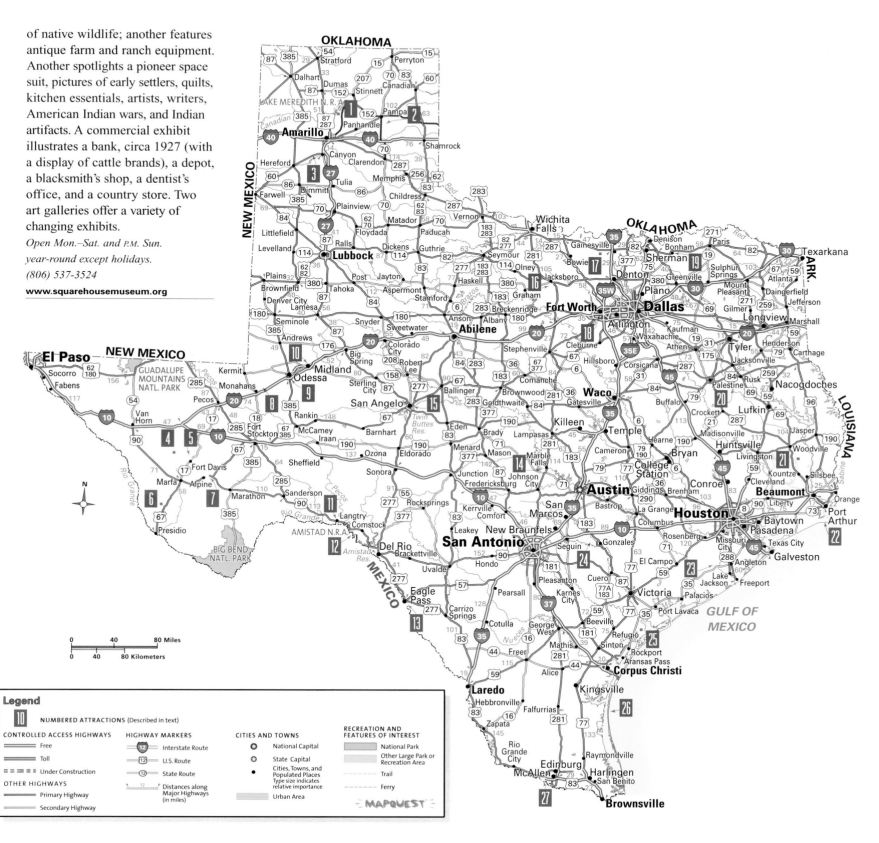

3 Panhandle Plains Historical Museum

15 minutes south of Amarillo on I-27, on the campus of West Texas A&M University, Canyon

The long and varied history of the northernmost section of Texas is captured in this well-conceived museum. One panoramic presentation, in chronological order, covers Paleozoic fossils, the culture of early man, the coming of the conquistadors, the American Indian-frontier era, ranching, the petroleum boom, and modern industry.

Ranch life in the Panhandle is represented by saddles, branding irons, an excellent gun collection, and a chuck wagon complete with the aroma of coffee on the campfire. In the Pioneer Village are reconstructions of buildings that were once essential to frontier towns; all are authentically equipped and furnished.

"People of the Plains" tells the story of human occupation of the southern Great Plains over the past 14,000 years. This state-of-the-art exhibit compares the various ways different cultures have solved their needs for water, food, shelter, trade, and transportation—from prehistoric creatures to modern-day cowboys.

A century-long parade of fashion (1850–1950) is presented in a series of realistic settings. These displays change, as do those in the center's art galleries. One building is devoted to buggies, sleighs, wagons, and automobiles. Also on the grounds is the headquarters of the T-Anchor Ranch, the oldest original structure in the Panhandle.

Open Mon.–Sat. and P.M. Sun. except Thanksgiving, Christmas, and New Year's Day. Admission charged.
(806) 651-2244
www.panhandleplains.org

4 McDonald Observatory
Fort Davis

The drive to this mountaintop observatory, home of one of the most powerful telescopes in the world, is exciting in itself. The steep but well-maintained road offers superb open vistas as it climbs to an elevation of 6,800 feet—the highest point in Texas accessible by public road.

At the summit a short self-guiding walking tour leads to the enormous white dome that houses the University of Texas's 107-inch reflecting telescope. The measurement represents the diameter of the telescope's primary mirror. (Three other domes house smaller telescopes.)

The main dome's viewing gallery, reached by climbing five flights of stairs, is dominated by the massive telescope. Driven hydraulically, it weighs 160 tons. Its giant mirror gathers some 250,000 times more light than the unaided human eye, and a great deal more than could be gathered by optical lenses. Also noteworthy are the large control console and the removable floor, which makes it possible to lower the mirror for a reapplication of its reflective aluminum coating. An enormous spectrometer used for studying free-floating gas and particles in the Milky Way occupies the third and fourth floors of the dome.

Doors in the dome ceiling are opened on clear nights (and sometimes for infrared observations during the day), and the telescope is rotated so that scientists can observe a particular part of the sky.

Indeed, this whole part of Texas is excellent for astronomical research. The air is clear and dry; the view is unobstructed; there are no city lights in the vicinity to compete with the luminosity of the stars. Nearby Mount Fowlkes is the probable site of a new 300-inch telescope that is projected to be the world's largest.

The visitors center at the base of Mount Locke offers colorful, well-designed exhibits and slide shows. One night a month, usually on Wednesdays nearest the full moon, the giant telescope is available for public viewing—an extraordinary opportunity for which reservations must be made six months in advance. Write to the observatory's Visitor Information Center, Box 1337, Fort Davis, Texas, 79734, and enclose a stamped, self-addressed envelope for confirmation. The least crowded months here are January and February.

A new, 12,000-square-foot visitors center features the Hobby-Eberly Telescope. Tours of the telescope take place two times daily.
Open daily except Thanksgiving, Christmas, and New Year's Day.
(877) 984-7827
(915) 426-3640
http://McdonaldObservatory.org

5 Fort Davis National Historic Site
101 Lt. Flipper Dr., Fort Davis

For nearly 40 years both infantry and cavalry troops from this frontier outpost protected mail and stagecoaches, freighters, emigrants, and travelers along the San Antonio–El Paso Road, fending off Apache, Kiowa, and Comanche raiders. The Apache leader, Victorio, surrendered in 1880, signaling an end to the American Indian wars in Western Texas, and the fort was decommissioned in 1891.

The restored fort stands with its face toward an open plain and its back against the cliffs of the majestic Davis Mountains. Fort Davis housed some 500 people in its more than 70 buildings, which included extensive living quarters, storehouses, a hospital, bakery, laundry, sawmill, and guardhouse. The corrals accommodated some 475 horses for eight troops of cavalry.

3 Panhandle Plains Historical Museum. *This chuck wagon, complete with the aroma of coffee cooking on the campfire, is just one of the museum's many representations of ranch life in the Panhandle.*

The fort is considered one of the most intact surviving examples of a post-Civil War frontier military post in the Southwest. Of the more than 20 structures that have been restored on the outside, five of these have had their interiors restored and are refurnished. During periods of high visitation, costumed interpreters give tours and conduct demonstrations in these buildings.

A former enlisted men's barracks houses a visitors center, museum, and an auditorium, where each half-hour a 15-minute video on the fort's history is presented. Museum exhibits highlight the roles played by both the U.S. military and their adversaries. There are several hiking trails, as well as a picnic area, in a historic grove of cottonwood trees.
Open daily except Christmas.
Admission charged.
(915) 426-3224, Ext. 20
www.nps.gov/foda

6 Shafter Ghost Town
20 miles north of Presidio, off Hwy. 67
Many a traveler has sped by Shafter, noticing only the dramatic view of the Chinati Mountains from the steeply banked road. Ghost towns like this one call for curiosity, initiative, and imagination.

There are no tourist facilities to beckon, nor do any interpretive signs tell the story of how a once thriving town came upon hard times and disappeared.

From about 1875 to 1942, Shafter was a rowdy silver-mining center, with about 3,000 residents and enough tough hombres to require the year-round presence of three Texas rangers. As its richest veins were mined out and the price of silver fell at home and abroad, the town of Shafter began its decline.

There remain only the evocative ruins of an old smelter, a church, a schoolhouse, and crumbling stone and adobe buildings. The old cemetery lies in the southeastern part of town across the creek. The ground here is so hard that it could be dug only to a depth of three feet; stones were piled up for the remaining three feet to make graves of the traditional depth.

The hillside, honeycombed with tunnels and holes, is dangerous for walking and should be observed only from a distance. There's still silver "in them-thar hills," and if silver prices increase, Shafter could rise again from its ghostly state.
(915) 229-3199
www.presidiotx.com

7 Museum of the Big Bend
Sul Ross State University, Alpine
In 1926 the West Texas Historical and Scientific Society was founded with the purpose of creating a museum for the Big Bend and Big Bend region. Today the museum continues to collect, preserve, exhibit, and interpret the materials that relate to the prehistory and history of the Big Bend of Texas and Mexico with an awareness of the region's cultural diversity.

Main exhibits include information concerning American Indians in the area through interpretive text and artifacts from the collection, the Spanish influence on both the Mexican and American cultures, specifically the evolution of the conquistador to the cowboy, and the impact of the mercury mining industry for those along the Rio Grande border.

⑧ Monahans Sandhill State Park. *Extending for several hundred miles, this table-flat landscape is a reminder of a sea that existed in the Permian period, some 280 million years ago.*

Temporary exhibits are designed to showcase materials from the collection or delve into a specific aspect of life and culture of the Big Bend. The museum annually hosts Trappings of Texas, which showcases the best in Western art and custom cowboy gear.

Visitors are invited to tour the Chihuahuan Desert Cactus Garden at the front of the museum. Designed and planted by the Sul Ross Biology Department, this garden illustrates the biodiversity of the region.
Open daily Tues.–Sat. and P.M. Sun.; closed on university holidays.
(915) 837-8143
www.sulross.edu/~museum

8 Monahans Sandhill State Park
Monahans
Undulating dunes rise to heights of 70 feet above a table-flat landscape, remnants of a sea that was here in the Permian period some 280 million years ago. Part of a vast dune field extending for several hundred miles into New Mexico, most of the 3,840-acre park is now stabilized by vegetation; many dunes, however, are still active—they are shaped and reshaped by the incessant winds.

An interpretive center displays local natural history, including the flora and fauna of the area, and an interactive exhibit features the variety of wildlife found here.

A self-guiding trail begins at the interpretive center. Among the highlights of this short walk are sand sagebrush, mesquite, and the useful prairie yucca. American Indians used yucca fibers for rope, the roots for soap, and other parts of the plant for food. Shin oaks, diminutive trees less than four feet tall when fully mature, spread out their roots as far as 70 feet to find water.

Scaled quail, Harris's hawks, cactus wrens, and other desert birds are seen year-round, and many migratory birds stop off. The park's field checklist includes some 80 species. Trailer sites and picnic spots are located among the dunes. It is the most crowded during Easter.
Open year-round.
(915) 943-2092
www.tpwd.state.tx.us/park/monahans

TEXAS

321

9 The Presidential Museum

662 N. Lee St., Odessa

Not long after President John F. Kennedy's assassination in November 1963, a group of Odessa citizens decided to dedicate a new museum to those who have held the nation's highest office. In the Hall of the Presidents there are portraits of each chief executive, along with personal memorabilia.

Exhibits show the evolution of ideas, techniques, and materials that have been used in campaigning for office, including banners, buttons, posters, and bumper stickers that feature the names and faces of winners—as well as losers all but forgotten today.

The important breakthrough of radio and television campaigning is documented. Another advance, not as obvious but important, was the advent of campaign buttons made of celluloid. With this then newfangled material it was possible to show the candidates' likenesses in color instead of black and white. An interesting curiosity was the use in 1896 of "soap babies": baby-shaped cakes of soap colored either silver or gold as reminders of an important monetary question.

America's first ladies are represented by a collection of exquisite, beautifully displayed dolls. Each is shown in her Inauguration ball gown, with matching jewelry, fans, and other accessories, and coiffed in the hairstyle worn on that memorable occasion. Of further interest to the fashion-conscious is a model of the official dress worn by the Texas "Ladies for Lyndon" (Johnson).

Open Tues.–Sat. year-round except major holidays. Admission charged.
(915) 332-7123
www.presidentialmuseum.org

10 The Petroleum Museum

Midland

This extraordinarily creative and surprising museum will fascinate people of all ages—whether or not they have an interest in the subject of oil. Exhibits move, talk, and invite participation. The persons in old photos recount in local accents anecdotes from their lives. A spin of a dial allows you to win or lose a theoretical fortune in oil wells. A fascinating film takes you on a plane ride, looking for leaks in a pipeline, while a full-size plane above, suspended from the ceiling, sways along with the film.

Highlights in one of the museum's three wings are the rooms that re-create the boomtown experience of the 1920s, and an enormous walkthrough replica of the Permian Basin Sea, with nearly 200,000 realistic models of coral, fish, and other marine creatures—all of which bear upon the geology of petroleum deposits. More than 200 million years of time and unimaginable pressure within the earth converted the materials in reefs like this one to the oil and natural gas we use today.

Displays in another wing feature the human history of the area and include branding irons, barbed wire, windmills, and tepees. Historical paintings by Tom Lovell are complemented by audiotapes. The North Wing shows an oil-well blowout that no visitor will ever forget.

Outside the museum, in the Oil Patch Exhibit, you'll find the world's largest collection of antique oil-drilling equipment. The rough-and-ready reputations of oilfield workers are understandable in light of such tools and equipment.

A new museum wing will feature seven of the Jim Hall Chaparral race cars, including the 1980 Indy 500 winner "The Yellow Submarine," The Chaparral 2E, and the Chaparral 2J Sucker Car.

Open Mon.–Sat. and P.M. Sun. except Thanksgiving, Christmas, and New Year's Day. Admission charged.
(915) 683-4403
www.petroleummuseum.org

11 Judge Roy Bean Center

Langtry

In the last decades of the 19th century this part of Texas was still very much the Wild West, and law enforcement was a continuing problem. A former Pony Express rider and saloonkeeper named Roy Bean was appointed justice of the peace and became known as the "Law West of the Pecos" (the Pecos River is about 10 miles distant).

Where Bean dispensed his quick version of justice along with hard liquor in his combination courtroom, billiard hall, and saloon, the modern visitors center now dispenses travel information and features dioramas with earphones.

Listeners hear about the life and times of the hard-bitten judge, including such colorful stories as that of the world championship Maher-Fitzsimmons prizefight he staged on an island in the Rio Grande in defiance of the governmental authorities in the United States, Texas, and Mexico.

Behind the visitors center is the restored courtroom-saloon, with its potbellied stove, antique bottles, and photographs of Bruno, the judge's pet bear. The saloon is named the Jersey Lilly for the English actress Lillie Langtry, whom Bean greatly admired. (She was called the Jersey Lily after her birthplace, and the misspelling of Lily is a sign painter's error.)

Actually, the town was probably called Langtry after a railroad worker of that name, but Bean convinced the actress that it had been named for her, and she accepted his invitation to visit in 1904. The judge died, however, months before she arrived. In addition to Bean's establishment and the visitors center, there's

9 The Presidential Museum. *Dedicated in the 1960s to the nation's chief executives, the museum features the evolution of ideas and materials that have been used both successfully and unsuccessfully in campaigning for office.*

⓬ Seminole Canyon State Park. *Best viewed by guided tour are the many spectacular rock formations created over the years by water erosion.*

a five-acre garden with more than 100 species of cacti and other native plants. The peak bloom is in April, but it is heavily visited in June, July, and August.

Open daily year-round except major holidays.

(915) 291-3340

www.dot.state.tx.us

🚶 🔭

⓬ Seminole Canyon State Park and Historic Site

Comstock

Water can erode rock into spectacular formations, and paradoxically, its effect may be most dramatic where it is scarce, as in this rugged area. Near the park a high bridge offers a magnificent view of the Pecos River Canyon, and visitors to the park can explore Seminole Canyon itself. The moderately strenuous hike down to the canyon floor should only be made on the guided tour. The streambed will most likely be dry, but the effect of its flow of water through the ages is evident in the width of the canyon and in the polished surface of its limestone.

Some of the oldest works of mankind are also in evidence here. Fate Bell Shelter is one of the oldest cave dwellings, housing layer upon layer of large, colorful pictographs that were painted on the rock walls 4,000 years ago. They depict animals, people, and some mysterious figures that may never be identified.

Exhibits at the visitors center, where the guided hikes begin, include a realistic, life-sized representation of a family living in a rock shelter; another reproduces pictographs painted in other caves.

Other displays depict local sheep- and goat-ranching, and history of the early railroad. Visitors can enjoy the desert area, especially attractive in spring, and a gentle three-mile walk to an overlook above the Rio Grande. The 2,173-acre park has a picnic area overlooking Seminole Canyon.

Open daily year-round. Canyon tours Wed.–Sun.

Admission charged.

(915) 292-4464

www.tpwd.state.tx.us

⓭ Fort Duncan

Eagle Pass. Follow Main St. toward toll bridge to Mexico; turn left on Adams St.; go one-half mile to Bliss St. and turn left into park.

Fort Duncan is in a pleasantly landscaped recreational park separated from the main part of Eagle Pass by Eagle Creek.

At the fort are nearly a dozen buildings that were part of a military garrison established in 1849 as a frontier outpost. For a time during the Civil War the fort was occupied by the Confederate army, and Eagle Pass was the only port open for the export of cotton from the South. Later, during American involvement in the Mexican Revolution in 1916-17, 10,000 U.S. troops were housed here.

The restorations include the blacksmith's shop, the commanding officer's headquarters, and the small, windowless powder magazine.

Inside the post headquarters is a small museum with a delightfully diverse collection of objects from the past. Some exhibits recall the military presence; others, such as an old-fashioned tuba, a hand-made baby carriage, and a glamorous dress from the 1890s, are mementos of civilian life.

Reminders of the American Indian heritage, primarily of the Kickapoo, include a fishing net made from bulrushes, and a jacket impressively beaded with a peacock design. The Kickapoos were forced into this area from their ancestral lands in present-day Illinois and Wisconsin.

Fort open daily year-round; museum open Mon.–Sat. year-round.

Admission charged.

(888) 355-3224

www.eaglepasstexas.com

⓮ Westcave Preserve

West of Bee Cave, on Hamilton Pool Rd., west of Austin

A 600-year-old bald cypress tree with Spanish moss hanging from its branches like wispy tentacles stands sentinel over this fragile 30-acre nature preserve in Travis County. Neighboring tall trees form a canopy that keeps moisture in and blocks out the sun.

The 35- to 125-foot sheer limestone walls of the canyon are a natural barrier to destructive intruders. Almost hidden along the banks of the Pedernales River, this place of profound beauty has been kept safe through the combined efforts of nature and man. A foundation has been set up to preserve the site and to educate future generations who will protect the land.

After centuries of erosion, a large limestone shelf collapsed into a streambed more than 100,000 years ago, creating the canyon. A spring-fed waterfall courses down 40 feet, nurturing the moss and maidenhair ferns that feed off the canyon walls.

Guided tours take place four times a day on weekends down to the canyon's semitropical bottom, where wild orchids grow in a cool emerald green grotto one-third of a mile down. It is a world away from the arid grassland at the top, with its cactus and ash juniper trees.

A Cooper's hawk builds her nest in treetops that drape over the waterfall. Dragonflies dart in and out of the stalactites and stalagmites, and a cliff-chirping frog hops about on the cave floor.

Open year-round.

(830) 825-3442

www.westcave.org

17 Grapevine. *In the Homestead winery, located in a restored late 1800s home, visitors can sample wines as well as get a taste of Texas history and folklore.*

15 Fort Concho National Historic Landmark

630 S. Oakes St., San Angelo
Established by the U.S. Army in December 1867, Fort Concho started as a tent city and later developed into a large military post, serving the vast territory of West Texas until 1889. Hundreds of soldiers, infantry, and cavalry—white and black (including the famed African-American Buffalo soldiers)—called Fort Concho home for 22 years.

The army built and staffed a wide range of forts west of the Mississippi after the Civil War to protect settlers from American Indian attack and to guard mail, stage, and railroad building lines, as well as to serve as a general police force in a wide-open region. Often the army found itself in the middle of competing interests among settlers, Indian tribes, buffalo hunters, and government/business interests back East.

Today the fort prospers as a National Historic Landmark owned and operated by the city of San Angelo, with 40 acres and 24 original, rebuilt and restored structures. Daily tours (except Mondays) show up to 10 of those buildings, including the visitors center, artillery exhibit, soldiers' barracks, headquarters, hospital, chapel, and an officers quarters.

The fort has special events, displays, and living history festivals all year.

There is also a special museum of communications equipment that is available on site, which should not be missed.
Open Tues.–Sat. and P.M. Sun. Admission charged.
(915) 481-2646
www.fortconcho.com

16 Fort Richardson State Park/ State Historic Site

Jacksboro
This is another of the forts in north-central Texas established for protection from Comanche and Kiowa raiders coming down from American Indian Territory (now Oklahoma) north of the Red River. The fort was named for Union Gen. Israel B. Richardson, who was killed at the battle of Antietam, and troops were first stationed here in 1867. Soon after they arrived, the small town of Jacksboro experienced a predictable boom as saloonkeepers, gamblers, and camp followers moved in to help relieve the troopers of their boredom—and their pay.

At the fort today, several of the original fieldstone buildings are preserved or restored. The officers' quarters, powder magazine, guardhouse, commissary, bakery, and the hospital and morgue can be viewed from the park grounds. These buildings, the parade area, and the displays in the barracks are reminders of the forces that had to be marshaled to wrest this land from the American Indians.

The park consists of approximately 454 acres, with three hiking trails. The Lost Creek Reservoir State Trailway is a 10-mile hike, bike, and equestrian trail that runs adjacent to Fort Richardson and along Lost Creek.
Park open year-round. Interpretive center open Wed.–Sun. Public tours available weekends; private tours by request. Admission charged.
(940) 567-3506
www.tpwd.state.tx.us

17 Grapevine

Northwest of Dallas, northeast of Fort Worth, Tarrant Cty.
Wild mustang grapes spilled over the black-land prairie in 1844, when this settlement, one of the oldest in North Texas, started its life under the Lone Star Flag. Statehood was just around the corner. Although it's in one of the busiest corridors in Texas, Grapevine holds on to its history with a tenacious grip. Main Street itself is a historic district, preserved by descendants of the original settlers. At the Heritage Center, artisans demonstrate and teach 150-year-old techniques.

The Historical Museum fits nicely into an old railroad depot that dates from 1901.

The Tarantula, a refurbished 1896 steam locomotive with open-air patio cars, heads daily from the Cotton Belt Depot to Fort Worth's historic Stockyard Station. Willie Nelson, Brenda Lee, and the Judds made country-western history when they graced the stage at the Palace Theatre, home of the Grapevine Opry.

Wineries like Cap Rock, La Buena Vida, and Homestead continue the tradition of producing fine vintages—started by the Spanish

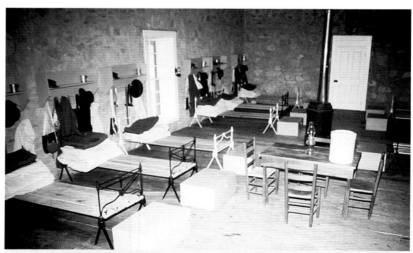

15 Fort Concho National Historic Landmark. *This military post, established in 1867, housed hundreds of soldiers, infantry, and cavalry who protected settlers from attacks by American Indians.*

in the 1600s–taking advantage of the area's grape-friendly climate. GrapeFest in September is a city-wide celebration.

Test your mettle on golf courses designed by Ben Hogan and Byron Nelson. Windsurf, fish, and sail on Lake Grapevine. Everybody can find something to do.

Open year-round.
(800) 457-6338
www.tourtexas.com/grapevine/
grapevine.html

18 The National Cowgirl Museum and Hall of Fame

Gendy St., Fort Worth
Golden girls of the golden West, all trailblazers in their own way, have a new building in which their achievements are honored. Almost 160 women, including U.S. Supreme Court Justice Sandra Day O'Connor, who is as comfortable in a saddle as she is on the bench, are in the Hall of Fame. Each year four to six women get the nod to enter the hall, joining the 400 women who are currently featured in the museum.

Bona fide ranch women, as well as more famous entertainers, rodeo competitors, artists, and writers, get their due here. Dale Evans and her stuntwoman, Alice Van Springsteen, are in the hall. The first pioneer woman to cross the Rockies, Narcissa Prentiss Whitman, and eight-time world-champion cowgirl Tad Lucas all possess the grit and spirit that make a true cowgirl.

The museum began in a library basement in Hereford and has made the move to Fort Worth's Western Heritage Center in the Cultural District. Housed in a 33,000-square-foot building, the word "Cowgirls"

is emblazoned across one side, and an impressive rotunda contains the women's stories.

You'll find interactive exhibits, with listening stations telling about how committed a cowgirl has to be. And for wannabe cowgirls and their sidekicks wanting to experience a simulated wild ride in a Wild West show, a bronco is raring to go.

Open year-round Tues.–Sun.
Admission charged.
(817) 336-4475
www.cowgirl.net

19 Sam Rayburn House, Fort Inglish, and Fannin County Museum of History

Both off Rte. 56, Bonham
Sam Rayburn, although Tennessee-born, was a dedicated Texas Democrat for a long political career comprising 25 consecutive terms in the U. S. House of Representatives—17 of those as speaker of the House. At the time of Rayburn's death in 1961 at the age of 79, no other person had served—in either capacity—for so long. Both records still stand.

Rayburn had this house built in 1916 and lived here the rest of his life. On view are many personal and family items, such as his famous 1947 Fleetwood Cadillac. The Rayburn Library, a large, imposing structure of Georgia marble, is also in Bonham. It contains a replica of the speaker's Washington office and a complete set of the Congressional Records.

Just down the road from the Rayburn House is a replica of the Fort Inglish stockade, which was built in 1837. Life on the early Texas frontier is vividly evoked here by the stark outbuildings and the primitive furnishings displayed in the blockhouse. Just three blocks south of the square is the Fannin County Museum of History, where two centuries of Texas legend come alive.

Sam Rayburn House open Tues.–Sat.
(903) 583-5558
Fort Inglish open Tues.–Sat. Apr.–Sept.
(903) 583-4811
Fannin County Museum of History
open Tues.–Sat. year-round.
(903) 583-8042
www.bonhamchamber.com

18 The National Cowgirl Museum and Hall of Fame. *The museum's impressive rotunda features 12 murals showcasing the lives of the spirited and courageous women of the American West, while giving the illusion of movement.*

20 Texas State Railroad State Historical Park and Rusk/Palestine State Park

The romance of the rails and the golden age of steam is colorfully captured in these unique parks.

The rails that run between the towns of Rusk and Palestine traverse typical East Texas pastureland and picturesque, unspoiled forests of loblolly pine and hardwoods. The line crosses some 30 wooden trestles, and the 25-mile right-of-way makes the Texas State Railroad one of the longest and narrowest state parks in the nation.

The Rusk/Palestine State Park includes the two terminals and provides picnic grounds at both places. But the facilities indicated by the symbols below refer to the Rusk unit, the larger of the two.

The Rusk depot, a handsome turn-of-the-century reconstruction built of native stone, has a park store and small theater featuring a film of the railroad's history.

The Palestine depot, of wood construction, is in keeping with the fine Victorian houses in this old railroad town.

Reservations should be made three to four weeks in advance. Trains start from each station at 11 A.M. The round-trip takes about four hours, including the one-hour layover for lunch.

Trains run Thurs.–Mon. June–Aug;
weekends only, Sept.–Oct., Mar.–May.
Fare charged. For reservations call
(214) 683-2561.
Rusk/Palestine State Park:
Open year-round.
(903) 683-5126
www.tpwd.state.tx.us

21 Big Thicket National Preserve

Visitor information station on Rte. 420, off Rte. 69/287, Beaumont

In the meadows and swamps and the pine and hardwood forests here, one is reminded of many different regions in the United States. Aptly described as "the biological crossroads of North America," the 12 units of this 97,000-acre preserve have overlapping habitats that support an extraordinary variety of flora and fauna.

Bogs and cypress trees of the Southeastern swamplands; grasslands and meadows of the Central Plains; Southwest desert cactus and yucca; and the trees of Eastern hardwood forests are all found within a 50-square-mile area. Nearly 1,000 kinds of flowering plants grow in the thicket, including four of North America's five species of insect-eating plants.

This ecological anomaly is a remnant of the continent's last major ice age, which ended more than 10,000 years ago. As the glaciers pushed south, they carried the seeds of numerous plants— and forced animals from northerly regions into this area. Many of these species adapted to their new environment, with its varied climate and soil, and continue to thrive here.

The preserve is referred to as "an American ark" for the diversity of wildlife it accommodates. Such unlikely neighbors as wood ducks, roadrunners, armadillos, and bobcats are seen here, as well as some 300 species of birds.

Fishermen enjoy the many creeks and sloughs, and hikers take to the trails. Those who prefer to see Big Thicket by car follow the self-guiding 74-mile auto tour, which has both paved highways and one-lane dirt roads and must be driven in a counterclockwise direction. Allow about 2 1/2 hours, plus time for stops, to explore this world of haunting beauty.

Open year-round except Christmas and New Year's Day.
(409) 246-2337
www.nps.gov/bith

22 Sea Rim State Park

Sabine Pass

With the Gulf of Mexico on one side and a vast stretch of salt marsh on the other, this park is truly a natural wonder. The name is derived from the so-called sea rim marsh, the section of the marsh grass that extends into the neighboring surf.

The park is composed of some 15,000 acres along Route 87, a vulnerable ribbon of pavement that occasionally disappears under the high tides spawned by tropical storms and hurricanes. Within its borders are three miles of sandy beach and more than 3,000 acres of marshland inhabited by alligators, muskrats, nearly 300 species of birds, and in spring and fall an amazing variety of waterfowl.

Along part of the coastline here, the tidal marshlands meet the waters of the Gulf to create an important nursery ground for shrimp, crab, and other marine life. The beach unit headquarters behind the dunes offers interpretive exhibits. The Gambusia nature trail, also in this section of the park, is a mile-long boardwalk that affords an intimate perspective of this fascinating environment.

The nearby Marshlands Unit provides access to boat trails in the marsh, and there are some platforms for observing the wildlife.

Open year-round except during hurricane threats. Admission charged.
(409) 971-2559
www.tpwd.state.tx.us/park/searim

23 Varner-Hogg State Historic Park

West Columbia

The aura of grace, charm, peace, and quiet that one encounters on this former plantation is surely a reflection of its long and productive past as part of Texas and Southern culture. In 1824 Martin Varner was one of 300 applicants granted land when Texas was still a province of Mexico. He built a cabin, worked the land, and raised stock for about 10 years before heading on to the less populated parts of northeast Texas.

Under a succession of subsequent owners, this remained a working plantation until 1901, when James Stephen Hogg, a former governor of the state, bought the place to use as a country estate. His belief that there was oil on the land was substantiated in 1917, nine years after his death. Income from the well goes to the University of Texas, which owns mineral rights.

In 1920 the main house was remodeled by Hogg's daughter, Ima, and his three sons. In 1958 the plantation was deeded to the state by Miss Hogg and named for its first and last owners. The house is furnished in the style of prosperous planters of the mid-19th century.

Near a grove of stately pecans, a large planting of paper-white narcissus blooms gloriously in December and January.

Open Tues., Thurs.–Sat., and P.M. Sun. year-round. Admission charged.
(409) 839-2689
www.nps.gov/bith

24 Palmetto State Park

Off Rte. 183, north of Gonzales

In this part of Texas, where the land is flat or gently rolling and the horizon is expansive, this park comes as a delightful surprise, with its unusual mixture of natural environments and its 550 species of Eastern and Western plants, including the dwarf palmetto.

21 Big Thicket National Preserve. *A reminder of the continent's last ice age over 10,000 years ago, this 97,000-acre preserve contains an extraordinary variety of flora and fauna.*

The two-mile scenic roadway from the park entrance to the San Marcos River climbs a small hill above a rich green pasture dotted with cattle and interspersed with woodland, in striking contrast to the sculptural forms of the cactus nearby. From the hilltop the road continues through a natural arcade of pecan, elm, and oak to the trails, campsites, and picnic grounds built on the banks of the river, which flows through the 270-acre park.

Birding is best in winter; more than 240 species have been spotted, including kingfishers, cardinals, red-shouldered hawks, and the caracara, or Mexican eagle. All three short hiking trails, none more than half a mile long, are gravel-surfaced and easy to walk. Swimming, tubing, and boating are enjoyed in the river, and fishermen appreciate the small oxbow lake for its bass, crappie, and catfish. The park is a checkpoint on the Texas Water Safari, a 419-mile canoe race held in July.

Open year-round. Admission charged.
(956) 585-1107
www.tpwd.state.tx.us

25 Aransas National Wildlife Refuge
Austwell
At this preserve on San Antonio Bay the plants, the birds, and the other Gulf Coast wildlife are protected from the incursion and depredation of mankind. Fittingly enough, the refuge has played a major role in the saving of the whooping crane, a magnificent bird that hunters had reduced to near extinction. Only 15 were here in 1940. By 1985 there were 69 adults and 14 young (a record number) on the refuge and from

26 Padre Island National Seashore. *Nearly 400 species of birds have been sighted on this 67-mile-long island, consisting of sandy beach and grass-covered dunes.*

150 to 180 in America. A platform with mounted telescopes provides an overview of the otherworldly waterscape and distant grassy islands.

The 54,829 acres are none too many for their purpose. Up to 350 species of birds winter here, and there are deer, javelinas, wild hogs, raccoons, armadillos, alligators, and turtles, while frogs thrive in the lakes and sloughs. Live oak, red bay, and hackberry are the dominant trees along the 16 miles of roadway through the preserve.

On the well-marked nature trails be sure to wear sturdy shoes and keep an eye out for rattlesnakes.

There are excellent wildlife displays at the visitors center, with weekend films of wildlife on the refuge. Whooping cranes linger from November through March. The refuge is least crowded in midweek in early spring and early fall. It is hot in summer, and mosquitoes are abundant. Insect repellent is recommended.

Open year-round.
(361) 286-3559
www.tpwd.state.tx.us

26 Padre Island National Seashore
Corpus Christi
Looking at the hard sand beach and grass-covered dunes of the 67-mile-long island, one might think that this is a stable environment. But as on all barrier islands, the scene is ever changing. And this, of course, is part of the attraction.

Also ever changing (but annually consistent) is the great variety of birds seen here in their season. Winter residents include sandhill cranes, snow geese, and redhead and pintail ducks, while in spring falcons and a variety of songbirds return from their winter sojourn to the south. Great blue herons, gulls, terns, and brown and white pelicans may be seen year-round. All in all, from 350 to 400 species have been sighted.

The northern part of the island, around Malaquite Beach, is sometimes crowded. Swimming is good here, and there are lifeguards on duty from June through August. Ordinary passenger automobiles can go several miles farther on the beach, but south of that point a four-wheel-drive vehicle is required. Beachcombing and fishing are

popular, and there are some good shell beaches between 10 and 20 miles south of the ranger station. Glass, nails, and the stinging purple jellyfish (Portuguese man-of-war) make bare feet inadvisable.

Open year-round. Admission charged.
(979) 345-4656
www.tpwd.state.tx.us

27 Bentsen-Rio Grande Valley State Park
Mission
The two oxbow lakes in the park recall the wayward past of the restless Rio Grande. They bring to the typical dry brush of mesquite and prickly pear a moist habitat of hackberry, cedar elm, and Mexican ash.

Professional naturalists and nature lovers are attracted by the remarkably varied flora and fauna in the park's 587 acres of river-bottom woodlands. The field checklist available at headquarters includes more than 270 species of birds. Some of the exotics are the chachalaca, pauraque, rose-throated becard, tropical kingbird, and Mexican crow.

Among the animals are the ocelot and jaguarundi (both endangered species in Texas) and the javelina, coyote, bobcat, and armadillo. Many plants and birds can be seen on the mile-long Singing Chaparral Nature Trail or on the longer hiking trail at the south end of the park. Many of the animals are nocturnal feeders and are most likely to be seen in the late evening or early morning.

Open year-round. Admission charged.
(361) 286-3559
www.aransaspass.org

Utah

There are few places in the world where so many different sculptural forms created by wind and water are so dramatically displayed.

Natural Bridges National Monument. *Formed by the erosive action of streams, this sandstone bridge can be viewed from a loop road or hiking trail (see page 333).*

Here you'll find spectacular cliffs and cathedrallike domes, soaring sandstone spires, monumental natural bridges, and a stunning panorama of a devastated land where wild mustangs roamed. The gooseneck meanders of the San Juan River must be seen to be believed.

Aspects of the ancient past are preserved in the fossilized bones of dinosaurs that once walked this land and in the petrified fallen timbers of a forest that stood here 140 million years ago.

From our own era is the historic site where the driving of two golden spikes tied a nation together with bands of steel. Here too there's an inviting variety of places for fishing, swimming, boating, hiking, and birding.

1 Bear Lake State Park
Garden City

There are two separate areas in this lakeside park, each of them offering access to the turquoise waters of Bear Lake, which covers 112 square miles and is surrounded by exquisite mountain scenery.

Sailing, powerboating, and fishing are the main attractions at the state marina in the northern section. On the south shore near Laketown, at Rendezvous Beach, the emphasis is on swimming, although here too boats may be rented or trailered in. Three campgrounds—Willow, Cottonwood, and Big Creek—are attractively situated along the shore.

Fishermen hook cutthroat trout here and Mackinaws that can weigh up to 30 pounds. Ice fishing for smelt—like ciscoes—is popular in winter. Sandhill cranes are common in the park's meadows and wetlands from late May to early June.

Open year-round. Admission charged.
(435) 946-3343

www.stateparks.utah.gov

2 Logan Canyon
Logan

The only thing that time has added to this scenic byway since the days of resident mountain man and trapper Jim Bridger is a smooth

2 Logan Canyon. *Nearly vertical limestone walls and rock formations laden with fossils greet travelers entering this canyon area along the Wasatch-Cache National Forest.*

two-lane highway—which makes exploring a lot easier for modern-day adventurers. The byway begins at the mouth of the canyon east of Logan, Utah. Visitors to this picturesque northern Utah town will also find the fully operational turn-of-the-century Jensen Farm, as well as modern cheese factories, and the resident Utah Festival Opera Company.

Deeply cut, nearly vertical limestone walls and rock formations laden with fossils greet travelers entering the canyon. The Logan River, popular for trout fishing, also parallels the route,

which explores the spectacular Wasatch-Cache National Forest.

A steady climb to the summit results in a sweeping view of the unique turquoise water of 20-mile-long Bear Lake, where marinas, beaches, cabins, and inviting bed-and-breakfast inns are available to enjoy. This route is popular among those traveling to Jackson Hole and Yellowstone National Park.

Elevations in the canyon range from 4,700 feet at the mouth to nearly 7,800 feet at the summit. This 41-mile drive requires approximately one hour. A recommended side tour is Tony Grove Lake, a

Legend

10 NUMBERED ATTRACTIONS (Described in text)

CONTROLLED ACCESS HIGHWAYS
- Free
- Toll
- Under Construction

OTHER HIGHWAYS
- Primary Highway
- Secondary Highway

CITIES AND TOWNS
- ⊛ National Capital
- ⊙ State Capital
- • Cities, Towns, and Populated Places Type size indicates relative importance

HIGHWAY MARKERS
- Interstate Route
- U.S. Route
- State Route
- Distances along Major Highways (in miles)

RECREATION AND FEATURES OF INTEREST
- National Park
- Other Large Park or Recreation Area
- Trail
- Ferry
- Urban Area

MAPQUEST

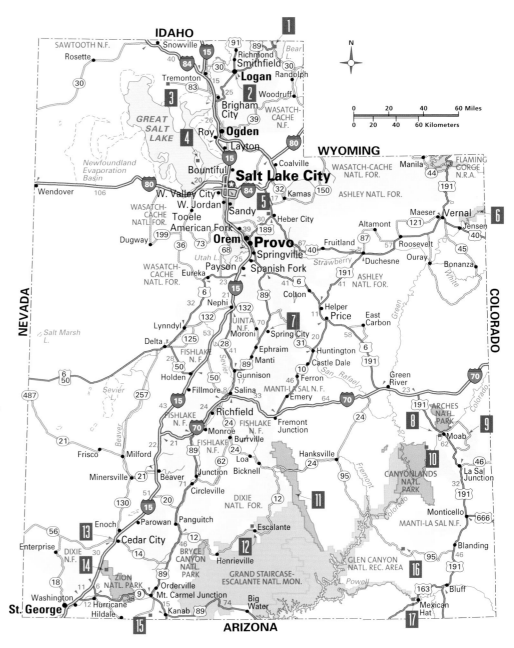

seven-mile offshoot leading to a spectacular glacial lake.

(435) 752-2161

www.utah.com

3 Golden Spike National Historic Site

Promontory Summit

Shortly past noon on May 10, 1869, two locomotives—Union Pacific's *119* and Central Pacific's *Jupiter*—met face to face here amid the barren hills at the summit of the Promontory Mountains.

Executives from both companies stepped forward and symbolically drove four ceremonial spikes into a polished laurel tie. Two of the spikes were gold (from which the site takes its name), one was silver, and one was an alloy of iron, gold, and silver. To conclude the ceremony a final, ordinary spike was driven into an ordinary tie.

Some people have called this the most significant event of the 19th century. The completion of the nation's first transcontinental railroad was a monumental achievement of engineering, willpower, and backbreaking work.

Although the entire enterprise took six years, most of the track was laid in four years by gangs of laborers toiling from dawn to dusk six days a week. The Central Pacific crew of Chinese laborers pushed eastward through the towering Sierra Nevada, with rock cuts, deep fills, trestles, switchbacks, 37 miles of wooden snowsheds and galleries, and 15 tunnels through 6,213 feet of solid granite.

The westward-driving Union Pacific workers, mostly Irishmen, had easier terrain but a no less hostile environment, for the Cheyennes and Sioux, well aware of what this railroad would mean to their territory and way of life, fought against it. These unsung heroes, who at best earned $2 or $3 per day ($10 to $15 if they provided their own horse or mule team), laid 1,776 miles of track, permanently linking America's East and West.

Replicas of the two engines, stand facing each other in the same spot as did the originals.

A visitors center offers a 20-minute film about the epic undertaking and displays artifacts, photographs, and a map of the transcontinental route. Nine miles of the original track bed can be toured by car, and a 1½ mile hiking trail leads to the remains of the Big Fill and Big Trestle, two structures that vividly evoke the heroic labor needed to complete the route.

Open daily May–Sept.; Wed.–Sun. Oct.–Apr. Closed Thanksgiving, Christmas and New Year's Day. Locomotives on display May–Labor Day. Admission charged.

(435) 471-2209, Ext.18

www.nps.gov/gosp

UTAH

4 Antelope Island State Park

*9 miles west of Syracuse/
Freeport Center on Antelope
Drive, Syracuse*

Rich in scenic beauty and natural features, Antelope Island is the perfect place to view the Great Salt Lake and experience the vast solitude of The Great Basin.

There are white sand beaches, hiking trails, and a sailboat marina. From the mainland, its 28,022 acres appear barren and deserted. But Antelope Island is home to a variety of flora and fauna native to the Great Basin region. The island was without its namesake antelope for many years, but they were reintroduced in 1993 and can now be seen in many areas of the park. Deer, bobcats, coyotes, many varieties of birds, and a small herd of elk also call the island home.

But most famous are Antelope Island's American bison, introduced to the island in 1893 and now numbering 600. The world-renowned herd is managed by the Utah Division of Parks and Recreation and visitors are welcome at the island's buffalo corral and management facilities. During the annual bison roundup at the end of October, visitors can get a close-up look at the bison and the techniques used on a working buffalo ranch.

Open year-round.
Admission charged.
(801) 773-2941
www.stateparks.utah.gov

5 Soldier Hollow Olympic Venue/ Wasatch Mountain State Park

6 miles southwest of Heber City

During the 2002 Olympic winter games, Soldier Hollow hosted 38 events in all, including cross-country, biathlon, Nordic combined, and paralympics. Athletes and officials proclaimed this one of the best-designed Nordic ski courses in the world because spectators rarely lost sight of competitors.

The 31-kilometer track now hosts a variety of activities and special events in an area that is typically 15 degrees cooler than temperatures in Salt Lake City. Now that the Olympics are history, this 600-acre corner of northern Utah's 23,000-acre Wasatch Mountain State Park has embarked on an ambitious plan to become a year-round travel destination as well as Olympic training ground.

One new summer offering for tourists is the biathlon, which is essentially a combination of Nordic skiing and target shooting. The event evolves into either a run-and-shoot or mountain bike-and-shoot exercise. And plans for future summer activities include an in-line skate-and-shoot and also a wheelchair-and-shoot.

For the winter, Soldier Hollow hosts Nordic skiing, snowshoeing, and tubing. A fully equipped shop rents cross-country skis, boots, and poles. A separate 700-foot tubing hill is also available.

Wasatch Mountain State Park, a Heber Valley landmark on the east side of the Wasatch Mountains, is home to one of Utah's best 36-hole golf courses. It has a second 36-hole course in the works.

Soldier Hollow:
(435) 654-2002
www.soldierhollow.org
Wasatch Mountain:
(435) 654-1791
www.stateparks.utah.gov

6 Dinosaur National Monument

*Fossil Quarry off Rte. 149,
7 miles north of Jensen*

One hundred forty-five million years ago, this now arid land was a low-lying plain inhabited by dinosaurs. When they died most of their skeletons decayed. But in one place flooding rivers buried many of their bones in sandbars, and in time these bones became fossilized. The north wall of the Quarry Visitor Center is actually the quarry face, which dramatically reveals fossils of turtles, crocodiles, and 14 species of dinosaurs, including some almost complete skeletons.

A few miles east, at Cub Creek, well-preserved petroglyphs may be seen. These animal, human, and geometric designs were pecked into the sandstone about 1,000 years ago by the Fremont People, whose prehistoric culture was first studied along the Fremont River.

A paved, self-guiding scenic drive begins at monument headquarters, 25 miles east of Jensen near Dinosaur, Colorado, and runs north for 31 miles through sagebrush-covered plateaus and verdant canyons.

More remote backcountry areas can be explored along several rugged, unpaved roads. In addition, opportunities exist for backpacking and river trips; information and the necessary permits can be obtained at monument headquarters or the Quarry Visitor Center. Two campgrounds and several backcountry camping areas are accessible by car.

*Quarry Visitor Center open year-round
except Thanksgiving, Christmas, and
New Year's Day; scenic drive generally
accessible May–Oct; campground near
Quarry Visitor Center open year-round.*
(435) 789-2115
www.nps.gov/dino/pphtml/facilities

6 Dinosaur National Monument. *Split Mountain rises in the distance as the Green River winds through miles of canyon here.*

7 Spring City

While many communities claim that they have been saved by being astride the interstate highway system, the fact that Interstate 15 bypasses Sanpete Valley has actually saved what has been described as the best concentration of houses, structures, and cultural elements reflecting 19th-century Mormon Utah in the state.

One of many small towns along "Heritage" Highway 89, Spring City is in the heart of what is called Little Denmark. Here, the influence of Scandinavian pioneers sent by Brigham Young to settle the area surrounds you.

Renowned for its many architecturally significant historic buildings, the entire town is listed on the *National Register of Historic Places*. If you want to see the inside of some of these remarkable buildings, mark the Saturday before Memorial Day on your calendar and come for Spring City Heritage Days and Home Tour.

Open year-round.

Tours: (435) 462-2211

http://heritageproducts.utah.org

⑧ Scott M. Matheson Wetlands Preserve

One-half mile from Moab on Kane Creek Rd.

The Scott M. Matheson Wetlands Preserve provides some of the best wetlands wildlife watching along the Colorado River in Utah. It is a critical "stepping stone" for migrating waterfowl, raptors, and shorebirds.

Beginning in the 19th century, ranchers grazed cattle among the thick vegetation of what they called the Moab Slough. Other settlers in the valley attempted to drain the slough and plant orchards and crops. Although ditches and canals are still visible, drainage efforts were abandoned when the Colorado River reclaimed this wetland in the floods of 1983 and 1984.

In 1990, The Nature Conservancy began to acquire land in the slough. Today, 875 acres are owned and jointly managed by the conservancy and the Utah Division of Wildlife Resources. In 1991, the preserve was named in honor of the late Scott M. Matheson, Utah's distinguished former governor and a conservation advocate.

Guided walks are held every Saturday morning, Mar.–Oct. Open daily.

(435) 259-4629.

www.discovermoab.com/wildlife.htm

🚶 🔭

⑨ La Sal Mountain Scenic Loop

6 miles south of Moab

Looming above the Moab Valley, the snow-capped La Sal Mountains were named by 18th-century Spanish explorers in the region. These dramatic mountains stand in sharp contrast to the fiery red sandstone rocks spread across the landscape, and offer cool retreat from high summer temperatures or endless backcountry snow adventures in the winter.

The La Sal Loop climbs from the desert environment of Spanish Valley up to the alpine meadows and beneath the 12,700-foot peaks. The 60-mile-long road is paved except for a few sections of gravel. The steep climb, much of it over narrow switchbacks, is slow-going and should not be attempted by cars towing trailers or recreational vehicles.

The high-country road is closed by snow in the winter, but during the rest of the year, it offers panoramic views of the Colorado Plateau and the Blue and Henry Mountains off in the distance.

The loop leaves Highway 191 six miles south of Moab and climbs the west side of the La Sals before descending through Castle

⑨ La Sal Mountain Scenic Loop. *Dramatic views of the La Sal Mountains, red rock canyons, and the Colorado River can be seen along this drive.*

Valley, which you can follow along the Colorado River back to Moab. Many classic Western films were shot in the Castle Valley area, and the visitors center in Moab offers information on self-guiding tours of these and other film sites.

Scenic drive generally accessible May–Oct.

(435) 259-1370

www.discovermoab.com/backways.com

⑩ Dead Horse Point State Park

Rte. 313, 31 miles southwest of Moab

Toward the end of the last century packs of wild mustangs roamed the mesas around what is now called Dead Horse Point, a stone promontory surrounded by high cliffs overlooking the Colorado River 2,000 feet below.

Cowboys fenced the narrow neck of land leading onto the promontory to use it as a natural corral for the mustangs. Once they had selected the best horses for personal use or sale, the gate was opened and the unwanted culls were allowed to find their way off the point and onto open range. One group never made it; according to legend, those broomtails died of thirst within distant view of the Colorado River.

Dead Horse Point is just one of the breathtaking overlooks in this 5,200-acre state park. Paved and primitive trails radiate outward from the visitors center to six points overlooking the river and the heavily eroded cliff walls, with their towering spires and steep bluffs.

The park offers self-guiding hikes and, in summer, short ranger-guided tours through a wilderness of pinyon pine, Utah juniper, single-leaf ash, and a wide variety of colorful wildflowers and cacti. Rock climbers and hang gliders occasionally pursue their sports along the precipice.

Open year-round.

Developed campground open Apr.–Oct.

Winter camping allowed on the point.

Admission charged.

(435) 259-2614 or

(800) 322-3770

www.stateparks.utah.gov

12 Escalante State Park. *Two sandstone arches, Metate and Mano, seem to balance on pedestals in Devil's Garden here.*

11 Capitol Reef National Park

Visitors center 10 miles east of Torrey on Rte. 24

Magnificent canyon landscapes, well-maintained hiking trails, and a 25-mile scenic drive make this desert park a backcountry enthusiast's delight. The primary feature of its rugged wilderness is a 100-mile-long ridge, or "reef," created by a buckling of the earth's crust as it was thrust upward by subterranean pressure.

Millennia of erosion and other geological forces have carved a stunning gallery of canyons, arches, towers, and buttes. One particularly striking dome, which is reminiscent of the U. S. Capitol in Washington, inspired the reef's name.

On the canyons' sandstone walls one can still see the glyphs carved by the Fremont People, who inhabited the area from A.D. 800 to 1200. Later the Paiute Indians lived here, and in the 1880s Mormon settlers planted orchards that were so successful their community eventually came to be called Fruita. Today the Mormons' 1896 schoolhouse can be toured, and the orchards, about a mile from the visitors center, are maintained by park personnel and are open to visitors in season.

A gravel road, following the path of a pioneer wagon trail, provides a scenic drive through the canyons into Capitol Gorge. A guidebook is available at the visitors center. Hiking trails also abound; bring plenty of water and insect repellent. A campground is maintained near the visitors center, and primitive sites are at Cedar Mesa in the park's southern wilderness.

Open year-round except Christmas. Admission charged.
(435) 425-3791
www.nps.gov/care

12 Escalante State Park

Escalante

The petrified forest in this 1,350-acre park is among the most remarkable in the country. In the late Jurassic Period 140 million years ago, the area was a wetland washed by streams powerful enough to transport whole fallen trees. The trees grew heavier as they became waterlogged and eventually sank to the river bottoms, where they were covered with gravel and silt. Over the ages water percolated through the soil, and as the wood cells dissolved they were replaced by silica as well as oxides of iron and manganese. The results can be seen in the startling reds, yellows, purples, and other colors in the petrified logs scattered throughout the park.

Hikers enjoy the moderately difficult one-hour climbs along the Wide Hollow and the Bailey Wash trails. Devil's Garden, with its arches and other curious sandstone formations, is worth a side trip. The 110-acre reservoir offers opportunities for swimming, wind surfing, and fishing for rainbow trout. Ice fishing is popular in the winter.

Open year-round. Admission charged.
(435) 826-4466
www.stateparks.utah.gov

13 Pine Valley Mountains Loop

North of St. George

The lowest elevations in Utah are in the southwestern corner, and therefore the area surrounding St. George is also generally the warmest in the state. And although the unique red rock country begs to be taken in, the summer months are just too hot to remain down low for too long.

A great way to escape the heat and still enjoy the red rock is to drive up into the Pine Valley Mountains north of St. George. Driving time for this back roads loop is under two hours, but give yourself twice that to get out and enjoy the sites along the way.

Three very different historical sites along the route will add interest to the drive that begins by following Highway 18 north out of St. George. Turn right at 25 miles out, and pass through the town of Central on Forest Road 035. The first site, Pine Valley chapel, is on the left just before connecting with Forest Road 011 to proceed along the loop. You can also go straight instead to enter the town of Pine Valley, or venture further into the campgrounds and hiking trails that lead deep into the Wilderness Area.

Back along the loop route, turn left at the quaint town of Pinto onto Forest Road 009 to close the loop to Highway 18. Just before reaching the pavement of Highway 18, you will pass the Hamblin Homestead Historical Site on the right. You will pass signs to the Mountain Meadows Massacre site on your right as you head south.

A must-see diversion on the way back to St. George is Snow Canyon State Park. Red rock canyons, sand dunes, lava flows, and volcanoes have all combined to form an amazing mixture of contrast and colors.

Admission charged for Snow Canyon. Snow Canyon: (435) 628-2255
www.stateparks.utah.gov

14 Kolob Canyons, Zion National Park

I-15, Exit 40, Springdale

Spectacular geological formations and a wide variety of environments make Kolob Canyons a place of exceptional beauty and interest. Within this less-used section of Zion National Park are the park's highest peak, 8,726-foot Horse Ranch Mountain, and the world's longest freestanding natural span known, the Kolob Arch.

A five-mile paved auto route into the five Finger Canyons of the Kolob is marked by 14 numbered stops keyed to an accompanying pamphlet available at the visitors center. The road winds between canyon walls of reddish Navajo sandstone sculpted by 13 million years of geological upheaval and erosion into the numerous buttes, arches, and ridges we see today.

Part of the road follows Hurricane Fault, a 200-mile-long fracture in the earth's crust, which elevated the land to the east nearly a mile. The change in altitude from valley to clifftop creates temperature differences averaging between 10° and 15° F. As a result, three distinct ecological zones can be observed in the canyons, from the valley's semi-arid juniper woodland to the lush forests of aspen, fir, and pine crowning Timber Top Mountain.

Mule deer, coyotes, and mountain lions frequent the area, as do peregrine falcons, ravens, and golden eagles. A strenuous hiking trail, requiring eight hours for a round trip, leads from the canyon road to Kolob Arch. Backcountry camping is allowed with a permit.

Open year-round.
(435) 772-3256
www.nps.gov/zion/pphtml/basics.html

⑮ Coral Pink Sand Dunes State Park

South of Mount Carmel Junction
You will hear the sound of revving motors here, because the 2,000 acres of rolling dunes in this 3,730-acre park attract dirt bike and dune buggy enthusiasts from far and wide. The sand is extremely fine, and off-road vehicles should have paddle-type tires.

The coral pink dunes are beautiful, especially just before sundown, when they come alive

with shifting shadows. Backpackers will find the campground here an excellent staging point for challenging, unmarked hikes through butte and mesa country. Be wary, however; rattlesnakes, black widow spiders, and scorpions thrive in this desert climate.

A 256-acre conservation area prohibits motorized vehicles in order to protect the coral pink beetle, found nowhere else in the world. Birders are likely to see scrub jays and hummingbirds. When winter snow cover is sufficient, the dunes are excellent for tubing.

Park and campground open year-round.
Admission charged.
(435) 648-2800
www.stateparks.utah.gov

⑯ Natural Bridges National Monument

Blanding
Until 1904 the three huge sandstone bridges here were called Caroline, Augusta, and Edwin, names given them by prospectors who explored the area in the 1880s.

They were given Hopi Indian names by President William Howard Taft in 1909 shortly after the site was designated a national monument. The oldest bridge is called Owachomo ("rock mound"); the longest is Sipapu ("the place of emergence"); and the youngest is Kachina, named for the masked divinities of the Hopi religion.

All three bridges were formed by the erosive action of streams as they flowed through the switchback bends of a canyon. A nine-mile loop road, suitable for bicycles as well as cars, links the starting points of the short trails to the three bridges and provides access to overlooks offering splendid views of the surrounding canyon scenery.

For those seeking longer hikes, nearly six miles of trail traverse the canyons' floors and connect the bridges. The terrain here, however, may be hazardous, and hikers should be alert for flash flooding. A campground near the visitors center has 13 sites.

Open year-round, but some trails may be

⑮ Coral Pink Sand Dunes State Park. *The eroding Navajo sandstone formations that surround this 3,730-acre park give the dunes their pink color.*

closed in winter. Closed major holidays.
Admission charged.
(435) 692-1234
www.nps.gov/nabr

⑰ Goosenecks State Park

Rte. 316 west off Rte. 261, north of Mexican Hat
The dramatic beauty of Utah's precipitous landscape is epitomized by the view from this 10-acre park set atop a towering mesa. From an overlook four "gooseneck" bends can be seen in the muddy San Juan River as it wends 1,000 feet below.

These bends, for which the park is named, are important examples of a geological phenomenon known as an entrenched meander: a curving streambed that by gradual water erosion or land upheaval is cut deep below the surface of the valley. Here the meanders have worn so deep that they have exposed layers of sandstone, shale, and limestone dating back more than 300 million years.

The mesa's vegetation has evolved to derive maximum moisture from the arid land. The Indian ricegrass, Mormon tea, prickly pear, and other sandy lowland plants provide cover and food that is too sparse to support much indigenous animal life; jackrabbits, skunks, and lizards are about the only creatures that manage to sustain a living in this landscape.

Birders will find the overlook rewarding, however, and it's an excellent place to stop for a picnic.

Open year-round.
(435) 678-2238
www.stateparks.utah.gov

Vermont

The fall color, white church steeples, maple syrup, cheese, and good skiing might well be enough—but there's more.

Missisquoi National Wildlife Refuge. *More than 200 species of birds can be seen in this area along the Atlantic Flyway.*

Among the surprises along the byways of the Green Mountain State are two attractions dedicated to the spirit: one is a shrine where healing is said to take place, the other a church built in the round to (perhaps) keep the devil from lurking in corners. More earthly concerns are recalled in a cheese factory and marble exhibit. Here are the homestead of a man who had a great idea for education and the boyhood home of our 30th president. Art is acknowledged in a petroglyph site and a display of works by a famous grandmother.

1 St. Anne's Shrine
Isle La Motte

Vermont's oldest white settlement was founded here at the water's edge in 1666, when a French officer, Capt. Pierre La Motte, built Fort St. Anne as a bastion against the Mohawk Indians. The fort was needed for only a short time, but soon afterward Jesuit priests built the first Christian chapel on the site in the woods.

Within the small cruciform chapel is a simple wooden altar with the figures of St. Anne and the Virgin Mary. To the left another altar is dedicated to St. Anne; on the walls near it hang abandoned crutches and plaster casts, evidence of the healings that are said to take place here. A rustic grotto near the chapel shelters a figure of the Virgin Mary. Also close by is an A-frame shrine that houses a marble statue of St. Anne. On the hill behind the chapel are other shrines that are dedicated to St. Anthony and Francis.

In a grove of pine trees on the site of the old stockade is the Gethsemane Garden, where the stations of the cross are inscribed on copper tablets. Beyond the Gethsemane Garden stands a granite statue of Samuel de Champlain, in a canoe with an Indian companion, marking the site of his landfall at Isle La Motte

1 St. Anne's Shrine. *An A-frame shelters a marble statue of St. Anne, the grandmother of Jesus, in a setting of tall pines. Jesuit priests built a chapel here in the 17th century.*

in 1609. Because of the crowds attracted to the shrine on weekends and holidays, it is best to visit the place on weekdays. Dock facilities are available for those who come by boat.
Open May 15–Oct. 15.
(802) 928-3362
www.islandsandfarms.com

2 Missisquoi National Wildlife Refuge
Swanton

The Indian name *Missisquoi,* meaning an area of "much water-fowl" and "much grass," well describes this place. Vast numbers of migratory waterfowl traveling the Atlantic Flyway stop to feed and rest here on some 6,600 acres of marsh, open water, and woodland. The best time to see them—black ducks, mallards, wood ducks, Canada geese, and many other species—is early fall, mid-September to early October. Among the nearly 200 species of birds observed here are osprey, bald eagles, and black terns.

The Black Creek and Maquam

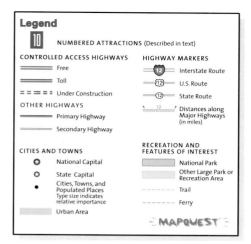

feet deep, and then continues wide and placid between banks set with hemlock and juniper.

There are no facilities for tourists here, but the falls may be seen at any time of the year. In wet weather they should be approached with extreme caution: the granite underfoot can be very slippery. The height and plunge of the falls could make one dizzy, and the spectacle is so attractive as to tempt the unwary viewer beyond a safe foothold.

(802) 525-4386

www.travelthekindgdom.com

4 Brighton State Park

2 miles east of Island Pond on Rte. 105. Go south on Lake Shore Drive 3/4-mile to park entrance.
The park is small but charmingly situated on the shore of Island Pond Lake.

Adjacent to the white sandy beach are picnic tables and a bath-house, fine views of the conifer-clad island from which the lake takes its name, and the surrounding hills.

The town of Island Pond, which would seem at home in the Swiss Alps, is attractively situated at the far end of the lake and adds to the appeal of the setting. It was the site of the first international railroad junction in the United States.

Open May–mid-Oct.; accessible year-round.
(802) 723-4360

http://vtparks.anr.state.vt.us/htm/ brighton.cfm

on the Missisquoi River.

White-tailed deer, red fox, raccoon, otter, and mink are in residence; and among the fish are northern pike, walleye, bass, salmon, and carp. But whether you fish or simply walk and look about you, the Missisquoi Refuge provides a fine opportunity to view nature as a network of interdependent communities.

Open year-round, but the trails may be flooded in spring.
(802) 868-4781

http://northeast.fws.gov

3 Big Falls

North Troy. River Road, off Rte. 105
The first pull-off on the left after you see the falls gives access to the best viewing spots, which are above the waterfall. Just upstream from the falls, the Missisquoi River divides around a rocky island topped by small conifers. The scene is elegant enough to have been designed by a Japanese gardener. Below this the river plunges, boils, fumes, and roars into a narrow chasm perhaps 60

Creek nature trails, together about 1.5 miles in length, are easily walked. They follow the course of two woodland creeks, where points of interest are numbered and described in the trail guide along the way, and include musk-rat burrows, woodpecker feeding

stations, and duck "loafing sites." Beavers are abundant here, along with signs of their activities— felled birch trees, wood chips, scent mounds, runs, and lodges. Kayaking and canoeing enthusi-asts will want to paddle the 11-mile loop that starts and finishes

5 North Hero State Park

North Hero, Lakeview Drive
Heroes from Vermont who fought in the Revolutionary War gave their name to the island this park is named for in Lake Champlain, the sixth largest lake in the country. Not too far from the bustling university town of Burlington, home of the University of Vermont, the peaceful, spacious campgrounds consist of three loops containing 99 wooded tent/trailer sites and 18 lean-tos, nestled in a heavily wooded forest over 399 acres, 13 miles from the Canadian border.

The level of the lake fluctuates from 95 to 100 feet above sea level, and about one-third of the park lies below 100 feet, so a fair portion of the park becomes seasonally flooded.

Chain pickerel and northern pike spawn in the flooded portions, map turtles nest on the beach, and white-tailed deer, poised to run, noiselessly observe the human activities. Ruffled grouse, American woodcock, and a whole variety of migratory waterfowl like wood ducks and mallards are common here.

Nearby attractions on the interconnected islands include the 1665 French settlement, St. Anne's shrine in Isle LaMotte, and a state-of-the-art hatchery, the Grand Isle State Fish Culture Station. Jedediah Hyde's log cabin, also in Grand Isle, is thought to be one the oldest in the United States.

With waters of the lake lapping the sides of your kayak, and the Green Mountains in the distance, you can inhale the near solitude. It's a perfect reason to be here.
Open mid-May–Labor Day.
Base rate charged.
(800) 252-2363

1 Groton State Forest. *Thousands of acres of hemlocks, birches, maples, and other hardwoods shelter beaches, a trout-fishing pond, hiking trails, and campsites here.*

(802) 372-8727 (summer)
http://vtparks.anr.state.vt.us/htm/north hero.cfm

6 Old Round Church

Bridge St, Richmond
From the time it was built in 1813, this remarkable 16-sided, two-story frame building has attracted comment. The reason for its shape is not certain. Local lore says it was to keep the devil from lurking in corners or to prevent an enemy from hiding around a corner. Another suggestion is that 16 men each built a side and a 17th added the belfry. A page from the account book of William Rhodes, the master builder, lists 17 workers in addition to himself. But the most likely explanation is that it was modeled after a round church in Claremont, New Hampshire, where Rhodes's parents lived.

The Old Round Church was built to serve as both a house of worship and a town hall. Five denominations cooperated to raise money for its construction by selling pews. Regular church services ceased around 1880, but town meetings were held here until 1973, when the church was declared structurally unsafe.

It was restored by the Richmond Historical Society and is a National Historic Landmark. Of special interest are the box pews, the handwrought hinges, and the hand-painted wood graining on both the pulpit and the horseshoe-shaped balcony.
Open daily July 4–Labor Day; weekends only late spring and early autumn.
(802) 434-4119
www.vmga.org/chittenden/ roundchurch.html.

7 Groton State Forest

West of Groton and Peacham
The nine recreation areas in this beautiful forest offer opportunities for a variety of outdoor activities, summer and winter. The forest, a mix of hemlocks, birches, maples, and other hardwoods, is threaded with trails for hiking, snowmobiling, and nature study. In several of the areas inviting campsites are to be found.

The Boulder Beach State Park is on Lake Groton, the largest body of water in the forest. Here the dense woods, which elsewhere come right down to the edge of the lake, have given way to a pleasant sandy beach studded with large boulders deposited by a glacier thousands of years ago. On your way to the beach, look for a massive boulder with a large paper birch growing from the top. A briskly bubbling stream runs alongside.

Dedicated trout fishermen may want to seek out Noyes, or Seyon, Pond in the Seyon Ranch State Park, where fly casting is permitted only from boats and canoes. ("Seyon" is "Noyes" spelled backward.) From Groton, go west on Rte. 32 for three miles. Turn right on Seyon Pond Road and go three miles to the park entrance.

Boulder Beach area open early
June–Labor Day; accessible year-round.
Seyon area open early May–Oct.
(802) 241-3670
www.wildernet.com

8 Kingsland Bay State Park
Ferrisburgh
This exceptionally pretty park is
set on an inlet on the east shore of
Lake Champlain, a place of quiet
green water and gray pebble
beaches strewn with small boulders and bleached driftwood.
Ledges of granite, clothed in
juniper and arborvitae, project into
the lake from miniature headlands;
far beyond are the peaks of the
Adirondacks.

The road into the park, running
along and above the shore, is
fringed on the lakeside by wild
grape, white pine, bittersweet, and
arborvitae; on the other side lie
open meadows. The road leads to
a picnic area where there are

8 Kingsland Bay State Park. *Visitors can picnic, swim, or sail at one of the pret-
tiest parks in the state, which is along the shoreline of Lake Champlain.*

tables and charcoal grills. There is
also a small beach where boats
can be launched.

If you continue a few hundred
yards beyond the park entrance
and take the first turn to the right,
you will come immediately to an
informal parking area at the head
of the inlet. From here, there are
fine views and access to the water.
*Open Memorial Day–Labor Day;
accessible year-round.*
Summer: (800) 658-1622
Year-round: (802) 877-3445
**http://vtparks.anr.state.vt.us/htm/
kingsland.cfm**

9 Button Bay State Park
Vergennes
Button Bay, a wide inlet on the
east shore of southern Lake
Champlain, is approached across
an alluvial plain that becomes a
patchwork of vivid green meadows and cultivated fields in the
spring. On the western side of the

lake are the undulating foothills
of the Adirondacks. At a distance
to the east rise the Green
Mountains—which from here take
on a lovely shade of blue.

The 253-acre park wraps
around the shore of Button Bay,
which is relatively open, with
conifer woods to the north and
south. There are well-arranged tent
and trailer sites and several lean-
tos, as well as a picnic area and
boat-launching sites. Nature trails
and a small nature museum add to
the park's appeal.
Open mid-May–Labor Day.
(800) 658-1622
http://vtparks.anr.state.vt.us

10 Floating Bridge
*Brookfield. Just off Rte. 14,
south of Williamstown*
Brookfield is a charming village
of white clapboard houses and
well-trimmed lawns nestled beside
the dark waters of Sunset Lake. In
1820 Luther Adams built a floating bridge across the lake here,
and since then people, animals,
carts, and cars have crossed the
water—a journey of about 100
yards—by this curious means.

The present bridge, built in
1978 by the Vermont Agency of
Transportation, is the seventh at
the site. Made of pressure-treated
timber, the bridge is supported by
380 floating polyethylene drums
filled with polyurethane foam. At
each end is a hinged ramp, and at
these points the water can be as
much as five inches deep. Driving
across the bridge is no longer permitted, but the area is a popular
spot for fishing and swimming.
www.easternvermont.com

11 The Justin Smith Morrill Homestead
Strafford
On July 2, 1862, President Lincoln
signed the Morrill Act, a measure
that contributed mightily to the
cause of higher education by
granting public lands to the states
to help finance colleges offering
courses in "agriculture and the
mechanic arts." Representative,
and later, Senator, Justin Morrill
worked on his far-reaching legislation here in the house he designed
and built from 1848–51. A wood
cottage painted rosy pink to simulate stone and adorned about its
windows, porches, and gables with
Carpenter Gothic trim, it seems
as visionary as the schools that
Morrill proposed.

The land rises to fields and
woods behind the house, and not
far up the hill are several farm
buildings, also pink. From the hillside may be seen the Strafford
Town House, erected in 1799 as
a meetinghouse for local officials,
and as a place of worship for all
denominations. The view is charming, as is a little man-made waterfall tumbling through the hole of a
lichened millstone. This small
detail evokes the kind of loving
care that Morrill gave to his home.

The furnishings include pieces
from Morrill's Washington home
as well as family memorabilia.
Among the intriguing features of
the house are the screens on the
parlor and dining room windows.
They have romantic landscapes
hand-painted on the outside to
keep people from looking in while
allowing those inside to see out.
*Open Wed–Sun., Memorial Day–
Columbus Day.*
Admission charged.
(802) 828-3051
www.historicvermont.org/morrill

12 Billings Farm and Museum
Route 12 & River Road, Woodstock

The gentle lowing of the Jersey herd blends with the bleating of the sheep at this working farm that harks back to the late 19th century. As the afternoon milking progresses, with guests invited to watch and learn, lives of Vermont farm families of 1890 are portrayed in exhibits of dairying, planting and the harvest, ice cutting and maple sugaring. The daily activities of that era are demonstrated: wood carving, rug hooking, butter churning, spinning, and wooden tool making.

The progressive dairy farm, which remains a working dairy to this day, was started by conservationist, lawyer, and railroad magnate Frederick Billings. Billings and his farm manager selectively bred the herd for optimum production and planted over 10,000 trees to restore the forest cover. One of

their cows came home from the Chicago World's Fair with the title "Champion Heifer of the World" in testament to the success of the methods used in the early years of the farm.

Billings's granddaughter, the late Mary French Rockefeller, and her husband, Laurance Rockefeller, established the farm and museum to interpret Vermont's rural life and agricultural history, and to ensure the continuation of the dairy, still acknowledged as one of America's best.

Open daily May 1–Oct. 31 and various weekends throughout the year.
Admission charged.
(802) 457-2355
www.billingsfarm.org

13 Vermont Marble Exhibit
Proctor

There are extensive deposits of marble in Vermont's Green

Mountains, and most of the stone quarried there is processed in the village of Proctor, the largest center for such work in North America. The Vermont Marble Exhibit, also the largest of its kind, documents every aspect of this remarkable stone and many of the ways in which it is used. An 11-minute movie details the history of the Vermont Marble Company.

Among the displays are walls of marble of different kinds from all over the world: Peru, golden vein, Carolina rose, Andes black, and many others—as varied, intriguing, and beautiful as their names. Exhibits include tabletops, baths, flooring, and a complete series of relief busts of the presidents of the United States. Other exhibits explore the geology of marble and quarrying and production methods.

In a sculptor's studio you can also watch marble being chiseled and carved and see an exhibition

of modern marble sculpture and statuary.

Open daily mid-May–Oct.
Admission charged.
(802) 459-2300
www.vermont-marble.com

14 Calvin Coolidge State Historic Site
Plymouth

In the early hours before dawn, on August 3, 1923, Vice President Coolidge, who was vacationing at his boyhood home in Plymouth, was awakened when a courier brought word that President Warren G. Harding had suddenly died. By the light of a kerosene lamp in the sitting room, Coolidge was sworn into office as the new president by his father, a notary public.

During his five years as chief executive Coolidge returned here for vacations. Content with the simplicity of the house and its air of peacefulness, it was not until 1932 that he installed electricity and other modern amenities. He was buried, as he requested, in the cemetery nearby in 1933.

The small white farmhouse stands in a spacious meadow at the edge of Plymouth village. Lovely period gardens and stands of ancient trees soften its spartan quality and complete the simple ambiance that make it so appealing—particularly when one considers the eminence of its owner.

Nearby is a handsome large barn that houses a Farmers Museum. The homestead, barn, and the white frame church that Coolidge attended now constitute a National Historic Landmark.

Open daily late May–mid-Oct.
Admission charged.
(802) 672-3773
www.historicvermont.org

12 Billings Farm and Museum. *A horse-drawn sleigh makes its way across snow-covered farm fields. Visitors can enjoy the ride from December through February.*

15 Crowley Cheese Factory
Healdville

At the country's oldest cheese factory, Colby (a kind of cheddar, but with a creamier, more open texture) is still made by hand, just as it was a hundred years ago. Visitors can see the curds being cut and raked in the big vats, then handworked and formed in hand-cranked presses. The tools, techniques, and product haven't changed.

The factory was built by Winfield Crowley in 1882, when his business outgrew the farm kitchen where he had by then been making cheese for almost 60 years. The establishment today is still redolent of the less hurried, more peaceful time when it got its start. A collection of old cheese-making tools—curd knives, a cheese press, and a centrifuge—is on display. You can sample the product or buy it at the gift shop, along with candy, maple syrup, jams, and baked goods.

Factory open Mon.–Fri.;
shop open daily.
(802) 259-2340
www.crowleycheese-vermont.com

16 Indian Petroglyphs
Bellows Falls

The best vantage point is about 10 feet downstream from the Vilas Bridge on the west side of the Connecticut River. Looking over the riverbank about 12 feet down on the south side, just beyond a white fence, you can see a boulder with yellow paint marks and several petroglyphs deeply incised in the rock, covering a surface about 15 feet in breadth and 6 feet in height, probably carved by the Pennacook Indians.

The petroglyphs represent heads, probably human, but per-

18 Molly Stark State Park. *Leafy trails lead hikers through a forest of hardwoods. One trail leads to the summit of Mount Olga, where your reward for the climb is a view of five states on a clear day.*

haps not. Several of them have a pair of horns, or feathers, projecting from the crown, and two are connected by a kind of cord. The most prominent figure in the group is a head adorned by six horns and supported by a neck and shoulders. If they represent humans, the carvings are a little larger then life-size. Possibly the petroglyphs commemorate periods when local tribes would suspend hostilities and gather here to fish for salmon on their spawning run up the Connecticut River. But what the staring-eyed faces represent, or when or why they were carved, we may never know. They may simply be an example of early American graffiti.

Accessible year-round.
(877) 887-2378
www.southernvermont.com

17 Grandma Moses Gallery and Schoolhouse
Bennington

A hardworking farm woman most of her life, Grandma Moses began to paint in oils in her 70s. Although she had no technical training, her

farm scenes and rural landscapes had a cheerful, naive quality that soon won her acclaim as a "primitive." She completed more than 1,500 works before her death in 1961 at the age of 101. The museum has the largest public collection of plates and tiles ornamented with scenes from her paintings and the tilt-top pine table she used as an easel (with side panels decorated in her inimitable style).

Adjoining the gallery is the schoolhouse Grandma Moses attended as a girl in Eagle Bridge, New York. It was also the school for four of her nine grandchildren and nine great-grandchildren. Built in 1834, the schoolhouse was moved to Bennington in 1972 and now serves as a museum of Grandma Moses memorabilia. In it is a stained glass window from the W. D. Thomas Pharmacy in Hoosick Falls, New York, where her work was first shown. The main part of the room re-creates the appearance of the old schoolhouse, with church pews (instead of benches) and antique desks.

The Grandma Moses Gallery

and Schoolhouse are part of the well-known Bennington Museum, which has fine collections of pottery, glass, furniture, paintings, uniforms, firearms, musical instruments, and early toys on display.

Open daily except Thanksgiving, Christmas, and New Year's Day. Admission charged.
(802) 447-1571
www.benningtonmuseum.com

18 Molly Stark State Park
Wilmington

Situated in a beautiful valley on the west side of Mount Olga, this small park has several appealing features. The local roads are favored by cyclists, and in winter the countryside is inviting for skiers and snowshoers. In addition, the forest of hardwoods and pines harbors deer, raccoons, Cooper's hawks, and other wildlife of interest to nature lovers. The park's campsites are set in the woods around a pleasant clearing dotted with apple trees.

Perhaps the main attraction, however, is the trail leading from the campground to the summit of Mount Olga. About three-quarters of a mile long, it is easy to follow, although it is somewhat steep near the summit. Your reward for going to the top of the fire tower is a 360-degree view of wooded hills and valleys with an occasional barn roof glinting in the sun. On a clear day you can see New York, Vermont, New Hampshire, Massachusetts, and Connecticut.

Open for camping mid-May–mid-Oct.
(802) 464-5460, June–Aug.;
(800) 299-3071, Jan.-May
http://vtparks.anr.state.vt.us/htm/ mollystark.cfm

Smithfield Plantation House.
Built in 1772, the interior of this white clapboard house is notable for its Chinese Chippendale staircase (see page 341).

Virginia

From the Tidewater to the Blue Ridge, the landscape of the Old Dominion is suffused with its historic past and gentle beauty.

Many facets of Virginia's long and varied history are revealed in out-of-the-way museums. A house that confirms the comfort and elegance enjoyed by a fortunate few in the plantation era also displays artifacts created by American Indians who roamed these hills and valleys more than 11,000 years ago. Another museum retains the character of a typical small farm and honors the black slave who labored there beside his master and went on to become an influential educator.

Aspects of the Civil War, which was heavily fought on Virginia soil, are memorialized. Among reminders of an earlier America are two gristmills, one of which belonged to a successful miller who was also a noted surveyor, soldier, and president of the United States.

1 Southwest Virginia Museum Historical State Park

Wood Ave., Big Stone Gap

Housed in a mansion originally built in 1895 by Rufus Ayers, a Virginia attorney general and southwest Virginia developer, this ornate four-story museum is constructed of sandstone and limestone, and its interior features native red oak woodwork, a grand staircase, and marble fireplaces.

The core of the museum's collection features items from southwest Virginia that were originally collected by C. Bascom Slemp, private secretary to President Calvin Coolidge, and his sister Janie Slemp Newman.

In 1946 this collection was bequeathed to the state, and the building was sold for its original 1800s building price of $25,000. The museum was officially dedicated as a Virginia state park in 1948. Over the years, the museum's collection has been added to, and today it features an extensive assortment of southwest Virginia history.

The first-floor exhibits feature the early development of coal boomtowns, like Big Stone Gap, and the coming of the railroads. Galleries on the second floor tell the story of southwest Virginia residents at the turn of the 20th century. Mail-order catalogs, photographs, Victrolas, clothing, and early

2 Wolf Creek Indian Village and Museum. *Dressed as American Indians in 1215, interpretive guides demonstrate skills of industry, artistry, and survival for 21st-century visitors.*

sporting equipment depict an interesting lifestyle. Two of the second-floor galleries chronicle the life of Slemp and his sister Janie's interest in telling the story of southwest Virginia.

The third-floor exhibits depict early American Indians and the flow of settlers along the Wilderness Road. Discover early pioneer life through woodworking tools, spinning wheels, a weaving loom, and a homemade whiskey still. The

ground floor features earlier pictures of the area. In addition, there is a gift shop of pioneer and Victorian-era items and local crafts.

Open Memorial Day–Labor Day. Closed Mondays Labor Day– Memorial Day. Also closed January and February and major holidays.
(276) 523-1322
www.dcr.state.va.us

2 Wolf Creek Indian Village and Museum

Off I-77, Bastian

In a tree-sheltered valley below the breathtaking mountains of southwest Virginia, archaeologists uncovered evidence of a thriving settlement of about 100 American Indians, dating back to the year 1215. That ancient community lives again—not far from its original home, still under excavation—in a living museum.

The painstakingly re-created village offers a fascinating trip back in time and into a distant culture, with opportunities for hands-on exploration. Dressed in the fashion of the day, interpretive guides go about the daily business of living like the Eastern Woodland Indians, happily demonstrating skills of industry, artistry, and survival for 21st-century visitors. Nearby, a more traditional museum showcases artifacts from the excavation site.

For those eager to learn more about the history and traditions of Virginia's earliest settlers, the well-stocked museum store offers a selection of educational books and videos.

Before returning to modern civilization, visitors can explore the pristine nature trails surrounding the village or enjoy a leisurely meal in the inviting picnic area.

Open daily year-round.
Admission charged.
(276) 688-3438
www.indianvillage.org

3 Smithfield Plantation House

Blacksburg

This white clapboard plantation house was built in 1772 on Virginia's western frontier by Col. William Preston, who at one time was a member of the Virginia House of Burgesses.

Named Smithfield in honor of Colonel Preston's wife, Susanna Smith, the plantation remained in the family for almost 200 years. In 1959 Mrs. Janie Preston Boulware Lamb, a great-great-granddaughter of the builder, presented the house and four acres of land to the Association for the Preservation of Virginia Antiquities, and the house was restored and opened to the public in 1964.

The interior of the one-and-a-half-story dormer-windowed house is notable for its Chinese Chippendale Staircase, its handsome drawing-room mantelpiece, and the dining-room corner cupboard, which was made on the plantation.

Reflecting the simplicity of the late 18th and early 19th centuries, the kitchen garden contains turnips, beans, herbs, and various fruits, along with primula and foxglove. The garden was restored in 1982 by the Garden Club of Virginia.

In the basement is the Michael-Schultz collection of American Indian artifacts, some from 9500 B.C., found in southwest Virginia.

Open Thu.–Sun., Apr.–early Dec.
Admission charged.
(540) 231-3947
www.visitroanoke.va.com

4 Virginia Museum of Transporation

303 Norfolk Ave., between 2nd and 5th St., Roanoke

From vintage locomotives to an official post-office bus, this museum celebrates the history and development of vehicles that have kept people and businesses moving in Virginia and throughout the world. Its impressive collection of rail and road veterans includes a Norfolk & Western Class J Locomotive, a 1942 Ford/American LaFrance Fire Engine, a DC Transit Company Streetcar—retired in 1945—and a classic Model T Ford.

In addition to celebrated trains, trucks, and cars, the museum offers an array of exhibits exploring the impact of the transportation industry on the region. Highlights include a continually expanding documentary honoring the contributions of African-Americans to the Norfolk & Western Railroad, from 1930 to 1970.

Visitors can also peruse more than 3,000 transportation-related photographs, including rare shots of early wagons, carriages, and airplanes in the Roanoke Valley; an eclectic assortment of railroad documents, including employee timetables; and over 1,000 samples of automobile sales pieces, including pioneering brochures heralding the coming of the horseless carriage.

Classic car enthusiasts can catch a monthly lecture on the art of automobile restoration and catch up on the progress of the museum's burgeoning automobile gallery. Kids and lifelong fans will delight in the huge model-train layout, with four tiers of track, swift-moving trains, and viewing levels to accommodate all sizes.

Open daily year-round. Closed major holidays. Admission charged.
(540) 342-5670
www.vmt.org/info.htm

5 Booker T. Washington National Monument

Rte. 122, between Bedford and Rocky Mount, Hardy

Burroughs Plantation, where Booker T. Washington was born in 1856 to Jane Ferguson, the plantation's cook, was a poor, small 19th-century farm with master and slave working side by side. At the end of the Civil War, when Booker was 9 years old, liberation came, and Jane and her two sons and daughter moved to West Virginia.

The plantation has been reconstructed, and once again it has the character and appearance that it had when Booker was a child. None of the original buildings remain, but the same chinked log construction has been used in the restoration. Racks of drying leaves hang in the tobacco barn; chickens and turkeys wander around freely; tansworth, a historic breed, occupy the hogpen.

A quarter-mile walking trail winds through the grounds, where you can experience the sights, sounds, and smells of the plantation. At the visitors center you will find a printed guide to the trail, which gives highlights of Washington's life and career.

Jack-o-Lantern Branch Trail, named for the small stream that flows through the fields and forests surrounding the plantation, is an easy walk. A detailed guide to the path is available at the Environmental Education and Cultural Center.

Open daily except Thanksgiving, Christmas, and New Year's Day. Admission is free.
(540) 721-2094
www.nps.gov/bowa

7 Natural Chimneys Regional Park. *Etched by the forces of nature, these chimneys are a reminder of a time, centuries ago, when the Shenandoah Valley was once covered by ocean.*

6 Red Hill Patrick Henry National Memorial

Brookneal

After many years of public life as one of the Founding Fathers of our country and a five-term governor of Virginia, Patrick Henry bought Red Hill Plantation in 1794 and retired there to continue his practice of law. He died five years later and was buried in a small cemetery on the grounds beside his second wife, Dorothy.

The plantation, now restored, is a complex of several buildings, including the main house, a two-story structure rebuilt on its old foundations; the kitchen; the carriage house; and the office where Patrick Henry practiced law.

Dominating the entire scene is an Osage orange tree. With an 85-foot spread and a height of 60 feet, it is said to be the largest and oldest Osage orange in the country. The American Forestry Hall of Fame lists it as both the Virginia champion and national champion of its kind.

At the visitors center a collection of Patrick Henry memorabilia is displayed, including his flute, cuff links, salt dishes, an ivory letter opener, wineglasses, his house keys, his law office desk, his telescope, and several letters written in his hand. A printed guide to a walking trail is available at the visitors center.

Open daily except Thanksgiving, Christmas and New Year's Day. Admission charged.
(800) 514-7463
www.redhill.org

7 Natural Chimneys Regional Park

Mount Solon

Soaring above the surrounding plain, the chimneys are a strange remnant of the time, countless centuries ago, when an ocean covered the Shenandoah Valley, leaving behind these rocks etched by the forces of nature.

It takes little imagination to see in these weathered, highly textured formations such shapes as turrets, gargoyles, distant cities, or perhaps menacing fortifications. Small junipers growing among the rocks help to create a curiously deceptive scale.

Since 1821, on the third Saturday of June and August, a jousting tournament has been held on the plains below the chimneys. Modern-day knights, with chargers galloping, try to spear three steel rings hanging from crossbars suspended over the 75-yard course in the meadow known as the National Jousting Hall of Fame.

Self-guiding nature and biking trails wander through the fields and woodlands. The park also has 145 tree-shaded campsites with electric and water hook-up, a swimming pool, picnic areas, and a children's playground.

Open year-round. Admission charged.
(888) 430-2267
http://home.rica.net/uvrpa/
Uppervalley.htm

8 Glen Burnie Historic House, Gardens and Galleries

801 Amherst St., Winchester
Framed by the Blue Ridge and Allegheny mountains, the Shenandoah Valley is renowned for its magnificent vistas. Housed in the homestead of a local founding father, a new museum focuses on the intimate side of this scenic region of Virginia.

For six generations Glen Burnie, a stately brick Georgian, was home to the descendants of Col. James Wood, founder of the city of Winchester. The public is now welcome to come in and admire the antiques, paintings, and adornments collected by the last resident family member. Outside, guests are invited to wander through the "yard"—25 acres of grand gardens, graced with sculptures and fountains.

In addition to celebrating the legacy and exquisite taste of one prominent family, Glen Burnie is also the site of the Museum of the Shenandoah Valley. Devoted to household tools, decorations, and ties, galleries celebrate the people—American Indian, African American, English, Scotish, and Irish—who have made the Shenandoah Valley their home.

The gallery's extensive eclectic collection includes clocks, quilts, pottery, chairs, tables, and folk art. Continuing the theme of "making a home," the Miniatures Gallery showcases grown-up doll houses, meticulously and beautifully furnished, complete with working crystal chandeliers. The

◨ Glen Burnie Historic House, Gardens and Galleries. *Visitors are welcome to stroll the 25 acres of grand gardens, graced with sculptures and fountains, that surround this historic museum.*

museum also offers hands-on views of home life, from demonstrations of pottery-making to interactive computer programs that give the whole family a chance to learn about the Civil War on the home front.

Open Apr.–Oct., six days a week.
Closed Mondays. Admission charged.
(540) 662-1473
www.glenburniemuseum.org

9 The Museum of Culpeper History

803 S. Main St., Culpeper
This new state-of-the-art facility contains collections ranging from dinosaur tracks to 21st-century technology. But it also focuses on an event of great importance in American history.

At various times during the Civil War both Union and Confederate forces occupied Culpeper, the site of some of the war's fiercest fighting. In 1861 the Battle of Brandy Station, with 19,000 mounted men, took place five miles from town. It remains the biggest cavalry encounter ever fought in the Western Hemisphere. The museum, founded in 1977, commemorates that battle and documents the town's involvement in the war.

Much of the museum's collection of bayonets, sabers, knapsacks, stirrups, firearms, and other items of warfare was found on the battlefields in the countryside surrounding Culpeper.

Paintings, 100-year-old maps, and many photographs decorate the museum's walls as well. An interactive topographical map of the Civil War battles in Culpeper is also featured.

Open Mon.–Sat. Feb. 1-Dec. 24;
open Sun. as well May 1–Oct. 31.
(540) 829-1749
www.culpepermuseum.com

10 George Washington's Grist Mill Historical State Park

Alexandria

This impressive reconstruction gives us a unique view of the private life and interests of our first president. Based on archaeological investigations and plans and papers found among his personal effects, the gristmill is a detailed replica of one Washington built and operated for almost 30 years.

Originally, Mount Vernon was the estate of Washington's half-brother, Lawrence. But Washington inherited the property in 1761 and with it a deteriorating and inefficient water mill.

Always a clever entrepreneur, the future president was sensitive to northern Virginia's agricultural transition from tobacco to wheat, and in 1770 he decided to abandon the old mill and build a new one in order to be better able to capitalize on the region's changing economy. Washington operated the mill successfully for the rest of his life, including the eight years of his presidency, and at his death willed it to a nephew.

A tour through the mill's five floors, from the 16-foot breast-shot waterwheel on the ground floor to the grinding, sifting, and packing areas above, provides a vivid picture of late 18th-century American industry—a picture made all the more intriguing by the thought that this busy enterprise was a product of the same insight, determination, and stamina with which our first president helped to forge a new nation.

Open daily May–Nov.
Admission charged.
(703) 550-0960
www.dcr.state.va.us

11 The Copper Shop

1707B Princess Anne St., Fredericksburg

Owned and run by coppersmiths Allen H. Green II and Allen III, the shop offers a fascinating look at how, in early America, simple tools and materials were used to create objects both beautiful and useful. It is one of the few places in the country where one can still see swell-bodied weathervanes and other copper objects being made.

The work is done entirely by hand, from making the pattern to cutting the copper sheets and hammering them to shape on hard sandbags. Traditional designs are used for many of the objects, and most are made to order.

One of the specialties of the shop is the Fredericksburg Lamp, an elegantly designed candleholder with a slim hurricane chimney created by the elder Mr. Green in 1976. It comes with or without a reflector in six different versions, including a patio lamp, a chandelier, and a table lamp. The Island Sconce, fashioned by Allen III, is also an impressive feature of the collection of copperware.

Open year-round.
(540) 371-4455
www.thecodger.com

12 Reedville Fishermen's Museum

504 Main St., Reedville

Overlooking a generous creek, this museum celebrates the maritime heritage of a proud historic town that remains one of the nation's most active fishing ports. In addition to tracing the birth, rise, and influence of the local menhaden fishing industry, specializing in catch used for bait, it honors the men who have mined the waters of the Chesapeake Bay for centuries.

The main building features intricate models of Chesapeake Bay workboats; authentic tools used by the area's watermen to harvest crabs, oysters, and wide-ranging fish; and detailed dioramas illuminating the trade, its practices, and its impact, from the earliest American Indian fishermen to today's dedicated purveyors.

Next door, the William Walker

12 Reedville Fishermen's Museum. *Overlooking Cockrell's Creek, this museum pays homage to the men who have mined the waters of the Chesapeake Bay for centuries.*

House—the oldest house still standing in Reedville, built in 1875—has been meticulously restored and appointed in the style of a typical waterman's home at the turn of the century. The museum also offers educational programs and rotating exhibits, including a summer tribute to skipjacks—distinctive sailboats known for their seasonal races on the bay. Amateur and vicarious fishermen will delight in the gift shop, stocked with books of regional interest, crafts made by local artisans, prints, maps, and children's toys.

For a final treat, a walk on the museum's deck offers views of the shimmering creek, stilled fished for its menhaden by modern fleets.

Open daily from May–Oct. and weekends year-round. Admission charged.
(800) 453-6529
www.rfmuseum.com

13 The Edgar Allan Poe Museum

1916 East Main St., Richmond

A building known as the Old Stone House, dating from the 1730s, is one of five houses devoted to the memorabilia, the life, and the times of author Edgar Allan Poe. Behind the stone house is the small, wall-enclosed Enchanted Garden inspired by two of Poe's poems, "To One in Paradise" and "To Helen." The garden is planted with evergreens, rhododendrons, and ivy-bordered lawns, with wrought-iron benches. Altogether, the atmosphere of the Poe Museum seems imbued with the spirit of its subject.

The museum's most elaborate display is a large painted clay model of Richmond as it was in the first half of the 19th century. Museum guides point out the places where Poe lived and worked.

Also on display are Poe's

walking stick, a pair of boot hooks, and his wife's trinket box and mirror—suitable mementos, perhaps, of a man whose life was that of a wanderer and whose temperament was insuperably romantic.

The collection contains a number of photographs and drawings of Poe and his circle of friends and includes a strange, ethereal sketch of his wife, Virginia. Facsimiles of the first editions of his works and of his manuscripts include a handwritten draft of his famous poem, "Annabel Lee." In an upper room the series of surrealist illustrations made in the 1880s by James Carling for "The Raven" is on display.

Open Tues.–Sun. except Christmas.
Admission charged.
(804) 648-5523
www.poemuseum.org

14 Chippokes Plantation State Park

Surry

In 1612 Capt. William Powell of Jamestown was granted 1,400 acres on the James River, a tract within Indian territory. He named it Chippokes in honor of Chief Choupouke, an American Indian who had befriended the settlers.

For more than 350 years Chippokes has been a working farm. Originally, corn and other grains, tobacco, and apple trees were grown here, but in the 19th century peanuts became the principal crop. The last owners, Mr. and Mrs. Victor Stewart, introduced dairy farming. (The plantation was given to the state of Virginia by Mrs. Stewart in 1967.) Today the farm produces corn, peanuts, soybeans, rye, barley, and beef cattle. Exhibits of antique farm equipment on the grounds and displays at the visitors center illustrate the story

 Great Dismal Swamp National Wildlife Refuge. *The wetlands and extensive waterways here provide habitats for black bears, bobcats, otters, deer, and hundreds of bird species.*

of farming here.

Of the many buildings—slaves' quarters, several barns, a large old river house—only the brick kitchen, built in the 18th century, and the mansion are open to the public. The handsome pale-hued brick house, constructed in 1854, is set in semiformal gardens with flowering trees, holly, boxwood, and crape myrtle and is elegantly furnished in traditional colonial style. There's also an old restored sawmill nearby.

Both walking and hiking trails wind through the farmland and meadows, and a picnic area sits on a bluff overlooking the James River. Visitors can rent historic cabins, decorated in period furniture, or choose from 32 campsites with electric and water hook-up. In addition, guests can enjoy an Olympic-size

swimming pool.

Cabin rentals and campsites are available year-round by calling (800) 933-7275. Museum open daily early Apr.–late Oct. Admission charged.
(757) 294-3625
www.dcr.state.va.us

15 Great Dismal Swamp National Wildlife Refuge

Suffolk

The heavily forested wetlands and extensive waterways of the refuge, a quiet, tranquil landscape of some 111,000 acres, spill over from Virginia into North Carolina, providing habitats for black bears, bobcats, otters, white-tailed deer, and hundreds of bird species. Birding is best during spring migration from April to June, when

the greatest diversity of species (particularly warblers) occurs. Two Southern species, the Swainson's warbler and Wayne's warbler, are more common in the Great Dismal Swamp than in other coastal locations. Two unusual natives here, the Dismal Swamp log fern and the Dismal Swamp short-tailed shrew, are found almost nowhere else.

Lake Drummond, a 3,100-acre, round natural lake in the heart of the swamp, is fed by many creeks whose mirrorlike black waters are colored and purified by tannic acid from the bark of various trees and other vegetation in the area. Remnants of a great cypress forest can be seen in the many "knees" encircling the lake.

To enter the swamp by water, you can launch your boat at the public ramp on U.S. Route 17 at Dismal Swamp Canal, which leads to Feeder Ditch. At the Feeder Ditch Spillway boats are carried by tram to the other side, where the creek continues its course to the lake. There is a 10-horsepower motor limit.

An interpretive three-quarter-mile-long boardwalk trail through the wilderness starts just beyond the parking lot at the entrance to Washington Ditch Road, south of Suffolk off Route 642. The ditch was named for our first president, who surveyed the area in 1768. Fishing, permitted only in Lake Drummond, by boat, is best in spring, when the sunfish, catfish, and crappie are plentiful.

Open year-round. Portions of the refuge may be closed in the fall during the white-tailed-deer hunt.
(757) 986-3705
www.greatdismalswamp.fws.gov

Washington

From wave-lashed Tatoosh Island to the lofty heights of Mount Rainier, you'll find historic sites, geologic marvels, and scenic wonders.

Baker Lake. *Highland lakes are fed by glacial streams in this wooded valley of the Pacific Northwest.*

The well-watered land and mild climate have long been hospitable to man. One excellent museum shows evidence of 9,000 years of habitation in the area, while on the Northwest Coast are the remains of an American Indian settlement that prospered more than 500 years ago. There are pioneer settlements of varying size and authenticity, a homestead that delineates the daily life of the early settlers, and a palatial art museum in an unexpected place.

The incomparable forces of nature are demonstrated in the devastation wrought by the eruption of Mount St. Helens and in the regeneration that has taken place. In other places are dramatic landforms sculpted by unimaginable torrents of water released during the last ice age. A limestone cave reveals fascinating formations, and a petrified forest invites inspection. There are scenic viewpoints and places for bird-watching, hiking trails to waterfalls and limpid lakes, and an inland cruise penetrating the North Cascades.

1 Neah Bay

U.S. Hwy. 101 to State Rte. 112 or 113

Famous for its scenery and salmon, Neah Bay also has one of the finest museums of American Indian culture in the United States. The $2 million Makah Cultural and Research Center houses the best of more than 55,000 archaeological items from the remains of Ozette, a nearby Makah Indian village that was buried and preserved by mud slides about 500 years ago. The exhibits—totem poles, seagoing canoes, a wealth of exquisitely crafted artifacts, clothes, household articles, and a reconstruction of a tribal longhouse—give a complete picture of an ancient and highly developed lifestyle.

Cape Flattery, the most northwestern point in the lower 48 states, is a comfortable half-hour hike from Neah Bay through dense forest on a cedar-planked boardwalk and groomed earthen trail with observation decks. The cape is noted for its rugged headlands and crashing surf. At the lookout from the end of the trail, you can see the rugged coastline, Tatoosh Island, and the Cape Flattery Lighthouse, which is unmanned. Koitlah Point and Hobuck Beach, each a short drive from Neah Bay, also offer stunning scenery. Whale watching is popular, and birding is excellent.

Museum open daily June–mid-Sept.;

 Neah Bay. *Boats moored in this fishing village are part of the seafaring economy that thrives on the coastline of the Olympic Peninsula.*

Wed.–Sun. mid-Sept.–May. Admission charged.
(800) 942-4042
www.olympicpeninsula.org

2 Deer Park Campground, Olympic National Park

Port Angeles. Exit south off U.S. Hwy. 101 at Milepost 253 onto Deer Park Rd. and continue 18 miles.

Among firs and pines at the end of a steep, tortuous dirt road, Deer Park has 14 primitive campsites near the summit of 6,007-foot Blue Mountain. A one-mile hike climbs from the camping area to the summit where there are superb views of the Olympic Range, the Strait of Juan de Fuca, Vancouver Island, and the Cascade Mountains. Other trails, steep and arduous in places, lead through valleys and meadows where one is likely to see Columbia black-tailed deer, for which the area is named, as well as Olympic marmots endemic to these mountains. Piper's bell-

flowers, Flett's violets, and a species of astragalus, all unique to the Olympic mountains, bloom here in the summer, as well as swaths of Indian paintbrush, lupines, and avalanche lilies.

In this fragile environment campfires and wood gathering are prohibited. A ranger station is staffed here during the summer.

Road generally open late June–Oct.
Campground open as snow permits.
Campground fee.
(360) 565-3130

www.nps.gov/olym

③ Baker Lake
North off State Rte. 20, near Concrete

Here is the essence of the Pacific Northwest: a land of dense, dark green aromatic forests, snow-capped mountains, large lakes lying in wooded valleys, and highland lakes fed by glacial streams.

Legend

⑩ NUMBERED ATTRACTIONS (Described in text)

CONTROLLED ACCESS HIGHWAYS
━━━ Free
━━━ Toll
═ ═ ═ Under Construction

OTHER HIGHWAYS
━━━ Primary Highway
━━━ Secondary Highway

HIGHWAY MARKERS
⑫ Interstate Route
⑫ U.S. Route
⑫ State Route
12 Distances along Major Highways (in miles)

CITIES AND TOWNS
⊛ National Capital
⊙ State Capital
• Cities, Towns, and Populated Places Type size indicates relative importance
Urban Area

RECREATION AND FEATURES OF INTEREST
National Park
Other Large Park or Recreation Area
--- Trail
--- Ferry

MAPQUEST

Although Baker Lake and Lake Shannon are man-made (created by power-company dams), they sit beautifully and naturally at the base of majestic Mount Baker. At nine-mile-long Baker Lake, which is the more accessible, boating and fishing are the main activities; prior to July 4 each year it is plentifully stocked with rainbow trout. Baker Lake is also one of Washington's best sources of sockeye salmon.

Hikes range from short strolls

to treks requiring several days into rugged backcountry and up the slopes of Mount Baker. Along the area's eastern edge, you can reach wilderness areas of North Cascades National Park.

For an introduction to the region's plant life, take the Shadow of the Sentinels nature trail (near the main entrance highway), which has interpretive signs along the way. Some of the Douglas firs you will see along the trail are more than 600 years

old. At the mouth of Swift Creek, near the north end of Baker Lake, agates and jaspers can be found. Several campgrounds are maintained along the access road. The area is heavily visited on summer weekends.

Access road open year-round, but check in winter for snow closings.
(360) 856-5700, Ext. 515

www.nps.gov/noca/challenger/ch8.htm

4 Stehekin Village and Rainbow Falls

Accessible from Chelan

Stehekin is an American Indian term for "the way through," and it aptly describes the narrow, fjord-like valley in which 50-mile-long Lake Chelan lies, providing a way through the almost impenetrable mountain barrier of the North Cascades.

At the upper end of the lake is the quiet, isolated village of Stehekin; settled in 1885, it has fewer than 100 residents. Even today there are no roads to Stehekin, but it can be reached by a delightful four-hour cruise from Chelan on a diesel-powered boat. Floatplane trips are also available. A shuttle bus runs up the valley from the village to campsites, trailheads, and Rainbow Falls, which plunge 312 feet.

Stehekin is a popular starting point for backpacking into the North Cascades; horses can be rented here, and there are numerous trails to explore. Motorbikes are also available.

Spring and fall are the best times to visit; summers are often crowded. Lodging is limited, and reservations are recommended.

Boat operates daily May–Oct. 31; Call for schedule rest of the year. Admission charged.
(800) 424-3526
www.stehekinvalley.com

5 Gardner Cave, Crawford State Park

12 miles north of Metaline

Shortly beyond the collapsed sinkhole that serves as the entrance to this 2,000-foot-long cavern, you will find a glistening world of flowstone, dripstone formations, and gours, which are dishlike basins in the cave floor. Their names—Christmas Tree, Queen's Throne, Fried Eggs—aptly suggest the strange shapes and effects created by rainwater laden with carbon dioxide as it slowly dripped through the 500-million-year-old metaline limestone here. Perhaps the most striking feature is a speleothem, a floor-to-ceiling column of calcite formed here by the union of a stalactite and a stalagmite.

About 500 feet of the cave is equipped with lighted stairways and walkways and may be viewed on guided tours conducted by the park staff. Wear warm clothing, since the cave temperature remains at about 40°F, and bring a flashlight to peer into darker corners.

To reach the cave, which is the featured attraction of the 49-acre park, you follow a 200-yard paved walkway up a small hill from the parking lot. The walk serves as a nature trail, with plaques identifying the flora.

Open Thur.–Mon., Memorial Day–Labor Day; closed in winter.
(509) 238-4258
www.parks.wa.gov

6 Sun Lakes-Dry Falls State Park

7 miles southwest of Coulee City

What gives this park its awesome beauty is an extinct waterfall. Long ago, as the glaciers of the ice age melted, Dry Falls was the largest waterfall in the world. Five times wider than Niagara and more than twice as high, the surging wall of water dropped 400 feet over a triple crescent 3 1/2 miles wide. As the glaciers that

9 Fort Nisqually, Point Defiance Park. *Tour guides in 1833 dress attempt to build a log cabin in a restored Hudson's Bay Company trading post.*

had dammed the Columbia River retreated and its waters returned to their original bed, the falls were left literally high and dry.

The interpretive center on the rim of the falls explains the geologic story of the Grand Coulee country and Dry Falls and also has exhibits detailing the flora and fauna of the area, including the elephants and rhinoceroses that once lived here.

Most of the park's 4,000 acres are within the canyon formed by the waters of Dry Falls, which left 400-foot-high cliffs on the east and 800-foot-high walls on the western side. Nine small lakes are contained within the park, as well as several natural springs and creeks. It has 15 miles of hiking trails, and bicycles and boats may be rented.

The park is especially lovely in early spring, when melting snows create a series of temporary waterfalls that tumble from the cliff tops.

Park open year-round.
Dry Falls Visitor Center open Wed–Sun., mid-May–mid-Sept. Camping fee.
(360) 902-8844
www.parks.wa.gov

7 Cashmere Pioneer Village and Museum

600 Cotlets Way, Cashmere

This museum and pioneer village traces life as it has been lived in this area for more than 9,000 years.

Touring the museum, one marvels at the ingenuity of the American Indians. Visitors learn, for example, that 5,000 years ago they practiced a form of brain surgery using fermented herbs similar to penicillin. No less impressive are the tiny beads carefully drilled with primitive stone tools, the basketry, and the fine leather and feather work.

The Hudson's Bay Company display gives a vivid view of what

went on in the fur business here in the early 1800s. You not only see an assortment of trade goods but also learn the rates of exchange: a 1-foot-high metal bucket, for instance, bought a 1-foot-high stack of fur pelts.

There are 20 authentic log cabins, all over 120 years old, in the village. Each is amazingly complete, down to the stacks of period-labeled canned goods on the shelves of the general store and the books and inkwells in the schoolhouse.

Many buildings have fascinating stories. The jailhouse was originally designed as a home by an escaped convict. The waterwheel used for irrigation, incorporating the drive shaft of an old Columbia River paddle steamer, is a nationally recognized symbol of the pioneers' ingenuity. There is so much to see here that you may wish to bring a lunch; a picnic area overlooks the village and a river. To avoid crowds, come in April, May, or October.
Open daily March–Nov. 15.
Admission charged.
(509) 782-3230
www.visitcashmere.com

8 Cle Elum Historical Museum
Corner of First and Wright Sts., Cle Elum
On April 5, 1901, when store owner Theron Stafford made the first phone call in Cle Elum, he had some 10 numbers to choose from. In 1966, when the dial system was installed—completing the transition to dial phones in the towns served by Pacific Northwest Bell—he would have been able to reach 96 million in the United States alone. To commemorate

this extraordinary development, the Pacific Northwest Bell Telephone Company gave the original telephone exchange building to the city, along with a fine selection of historic equipment ranging from an 1894 model with a crank to the Touch-Tone designs of today.

The museum, however, is not solely devoted to the telephone. A collection of photographs from newspapers and other sources depicts the life and times of this small coal-mining town. One oddity is a camera owned by Etta Place, who, with Butch Cassidy and the Sundance Kid, tried to rob a nearby bank.
Open Mon.–Fri. and P.M. weekends, Memorial Day–Labor Day; P.M. Tues.–Thurs. the rest of the year.
(509) 674-5702
www.pe.net/~rksnow/wacountycleelum

9 Fort Nisqually, Point Defiance Park
Take the Sixth Ave. exit off Hwy. 16 and continue north on Pearl St., Tacoma
In the deep wilderness where beaver trapping was a lucrative business and the arm of the law was remote, the British Hudson's Bay Company built forts to trade with the Puget Sound Indians and safeguard its money and stock of furs. Such was the case in 1833 when Fort Nisqually was built, a lonely post on Puget Sound.

The fort here today is a reconstruction of one that stood about 17 miles to the south, and it has an authentic look and feeling. Some of the original buildings have been restored and moved to this site. Of the 10 buildings inside the stockade, 3 can be toured: the 1843 Granary

(the oldest standing structure in Washington State), the blacksmith's shop, and the Large House, a reconstruction of the factor's quarters displaying artifacts from the old fort. You can climb the stairs inside the three-story bastions and see a six-pound cannon with the British Royal Crown markings of the 1830s.
Park open year-round. Large House open daily Memorial Day–Labor Day; Wed.–Sun. the rest of the year.
Admission charged.
(253) 591-5339
www.traveltacoma.com

10 Steilacoom
Pierce County, on the shores of Puget Sound
Founded by a sea captain and officially born in 1854, Steilacoom has the distinction of being the oldest incorporated town in the state of Washington. Just strolling

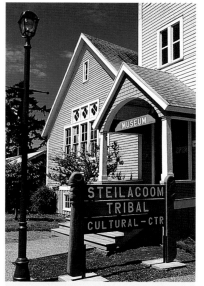

10 Steilacoom. *The American Indian legacy of the Chambers Creek area is celebrated in this Tribal Cultural Center and Museum.*

its streets is a trip back to the past; the small town has 32 buildings and landmarks named to the *National Register of Historic Places.* Lovely historic homes abound, including the Nathaniel Orr Home and Pioneer Orchard, decorated with original furnishings and artifacts. For an old-fashioned treat, visitors can drop in at Bair Drug & Hardware Store. Established in 1895, it now displays patent medicines, hardware relics, and an early town post office, along with a 1906-vintage soda fountain serving up milkshakes and sundaes in style.

Complementing its historic aura, the town has two museums. Steilacoom Historical Museum on Lafayette Street focuses on the years from 1860 to 1900, with fascinating artifacts of local pioneer life. Features include original volumes from Washington Territory's first library, a blacksmith shop, a Victorian parlor, and a barbershop with a unique collection of shaving mugs.

A few blocks away on Main Street, in a former church, the Steilacoom Tribal Cultural Center and Museum celebrates the area's American Indian legacy. Exhibits trace the history of the Steilacoom tribe, with a collection of items ranging from hunting tools to clothing made from cedar bark.

The historic town also hosts several annual events. At the fall Apple Squeeze, visitors can enjoy apple cider fresh off the presses.
Open year-round. Admission charged. Historical Museum: (253) 584-4133
www.steilacoom.org/museum
Tribal Cultural Center and Museum: (253) 584-6308
www.ohwy.com/wa/t/tribaccm.htm

11 Queets Valley Rain Forest, Olympic National Park

The cooling of moisture-laden ocean air as it is driven upward by mountain slopes is responsible for the unusually heavy annual precipitation—about 145 inches—in this remote part of the Olympic National Park. The result is a temperate rain forest that grows with almost tropical intensity. Sitka spruces and Western hemlocks are the dominant trees, along with Douglas firs and Western red cedars. Club moss hangs everywhere in festoons, and licorice fern grows in the shade of big-leaf maples. There is scarcely a square inch of soil that does not support vegetation of some kind. A well-maintained 14-mile dirt road following the Queets River gives access to the valley.

The most famous inhabitants here are the noble Roosevelt elk, frequently seen in meadows along the easy three-mile loop trail, which begins at the campsite at road's end. You might also glimpse black-tailed deer or a pileated woodpecker. Other hikes involve fording the river, but this should be done only in summer when the water is low.

Trout and salmon fishing is good, and visitors can see salmon spawning in the fall and winter. Float trips are popular from April through June. Be careful of submerged logs and overhanging boughs, however. There are launching places for boats, canoes, and rafts along the access road and at the campsite.

Park and campground open year-round; call for conditions. Camping fee.
(360) 565-3130
www.nps.gov/olym/queets.htm

12 Leadbetter Point, Willapa National Wildlife Refuge

Stackpole Rd., Oysterville
The three-mile-long refuge at the tip of Long Beach Peninsula is a world of mud flats, sand dunes, saltmarsh, and oyster beds—a home or way station for more than 200 species of birds, especially during the migratory seasons. Virtually every kind of shorebird in Oregon and Washington congregates here at some time during the year. Black brants by the thousands stop on their way north from Mexico in April and May, and scores of sooty shearwaters en route to New Zealand drop by in August. In January the point is a good place to glimpse such rarities as gyrfalcons and snowy owls.

On the ocean side of the point, you may see seals sunning themselves. In summer the 500-acre Salicornia salt marsh, which has never been dredged, produces a rich display of grindelia, jaumea, asters, and other wildflowers. The refuge is accessible only by foot trails from the parking lot. Mosquitoes are numerous and repellent is recommended.

Open year-round.
(800) 451-2542
www.funbeach.com

13 Cowlitz County Historical Museum

405 Allen St., Kelso
This well-organized museum chronicles the main themes of 19th and 20th century life in the Pacific Northwest. Canoe anchors, arrowheads, and carrying baskets reflect the American Indians' mode of survival in this abundant land. The hardships of pioneers on their overland journey and the struggles of early settlers are recalled by displays of early-day tools and equipment, as well as an 1884 cramped but sturdy log cabin lived in by a Toutle River settler.

The all-important logging industry is also portrayed. The rapid changes in lifestyles of the Northwest are depicted in colorful tableaux of a general store, with a stereoscopic viewer on the premises, a steamboat dock, and a railroad depot. An exhibition of local bird life completes the collection.

Open Tues.–Sun. Closed major holidays.
(360) 577-3119
www.co.cowlitz.wa.us/museum

14 Lewis County Historical Museum

Off Interstate 5, Chehalis
Tucked inside a classic brick train depot, built in 1912 and spanning about a block in length, this charming museum evokes pioneer life in Lewis County, the first official county in Washington State. Four galleries provide a trip back in time, starting with displays celebrating the region's original settlers, the Cowlitz and Chehalis Indians. Visitors are also invited to step inside a blacksmith shop and a vintage second-hand store, as well as ponder typical farming, logging, and mining tools.

Child-friendly attractions include a bygone mercantile store and the "Home Sweet Home" house, stocked with old-time dress-up clothes and pretend cooking utensils. Grown-ups can arrange for a guided tour of the museum or sign up for one of the periodic classes offered in pioneering crafts and skills, like soap making.

Nearby, the Chehalis-Centralia Railroad offers rides on a splendidly restored 1916 steam locomotive. Complete with toots and whistles, the train ride traverses a nine-mile section of track through the Chehalis River Valley, past verdant pastures and rolling hills. Dinner

15 Mount St. Helens National Volcanic Monument. *The Independence Pass trail, near Norway Pass, offers a sense of the scope of the volcano's eruption, with Spirit Lake in the background.*

excursions are offered twice a month from June through September.

Open year-round Tues.–Sun. Closed Mondays and major holidays. The train operates May–Sept., weekends only. Admission charged for both.

(360) 748-0831

www.lewiscountymuseum.org

(360) 748-9593

www.ccrra.com

15 Mount St. Helens National Volcanic Monument

Exit 49, off Interstate 5 in Castle Rock, to State Hwy. 504

On May 18, 1980, a volcanic eruption blew out the northern face of Mount St. Helens. The stupendous explosion displaced nearly a cubic mile of material and threw rock and ash over 14 miles into the atmosphere; devastated 240 square miles of forest, river, and lake; and took 57 lives.

The easily accessible Johnston Ridge Observatory is in the heart of the blast zone and offers state-of-the-art interpretive displays and a walk on the Eruption Trail.

Another dramatic view of the destruction is from Windy Ridge. On the way the road passes through dense forests of Douglas fir and then abruptly enters the devastated area of blown-down timber and valleys filled with ash. At Windy Ridge (south of Randle, Forest Service Roads 25 and 99), you are only four miles from the crater; directly below you lies Spirit Lake, choked with logs.

For an even closer look into the crater and at the growing lava dome, stop at Norway Pass, just off Forest Service Road 26, and take the 2 1/2-mile hike leading through the downed forest to a

16 Sunrise, Mount Rainier National Park. *Blue lupines carpet the meadows in summertime at the foot of breathtaking Mount Rainier.*

fine viewpoint. Along the way you'll notice evidence of the recovery process as lupines, fireweed, and pussytoes grow up through the blanket of ash.

Naturalists at Johnston Ridge give interpretive lectures several times a day during the summer. Further information is available at the Iron Creek Information Station on Forest Service Road 25, south of Randle, and there are explanatory displays at the Mount St. Helens visitors center on Silver Lake, east of Castle Rock. The Coldwater Ridge visitors center invites sightseers to discover the fascinating ways that plants and animals have reappeared.

Forest Service access roads generally open June–Oct. Forest pass required.

(360) 577-3137

www.fs.fed.us/gpnf/mshnvm

16 Sunrise, Mount Rainier National Park

State Hwy. 410 east of Tacoma

Among America's most ravishing sights is the 14,411-foot volcanic peak of Mount Rainier with its 27 glaciers reaching down like fin-

gers to subalpine meadows carpeted in summer with wildflowers.

The Sunrise area, 7 miles east of the summit at an elevation of 6,400 feet (the highest point you can reach in the park by car), is an excellent place to admire this majestic mountain and to explore a region where a variety of plants and animals manage to survive in extremely marginal circumstances. The 14-mile paved access road to Sunrise climbs through breathtaking mountain scenery.

Hiking trails start at the Sunrise visitors center and lead through subalpine firs, whitebark pines, and Alaska cedars. At the timberline are gnarled and dwarfed trees, some of which may have taken 75 years to reach a height of 18 inches. Rainier's famous meadows of wildflowers bloom in two stages on the eastern slope. In late June or early July you can expect to see pasqueflowers and avalanche lilies; these are followed by cinquefoils, blue lupines, asters, and Indian paintbrush.

There are no accommodations at Sunrise; the nearest campsites are nearby at White River Campground.

Open Memorial Day–Labor Day.

Admission charged.

(360) 569-2211

www.nps.gov/mora

17 Fort Simcoe State Park

White Swan

Work on Fort Simcoe began in the summer of 1856 amid growing hostility between the local Yakima Indians and the settlers and gold seekers whose quest for a better life often led them to encroach upon tribal lands. After the defeat of the Yakimas in the war of 1858, the fort served as an Indian agency headquarters for 63 years.

Of the original 35 buildings, 5 still stand: 3 captains' dwellings, a squared-log blockhouse, and the quite unmilitary-looking commander's house, which is restored and furnished as it was in 1858. A log barracks and 2 additional blockhouses have been reconstructed. A small museum has displays about the history of the fort and the Yakimas, including a life-size diorama of a Yakima winter house.

The fort occupies a commanding rise where the foothills of the Cascade Mountains yield to the plain along Toppenish Creek. Traditionally the site was a meeting place for the Yakimas, who called it *mool-mool,* meaning "bubbling water," because of the nearby spring. As you stroll through the oak groves of the 200 acres here, don't be surprised if you hear a rat-a-tat-tat overhead.

This area is also a favored breeding site for Lewis's woodpeckers.

Open daily Apr.–Sept.; weekends only, Oct.–Mar.

(509) 874-2372

www.parks.wa.gov

 Maryhill Museum of Art. *This art-filled chateau sits in majestic solitude on a remote bluff overlooking the Columbia River Gorge.*

Maryhill Museum of Art

Washington Scenic Hwy. 14, south of Goldendale

The palatial stone mansion set high on a remote spot overlooking the Columbia River, surrounded by 26 acres of parklike gardens, was built by the multimillionaire Samuel Hill, the son-in-law of railroad magnate James J. Hill and an international peace promoter, world traveler, and friend of royalty. Sam Hill, of Quaker parentage, had intended to start a Quaker agricultural community here with Maryhill as his residence. The colony did not materialize, and he was persuaded by Loie Fuller, an avant-garde dancer, to turn the building into a museum. Later his friend Queen Marie of Romania dedicated the museum to beauty and peace as a symbol of her gratitude for American aid after World War I. In 1935, four years after Hill's death, the wealthy art patroness Alma Spreckels donated part of her own art collection to the museum.

The centerpiece of the museum is Sam Hill's collection of "Rodin's Rodins"—bronzes, plasters and sketches that the famous sculptor

kept in his studio for reference. Among them is a plaster cast of a reduced version of "The Thinker," the only one in existence.

Other displays include 19th-century American and European paintings, weaponry, icons, American Indian baskets, antique chess sets, 1940s French fashion mannequins, and the Queen Marie Room, where you'll find her throne, a coronation gown, and many of her personal belongings. There is also an outdoor sculpture garden.

Maryhill is as much a curiosity as it is a museum of fine art. Nothing really quite prepares you for this imposing structure—filled with priceless art and artifacts— literally in the middle of nowhere. An eccentric added attraction is a concrete model of England's Stonehenge, visible from the highway leading to Maryhill: It was built by Hill as a memorial to the men of Klickitat County who died in World War I.

Museum open daily mid-Mar.–mid.-Nov. Admission charged.
(509) 773-3733
www.maryhillmuseum.org

Olmstead Place State Park

Ellensburg. Take Exit 109 off I-90 and continue north to Mountain View Ave. Turn east on Mountain View, which becomes Kittitas Hwy., and continue to North Ferguson Rd.

Samuel and Sarah Olmstead, attracted by the grasslands and rich soil of the Kittitas Valley, arrived here in 1875, built a 40- by 30-foot cabin, and began farming a 160-acre homestead. Their family lived here for two generations, including the year 1878, when the cabin was used as a fort in the Nez Perce War.

Today this historical park offers an intriguing opportunity to see how a Kittitas Valley family farm developed from the 1870s through the 1950s. Touring the four rooms of the original cabin, you'll see a long rifle owned by a neighbor and the saddles, crockery, cookware, china, storage chests, organ, stove, and desk that were the stuff of the family's daily life.

A house built in 1908 is more

Olmstead Place State Park. *Most of the original furnishings are still inside this cabin, built in 1875, and home to the Olmstead family for two generations.*

elegantly appointed, with wrought-iron lamps, carved desks, and a library furnished with a red plush velvet love seat. The renovated red barn—originally used for grain storage—now houses hands-on farm activities and exhibits. Much of the vintage farming equipment seen on the grounds is operated during the threshing bee held the second weekend after Labor Day. You can also tour the granary, wagon shed, and dairy barn.

The three-quarter-mile Altapes Creek Trail leads along the tree-lined creek to the picturesque Seaton schoolhouse, a small log cabin built more than 100 years ago. Altapes is a Kittitas word meaning "most beautiful creek in the valley."

Open year-round for day use. Guided tours of historic buildings on weekends Memorial Day–Labor Day and by appointment all year.
(509) 925-1943
www.parks.wa.gov

Ginkgo Petrified Forest State Park

Vantage

Specimens from one of the world's most spectacularly varied fossil forests can be seen here on a 7,470-acre site that encompasses prehistoric swamp and lake beds repeatedly inundated by lava. Felled trees from the dense forests of the Miocene Epoch—not just the ginkgo for which the park is named, but some 200 other species—were preserved beneath the solidified basalt, gradually turning to brilliantly colored stone as mineral deposits replaced their cell structure. Ice age erosion brought them to light again.

Now cross-sections of the fossilized logs can be seen in the park's Heritage Area Interpretive Center along with an array of intelligently planned explanatory exhibits. The area also contains a number of delicate American Indian carvings incised in black basalt. You can see logs in their original setting by taking either of the hikes through the Natural Area, the first a three-quarter-mile interpretive trail, the second a 2¹/₂-mile trek.

It's a good idea to make your camping headquarters at Wanapum Recreation Area, which is located within the park three miles south of Vantage on the shore of the Columbia River. Wanapum provides excellent facilities for fishermen and other outdoor enthusiasts.

Park open year-round. Camping fee. Interpretive Center open daily, Memorial Day–Labor Day.
(509) 856-2700
www.parks.wa.gov

21 Palouse Falls State Park
Southeast of Washtucna
The grace, beauty, and power of Palouse Falls as it drops 200 feet into a horseshoe-shaped basin create one of Washington's most spectacular sights. From the park viewpoint you can photograph the awesome surge of water and the rainbows created by its sunstruck mist. Surefooted visitors hike 250 feet down to the basin for a water-level view (or to try for catfish, which spawn in the canyon pools). Others walk the path that meanders around the bluffs above the falls for a bird's-eye view. The hike takes about 20 minutes. Below the falls the wild waters of the Palouse rush through its nat-

ural canyon, which extends for eight miles, and then wind among rolling bluffs to empty into the Snake River.

The falls and canyon have a long history. Twenty thousand years ago a glacial lake spread from northern Idaho to northwestern Montana, covering more than 3,000 square miles. As the climate warmed, the ice dam burst and a tremendous flood of water and debris roared down the Snake and Columbia rivers, rearranging the landscape as it went.

The canyon attracts many bird species, including owls that nest in the cliffs. Picnic tables and a small campground are available here.

Open year-round. Camping fee. Closed to camping Sept. 25–Mar. 15.
(360) 902-8844
www.parks.wa.gov

22 Whitman Mission National Historic Site
Walla Walla
This pastoral setting of open fields with a millpond, a memorial obelisk, a reconstructed covered wagon, some ruins, and a grave site is the scene of a tragic conflict of cultures that took place in 1847.

Marcus and Narcissa Whitman, along with their companions, Henry and Eliza Spalding, came west in 1836 to convert American Indians to Christianity. The mission that they built here at Waiilatpu soon became an important way station for thousands of other immigrants. Whitman's efforts at conversion, however, achieved far less success. The Cayu didn't want to give up their long-standing traditions and centuries-old spiritual and religious

 Whitman Mission National Historic Site. *This covered wagon was used by pioneers traveling west on the Oregon Trail.*

beliefs. Their tenuous trust of settlers collapsed when an epidemic of measles killed half the tribe. The Indians had less resistance to the disease, while many of the non-Indian settlers survived. Believing they were being poisoned, a band of desperate Cayuses attacked the mission on November 29, 1847, killing the Whitmans and 11 others and taking 50 captives who later were ransomed. About 250 members of the Cayuse village died as well. The immigrant's punitive campaign against the Cayuses drove them from their land and into the mountains.

The visitors center at this 98-acre site displays implements belonging to the Whitmans and some beautiful Cayuse garments, including a feathered headdress, a beaded leather shirt, and dresses ornamented with shells. A short audiovisual show describes the mission's history. In summer, craft demonstrations are presented.

Open year-round except Thanksgiving, Christmas, and New Year's Day.
(509) 522-6360
www.nps.gov/whmi

23 Fields Spring State Park
Anatone
Named for an early homesteader who developed a spring as a water supply for his nearby ranch, this pleasant 742-acre park is situated on a trail once used by the Nez Perce Indians. The prime attractions today are the splendid view of three states from the top of Puffer Butte and the excellent birding. Seven kinds of woodpeckers have been observed, and ruffed grouse, hawks, great horned owls, and various warblers are common.

Puffer Butte is aptly named, since the mile-long trail to the 4,500-foot summit is fairly strenuous as it climbs through meadows and woodlands of fir, spruce, and ponderosa pine. Deer and elk are occasionally seen along the trail. From the top of the butte, you can look directly down into the canyon of the Grande Ronde River 3,000 feet below. To the west lie the forests and rolling hills of Washington, to the south Oregon's Wallowa Mountains, and to the east the Snake River and the mountains of Idaho.

The park has a campground and recreation areas. In winter a sled run provides downhill thrills, and the park is a popular departure point for cross-country skiers.

Open year-round. Camping fee.
(360) 902-8844
www.parks.wa.gov

Cathedral State Park. *These giant hemlocks stretch 90 feet into the sky and are about 350 years old.*

West Virginia

Deep in the forested hills and valleys are rewarding encounters with nature— and with the vibrant history of a hard-won land.

Spectacular waterfalls, a great hemlock forest, and a high plateau accent the dramatic natural scene in this mountainous state. The abundant game that made this rugged land a favorite hunting ground for many American Indian tribes is still appreciated—and has been protected in a wildlife center and fish hatchery. The demanding life of the early pioneers is depicted in two excellent farm museums. The prehistoric Mound Builders, who were the first inhabitants of this land, left behind invaluable treasures for us to explore 2,000 years later.

1 Grave Creek Mound Historic Site

Moundsville. Take 8th St. off Rte. 2 and continue to Jefferson St.
The largest conical mound in the Americas, Grave Creek Mound rises impressively to a height of 69 feet from a base 295 feet in diameter. It contains an estimated 60,000 tons of earth, all of it carried in baskets from the encircling moat and the nearby borrow pits. At an average load of 40 pounds per basket, the construction required 3 million basketfuls.

Built about 2,000 years ago by American Indians of the Adena culture (which blossomed in the Ohio Valley), the structure was discovered in the early 1800s by white settlers. Its first excavation, in 1838, revealed two burial chambers containing human remains, ornaments, tools fashioned of bone, stone, and shell, and a small tablet of sandstone inscribed with signs that have been interpreted as a kind of pre-Columbian writing.

On climbing the spiral path to the top and looking down upon the Ohio River and the surrounding hills, one can't help wondering what inspired the Mound Builders to create their massive works. The mound provokes a perplexed melancholy over a mystery that may never be solved and a people lost forever.

2 Valley Falls State Park. *The flat rocks, beaten smooth by a relentless stream of water, are a reminder of nature's force and of the geologic passage of time.*

Adjacent to the mound is the Delf Norona Museum which contains artifacts and other displays dealing with the mound, the Adena, and associated cultures in the vicinity. The modern facility, with its natural brick façade and pyramid-shaped skylights, is an architectural tribute to a prehistoric era. It also features a fine-art gallery and a small theatre, which offers musical and theatrical performances.
Open daily year-round except major holidays. Admission charged for

Adena culture exhibits.
(304) 843-4128
www.wvculture.org/sites/gravecreek. html

2 Valley Falls State Park
Fairmont
This was once the site of the largest Cherokee village in the area. The Indians called the place Evil Spirit Falls; white explorers called it Hard Around Falls, and later, Falls of the Big Muddy (or

Monongahela). Still later, the falls took the name of David Tygart, a pioneer settler.

At the head of a long canyon a series of four falls flows over beds of rock, as smooth as if they had been cast from a mold, into a large pool below. From the broad, flat rocks on the riverbank you can get an eye-level view of the upper falls: thin tongues of polished rock, over which a filigree of water and air rushes in a billowing curve, to surge against the rocks at your feet in a churning swirl of pale, glass-green waves and sparkling bubbles. The roar and flow of the falls is hypnotic, and you soon wonder whether the water or the rock you stand on is moving.

You can also see the grooves where rock was cut for a millrace in 1837. In the past 150 years the rock has hardly worn at all. Its comparison with the slick, smooth surface at the lip of the falls is a reminder of the incomprehensible span of geologic time. A bridge crosses the millrace to the remnants of a gristmill built about the same time.

The 1,145-acre park offers a small picnic ground near the falls and eight hiking trails in woodlands where wild turkeys, white-tailed deer, and red foxes may be seen. Walleyed pike, channel catfish, and smallmouth bass are likely catches in the stream. Spring is the best time to visit for good weather and the greatest volume of water.

Open year-round.
(304) 367-2719
www.wvparks.com

▌3 Cathedral State Park
Aurora
The name of the park is fully justified by the great upward loom of the giant hemlocks, the subdued light, and the enduring silence here. The majestic trees, estimated to be 350 years old, reach up to 90 feet in height with trunks 21 feet in girth. Among them is the largest hemlock in the state. One of the last living stands of the virgin hemlocks that once flourished in the highlands, the forest was proclaimed a natural history landmark in 1966.

Cathedral Trail makes a loop through the 133-acre park. For part of the way it follows the course of fern-bordered Rhine Creek. Pathways wander off to the side and then return to the main trail, allowing one to explore further. In the grove of huge trees the light is a soft, subaqueous green, and the understory is spacious.

Each tree is in its own clearing, and many are encircled at a respectful distance by rhododendrons. A wide variety of wildflowers add beauty to the scene. Nature is allowed to take its course in the park with little human intervention. At least one giant has become entirely stripped of bark and stands like a skeleton among its living relatives. Here and there one finds a fallen tree clothed in soft green moss.

The park provides charcoal grills and a shelter in the picnic area and a playground. Spring and summer are especially lovely here, but the park is also inviting in the fall, when it is less frequented.

Open year-round.
(304) 735-3771
www.cathedralstatepark.com

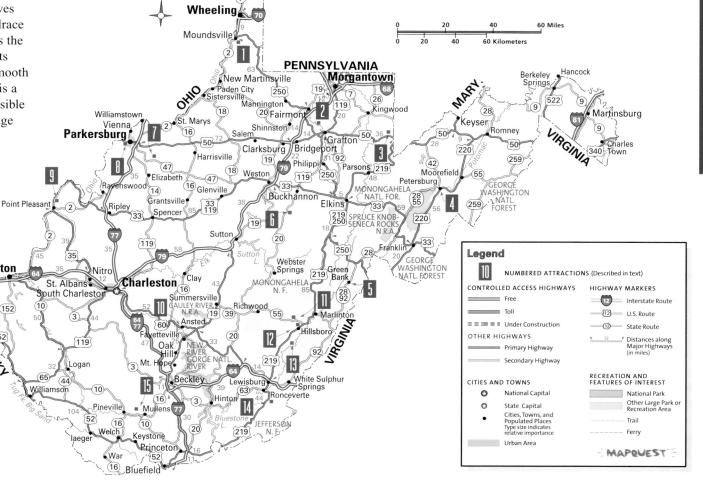

4 Petersburg Trout Hatchery
Petersburg

Regardless of whether you prefer trout in a stream or on a dinner plate, it is fascinating to see how the demand for that prized fish is met. At this hatchery (one of 10 in the state) 1 million trout, rainbow and golden, are raised every year for introduction into West Virginia's streams.

The golden trout were bred selectively in Petersburg from a gift of 10,000 rainbow fry given to the hatchery in 1949, and were introduced on a large scale into West Virginia's rivers in 1963, the state's centennial year. The golden is indeed a shining gold color with red-striped sides and red-veined fins and tail.

The grown fish and breeding stock are kept in four large, dark pools constantly aerated by fountains, side sprays, and a stream flowing through.

The trout can be seen swimming in shoals, darting, or resting. Younger trout—which are 1 1/2 to 2 inches long and dark brown in color—are kept in two raceways, each holding some 100,000 of the fish. The fry that grow into these fingerlings are raised indoors in shallow tanks about 15 feet long.

The trout to be released in streams are transported in stocking trucks through which water is constantly circulated by an electric pump. About 90 percent of the fish will be caught by appreciative anglers enjoying a day out on the water.

Perhaps the most interesting time to visit the hatchery is late September–early October, when spawning and hatching occur.

Open year-round.
(304) 257-4014

5 The National Radio Astronomy Observatory
Green Bank

The radio dishes and antennas of this observatory loom from the valley floor to tune in to distant galaxies, quasars, and pulsars. Operated by a private consortium of universities, the observatory also maintains research facilities in Arizona and New Mexico. It chose this secluded valley, which is part of the National Radio Quiet Zone, for one of its sites because the surrounding hills provide a shield from harmful radio interference.

The site is home to one of the most advanced astronomical instruments on Earth, the Robert C. Byrd Green Bank Telescope (GBT). The GBT is the world's largest fully steerable radio telescope, amd the largest moving structure on land. At 485 feet in height, it is taller than the Statue of Liberty. Other equipment here includes a 140-foot equatorially mounted telescope, and the interferometer, which makes use of three telescopes together.

The center also has several historical telescopes and antennas, including an exact replica of the Jansky telescope. Karl Jansky's study of the Milky Way in 1930–32 led to the recognition that radio signals are produced by natural processes in space.

Learning of the mind-boggling work that goes on here and seeing the sci-fi landscape and equipment, you get a thrilling and yet eerie awareness of remote worlds. A 30-minute narrated bus tour of the site, following a 15-minute movie on radio astronomy, is offered. The tours begin on the hour and depart from the observatory. Cameras are permitted.

Open daily mid-June–Labor Day; weekends only Sept.–Oct.
(304) 456-2011
www.gb.nrao.edu

5 The National Radio Astronomy Observatory. *Visitors will be starstruck by the Robert C. Byrd Green Bank Telescope, one of the most advanced astronomical instruments on Earth.*

6 West Virginia State Wildlife Center
On Rtes. 4 and 20, French Creek

At this well-kept, parklike zoo you can see the wild animals and birds that once were—and mostly still are—native to West Virginia. The 329-acre farm was started in 1923 to protect diminishing wildlife and to pen-raise animals and game birds for release into the countryside. That program was eventually discontinued, and in recent years the place has been devoted to education and recreation. Native wildlife wander freely in the fenced natural habitats arranged along a mile-long loop walk.

The most spectacular of the creatures to be seen are the mountain lion of formidable size, black bears, elks, river otters, and bison. Among the more engaging specimens are white-tailed deer, coyotes, raccoons, and showy ring-necked pheasants. Wild turkeys, foxes, timber wolves, opossums, and other species are also at home here. In addition, the Wildlife Center maintains a stocked trout pond, open to fishermen, and a spacious picnic area.

Open year-round; admission charged Apr.–Nov.
(304) 924-6211
www.dnr.state.wv.us

7 North Bend State Park
Cairo

In this beautiful 1,405-acre park one has the sensation of wandering a high plateau. The central area lies on a bluff at a horseshoe bend in the North Fork of the Hughes River, flowing placidly several hundred feet below. A scenic trail, overhung by large sycamores and hemlocks, skirts the rim of the escarpment, sometimes descending into and climbing out of the miniature valleys that score the sides of the bluff and run down to the river's edge. Other trails through the woodlands lead to a variety of overlooks and dramatic rock formations. The 72-mile North Bend Rail Trail is designed for hiking, mountain biking, and horseback riding. The woods are inhabited by white-tailed deer that are remarkably unafraid.

In addition to the accommodations provided by the North Bend Lodge, which is situated on a ridge overlooking the river valley, the park offers vacation cabins and tree-shaded campsites.

A nature trail for the handicapped with information stations in print and braille, outdoor games and equipment for the blind, a swimming pool, and playgrounds are among the many facilities found here. Bicycling can be enjoyed along the roads and three of the trails.

Open year-round.
(800) 225-5982
www.northbendsp.com

 Blennerhassett Island Historical State Park

In the Ohio River, 2 miles west of Parkersburg
A scenic, 20-minute ride on a vintage 19th-century riverboat is the perfect way to begin a day at this quaint, tranquil island—and just about the only way to get there. Sternwheeler ferries depart from the docks of downtown Parkersburg, just outside a museum devoted to the island's colorful, turbulent history.

On the island, visitors can wander through craft and specialty shops, catch a horse-drawn carriage ride, stroll along sandy beaches and tree-shaded paths, or sit and enjoy a picnic in one of the many inviting sheltered spots. Of course, no one can miss the island's centerpiece and namesake: Blennerhassett Mansion.

Originally built in 1798, it was the proud homestead of Harman Blennerhassett, a wealthy Irish aristocrat. Seven years later, he was forced to flee the island due to charges of complicity in a treason plot with the infamous Aaron Burr. In 1811, the magnificent mansion burned to the ground. More than 150 years later, archaeologists unearthed its foundations and inspired its glorious rebuilding. Today, guides in period garb conduct tours through the reconstructed mansion, as work on furnishing and adorning its interior continues.

Harman Blennerhassett was not the island's only notable resident. Tracing the island's roots back to the ice age, it was claimed by American Indian tribes. During the 1760s, the celebrated Delaware

Indian Chief Nemacolin made his home here, and it was in the 1780s that the white settlers came. In its pioneer heyday, Blennerhassett was visited by such legendary figures as Walt Whitman, Henry Clay, and Johnny Appleseed.
The museum is open year-round, but the island is only reachable when the sternwheeler ferry runs, from the first weekend in May through the last weekend of October. Separate admission fees for each.
(304) 420-4800
www.blennerhassettislandstatepark. com/history.html

West Virginia State Farm Museum

Just off Rte. 62, 4 miles north of Point Pleasant
This memorial to America's early-day farmers and pioneers takes one back to the time when there were no shopping malls, and do-it-yourself was a way of life. The demonstrations of broom making, quilting, and other such activities (given at special times) bring the scene to life. In early autumn you can see the steam engine and belt-driven threshing machine in action and buy the cider, apple butter, and molasses made here.

Among the 31 buildings on the farm's 50 acres are an 1805 log cabin, a one-room schoolhouse, an operating blacksmith's shop, a country store that is stocked with nostalgic items, and a replica of a Lutheran church built in 1815. The church, a simple log cabin, has a safety balcony for women and children and a musket rack by the entrance—reminders of the conflicts between the Indians and the encroaching white settlers.

Also found here are fascinating collections of household and farm equipment of the 1800s, barnyard animals, and a museum with a taxidermic collection of birds and animals. With advance notice groups can arrange to purchase a special "pioneer" lunch here.
Open Tues.–Sun. Apr. 1–Nov. 15. Admission free; donations encouraged.
(304) 675-5757
www.pointpleasantwv.org

7 North Bend State Park. *Visitors can stay in one of these deluxe cedar cabins, tucked away in a white pine forest.*

10 Contentment Museum
On Rte. 60 in Ansted

The antebellum house, restored one-room schoolhouse, and small museum that make up this complex provide an insight into the quiet rural life of 19th-century West Virginia.

The house, built about 1830 with a white-columned veranda across the front, was named Contentment by the wife of the ex-Confederate officer who acquired the property in 1872. One can easily imagine the serenity the couple found in this setting. Among the modestly elegant antique furnishings one particularly charming piece is the fainting sofa, popular generations ago, when ladies were expected to be creatures of delicate sensibilities.

The schoolhouse, with its benches, desks with inkwells, Burnside stove, and bell tower, evokes the days of blue-back spellers and *McGuffey's Readers*. At the back of the building are the privies that were required before the advent of indoor plumbing. Among the museum displays are moonshiners' copper stills, confiscated by the revenuers, an 1880s wedding gown, a quaint Godey trunk, old pictures of the mining camps, Civil War memorabilia, and American and Indian artifacts.
Open Mon.–Sat. and P.M. Sun., June–Sept. Admission charged; those under 12 free.
(800) 927-0263
www.newrivercvb.com/ansted

11 Cranberry Glades Botanical Area
Elkins. Reached by Forest Road 102, one-half mile west of the nature center on Rte. 39/55.
One walks in wonder here in an open, treeless basin completely

11 Cranberry Glades Botanical Area. *This unusual 750-acre ecological preserve contains many unique plants, some descended from seeds that took root here more than 10,000 years ago.*

out of character with the dense surrounding forest of evergreens and hardwoods.

In the four bogs that make up the glades are species of cranberries, bog rosemary, mosses, lichens, and deep layers of peat that are native to the Canadian muskeg some 800 miles to the north.

The major theory about how this intriguing island of botanical nonconformity came to be is that the deep layers of sphagnum moss developed over the centuries in shallow basins created by the shifting sedimentation of the local streams; plants able to tolerate the extremely acid conditions eventually became established.

The glades are here to be enjoyed. In the botanical area, which encompasses 750 acres, a half-mile-long loop boardwalk with interpretive signs gives you a close view of two of the bogs, with their cranberry vines, thickets of chokeberry, wild raisin, speckled alder, spongy mosses, grasses, sedges, and flowers. Among the latter are swamp candle, orchids, trilliums, monkshood, swamp buttercups, jewelweed, and the carnivorous sundew.

The adjacent 35,864-acre Cranberry Wilderness Area (which is within a black bear sanctuary) offers more than 70 miles of trails varying in length from 1 1/2 to 13 1/2 miles and primitive campsites for backpackers. Adjoining the wilderness area is the Cranberry Back Country, where 20,000 acres are laced with trails, and abandoned roads are suitable for hiking, riding, and cross-country skiing. The nature center has information on all three areas. Accessible year-round, weather permitting.
Nature center open daily Apr. 1–Nov. 30.
(304) 653-4826
www.fs.fed.us/r9/mnf/sp/
cranberry_glades.html

12 Pearl S. Buck Birthplace
Hillsboro

Pearl Comfort Sydenstricker, who is better known under her married name, was born here on a small farm in 1892. The writer, who won acclaim in the 1930s for her novel about China, *The Good Earth,* became the first American woman to receive both the Pulitzer Prize (in fiction) and the Nobel Prize (in literature).

The gracious white frame homestead, with its balconied portico, built in the 1840s by her mother's family, the Stultings, is furnished approximately as it was in 1892. Much of the furniture was built by Mrs. Buck's grandfather. The memorabilia displayed include photos of the author during her years in China and the Bible that her father, a missionary, had transcribed into Chinese.

On the property is the Stulting barn, which has been restored and contains an assortment of farm implements of the same period. The Sydenstricker house, in which Pearl Buck's father was born 40 miles away, has been relocated here as part of this interesting historical farm complex.
Open May–Oct.
(304) 653-4430
www.wvnet.edu/~omb00996

13 Beartown State Park
Hillsboro

Except for the boardwalk, this area of unusual rock formations is entirely the creation of nature. The rock is Droop sandstone, which tends to break up into huge blocks along nearly vertical planes. As the result of erosion, these blocks have shifted downward, causing deep fissures of varying width and sheer cliffs.

Some of the cracks are two or three feet wide with flat floors, suggesting streets running between buildings. Colonies of black bears are said to have lived among these rocks because they contained many cavelike openings—hence the name.

To see this fascinating place, one goes by a sturdily-railed boardwalk over torrents of fallen rock and deep, mossy, straight-walled crevasses. Tall, feathery hemlocks grow from towering wedges of rock as though from the prows of ships; the roots of the trees are sometimes high above you, sometimes below, and often crawling down the sides of the rock like writhing snakes. Rockcap ferns, light green and heavy-textured, grow like small trees on many rocks, bewildering one's sense of scale. In accompaniment to this grandeur, windsong fills the air in the trees and crevasses and among the boulders.

The boardwalk crosses miniature canyons and valleys in the rock, their sides occasionally blushed with patches of pale red, yellow, and orange and streaked with mineral deposits. Then, at ground level, the boardwalk ends, and you stroll through a deep crevasse, its rock walls pocked with skull-like depressions and erosion holes and worn into soft pleats, folds, and bony skeletal formations.

The way out connects with the boardwalk and then back to the parking lot, where you can have a refreshing drink of water from a hand-pumped fountain. The half-mile walk has interpretive signs. The best time to visit the park is in the autumn, when the crowds are not as large.

Foot travel welcome year-round; gate opened by request only Nov.–Apr.
(304) 653-4254

www.beartownstatepark.com

14 Organ Cave
Rte. 63, between Rtes. 60 and 219

This national natural landmark is distinguished for its geological and archaeological features, its historical significance, and its impressive length (40 miles) and depth (486 feet). For centuries, long before it was officially opened as a commercial cave in 1835, explorers have been mesmerized by its massive passageways, now meticulously mapped.

Throughout, stunning limestone sculptures, formed from the bones of prehistoric animals and forces of water, date back hundreds of millions of years and continue to evolve today. The name Organ Cave was inspired by the largest, and arguably most awesome, of all the calcite formations, evoking a grand church organ.

In addition to its astounding natural architecture, the cave contains the largest collection of saltpeter vats in the United States, mined during the Civil War for making gunpowder. Beyond its practical value, the cave also served the spiritual needs of soldiers: religious services for over 1,000 of Gen. Robert E. Lee's men were held in the shelter of its huge underground entranceway.

Avid spelunkers can sign up for a variety of specialized guided tours. For those ready to climb and crawl, there are "wild" tours which lead you deep underground and bring you face-to-face with such wonders as a trio of breath-taking waterfalls that cascade over a 90-foot drop, or a rare growth of gypsum flowers, or bustling communities of bats. On weekends, Organ Cave resounds with gospel singing, showcasing talented voices from surrounding counties.

Open daily year-round.
Admission charged. Additional fees for specialized tours.
(304) 645-7600

www.organcave.com

15 Twin Falls State Park. *This 3,775-acre park has an immense variety of natural wonders, from two waterfalls to an awe-inspiring gorge.*

15 Twin Falls State Park
Mullens

Woodland streams, two waterfalls, a beautiful gorge, forests carpeted with ferns and mosses, rhododendron thickets, old fields, a rustic pioneer farmhouse, rural peacefulness, and a small museum are among the remarkably varied offerings in this splendid 3,775-acre park.

To take the Falls Trail, which is lovely during any season, you can park a short distance from Cabin Creek Falls. About 20 feet high, the falls tumble down overhanging ledges to a green pool rimmed by rhododendrons. The path continues along Marsh Fork stream through a lightly wooded valley and then follows a climbing course above Black Fork stream to Black Fork Falls, a fine outfling of water more spectacular than the first falls. The trail, about 1 1/2 miles long, is not a loop and requires backtracking.

If you are in the mood for a shorter walk, try the Twin Oaks Trail, which offers a three-eighths-mile loop around a clearing in a woodland of oak and beech.

The Pioneer Farm, a restored log-and-chink farmhouse with out-buildings and small fields enclosed with split-rail fences, is marvelously picturesque. The farmhouse is occupied and not open for inspection, but you can lean on the fence and contemplate the charms of rural life.

The park also has a lodge with a restaurant, tennis courts, a golf course, a pool, a playground, camping areas, and picnic spots.

Open year-round.
(304) 294-4000

www.twinfallsresort.com

Horicon National Wildlife Refuge. *Birds take flight along the great Mississippi Flyway (see page 366).*

(see page 366)

Wisconsin

Variety abounds in the Badger State—in the superb parks and wildlife areas, in the arts and architecture, and in historic places.

The hard-working pioneers who laid the foundation for a prosperous state are honored here. A logging museum, exhibition farm, gristmill, old inn, and the re-creation of a typical small town provide the honest flavor of a vigorous past.

Nature lovers will find good birding, hiking in a blessedly quiet wilderness, and a refuge with spectacular visitations of waterfowl. Other attractions include folk art cast in concrete, art inspired by nature, Victorian furnishings and 19th- and 20th-century art all under one roof, a world-class paperweight collection, and unusual period homes.

1 Madeline Island Historical Museum

3 miles from the city of Bayfield on northern Wisconsin's Apostle Islands

Just a short ferry ride from the mainland takes visitors to the enchanting Madeline Island of the Upper Great Lakes. Since 1659, the date marking its first foreign visitors, the island has attracted dreamers and schemers.

Built on a partnership between French fortune-seekers and the Ojibwe people, the island's fur trade flourished for 200 years. Over the centuries, Madeline also has attracted fishermen, loggers, missionaries, and, beginning in the 1890s, summer residents.

In 1955, Leo and Bella Capser, a couple who had been faithful summer residents for more than 50 years, embarked on a mission to give the island a special place to preserve its colorful history.

Rallying other residents—seasonal and year-round—they amassed a collection and pieced together a complex from part of a surviving American Fur Company building, the former town jail, a memorial to a drowned seaman, and an old barn. On June 15, 1958, the Capsers proudly opened the museum to the public.

Now managed by the Wisconsin Historical Society and substantially expanded with the addition of a

2 Amnicon Falls State Park. *The water rushing over the falls here is a creamy root-beer brown thanks to the tannic acid in the nearby vegetation.*

modern exhibit hall, the museum tells the island's unique story—from its prehistoric beginnings to the present day.

The museum also features objects that reflect the life and spirit of the Ojibwe people.

Open daily Memorial Day through the first weekend in October. Admission charged.

(715) 747-2415

www.madeline.wisconsinhistory.org

2 Amnicon Falls State Park

Superior

The Amnicon River, which courses through this pleasant park, has a dramatic series of waterfalls and cascades. And surprisingly, the water rushing over them is a rich, creamy, root-beer brown—a color imparted by tannic acid from vegetation. But the waterfalls are more than a scenic attraction. They also make it possible to see the park's other interesting feature, a geological fault line running through the area.

WISCONSIN

The Douglas Fault, visible at the foot of the Upper Falls, was created about 500 million years ago, when a deep layer of volcanic basalt rock began to push its way through the thick sandstone bed on which the park rests. Today at the falls the river flows through a smooth channel in an upthrust cliff of dark basalt before tumbling into a plunge pool and proceeding on to red sandstone cliffs even more eroded and smoothed by the water. Just below the falls, a 12-foot-wide zone of brownish red rocks and pebbles (fault breccia) marks the point where the basalt and sandstone ground against each other.

A covered bridge leading to a charming pine-covered island in the river offers excellent views of the falls. The river can be followed on trails that extend along its bank and circle the island. Swimming in the river is a great adventure. However, jumping or diving off the cliffs isn't allowed. During the long Wisconsin winter, the park provides a tranquil setting for snowshoers.

Open year-round. Admission charged.
(715) 398-3000

www.wiparks.net

2 Amnicon Falls State Park. *Tent camping can be enjoyed here, along with fishing, swimming, and hiking.*

🏕 Crex Meadows Wildlife Area. *Canada geese flock to this nature preserve, which ranks as one of the most appealing in the country.*

3 Lucius Woods County Park

U.S. Hwy. 53, Solon Springs
Tucked compactly between U.S. Hwy. 53 and St. Croix Lake, this park has only 41 acres. But it is enjoyable to visit for its pleasant swimming beach and its tall stands of ancient red and white pines—and in winter, for its variety of winter sports.

The beach is a small half-moon of sand nestled in the wooded shoreline of the invitingly spacious lake. A picnic area and a playground are nearby. The lake also offers fishing and boating.

The white pines with their deeply furrowed bark and the red pines with their scaly plates of ruddy bark are best seen along the hiking trail that follows the creek through the grounds.

An amphitheater is the summer home to a local symphony and serves as the stage for summer music shows, ranging from jazz to

country and western.

Winter activities center on ice fishing. Cross-country skiing is also permitted, but trails are not cleared.

Open mid-May–Sept. Fees charged for music shows.
(715) 378-2219
www.douglascountywi.org

🏕⛺🚐🏊🚶🎣⛸❄

4 Crex Meadows Wildlife Area

Grantsburg, at County Hwys. D and F
Uncommonly beautiful and richly endowed with wildlife, this nature preserve ranks among the most appealing in the country. Its open landscape encompasses 30,000 acres of grassy meadows, prairie and heathlike terrain, open pools and lakes, and reedy marshes. There are small stands of scrubby oak and willow as well.

Sandhill cranes and white-

tailed deer are often sighted in the areas planted with corn to feed wildlife, and one might see a black bear wandering in the marsh grass. More than 150 species of birds nest here, and some 270 species have been observed. Spring and fall are the best viewing times, but bald eagles, ospreys, and sharp-tailed grouse can be seen from April to October. The wildlife area is also home to a wolf pack since 1995 called the Crex Pack.

Gravel roads provide excellent access, but they are not suitable for bicycles with narrow racing tires. There are two trails developed specifically for hiking. In winter cross-country skiers have free run of the trails, and snowmobilers can swoosh along a 15-mile groomed trail. To avoid disturbing birds during their crucial nesting period, camping is permitted only from September through December. A brand-new wildlife education and visitors center is now open, featuring displays and dioramas of the brush prairie and wetlands.

Open year-round.
(715) 463-2896 or (715) 463-2739
www.crexmeadows.org

🏕⛺🚐🚶🚴🔭⛸❄

5 Wisconsin Concrete Park

State Hwy. 13 south of Phillips
Fred Smith and his amazing, colorful concrete sculptures are a part of the lore and legend of this part of Wisconsin. A lumberman, Smith retired at the age of 64 in 1950 and immediately began to make his folk-art sculptures—an impulse that, he said, "just comes to me naturally." By the time a stroke disabled him 15 years later, he had created more than 250 figures. And he steadfastly refused to

sell to collectors, choosing to leave his work "for the American people."

Smith's farm is now a public park, and his artistic endeavor preserved there is a strange but delightful collection of concrete figures: giant Indians, folk heroes, scenes from movies and history, life-sized deer, bears, and other animals, and local characters whom Smith knew, such as Mabel the Milker milking a cow. Some pieces incorporate real buggies and wagons. His last work portrayed a beer wagon drawn by a team of eight Clydesdale horses.

Smith applied his concrete over a frame of wood and chicken wire, and then embedded bits of glass and other materials in the surface for decoration. The resulting figures are storybook primitives with a rigid, straight-armed stance. The

🏕 Wisconsin Concrete Park. *One of Fred Smith's 250 colorful concrete-and-glass sculptures decorates this park.*

effect is at once outrageous, touching, funny, and charming.

Open year-round, but partly inaccessible when snow is deep. Admission free but donations encouraged.
(800) 269-4505
(715) 339-6371
www.pricecountywi.net

Rhinelander Logging Museum

Off Business U.S. 8 in Pioneer Park, Rhinelander
In the 1870s the town of Rhinelander was established as a supply center for the logging camps that were clearing the last of northern Wisconsin's virgin wilderness. This museum, with its reconstructed log cookhouse and bunkhouse, re-creates a logging camp of that era.

In the authentically furnished cookhouse are a period stove, sink, cookware, and long tables set with enamel plates and cups. Here, too, is the horn used to call the men to dinner.

The rest of the museum displays ox yokes, pulleys, saws, axes, peavies, pike poles, and the spiked shoes lumbermen wore when they were floating logs downstream.

The exhibits continue outdoors under tall pines, with a combination blacksmith's and carpenter's shop, a boat shed, and a rural schoolhouse. Most notable, however, is the collection of heavy equipment, which includes vintage fire engines, locomotives, log-hauling equipment, a water truck used to ice roads for log sleds, and boom sticks, the huge, chain-linked logs used to raft pulpwood across Lake Superior.

The 500 Line Depot was built in 1892 and moved to the museum complex. The depot has been restored to its original design and paint scheme. In the basement

you'll find a model railroad display of the trains operating in the area in the 1920s–40s.

Open daily Memorial Day–Labor Day. Donations accepted.
(715) 369-5004
www.rhinelanderchamber.com

⑦ The Farm

State Hwy. 57, 4 miles north of Sturgeon Bay in Door County
On the signs for The Farm, the word "The" is underlined, and rightfully so, for this sample of American rural life is as close to the real thing as any re-created homestead can be.

The emphasis here is on animals, especially young ones that can easily be petted and fed. Children will likely be charmed, entertained, and educated.

Breeding is scheduled so that various animals will be born throughout the summer, when the farm is open. Although the cast of animals is ever-changing, the visitor is likely to encounter calves, kids, kittens, puppies, chicks, lambs, rabbits, and piglets. Bottles of milk to feed to the animals are on sale. Chickens, ducks, and turkeys await a handout of corn. There are nanny goats to milk, and many larger animals, such as horses, donkeys, and cows.

Besides the hutches, coops, stables, barn, paddock, and pastures for animals, the 40-acre farmstead has about half a dozen century-old log cabins and outbuildings that were relocated here. Most of them contain antique farm tools, equipment, and domestic utensils.

Open daily Memorial Day–Oct. Admission charged.
(920) 743-6666
www.ohwy.com/wi/t/thefarm.htm

⑧ Leigh Yawkey Woodson Art Museum

Franklin and 12th Sts., Wausau
Artwork inspired by nature is the specialty of this museum, which is housed in a gabled brick residence resembling a comfortable country house in England's Cotswolds.

Visitors can stroll through the Margaret Woodson Fisher Sculpture Gallery, a beautifully landscaped 1 1/2-acre garden dotted with more than a dozen works.

Prominent among the museum's permanent displays are the Royal Worcester porcelain birds collected by Leigh Yawkey Woodson, whose daughters established the museum as a memorial to their mother.

The collection contains complete sets of both American and English birds, all delicately detailed annually by the artist Dorothy Doughty. The museum sponsors an exhibit called "Birds in Art" and gathers all forms of art relating to birds. Approximately 100 works are then selected to be showcased. Other ceramics include 18th-century Worcester lusterware by Leeds and Wedgwood. A glass collection features Victorian baskets as well as art nouveau and modern pieces.

The museum's wildlife art collection concentrates on birds, ranging from 18th- and 19th-century prints by John Gould and John James Audubon to more recent paintings by Roger Tory Peterson. It also includes duck decoys and bronze sculptures. The museum has changing exhibits as well; nature is usually—but not always—the theme.

Open Tues.–Fri. and P.M. weekends except major holidays.
(715) 845-7010
www.lywam.org

⑧ Leigh Yawkey Woodson Art Museum. The Heavyweight, *a sculpture of a hippopotamus at rest, adorns the outdoor gardens here.*

9 Dells Mill

Off Rte. 27, 3 miles north of Augusta

Today Wisconsin is famed as the dairy state, but during the second half of the 19th century, the chief agricultural product was wheat, and it was an important part of the nation's breadbasket. Dells Mill, opened in 1864, was one of hundreds of gristmills that sprang up to grind the grain into flour and feed.

Rising high above a rocky streambed (terrain called dells in Wisconsin), the mill is an impressive five-story structure built by German millwrights with hand-hewn pine timbers secured with pegs of oak. The well-preserved mill is still capable of doing a good day's work, but it is now primarily a museum reflecting country life in bygone days. The exhibits include plows, scythes, harnesses, a rope-making machine, sleighs, buggies, a reconstructed prairie schooner, and Civil War artifacts.

The most intriguing exhibit, however, is the mill itself, with its old overshot waterwheel, its drive shaft and cogged wheels with hard maple teeth, its grain bins, and its complexities of beams, pipes, and more than a half-mile of leather belts that drive the roller mills.

Open daily May–Oct. Admission charged.
(715) 286-2714
http://timbertrails.com/dmhlm1.htm

10 Octagon House

Third St., Hudson

In 1855, when this distinctive eight-sided, stuccoed dwelling was built, such structures were in vogue partly because the octagonal shape was believed to endow the building with certain spiritual powers. Most such houses were built in the Northeast by followers of the phrenologist Orson Fuller, who published a book

on the subject. A former New Yorker, John Shaw Moffat, brought the idea with him and built this house with a commanding view of the St. Croix River.

Today that vista is blocked by surrounding structures. But the house, which can be seen by guided tour, has been lovingly restored and furnished with heirlooms from local families and is now owned by the St. Croix County Historical Society. Many items, such as the black walnut dining set, came to the area by riverboat. The piano in the lace-curtained parlor survived two river dunkings but still plays. Other items are of local origin, such as the parlor's cherry log table and the kitchen's Civil War–era pot holder, boldly embroidered "Any Holder But A Slave Holder."

The upstairs porch displays a collection of dolls with examples from the 1830s through the Shirley Temple era. The Garden House and the Carriage House also contain

collections of miscellaneous memorabilia.

Open Tues.–Sat. May–Oct.
Admission charged.
(715) 386-2654
www.hudsonwi.org

11 Mid-Continent Railway Museum

West Walnut Street in North Freedom

Commemorating and reviving the "Golden Age of Railroading," this outdoor living museum features an extensive collection of vintage trains and equipment, plus its own classic operating railroad. Just stepping onto the grounds recalls a bygone way of life.

Authentic turn-of-the-century structures stand beside new buildings based on old design plans. The museum's signature depot was originally built in 1894 by the Chicago & North Western Railway—in a town three miles away. The antique depot, among several

10 Dells Mill. *One of hundreds that sprang up a century ago to grind Wisconsin's wheat, this mill is primarily a museum now.*

attractions, was painstakingly transported to the museum site for restoration and permanent residence.

Spanning the years 1880 to 1916, the museum's collection reflects a time when steam locomotives ruled—moving 90 percent of the nation's passengers. In addition to more than a dozen steam locomotives, it includes 36 passenger cars and 34 freight cars, both wooden and steel; 20 cabooses; and an assortment of service equipment, from snowplows to crane-wreckers.

Beyond gazing at genuine articles of the famed iron horses in all their might and glory, visitors can climb aboard for a nostalgic ride. Each day, authentic diesel-powered locomotives make repeated runs around the museum's miles of restored rolling track.

Open daily mid-May to Labor Day; weekends Sept.–Oct. Admission charged.
(608) 522-4261
www.midcontinent.org

12 Bergstrom–Mahler Museum

165 N. Park Ave., Neenah

Evangeline Bergstrom, who lived in this lakeside Tudor-style house until her death in 1958, was one of the world's leading collectors of glass paperweights. Indeed, her 1940 book on the subject did much to spark renewed interest in this form of art glass.

The 1,500 weights and other glass pieces that Mrs. Bergstrom gathered form the museum's primary permanent collection. The display is so wide-ranging and comprehensive that it is hard to imagine any style, period, or major maker of paperweights that is not included. Not only do the paperweights vary enormously but many are embedded with items ranging from delicate glass flowers to working compasses.

The museum also includes mantel ornaments, doorknobs, vases, and prize marbles, augmented by some modern French portrait pieces by Baccarat, Cristal d'Albret, and St. Louis.

Another permanent exhibit is the Mahler Germanic Glass Collection, which consists primarily of drinking vessels made in central Europe from the 16th through the 19th centuries. These elaborately decorated tumblers, beakers, decanters, and goblets encompass a wide array of glass types, and many are colorfully enameled with heraldic crests, scenes, and sovereigns' portraits. Some have gold and ruby overlay, delicate scrollwork, and cut ornaments.

The museum also shows traveling exhibits of glassware and other artwork.

Open Tues.–Sat. and P.M. Sun.
Closed major holidays.
(920) 751-4658
www.paperweightmuseum.com

13 Rahr–West Art Museum
Park St. at N. Eighth St., Manitowoc
Consistent with its two-part name, this museum has a split personality. The original building, given by the Rahr family, is a shingled Queen Anne–style mansion built by

Joseph Vilaf in 1891. It is filled with authentic Victorian furnishings and 19th-century art, including works by such noted painters as Rembrandt Peale, Adolphe Bouguereau, and George Paxton. The mansion also has collections of contemporary porcelain, American Indian artifacts, antique dolls, and most notably, rare Chinese ivories.

In striking contrast, the museum's sleek, modern exhibition wing, a gift of John and Ruth West, is home to a collection of 20th-century art with more than 150 canvases. Most of the painters are Americans, ranging from abstractionists such as Frank Stella, Joseph Raphael, and Sam Francis, to more representational artists such as Neil Welliver, Milton Avery, and Jane Freilicher. The new wing also devotes a large space to traveling exhibits.

Open Mon.–Fri. and P.M. weekends.
(920) 683-4501
www.rahrwestartmuseum.org

14 Wade House State Historic Site
Off State Hwy. 23, on Plank Road, Greenbush
This attractive Greek Revival inn, built in 1851 by Sylvanus Wade, is part of a group of preserved

14 Wade House State Historic Site. *A Civil War re-enactment is held every September on the grounds here.*

buildings here that give an intriguing insight into life and travel in 19th-century America.

Wade, an optimistic entrepreneur from the East, built the inn in the Wisconsin wilderness to cater to travelers making the bone-rattling stagecoach journey along the plank road between Sheboygan and Fond du Lac. Tours of the 27-room structure reveal that Wade entertained his guests in a simple barroom and a parlor with a pump organ. He fed them family-style on long pine tables in the dining room, with dishes prepared in a large winter kitchen.

Upstairs, the Wade family lived in rooms furnished with wash-stands, chests, and trundle beds, while the servants got by in more modest quarters near the back stairs. Resident guests also lived modestly in eight tiny rooms squeezed onto the third floor, sleeping on corn-husk mattresses.

Amazingly, 60 percent of the inn's original furnishings remains intact.

Also located here are a re-created blacksmith's shop with a working forge. Even more interesting is the Wesley W. Jung Carriage Museum, which has an outstanding collection of more than 120 antique horse-drawn vehicles. Among them are farm wagons, a butcher's wagon, a self-unloading coal wagon, fire engine pumpers, a 10-passenger sleigh, public omnibuses, a circus calliope, and children's play carriages, as well as elegant carriages and everyday buckboards.

The cost of admission includes a ride in a horse-drawn carriage from the visitors center to the inn and the carriage museum.

Open Tues.–Sun., Memorial Day–Labor Day; Wed.–Sun. Labor Day–mid-Oct.
Admission charged.
(920) 526-3271
www.shsw.wisc.edu/sites/wade

12 Bergstrom–Mahler Museum. *This Tudor-style house holds one of the world's most comprehensive collections of glass paperweights.*

15 Horicon National Wildlife Refuge. *A marsh bird known as a sora can be seen here during the spring, summer, and fall.*

15 Horicon National Wildlife Refuge

County Rd. 2, Mayville
Millions of waterfowl migrate along the great Mississippi Flyway, and this federal wildlife preserve of 21,000 acres and an adjoining state wildlife area with 11,000 acres were established primarily to provide them with a refuge. Careful management has turned this into one of the nation's greatest areas for wildfowl—and for people who enjoy seeing them.

The marsh is best known for the big black-necked Canada geese that touch down here by the tens of thousands in the fall—and unfortunately attract thousands of viewers. But at other times of the year, the marsh is a quiet refuge for the visitor as well as for the plentiful wildlife.

In the spring northbound geese and ducks stage a smaller migratory show. And during the summer the marsh teems with nesting egrets, blue-winged teals, coots, great blue herons, mallards, wood ducks, and redheads. An occasional white-tailed deer and red fox may be seen as well.

Six miles of interconnecting trails wind through the marsh and along the impoundments around the edges. They traverse a beautifully austere landscape of lush reeds and rough marshlands mingled with clear lakes, sparse pockets of brush, and small stands of trees. Some areas can be seen by car along perimeter roads. Fishing is allowed on designated areas from the banks of the lakes and ditches. Northerns, bullheads, and crappies are likely catches.

Most areas open and accessible year-round.
(920) 387-2658
http://midwest.fws.gov/horicon/ index.htm

16 Villa Louis

On St. Feriole Island in Prairie du Chien, 62 miles south of La Crosse
Built in 1870 by H. Louis Dousman, a prosperous frontier entrepreneur, and impeccably appointed by his wife, Nina, this stately hilltop estate is now one of the most authentically restored Victorian homes in the United States.

Under the auspices of the Wisconsin Historical Society, it has been painstakingly and strikingly re-created in the style Mrs. Dousman selected for her 1885 redecoration: British Arts and Crafts.

Atypical for a Midwestern home, even for a mansion of its time, the furnishings feature ornate brass filigree, hand-wrought faux grain woodwork, and lush fabrics. Throughout the magnificent home, visitors will also find priceless family heirlooms, collectibles, and artwork.

While distinguished for its Victorian splendor, this expansive country estate also enjoyed a brief heyday as a hub for harness racing. Passionate about the popular sport, Dousman transformed his homestead into a breeding ground and finishing school for thoroughbred trotters called the Artesian Stock Farm. Hailed for its elegant setting and enviable stable of 75 trophy-winners, the racing enterprise flourished until 1886, ending with Dousman's sudden death. The estate was renamed Villa Louis in his honor.

Each September, Villa Louis celebrates the memory of the Artesian Stock Farm when it opens its grounds to the Midwest's largest and most classically stylish competitive carriage driving event.

The mansion also hosts popular Victorian cooking workshops, ghost tours by lamplight, and a historic battle re-enactment: In its premansion days, the estate's sprawling lawn had served as Wisconsin's sole battlefield in the War of 1812.

Open May through Oct.
Call for hours. Admission charge.
(608) 326-2721
www.shsw.wisc.edu/sites/villa

17 Stonefield

Cassville, off Hwy. 133 on County Road VV
Centered around a classic village square with bandstand and apple trees, Stonefield re-creates the small-town Wisconsin of nearly a century ago. The 30-odd mostly clapboard structures are constructed in a turn-of-the-century style, and most are filled with authentic period furnishings.

The law office has leather volumes and wooden file cabinets; the doctor's office, an examination table and surgical tools. The butcher shop has a marble counter and scales, while the ladies' hat shop is an oasis of feathers, lace, and satin. The goods in the Farmers' Store include corsets, shirt collars, and chewing tobacco.

A wonderful array of patent medicines and toiletries line the drugstore's shelves. The cheese factory, newspaper printing shop, cigar factory, and photography studio all display period equipment. Other buildings include a train station, bank, church, creamery, stables, school, firehouse, and

17 Stonefield. *The small-town Wisconsin of nearly a century ago comes alive in this classic village square.*

saloon. There is even a furniture-undertaker's shop (a common combination at the time) with cabinetmaking tools in front.

A visit to the village should include the adjoining State Agricultural Museum—formed by the walls of a former sheep barn—which has displays devoted to the settlement of Wisconsin and the evolution of agriculture here. Especially interesting are the beautifully crafted scale models of reaping machines complete with horses and humans.

The ticket to the village also admits the visitor to another Stonefield, the mansion which gave its name to the village. The restored brick structure, which stands just across the highway in the Nelson Dewey State Park, was the home of Wisconsin's first elected governor.

The 739-acre park, which is open year-round, offers quiet beauty, camping sites, nature trails, and excellent bird-watching. More than 85 species nest here in summer. The overlook on the bluffs above the village provides fine views of the Mississippi meandering through a wide valley.

Open Tues.–Sun. Memorial Day–Labor Day, then weekends only until Oct. 31. Admission charged.
(608) 725-5210
www.shsw.wisc.edu/sites/stone

18 Lincoln Tallman House
440 N. Jackson St., Janesville
In the late 1850s land speculator William Tallman paid the princely sum of $42,000 in gold to build his family estate here. Styled after an Italian villa, the house has 26 rooms on five levels: a basement, three main stories, and a small rooftop observatory. No effort has

19 Kenosha Public Museum. *The Ice Age exhibit here features a replica of a woolly mammoth and its Paleo-Indian hunter.*

been spared to make the rooms look not only authentic but lived in. More than half of the home's furnishings are original, including the bed upon which Abraham Lincoln slept.

In the brick-floored basement, the kitchen has a stone fireplace and a dumbwaiter and is outfitted with cutting boards, meat grinder, and period utensils. The adjoining pantries are equipped for canning, churning, and butchering, and the laundry has a cradle washer and a coal-heated steam iron.

The ground floor has both a formal parlor and dining room (with the table set for a meal) and more comfortable smoking, sewing, and breakfast rooms. When Tallman entertained Lincoln here in 1859, the future president reportedly found the parlor too fancy for his taste and

moved to the sewing room.

Upstairs, the second floor contains bedrooms, servants' quarters, and an office with Tallman's pigeonhole desk. The third floor has large, gallery-like rooms where children played and the visiting seamstress prepared new spring and fall wardrobes. The observatory looks out across the lead roof to the leafy grounds.

Another smaller, restored and refurbished home can also be visited. It is an 1842 Greek Revival stone house that was moved here to save it from demolition. It contains the archives of the Rock County Historical Society, where people can do genealogical research.

Open daily June–Sept., weekends year-round. Admission charged.
(608) 756-4509
www.lincolntallman.org

19 Kenosha Public Museum
5500 First Ave., Kenosha
A striking new building overlooking Lake Michigan has opened its doors to accommodate the growing collection of natural history and art exhibits at this museum, which first opened in 1937. Visitors walk into a towering atrium lobby that resembles the glacier that first sliced through southeast Wisconsin 15,000 years ago.

At the Ice Age exhibit on the first floor, you'll find a replica of the Hebior mammoth, the largest, most complete mammoth ever found in North America. In 1992, a Kenosha Public Museum archaeologist began excavating a woolly mammoth skeleton just 10 miles away. Cut marks on the bones indicated the animals were butchered by humans using stone tools, and carbon dating indicated the bones were 12,500 years old. They are displayed as they were found at the excavation site.

Featured on the second floor are works by the world's greatest artists, such as Picasso, Renoir, and Chagall.

Also not to be missed is an unusual collection of small dioramas presenting the studios and works of the world's greatest sculptors. One shows Michelangelo with the *Pietà* and his statues of *Moses* and *David*.

At rotating areas at the Field Station, visitors are invited to dig in with hands-on activities and take a closer look at insects, fossils, and shells; create American Indian beadwork design; or identify neighborhood birds.

Open daily year-round.
(262) 653-4140
www.kenosha.org

Medicine Lodge State Archaeological Site. *This area is rich in petroglyphs etched into the surrounding sandstone (see page 370).*

Wyoming

Here is the essence of the Old West, where Indians, cowboys, trappers, miners, soldiers, and settlers all had their day—and are still remembered.

American Indians dominated this land long before the coming of the white man, and their clothing, weapons, and ceremonial objects can be admired in a variety of excellent museums. Also recalled, in museums, historic forts, and an (almost) ghost town, are westward-bound pioneers, miners who stayed while the digging held out, ranchers and farmers who settled down, and the soldiers sent to protect them all.

The prehistory of this land is documented by dinosaur footprints, the fossils of ancient birds and fish, and an archaeological dig. Wildflowers abound in their season, many parks have inviting trails, and in an understatement unusual for scenic attractions, Hell's Half Acre is 640 times that size. There are remarkable on-again, off-again waterworks to ponder as well as natural splendors.

1 Teton Canyon Campground

Caribou-Targhee National Forest, 7 miles west of Alta

This campground is nestled picturesquely along Teton Creek at the base of striking mountain vistas. Several trails, ranging from easy to difficult, are accessible nearby.

The Devil's Stair, beginning about 2 1/2 miles up the south fork of Teton River, climbs steeply along cliffs to the wide, flat area called Death Canyon Shelf, offering spectacular views of the Teton Mountains. A less difficult route includes a hike up South Teton Creek, which affords a breathtaking view of waterfalls and even offers a cliff-climbing area. Both North and South Teton Trailheads bring hikers to the Jedediah Smith Wilderness Area.

Deer, elk, and an abundant population of moose roam the area year-round. In midsummer hundreds of hummingbirds flock to the myriad wildflowers, and the creek offers excellent trout fishing. Insects can be annoying, however, so bring a repellent. Snowmobiling and cross-country skiing attract winter visitors.

Park open year-round; water shut off Oct. 1.
(208) 354-2312
Reservations: (877) 444-6777
www.reserveusa.com

4 Bighorn Medicine Wheel. *This mysterious circle of limestone slabs and boulders was discovered by Crow Indians in 1766.*

2 Buffalo Bill Historical Center

720 Sheridan Ave., Cody

Dubbed "the Smithsonian of the West" by author James Michener, this place is famous for celebrating America's frontier heritage. Inspired by its flagship Buffalo Bill Museum, established in 1927, the 237,000-square-foot complex has expanded its focus through the decades to house the Whitney Gallery of Western Art, the Plains Indian Museum, and the Cody Firearms Museum.

The center has now entered a new frontier with its $17 million state-of-the-art Draper Museum, showcasing the biological and geological wonders of the Greater Yellowstone ecosystem. Using cutting-edge technology, this museum leads visitors down an interactive trail through the sights, sounds, and sensations of the West's natural world. Visitors get to delve into exhibits such as ranching, logging, and oil development.

Open daily Apr.–Oct.;
open Tues.–Sun. Nov.–Mar.
Admission charged.
(307) 587-4771
www.bbhc.org/dmnh/index.cfm

3 Pryor Mountain Wild Horse Refuge and Red Gulch Dinosaur Tracksite

In Big Horn County, near Lovell and near Greybull, respectively
Just up the road from Yellowstone National Park, Big Horn County is home to mountains, waterfalls, and hundreds of miles of scenic trails. At the Pryor Mountain Wild Horse Refuge, visitors might spy as many as 160 wild mustangs on a 40,000-acre sweep of land. First admired and prized by American Indians, the distinctive stallions are direct descendants of breeds cultivated in ancient Spain, Portugal, and Africa, including Barbary, Andalusian, and Arabian.

Nearby at Red Gulch, covering 40 acres of publicly guarded ground, visitors can trace the footsteps of dinosaurs dating back some 160 million years to the Middle Jurassic period. Until 1997, when the prehistoric footprints were uncovered, most scientists viewed Big Horn County as the former home of a huge ocean, inhabited exclusively by sea creatures. Yet, as the tracks of gigantic mammals attest, the area was once covered by soft mud. Over the eons, the mud hardened, leaving whole footprints preserved beneath. Today visitors can easily spot over 100 footprints and other fossil traces. Visitors are permitted to take home petrified wood and plant fossils they find but must leave any animal vertebrae for the local experts to study.

Open year-round. Free.
Pryor Mountain: (307) 548-2251
Red Gulch: (307) 347-5100
www.bighorns.com

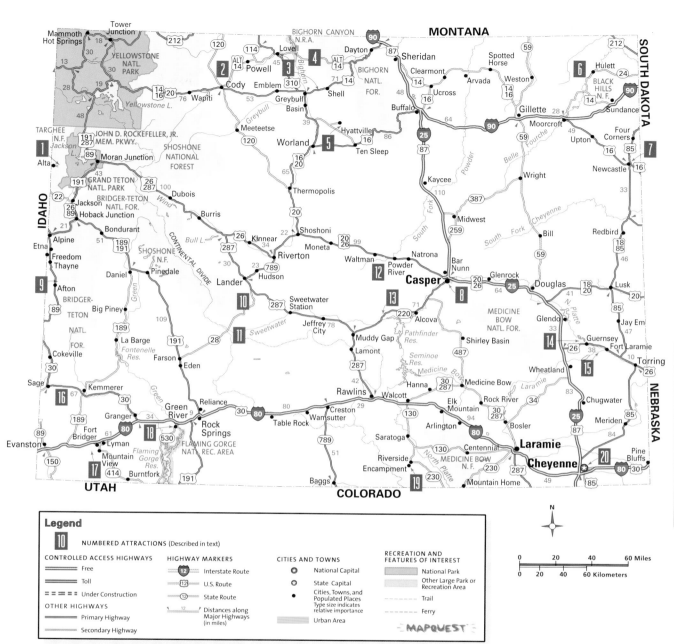

Legend

	NUMBERED ATTRACTIONS (Described in text)

CONTROLLED ACCESS HIGHWAYS
— Free
— Toll
=== Under Construction
OTHER HIGHWAYS
— Primary Highway
— Secondary Highway

HIGHWAY MARKERS
Interstate Route
U.S. Route
State Route
Distances along Major Highways (in miles)

CITIES AND TOWNS
National Capital
State Capital
Cities, Towns, and Populated Places
Type size indicates relative importance

RECREATION AND FEATURES OF INTEREST
National Park
Other Large Park or Recreation Area
Trail
Ferry
Urban Area

MAPQUEST

0   20   40   60 Miles
0   20   40   60 Kilometers

4 Bighorn Medicine Wheel

Off Alt. Rte. 14, east of Lovell
In 1776, when the Crow Indians first occupied this mountain on the western edge of Bighorn National Forest, they discovered the great Medicine Wheel, a circle of limestone slabs and boulders with a circumference of 245 feet, 28 stone spokes, and a round pile of stones about 3 feet high as a hub.

Its origin and purpose remain a mystery. Speculation is that a sun-worshiping people built the wheel. The hub supposedly symbolizes the sun, and the spokes indicate the 28 days of the lunar month. Radioactive carbon dating by the University of Wyoming of wood found inside a rock pile puts the construction of the wheel at 1760, but it may be quite a bit older.

The wheel is reached by a steep and winding three-mile dirt road offering glorious views of surrounding mountains and valleys.

Open year-round; entrance road may be impassable in winter.
(307) 674-2600
www.fs.fed.us/r2/bighorn

5 Medicine Lodge State Archaeological Site

6 miles NE of Hyattville off Cold Springs Road

Ten thousand years of human habitation have been documented at this location—a sheltered valley on the western slope of the Bighorn Mountains, near the confluence of Medicine Lodge and Dry Medicine Lodge creeks.

The prehistoric site had long been recognized as an important one because of the outstanding petroglyphs and pictographs that had been incised and etched on a sandstone bluff here.

But in the early 1970s even more significant finds were made. Digging at the base of the bluff, through approximately 26 feet of soil and rocky material, a team of archaeologists, led by Dr. George Frison, uncovered more than 60 cultural levels and thousands of artifacts, ranging from bones and projectile points to hearths and food storage pits. The finds are helping scholars to reconstruct the lifeways of man from the end of the ice age to today.

In 1972 the area was purchased by the Wyoming Game and Fish Department to provide winter refuge for the elk and deer herds. Campgrounds and picnic tables and grills are set among the willows and cottonwoods. The Medicine Lodge Creek is an excellent brown trout fishery and the nearby nature trail is ideal for bird-watching.

Open year-round, but roads may be impassable in winter snow. Call ahead for conditions. Admission charged.
(307) 469-2234

http://wyoparks.state.wy.us/ mlodge.htm

 Devils Tower National Monument. *Established as the nation's first national monument, dedicated in 1906 by President Theodore Roosevelt, the area is regarded as hallowed ground by many American Indian groups.*

6 Devils Tower National Monument

Devils Tower

About 60 million years ago, molten magma from the earth's core forced its way upward into the softer sedimentary rock here. The magma cooled underground and formed a huge stock of hard igneous stone. Slowly the sedimentary rock eroded away by the Belle Fourche River, exposing the stock. Known as Devils Tower, it rises abruptly from its base and looms 1,267 feet above the river. The tower formed into a network of 4-, 5-, and 6-sided columns, each 8 to 15 feet in diameter, separated by the thermal gradient cracks, as the entire mass began to cool. In 1906 the imposing formation was designated the nation's first national monument. Each year expert climbers edge their way to the top, a domed area of 1½ acres.

The surrounding park offers hiking trails, tent and trailer campsites, and picnic grounds. Birding is also quite good, since the park is at the juncture of wooded mountains and plains. More than 100 bird species have been sighted here, including bald and golden eagles and prairie falcons. White-tailed and mule deer inhabit the woodlands, and inquisitive prairie dogs pop up from their town near the park entrance to pose for photographers.

Park open year-round; campground open mid-May–Sept. Admission charged.
(307) 467-5283

www.nps.gov/deto

7 Accidental Oil Company

4 miles east of Newcastle on Rte. 16

Al Smith, a lifetime oilman, was convinced that oil could be found at shallow depths as well as at the usual depth of 4,000 feet or more. Seeking oil on land he had leased from the government in 1966 and unable to find a rig, he began to dig by hand, using only a pick and a shovel and a few sticks of dynamite. About four weeks later he astounded the experts by striking oil at a depth of 24 feet. At the peak of its production, the well yielded a little more than five barrels of crude oil per day.

A 120-foot ramp leads to a viewing room at the bottom of the 24-foot well. In the ultraviolet lighting the oil oozing from cracks in the 100-million-year-old rock appears to be a bright fluorescent yellow, and the process of seepage is easy to see.

Antique drilling equipment, including a 1912 steam-powered cable-tool drill rig, is displayed on the grounds. An 1880 derrick stands on a hill above the gift shop, which is located in an oil storage tank.

Open year-round. Admission charged. (307) 746-2042

http://w3.trib.com/~debran/map.html

8 National Historic Trails Interpretive Center

Off I-25 at Exit 189, Casper

Here visitors can literally walk in the paths of the American pioneers. Many sections of westward trails forged more than 150 years ago remain intact and open to foot traffic, enhanced only with historic markers.

Operated by a unique partnership among the Bureau of Land Management, the National Historic Trails Center Foundation, and the city of Casper, the 27,000-square-foot interpretive center captures the stories—geographic, national, and personal—of the Oregon, Mormon, California, and Pony Express trails in the 1800s. It also pays tribute to the pivotal role of lesser-known regional trails, Bozeman and Bridger, and explores the everyday life of local American Indians.

State-of-the-art interactive exhibits follow arduous journeys across the desert in wagons and on horseback. Highlights include the westward mission of religious freedom embraced by some 70,000 members of the Church of Latter-day Saints and the frenzied California Gold Rush years.

Open daily Apr.–Oct.; open Tues.–Sat. Nov.–Mar. Closed major holidays. Admission charged.
(307) 261-7600
www.wy.blm.gov/nhtic

9 Periodic Spring
Off Second Ave., 5 miles east of Rte. 89, Afton

Known locally as the Geyser, this frigid mountain spring seems truly magical. For several minutes it gushes torrentially from a 10-foot-wide opening in the wall of Swift Creek Canyon. Then suddenly it stops, and the streambed, 7,100 feet below, dries up. A few minutes later the water bursts forth from the rock again with all its earlier vehemence.

The duration of these cycles varies with the level of the water table. During dry months—particularly August, September, and October—the spring flows for perhaps 8 to 18 minutes, shuts off for a similar interval, and then flows again. During the snowmelt in May and June, however, or after heavy rains, it flows continuously with only minor changes in volume. No one is certain what causes this phenomenon, but geologists believe the water is drawn and discharged by a natural siphon from an underground lake.

The spring can be reached only by a narrow trail that offers stunning views of soaring chimney rocks. It is in the Bridger-Teton National Forest, where you'll also find several glaciers and the highest mountain in Wyoming—Gannett Peak. A five-mile road leads to the trailhead. Campsites and picnic areas are located nearby.

Trail open June-Oct.; campground open late May–early Sept.
(307) 739-5500
www.fs.fed.us/btnf

10 Sinks Canyon State Park
Lander

This ecologically diverse park takes its name from its most noted natural phenomenon. The Popo Agie River "sinks" here into a limestone cave, proceeds underground for half a mile, and resurfaces into a pool known as The Rise. The area around The Rise contains two strikingly different ecosystems, reflecting the amount of sunlight received on the canyon's slopes. The shadier north-facing slope is a forest of Douglas fir, limber pine, and aspen, while the arid south-facing slope supports juniper and sagebrush.

Black bears, beavers, mule deer, moose, and bighorn sheep range the hillsides, and the river abounds in trout. A nature trail with 21 stops can be walked easily in an hour. The park road is part of a 60-mile loop through scenic mountain backcountry between Lander and South Pass City. Pamphlets describing highlights of the drive are available at the park.

Park open year-round, weather permitting; visitors center open Memorial Day–Labor Day.
(307)332-3077
www.wyobest.org

11 South Pass City State Historic Site
South Pass

Situated at the southern end of the Wind River Range, where the Oregon Trail crosses the Continental Divide, South Pass City is one of the scores of communities established during the search for "the yellow metal that drives the white man crazy," as one wise American Indian put it. Gold was discovered here in 1867; within a year 28 mines were established, and the area's population boomed to about 3,000. But five years later no one had yet hit a mother lode; discouraged, the miners moved on to more promising locations, and the town rapidly declined.

Now restored, South Pass City is a living ghost town with a handful of residents. Its bustling past is still visible in 30 or so buildings that were once of vital importance, such as the 1868 Sherlock Hotel, the South Pass Hotel, and the Miner's Exchange Saloon. Giving authenticity to the scene, a few optimistic prospectors still work the mines.

Visitors center open daily May 15–Sept. 30.
(307) 332-3684
http://spacr.state.wy.us/sphs/index1.htm

12 Hell's Half Acre
East of Waltman off Rte. 20-26

The pioneers who named this region rather underplayed its size, but its hellish aspects obviously impressed them. Hard rains and winds have carved a 320-acre chasm in an otherwise flat terrain, sculpting pinnacles, gulches, and fantastic shapes out of the bed of white clay and shale. The freakish landscape was regarded with superstitious awe by both American Indians and trappers, who often avoided the area. But it is also a scene of striking beauty, with bands of yellow, pink, white, and orange striating the canyon walls.

A restaurant at the rim of the chasm has viewing platforms open to the public, and there are hiking trails down into the canyon. But be careful: what may appear to be hard rock underfoot is crumbly baked clay.

Park open year-round, weather permitting.
(307) 473-7773
www.hellshalfacrewyo.homestead.com/

12 Hell's Half Acre. *Contrary to its name, this spectacularly colored chasm, filled with caves, gulches and jutting rock formations in the midst of the Wyoming prairie, actually encompasses 320 acres.*

13 Independence Rock State Historic Site

West of Alcova off Rte. 220, Evansville

A famous landmark on the Oregon Trail, the huge granite mound found here reaches 136 feet above the Sweetwater River Valley and extends over 24 acres. William Sublette, fur trader and guide, is generally credited with naming the rock on July 4, 1830, in honor of the anniversary of the Declaration of Independence.

Wagon train travelers found Independence Rock a convenient resting and camping stop on the trail. The names and dates carved on its face by these early pioneers prompted the Jesuit missionary Pierre Jean De Smet to dub the rock "the Great Register of the Desert" as early as 1841. More than 5,000 inscriptions were carved here, and many of them are still visible. A paved path takes visitors from the parking lot to the rock and a picnic area.

Open year-round. Admission charged.
(307)577-5150

http://spacr.state.wy.us/sphs/index1.htm

14 Guernsey State Park

1 mile NW of Guernsey, on the North Platte River

In 1927 the Bureau of Reclamation dammed the North Platte River here. The resulting 2,400-acre Guernsey Reservoir is the centerpiece of this lovely park. Ancient sandstone cliffs rise defiantly from the placid shorelines, surrounded by rolling, grassy hills dotted with stands of juniper and pine. The four-mile Lakeshore Drive offers outstanding panoramic views and provides access to four of the park's seven campgrounds.

The other camping areas are in the park's backcountry, where deer, antelope, bobcats, and coyotes occasionally may be spotted. A sandy beach can be used by swimmers, and picnic areas and three boat ramps are available. Fishing, however, is poor because the reservoir is drained annually to remove silt.

The park buildings and other facilities are an added attraction. These sturdy sandstone masonry structures, built during the Great Depression of the 1930s, are excellent examples of the Civilian Conservation Corps's skill and craftsmanship. The most impressive building (with heavy cypress doors and hand-wrought iron lighting fixtures) is the visitors center and museum, where there are displays about regional geology, archaeology, and history. Another building in the park, fashioned in a style similar to that of the museum, is the castle, with a giant fireplace and winding steps that lead to an observation area and picnic shelters.

Park open year-round; visitors center open P.M. mid-May–mid-Sept.
(307) 836-2334

http://spacr.state.wy.us/sphs/index1.htm

15 Fort Laramie National Historic Site

3 miles SW of Fort Laramie off Rte. 26

In 1834 William Sublette and Robert Campbell, two fur traders, established their headquarters and a trading post here near the confluence of the Laramie and North Platte rivers. As more and more wagon trains creaked westward, the American Indians who lived in the area became increasingly angry, and the settlers' need for protection along the Oregon Trail grew. Finally in 1849 the U.S. government bought the trading post and turned it into a military fort. In 1938 it became a national historic site.

Several buildings have been restored, including the commandant's home, the surgeon's quarters, the bakery, the guardhouse, the post store, and "Old Bedlam," Wyoming's oldest surviving military structure, which provided housing for the post's officers. Park staff members in period clothing of the 1800s demonstrate cannon firing, baking, and other fort activities. Displays in a small museum include 19th-century U.S. Army uniforms, weapons, and saddles. Park rangers conduct tours and programs daily during the summer months.

Open daily.
(307)837-2221

www.nps.gov/fola

16 Fossil Butte National Monument

11 miles west of Kemmerer off Rte. 30N

Violent land upheavals here 50 million years ago created a lake where ancestors of many modern mammals, birds, fish, and reptiles flourished in a subtropical climate. When these creatures died, their remains were protected by layers of sediment. Later, under enormous pressure, the sediment turned to limestone, preserving the animals' fossilized skeletons in almost perfect condition.

At the visitors center of this 8,198-acre monument, fossils of fish resembling gar, paddlefish, and herring are exhibited along with rare fossils of a stingray, a 13-foot crocodile, a boa constrictor, a bird, and a bat. There are video presentations as well as a Junior Ranger program available year-round; Ranger programs are only offered during the summer months.

16 Fossil Butte National Monument. *Perfectly preserved in limestone, the fossils found at the monument, such as this prehistoric fish skeleton dating back millions of years, offer scientists a close look at the ancestors of today's mammals, reptiles, birds, and fish.*

On weekends between Memorial Day and Labor Day, visitors may hike to a small research quarry and assist monument staff with the digging of fossils. Two moderately strenuous trails (1 1/2 and 2 1/2 miles) and interpretive signs help visitors explore the Monument and understand its geology, paleontology, and ecology.

An auto route winds for several miles through native sagebrush and grasslands to a picnic area in an aspen grove.

You may have cows for company in this open range country, and you may see a few mule deer. In winter the monument may be explored on cross-country skis or snowshoes, but there are no groomed trails. Fossil Butte is one of the least visited national parks and is a good place to find solitude.

Park open year-round; visitors center open daily May–Sept., staff availability and weather permitting.
(307) 877-4455
www.nps.gov/fobu

17 Fort Bridger State Historic Site

Fort Bridger, Exit 34 on I-80
Jim Bridger, justly famous beaver trapper, trader, and guide, established a trading post here in 1843 with his partner Louis Vasquez and supplied the needs of wagon trains on the Oregon Trail. Twelve years later the Mormons bought the post as a resting place for their people emigrating westward, but after a dispute with the federal government they burned it and went on to Salt Lake City. United States troops arrived in 1857 and built what was to remain an important fort until 1890, putting up 29 buildings.

20 Wyoming State Museum. *The life-size cast of a camptosaurus dinosaur is the highlight of the museum's paleontology gallery.*

Today visitors can see the stables, which were used by the Pony Express, and the sutler's complex (post store), stocked with goods from the 1880s. Army uniforms, buffalo robes, and the evidence of a poker party are shown in the officers' quarters. The commandant's residence has been restored with period furnishings, including a moose-horn chair.

Open daily May 1–Sept. 30; weekends the rest of the year. Admission charged.
(307) 782-3842
http://spacr.state.wy.us/sphs/index1.htm

18 Sweetwater County Historical Museum

3 East Flaming Gorge Way, Green River
Through the ages Sweetwater County has had a series of inhabitants, from dinosaurs and other prehistoric creatures to American Indian tribes, white settlers, and the European and Asian laborers who came in the 1870s to work in the mines.

The museum illustrates this stream of history with such exhibits as a rare fossil of a palm leaf, a dinosaur footprint, and the mounted heads of buffalo, deer, and a trumpeter swan. Excellent examples of Sioux quillwork and beadwork may be seen, as well as carved jade, pottery, garments, and other items that belonged to the Chinese immigrants.

The large collection of historic photographs shows early miners, mining sites, mountain men, pioneers, and the coming of the railroad.

Open Mon.–Fri. year-round except holidays. Also open P.M. Sat., July–Aug.
(307) 872-6435
www.sweetwatermuseum.org

19 Grand Encampment Museum
Encampment
The discovery of a copper lode in 1897 brought affluence to the ranch town of Grand Encampment. However, the prosperity lasted only 11 years—the mines were closed in 1908, when the owners were accused of fraud. Although the town survived, the "Grand" was dropped from its name for the sake of honesty.

The aura of the mining community has been re-created at this

museum complex—a cluster of 14 weather-beaten buildings almost overtaken by the desert. On a guided tour you can inspect an 1870s stagecoach station, a saloon, and a general store equipped with a huge coffee grinder and a brass cash register. The Doc Culleton Building displays a variety of artifacts, old-time photographs, and the Oldman research center. Also of interest is the Mosley folding bathtub and a two-story outhouse designed for use when deep snow and drifts buried the lower unit.

Open Memorial Day–Labor Day. Mon.–Sat., P.M. Sun. Donations accepted.
(307) 327-5308
http://encampment.1wyo.net/gemuseum

20 Wyoming State Museum
Barrett Building, 2301 Central Avenue, Cheyenne
Cheyenne was founded in 1867 as a major depot along the Transcontinental Railway, and less than a year later the Territory of Wyoming was created by Congress. The museum itself was started in 1895, just five years after Wyoming was granted statehood.

Remodeled in the late 1990s, the museum's new exhibits encompass a wide range of subjects, including wildlife, mining, dinosaurs, art, American Indians, ranching, agriculture, the military, state traditions, and noted state citizens, both famous and infamous.

The Hands-on History Room allows visitors to experience interactive exhibits. The museum also hosts several temporary exhibits throughout the year.

Open Tues.–Sat. year-round. Closed state and federal holidays.
(307) 777-7022
http://wyomuseum.state.wy.us

ACKNOWLEDGMENTS

It takes a large team of people to compile, research, and fact-check the information for a book of this size. To all those who responded so enthusiastically to our many requests for information, we thank you. We couldn't have done this book without you. Special gratitude goes to:

Alabama—Mary E. Gaines, Public Affairs Officer for the National Forests in Alabama
Alaska—Amy Cockerham, Alaska Travel Industry Assn.; Mark Morones, Communications Director, Alaska Travel Industry Assn.
Arizona—Kristin Jarnagin, Arizona Office of Tourism
Arkansas—Kerry Kraus, Arkansas Dept. of Parks & Tourism
California—John Arnold, California State Parks
Colorado—Christy Nielson, Tourism Account Manager, PRACO, Ltd./Colorado Tourism Office
Delaware—Carolyn White, Delaware Tourism Office
Florida—Susan Duncan, Curator, Elliott Museum
Georgia—Trish Croll, Georgia Dept. of Industry, Trade and Tourism
Hawaii—Lisa Mock, O`ahu Visitors Bureau
Iowa—Jim Liechty, Madison County Conservation Board
Kansas—Beverly Hurley, Leawood
Louisiana—Bruce Morgan, Louisiana Office of Tourism; Debbie Munson, Schriever
Maryland—Mindy Bianca, Maryland Office of Tourism Development

Michigan—Robin Peebles, Marketing Manager, Travel Michigan, Lansing
Missouri—Angela Lower, Account Executive, MMG Worldwide, Kansas City
Nebraska—Mary Ethel Emanuel, Nebraska Division of Travel and Tourism
New Hampshire—Margaret Joyce, Director of Communications, New Hampshire Division of Travel and Tourism Development
New Mexico—Dan Monaghan, New Mexico Dept. of Tourism
New York—Mary Ellen Walsh, New York State Tourism Office
North Carolina—Greer Beaty, North Carolina Dept. of Commerce
North Dakota—Scooter Pursley, North Dakota Tourism Division, Dept. of Commerce
Oklahoma—Lori Nelson, Director of Public Relations and Promotions, Travel and Tourism Division, Oklahoma Tourism and Recreation Department
Oregon—Tori Benson, Oregon Tourism Commission; Frank Howard, Oregon Parks and Recreation Dept.
South Carolina—Anna Lock, South Carolina Parks, Recreation & Tourism
South Dakota—Leah Mohr, South Dakota Tourism Office
Tennessee—Lorene Lambert, Tennessee Tourist Development
Texas—Kimberley Baker, Texas Dept. of Economic Development
Wyoming—Dave Troyankek, Wyoming Travel & Tourism Office

National Park Service—Dennis Latta

PHOTO CREDITS

119 Michael Whye 120 *Left* Michael Snell 120 *Right* Donna Dannen 122 Michael Snell 123 Kansas Department of Wildlife & Parks 124 Michael Snell 125 Forest Service,U.S. Department of Agriculture 126-135 *All* Courtesy of Kentuckytourism.com 136 *Left* Ian Adams 136 *Right* Brian Miller 138 Jack Olson 139 Brian Miller 140 Ian Adams 141 The Image Finders/David Haas 142 *Left* David Muench 142 *Right* Voscar 143 *Left* Maine Office of Tourism/Jeff Greenberg 144 Maine Office of Tourism 145 Voscar 146 *Top* David Muench 146 *Bottom* Maine Office of Tourism 147 Abbe Museum/Stephen Bicknell 149 *Top* The Image Finders/Jim Baron 149 *Bottom* Image Finders/Jim Baron 150 *Left* Richard Cummins 150 *Right* Courtesy of New Germany State Park 152 *Top* Russell C. Poole 152 *Bottom* M.E.Warren 153 *Top* Van Bucher 153 *Bottom* Van Bucher 154 Russell C. Poole 155 M.E. Warren 156 *Left* Lowell National Historic Park/James Higgins 156 *Right* Elliot Cohen 158 Trustees of Reservations/Wendy Jones 159 Trustees of Reservations/Wendy Jones 160 Elliot Cohen 161 Lowell National Historic Park/James Higgins 162 Jeff Gnass 163 Roger Archibald 164 *Left* Greg Ryan & Sandy Beyer 164 *Right* Terry Donnelly 166 David Muench 167 Courtesy of Iron County Historic Museum 168 David Muench 169 *Top* Andre Jenny/Unicorn Stock Photo 169 *Bottom* Wolf Marz 170 *Both* Dennis Cox 171 Frederik Meijers Gardens/Chuck Heiney 172 *Left* Greg Ryan & Sally Beyer 172 *Right* National Park Service 174 Layne Kennedy 175 *Top* John Elk III 175 *Bottom* Richard Smith 176 Greg Ryan & Sally Beyer 177 Greg Ryan & Sally Beyer 178 *Both* David Muench 179 John Elk III 180 *Left* Robert P. Falls 180 *Right* Buddy Mays Travel Stock 182 Robert P. Falls 183 National Park Service 184 Franke Keating 185 Photo Researchers/Garry McMichael 186 *Left* David Muench 186 *Right* Missouri Department of Natural Resources 188 *Top* Unicorn Photos/Martha Mcbride 188 *Bottom* Kent & Donna Dannen 189 John Elk III 190 *Both* Missouri Department of Natural Resources 191 Missouri Department of Natural Resources 192 Missouri Department of Natural Resources 193 *Top* David Muench 193 *Bottom* Missouri Department of Natural Resources 194 *Left* John Elk III 194 *Right* David Muench 196 David Muench 197 David Muench 198 *Top* Montana Fish and Wildlife 198 *Bottom* Jeff Henry 199 Montana Fish and Wildlife 200 *Left* Bruce Coleman/Lee Rentz 200 *Right* David Muench 202 Jack Olson 203 Kent and Donna Dannen 204 Michael Forsberg 205 Fort Hartsuff 206 Heartland Museum 207 David Muench 208 *Left* Las Vegas News Bureau 208 *Right* Dennis Parks 210-213 *All* Nevada Commission on Tourism 214 *Both* Alan Briere 216 Canterbury Shaker Village 217 *Top* Alan Briere 217 *Bottom* Russell C. Poole 218 both Alan Briere 219 George Barker/Strawberry Banke 220 *Left* Bruce Coleman/Gene Ahrens 220 *Right* Mark Muench 222 David Muench 223 *Top* David Muench 223 *Bottom* Mark Muench 224 Jeff Gnass 225 Tom Till 225 Paul Rezendes 226 Bruce Coleman/Gene Ahrens 227 Batsto Village 228 *Top* JP Foster 228 *Bottom* J. Goerk Lyden 229 Bill and Nancy Erickson/New Wave Photography 230 *Left* New Mexico Department of Tourism 230 *Right* David Muench 232 New Mexico Department of Tourism 233 David Muench 234 *Both* David Muench 235-237 *All* New Mexico Department of Tourism 238 *Both* Elinor Osborn 240 Griffis Sculpture Park 241 NY State Office of Parks 242 *Top* Tony Ingraham/Fingerlakes SP 242 *Bottom* Lee Snider/Photo Images 243 National Bottle Museum 244 Laurie Platt Winfrey 245 Huguenot Historical Society 246 *Top* G. Clemonts/Center of Tibetan Art 246 *Bottom* Angus Oborn/Lonely Planet 247 U.S. Department of the Interior 248 *Left* David Muench 248 *Right* Ernest H. Robel 249 *Bottom* David Muench 250 *Both* NC Department Natural Resources 251 Alamance County Visitors Bureau 252 *Top*

Bruce Coleman/Ronald Thomas 252 *Bottom* Carol Shanks/Transparencies 253 NC Department Natural Resources 254 *Top* Outer Banks Visitors Bureau 254 *Bottom* NC Department Natural Resources 255 *Both* NC Aquarium at Fort Fisher 256 *Left* Jack Olson 256 *Right* ND Department of Tourism 258 ND Department of Tourism 259 Marc Muench 260 ND Department of Tourism 261 Francis Caldwell/Affordable Stock 262 *Left* David Muench 262 *Right* Randall Schieber 264 Bicycle Museum of America 265 *Top* Randall Schieber 265 *Bottom* Donald Voelker 266 Warther Museum 267 Aaron Keirnes 268 H. Armstrong Roberts/R.Krubner 269 David Muench 270 *Left* H. Armstrong Roberts/W. Metzen 270 *Right* Lee Foster/Lonely Planet 272 Marylin Angel Wynn/Native Stock 273 Dennis Peterson/Spiro Mounds 274 David Muench 275 David Muench 276 *Left* Historic Columbia River Highway 276 *Right* David Muench 278 David Muench 279 David Muench 280 David Muench 281 *Top* David Muench 281 *Bottom* John Day Fossil Beds 282 David Muench 283 Sumpter Valley Railroad 284 *Left* H. Armstrong Roberts/Rick Dunoff 284 *Right* George Ostertag 286 Bruce Coleman/Kate McDonald 287 *Top* George Ostertag 287 *Bottom* U.S. Forest Service 288 PA Fish Commission 289 Tom Till 290 Reptile Land 291 Hawk Mountain Association 292 Laura Zito 293 *Top* Mutter Museum 293 *Bottom* H. Armstrong Roberts/J. Irwin 294 *Left* Lee Snider 294 *Right* Paul Rezendes 295 *Right* Rhode Island Historical Society 296 Lee Snider 297 Barbara Money/Audubon Society 298 *Left* David Muench 298 *Right* Allen Davis Market Corner 300 SC Department of Parks 301 Sumter County Museum 302 SC Department of Parks 303 SC Department of Parks 304 *Left* David Muench 304 *Right* Tom Bean 306 SD Cultural Center 307 SD Department of Game 308 David Muench 309 David Muench 310 *Left* National Park Service 310 *Right* Chucalissa Museum 312 National Park Service 313 Photo Researchers/Will McIntyre 314 Dennis Keim 315 Courtesy of Rugby 316 Museum of Appalachia 317 Courtesy of Jonesborough 318 David Muench 318 Carson County Square House 320 Panhandle Plains Historic Museum 321 David Muench 322 The Presidential Museum 323 David Muench 324 *Top* Texas Visitors Bureau 324 *Bottom* Fort Concho 325 Rhonda Hole/Cowgirl Hall of Fame 326 David Muench 327 David Muench 328 *Left* David Muench 328 *Right* Bruce Coleman/John Flannery 330 David Muench 331 David Muench 332 David Muench 333 David Muench 334 *Left* U.S. Fish and Wildlife 334 *Right* St. Anne's Shrine 336 Vermont State Parks 337 Vermont State Parks 338 Jon Gilbert Fox 339 Vermont State Parks 340 *Left* Terry Keith Nicholson 340 *Right* Virginia Tourism Corporation 342 Virginia Department of Tourism 343 Courtesy of Glen Burnie Historic House, Gardens and Galleries 344 Virginia Tourism Corporation 345 Photo Researchers/Van Bucher 346 *Both* David Muench 348 Tacoma Regional Visitors Bureau 349 Tacoma Pierce County Visitors Bureau 350-351 David Muench 352 *Top* Mary Hill Museum 352 *Bottom* Olmstead Place 353 Whitman Mission 354 *Both* West Virginia Department Natural Resources 356 Photo Researchers/Larry Mulvehill 357 West Virginia Department Natural Resources 358 David Muench 359 West Virginia Department Natural Resources 360–362 *All* Wisconsin Department of Tourism/Bob Queen 363 Don Frisque 364 Dells Mills 365 *Top* Bergstrom-Manler Museum 365 *Bottom* Wisconsin State Historical Society 366 *Top* Fon Du Lac 366 *Bottom* Julia Hertel 367 Kenosha Public Museum 368 *Left* Courtesy of Medicine Lodge State Archaeological Site 368 *Right* David Muench 370 David Muench 371 Gregory K. Scott 372 National Park Service 373 Wyoming Department of State Parks

Picture Research by Carousel Research, Inc.

INDEX

INDEX

INDEX

INDEX

INDEX

INDEX